Cusco
& Machu
Picchu

1st Edition
January 2011

Cusco, Machu Picchu, Sacred Valley, Lima

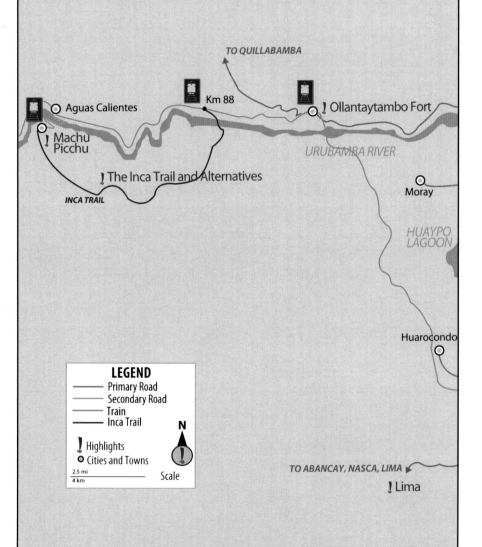

Sacred Valley

TO QUILLABAMBA

Aguas Calientes

Km 88

Ollantaytambo Fort

Machu
Picchu

URUBAMBA RIVER

! The Inca Trail and Alternatives

Moray

INCA TRAIL

HUAYPO
LAGOON

Huarocondo

LEGEND
Primary Road
Secondary Road
Train
Inca Trail

! Highlights
○ Cities and Towns

2.5 mi
4 km

N

Scale

TO ABANCAY, NASCA, LIMA

! Lima

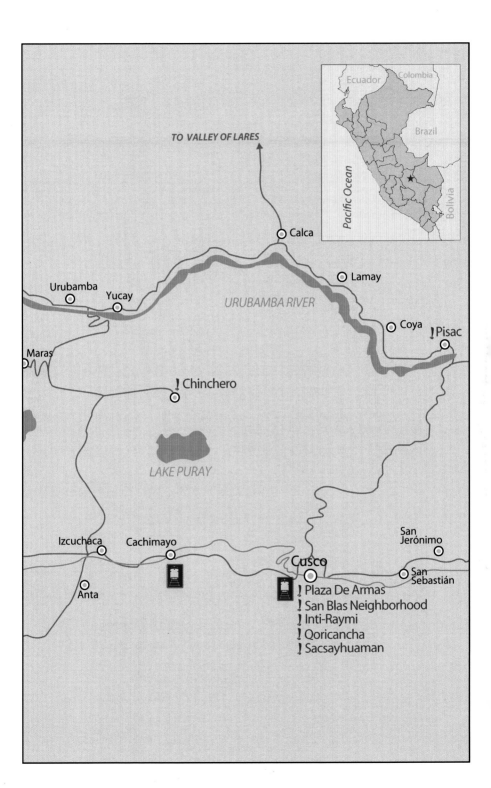

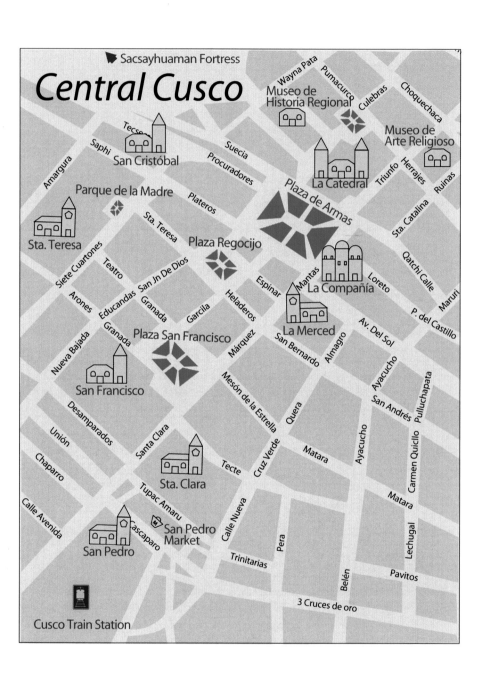

Central Cusco

◣ Sacsayhuaman Fortress

Wayna Pata
Pumacurco
Culebras
Choquechaca

Museo de Historia Regional

Museo de Arte Religioso

Tecse
Saphi
San Cristóbal
Suecia
Procuradores

Amargura

La Catedral
Triunfo
Herrajes
Ruinas

Parque de la Madre
Plateros

Plaza de Armas

Sta. Catalina

Sta. Teresa
Sta. Teresa

Plaza Regocijo

Qatchi Calle

Maruri

Sta. Teresa

Siete Cuartones
Teatro
Espinar
Mantas
La Compañía
Loreto
P. del Castillo

Arones
Educandas
San Jn De Dios
Granada
Garcila
Heladeros
La Merced
Av. Del Sol

Nueva Bajada
Granada
Plaza San Francisco
Márquez
San Bernardo
Almagro
Ayacucho
Pulluchapata

San Francisco
Mesón de la Estrella
Quera
Matara
Ayacucho
San Andrés
Carmen Quicllo

Desamparados
Santa Clara
Cruz Verde

Unión
Tecte
Matara

Chaparro
Sta. Clara
Calle Nueva

Calle Avenida
Tupac Amaru
Pera
Lechugal

Cascaparo
San Pedro Market
Trinitarias
Belén
Pavitos

San Pedro
3 Cruces de oro

Cusco Train Station

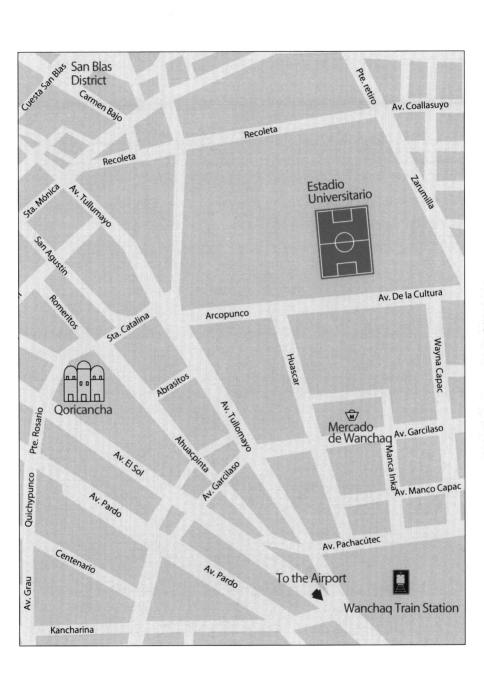

▶ Plaza De Armas

Plaza de Armas is a lively central hotspot for travelers and residents, which makes for an ideal hangout whether you're traveling through or planning to stay for a while. You can spend an afternoon resting by the fountain, trying street food or admiring the beauty of the Iglesia de Matriz. Don't forget to stop by the Casa de Fierro, a house made of iron, designed by Gustave Eiffel. In the evening, meet some friends for dinner or a drink at one of the many restaurants that line the plaza.

◀ San Blas Neighborhood

San Blas, one of the oldest and most charming neighborhoods in Cusco, is a great place to spend the day. Famous for its art scene, its narrow streets filled with studios, this neighborhood will give you plenty to see and do. The lovely colonial buildings are perfect for photos, so don't leave your camera behind. Stop off at Iglesia San Blas, one of the oldest churches in Cusco. It houses some of the most impressive wood carvings in the world.

▲ Qoricancha

Qoricancha, or the Temple of the Sun, is an extraordinary example of Incan architecture and considered by many to be one of the most respected and important temples of the Inca Empire. The temple was used by the Incas as the main observatory for astronomical study. During Spanish control, it was stripped of golden adornments that were once intended to reflect sunlight through the courtyards of Qoricancha. Today the site offers archeologists a wealth of information about the Incan empire. To date, excavations have uncovered chambers, gold and silver figurines and several types of plants.

◀ Inti Raymi

Inti Raymi, an Incan celebration honoring Inti, the god of the sun, marks the winter solstice and new year. On June 24, a play is preformed in Cusco to represent the ancient celebration of Inti Raymi. As a kick off to the celebrations, a local man is chosen to represent an Incan ruler. He is adorned with a colorful feathered headdress and carried to the center of town, where locals perform rituals that start nine days of celebrations.

▶ Machu Picchu

Known as The Lost City of the Incas, Machu Picchu is considered one of the most well-known symbols of the Incan Empire. In 1983, it was named a UNESCO World Heritage Site and has become one of the most-visited destinations in South America. Perched high above the Río Urubamba, surrounded by jungle and Andean peaks, this stunning archeological achievement is only accessible by trail or train—it's worth the trip.

▲ The Inca Trail and Alternatives

This world-famous path to The Lost City of the Incas is part of the Sanctuario Histórico de Machu Picchu, an area of over 32,000 hectares (79,000 ac). Distinguished by its steep ascents and pristine beauty, the Inca Trail offers magnificent views of Andean scenery. Hikers pass through cloud forests and ancient archaeological sites until they reach Machu Picchu. The Inca Trail is perhaps the most sought after of South American experiences.

▲ Chinchero

Located only 28 kilometers northwest of Cusco, this small Andean town provides stunning views of the Sacred Valley below and the snow-capped peak of Salkantay above. Local folklore holds Chinchero as the mythical birthplace of the rainbow. Known for its textiles, on Sundays the market is bustling with artisans dressed in traditional clothing who will barter for hats, gloves and their famous handmade fabrics.

▲ Ollantaytambo Fort

The Ollantaytambo Fort is one of the most visited sites in the Sacred Valley. With 16 terraces, it spreads across the mountainside and once served as an Inca stronghold against the invading Spanish. The terraces and accompanying temples were built using some of the finest stonework in the Inca Empire, and the irrigation and waterworks systems stand as impressive examples of ancient infrastructure. Climb all the way to the top of the complex and you will be rewarded with incredible views of the town and surrounding ruins.

▲ Pisac

Pisac is a popular destination for ruin-seekers and for those looking for more modern comforts. Spend the day exploring ancient temples and palaces and the evening eating traditional Peruvian food at one of the many restaurants. The Pisac market is generally on the top of the must-see list for those visiting the Cusco region. Every Tuesday, Thursday and Sunday, the streets become crowded with artisans selling textiles, jewelry, carved gourds, ceramics, felt hats and antiques. On Sundays, a market for locals sells vegetables and products that are not always found on other days, which makes Sunday a good day to visit.

▲ Sacsayhuaman

Located on the hillsides rising over the city of Cusco, the fortress ruins of Sacsayhuamán are some of the most impressive in the area. Although few structures now remain inside, the massive 20-meter-high outer walls have stood against past battles, earthquakes and time. Sacsayhuamán is an example of the Inca's extraordinary architectural prowess; today engineers are baffled by the scope and scale of the ruin's stonework, which fits together perfectly without mortar.

CUSCO

▲ Ausangate Trek

Avoiding tourist trails, the Ausangate trek goes through the most preserved areas of the Cordillera Vilcanota. Along the way, trekkers can take in impressive views of glaciers that rest against the peaks of Colquecruz and Jampa. Passing through some of the more remote areas in Peru, the trail also offers glimpses of Andean llama herders and weavers.

▲ Lima - Surfing

The long coastlines of Lima offer great spots for surfing at all levels. The waves of Costa Verde call in surfers from all around Lima, where hundereds of people ride the area's most popular waves. In La Herradura, the waves are big and the rewards equally so, if you're patient. Pico Alto and Kon Tiki also attract the big-wave riders, while Punta Rocas and Cerro Azul are a bit more tranquil but equally popular. The summer is the time for board shorts and crowded beaches, while in winter you might need a wet suit, but you'll have more waves to yourself.

▼ Lima - Ceviche

Lima is a food city, so much so that is was named the Gastronomic Capital of the Americas. While Lima is well known for its delicious international cuisine, it's especially famous for ceviche, a seafood dish where raw fish is marinated in citrus (usually lime juice) until it is essentially cooked by the citric acids. Cevicherías are located all over the city and are popular with many limeños. The Peruvian dish requires fresh fish, onions and peppers tossed together to make what is genuinely considered the best ceviche in Latin America.

▲ Lima - Larco Museum

The Larco Museum is considered one of the most extensive collections of Peruvian pre-Colombian artifacts in the country, if not the world. Housed in an 18th century vice-royal mansion, which was built over a seventh century pyramid, the exhibits range from religious statues made from gold to erotic pottery that dates back 3,000 years. Larco Museum is one of the only places in the world that allows visitors to tour its storage area, which holds more 45,000 classified archeological artifacts.

RECOMMENDED ITINERARIES

Cusco - One day walking tour in the city, including Sacsayhuamán

One of the best ways to experience Cusco in a day is by taking a walking tour between the two towering statues that look down on the city from opposite hills.

The walk begins at the Cristo Blanco statue, which you can either reach by taxi or stroll through cobbled streets, up the hill, and past the Sacsayhuamán Inca ruins. The ascent to the statue from the road is somewhat difficult. It will take you up steps and then a steep trekking path, but the view at the top is worth it.

The path back down follows more quaint cobbled streets before it reaches the San Blas square, a vibrant haven of Peruvian artesanía. The area is filled with art shops, where you can buy modern art paintings, t-shirts and embroidered goods.

After scouting for art and exploring the never-ending streets that zigzag across the colonial buildings in this picturesque area of Cusco, head to the Plaza de Armas. You will pass through other small and pretty squares on your way. Plenty of lovely lunch spots provide a welcome rest from the long stroll. After a look at the cathedral and the churches of Jesus Maria and El Triunfo, located in the plaza, head to the lively craft market that backs onto one of the city's many old Inca walls.

From here, it is easy to find the main road where you will find an occasionally working fountain and a towering monument to the ninth Inca. This area is home to many of the stray dogs that roam the city, so you will quite probably attract a new friend to accompany you on the walk up the second hill to your final destination.

The statue of another Inca warrior appears as you head across the road through twisting streets that climb into the hills. When the streets eventually lead you to your final destination, another fantastic birds-eye view of the city is unveiled. If timed right, this makes the perfect spot to take in the sunset.

Cristo Blanco Statue

Cusco and The Sacred Valley in 7 days

Day 1: Arrive in Cusco before lunchtime. Buy a Tourist Ticket and check out some of the in-town attractions, such as the Cusco Cathedral and Museo Histórico Regional. Later, head to one of the many cafés overlooking the Plaza de Armas for a coffee and a stint of people-watching.

Day 2: Take a bus from Cusco to Pisac. From this pretty market town, hike up for an hour or so to the Pisac Fort, overlooking much of the Sacred Valley. Spend an hour or two wandering the ruins and then head back down to Pisac either on foot or in a taxi. Take a bus to Ollayantaytambo and stay overnight here.

Day 3: Get up early and head to the Ollantaytambo Fort before breakfast, to miss the tour buses. Take an hour or so to check out this fort and grab brunch in Ollantaytambo. Afterward, wander the town for a while and pick up some souvenirs or gifts. Later, take a bus back to Cusco, and if there's time, check out another place from the Tourist Ticket.

Days 4 to 7: Hike to Machu Picchu, either on the Inca Trail or one of the many alternatives, such as Lares. The Inca Trail and Lares Trek leave travelers at Machu Picchu on the fourth day (Day 7). Take several hours on a guided tour of the ruins. If you want to climb Huayna Picchu, recommended for the view from the top, it is necessary to head up there early. After your visit to Machu Picchu, return to Cusco in the evening.

Machu Picchu with Huayna Picchu in the background

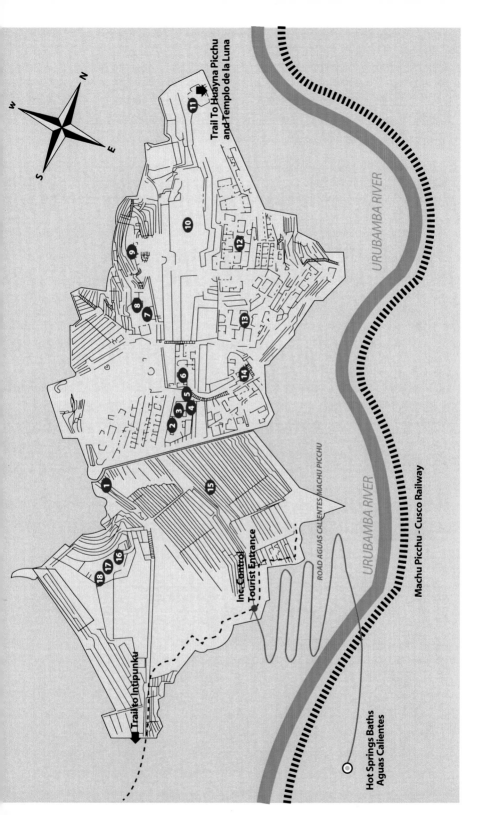

MACHU PICCHU

The Main Square

1. The City Gate
2. Ñusta's Bedroom
3. The Temple of the Sun
4. The Royal Tomb
5. Ritual Fountains
6. The Royal Palace
7. Temple of the Three Windows
8. The Main Temple
9. Intihuatana
10. The Main Square
11. The Sacred Rock
12. Houses of Factories
13. Industrial Zone
14. The Prisoner's Area
15. Cultivation Terraces
16. The House of the Guardians
17. Funerary Rock
18. Cementery

Temple Of The Sun

View of Machu Picchu from the Sungate

The Main Temple

Cultivation Terraces

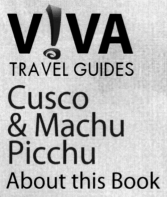

V!VA TRAVEL GUIDES

Cusco & Machu Picchu

About this Book

At V!VA, we believe that you shouldn't have to settle
for an outdated guidebook. You can rest assured that in your hands
is the most up-to-date guidebook available on Cusco because:

-- The final research for this book was completed on December 16, 2010.
-- Each entry is "time stamped" with the date it was last updated
-- V!VA's hyper-efficient web-to-book publishing process brings books to press
   in days or weeks, not months or years like our competitors
-- V!VA's country guides are updated at least once per year.

When you buy a V!VA Guide, here's what you're getting:

-- The expertise of professional travel writers, local experts and real travelers
   in-country bringing you first-hand, unbiased recommendations to make the
   most out of your trip
-- The wisdom of editors who actually live in Latin America, not New York,
   Melbourne, or London like other guidebook companies
-- Advice on how to escape the overly-trodden gringo trail, meet locals and
   understand the culture
-- The knowledge you'll need to travel responsibly while getting more for your money

Contribute to V!VA

V!VA is an online community of travelers, and we rely on the advice and opinions of
vagabonders like yourself to continuously keep the books accurate and useful.

Take a part in this ongoing effort by reviewing the places you have been on the
website, www.vivatravelguides.com.

Other travelers want to know about that rarely visited town you stumbled upon, about
that bus company you will never take again, about that meal you just can't stop
thinking about.

Together, we can help enhace each other's travel experiences and share in our love and
passion for exploring Latin America.

Go ahead! Log on and create a free user account to help make the best guidebook
series to LatinAmerica even better.

Machu Picchu Highlights

Intihuatana

A brief walk uphill from the Principal Temple will bring you to one of the most important shrines at Machu Picchu. Intihuatana, or Hitching Post of the Sun, is an intriguing carved rock whose shape mimics that of Huayna Picchu, the sacred peak rising beyond the ruins. Though the Incas created rocks like this for all their important ritual centers, Intihuatana is one of the few not destroyed by the Spanish conquistadores. Overlooking the Sacred Plaza, this sundial-like rock served as an astronomical device used to track constellation movements and to calculate the passing of seasons. Given its shape and strategic alignment with four important mountains, many scholars have conjectured that Intihuatana is symbolically linked to the spirit of the mountains on which Machu Picchu was built. If you follow the steps down from here, past the Sacred Plaza and towards the northern terraces you'll arrive at the Sacred Rock, gateway to Huayna Picchu. Updated: Jul 17,2007.

Temple of the Sun

Upon entering the main ruins you'll cross over a dry moat and come across the first site of major interest, the Temple of the Sun. Once used as a solar observatory, this unique complex is the only round building at Machu Picchu. At sunrise during the summer solstice, the sun's rays flood through the window and illuminate the tower with a precision only the Incas could have executed. Also known as the Torreón, the temple presents a spectacular, semicircular wall and carved steps that fit seamlessly into the existing surface of a natural boulder, forming some sort of altar. Although access inside the temple is not permitted, the outside architecture is spectacular in and of itself. The temple displays some of Machu Picchu's most superb stonework, and has a window from which the June solstice sunrise and constellation of Pleides can be observed. In Andean culture the Pleiades continues to be an important astronomical symbol, and the locals use the constellation to calculate the arrival of the rains and to determine the best time of year to plant crops. Next to the Temple of the Sun is the Chamber of the Princess, and below the temple is The Royal Tomb. Updated: Jul 17,2007

Royal Tomb

The Royal Tomb is a bit of a misnomer due to the fact that neither graves nor human remains have ever been encountered here. Though it may lack the macabre history that some travelers may expect, this cave-like structure is an excellent example of the Inca's stonemasonry genius. Located inside is a magnificent stepped altar and a series of tall niches, once used to present offerings, which capture the sun's rays to produce brilliant patterns of morning shadows. Just down the stairs leading from the Royal Tomb is a series of interconnected fountains and a still-functioning water canal. Updated: Jul 17,2007.

Chamber of the Princess

The two-story structure sitting adjacent to the Temple of the Sun is the Chamber of the Princess. The building was most likely used for Inca nobility, which may explain why Yale archaeologist Hiram Bingham chose its name. A three-walled house standing next to the chamber has been restored with a thatched roof and provides a good illustration of how Inca buildings might have once looked. From here you can follow a staircase that leads upwards past the Royal Area (denoted by characteristic imperial Inca architecture) and to the two most impressive buildings in the city: the Three-Windowed Temple and the Principal Temple. Updated: Dec 09,2009.

Three-Windowed Temple

Not far from the Chamber of the Princess is the spectacular Three-Windowed Temple. It is part of a complex situated around the Sacred Plaza, a ceremonial center that some argue is the most captivating section of the city. The temple's unusually large, trapezoidal windows perfectly frame the mountains unfolding beyond the Urubamba River valley. To your left as you face the Three-Windowed Temple is another popular Machu Picchu attraction, the Principal Temple. Updated: Dec 09,2009

Principal Temple

Situated next to the Three-Windowed Temple, this magnificent three-walled building derives its name from the immense foundation stones and fine stonework that comprise its three high main walls. The wall facing furthest east looks onto the Sacred Plaza. In contrast to most ancient temples in the Americas, whose entrances face east, the Principal Temple's entrance faces south. White sand found on the temple floor suggests that the temple may have been tied symbolically to the Río Urubamba, a theory that is not too farfetched considering the importance of water in the ancient Inca culture. The kite-shaped sacred stone sitting in the small square around the temple is thought to represent the Southern Cross constellation. A short stroll uphill from here brings you to one of the most spectacular sites of Machu Picchu, the Intihuatana, or Hitching Post of the Sun. Updated: Dec 09,2009.

Huayna Picchu

Just down the steps from Intihuatana and across the Sacred Plaza is the Sacred Rock, a massive piece of granite curiously shaped like the Inca's sacred mountain of Putukusi, which looms on the eastern horizon. Little is known about this rock, except that it serves as the gateway to Huayna Picchu. Access to the sacred summit is controlled by a guardian from a kiosk behind the Sacred Rock. The trail is open daily 7 a.m.-1 p.m., with the last exit by 3 p.m. The steep walk up to the summit takes about one to two hours and includes a 20-meter climb up a steep rock slab using a ladder and rope. (Those afraid of heights may want to pass on this climb.) Your physical labors will be rewarded, however, with a spectacular panoramic view of the entire Machu Picchu complex and the Andean mountains and forests which cradle it. About two-thirds of the way down the trail behind the summit, another trail leads to the right and down to the exquisitely situated Temple of the Moon. Updated: Dec 09,2009

Temple of the Moon

Situated about 400 meters beneath the pinnacle of Huayna Picchu (about a 45-minute walk each way from the summit) is The Temple of the Moon, another spectacular example of Inca stonemasonry. The temple consists of a large natural cave with five niches carved into a massive white granite stone wall. Towards the cave's center is a rock carved like a throne, next to which are five carved steps that lead towards darker recesses where even more carved rocks and stone walls are visible. The temple's name originates from the way it radiates with moonlight at night, but many archaeologists believe that it was also symbolically aligned with the surrounding mountains. Steps on either side of the small plaza in front of the temple lead to more buildings and some interesting stone sanctuaries below. For equally incredible views of Machu Picchu and Huayna Picchu you can take the other trail leading down from the guardian's kiosk behind Sacred Rock. The thirty minute climb to Intipunku, the main entrance to Machu Picchu from the Inca Trail, is slightly less demanding and a good option for anyone lacking in time or energy. Updated: Dec 09,2009

Intipunku

If you don't have the time or energy to make the climb up to Huayna Picchu and Temple of the Moon, then you may prefer to take the trail leading from the guardian's kiosk behind the Sacred Stone to Intipunku, the main entrance to Machu Picchu from the Inca Trail. Intipunku, also known as the Sun Gate, consists of two large stones that correspond to the winter and summer solstices, and on these dates the gates are illuminated by laser-like beams of light. In addition to their symbolic importance, the gates also provide remarkable views of Machu Picchu and Huayna Picchu. Updated: Dec 09,2009.

VIVA Travel Guide to Cusco, Machu Picchu and the Sacred Valley

ISBN-13: 978-0-9825585-2-2

Copyright © 2010, Viva Publishing Network.

Voice: (970) 744-4244

Fax: (612) 605-5720

Website: www.vivatravelguides.com

Information: info@vivatravelguides.com

www.vivatravelguides.com

◊ Cover Design: Jason Halberstadt, 2009 ◊
◊ Cover Photo: Douglas J. Klostermann, " Inca King at Inti Raymi," 2007 ◊
◊ Cover Photo: Mark Green,"Machu Picchu," 2009 ◊
◊ Back Cover Photo: Bernardo Carbajal, "_BER5731," 2009 ◊
◊ Title Page Photo: Boring Lovechild, "Cusco, Plaza de Armas" 2009 ◊

Photo Credits:
Color Insert Photos: "San Blas Neighborhood" by Paula Newton, 2010; "Pisac" by Paula Newton, 2010.

The following photos are licensed under the Creative Commons license (see http://creativecommons.org/licenses/by/2.0 and http://creativecommons.org/licenses/by/3.0 for details):

La Catedral by Geoced, 2009, http://www.flickr.com/photos/geoced/4523759334/; "Coricancha, Cusco, Peru." by Håkan Svensson, 2002, http://en.wikipedia.org/wiki/File:Imagen-Cusco_Coricancha_view1.jpg; "DSC_0367" by Fred Lam, 2008, http://www.flickr.com/photos/fredlam/2608282091/; "Machu Picchu from the Guard House" by Alex E. Proimos, 2009, http://www.flickr.com/photos/proimos/4015248297/; "Winaywayna, Inca Trail (Fourth Day), Peru" by Emmanuel Dyan, 2009, http://www.flickr.com/photos/emmanueldyan/4288786967/; "Chinchero Market - Sacred Valley – Peru" by David Berkowitz, 2010, http://www.flickr.com/photos/davidberkowitz/4872564523/; "Ollantaytambo, Peru" by Bernard Gagnon, 1984, http://en.wikipedia.org/wiki/File:Ollantaytambo,_Peru.jpg; "Sacsayhuaman" by Chris Palmer, 2010, http://www.flickr.com/photos/ginsnob/4645445776/; "besthike.com Ausangate Circuit, Peru" by Rick McCharles, 2005, http://www.flickr.com/photos/rickmccharles/188363122/; "Eating Ceviche in Lima" by Christian Haugen, 2009, http://www.flickr.com/photos/christianhaugen/3666567936/; "Surf" by Cristóbal Alvarado Minic, 2009, http://www.flickr.com/photos/ctam/4157061804/; "Storage Gallery of the Larco Museum" by Lyndsay Ruell, 2006, http://en.wikipedia.org/wiki/File:Storage_Gallery.jpg; "Cristo Blanco Statue" by Imke.stahlmann's, 2010, http://www.flickr.com/photos/11264282@N02/4891702790/; "View over Machu Picchu with Huayna Picchu in the background" by Jimmy Harris, 2009, http://www.flickr.com/photos/jimmyharris/3839634998/; "The Main Square" by Nick Jewell, 2009, http://www.flickr.com/photos/macjewell/4236522891/; "Temple of The Sun" by Teo Romera, 2010, http://www.flickr.com/photos/teosaurio/4532652867/; "Cultivation Terraces" by Nick Jewell, 2009, http://www.flickr.com/photos/macjewell/4237286436/; "The Main Temple" by Teo Romera, 2010, http://www.flickr.com/photos/teosaurio/4533883747/; "View of Machu Picchu from the Sungate" by Ethan Lindsay, 2004, http://www.flickr.com5.

INTRO & INFO

CONTENTS

Geography	12
Flora & Fauna	12
History	13
Politics	14
Economy	15
Population	15
Language	16
Religion	16
Holidays and Fiestas	18
Culture	19
Painting and Sculpture	20
Music	20
Dance	21
Theater	21
Social & Environmental Issues	24
Visas	26
Embassies and Consulates	27
Getting To and Away from Peru	29
Border Crossings	30
Getting Around	31
Types of Tours	34
Adventure Travel	35
Hiking	36
Horseback Riding	37
Mountain Biking	38
Mountain Climbing	39
Sandboarding	40
Sport Fishing	41
Rock Climbing	41
Surfing	41
Whitewater Rafting	42
Studying in Peru	42
Volunteering or Working	43
Lodging	44
Food and Drink	46
Shopping	50
Health and Safety	52
Media	54
Mail and Packages	54
Telephones and Calling	55
Money and Costs	56
Banks	57
Etiquette and Dress	58
Responsible Tourism	58
Photography	59
Travel Tips	59
Women Travelers	59
Gay and Lesbian Travelers	60
Disabled Travelers	60
Senior Travelers	60
Travelers with Kids	60

INTRO & INFO

Cusco Introduction 62
When to Go 62
Safety 62
History 62
Getting To and Away 64
Getting Around 66
Holidays and Festivals 66
Services 72
Tours 72
Best of Cusco 75

Cusco Guide 78
Things to See and Do 78
Lodging 86
Restaurants 94
San Blas **100**
Lodging 100
Restaurants 102
Nightlife 105
Andahuaylillas and San Pedro 107

Sacred Valley 108
History 108
When to Go 108
Acclimatization 108
Things to See and Do 109
Safety 109
Trekking 109
Tours 113
Chinchero 114
Pisac **114**
Getting To and Away 114
Lodging 117
Restaurants 118
Urubamba **119**
Getting To and Away 119
Services 119
Things to See and Do 120
Lodging 120
Restaurants 120
Ollantaytambo **121**
History of Ollantaytambo 123
Getting To and Away 123
Things to See and Do 124
Lodging 125
Restaurants 128
Aguas Calientes **130**
Getting To and Away 130
Services 130
Things To See and Do 132
Lodging 132
Restaurants 134
Machu Picchu and The Inca Trail **136**

When To Go   137
What to Bring   138
What to Expect   138
Getting There   139
Machu Picchu History   141
Machu Picchu Activities   141
Machu Picchu Tours   143
Machu Picchu Lodging   144
Machu Picchu Restaurants   144

Lima Introduction   **146**

History of Lima   146
Getting To and Away   147
Banks in Lima   151
Emergency Medical Care   151
Services   151
Lodging   152
Tours   152
Things to See and Do   154
Lima Museums   154

San Isidro   **158**

History of San Isidro   158
Things to See and Do   160
Lodging   160
Restaurants   162

Central Lima   **166**

History   166
Services   168
Things to See and Do   169
Lodging   173
Restaurants   175

Miraflores, Barranco
and Chorillos   **180**

Miraflores   **180**
History   180
Services   181
Things to See and Do   182
Tours   185
Lodging   185
Restaurants   190
Nightlife   195
Barranco   **196**
Barranco   196
Services   197
Things to See and Do   198
Lodging   198
Restaurants   200

Nightlife   201
Chorrillos   **202**
Services   202
Things to See and Do   202
Chorillos Lodging   203

Elsewhere in Lima   **204**
Lima Airport   204
Neighborhoods   204
Callao   204
Magdalena del Mar   205
Monterrico   205
Pueblo Libre   206
San Borja   208
Around Lima   209
Things to See and Do   209

Peru Living   **212**
Housing and Real Estate   212
Moving   214
Services   215
Money and Costs   217
Living Abroad   217
Work and Business   218
Education   228
Long-Term Health   236
Safety   241
Shopping   242
Packing for Peru   246
Driving/Buying a Car   246
Leisure Time   248

Index   **252**
Packing Lists   261
Useful Spanish Phrases   263
Embassies and Consulates   266

INTRO & INFO

ABOUT THE WRITERS

Dr. Christopher Minster, PhD is a graduate of Penn State University, The University of Montana and Ohio State. He is V!VA Travel Guides' expert on ruins, history and culture, as well as spooky things like haunted museums. "Crit" worked for the U.S. Peace Corps in Guatemala as a volunteer from 1991 to 1994 and has traveled extensively in Latin America.

Rachel Griffiths is originally from New Zealand but currently enjoying living in Peru and travelling around South America. She has a Bachelor of Business and has developed a love of writing and communications, particularly for telling interesting travel stories. Her passion for going places she's never been before has taken her throughout Southeast Asia, India, Mexico, and Central and South America. She loves to travel freely in order to discover new places.

Challen Clarke has an MFA in nonfiction writing from St. Mary's College of California and a B.A. in English from the University of San Francisco where she graduated Summa Cum Laude. Her passions are writing and traveling and she feels lucky to have discovered a way to do both. She has lived in Italy, Hungary, and Ecuador, sailed from San Francisco through the Panama Canal, and explored more than 18 countries.

Zach Demby graduated from Syracuse University with a degree in philosophy, resigning him to a life of unemployment and unsolicited analysis. He went on to study creative writing at Saint Mary's College of California. He has worked as a freelance writer and editor on several literary magazines and websites , but was unfulfilled. A chance meeting with a beleaguered pirate inspired Zach to see the world, and since then he's been to more than ten countries and doesn't plan on stopping anytime soon.

Rick Segreda graduated with Departmental Honors from Manhattanville College in Purchase, New York, earning a B.A. in Religious Studies and Literature. Following a spell managing a hostel for Hostelling International in Washington State, and serving on its Board of Directors, Segreda relocated to Ecuador. In Quito, he divides his time between film critiquing for Ecuador's largest daily, La Hora and serving as a staff writer for V!VA. He pounded the streets of Peru to take a leading role in the production of this book.

MANY THANKS TO:

Natalia Cohen and **Philippa Jephson** contributed content for Cusco. **The South American Explorers clubs** in both Lima and Cusco were also a great help in pointing us in the right direction.

We thank our VIVA intern superheroes: **Clemence Duron, Eli Mangold** and **Jennifer O'Riordan** and also **Jesua Silva**, VIVA's staff cartographer. Thanks also to **Rigoberto Pinto, Cristian Avila and Tania Morales**, the programming masterminds who keep www.vivatravelguides.com running smoothly and are always willing to lend a hand to the not-so-computer-savvy staff; and an additional thanks to the whole **Metamorf** team for their support.

Last but not least, thanks to the hundreds of Peruvians who taught us about the culture, history & beauty of their country.

ABOUT THE EDITORS

INTRO & INFO

Paula Newton is V!VA's operations expert. With an MBA and a background in New Media, Paula is the Editor-in-Chief and the organizing force behind the team. With an insatiable thirst for off-the-beaten-track travel, Paula has traveled extensively, especially in Europe and Asia, and has explored more than 30 countries. She currently lives in Quito.

Nick Rosen is a staff writer and editor for VIVA. He holds a BA in International Development from Montreal's McGill University and has worked on public health projects in Kenya and Ghana. He maintains that nothing compares to the sublime beauty of his native New Jersey.

Libby Zay is a staff writer and editor at V!VA Travel Guides. She grew up in Cleveland, Ohio and earned degrees in Popular Culture Studies and Women's Studies from The Ohio State University, where she also minored in Film. Her wanderlust has led her to circle the U.S. in a smelly conversion van, as well as journey to the far reaches of Moldova. Before moving to Quito, Ecuador, Libby worked as an editorial assistant at AOL Travel in Washington DC.

Desiree Andrews has worked as a writer and editor since 2006. She received a BA in Creative Writing at Prescott College. She has worked as a journalist in Reykjavik, Iceland, rescued sea turtles in Hawaii, and served as an editorial assistant and marketing assistant at Tin House Books in Portland, OR. She currently lives in Quito, Ecuador and works full-time as a staff writer for V!VA Travel Guides.

About VIVA Travel Guides

VIVA Travel Guides pioneers a new approach to travel guides. We have taken the travel guide and re-designed it from the ground up using the Internet, geographic databases, community participation, and the latest in printing technology, which allows us to print our guidebooks one at a time when they are ordered. Reversing the general progression, we have started with a website, gathered user ratings and reviews, and then compiled the community's favorites into a book. Every time you see the V!VA insignia you know that the location is a favorite of the V!VA Travel Community. For you, the reader, this means more accurate and up-to-date travel information and more ratings by travelers like yourself.

Community and Free Membership:

The accuracy and quality of the information in this book is largely thanks to our online community of travelers. If you would like to join them, go to www.vivatravelguides.com/members/ to get more information and to sign up for free.

Your Opinions, Experiences and Travels:

Did you love a place? Will you never return to another? Every destination in this guidebook is listed on our web site with space for user ratings and reviews. Share your experiences, help out other travelers and let the world know what you think.

Corrections & Suggestions:

We are committed to bringing you the most accurate and up-to-date information. However, places convert, prices rise, businesses close down, and information, no matter how accurate it once was, inevitably changes. Thus we ask for your help: If you find an error in this book or something that has changed, go to www.vivatravelguides.com/corrections and report them (oh, and unlike the other guidebooks, we'll incorporate them into our information within a few days).

If you think we have missed something, or want to see something in our next book go to www.vivatravelguides.com/suggestions and let us know. As a small token of our thanks for correcting an error or submitting a suggestion we'll send you a coupon for 50 percent off any of our E-books or 20 percent off any of our printed books.

Coming soon on www.vivatravelguides.com

This is just the beginning. We're busy adding new features that our users have requested to our books and website. A few coming attractions to improve community functions include the ability to: join specialized groups, find travel partners, participate in forum discussions, write travel blogs, add maps, and much more!

How to Use This Book:

This book is a best-of Cusco taken straight from our website. You can check out www.vivatravelguides.com to read user reviews, rate your favorite hotels and restaurants, and add information you think we are missing. The book also features highlighted sections on Inca Trail hikes, ecotourism and adventure travel. While you are out and about in Peru, use our helpful tear-out sheet in the back of the book, complete with emergency contact details and helpful numbers.

Travelers' discussions. User reviews. Feedback. Photo contests. Book updates. Travel news. Apps. Writing contests. Give-aways.

V!VA
TRAVEL GUIDES

Follow us online
www.facebook.com/vivatravelguides
www.twitter.com/vivatravelguide
www.vivatravelguides.com

Introduction

In Quechua, the language of the Inca, Peru means the "land of abundance." Peru is full of extremes. Its landscapes vary from lush, towering Andean peaks to rolling sand dunes on the coast to the Amazon— the largest, most diverse rainforest in the world. Peru is also rich in pre-Columbian culture. There are millions of Peruvians in the Andes mountains who still live the way their ancestors did thousands of years ago. For the archeology buff, the mountaineer, the surfer and the jungle explorer, Peru truly is a land of abundance. Updated: Jan 19, 2009.

Geography, Climate, Flora and Fauna

Peru features a diverse array of flora and fauna, thanks to its climactic and geological diversity. One of Peru's leading scientists, Dr. Javier Pulgar Vidal, completed extensive studies of the country in the 1930s and identified no less than eight climatological zones and 96 sub-zones, each of which represents a different biological niche. The eight zones are Chala, or coastland, Yunga, lowland valleys, Quechua, a temperate, middle-altitude zone, Suni, highlands, Puna, inhospitable highlands, Janca, snowy mountain peaks, Omagua, high interior jungle, and Rupa-Rupa, lowland jungle.

The Chala, or coastal, region features islands, mangroves, beaches, some marshes and inland areas up to about 500 meters (1,600 ft.) above sea level. The flora of the Peruvian Chala region is marked by palm trees, coconuts, olive trees, papayas, mangroves and the variety of grape from which Peruvian pisco is made. The region is also home to certain reeds and rushes that are used commercially by local residents to make baskets, mats and other handmade goods. Chala means "maize plant" in Quechua. The fauna includes all sea animals, such as fish and sea lions, as well as marine birds such as frigates and boobies.

The lowland valleys and hills that make up the Yunga ("warm valley") region (500-2,300 meters / 1,600-7,500 ft. above sea level) are marked by food bearing trees such as the avocado, plum and citrus trees including orange, grapefruit and lime. Peru's extensive sugarcane fields are found in the this region. The Yunga is famous for its orchids; more than 200 species are thought to exist here. It also features many species of birds,

including the rare white winged guan. The region is also home to some small species of wild cats, exotic reptiles, including boas and several types of lizard, as well as the Andean spectacled bear. The Yunga is currently considered a highly endangered ecosystem; a great deal of damage is being done by agriculture and deforestation.

The temperate Quechua region (2,300-3,500 meters / 7,500 ft.-11,500 ft. above sea level) is the most important agricultural zone for Peruvian grains, such as maize and wheat. Tomatoes, papayas and peaches also grow well in this region.

The Suni region (3,500-4,100 meters / 11,500-13,500 ft. above sea level) is a cold, dry region which includes some glacial lakes. "Suni" means "high" in Quechua. The flora characteristic to this region are tough, hardy plants and bushes, with very few trees. Little agriculture takes place in the Suni region, but quinua (a local grain) does well, as do some potatoes, barley, oats and the broad bean. The famous guinea pig, long a staple of Andean cultures, is native to this region. The Lake Titicaca basin is considered to be a combination of Suni and Puna regions.

The Puna zone is the highest zone that supports human populations: the Janca region is too inhospitable for people to stay there for long. The Puna ("Puna" means "altitude sickness" in Quechua) is home to iconic Andean creatures such as the llama, vicuña, guanaco and alpaca. Sheep, which are not native, also thrive in this region. The Puna is home to several highland lakes that are important stopovers for migratory birds. Potatoes grow well in this zone, as do certain cacti.

The Janca ("white") region is the highest in Peru, and is characterized by glaciers and snow-capped peaks. Some hardy grasses, moss and lichens thrive there, but little else. There are some animals and birds that reside here as well, including the endangered Andean condor.

The Omagua region, or high jungle, gets its name from an indigenous word meaning "region of the fresh water fish." In Peru, there are vast stretches of virgin rainforest classified as Omagua. It is home to several species of mammal and reptile as well as many birds and insects. There are also, naturally, several species of fish that thrive in this climate zone, the largest of which is the paiche. There are several important species of plants, including the Brazil nut tree, mahogany and the hallucinogenic *ayahuasca*.

Peru's steamy interior jungle lowlands are classified as Rupa-Rupa, from a Quechua word meaning "ardent." It is a thriving, vital ecosystem, and is home to countless species of plant and animal life. Many trees from this region are considered of commercial value, including the balsawood, rubber and oil palm trees. Updated: Jan 27, 2010.

History

The area now known as Peru was inhabited long before the arrival of the Spanish. Various smaller ethnic groups controlled regions and cities before the ascendance of the Inca from the Cusco area in about 1440. The Inca conquered the region and established Cusco as the center of their Empire.

The Inca were talented mathematicians and stonemasons. They built formidable cities and fortifications, and they were skilled rulers. Interestingly, their civilization was not familiar with the wheel and axle, and all of the heavy stones for their cities were transported by sled or rolled on logs. They did not have a written language. Instead the Inca used *quipus*, which are complex sets of colored cords knotted in patterns to express numerical values. In terms of mathematics, these cords were just as accurate as writing. Although some quipus still exist in museums, the art of deciphering them has been lost.

When a Spanish expedition arrived in 1532 under Francisco Pizarro, they found an Inca Empire in chaos. A bloody civil war had torn the empire apart, with two brothers—Atahuallpa in the north and Huascar in the south—fighting for dominance. Not long after the arrival of the Spanish, Huascar was captured by Atahuallpa's forces. When Atahuallpa, in turn, was captured by the Spanish at Cajamarca, he ordered Huascar executed so that he alone would be the Inca. Unfortunately for Atahuallpa, Huascar was the elder brother, which under the European system of inheritance made him Inca. The Spanish branded Atahuallpa as a usurping traitor, and murdered him. Subsequently, the Spanish would base their legal claim to Andean lands on the notion that since they had taken them from a 'usurper,' their continued occupation was just and legal.

In the 1540s, the Spanish conquistadores fell to warring among themselves in a series of civil wars that were every bit as brutal as the conquest had been. Francisco Pizarro himself was hacked down in the street. It wasn't until the arrival of a series of Viceroys in the latter half of the century that the situation calmed down. The most notable of the Viceroys was Francisco de Toledo, who ruled from 1569 to 1581. Toledo toured the vast lands of Peru, taking with him mapmakers, historians and bureaucrats. He often kept Inca policies and legal precedents in place when he could.

By the latter half of the 16th century, precious metals had been discovered in abundance in parts of Peru, and gold and silver from the region was shipped to Spain for more than two centuries. In the early 1800's, Peru was one of the last countries to declare independence from Spain, largely because the capital city of Lima was very loyal. Even so, Peru declared itself independent in 1821. What followed was a long period of instability: Peru had 59 presidents from 1821 to 1900. Although it fared a little better in the twentieth century, there was still a great deal of chaos; Peru had five different presidents in 1931 alone. As recently as 1980 Peru was ruled by the military, although in recent years a fragile democracy has taken root.

During the 1980s, Peru was plagued by the twin evils of cocaine production and insurgency. The Maoist Shining Path insurgent group controlled huge areas of the Peruvian countryside and operated with impunity in Lima at the height of its power. Atrocities were committed on both sides as the government sought to put down the rebellion. In the 1990's the administration of Japanese-Peruvian mathematician Alberto Fujimori was successful in bringing the economy under control and in eliminating the terrorism of the Shining Path. The Shining Path's leader, Abimael Guzmán, was captured in Lima in 1992, and the group never recovered. Although he was re-elected in 2000, Fujimori was forced to flee to Japan in order to avoid being indicted for corruption.

In the run-off election, the people of Peru elected Alejandro Toledo, one of 16 children and a former shoeshine boy who also happens to be an indigenous native from the Andes. This marked the first time since Atahuallpa that the area of Peru was ruled by a non-European. The Toledo administration was also marked by several scandals, including everything from forging registration signatures to an illegitimate daughter. International observers, however, Toledo deserves some credit for sparking the country's economic growth. In June, 2006, Alan García Pérez, who had served as president from 1985 to 1990, was re-elected president. Updated: Apr 29, 2009.

INCA

The ancient and modern people of the Andes are often incorrectly referred to as the "Inca." In fact, only the kings and ruling family were referred to as Inca. The closest translation for the word "Inca" is "king," at least in the way the people of the ancient Andes used it. They called their empire "Tawantin-suyu." Updated: Jul 20, 2007.

Politics

The Republic of Peru operates as a presidential representative democratic republic and is based on a multi-party system, whereby the president (Alan García, as of 2010) is elected for a five year term and serves as both head of state and head of government. The legislative body is a 120-member elected unicameral Congress. Although it used to be a largely toothless body, it has seen a notable increase in powers in recent years and serves as an important counterbalance to the executive branch. The judiciary is independent of both the executive and legislative branches, and new efforts have been made to reform its notoriously obsolete and corruption-riddled practices.

Peru's modern political history has been more a series of personality showdowns and power struggles than an institution based on party platforms, though parties spring up and have maintained a prominent status since the 1950s.

Peru is in an ongoing state of democratization, but has struggled to achieve the development progress enjoyed by its neighboring countries. This is largely due to corruption and poor leadership, which renders the nation gravely impoverished and disposed to increased inequality. Peruvian politics have been continually compromised by corruption, with two of the last three presidents currently under investigation.

Remnants of the first major disappointment still linger after the erratic presidency of Alberto Fujimori, who was elected in 1990. Though the early years of his term looked hopeful and inspired a dramatic economic turnaround and a significant reduction in guerrilla activity, the president's increasing reliance on harsh authoritarian measures and economic decline in the late 1990s spawned rising dissatisfaction, contributing to its rapid decline. Fujimori resigned from office in 2000, fleeing to his native Japan as charges of diverting vast government revenues closed in on him. He later returned to South America and based himself in Chile during the 2006 Peruvian elections in an attempt to clear his reputation, but was quickly taken into custody by authorities.

Alejandro Toledo, García's immediate predecessor and the first democratically elected Peruvian president of indigenous descent, also failed to make good on promises to meet the needs of the poor and bring the country up to speed in terms of globalization. Topping off his apparent inability to make any sort of progress, he is still under investigation for nasty scandals exposed during his term as president.

The presidential election of 2006 saw the return of García who, after serving a less than impressive presidential term during the turbulent 1980s, returned to office with promises of social reform and major economic improvements. Thus far the government led by García seems far more interested in promoting neo-liberal strategies such as free trade, than in adopting policies aimed at reducing poverty and advancing the UN's Millennium Development Goals.

In the 2006 election, populist candidate Ollanta Humala showed greater interest in pro-poor policies and campaigned on the premise of bringing about a "revolution for the poor." García, however, cited Humala's radical rhetoric and open support of Venezuela's leftist president Hugo Chávez as dangerous for the independence of the nation and took the seat.

Poverty has been further exacerbated by the diversion of much needed national resources to deal with internal conflict caused by rebel groups such as the Maoist Shining Path and the Tupac Amaru Revolutionary Movement (MRTA). Though huge progress in curbing violence was made during Fujimori's presidency, the campaign was expensive and sporadic insurgencies have since plagued the nation. Drug trafficking and drug-related crime also remains a problem in Peru and involvement is often attributed to former members of these revolutionary groups. Updated: Oct 26, 2007.

Peru Quick Facts

Area: 1,285,216 sq km (496,224 sq. mi)

Population: 29,907,003

Capital: Lima

Religion: Roman Catholic 81%; Evangelical 12.5%, other 3.3%; unspecified or none 2.9%

Languages: Spanish and Quechua (official); Aymara, and a large number of minor Amazonian languages

Literacy: 92.9%

Life Expectancy: 71

Currency: Nuevo Sol (PEN)

GDP Per Capita: U.S. $8,600

Industry: mining of metals, petroleum, fishing, textiles, clothing, food processing.

Agriculture: coffee, cotton, sugarcane, rice; poultry; fish.

Exports: fish and fish products, gold, copper, zinc, crude petroleum and by-products.

Electricity: Peru uses a 220v system. Updated: Jul 06, 2010.

Economy

When the Incas came to the region of Peru in the 15th century, they found several small tribes engaged in basic crop cultivation, notably corn and cotton. When the Incas conquered the region, they added limited mining and other agricultural practices to the region. When the Spanish arrived in 1531, they defeated the Inca Empire and established their own rule in the region. Using native labor, they greatly increased mining operations. The city of Lima was founded in 1535, in part, as a port city from which gold and silver could be shipped back to Spain.

During the colonial and republican eras, the economy of Peru remained based on mining, agriculture and fishing. In the 1840s, it was discovered that there were great deposits of saltpeter (in the form of eons' worth of accumulated bird guano) on some islands off the coast of Peru. The guano made excellent fertilizer and saltpeter is an essential ingredient for explosives. Harvesting the guano brought in a great deal of revenue for Peru. The islands were so rich that Spain seized them in 1864, but the Peruvians eventually drove them off. By 1874 almost all of the accumulated guano had been harvested.

In the 1980's, Peru's economy was in dire shape, and the inflation rate was skyrocketing. President Alberto Fujimori instituted several reforms and encouraged foreign investment, and in the 1990's the economy stabilized. From 1994 to 1997, the economy did particularly well, and GDP increased dramatically. After a few years of stagnation, the economy is again growing under the fiscally sound policies of successive administrations.

Today, Peru's economy is very diversified. Mining, fishing, metals, textiles, food, chemicals and tourism are all important sectors of their growing economy. Peru's main exports include coffee, minerals and fish. The US, China and Great Britain are Peru's largest trading partners.

Tourism is a steadily growing and increasingly important part of Peru's economy. The ruins of Machu Picchu, Cusco, Lima as well as the Amazonian and Andean mountaineering expeditions have made Peru one of South America's top tourism draws, especially now that the Shining Path threat is no longer an issue. Updated: Jul 20, 2007.

Population

Peru has a population of nearly 30 million. The annual growth rate of the population is reported to be 1.19 percent in 2010. The population is fairly young —28.5 percent of the people are estimated to be under the age of 15. Ethnicity is divided into four main groups: Amerindian (45 percent), *mestizo* or mixed (37 percent), white (15 percent) and other, including those of African, Japanese and Chinese descent (3 percent). Updated: Jul 06, 2010.

Language

Spanish was brought to Peru in the 16th Century by the conquistadors and today it is the most widely spoken language, spoken in most cities and towns. The majority of Peruvians speak at least some Spanish. English is not common, although most tourism professionals do speak English. Various dialects of Quechua are spoken across Peru, particularly in the Andean regions. Some of these forms are very markedly different from one another. The use of Quechua has been declining over the past century, although there are some initiatives underway in some areas to bring it back into the classroom, to maintain traditions. Aymara is spoken largely in the Lake Titicaca area, in and around Puno. Updated: Jul 16, 2007.

SPANISH, QUECHUA AND AYMARA

In April 2006, two Peruvian congresswomen from Cusco proclaimed that they would communicate only in Quechua during plenary sessions in congress. Thus another salvo had been fired in Peru's century's old struggle in the use of language to determine national identity and culture. Since 1975, Peru's constitution has recognized Quechua and Aymara along with Spanish as official languages of the Republic. However, since Spain's conquest of South America, Spanish has served as the dominant language of Peru, after the conquistadors excluded all indigenous languages from cultural and political discourse. Despite this, a significant portion of minorities (estimates range up to ten million) are very proudly bilingual, speaking some strain of Quechua or Aymara.

The word "Quechua" is used to denote both a people and a wide variety of dialects that pre-date the Incan empire by at least a millennium. Peru itself can lay claim to being the birthplace of Quechua, which then became the lingua franca of trade throughout the Andes. But the language of Quechua itself has at least forty separate dialects that have evolved with wide variations according to geography. Indeed, within Peru, northern Quechua and southern Quechua can not use their respective languages to communicate.

A commonly held belief has evolved that the Cusco Quechua is the most authentic and complete Quechua, but some historians argue that was more due to Cusco being the seat of the Incan empire which arose in the early 15th century. It mandated Quechua as the official language of the realm, though the Incans tolerated the use of other idioms. Ironically, it was primarily the Spanish who actually spread the use of Cusco Quechua, co-opting it as a tool for mainting order, even while curtailing its ability to serve the needs of its native speakers.

Quechua words that have become incorporated into the English language through Spanish include: coca, condor, gaucho, jerky, llama, potato, puma, and quinoa. Huttese, the language of the Huts in the Star Wars series, is largely taken from Quechua. Updated: Jul 20, 2007.

Religion

When the Spanish arrived in the region in the early 1530s and set about conquering the Inca Empire, they brought their Catholicism with them. Churches and cathedrals sprang up in every new Spanish settlement. During the colonial period, the mendicant orders—the Dominicans, Franciscans, and Augustinians—were prominent in colonial Peru's society. Today, many important cities dating from the colonial period have cathedrals, monasteries and squares dedicated to San Francisco and San Agustín, perpetuating this colonial legacy.

Before the arrival of the Spanish, the native Andeans had a complex pantheon of deities that they worshiped. The greatest of the Inca deities was Vira Cocha, and some early Spanish missionaries saw in Vira Cocha an embodiment of their own Christian God (while other missionaries saw him as Satan incarnate). For a fascinating look at pre-Columbian Andean religion, check out The Huarochiri Manuscript, one of very few documents that deal with pre-Hispanic religious beliefs that survived the colonial era.

In 1586, Isabel Flores de Oliva was born in Lima. She would later adopt the name Rosa, because of her extreme beauty as a child. An extremely devout young woman, she refused to marry and eventually entered a Dominican convent. She was known for her acts of charity as well as extreme self-mortification, including constantly wearing a spiked crown, long fasts and sleeping on a bed full of stones, thorns and broken glass and pottery. Perhaps not surprisingly, she died at the young age of

Lori Berenson: American Behind Peruvian Bars

A panel of hooded military judges delivered the announcement through voice-distorting microphones. Their verdict; guilty as charged. Twenty-six-year-old Lori Berenson's fate was sealed. She was sentenced to life in prison on January 11, 1996 for treason against the fatherland, Peru.

Lori Berenson grew up the daughter of university professors in New York, attending high school with Jennifer Aniston and Cher's daughter, Chastity Bono. But eventually this upper-middle class girl would trade in her anthropology classes for social causes. Berenson dropped out of MIT and headed to Central America where she picked up a different kind of education, losing friends to the brutality of El Salvador's National Guard and working with the Committee in Solidarity with the People of El Salvador (CISPES) and the Salvadoran Popular Forces of Liberation.

Her curiosity about different cultures eventually led her to Peru in 1994. Her traveling companion was Pacifico Castrellon. He was deeply involved in the Tupac Amaru Revolutionary Movement (MRTA), one of the most wanted and watched terrorist groups in Peru. Berenson would later claim he was a Panamanian whom she met by chance in an art gallery in Panama City. Castrellon would claim their trip to Peru was arranged by the MRTA rebels and on their way to Peru they met with MRTA leader Néstor Cerpa in Ecuador.

In Peru, Berenson leased a large house in the suburbs of Lima with Castrellon. This house would be the headquarters for the MRTA, and a storing place for seven automatic rifles with over 8,000 rounds of ammunition, 100 hand grenades and over 2,000 sticks of dynamite. Berenson claimed she knew nothing of this. She also claimed that she knew nothing of the members' involvement with the MRTA who lived in her house. In August 1995, she moved out of the house, and rented her own apartment in Lima. Guards say they do not recall seeing any MRTA members enter her new residence, and her activity appeared to be normal.

Berenson was able to obtain assignments from two U.S. publications, Modern Times and Third World Viewpoint, to work as a freelance journalist. She secured appropriate press credentials in Lima. However, Berenson actually never wrote anything for these publications, and some think she set up these assignments as a cover for what she was really doing—terrorist activities.

On November 30, 1995, Berenson was arrested along with Nancy Gilvonio, the wife of the MRTA leader Cerpa, while riding a bus in Lima after leaving Peru's Congress. The day after her arrest, Berenson's house was raided by security forces and a coded floor plan of Congress allegedly sketched by Berenson, along with a forged Peruvian election ID card bearing her photo were among the evidence seized.

Thirteen months later, Cerpa led a takeover of the Japanese Ambassaor's Lima residence. The MRTA rebels held 72 hostages for four months. They demanded freedom for hundreds of imprisoned comrades, with Berenson being number three on their list.

After Berenson's original trial in 1996, she was retried under lesser charges, due to international pressure. She was found guilty of collaboration. In prison, Berenson was subjected to horrific living conditions and became chronically ill. She was eventually moved to a lower elevation prison where her health problems seemed to improve.

In 2003, she married Anibal Apari, a paroled MRTA member whom she met when both were serving time at Yanamayo prison. Berenson currently spends her days working in the prison bakery and speaking out against human rights violations.

"I have nothing but love for the Latin American and Peruvian people. I've been in jail many years now because of my beliefs, but I still have great hopes and I'm still convinced that there will be a future of justice for the people of Peru and all humanity."

Berenson's case went to the Inter-American Court of Human Rights, based in Costa Rica, in 2002. Even though she experienced many injustices during her trials, such as double jeopardy and a lack of due process, the court upheld the second ruling of the Peruvian Supreme

Court. Former U.S. Ambassador to Peru, Dennis Jett, said the reason is simple: "She isn't innocent."

In May 2010, Berenson was released from prison on parole. The conditions of her release require her to stay in Peru until 2015, when her prison term is set to expire. Protesters have gathered daily since then outside her apartment in the Lima neighborhood of Miraflores.
Updated: Jul 23, 2010.

31, and her funeral was attended by all of the city leaders of Lima. Many miracles have been attributed to her, and she was canonized in 1671 as Saint Rose of Lima. She is the patroness of the Americas as well as Lima, which remembers her with a holiday on August 30. St. Martin of Porras (1579-1639) was also born in Lima, and St. Turibius of Mongrovejo (1538-1606), although born in Spain, was Archbishop of Lima from 1579 until his death.

Over the centuries, Spanish priests managed to stamp out most of the traces of native religion, but some structures and beliefs remained. Cusco's temples were built over but not totally destroyed, and some of the foundations can still be seen. In a religious melding process known as "syncretism," some churches combine elements of native religion with Christianity.

Today, Peru is still predominantly Roman Catholic (about 75 percent) but there are other religions as well. Mission-oriented groups such as the Church of Latter Day Saints (Mormons) and Jehovah's Witnesses are growing, and there are communities of Muslims, Buddhists, Hindus, and other faiths. The reclusive Los Israelitas del Nuevo Pacto Universal (Israelites of the New Universal Pact) often put forth candidates for major elections from their compound in the hills near Huarochirí, but little is known about them and their mysterious founder, Ezequiel Ataucusi ("the illuminated one"). One of their candidates, Javier Noriega, was elected to the Peruvian congress.

Peru is often a destination for new age spiritual pilgrims. Shamans (both real and fake) in the Amazon offer experiences with *ayahuasca*, a hallucinogenic vine that is often credited with giving visions. Cusco is also considered a center for new age "energy." Updated: Jul 06, 2010.

Holidays and Fiestas

January 1: New Year's Day (Año Nuevo).

January 6: Epiphany.

February 2: Virgin de la Candelaria, Puno. The Virgin de la Candelaria is the Patron Saint of Puno. The statue of the Virgin is paraded around the town accompanied by people of all ages dancing.

Carnival: Celebrated the weekend leading up to Ash Wednesday, Carnival is the ultimate party in Latin America, and in Peru it is celebrated in most of the Andes. A popular custom is to throw water at people. As a gringo you are likely to be a popular target! In Cajamarca, a Carnival queen is elected and there are competitions of friendship and song.

Semana Santa: (Easter / Holy Week). Semana Santa is celebrated all over Peru, but Ayacucho is a special place to spend this period because it hosts one of the most important Holy Week festivals in all of Peru. In the days leading up to Easter Sunday, Ayacucho transforms into a city of flowered streets, processions, fireworks, dancing, and more.

May 1: Labor Day

Corpus Christi: (May / June). This Catholic celebration is celebrated fairly widely in the Andean regions.

June 24: Inti Raymi, Cusco. In June, Cusco turn into one big party in the period preceding this important Incan festival (see box).

June 29: Day of San Pedro and San Pablo. Peruvian holiday.

July 16: Virgen del Carmen, Paucartambo, near Cusco. This celebration is in honor of the Virgen del Carmen, the patron saint of Paucartambo. Folk stories are acted out by local dance groups and there are processions through the steets to scare away demons.

July 28-29: Independence (Fiestas Patrias). Independence day is an important public holiday for Peruvians, with many traveling during this period, and corresponding price hikes for accommodation. In Lima there are both military and civilian parades. Independence Day itself is July 28, while most of the celebrations take place on July 29.

August 30: Saint Rose of Lima.

October 8: Battle of Angamos, commemorating a decisive Chilean victory on this date in 1879, during the War of the Pacific.

October 18-28: Señor de los Milagros (Lord of the Miracles). This is a very important Peruvian celebration for the Patron Saint of Lima, with huge processions through the streets, led by a select few who carry the statue.

November 1: Todos los Santos (All Saints Day).

November 2: Dia de los Muertos (Day of the Dead). Offerings of food, particularly of bread shaped like peope and animals are made for the dead.

December 8: Day of the Immaculate Conception. Although this festival is celebrated throughout Peru, Chivay is perhaps the most interesting place to observe this festival.Men dress in drag and pretend to snatch the women!

December 24-25: Christmas. Celebrations start on 24th. Families will gather to celebrate together with a big meal on December 24 and will spend Christmas together. December 25 is a national holiday.

December 31: Año Viejo (New Year's Eve).

Culture

The arts have played a prominent role in Peruvian history and culture, coloring the nation with a wide variety of styles that can be seen across its regions in everything from literature and architecture to painting, crafts and dance.

While Spanish influence cannot be denied, the indigenous heritage of Peru is one of the richest in South America, with traces of Inca tradition prominent throughout Peruvian culture. All types of art, from architecture to handicrafts, are a unique fusion of Spanish and indigenous forms and styles. Descendants of the Quechua and Aymara peoples who populate much of the Andean highlands have preserved

Inti Raymi

Every year in June, there is an opportunity to witness Inti Raymi, or the Festival of the Sun, a beautiful exhibition of Peruvian culture and tradition.

The Inti Raymi festival originated as a celebration to honor the Sun God as insurance for good crops in the harvest season. Each Winter Solstice, when the sun is farthest from the earth, ancient Incas would gather out of fear of the lack of sun, beseeching its return. In 1572, the colonial Spaniards banned the tradition because of its pagan rituals.

The festivities were forced underground, but today it is considered one of the largest festivals in South America, second only to the Carnival of Rio. Every year, hundreds of thousands of people gather in Cusco for the weeklong festivities. From live music to street vendors to daytime fairs, the festival consists of different daily activities. Free concerts, put on by the best Peruvian musical troupes, are held in the Plaza de Armas nightly.

All activities lead up the June 24, the climax of the festival and the actual day of Inti Raymi. Scientifically speaking, the winter solstice begins June 21, but Peruvians follow the Pacha Unachaq, a sundial used by the Incas.

Over 500 actors are selected to enact the day-long ceremony. It is considered a great honor to be cast as Sapa Inca or his wife, as they are the two main characters for the day. Ceremonies commence in the Qorikancha square in front of the Santo Domingo church, which is built over the Temple of the Sun. Here, Sapa Inca calls on blessings from the sun. Afterwards, he is carried on a golden throne to Sacsayhuamán, a fortress in the hills above Cusco. Thousands of people await his arrival, upon which he climbs the sacred altar. A white llama is sacrificed to ensure the fertility of the earth.

At sunset, strawstacks are set on fire and revelers dance around them to honor the Empire of the Four Wind Directions. The ceremony ends with the celebrants returning to Cusco, watching as Sapa Inca and Mama Occla are carried on their golden thrones. And so the sun's new year begins! Updated: Jul 23, 2007.

and continue to emulate the folklore and traditions of their ancestors, while other regions have incorporated these customs into a more modern context. As a result, Peruvian culture enjoys a vibrant and eclectic mixture of old and new. Updated: Apr 23, 2010.

PAINTING AND SCULPTURE
Spanish colonization brought European art into the New World and its influence spread rapidly throughout Peru. Religious paintings were used to teach Christianity to the natives. By the 17th century, native artists began combining the imported artistic influences with local tradition and style, leading to the Cusco School of the 17th and 18th centuries. The Cusco School was the most significant movement in Peru's art history, made up of mestizo painters and sculptors who produced countless depictions of religious figures adorned in gold. Artists of the era were largely influenced by Spanish and late-Gothic works.

During the 19th century, artists began following the lead of the Mexican muralists, which led to a new Peruvian movement that incorporated Andean accents with depictions of the life and hardships of the nation's indigenous. An indigenous movement led by painter José Sabogal (1888-1956) in the 20th century sought to integrate pre-Columbian influence with more contemporary Peruvian style and tradition. The majority of these works depicted indigenous women and incorporated ancient motifs from weavings and pottery. By the mid 20th century, artists began experimenting with abstract art, though works today still maintain pre-Columbian and Peruvian styles. Updated: Apr 23, 2010.

ARCHITECTURE
While much of Peruvian architecture is of Creole style (a blend of Spanish and indigenous influences), there is also a prominent Moorish influence that originated in North Africa, traveled to Spain and was then brought to the Americas. Of course Peru's numerous pre-Columbian ruins, including Machu Pichu and Moche, are also a significant part of the country's architectural heritage. Updated: Apr 23,2010.

CRAFTS
Peru is a haven for folk art and high quality handcrafts, boasting one of the largest variety of arts and crafts in the world. Folk art is not only a fundamental activity for the cultural identity of Peru, but a way of life for many communities. A diverse array of brightly colored textiles—particularly from the highlands in Ayacucho and Huancayo—depict local Andean and coastal life, with large graphic pre-Columbian shapes of animals and indigenous life, with some hints of Spanish influence. Pottery, woodwork, woven baskets, worked gold and silver jewelry as well as hand-tooled leather goods are also prevalent across the country. The Paracas region is renowned for its long tradition of unique weavings. Updated: Apr 23, 2010.

MUSIC
Music in Peru presents an eclectic mix of sounds, beats, and styles with roots in the Andes, Spain, Africa and elsewhere. Much of the country's musical influences and instruments can be traced back to pre-Incan times, particularly the panpipes, flutes and drums that are synonymous with Andean music. Archeological discoveries show that music has been played in what is now Peru as far back as 10,000 years ago.

Native music consists primarily of strummed string instruments reminiscent of mandolins and Spanish guitars, including the *charanga*—Peru's national instrument. Though once considered music of the rural poor, the resurgence of the indigenous movement in the art world and the post-revolutionary environment after 1959 made native music and the charango popular among performers across classes. Music in the Andes has maintained much of its native tradition, incorporating Spanish touches with stringed instruments and vocals. The *Huayno* is a soulful, chant-like style of music most popular in the southern Andean region. It spread from the interior mountainous regions to the coast in the mid-20th century, taking off throughout Peru and other Andean nations.

In the Arequipa region, traditional Andean music is heavily accented with Spanish melodies, particularly in the *Yaraví* style, characterized by sad and soulful vocals accompanied by a Spanish guitar. Music in Puno, Cusco and surrounding regions is similar in its soulful, melancholic style, but often incorporates violins and other stringed instruments into traditional Inca rhythms. Heading into the Central Andes, music becomes more lively and upbeat, particularly that of the *Huaylas* style around the Huanuco, Huaraz region.

Coastal music—*la música criolla*—exhibits a myriad of rhythms with a generally livelier feel than those of the Andes, with beats rooted in traditional Spanish, African and Gypsy music. A significant number of slaves was brought to the Peruvian coast, which makes for a strong African cultural influence in the area. By the 1950s, Afro-Peruvian music began being recorded in earnest and incorporated the Spanish guitar, the *quijada* (an instrument made from the jawbone of a mule) and the *cajón* drum (a percussive wooden box). The *landó* and the *festejo* are two of the most popular forms of up-beat Afro-Peruvian music, often played to accompany frenetic dances.

Rock music from North America was introduced in the mid-1950s, paving the way for the first Peruvian rock bands. The 1960's saw new trends, including the raw sounds of garage rock. Rock music saw a lull in the late 1960s and 70s during the reign of a military dictatorship, which considered the music alienating and banned most concerts. Though rock bands lost momentum, several were able to endure in an underground scene into the 1980s. Rock became more diversified in the 1990s, and bands slowly became recognized in the mainstream later in the decade. Today rock music enjoys a thriving scene in Peru and has even had some commercial success on the international stage. Updated: Jul 06, 2010.

MUSEUMS

Peru's museums showcase the diversity of the country's art and culture, its natural wonders and its long history.

Peru has some of the finest archeological museums in the world, displaying precious and beautiful artifacts from the many ancient cultures that called this land home. In Lima, the Museo Rafael Larco, Museo de Oro and Muse de la Nación are must-sees. Outside the capital, Lambayeque's Museo Bruning Museo de las Tumbas Reales are extraordinary, while a number of archeological museums in Cusco display Inca artifacts.

The finest art museum in the country is Lima's Museo de Arte, though there are many museums focusing on colonial art in Lima, Arequipa and Cusco. For the nature-minded, the Javier Prado and Ricardo Palma natural history museums give a worthy introduction to Peru's geology and biodiversity. Updated: Jul 23, 2007.

DANCE

As with music in pre-Columbian Peru, so too was dance assimilated into the undertakings of farming, hunting and combat. There is the *llamerada*, for example, a dance that imitates the act of llama herding as a means of ensuring the successful realization of the task that is still performed in parts of Peru. The symbolic significance of these dances is similar to the "sun dances" of Native North Americans, because both cultures consider dance as a religious ritual with the ability to improve quality of life.

Dances that can trace their origins to pre-Columbian times include the *huayno*, the most representative of Andean folkloric dances. Quite possibly, it began as a ritual dance performed at funerals, but now serves as a purely-celebratory function in the community. The dance is performed by couples wearing embroidered vests and brightly colorful dresses—the national hues of yellow, red, and blue predominate—who circle the musicians while doing abrupt spins, hops, and tap-like movements to keep time with the drums, harps, guitars, and violins. Some variations include wind instruments such as trumpets and saxophones.

The *Marinera* is Peru's most famous dance, a *pas de deux* in which both partners elegantly wave silk handkerchiefs and execute graceful and precise movements to the accompaniment of Spanish guitars, a Creole *cajón* and bugles. The barefoot woman, with her flowing, pleated, and striped skirt, marks the rhythm and guides her male partner, who is sharply attired with a wide-brimmed hat. The name refers to the coastal region where it originated, and the dance traditions of Spain, Africa, and indigenous Peru all contribute to a dance that is associated with national pride. Updated: Jul 23, 2007.

THEATER

There are several theatrical traditions in Peru, which have at times both conflicted and merged with one another. This has resulted in provocative contemporary work that has received worldwide acclaim.

Before conquest and colonization, theater was religious ceremony, celebrating such deities as the sun god Inti in the festival of Inti Raymi. Following the Spanish conquest, it was banned by the Catholic Church due to its pagan ceremonies. Ironically, the Church incorporated many pagan elements into its own religious pageants, despite banning many rituals. The Inti Raymi celebration did not return until the 20th century, when a renewed appreciation of indigenous culture revived Inti Raymi as theater, proudly presented in the Quechua language. The show is performed in the city of Cusco, where a local is chosen to represent an Incan ruler, adorned with helmet-like feathered crown. The lucky actor bears a war hammer, and is born aloft in his throne to the town center, where rituals and prophecies initiate nine days of celebrations. Other religious festivals integrate elements of both the Catholic veneration of saints and the Virgin Mary with Andean ceremonial traditions and archetypes.

For its part, the Church introduced the theatrical-theological traditions of Old Spain to the New World, with the first play being performed in 1568 in Lima's Plaza de San Pedro. Over the centuries Peru secularized, allowing it to obtain wealthy patrons outside the Church. By the 20th century playwrights such as Sebastian Salazar Bondy and Enrique Solari Swayne brought literary prestige and social conscience to the Peruvian stage.

However, Peru's most highly-regarded contribution to the art of theater is the innovative company Yuyachkani. Formed in the early 1970's, Yuyachkani, heavily influenced by the modernist, avant-garde philosophy of European directors such as Peter Brook and Jerzy Grotowski and brought about a renewed focus on the actor as the catalyst for stirring the political and spiritual conscience of the audience. The group itself survived through Peru's volatile political and social history to serve as a sort of Greek chorus for the country. The company's name is derived from the Quechua expression for "I am thinking and I am remembering." The company has not been afraid to tackle some of the most socially-ravaged aspects of Peru, addressing issues of terrorism and social injustice through a style that is abstract yet accessible to all Peruvians. A production of Sophocles' *Antigone* performed in Quechua and Spanish serves a pointed commentary on the abuses of governmental power. The group's has influenced a generation of theatrical artists not only in Peru but also in neighboring Andean countries.

The active theater scenes in Lima, Cusco and other Peruvian cities offers visitors a wide range of creativity, from the classics to post-modern works. Notable theaters in Lima include the Teatro Municipal, the Centro Cultural de La Catolica, and the Teatro Britanico. Updated: Jul 23, 2007.

COMEDY

Peruvian comedy, at least in the post-colonial era, began in the 19th century with Manuel Ascensio Segura, a journalist and playwright whose work tweaked and satirized the institutions and customs of his society. Peruvian militarism was a frequent target of his work. He also poked fun at partisan politics, libelous journalism and Lima's provincialism. Though classified technically as "comedy," today Segura's work, like Molière's, is more likely to evoke a knowing approval from a sophisticated audience for the acuity of his observations rather than belly laughs.

In terms of humor for laughs as opposed to humor as social comentary, the comedy troupe Los Cómicos Ambulantes (The Walking Comics), has been making Peruvians laugh since the 1970's. It's a rag-tag, loosely assembled association of performers. Some had backgrounds as professional circus clowns, and others were simply naturally funny. They do great street theater, attracting crowds by parodying behavior and attitudes indigenous to cities like Lima and Cusco, where they call themselves the Incas of Laughter.

A turning point for Los Cómicos Ambulantes came when they were invited to perform on popular Peruvian talk shows such as Talking Straight and Between Us, where their perceptive pokes at Peruvians struck a chord with a popular audience. The result was their own programs, "The Walking Comics Show and The Kings of Laughter." As with American comedy shows such as Saturday Night Live, the show served as a launching pad for individual careers such as Kike and Lonchera. Other cast members did less well and wound up in poverty. In the meantime, local street performers and comedy troupes, such as La Banda del Choclito continue to amuse the local citizenry.

Yma Sumac-The Life of an Andean Princess

Singer Yma Sumac stands alone as the most famous Peruvian in the world. Only novelist Mario Vargas Llosa approaches a comparable degree of international recognition. Unlike Llosa, however, her cachet isn't highbrow art, but rather more pop culture kitsch. Appropriately, she is the only Peruvian with a star on the Hollywood Walk of Fame. She came into her own, globally, during the 1950s and could be described as a cross between the high art of Maria Callas and the high camp of Brazilian diva Carmen Miranda.

"Exoticism" and novelty songs were an ongoing selling point in the pre-Elvis era of American music. With her exotic Andean looks (she is reportedly a direct descendent of the last Incan king Atahualpa) and her four-and-a-half octave reach, Yma Sumac found her niche with a wide audience.

Yma Sumac was born in 1922 in Ichocán, Perú, with the name Zoila Augusta Emperatriz Chávarri del Castillo. Biographical data claims that she practiced singing by imitating the sounds of the many exotic birds of Peru. By the age of thirteen she was already singing before crowds of thousands, and her vocal range attracted the attention of the Minister of Education, who sent her and family to Lima so she could attend a Catholic boarding school. By 1942 she adopted the stage name Imma Sumack, later modified to Yma Sumac, and was singing on the radio. Years later a rumor spread that "Yma Sumac" was an anagram for "Amy Camus" and that she hailed from Brooklyn, to which Yma jokingly responded "Must all talent come from Brooklyn?"

During the Latin music boom of the 1940s she moved to New York and few years later was signed by Capitol Records. Working with such pop music legends as Billy May and Les Baxter, she hit the charts offering slick, Hollywoodized versions of Andean and South American folk tunes, as well as mambo songs in sync with the cha-cha-cha zeitgeist of the times. Her albums—now popularly sought after as pop and camp items—also featured covers of other people's novelty hits, such as "Wimoweh," also known as "The Lion Sleeps Tonight," but all arranged to showcase her famous bass-to-coloratura voice.

Her exotic allure, complete with elaborate "Incan Princess" costumes, attracted a lot of attention, and she appeared in major motion pictures such as "Secret of the Incas," which starred Charlton Heston and was filmed in her native Peru. She also recorded the song "I Wonder" for Walt Disney's "Sleeping Beauty."

Though her popularity peaked in the 1950s, she continued to perform in concert halls worldwide throughout the 1960s. She attempted to reach a new audience with a pop-rock album in 1971, and then returned to Peru in semi-retirement. She began to make a comeback in the 1980s, which included a turn in the Stephen Sondheim musical Follies in Long Beach, California, as well as recitals in New York and San Francisco.

But it wasn't until the late 1990s and early 2000s that a substantial interest was renewed in Yma Sumac's work, with her songs featured on the soundtracks to such movies as "Men with Guns," "The Big Lebowski," "Happy, Texas," "Ordinary Decent Criminal," "Confessions of a Dangerous Mind" and "The In-Laws."

Now living in Los Angeles, Yma Sumac receive the Orden del Sol (Order of the Sun) award in 2006 by the President of Peru, Alejandro Toledo, as well as the Jorge Basadre Medal by the Universidad Nacional de San Marcos. Her return to her native Peru was one of the biggest media events in the country's history.

Yma Sumac died on November 1, 2008 in Los Angeles. She was 86. Updated: Nov 05, 2008.

Social and Environmental Issues

SOCIO-ECONOMIC CLIMATE

In Peru, as in all Latin American countries, social issues revolve around the economy. The issue is intertwined with racial tension relating to Peru's colonial heritage. Eighty-two percent of the country is of either indigenous or of mixed indigenous-Spanish descent, while 15 percent of populace is Caucasian of purely Spanish heritage, yet that same 15 percent continues to make up the majority of Peru's upper-class with its attendant domination of industry and politics.

This, in turn, has led to ongoing civil unrest resulting from large-scale poverty and resentment among the mostly disenfranchised non-white majority. The tenions are further exacerbated by a lingering racism that originated in the arrival of the Spanish and pervades popular culture, such as in television shows and advertising, which presents Caucasian Peruvians as closer to an ideal of physical desirability.

This came to a head with the emergence of two separate radical factions during the early 1980's: the Shining Path, which was Maoist, and Túpac Amaru, which was Marxist-Leninist. Both organizations recruited among the poorest in Peru's rural areas and used violence and terror to achieve their aim of taking over the country. For some time it seemed that the Shining Path movement might succeed; at one point 60 percent of the country, mostly the countryside, was under its control.

Although the authoritarian regime of Alberto Fujimori largely ended the armed conflict in the country, the underlying tensions remain to this day. During the 2006 election, the candidacy of Ollanta Humala drew on the frustration of poor, indigenous Peruvians who felt they had not benefited from the economic growth of the Fujimori and Toledo years. Although Humala was defeated, the campaign demonstrated that significant socio-economic divisions remain.

GAY PERU

Throughout most of Latin America, notions of gender have been experiencing significant upheaval over the years. For example, despite traditional machista notions that men should be providers and physically strong, and women as obedient mothers and wives, over the last thirty years women who can afford it are now routinely obtaining education and

pursuing careers. Similarly, despite traditional homophobia, homosexuality was officially decriminalized in 1999, and the past decade has seen growing prominence for gay businesses along with a gay subculture in Lima, Arequipa, and other cities with both a large population and a notable urban culture.

However, while urban culture might be moderately gay-tolerant, it is still not gay-friendly and many men and women lead closeted, double lives. Within certain areas, such as theater or the arts, it is easier to be "out" than in business or politics. Many gays and lesbians chose not to come out to their families. Still, the anonymity of the Internet has facilitated the promotion of a gay culture, and visitors can check out websites such as www.gayperu.com for where they can safely find gay bars, clubs, hotels, and restaurants.

THE MACHU PICCHU VS YALE UNIVERSITY

CONTROVERSY

President Alan Garcia has been fortunate to seize upon a nationalist and patriotic issue, one especially relevant to Peru's indigenous population. The controversy surrounds relics removed by National Geographic explorer Hiram Bingham from Machu Picchu after his discovery of the historic city in 1912, and whether or not they should me repatriated to Peru. They have been residing at Yale University ever since Bingham brought them to the United States. Yale claims that the government of Peru legally signed off on the artifacts, which comprise everything from crockery to clay deities, while Peru maintains that Yale's custody of them was only for the sake of research and with the understanding that they would eventually be returned.

In the nearly one hundred years since Bingham's discovery, generations of Peruvians have lived and died without access to some of the most valuable tokens of their ancestral heritage. However, how much access they would have had if the items remained in Peru is an open question. In an investigative piece by Arthur Lubow in The New York Times, Lubow noted that "Peru's record in safeguarding archaeological treasures...is spotted with the traces of disappearing objects." For example, in 1979, literally hundreds of pieces of Incan and pre-Incan pieces went missing from the National Museum of Archaeology. In 1993 almost the entire gold collection from Cusco's Museo Inka disappeared. There is also the fact that, visually, much of what is in Yale's Peabody Museum is less interesting and less impressive than is on already on display on museums throughout Peru. Garcia is threatening to take up the issue, nonetheless, in an international court.

Environmental Issues

Peru has some of the richest and most abundant natural resources of any country in the world, but with the economic crises and political turmoil of the last several decade, the country's environment has been exploited more than it has been protected. As a result, Peru is experiencing panoply of ecological problems that have raised concerns of environmentalists around the world. These include air and water pollution, soil contamination and erosion as well as deforestation.

Industrial and vehicle emissions in Peru create over 26 metric tons of carbon dioxide a year, while in the rural areas, due to industrial, sewage, and petroleum-drilling waste, only 62 percent of the population has access to pure drinking water. Overgrazing in the sierras and the coasts, meanwhile, has brought about soil erosion.

Half of Peru is forested, but experiences a deforestation rate of 0.35 to 0.5 percent that is largely a consequence of subsistence farming. Due to a squatter's law, migrant farmers are allowed to obtain possession of public land if they can prove they have lived in it for at least five years, and so many forests are cut down for farms. The greater degree of deforestation, however, is wrought by commercial logging, both legal and illegal, as well as mining, petroleum drilling, and road development.

Most of the logging in Peru going on is illegal; estimates are that up to 95 percent of the country's mahogany is unlawfully cut and sold, much of it from national parks and federal reserves. With law enforcement agencies underfunded and vulnerable to bribery, almost no commercial loggers are either charged or prosecuted.

Then there is the deforestation brought about by the oil extraction industry. In 2005 a contract was granted to the China National Petroleum Corporation in the Madre de Dios region of southern Peru, an area that is home to more then 10% of the world's bird species. Coca production, both legal and illegal, has taken its toll as forests have been cleared in order to make way for coca plantations.

Gold mining also contributes substantially, since the process involves destroying river banks and clearing floodplain forests. Furthermore, this creates an incentive to bring independent miners who then cut trees for firewood and housing. Mercury is a necessary component of the mining process, but it poisons the soil and water.

A very controversial construction project in Peru's Amazon basin is the proposed construction of a superhighway across the jungle, the country to Brazil. There are concerns that the road will essentially urbanize everything along its path, endangering all flora and fauna in the area.

Peru has up to 2,937 varieties of amphibians, birds, mammals, and reptiles, and 17,144 species of plants. Currently, Peru's endangered species list includes 46 mammal varieties including the yellow-tailed woolly monkey and the black spider monkey, 64 types of birds including the tundra peregrine falcon and the white-winged guan, and 653 categories of plants. Many of these are endemic, that is, they are native only to Peru. There are a number of reptiles at risk as well, including the hawksbill turtle, the leatherback turtle, the spectacled caiman as well as the Orinoco and American crocodiles. Updated: Jul 06, 2010.

Travel Insurance

To protect yourself financially while visiting Peru, travel insurance is a very good idea. Travel insurance will reduce or remove your financial costs from medical bills, lost or stolen items and unexpected cancellations incurred while traveling.

There are many sources for travel insurance in Peru, all offering a variety of plans. There are differences in deductibles, benefit caps, coverage for stolen goods and exclusions for certain risky activities. Once you know what you will be doing in Peru, travel insurance plans can be crafted to meet your needs.

MEDICAL INSURANCE
Unexpected medical expenses can be a

huge cost, so your travel insurance policy in Peru should include coverage for medical care. There are three things to look for in medical coverage; the deductible (the part of the claim that insurance will not cover), the ceiling or cap (the maximum amount the insurance company will pay) and provision for medical evacuation, should you need special treatment back home. As a general rule, Peruvian hospitals will want payment up front; in rural areas, they will ask for cash, rather than a credit card. You should get a receipt for any payment you make, as you will need this to get the reimbursement from your insurer.

Before you leave, check which activities are covered and which are not. In many insurance policies, medical costs sustained as a result of rock climbing, mountaineering and other adventure sports common in Peru are not covered.

LOST OR STOLEN ITEMS
If you are going to bring expensive gadgets like laptops, cameras or smartphones with you to Peru, it's probably a good idea to get some coverage for your possessions. Bare-bones policies do not usually cover lost or stolen goods, but if you're willing to pay a bit more, you can find policies that will protect you from such losses.

If something of yours is stolen, you should go to a police station within 24 hours to get a written report. You will need to submit this report in order to get a reimbursement.

INSURANCE TIPS
Keep these travel insurance tips in mind when you are heading to Peru:
* Always carry the phone number for your 24 hour insurance hotline. It is also wise to give a copy of your plan to someone back home and to keep the information saved in an E-mail account.
* Carry a list of your prescriptions with you, ideally translated into Spanish.
* Also have a list identifying any major allergies you have.

Visas
Citizens of the following countries can travel to Peru for up to 90 days without a tourist visa.

South America: Argentina, Bolivia, Brazil, Colombia, Chile, Ecuador, Guyana, Paraguay, Surinamés, Uruguay, Venezuela.

North America: Canada, USA, Mexico.

Central America: Antigua & Barbuda, Bahamas, Barbados, Belize, Costa Rica, Dominicana, Dominican Republic, El Salvador, Grenada, Guatemala, Haiti, Honduras, Jamaica, Nicaragua, Panama, Saint Kitts & Nevis, Saint Lucia, St. Vincent & the Grenadines, Trinidad & Tobago.

Europe: Germany, Andorra, Austria, Belgium, Belarus, Bulgaria, Cyprus, Croatia, Denmark, Slovenia, Slovakia, Spain, Estonia, Russian Federation, Finland, France, United Kingdom & Northern Ireland, Greece, Hungary, Ireland, Iceland, Italy, Latvia, Liechtenstein, Lithuania, Luxemburg, Macedonia, Malta, Moldavia, Monaco, Norway, Netherlands, Poland, Portugal, Czech Republic, Serbia & Montenegro, San Marino, Vatican City, Sweden, Switzerland, Ukraine.

Asia: Brunei Darussalam, Philippines, Indonesia, Israel, Japan, Malaysia, Republic of Korea, Singapore, Thailand, Hong Kong, Taiwan. Oceanía: Australia, Fiji, Cook Islands, Marshall Islands, Salomón Islands, Kiribati, Micronesia, Nauru, Niue, New Zealand, Palau, Papua New Guinea, Samoa, Tonga, Tuvalu, Vanuatu.

Africa: South Africa

All citizens of countries NOT listed are required to obtain a travel visa prior to entering Peru. These can take a few weeks to process.

Passports are required of all countires regardless of visa status. If you are entering Peru for business, or to study at a Peruvian university, you must obtain a buiness or student visa regardless of the country you are from. Business and student visas are only good for 90 days, but renewals are allowed and are determined upon an individual basis.

All visitors entering via plane or border crossings can stay in the country will recieve a tourist card vaild for either 30, 60 or 90 days. It depends upon where you enter the country and what that border crossing offers, but your best bet is to ask for the 90 day card, otherwise you may have to exit the country and re-enter again. You must also get a new tourist card upon each reentry and always present it when you exit the country.

If your tourist card is stolen or lost, a new one needs to be obtained at Migraciones

Av. España 700 and Av Huaraz, Brena, Lima from 9 a.m. to 1 p.m. Monday through Friday. Otherwise, when you exit the country you will be fined.

BUSINESS VISAS

Business travelers are issued three-month visas and they must be renewed quarterly at the Oficina de Migraciones in Lima. Your passport must have a remaining validity of at least the length of the trip.

Application process:
- Fill out the visa form
- Obtain a letter from your employer indicating the motive and the length of your stay
- You must gather one passport picture, copy of the flight ticket, money order payable to Consulado General del Peru for US $ 30.
- Bring it to the nearest Peruvian consulate office, or if you are mailing your application, you must send a FedEx pre-paid envelope with your name and complete address to return the documents.

STUDENT VISAS

Students are issued visas for three-month stays through a Peruvian Consulate in their home country. Passports must have a remaining validity of at least the length of the trip.

Application Process:
- Fill out the visa form
- Obtain a letter from your university or educational institution in Peru, indicating the motive and the time of your stay.
- You'll need to gather one passport picture, copy of the flight ticket, money order payable to Consulado General del Peru for $30.
- Bring your application to the nearest Peruvian Consulate, or if this procedure is done by mail, you have to send a FedEx pre-paid envelope with your name and complete address to return the documents.
- Once you have been enrolled in a Peruvian school, Student visas may be renewed at the Oficina de Migraciones.

IMMIGRATION

Duty Free: When leaving Peru, any one person is allowed to exit with 400 cigarettes, or 50 cigars or 500 grams of tobacco, three liters of Alcohol, new articles for personal use or gifts up to value of $300.

Archeological Items and Art: The government of Peru prohibits the exportation of archaeological artifacts and colonial art. These restrictions include archaeological material from the pre-Hispanic cultures and certain ethnological materials from the colonial period of Peru. Many countries outside of Peru including the USA and UK have the authority to take action if you are found with any of these possessions.

Embassies & Consulates

Argentina
28 de Julio 828, Lima, Tel: 51-1-433-3381/ 9966 / 4545, Fax: 51-1-433-0769, E-mail: embajada@terra.com.pe

Bolivia
Calle Los Castaños 235 San Isidro, Lima 27, Tel: 51-1-442-3836 / 51-1-440-2095, Fax: 51-1-440-2298, E-mail: jemis@emboli.firstcom.com.pe

Brazil
Ave José Pardo, 850, Miraflores, Lima 18, Tel: 51-1-421-5660 / 5650, Fax: 51-1-445-2421, E-mail: embajada@embajadabrasil.org.pe, URL: www.embajadabrasil.org.pe

Canada
Libertad 130, Miraflores Lima 18, Tel: 51-1-444-4015, Fax: 51-1-242-4050, E-mail: lima@dfait-maeci.gc.ca, URL: http://geo.international.gc.ca/latin-america/peru/

Chile
Javier Prado Oeste 790, San Isidro, Lima, Tel: 51-1-221-2221 / 2080 / 2081, Fax: 51-1-221-1258, E-mail: emchile@terra.com.pe

Colombia
Av. Jorge Basadre 1580 San Isidro, Lima, Tel: 51-1-442-9648 / 441-0530 ext. 15 or 16, Fax: 51-1-441-6922

Costa Rica
Calle Baltazar La Torre 828, San Isidro, Lima, Tel: 51-1-264-2999 / 2711, Fax: 51-1-264-2799, E-mail: Costarica@terra.com.pe

Cuba
Coronel Portillo No. 110, San Isidro, Lima, Tel: 51-1-264-2053, Fax: 51-1-264-4525, E-mail: embcuba@chavin.rcp.net.pe

INTRO & INFO

Dominican Republic
Av. 28 de Julio 779, Piso 2 letra F, San Isidro, Lima, Tel: 51-1-433-2856

Ecuador
Las Palmeras 356, San Isidro, Lima, Tel: 51-1-212-4171, Fax: 51-1-422-0711, E-mail: embajada@mecuadorperu.org.pe, URL: www.mecuadorperu.org.pe

Finland
Av. Victor Andrés Belaunde, 147 Edificio Real Tres, Oficina 502, Centro Empresarial Real San Isidro, Lima, Postal address: Embajada de Finlandia Apartado Postal 270155 Lima 27 Peru, Tel: 51-1-222-4466 / 4480 / 1487, Fax: 51-1-222-4463, Email: embajada@finlandiaperu.org.pe, URL: barrioperu.terra.com.pe/finlandia and www. finlandiaperu.org.pe

France
Avenida Arequipa 3415, San Isidro, Lima, Tel: 51-1-215-8400, Fax: 51-1-215-8410, E-mail: france.embajada@ambafrance-pe.org, URL: www.ambafrance-pe.org/

Germany
Avda. Arequipa 4210, Miraflores, Tel: 51-1-212-5016, Fax: 51-1-422-6475, E-mail: kanzlei@embajada-alemana.org.pe, URL: www.embajada-alemana.org.pe

Greece
Av. Principal 19, Urbanización Sta. Catalina, La Victoria, Lima, Tel: 51-1-476-1548 / 1643, Fax: 51-1-476-1329

Guatemala
Calle Inca Ripac 309, Jesús María, Lima, Tel: 51-1-460-2078 / 462-0920, Fax: 51-1-463-5885, E-mail: embperu@minex.gob.gt

Honduras
Ave. Las Camelias 491. Oficina 202, San Isidro, Lima, Tel: 51-1-422-8111 / 8112, Fax: 51-1-221-1677

India
Av. Salaverry 3006, Magdalena del Mar - Lima 17, Tel: 51-1-460-2289, Fax: 51-1-461-0374, URL: www.indembassy.org.pe, E-mail: hoc@indembassy.org.pe

Israel
Natalio Sanchez 125, Piso 6, Santa Beatriz, Tel: 51-1-418-0500, Fax: 51-1-418-0555, E-mail: info@lima.mfa.gov.il, URL: http://lima.mfa.gov.il

Italy
Venida Gregorio Escobedo 298 Jesus Maria, Lima, Tel: 51-1-463-2727 / 2728 / 2729, Fax: 51-1-463-5317, E-mail: italemb@chavin.rcp.net.pe

Japan
Av. San Felipe 356, Jesús María, Lima 11, Tel: 51-1-218-1130, Fax: 51-1-463-0302, URL: www.pe.emb-japan.go.jp/

Mexico
Av. Jorge Basadre 710 (San Isidro), Lima, Tel: 51-1-221-1100, Fax: 51-1-440-4740, E-mail: info@mexico.org.pe

Netherlands
Torre Parque Mar, Av. José Larco 1301, Piso 13. Miraflores, Lima 18, Tel: 51-1-213-9800, Fax: 51-1-213-9805, E-mail: info@nlgovlim.com

Panama
Av. Emilio Cavenecia N° 329 oficina 2A, San Isidro, Tel: 51-1-421-4762, Fax: 51-1-421-2836, URL: www.consuladopanamalima.com.pe

Portugal
Av. Central, 643 Piso 4, San Isidro, Lima 27 , Tel: 51-1-440-9905, Fax: 51-1-442-9655, URL: www.argentinische-botschaft.de

Russia
Avenida Salavaerry, 3424 San Isidro, Lima, Tel: 51-1-264-0036 / 0038, Fax: 51-1-264-0130, E-mail: embrusa@amauta.rcp.net.pe

South Korea
Av. Principal No. 190, Piso 7, Urb. Santa Catalina, La Victoria Provincia, Lima, Tel: 51-1-476-0815 / 0861 /0874 / 51-1-225-0772, Fax: 51-1-476-0950, E-mail: koremb-pu@mofat.go.kr

Sweden
La Santa María 130, San Isidro, Lima, Tel: 51-1-442-8905, Fax: 51-1-421-3295, E-mail: konslima@speedy.com.pe

Switzerland
Avda. Salaverry 3240, San Isidro, Lima 27, Tel: 51-1-264-0305, Fax: 51-1-264-1319, URL: www.eda.admin.ch/eda/es/home/reps/sameri/vper/emblim.html

Spain
Calle Los Pinos, 490, San Isidro, Lima 27, Tel: 51-1-513-7930, Fax: 51-1-422-0347, E-mail: cog.lima@mae.es

Uruguay
José D. Anchorena N 084, San Isidro, Lima, Tel: 51-1-264-0099 / 1286, Fax: 51-1-264-0112, E-mail: uruinca@embajada-uruguay.com

United Kingdom
Torre Parque Mar, 23rd floor, Av. Jose Larco 1301, Miraflores, Lima, Tel: 51-1-617-3050, Fax: 51-1-617-3055, Consular: consular.lima@fco.gov.uk, URL: www.britishembassy.co.uk

United States of America
Avenida La Encalada, Surco, Lima 33, Tel: 51-1-434-3000, Fax: 51-1-618-2397
Updated: Jul 23, 2007.

Extra Passport Photos: For your own convenience, bring an extra set of passport photos. If your passport is stolen, if could take several days to get a photo of the appropriate size taken. By already having additional passport-sized photos, you'll save your self lot of time and frustration. Updated: Jul 23, 2007.

Getting To and Away from Peru

BY AIR

The peak season for traveling via airplane to Peru runs from July to August, coinciding with summer vacations for teachers and students. Tickets in September sell out rather quickly, however, because ticket prices drop, and December is a busy time due to the high number of Peruvian immigrants returning home to visit their families. During anytime of the year, there is a departure tax of approximately $30.

The main carriers offering flights from North America are Delta, Continental, American Airlines and four Latin American-based airlines: Lan Peru, TACA, LACSA and Copa. TACA and LACSA offer flights from Miami to San Jose, Costa Rica, and from there to Lima, while Copa stops first in Panama City.

The main carriers from the UK are Lufthansa (via Germany), American Airlines, Continental Airlines, Delta Airlines, United Airlines (all via the US), Iberia, (via Madrid) and KLM (via Amsterdam).

Australia and New Zealand are serviced by Air New Zealand, Aerolineas (an Argentine airline), Lan Chile, Quantas, and United Airlines. Updated Jul 23, 2007.

Departure Tax

As of April 2006 the international departure tax for Peru is $30.25, which can be paid in dollars, solés, or both. The departure tax for flights inside Peru is $6.05, but both rates are subject to change. There is no departure tax for leaving the country by bus, car, bicycle, or foot. Updated: Jun 20, 2007.

BY LAND

From Ecuador
If you are accessing Peru by land from Ecuador, there are Transporte Cifa has buses leaving from such cities as Guayaquil, Loja, and Cuenca that head south to the border towns of Huaquillas in Ecuador and Tumbes in Peru. Your bus will stop at the migration office, where you will be expected to show your passport, tourist visa, and, perhaps, some proof of financial independence. Resist "help" from anybody who is not an official public servant.

From Colombia
The U.S. State Department warns that "the entire Peru/Colombia border" is highly dangerous due to narcotics trafficking and armed guerilias.

From Brazil
Land travel between Brazil and Peru has been very sparse due to the limited and poor quality roads. There are, however, plans underway to construct major roads connecting Sao Paolo to Lima, and Iberia in Brazil to Puerto Maldonado in Peru. In the latter region there already is a (muddy) road going to the Brazilian border, which you can access via a few minibuses and trucks, but most people prefer to be ferried by boat.

From Bolivia
The most common entry point into Peru from Bolivia is the road heading west from La Paz, which will take you to the border towns of Guaqui and Desaguadero. Some travelers will

also depart via boat from the Bolivian coastal town of Puerta Costa on Lake Titicaca to Copacabana, and from there enter Peru.

From Chile

There are buses, trains, and taxis that will take you along the Coastal Highway to the Peruvian border town of Tacna. Updated Aug 14, 2009.

BY WATER

Many travelers dream of sojourning up the Amazon and its tributaries by boat, from one country to another. Although not as common as it once was, you can still choose this adventure. It's a slow journey, stopping at villages along the way to drop off, pick up passengers and cargo. Here are a few things to keep in mind:

- Speak only with the captain of the boat; confirm departure date and time, and prices.
- Compare prices with different boats; inspect the vessel for cleanliness. Pay only the captain or another authorized person, and obtain a receipt.
- Larger boats have cabins (some even with air conditioning); however, these are more expensive than hammock space on the deck, and tend to be hot and stuffy. If you opt to travel swinging along in your hammock, be sure to choose a spot away from the fumes and noise of the engines, the insect-attracting lights and the bathrooms. Have rope not only to hang your hamaca, but also to hang cloth for privacy. Board early (often it is possible to do so the night before) to land a choice spot.
- Use a mosquito net and repellent, and don't forget to take your malaria medication.
- Be sure secure your belongings very well; lock your berth or bags, and always keep the key with you.
- Food will be provided, as will drink (often made with river water). Bring along some fresh fruits and comfort foods—and purified water. Have your own cup and some diarrhea medication, just in case.
- It gets remarkably cool at night on the river; light, warm clothing and a blanket (or cloth hammock) will keep you warm.

From Ecuador

Twice a week, motorized canoes ply the Napo River from Coca to Nuevo Rocafuerte, Ecuador (full day, $30). Ecuadorian immigration is in Nuevo Rocafuerte, and Peruvian in Pantoja. Another canoe takes you to Pantoja, Peru (two hours, $10 per person). Irregular boats go to Iquitos (four to five days, $20). Check in Coca for immigration and boat details before beginning this journey.

From Colombia

In the middle of the Amazon jungle is a triple border—Leticia, Colombia; Tabatinga, Brazil; and Santa Rosa, Peru—where the respective countries' immigration formalities are performed. Take a boat across the Amazon from Leticia to Santa Rosa ($1). Vessels leave the Peruvian port for Iquitos (speedboat, 11-12 hours, $50; slow launch, two days, $20 hammock, $30 cabin; buy your ticket the day before).

From Brazil

Many boats make the long journey up the golden Amazon River from Manaus to Benjamin Constant and Tabatinga. (It may be quicker to take the boat just to Benjamin Constant, then a fast local ferry to Tabatinga, 2 hours, $1.50.) This route takes seven to eight days upriver and costs $60 for hammock and $120 for a double cabin. For immigration information, please see above.

From Bolivia

This sojourn is only for the most hardy (and patient) of souls. Three days or more can pass between boats. From Riberalta, Bolivia, you take a boat to Puerto Heath (three days, $15-20), and from there a canoe to Puerto Pardo, Peru (five hours, $5) and then to Puerto Maldonado. Check locally for the most accurate information, as it is quite scarce from the outside. Updated: Dec 03, 2009.

Border Crossings

For tourists from most non-Latin American countries, all you need to enter Peru from its official entry points with Ecuador, Colombia, Brazil, Bolivia, and Chile is current and valid passport. However, if you have been residing in any of these countries for more than 90 days, it is expected that you will present an official "permission to leave" slip, usually obtained at your host country's immigration office. Due to Peru's limited public service budget, none of the terrestrial entry ports are open 24/7, so it is best to plan your arrival at these borders accordingly.

A word of caution; the moment you get off your bus or step out your taxi, any number of locals will aggressively offer you help, and explain all sorts of "fees" and "taxes" you will need to pay, and how they will serve as your guide. They will also be willing to change money for you. Use common sense and deal only with recognizable and verifiable border guards and immigration officials, and change your money only at banks or other legitimate businesses. Updated: Jul 23, 2007.

Getting Around

BY AIR

There are currently 64 airports in Peru, and five major domestic airlines; Wayra, StarPeru, Aero Condor, LAN Peru and LC Busre, all of which fly out of Peru's main airport, Jorge Chávez International in Lima (the only international airport in Peru). As for the airports, approximately 13 receive commercial airlines; the rest serve private charter and military craft. All major tourist destinations in Peru, such as Cusco, Iquitos, Huaraz, Arequipa, Puno, and Puerto Maldonado have airports and at least one major carrier to take you there. Domestic flights average about $100 for flights between major Peruvian cities.

Follow some common sense rules when getting around Peru via airplane: confirm your flight at least 72 hours in advance, get to the airport at least three hours early, have enough cash on hand to pay departure and other taxes, only deal with official personnel at airports (you will be hounded by so-called "helpers"), accept nothing from strangers and keep your money and passport safe. Updated: Jul 13, 2010.

BY BUS

Due to the country's poor economy, Peruvians travel by more by bus than other form of transportation, and so do most of the country's tourists. Bus travel is inexpensive, but the quality of the buses varies, as do rates according to season. Cruz del Sur, Ormeño, and Movil are three of the lines that offer more comfortable seating, faster service, and a cleaner, safer environment. Some of the most luxurious buses show movies and have sandwich bars.

For long stretches, whenever possible, pay the extra money for the most comfortable buses as squishier seats and a working bathroom can make a 24-hour ride much more pleasant. Keep in mind that even on the higher-priced buses passengers should be wary of theft and guard their possessions. Use common sense like putting your valuables in the center of your carry-on rather than front or side pockets, and secure the bag to your body while you sleep.

Buses traveling between large cities routinely sell-out so it is recommended that you purchase you ticket at least a day in advance, especially on the routes between two major cities like those that run from Lima to Cusco. Almost every town in Peru has at least one terminal in the center of town and most buses run punctually. Savvy travelers often bring a blanket, toilet paper, and hand sanitation with them in their carry-on. Many of the buses leave at night and can get chilly, and even if the bathroom on the bus is functioning, there often is no paper. If your bus does not have a bathroom, make use of the stops the bus does make to use a public bathroom and in emergencies the bus driver can normally be persuaded to make a stop for you.

The cost of journeys will depend on type of bus, service and distance to be travelled. Average costs can be said to be $1.50 an hour of travel time, but an example of approximate travel costs are: Cusco to Puno (6-7 hours, $5) and Cusco to Lima (22 hours, $30). Updated: Jul 13, 2010.

BY TRAIN

Due to their high-maintenance cost compared to buses, there are only a few number trains running in Peru. Most of these cater to tourists, providing beautiful vistas along the route. The more popular routes travel between Cusco to Machu Picchu, Lima to Huancayo and Arequipa to Lake Titicaca, which then goes through the Urubamba Valley to the edge of the Amazon. Tickets should be purchased at least a day in advance. The companies range from Económico (which the locals take) to Pullman (the most popular with tourists) to Inca, for the wealthy. A local train still runs several times a day between Huancayo and Huancavelica. Updated: Jul 13, 2010.

BY TAXI

Within cities, taxis, excluding Lima, are on average about $1-$1.50 for any short journey. You will be paying more in Lima for a journey within the Capitol but still not horrendously priced. A popular mode of intercity transport are the combi vans (shared minivans with set routes) which are very reasonably priced, if a little uncomfortable, from $0.20-$2.00 per journey depending on destination and also colectivos (shared taxis) which are also a

INTRO & INFO

very economical way to travel around Peru. Bus is by far the most popular and safer way to travel larger distances between cities.

Unlike Ecuador and other countires, taxis in Peru do not have meters to provide an objective price. With poverty and low wages being what they are in this country, even the most congenial taxi driver will not be above trying to pull a fast one on an inexperienced tourist, though the majority will be honest.

Your best bet is to inquire what the estimated price from point A to point B will be even before you hail a cab, so you have a starting point for bargaining. Peru's tourist police are very strict about curtailing unlicensed cabs, and they can tell you what sort of identifying sticker for legal cabs you should look out for. It is not uncommon for travelers in groups to take cabs from one town to another because the fare, when divided, is often similar to a minibus (but considerably more comfortable). Updated: Jul 13,2010.

BY HITCHHIKING

As with most places in Latin America, some common-sense precautions should be used if you are going try hitchhiking as a means of getting around. A woman traveling alone should never hitchhike, and even men are better off traveling with a partner, in terms of both safety and getting rides. The safety factor increases with the number of fellow travelers. Traveling during the day is preferred, and most drivers expect some compensation. Updated: Jun 14, 2007.

BY CAR

Most travelers choose to explore this large country using a combination of air and bus travel rather than renting a private car for numerous reasons. Renting a private car is expensive, especially if you want a 4X4, the roads frequently have expensive tolls, and the vastness of the country makes for time-consuming drives.

In addition, driving in Peru can be hazardous to those unfamiliar with the rules of the road, and actually even for those who do know the rules. Car accidents are frequent and drivers are aggressive in general. Theft and vandalism of the vehicle are also justified concerns.

The pros of renting a car are that with your own vehicle you are free to explore the country at your leisure and you can visit towns,

roads, and sites that are well off the beaten path. Most people who do rent cars, tend to rent them in Lima, as that is where most international flights arrive. Keep in mind, however, that if you do rent a car in Lima, you may have quite a drive ahead of you in order to get to most of the major attractions in Peru. Traffic in Lima is dense and difficult to navigate and driving rules may be very different than what you are used to.

No matter if you are driving in the cities or the country, be prepared to share the road with taxis, buses, tractors, moto-taxis, scooters, and pedestrians. Automatic transmissions are difficult to find and any driver should be fully capable of driving a standard transmission. If you must rent a car in Peru, it's best to stick with one of the major international rental car companies. There have been complaints that the smaller companies often overcharge credit cards, attach hidden fees, and rent vehicles that are poorly maintained. The following rental car companies are located in Lima: Budget - locations at Jorge Chavez International Airport, Miraflores, and San Isidro. Hertz – locations at Jorge Chavez Int'l Airport, and in Miraflores. Dollar Rent a Car - locations at Jorge Chavez Int'l Airport, and in Miraflores. Updated: Jul 13, 2010.

BY BIKE

With the increasing political stability that has developed in Peru over the last ten years, more and more adventure cycling enthusiasts attempt to see the width and breadth of this country on two wheels. For those who desire such an adventure, there are a few important recommendations. A steel-frame bike will be the most durable. Bring a bike that has a 26 inch wheel, since such wheels are standard here and thus finding replaceable parts for them will be easy. However, you should also bring your own tire replacements for long trips, since the quality of such is generally poor in Peru. One should also bring additional, and high quality, spokes and tubes for long trips. A mountain bike is best for making it across Peru's challenging geography.

To avoid accidents, always ride with a rear-view mirror, and avoid major highways, which have little to offer in terms of scenery or culture anyways. Since they share the road with horses, llamas, or donkeys, drivers on smaller roads are more conscientious. Use sun block, and wearing long sleeves and riding pants will reduce your exposure to dirt, bugs, and sun. Go slowly to adjust to different climates and altitudes, and when arriving in a high-altitude city like Cusco, spend a few days acclimatizing before you move on. Connect with other cyclists as well as hostel and campground owners to keep current on what routes have higher crime possibilities. Many cyclists stop at Casa Ciclista in Trujillo, where the owner Lucho Ramirez welcomes and registers all cyclists. The best times to go are from July through September, and one can make this trip for as low as $20 a day. In terms of taking your bike to Peru, you can have it boxed before boarding and reassembled in Peru, all for less than $100. Updated: Sept 25, 2008.

BACK ROADS CUSCO TO QUITO

Are you ready for an adventure few will ever take, through landscapes that sing to your soul and villages and mining towns that prick your conscience? Then pack your bags for the rollercoaster journey from Cusco to Quito via Andean back roads. The roads take you to heights of 4,330 meters (14,206 ft) and dips to 740 meters (2,428 ft), without descending to Lima or the coast. The trip takes several weeks, due to mostly unpaved, hair-pinning roads, infrequent transportation and daytime-only travel. It is best during the dry months (May-September); frequent landslides during the rainy season that cause delays and cancellations. Be warned in some areas, especially Huánuco-Cerro de Pasco, miner and cocalero strikes may disrupt transit. Keep your eyes on the news and ear to the ground.

Lodging and restaurants exist in all the transfer towns. All transportation is daily, except where noted.

Your journey begins in Cusco. The unpaved road to Abancay, Andahuaylas and Ayacucho wends across barren puna surrounded by glacier-blanketed mountains, scattered with flamingo-lined lagunas (399 kilometers, 24 hours, $15).

From Ayacucho to Huancayo a poor road meanders through breathtaking scenery (319 kilometers, 9-10 hours, $8-10). Several companies leave Huancayo for La Oroya and Cerro de Pasco (five hours, $5), a bleak town at 4,330 meters (14,206 ft) scarred by a gaping open mine. Frequent buses and colectivos depart Cerro de Pasco for Huánuco, a charming city at 1,894 meters (6,214 ft, 2-3 hours, $3-5).

From Huánaco, the coarse road soars to La Unión at 3,204 meters (10,512 ft, colectivos and buses 5-6 hours, $8-10). From La Unión's market, combis leave half-hourly for Huallanca (Húanuco) (1 hour, $1); a paved road continues to Huaraz (three daily buses, 6 hours, $7).

The route from Huaraz rambles northward into the upper Marañón River valley and to the rarely visited Parque Nacional Río Abiseo. Travel to Sihuas (8 hours, $9; 8:30 a.m. and 11 a.m.), where buses depart for Tayabamba at 3,300 meters (10,826 ft, 7-8 hours, $8; Monday, Wednesday, Saturday, midnight-2 a.m). The journey to the uninviting mining town Retamas lasts three hours (colectivos and combis, $6, 7 a.m.-5:30 p.m.); quaint Llacuabamba (15 minutes, $1) offers a better night's sleep. Thrice-weekly buses travel from Retamas to pleasant Huamachuco (12 hours, $9; Monday, 8 a.m., Thursday, 8 p.m., Saturday, 4 a.m.; also daily combis, 10 hours, $12). The trip passes through Chahual, with an altitude of 1,450 meters (4,757 ft). From nearby Los Alisos you can make the ten day trek to the Chachapoya ruins of Pajatén in Parque Nacional Río Abiseo (guide and permits needed). The road then climbs to a 3,900-meter (12,795 ft) pass before arriving at Chugay and then descends to the Río Grande and Huamachuco.

Frequent combis depart Huamachuco for Cajabamba (2.5 hours, $2), from where you then catch one for Cajamarca (4 hours, $4). The trip from Cajamarca into the mysterious Chachapoyas region is arduous. It first jolts along to Celedín (112 kilometers, 4 hours, $4; four buses daily; also combis from Avenida Atahualpa, 300 block). Microbuses leave Celedín for Leymebamba only three times per week ($6.60), and buses direct to Chachapoyas on Thursday and Sunday at 11 a.m. ($10). Combis leave early mornings from Leymebamba for Chachapoyas.

From Chachapoyas, you forge northward along the Andean cloud-forested slopes, descending to 740 meters (2,428 ft) at Jaén, to the La Balza, where you cross into Ecuador.

Upon entering Ecuador, you pass through fascinating Andean towns including Vilcabamba, Loja, Cuenca and Riobamba before reaching your destination, Quito, the second-highest capital in the Americas. Updated: Aug 17, 2007.

Types of Tours

Organized tours are available to a wide range of attractions, landscapes, climates and cultures. A slew of reputable agencies offer a number of excursions, from scenic day trips to Lake Titicaca—the world's highest navigable lake—to mystical multi-day hikes through Machu Picchu and along the Inca Trail. Peruvian Amazon tours explore one of the most bio-diverse areas of the planet and highlight the unique flora and fauna in the rainforest, while Andes trips will take you high into the picturesque peaks. Choose an adventure trekking tour, or sit back and take it all in by bus. Either way, there are trips for every spirit of traveler, with expeditions that can include hiking, mountain biking, rafting, culture tours, and shopping. A wide range of itineraries means there is something to fit your interests, timeframe and budget. Tours can easily be booked internationally or in all major cities once in Peru.

Photo by: Anthea Okereke

ANDES TOURS

The snowcapped peaks and glacial lakes of the Peruvian Andes offer some of the most incredible scenery in the hemisphere, and a wide range of tours cater to both expert mountaineer and greenhorn trekker alike. It is not necessary to be "super fit" to hike in the Andes, but you do need to be of generally good fitness and a regular walker. Tours are rated by level of difficulty and often last a couple of weeks or more, though many several-day trips are also available. The majority of Andes tours depart from Huarez, though trips can be taken from several of the country's other mountain towns.

AMAZON TOURS

Amazon tours allow you to explore one of the most bio-diverse areas on the planet via boat trips down the Amazon tributary rivers, eco-lodge stays or often a combination of the two. Typically capable guides take you deep into the rainforest in search of the more than 1,500 species of birds,

2,500 species of fish and more than 50,000 species of plants. Tours can last anywhere from two days to two weeks and offer a wide range of accommodation.

LAKE TITICACA TOURS

Tours of the world's highest navigable lake offer a variety of single and multiple-day tours of the waters and the communities living on its shores and islands. Tours range from a few hours of island exploration to days of getting to know lakeside villages. Most travel agencies in Puno handle the conventional tours of Lake Titicaca and Sillustani, along with a handful of other ruins programs that can extend trips by a few days.

INCA TRAIL TOURS

Hiking the Inca Trail is by far one of the most popular activities in Peru, and there are a host of tour possibilities to guide you. Shorter jaunts of a few days touch in on the sites, while trips of three days to more than a week will take you winding through an array of scenery, altitudes, climates and ecosystems, ranging from high Andean plains to dense cloud forests. Many excursions end with a climactic arrival at the breathtaking Machu Picchu site. Most trips depart out of and return to Cusco, and if you haven't had time to acclimate to high altitudes it may be worth hanging out here for a few days before hitting the trail. Look around; trips vary greatly in levels of difficulty and price.

ORGANIZED TOURS

There are a number of Peru-based operators who can provide guided tours of the country. Alternatively, there are tour operators based in North America, Europe and Australia that offer a variety of tours that contain most of the Peru's highlights. Companies such as G.A.P. (www.gapadventures.com) based out of Canada, or UK based Tucan Travel (www.tucantravel.com) offer a variety of options, from short duration trips that visit just one or two destinations to tours that explore the country pretty thoroughly. There are also multi-country tours available, that include Peru as part of a trip that may take up to six months and cover all of South America. These types of tours are often group trips where you will be traveling with a number of others from different countries and backgrounds from all over the world. They are more costly than going it alone, but for those short of time who like to have everything organized upfront they can be a good option. Updated: Jul 23, 2007.

Some tour operators and options are detailed below. Alternatively, check out the other sections of this book to find more information about tour operators in specific locations.

Andex Adventure
Tel / Fax: 51-1-251-6530
E-mail: info@andex-adventure.com
URL: www.andex-adventure.com

Alpamayo Climbing
Tel: 51-4-342-5661
E-Mail: santacruztrekking@yahoo.es
URL: www.santacruztrek.com

Aventuras de Oro
Tel: 51-1-243-4130, Fax: 51-1-241-9172
E-mail: info@aventuras-de-oro.com
URL: www.aventuras-de-oro.com

Sun God Expedition Tours
Tel: 51-8-423-2765
E-mail: info@sungodperu.com
URL: www.sungodperu.com

Peru Adventures Tours
Tel / Fax: 51-5-422-1658
E-Mail: info@peruadventurestours.com
URL: www.peruadventurestours.com

Sports and Recreation

Like much of South America, soccer (fútbol) is something like religion in Peru. Kids play in the street, adults play in the parks and when the national team is playing, the country shuts down. Be sure to take in a game if you can: it's an unforgettable experience. Many of Peru's best players play for teams in other countries because they can earn a great deal more money, but fans back home still like to follow their careers. While the peruanos are playing soccer, active visitors will notice that Peru is a paradise for adventure sports. Hiking, trekking, rafting, paragliding, sport fishing, rock climbing—you name it. Some sports, such as sandboarding (cross a snowboard with a sand dune and you get the idea) are best done in Peru. Updated: Jul 23, 2007.

Adventure Travel

Jagged mountains of the Andes, dense Amazonian jungle, endless desert sands and a rugged coast make Peru a dreamscape for the outdoor enthusiast. From world-class mountain climbing and multi-day treks into ancient ruins, to whitewater rafting, horseback riding and surfing; there's an adventure to suit every taste and season. Hike into deservedly-famous Machu Picchu, or break off the tourist-trodden path on the high mountain Ausangate Circuit. Challenge the surf of the north coast, then dry your bones sandboarding in the monstrous dunes at Huacachina. Peru is definitely an adventure playground. Updated: Apr 05, 2010.

Birdwatching

Peru ranks with Colombia as having the highest number of bird species in the Western Hemisphere—over 1,800 in fact, and second only to Brazil in its number of birds endemic to the country itself (nearly 300). The range of birds extends from tiny antbirds to magisterial condors, with macaws, parrots, owls, hummingbirds and nearly everything else imaginable. There are more impressive statistics: 85% of Peru's birds are permanent residents; of the endemic species living within Peru, 120 cannot be found anywhere else. Peru is a record-holder for the highest number of species living in a single location—925 species in the Manu Biosphere Reserve. Peru in fact contains an impressive 20 percent of the world's bird population. The government of Peru, in recognition of this, has set aside 13 percent of its territory for the protection and preservation of its environment, with 58 reserves and natural habitats. While on your birding expedition, you are well advised to employ a local tour guide. They have an experiential and native knowledge of the region that can make all the difference in your viewing venture. Take your camera and binoculars along and get ready!

MANU BIOSPHERE RESERVE

The Manu Biosphere Reserve has the largest concentration and largest variety of bird life in the world: a staggering 925 species discovered so far, with the number possibly soon to go as high as 1,000. Manu holds one in every nine species found on the planet.

The Biosphere Reserve encompasses a great variety of altitudinal zones and habitat types. Altitudes vary from over 4,000 meters above sea level in the high Andes down to 350 meters in the lowland Amazonian rain forest. For every 1,000 meters gained or lost, the structure of the bird communities differs. This altitudinal variation, coupled with the variety of forest types, grasslands, lakes, and micro-habitats such as bamboo stands, reedbeds, and treefalls, has produced the highest bird count for any area in the world.

On a two to three week birding trip to Manu, from the highlands to the lowlands, birdwatchers regularly record 450-500 species, a truly staggering number. Among the birds one will see are the Grey-breasted Mountain-toucan, the Mountain Cacique, the Swallow-tailed Nightjar, the Barred Fruiteater, the Collared Jay and most especially, the Andean Cock-of-the-Rock.

TAMBOPATA & MADRE DE DIOS

The Tambopata and Madre de Dios regions, the least developed and least populated in all of Peru, feature over a 1,000 bird species as well as 200 mammals, 1,230 species of butterfly, and up to 3,000 plant species—a higher concentration in one area than anywhere else in the world. The bird species to be found here include the Russet-backed Oropendola, the Yellow-rumped Cacique, Sand-coloured Nighthawks, Horned Screamers, Large-billed Terns, Sunbitterns and of course, macaws. Indeed, Tambopata offers the largest known assemblage of macaws in the world, and this area is also home to the Tambopata Research Center, dedicated to the study and preservation of the macaw.

ABRA MALAGA (CUSCO)

This famous birdwatching spot near the Cusco-Quillamba road provides an opportunity to appreciate such critically endangered bird species as the Ash-breasted Tit-Tyrant, the Royal Cinclodes and the White-browed Tit-Spinetail.

The area itself, ten hectares of Polylepis woodland at 4,000-4,300 meters, is divided into three regions; the Peñas, the Pass and the Canchayoc. The Peñas offers a spectacular variety of hummingbirds, including the Great Sapphirewing, Black-tailed and Green-tailed Trainbearers, Purple-backed Thornbill, Giant Hummingbird. The Pass, the most popular section, offers the Tawny Tit-Spinetail, Puna Tapaculo, Stripe-headed Antpitta and Line-fronted Canastero. The Canchayoc features the Unstreaked Tit-Tyrants, the Pale-edged Flycatcher, the Puna Thistletail, the Chestnut-bellied Mountain-Tanager and the Scarlet-bellied Mountain-Tanager.

BALLESTRA ISLANDS

The Ballestra Islands features over 160 species of marine birds, such as cormorants, boobies, flamingos, pelicans and the most northern penguins in the world. Cold currents from Antarctica carry nutrients that feed fish, which in turn bring on the sea birds. During the months of February and March condors will also visit the islands to feast on carcasses of sea lions. The large bird population here produces and, due to little rain, stores a high quantity of bird droppings. These droppings turn into guano, which sustained Peru's 19th-century economy when it was exported to Europe as a fertilizer. The birds on Ballestra include the Humboldt Penguin, the Wilson's Storm-Petrel, the Peruvian Pelican, the Peruvian Booby, the Guanay Cormorant, the Red-legged Cormorant, the Blackish Oystercatcher, the Tawny-throated Dotterel, the Chilean Skua, the Gray Gull, the Kelp Gull, the Band-tailed Gull, the Gray-hooded Gull, the Inca Tern, and even the land bird, the Seaside Cinclodes.

IQUITOS

Deep in the heart of the Peruvian Amazon, the Pacaya-Samiria National Reserve is home to an iridescent array of hawks, herons, and jacamas. Updated: Jul 06, 2010.

Hiking

Peru is one of the most mountainous of the South American countries, yet it boasts diverse ecosystems ranging from its western beaches to its tropical jungle lowlands. The most famous hiking route in the Americas—the Inca Trail—covers much of the highlands, although the most famous section is definitely from Cusco to Machu Picchu, which draws thousands of trekkers every year. The Salkantay loop, the Huayhuash mountain range and the Cordillera Blanca are other popular hiking areas. For experienced mountaineers, there are literally dozens of spectacular peaks. The highest mountain in Peru, Huascarán, first climbed in 1932, is particularly popular.

HIKING THE INCA TRAIL

The most famous hike in Peru, perhaps in the world is the Inca Trail and thousands travel to Peru each year to trek this route and enjoy its final reward—Machu Picchu. However, with an Inca Trail bursting under the strain of the volumes of hikers, a number of other, alternative hikes are gaining in popularity, so don't limit yourself to the well-trodden path, perhaps try something new instead. Consider doing the Lares Trek which ends at Machu Picchu, passing through remote Quechua communities and a glacial landscape. Note that only 500 people per day area allowed to hike the trail (porters and guides included), so to avoid disappointment it is recommended to register at least three months ahead of the trek. Be aware that the Inca Trail is closed during the month of February. You will need to hike with a guide.

SACRED VALLEY HIKING

There is also great hiking in the Sacred Valley region. Ollantaytambo makes a good starting out point. If you're a hiker that also appreciates history, you'll love the hiking options in this area, as many of them take you to ancient Inca ruins or agricultural terracing. Hikes that you might want to try include those of Pumamarca, Pinculluna, Salcantay, Ausangate, Vilcabamba and Choquequirao.

HIKING IN THE CORDILLERAS

The Cordilleras offer an array of hikes and treks for varying abilities, but all guarantee views of breathtaking landscapes—jagged peaks and sweeping valleys. If you want to hike in this region, Huaraz makes for an excellent base camp. It is better to hike in the dry season, between May to September, although April, October and November can be fine for hiking too. Some trekking highlights include the Santa Cruz to Llanganuco route, which arrives at stunning blue lakes, the Olleros to Chavín trek which finishes at the Chavín de Huantar fortress temple, Huayhuash and Alpamayo.

HIKING IN THE COLCA CANYON

The Colca Canyon is another part of Peru where hikers will be spoiled for choice, with spectacular hiking in one of the world's deepest canyons and the possibility of spotting a majestic condor or two. Hikes in this area include steep forays into the canyon, levelling off at lush oases. In the countryside surrounding Arequipa, hiking opportunities also abound. Great hikes can be had on El Misti and Chachani, two of the mountains surrounding the city.

ALTITUDE SICKNESS

When you are hiking in Peru, be aware of altitude sickness. Don't plan on doing long hikes within your first few days. It is important initially to rest for a few days and drink lots of bottled water. Once acclimatized and hiking, be on your guard for symptoms of altitude sickness, which include severe headaches, drowsiness, confusion, dry cough, and/or breathlessness. If symptoms continue, it is important to get to a lower altitude and rest. Altitude sickness can come on suddenly if you experience a sudden change of altitude.

HIKING EQUIPMENT

In addition to altitude sickness, make sure that you are appropriately equipped with a decent pair of hiking shoes, a wind / waterproof jacket, hat, scarf, gloves, quick-drying pants and plenty of warm gear. It gets really cold at these high altitudes; don't head out unprepared, even if it looks nice and sunny. Don't forget your sunscreen—despite the cold, the sun can burn you more quickly at these altitudes. Be sure to take lots of water and snacks too. Updated: Jul 23, 2007.

Horseback Riding

Peru is a country of spectacular vistas and incredible natural diversity, and one of the best ways to experience it is on horseback.

The Peruvian Paso horse is a specific breed, descended from the original horses brought over by the conquistadores over 400 years ago. The Paso horses feature a four-beat gait (called the paso llano) that makes them exceptionally smooth to ride. They are spirited, but well-trained Paso horses are easy to handle. The Paso horses are a Peruvian breed and a source of pride to many Peruvians.

Paso horses are often trained differently than in other parts of the world; if you're an experienced rider, you may find that your horse does not respond to the commands you're used to. If this is the case, simply take a little time to become accustomed to the proper commands and ask the guide if you have any problems.

TIPS

Most horseback tour operators in Peru are reputable and take excellent care of their horses, particularly those that offer multiday excursions. However, some of the smaller operators and those specializing in day trips don't take as good care of their horses as they should. If you think your operator is a little sketchy, ask to see the horses beforehand. If they look unhealthy or have saddle sores, you may want to find a different operator: nothing can ruin a riding trip like thinking your mount has been abused. Please advise Viva Travel Guides if you find inhumane situations at any stables.

Some of the horses are tamer than others, and some can be downright squirrelly. If you feel like you have no control over your horse, don't hesitate to ask for a change. If the tack (saddle and bridle) looks old, cracked, or too worn, ask to have it changed.

A fall can lead to serious injury. Be sure the girth band is tight and make sure the stirrups are the right length: if they're too short or too long it will make your ride difficult.

Your guide will usually be the person who takes care of the horses, and chances are he will know more about horses than local culture, flora or fauna, and may not say much during the trip. If the horses are healthy, clean and well-behaved, be sure to tip at the end of the ride. A couple of dollars per rider should suffice.

PLACES TO RIDE

In the north of Peru, the Cajamarca-Trujillo-Chiclayo area is a popular one for multiday horseback trips. Northern Peru receives significantly fewer visitors than the Cusco and Machu Picchu in the south, and the rides are therefore more rustic. There are still ruins to ride through, and many museums and hot springs to visit.

The Ayacucho area is also popular, as it offers stunning Andean vistas along with good markets for shopping. Many multiday horseback trips in the Ayacucho area go from the highlands to the coast, and take little trips to Ica and the Nasca lines.

The Sacred Valley, with its picturesque towns, Andean culture and ancient ruins is another favorite horseback riding destination. There are many nice hotels as well where you can spend the night. Many of the longer tours include side trips to Machu Picchu and Cusco. Expect to see fields of wildflowers, smiling children herding sheep and goats and spectacular mountain vistas.

The Inca Trail is generally considered a hiking trail, but it is possible to find outfitters and tour companies who do it on horseback.

In the far south, Arequipa is also a popular destination for horseback riding, and it is easy to find trips into the nearby Colca Canyon. There are several travel agencies in town that can hook you up with a reputable horseback tour. Updated: Jul 23, 2007.

OPERATORS

Hotel Las Dunas in Ica (www.lasdunashotel.com)
Hotel Ocucaje Sun and Wine Resort outside of Ica (www.hotelocucaje.com)
Hotel Incatambo Hacienda, outside of Cusco.
Hotel Royal Inka Pisac, in the Sacred Valley (www.royalinkahotel.com/hpisac.html)

Mountain Biking

Mountain biking is relatively new to Peru but due to nearly unlimited numbers of trails and routes it is quickly growing in popularity. The two major mountain biking centers are Huarez in the Cordillera Blanca Range and Cusco around the Sacred Valley, neither of which have a shortage of tour operators. Trips from one day to two weeks are available and most multiday excursions include a support vehicle to transport your food, clothing etc. Rentals are available in both locations but if you are planning a trip to Peru solely for biking it's best to bring your own. As with any rental, you get what you pay for. Cheaper bikes will cost about $15/day, but to get a decent bike with front suspension will cost closer to $25/day. All rentals should come with a helmet, puncture repair kit, pump and a first-aid kit. Below are the brief descriptions of the main riding destinations.

HUARAZ AND THE CORDILLERA BLANCA

Huaraz is the primary location for mountain bikers in Peru. Experienced riders, especially those looking for a more physically challenging experience, tend to gravitate towards Huaraz.

The most popular trip is the Huascarán Tour. Offered by most major tour companies this trip is anywhere from 5 to 14 days and includes extensive touring of the Cordillera Blanca Range and of Huascarán National Park. The vistas in the Cordillera Blanca are stunning and many consider it the most beautiful range in the world.

Huaraz has some of the more challenging riding in Peru, but most companies offer a range of options depending on ability and fitness level.

Given that many of the rides are in the Cordillera Blanca, there is loads of technical singletrack to be ridden. If you're looking to burn your quads you can ride to the top before barreling down, but if you're only looking for the exhilaration of the downhill ride many companies will drive you and your bike to the top.

CUSCO AND THE SACRED VALLEY

Cusco is the best choice for mountain biking tours for less-experienced riders, or those looking for an easier ride. Mountain biking tours from Cusco range from one

INTRO & INFO

day to over a week. There are numerous options for those looking to get out and spend a day on a bike to see the beautiful Sacred Valley. Most of the day trips are straight-forward, downhill cruises taking riders past Inca ruins and through the striking surroundings of the Sacred Valley.

Photo by: Rebecca Herrera

AREQUIPA

Many of the trekking and rafting companies based in Arequipa also offer mountain biking. The Colca Canyon is the deepest in the world and is a popular destination for riders of all abilities. Another option is a downhill or cross-country ride on the sides of the snow-capped Misti Volcano. Most companies drive you to the highest point of the trip and from there you get on your bike and begin to cruise downhill.

Mountain Climbing

If summiting some of the world's grandest and most beautiful peaks is your thing, then Peru is the place for you. Peru boasts an incredible 32 mountains higher than 6,000 meters, the pinnacle of which is Huascaran, giving experienced climbers a plethora of options. However, many of the lower mountains can be tackled by relative amateurs and there are plenty of challenging peaks for aspiring climbers.

Some of Peru's mountains can be climbed year round but for the highest mountains, June to September is the only time a summit can be attempted. For attempts at Peru's grandest peaks be sure to plan your trip well in advance as guides are required and last-minute planning can limit your options.

The range with the highest concentration of peaks (and climbers) is the Cordillera Blanca, near Huaraz. Here there are countless mountains for climbers of all ability levels. Further south are Arequipa and Cusco,

which are the country's second best mountaineering areas after the Cordillera Blanca.

For all three areas, acclimatization periods of 4-7 days are recommended. Often these days can be filled with less-challenging day hikes giving climbers a chance to get used to the altitude as well get their legs ready for the days ahead.

Every tour company has English and Spanish guides, but you will pay a little more for the English speakers. They are in high demand and language education is expensive.

CORDILLERA BLANCA

The Huaraz area in Peru attracts some of the world's best mountaineers each year to attempt the breathtaking peaks of the Cordillera Blanca Range. It is unquestionably the climbing capital of Peru, and has a several world-class mountains. Climbers traveling to Peru solely to conquer 6,000+ meter peaks often complete several in a couple of weeks. Many of mountains are located within Huascarán National Park, meaning the climbs take place in protected and unspoiled nature. The Cordillera Blanca is also considered to be one of the most accessible climbing areas in the world, in addition to being one of the best places to climb.

The highest peak in the range is Huascaran (6,768 m) making it a favorite of climbers. Alpamayo (5,947 m) is the most climbed mountain in the Cordillera Blanca and is considered by many to be the most beautiful mountain in the world due to its near perfect pyramid shape.

The Ishinca Valley is another popular destination in the region because it offers climbs ranging from easy (by mountaineering standards) to difficult. The primary peaks in the Ishinca Valley are Urus (5,430 m), Ishinca (5,530 m) and Tocllaraju (6,034 m). Ishinca and Urus are considered easy and can be attempted year-round. Tocllaraju is rated moderate/difficult and can only be climbed from May through September.

Another favorite climb in the region is Chopicalqui (6,354 m). This mushroom shaped peak is moderately difficult but from the summit treats climbers to one of the best panoramic views of the Cordillera Blanca including a look straight across at Huascaran. The climbs listed above take from 5-7 days each, depending on ability and fitness.

Huaraz and the surrounding area also hosts the Semana del Andinismo in June of every year. This festival, celebrating all things mountain, attracts some of the best climbers, skiers and snowboarders from around the world. They descend on Huaraz for a week of intense, friendly competition with Peruvian locals and others from around the world.

AREQUIPA

Although it doesn't have the number of peaks the Cordillera Blanca has, Arequipa offers beginners a few choices to try out mountain climbing. The three most popular climbs in Arequipa are Volcan Misti (5,825 m), Chachani (6,057 m) and Ampato (6,318 m).

Volcan Misti looms as a backdrop within sight of Arequipa, while the others are further away. Reaching the summit of Misti is a straightforward 2-day climb, and you will likely leaving your hotel in the morning of the first day and return the evening of the second.

Chichani is considered one of the easiest 6,000 meter peaks in the world, so if you simply want to notch one in your belt this is the place to do it. Like the Misti climb, this two day tour departs Arequipa in the morning of the first day whereupon you are driven up to the base of Chichani at over 5300 m. The following morning the summit trip begins early and after a full day of travel up and down the mountain you return back to Arequipa that evening.

Reaching the summit of Ampato is the most challenging of the three primary expeditions operating out of Arequipa. This trip requires a commitment of four days and entails many more kilometers covered on foot than the other two. Three days of intense climbing and descending and multiple camps make this climb more strenuous and reflective of a real mountain expedition than the others. The peak of Ampato has added historical significance because Mommy Juanita, the superbly preserved Peruvian mummy, was found there in 1995.

CUSCO

The two most intimidating mountaineering expeditions from Cusco are the summits of Salcantay (6,271m) and Ausangate (6,372m). The only time for a summit of these peaks is between June and September. Salcantay takes 8-10 days to summit while Ausangate takes at least 10 days. Neither of these climbs is appropriate for beginners and they should not be attempted without an experienced, certified guide. Updated: Jul 23, 2007.

Sandboarding

Sandboarding is a specialty in Peru, particularly in the Ica Desert region. Many of the hotels and hostels at the Huacachina Oasis rent or provide sandboards, and most of the local tour companies offer trips as well.

Sandboarding is a lot like snowboarding, only on sand instead of snow. Typically, groups of tourists will select battered boards from a selection provided by the tour operator of their choice, and then pile into a questionable-looking dune buggy for a quick ride out into the desert. When a good-looking dune is identified, the car will drop you off at the top. Helpful guides will show you how to "surf" down the dune without killing yourself. Before long, everyone will reach the bottom; the guide, who has effortlessly glided down on his board, and the tourists, who have either rolled ass-over-head after taking a sandy tumble or walked because there is no more wax on their board.

Boards should be waxed between runs, and your guide will show you how as the buggy brings you to another dune. On a typical day, you may get in about a half-dozen different runs before heading back to Huacachina.

If you're near Nazca and up for a challenge, you may want to check out Cerro Blanco, or "White Mountain." At 2,070 meters, it is one of the tallest sand dunes in the world (if not the tallest). It is certainly the most massive peak in Peru available to sandboarders. Dune buggies can only get you so close to the top of Cerro Blanco: you'll have to leave your hotel early, drive for a while, and then walk three hours to get to the top, carrying your board, water, sunscreen, etc. The descent usually takes about an hour. Cost depends on the tour agency you choose, but averages about $50-60.

What to bring: a lot of water, perhaps three liters or so. Sunscreen, hat, strong, comfortable shoes, sunglasses and a camera.

Every year, the Dune Riders International World Tour of Sandboarding sponsors the Copa Sudamericana in Peru, a sort of South American championship of sandboarding. Contestants come from around the world to compete in categories like Boarder Cross and Parallel Slalom. The competition is still in its initial years, so it often changes dates, venues and events. A good place to find information on this event is: www.sudamericansandboardcup.com. Updated: Jul 23, 2007.

Sport Fishing

The world's largest black marlin, weighing a staggering 1,560 lbs. (702 kilos), was caught in Peruvian waters. Still need a reason to come try your luck? Peru offers excellent saltwater fishing on the coast in addition to excellent freshwater fishing in the Amazon. Trout fishing is good in the highlands.

Rock Climbing

Peru is full of rocks, many of which are suitable for climbing. The big cities of Lima and Cusco both have good rock climbing locations nearby. Many travel agencies in these cities specialize in this sort of adventure tour. Updated: Jul 23, 2007.

Surfing

Some archaeological evidence suggests that the first surfers were not Polynesian, but Peruvian. Regardless, Peru features several top-notch surf spots, including Punta Rocas and Cabo Blanco, both spots on the world surfing championship circuit. There are good waves year-round in different areas of Peru's long Pacific coast. Although surfing is catching on in Peru, it is still not as big a surf destination as, say, Brazil, and it is easy to find a secluded spot where you'll have the waves to yourself.

Surfing has been a staple in Peru since the beginning of its civilization. The sport was revered because of its spiritual ambience,. Wave riding was also a daily part of the fisherman's routine, when they surfed on their *totora*, or reed boats.

Since then, both the styles and methods of surfing in Peru have evolved, with synthetic surfboards replacing the wooden boats. However, Peruvian esteem has not diminished. The country has turned out many legendary surfers, such as Sergio "Gordo" Barreda, a four-time Peruvian national champion and two-time international champion. Needless to say, many young locals take inspiration from him, beginning their surfing careers early.

Peru is blessed with consistent surf and good weather along its 3,000 kilometer coast,

unlike many of the countries in the world, where surfing is limited to a short season. The country also hosts one of the surf world's most sought-after waves—Chicama.

Chicama, the world's longest wave, provides rides of over 4 kilometers. The wave embodies the "go big or go home" surfer mentality, because after paddling out, surfers are denied the chance of going back. The wave is definitely on every professional surfer's "to-do" list.

Reportedly, Chicama was discovered by Hawaiian surfer Chuck Shipman from the window of a plane on his way home from the world surfing championships in Peru. Barreda's brother Sergio later returned to the wave with a few friends to film the phenomenon, but the film actually ran out before the ride was even completed.

There are dozens of other prime surfing beaches, ranging from undiscovered stretches to always-happening hippie towns. Some beaches are specified for experts, and dangerous for those who don't know what they are doing. Others are perfect beginning points for novices, though. The cold Humboldt Current and the warm Nino Current feed the waves year-round, thus creating huge temperature differences along the coast. It is best to check out surf reports online before heading out to a chosen destination.

Cabo Blanco, for those in the know, has the best waves in all of Peru. It was discovered, unsurprisingly, by Gordo Barreda in 1979. Advanced surfers that can handle the left reefbreak are rewarded with perfect tubes, when conditions are right—waves can get up to 10 feet tall here! Mancora, known for its gorgeous coastline and good waves, is the most common surfing destination. Supposedly, this beach is sunny 365 days a year. During the early months of the year, a swell from the Pacific builds long waves. However, if the surf isn't to your liking, there are always the captivating white-sand beaches (great for tanning!) and lively bars to keep you busy.

Although the Peruvian surf scene offers so much, it is relatively unoccupied compared to other top surf spots, and well worth the time spent. After all, the Beach Boys mentioned Cerro Azul in their '60s hit "Surfing Sufari" and the film adaptation of Ernest Hemingway's "The Old Man and the Sea" was shot near Cabo Blanco. Perhaps you'll be inspired too. If not, you'll still encounter some unforgettable breaks and undiscovered waves.

There are limitless choices to how you want to approach your surf journey through Peru. It is possible to book a surf tour through the numerous operators, many of which are based in Lima. There is also the opportunity to find a private guide to drive you along the coast to great spots; this is a good way to find the beaches that only locals know of. Or you can take a chance, and rough it on your own! Updated: Aug 06, 2008.

Whitewater Rafting

Whitewater rafting is soaring in popularity in Peru largely because of the abundance of world-class rivers in the country. Adding to the convenience, many of these rivers are located near two of the country's most-visited tourist destinations, Cusco and Arequipa. Peru has whitewater options for every level of experience, from beginner Class II and III water to Class IV, V and beyond. Although some rafting companies offer kayaking trips, it is less common than rafting. Experienced kayakers should contact the tour operators in the whitewater areas for information. Some companies in Arequipa offer inflatable kayak trips down Class III water.

Cusco is Peru's rafting capital. The most popular trips are day trips on the Río Urubamba. These trips leave the city at 9 a.m. and return at 3 p.m., giving visitors about three hours on the river. Many companies also offer three-or-four-day trips on the Río Apurímac, which is probably the best known rafting destination in Peru. Despite operating out of Cusco, these trips require a four-hour drive before actually getting on the river. The Apurímac is a special river because it is the largest contributor to the Amazon, so some consider it the longest river in the world. Another popular choice is rafting trips down the Río Tambopata in southwestern Peru, which

begins on Lake Titicaca. These trips generally last over a week and meander through the Tambopata Candamo Reserved Zone in the Peruvian Amazon. While an excellent adventure, be sure to ask how many days of your trip will include whitewater. Once you reach the Amazon the water gets much tamer and involves more "floating."

Arequipa offers several rafting destinations. The most common are day trips to the Chili and Majes rivers. These trips include 3-5 hours on the river and return to Arequipa in the evening. Some companies also offer multi-day trips down the Colca Canyon, the deepest canyon in the world.

Expeditions down the Río Cotahuasi are also available in Arequipa. This trip takes rafters down what is considered to be one of the finest and toughest stretches of Class IV and V whitewater anywhere. The trip starts with a grueling high-altitude drive to the river followed by a strenuous hike around Sipia Falls. Over the next 120 kilometers, paddlers will encounter not only huge whitewater but also spectacular campsites and Inca ruins. Advance research and booking is a must, because these trips are offered infrequently. Mayuc Tours and Condor Journeys & Adventures are two outfitters that offer this tour.

When choosing a rafting company make sure all the necessary safety equipment is provided. All guides should be certified, and lifejackets, throw-bags and helmets should be included. Most companies go beyond the requirements to ensure a safe, comfortable experience, but it's still important to take care that the safety standards meet your expectations. Updated: Jul 23, 2007.

Studying in Peru

STUDYING SPANISH

Peru is home to a number of excellent Spanish schools, most of which are centered in cities with thriving tourist scenes such as Lima, Cusco, and the area around Lake Titicaca. Arequipa, Huancayo, and Hauraz are also growing in popularity as good places to learn Spanish. Combined with the host of other things the area has to offer—mountains, jungle, rafting, history and so on—Peru is an ideal locale to hunker down and habla español. Updated Mar 13, 2008.

STUDYING QUECHUA

For those looking to live and work in certain Andean areas, or for those who simply want to try something different, you may want to take some classes in Quechua while visiting Peru.

Quechua, the official language of the Inca Empire, is still spoken today by some 13 million people, most of whom are located in Peru, Bolivia and Ecuador. For English speakers, Quechua is fairly easy to learn, because the verbs are regular and there are few exceptions to the grammatical rules. The hardest part, according to those who have learned it, are the prefixes and suffix that can be added to words to change or modify their meaning.

There are several schools in Peru where you can learn Quechua. The best ones are in areas with a higher indigenous population, naturally. Cusco is a good place to learn Quechua. Some of the Spanish schools offer classes in introductory and intermediate Quechua in addition to their normal Spanish classes.

Quechua classes tend to focus on conversational language skills; there are relatively few books written or printed in Quechua, and therefore written/reading skills are less important than speaking. The courses also tend to offer a great deal of culture as well, as tradition and history are important aspects of the indigenous Andean cultures. Some of the better schools offer organized excursions where students can practice Quechua in a real-life environment.

Is a course in introductory Quechua for you? If you're very interested in Andean culture, if you have some time to spend, if your Spanish is already pretty good and if you want to learn a language that has centuries of tradition, you may want to try it! Updated: Oct 21, 2009.

Volunteering or Working

If you would like to have a different experience in getting to know Peru, beyond the tourist veneer, consider volunteering. Projects with street children are common in Lima and the Cusco-Sacred Valley region, calling upon you to just spend time with the children and teach them basic living skills and English. A few projects provide room and board; however, many charge a fee. You can check with the South American Explorers Club in Lima for opportunities, or with language schools.

If you are a medical or other professional, check with organizations like Doctors Without Borders or Maryknolls for long or short-term opportunities. Some have two and three-year stints, with expenses covered and a stipend provided.

You can also try the old standby; teaching English. Visit English language centers, résumé in hand, to find a job. Be wise, though, and research any prospective employer, as some schools have earned a reputation for not paying their teachers. Also, many high schools look for teachers; frequently they ask for no certification and will arrange for your work visa. You can also tutor privately, putting up signs around and relying on word-of-mouth. Pay would, of course, be higher in Lima and Cusco.

Another option, requiring a good command of Spanish, is in tourism; translators for tour groups, guides or restaurant, bar and hotel help are in fairly high demand. Keep your ear to the ground for these opportunities and ask around. Often you'll receive room and board; wages, if any, will be low.

Whether for volunteer or work positions, check websites such as: www.goabroad.com, www.workingabroad.com, www.idealist.org, and www.gapyear.com. Updated: Jul 23, 2010.

Photo by Seattle Miles

Teaching English

As more and more Peruvians are studying English, there is a greater need for English teachers. Although many people coming to Peru for a short time look for work in language institutes, if you are thinking of staying for a longer time, look for work in universities or schools. Not only is the pay better, (typical pay is $500–700 per month, plus benefits, which, compared to about $5 an hour at language institutes with no benefits is a better option), but it's more stable and the working environment is often more organized.

If you want to teach in a language institute, you should be a native speaker or have an appropriate English level. You will also be expected to commit a certain amount of time to the language institute, usually between three and six months, be willing to work split-shifts, and some Saturdays. Often these jobs will be under the table, so you will have to border hop or go to Immigrations in Lima to get visa extensions. The majority of these jobs can be found in touristy cities, such as Lima, Cusco, Arequipa, and Trujillo. Occasionally job openings will be advertised on TEFL websites, but you'll probably be better off looking at the Yellow Pages (www.paginasamarillas.com.pe) or going to the city centre and presenting your CV or resume at Institutos de Idiomas. Language institutes usually hire year-round and classes last between one and three months.

To get a job with a school or university, you may be required to have a TEFL Certificate, a degree in Education, a valid license in Education or teaching experience in addition to having the appropriate English level. You will also have to be available for the entire school year (March to December) and some schools have training in February. Some places will arrange the appropriate working visa and others (usually universities if you work part-time) will require you to have all your papers in order before they hire you. Job advertisements can be found in El Comercio, the national newspaper or on the schools' website. As many jobs are found word-of-mouth, try sending your CV or resume out in November to School Directors or Directors of the Centro de Idiomas in universities.

If you are a qualified teacher and can commit two years to living in Peru, try International Schools. Often you can arrange a job before you arrive and the pay is similar to what teachers get paid in their home country. There are International School Job Fairs held throughout the year and you can also look the following:
Remember that the school year starts in March, so plan to start sending out your resume or CV (with a recent photo) in November.

Lodging

Hotels in Peru are as varied as the country's landscapes and people. Luxury five-star hotels are available in Lima. Stately boutique and historical hotels, monasteries and haciendas are a rewarding way to visit Cusco and Machu Picchu. Eco-lodges in the Peruvian Amazon provide a comfortable, up-close look into the wildlife of the world's largest rainforest. Some family-run hotels are perhaps the most intimate way to get to know the country, that is, except for an adventurous home stay where you'll come to understand the culture of Peru first hand with a Peruvian family.

In the major cities, tourist attractions and national parks of Peru, luxury hotels and resorts abound. Lima, Arequipa, Cusco, Machu Picchu and the Amazonian parks all have world-class accommodations. If you are willing to shell out $150-400 for a room while in Peru, resorts and fancy hotels usually have richly-furnished rooms, professional, English-speaking staff, and varied amenities. For a more relaxed setting, you should check out the luxury options on the outskirts of major cities. Business hotels cluster in downtown areas.

Of course, you do not have to spend a bundle to get a good night's sleep in Peru. Hostels can be found in every city and most smaller towns, and most charge $7-20 per person. Many will have a range of options, such as private and dorm rooms, and rooms with shared and private bathrooms. In the warmer parts of Peru, budget hotels should still provide mosquito nets for guests, as the presence of malaria and dengue fever make it a matter of safety. Updated: Jun 30, 2010.

SPAS

Spa and relaxation tourism is growing internationally, and Peru is no exception. Many travelers come to Latin America from the United States and Europe who are eager to spend a night or two at a nice spa, where a day of massages, Jacuzzis, mud baths and more costs a mere fraction of what it would at home.

The best spas in Peru are currently found in the most important tourism centers, such as Lima, Cusco and Nasca. More re-mote locations such as Iquitos do not have as much to offer as of yet.

Most spas in Peru offer a variety of mas-sages, steam rooms, aromatherapy and Jacuzzis. Some offer yoga, specialized treatments, sound therapy, mud baths and more. Every spa has its own special-ties, so check what services they feature before you go. Generally, massages and other services can be ordered individu-ally, or as part of a package.

Some of Peru's better spas include:

Cantayo Hotel Spa and Resort, Nasca
The Cantayo Hotel, one of the most elegant in dusty Nasca, is expanding its spa services. Currently, it offers massages and yoga, and will feature steam rooms, pools and hydro-massage facilities soon.

Kallpa Wasi Spa, Yucay, Sacred Valley
About an hour from Cusco, those looking to relax after spending a few days hiking the Inca Trail or exploring Machu Picchu might want to head here. It's part of the Sonesta Posada del Inca Hotel.

Stilos Spa, Cusco
This spa is not affiliated with any hotel: you can't spend the night. It does have a good reputation and a wide variety of massages and treatments.

Miraflores Park Hotel, Lima
Features the Zest spa, one of the best in Lima. It's expensive, but the hotel is run by the prestigious International Orient Express group, so you know you'll get top-notch ser-vice. Updated: Oct 21, 2009.

HACIENDAS
Like the rest of Latin America, Peru was once home to many haciendas, elegant country estate homes owned by wealthy citizens during the colonial and republican periods. Some haciendas were adminis-trative centers from which a single family could rule up to dozens of indigenous vil-lages like medieval dukes. Although histori-cally linked to oppression and exploitation of indigenous society, there is no denying that the stately buildings, often with balco-nies, gardens, stables and courtyards, are tranquil, beautiful and well worth a visit.
In some countries, such as Ecuador, many old colonial and Republican haciendas have been turned into first-rate guest homes, of-fering horseback riding, traditional food and elegant accommodations. Unfortunately for Peru, many of the country's most attractive haciendas were taken over by the govern-ment between 1968 and 1972, during the agrarian reforms of President Juan Velasco. Many of the best haciendas were given over to cooperatives, which allowed them to de-teriorate into rubble, and some were looted and burned. In the best of cases, the marvel-ous old buildings were merely neglected.

A few haciendas have survived, however, and their owners are learning what Ecuador learned decades ago; restored haciendas make great hotels. One of the best is Haci-enda San José in Chincha, first established as a sugarcane plantation in 1688. Its own-ers managed to keep it during the Velasco administration and converted it into a hotel and restaurant soon after.

Due to the booming tourism industry in Peru, many old haciendas are being refur-bished and marketed as hotels. Areas of high tourist traffic are seeing more and more of them, especially the Sacred Valley near Cusco.

A stay at a converted hacienda can be a highlight of any trip to Peru. There is some-thing magical about staying at a place that has been around for centuries, especially if it has been nicely refurbished. Most of the haciendas in Peru are in the upper-middle price range; expect to pay roughly $70/night for a double. Many offer a wide range of activities, from mountain biking to horseback riding, and all offer tranquil garden paths, beautiful rooms and scenery, terraces and gardens. If a stay at a colonial hacienda is within your budget, it is certain-ly worth it to check one out. Oct 21, 2009.

CAMPING
Peru, being the hiking and trekking mecca that it is, has a ton of camping opportunities. In general, travelers will not be responsible for their own equipment (tent, sleeping bag, camping stove etc) as most camping trips are organized through tour operators who provide (or rent) all types of gear. However, if you are planning on doing a lot of camping it's not a terrible idea to bring some of your favorite (or most personal) items. In the Huaraz and Cusco regions the number of options for trekking or climbing in combination with camping is almost unlimited. Camping is

INTRO & INFO

commonly combined with other multi-day outdoor activities such as biking or white-water rafting.

The majority of the camping is done in the Cusco region, where the combination of the jam-packed Inca Trail and the accompanying Sacred Valley provide visitors with a multitude of camping possibilities. Most treks in the region can be organized through guiding companies in Cusco.

Huaraz, Peru's climbing capital, predictably has lots of camping as well. However, the camping is merely a necessary element of summiting one of the several nearby peaks. For those not going up the mountains, there are also camping and trekking options throughout the Cordillera Blanca.

Peru's multi-day whitewater rafting trips include camping as well. Most of them leave from Cusco, although you will put-in the river hours from the city. The outfitter will provide all necessary equipment.

Along the coast and in the mountains there are camping options as an alternative to pricier hotels. If you plan on this style of camping you will want to make sure you place your tent in a safe place and that (ideally) the campground has a place to lock up valuables. People have been known to camp on the beach in Peru, but ask around before to make sure it's safe. Updated: Jul 03, 2007.

ECOTOURISM
Ecotourism in Peru has boomed in the last decade. There are many valid eco-lodges that have little to no negative effect on the environment and help you truly appreciate Peru's natural beauty. However, many hotels claim to be eco-lodges (many simply by adding the prefix "eco" to all goods and services) without following basic steps to guarantee ecological protection. All good eco-lodges should follow a few basic guidelines:

1. Minimal environmental impact should be the fundamental goal of every eco-operator. How a hotel or tour operator manages its impact will tell you immediately if it is truly ecologically minded. Ecologically-responsible businesses recycle, conserve water and energy, manage waste properly (i.e. implement composting and gray water projects), and allow guests to choose whether or not to change linens or towels daily. These simple efforts make a huge difference in the long-term environmental impact of tourism.

2. Conservation may be practiced in many different ways. Habitat preservation is one of the principal forms of conservation. Habitats may be preserved by establishing private reserves, supporting established national parks and reserves or funding native tree reforestation projects. Although protected areas may be visited by tourists, it is important to recognize that their primary purpose is preservation. Whenever visiting a protected area, your visit should be made with minimal impact.

3. Sustainability is vital to the long-term success of ecotourism. The majority of products consumed at an eco-facility should be locally produced. Furthermore, construction should be done using local materials and methods, and local organic gardens should be the source of the majority of the food served. Ultimately, sustainability means that a lifestyle that is in balance and that can be maintained indefinitely without depleting the earth's resources.

4. Community involvement is a crucial aspect of ecotourism. Ecotourism should generate revenue for the local economy without harming the environment. Ideally, the community should own the establishment. If this is not possible, the operation should at least employ local labor. Moreover, in addition to generating revenue and providing employment, eco-establishments should sponsor community development projects.

5. Environmental education teaches others to be ecologically responsible. Every guest should leave an eco-facility having learned something about environmental preservation and cultural sensitivity. This ensures the continued growth of environmental and cultural awareness.

Food and Drink
Peruvian food has begun to win international acclaim in recent years, but the locals have known about, and celebrated, its unique ingredients, diverse flavors and interesting fusions for ages. In Peru, food is a window into the society as a whole; Peruvian recipes reflect the country's unique geography, openness to blend races and cultures and its use of ancient cooking techniques in modern

Culinary Vocabulary

Aji: Ají is the Spanish word for chili pepper. It is a staple in Peruvian cuisine.

Arroz con Leche: A rice and caramel pudding flavored with cinnamon and vanilla.

Arroz con Pollo: A rice and chicken stew with ají amarillo and cilantro flavoring.

Arroz Tapado: A sauté of meat, garlic, tomatoes, raisins, olives, egg and parsley, served in between two layers of rice.

Ceviche: One of the most popular Peruvian dishes, ceviche is the combination of raw fish or shellfish, lime juice, ají, onion, sweet potato and corn.

Charqui: Traditionally, dried llama meat used in Andean cooking, however today beef tends to be more commonly used.

Chifa: The name given in Peru to Peruvian Chinese cuisine. Chifas are what Chinese restaurants are called in Peru.

Cuy: Guinea Pig, a Peruvian delicacy. They are usually roasted with garlic, or served with a peanut sauce.

Criollo or al la criolla: Types of spicy food, "Creole."

Lomo Saltado: Sautéed beef and potatoes with ají and soy sauce, this is a good example of a combination of Peruvian and Chinese cuisine.

Pachamanca: A popular dish in the highlands that symbolizes the relationship between the Andean people and the Earth. It generally consists of several ingredients, usually including chicken, cuy, potatoes and corn. It is cooked inside a hole filled with stones covered in herbs.

Pisco: Pisco is a brandy distilled from fermented grape juice. It is considered to be Peru's national drink.

Pisco Sour: The cocktail of Peru. It is a mix of pisco, lemon, egg whites, syrup and bitters.

Queso Fresco: A typical Peruvian cheese, white and soft.

Salsa Criolla: A sauce that is usually served with meals, consisting of onions, ají, lime juice, and cilantro.

Tiradito: A dish similar to ceviche, but with a more subtle taste. Its main differing point from ceviche is its lack of onions.

La Trucha: Trout

Updated: Jun 11, 2009.

dishes. Luckily for travelers, this gustatory tour through the history and culture of Peru is quite affordable, with even a fancy dinner rarely running much more than $20.

TRADITIONAL FOOD OF PERU

For the indigenous cultures of Peru, like the Moche, Chimu and Inca, food centered around the crops, animals and fish that could be found locally, and much of that sentiment still remains. The Andes region yielded hundreds of varieties of corn and potatoes, many of which are still available in Peruvian restaurants today. The lucuma fruit, revered by the ancient Moche, remains Peru's favorite flavor of ice cream. Even the humble lima bean, called a pallar, has been cultivated for thousands of years in Peru, its country of origin (and from whose capital the bean takes its name). Though these ingredients can be found anywhere in Peru now, many of Peru's traditional dishes are still associated with particular regions of the country.

FOOD OF THE PERUVIAN COAST

The quintessential Peruvian coastal dish is ceviche, raw seafood (often fish) marinated in chiles and lime juice and served with sweet potatoes, toasted corn and seaweed. Other typical coastal foods include causa and papa rellena, both of which involved mashing and stuffing a potato; escabeche, in which chicken or fish is cooked in a tangy vinegar and onion sauce; and aji de gallina, which features shredded chicken in a spicy, creamy sauce.

FOOD OF THE ANDES

In the Peruvian mountains, the diet of indigenous people remains nearly the same as it has been for hundreds of years. Staples include corn, potatoes and the meat from animals such as alpacas and guinea pigs (*cuyes*). The idea of eating a furry little animal may seem repulsive to many foreigners, but cuy is a common food that is considered a delicacy by many in the region. When in the area, you are sure to walk down a street and see restaurant after restaurant roasting up guinea pig. If you are feeling brave, try one; it definitely will be an experience you'll never forget.

A pachamanca is a special highland meal, usually reserved for celebrations. It is made from a variety of meats, herb and vegetables, which are slowly cooked underground on heated stones. It is a rather tedious process, which requires a very skillful cook.

FOOD OF THE AMAZON

Fruits and vegetables make up the basis of the jungle diet. If you make the trip to the Amazon basin, you are sure to encounter many foods that are foreign to you, such as turtle and game animals. A popular fruit is *camu camu*, which is a small reddish, purple fruit that resembles a cherry and has an extremely high Vitamin C content.

PERUVIAN FUSION FOOD

Peru has experienced mass immigration from places such as Spain, China, Africa, Japan and Italy. These immigrants brought their own techniques and tastes and combined them with traditional Peruvian cooking. This has yielded a cuisine that fuses together the food of four continents. One of the most popular mixed cuisine types in Peru is chifa, or Peruvian-influenced Chinese food. You will also find many "Peruvian" meals, such as lomo saltado, a dish of beef stir-fried with vegetables, spices, soy sauce and potatoes, which combines traditional Peruvian food with Chinese influences. A popular dish called tiradito, raw slices of fish marinated in lime and ginger, shows the role that Japanese cooking has played in Peru.

PERUVIAN DESSERTS

Those with a sweet tooth will not be disappointed with the desserts and sweets of Peru. There are many very popular and delicious choices from which to select. Helados, or ice creams, are one of the most popular treats. Besides traditional ice cream flavors, such as chocolate and vanilla, you can often find exotic flavors made with local fruits. Another common dessert option is alfajores, lemon-flavored pastries with a sweet, creamy filling. Turrones, similar to fudge, are also very popular. They are most commonly made from almonds, although some are made from honey.

INTERNATIONAL FOOD IN PERU

If your time in Peru leaves you a bit homesick, you will be glad to know that many fast food establishments are present in major cities. Kentucky Fried Chicken is particularly popular in Peru. There is even Starbucks in Lima, if you simply must have a Frappuchino. Major cities like Lima and Arequipa, as well as tourist centers like Cusco, are littered with international restaurants serving food from pizza to pad thai.

WHAT TO DRINK IN PERU

The most popular drink in Peru is, by far, the pisco sour. It is made with pisco, which is a type of brandy distilled from grapes. The brandy is then mixed with egg white, lemon, sugar syrup and spirits to make a pisco sour. Chicha is a popular drink in the Andes. It is made with fermented corn and herbs.

For those looking to stay sober, soft drinks are very popular, especially Inca Kola, Peru's bright yellow answer to Coca Cola. Fresh juices are also widely available, but be careful, because they are often prepared with tap water. Most restaurants in touristy areas know to make the juice with purified

Inca Kola

During your time in Peru you are sure to encounter this sweet, yellow soft drink. Its flavor resembles bubble gum, and most in Peru enjoy it at room temperature from a glass bottle.

Launched in 1935, the cola has seen great success in Peru. It has consistently had higher sales then both Coca Cola and Pepsi, declaring itself the drink of Peru. During the 1970s and 80s the drink often used the slogan "Made of National Flavor!" Both Pepsi and Coke strove to catch up with Inca Kola's sales during the 90s, but to no avail. A major hit for Coke during this time was when McDonalds forced them to allow Inca Kola to be sold in their restaurant.

In 1997 Coca Cola began to look into buying out Lindley Corporation, who produced Inca Kola. By 1999 a deal had been worked out. Coca Cola bought 59% of the Inca Kola Corporation and 30% of the Lindley Corporation for $300 million. In return, Lindley Corporation was given the rights to bottle all Coca Cola products in Peru, and Coca Cola was given permission to bottle and sell Inca Kola in other countries. However, Coca Cola only bottles and sells Inca Kola in Ecuador and the Northeast part of the United States. Today Inca Kola continues to dominate the soda market in Peru. Be sure to give it a try, and see why its flavor has experienced such popularity in Peru. Updated: Jul 23, 2007.

Pisco Sour

Want to see the gloves come off? Gather a Peruvian and a Chilean, then ask them where the best Pisco comes from. Make sure you stand far back, because the fight could get dirty; a huge controversy surrounds this grape brandy.

The history of Pisco production dates back to the beginning of the colonial era and the early wine-producers in what would become southern Peru. In order to supplement their income, these viticulturists produced a stronger, cheaper drink, which they sold at the port of Pisco. Today, Peruvian Pisco production is highly sophisticated and heavily regulated. The spirit comes in several varieties, including Pisco puro, made from a single grape (usually Quebranta or Italia), and Pisco acholado, made from a blend of several grapes. Pisco can be found throughout the Andean region in the form of Pisco Sour, a cocktail made with Pisco, lime juice, sugar, egg whites, and angostura bitters. This delicious drink, an excellent accompaniment to ceviche, is deceptively mild and famous for sneaking up on the unwary.

A veritable war is now being fought between Peru and Chile over the rights to claim Pisco as their respective national drink. While Peru claims its historic origin, Chile was the first to expand its production and create a massive export market. Chileans argue that foreign taste buds recognize their product as the "authentic" version. Peruvians counter that the Chilean version, which allows additives and is yellow in color as opposed to clear, is not "authentic" because it deviates from the traditional method of production. The Pisco battle is not likely to be settled anytime soon. In the meantime, perhaps each side could try to kick back, and have a strong Pisco Sour—made with Pisco from their origin of choice.
Ingredients: 2 oz. Pisco; ¾ oz. lime juice; ½ oz. simple syrup (granulated sugar melted in water); 1 egg white; 3 oz. ice or enough to fill a cocktail shaker; a few dashes of Angostura bitters.

First make the simple syrup. Then, blend together Pisco, lime juice, simple syrup, and egg white with ice. Take an old-fashioned or highball glass, dip the rim in egg white and then sugar. Strain the drink into the glass and sprinkle with a few drops of Angostura bitters. Salud. Updated: Jul 23, 2007.

or boiled water, but a hole in the wall probably won't. Updated: Apr 27, 2010.

WINES OF PERU

Few foreigners realize the tastiness and quality of wines produced in Peru, or the deep history of wine grape cultivation in the country. Though the grape growing region is quite small and doesn't boast the production scale or reputation of larger markets in neighboring Chile or Argentina, the quality of wines is comparable. Also produced in the area and receiving far more fame is the country's national drink, Pisco, a strong traditional beverage extracted from white grapes. Wine grapes were first introduced in the 16th century when Spanish conquistador Marquis Francisco de Caravantes brought wine vines from the Canary Islands and initiated wine production in the region. As production

expanded and Peru began exporting wine to other colonies, Spanish wine producers became nervous and negotiated a ban on wine trade with the king. They successfully shifted focus away from the Peruvian wine trade and towards increased production of grape liquors using pre-Inca style earthenware containers called *piscos*.

These early endeavors of Jesuit monk farmers established the foundation for the trading of Pisco and new centers of production, particularly within the province of Ica, today's center for Peruvian wine culture. The Ica region enjoys fertile soils and the cool air of the Humboldt Current, much like the Napa Valley. The area is blessed with ideal conditions for the cultivation of wine grapes. Peru's best wineries—or *bodegas*—are located here, such as the larger Bodegas Tacama and Ocucaje.

Grape harvest is annually celebrated with lively parades, marching bands, and tastings in Ica every March during the colorful National Vintage Festival. Updated: Oct 26, 2007.

Shopping

Every country has its textile, pottery or art that it's famous for. But Peru is an exception. It has so many quality choices—almost too many. But if you're a shopper, you'll enjoy Lima and Cusco, and not only for cheap prices. From hand-woven tapestries, beautiful crafted silver jewelry, knitted sweaters, scarves, gloves and clothing boutiques—it's a challenge to choose. Traditional folk art or modern contemporary painting? Antique tapestries or newly woven weavings? Ceramics or CDs?

Photo by: Catherine Hofler

Soft, cozy, finely knit Alpaca sweaters are one of the best buys in Peru. While they might be really expensive by Peruvian standards, the cost would still be much higher in Europe or the United States. Alpacas are descendants of camels and cousins to llamas, They evolved thousands of years ago developing a fine hair with remarkable softness, fineness, length, warmth, and strength. But finding the right Alpaca sweater or product is worth a little shopping around.

Alpaca products, from sweaters to gloves to hats to ponchos are abundant

throughout Peru, and especially in Cusco. There are 22 different natural colors of Alpaca. Baby Alpaca makes the most luxorious and soft products. Alpaca became the fiber used to clothe the wealthy Incans. It is said that Baby Alpaca, the first-shorn fiber produced by a juvenile alpaca, was reserved for royalty only. Anyone else found donning the cashmere-like product were penalized, sometimes even killed.

While there are many high-end stores where you can get gorgeous sweaters at a hefty price—over 225 solés—acrylic fakes are abundant as well. Many stores and kiosks (especially in Cusco) advertise real baby alpaca or real 100 percent pure alpaca products for 60 or 70 solés. In all likelihood, these are fakes, even if the store owner says it's real and gives you a long story about who made it. Don't get duped. Real alpaca is beautifully made; the texture is super soft and feels like cashmere. If it's too silky though, it's probably been spun with polyester and if the texture is too rough, it's been spun with sheep's wool. The label also makes a difference. A real alpaca sweater will have the label of the person who made it, or company. Most often, true alpaca items are found in mid-to-high end stores in Cusco and Lima. As always, don't wait for the airport to buy alpaca products; while well-advertised, they are also way overpriced.

Since you are in the land of the Incas, artists have designed some exquisite pre-Colombian art work that you can purchase nearly anywhere, from street markets to museums. A range of Incan designs are painted in a variety of colors from bright oranges and reds to earthy browns and stone blues. Relatively cheap and beautiful, they make a great wall hangings and souvenirs. Most artists and galleries have suitable packaging so that you can take it home without damaging it.

If you're looking for textiles, you won't be disappointed by Peru's numerous indigenous markets. Antique tapestries, which many indigenous Peruvians still use to carry children or food, can be found in the crowded, winding marketplaces of

Cusco, Lima and elsewhere. There is a store on the southwest side of Plaza De Armas that sells beautiful tapestries in a range of colors. Also, Lima's Avenida la

Is it the Real Thing?

You zone out the bustling hum of the surrounding market. You have found the perfect beautiful sweater to keep you warm in the chilly Andes. "Oh, yes, it's wool," the vendor says with a friendly smile.

Ah, but the nagging doubt lingers in your mind; is it the real thing—or synthetic?

You can still rely on touch to tell you—to some degree. Sheep wool is thick and itchy. Alpaca wool is fine, cashmere-soft. It rolls down compactly, yet springs back to its original density when unrolled. Synthetics—polyester the imposter, nefarious nylon—are easily identified, right? Not anymore. Increasingly, these fibers have become almost equal in feel to their authentic counterparts.

But there is still one fool-proof way to know for sure whether that sweater is the real, all-natural, 100% thing. The secret is always to carry a pack of matches in your pocket when you head out to the market to shop for textiles. A lighter will work, also. First, pick a bit of fuzz off the sweater, being careful not to pull the yarns of the garment. Twirl the fuzz to make a strand. Strike a match and burn your strand.

Plant fibers—cotton, linen, ramie and even silk (after all, it comes from mulberry leaves)—will turn to a fine, light-colored ash. Animal fibers—whether from lamb, sheep, alpaca, llama or even critters like qiviut and yak (yes, this test will work on any continent)—will singe and smell like burnt hair. Synthetics will melt into a small black ball and smell like burnt plastic. If the sweater is a combination of animal and synthetic fibers, it will both singe and melt. Depending on how much it does of one or the other, can help you calculate the percentage of blend. Updated: Aug 8, 2007.

Paz Market in Miraflores has many kiosks that sell antique tapestries. These are authentic, so they may be used. However, if you don't a few stains and a musty odor, you'll find authentic textiles at great prices.

The closer you get south towards the silver mines of Bolivia, the more you will begin to see more stores that sell silver, or *platerías* as they are called in Spanish. Earrings, rings, necklaces, bracelets, jacket pins, hair pins, silverware, serving plates, candle stick holders and frames can all be found in both Lima and Cusco. Many are one-of-a-kind and most are handmade in Lima, silver tends to be more expensive, but there are a slew of exceptional silver stalls at the market on Avenida La Paz in Miraflores. Unique designs can be found, and many are actually wrought into Incan symbols, complete with red, blue and green precious stones.

Cusco on the other hand—despite the fact that it is most definitely a tourist town—tends to have more competitive prices due to its proximity to Bolivia. In Cusco there are many *platerías* along Plaza de Armas, which offer variety, but plata of questionable quality. You might also want to head up towards Calle San Blas, where you will find many funky, independently-owned jewelry boutiques that have some incredibly exciting finds.

The guidelines below provide some tips on how to best acquire Peruvian products, regardless of which town you are in:

First trick of the trade: From September to May is considered low season, and many shopowners are likely to cut you a deal

Second: As in all of South America, bargaining is ubiquitous and essential. Don't feel bad or feel like you should give more because they are small shopowners. They expect you to bargain, and if you don't, many locals will actually be offended.

Third: Try to pay in cash. You are likely to get a better deal on the items you are purchasing. This includes even high-end stores where credit cards are common, and readily accepted. The fees associated with credit-card payments tend to be higher than the discounts, so it's worth their while. Updated: Jul 23, 2007.

South American Explorers Club

The South American Explorers' Club has a fairly strong presence in Peru, with clubs in both Lima and Cusco. The club houses have a lot to offer to both travelers and expats and are usually a great place to meet other like-minded people. For travelers, the club is an excellent source for maps, guidebooks and general up-to-date safety and travel information. Sometimes excursions are organized, and there are regular weekly events too. Club members get discounts on all of this, plus cheaper deals in many bars, restaurants and tour agencies in Peru. Note: The SAE Clubhouse is closed on Sundays.

Lima contact details: Calle Piura 135, Miraflores, Lima. Tel / Fax: 51-1-445-3306, E-mail: limaclub@saexplorers.org.

Cusco contact details: Atocsaycuchi 670, San Blas. Mailing Address: Apartado 500, Cusco, Peru. Tel: 51-84-245-484, E-mail: cuscoclub@saexplorers.org. Updated: Apr 24, 2009.

Health and Safety

While traveling in Peru, it is important to feel safe and at ease. It is best to avoid focusing on all the potential diseases you could contract. Instead, just follow our preparation guidelines and you should be fine.

Pharmacies in Peru are conveniently located and are common. As with most Latin American countries, if you tell the pharmacist your symptoms, then he/she will often be able to recommend what you need, helping to avoid a costly visit to the doctor. Reliable national chains are Inkafarma and Fasa. Updated: Mar 25, 2009.

MINOR HEALTH PROBLEMS

Altitude Sickness

When traveling at a high altitude, it is important to rest the first few days and drink lots of bottled water. Should you feel a severe headache, drowsiness, confusion, dry cough and/or breathlessness, drink lots of water and rest. If the symptoms continue, you may want to move to a lower altitude. Anyone planning to hike at high altitudes is advised to relax in a high-altitude city, like Cusco, to get acclimatized for a few days before any physical exertion. Note that altitude sickness, locally called *soroche*, can come on quickly if you experience a sudden change of altitude.

Sunburn/Heat Exhaustion

Peru's high altitudes, where cool breezes constantly blow and snow can accumulate, can be deceptive, but the sun is incredibly strong. Apply sunscreen with at least an SPF of 30 every few hours you are outside. If you get a severe sunburn, treat it with a cream and stay out of the sun for a while. To avoid overheating, wear a hat and sunglasses and drink lots of water. Overweight people are more susceptible to sunstroke. The symptoms of heat exhaustion are profuse sweating, weakness, exhaustion, muscle cramps, rapid pulse and vomiting. If you experience heatstroke, go to a cool, shaded area until your body temperature normalizes and drink lots of water. If the symptoms continue, consult a doctor.

Motion Sickness

Even the hardiest of travelers can be hit by motion sickness on the buses in the Peruvian Andes. Sit near the front of the bus or stay above deck on the boat and focus on the horizon. If you are prone to motion sickness, eat light, non-greasy food before traveling and avoid drinking too much, particularly alcohol. Over-the-counter medications such as Dramamine can prevent it. In Peru, go to a pharmacy and ask for Mareol, a liquid medicine similar to Dramamine. If you suffer from severe motion sickness, you may want to get a prescription for something stronger, like the patch. Ginger is good for mild motion sickness and can be bought in pill form but might be hard to find in Peru.

Traveler's Diarrhea

This is probably the most common disease for travelers. There is no vaccine to protect you from traveler's diarrhea; it is avoided by eating sensibly. Contrary to popular belief, it is usually transmitted by food, not contaminated water. Eat only steaming hot food that has been cooked thoroughly in clean establishments. Avoid raw lettuce and fruit that cannot be peeled, like strawberries. Vegetables are usually safer than meat. An inexpensive vegetable wash (known as vitalín) can be purchased at any supermarket and is a good way to ensure clean fruit and vegetables if you are cooking your own meals.

Make sure any milk you drink has been boiled. Avoid ice cream that could have melted and been refrozen, such as anything for sale in the street. *Helado de paila*, which is made from natural fruit juices and egg whites, is safer since it doesn't contain milk. If you do get diarrhea, the best way is to let it run its course while staying hydrated with clear soups, lemon tea, Gatorade and soda that has gone flat. Bananas are also a good source of potassium and help stop diarrhea. If you need to travel and can't afford to let the illness run its course, any pharmacy will give you something that will make you comfortable enough for a bus trip. If the diarrhea persists for more than five days, see a doctor. Updated: Mar 24, 2009.

MORE SERIOUS HEALTH PROBLEMS

Hepatitis

If you are planning to live in Peru for more than six months or work in a hospital, it may a good idea to get a vaccination against hepatitis. However, this is not considered necessary for short-term travelers. Avoid situations where you could be subject to being punctured by a dirty needle. Needless to say, it is a good idea to stay away from any sort of questionable injection. It is also not a good idea to get a piercing while traveling, especially at the popular outdoor markets.

Malaria

Some doctors around the world will tell you that if you travel anywhere in South America, you must take pills to prevent malaria. This is not true. Malaria is only found on the Pacific Coast and in the Amazon Rainforest. If you are only traveling in the Andes, you run no risk of contracting malaria. However, if you plan to spend a lot of time along the Pacific Coast or in the Amazon Rainforest, it is a good idea to take the proper measure to prevent the disease. Mosquitoes carrying malaria are evening and nighttime biters.

If you are planning to go to the Amazon Rainforest for a couple of days, you may want to ask the staff of the lodge for recommendations. Many areas of the Amazon are relatively mosquito-free because black-water rivers are inhospitable breeding grounds for mosquitoes. Thoroughly apply insect repellent with at least 30 percent DEET. Applying to your hair is good way to make the scent stay on your body longer. Sleep under a mosquito net, wear light colored clothes and avoid shiny jewelry. Also, avoid using scented soaps or perfumes.

Rabies

There are stray dogs throughout Peru that are usually harmless. However, many homeowners train guard dogs to attack trespassers. On long hikes in rural areas, always carry a walking stick to defend yourself if a dog starts to attack. In case you are bitten by a dog, rabies vaccinations are readily available in Lima and other major cities.

Typhoid

An oral capsule or injection should be taken if you are planning to travel in Peru or South America for an extended period of time (six months or more). The injection needs boosting every three years.

Yellow Fever

This mosquito-born disease is endemic to Peru and many other parts of South America. Talk to your doctor before taking the vaccine, as it is not recommended for people with certain allergies, pregnant women and other special cases. The vaccine is good for ten years. Updated: Feb 26, 2009.

SAFETY

As is true in most Latin American countries, travelers tend to stand out in Peru. There is a good chance you will stand a head taller than the crowds on rural buses throughout the country, and people will notice that you're foreign. As a result, travelers are easy targets for petty crime. Although crime in Peru is rarely violent, good street sense and awareness must be exercised. In crowds, always hold your bag close to your body and in front of you where you can see it. Most thieves work in teams; one will distract you while the other slashes your bag or picks your pocket. If you are approached by a suspicious person asking for money or the time, just walk away quickly. Don't let yourself get cornered.

Distribute important documents into at least two stashes. Keep your passport, at least one credit card and most of your cash well protected under your clothes—either in a money belt, in-sewn pocket or other contraption. Keep a wallet or coin purse within easy reach (but NOT in a hip pocket) with a small amount of money and perhaps a second credit card for daily food and shopping, so that you don't have to reach into your main reserve when you aren't in a comfortable space.

In most cities in Peru, the dodgy neighborhoods are easy to identify; they are around bus stations and major outdoor markets. Lodging is usually slightly cheaper in these areas, but for a dollar or two more a night, you can get a substantial upgrade worth the peace of mind. Researching the perfect spot beforehand is the best way to avoid being stuck in a neighborhood that makes you uncomfortable.

Prominent Press in Peru

Daily Newspapers:
El Comercio
El Peruano
Expreso
La Republica
Gestion
Ojo
Liberación
Correo

TV Channels:
Frecuencia Latina
America Televisión
Panamericana Televisión S.A
Nacional del Perú
ATV, Andina de Televisión

Magazines:
Caretas
Gente
Cosas
Semana Economíca
Agro Noticias
Minas y Pozos
Diplomacia & Negocios Internacionales
Viceversa
Empresa Privada
Empresarial
Bussines
Comercio y Produccion
Medio Empresarial
Caucus
Rumbos de Sol & Piedra

Radio Stations:
Radioprogramas del Perú (RPP)
Cadena Peruana de Noticias (C.P.N)
Radio Nacional del Perú
Radio "El Pacífico"
Radio "Santa Rosa"
Radio Milenia
Radio R/C-Comas
Radio Canto Grande
Radio Latina
Radio Libertad
Coordinadora Nacional de Radio CNR
Radio "Miraflores"
Radio "Stereo Lima 100"

Media

The government of Peru officially recognizes free mass media. Unfortuately, from 1968 until the rule of Alberto Fujimori during the 1990s, the country saw little media independence. Ironically, it was the media that brought the Fujimori scandal to light. The government continues to exert power over media outlets by purchasing advertising that promotes pro-government views, but there is much more freedom of expression attained by journalists in the press today.

Privately owned and operated broadcasting and newspaper companies control the media scene in Peru. State-run stations have a home on the air and TV waves, but are not popular.

The leading Lima daily newspapers are El Comercio, Ojo, and Expreso, distributed throughout the nation. Official government decrees are published in the official government newspaper, El Peruano.

Mail and Packages
Peru's postal service is reasonably efficient, especially now that it is managed by a private company (Serpost S.A.).

SENDING MAIL LOCALLY
When addressing local mail, note that "Jr." doesn't mean "junior"; it is a designation meaning "Jirón," or street. Sometimes in place of a number for a street addresses is "s/n." This abbreviation simply means "sin número," or no number. The house or building with such an address is unnumbered.

SENDING MAIL ABROAD
Letters and postcards to North America take between 10 days and two weeks. If you are purchasing large quantities of textiles and other handicrafts, you can send packages home from post offices, but it is expensive.

UPS is found in Arequipa and Lima, but its courier services cost nearly three times as much as those of DHL. Another option, if you have computer access, is L-Mail. Through this ingenious website, you can write a letter, create an audio letter, and the company will print it out and post it for you from a location close to your mailing destination.

All overseas mail is sent first class, airmail (SA=South America, NA=North America, E=Europe, A/O=Asia/Oceania).

RECEIVING MAIL
You can have mail sent to you, care of any main post office (Correo Central). Have letters addressed with your full name (last

name in capitals), Poste Restante, Lista de Correos, Correo Central, city or town, Peru. The South American Explorers' Clubhouses in Lima or Cusco are also places where members can receive mail and packages. Membership is $50 a year for all four locations (Lima, Cusco, Quito and Buenos Aires).

Mailing Address SAE Lima: Ca. Piura 135, Miraflores, Lima
Mailing Address SAE Cusco: Apartado 500, Cusco.

CUSTOMS AND MAIL FEES

Letters to North America cost around $1 to send, while those to Europe will cost around $1.20. When sending packages, you will pay more than $100 for 10 kilograms (22 lbs.), similar to what it costs to use DHL, which will probably get your package to your destination faster.Updated: Jun 30, 2010.

Telephones and Calling

PERU CELL PHONES

Upon arrival to the airport you may find vendors renting cell phones for the duration of your stay in Peru. Many travelers have had a positive experience with the Peru Rent, a ceullar telephone company. In general, all incoming calls are free, long distance rates are lower, there are no international/roaming charges, there is a free concierge service and rates are lower than prepaid rates. There are a couple of plans to choose from.

Plan A has an activation fee of $9.99 and the rate is $1.49 per minute, with no charge for incoming calls.

Plan B has no activation fee, a daily charge of $9.99 and a rate of $0.99 per minute.

Global Systems for Mobiles (GSM) is the wave of the future in the cell phone world. You need both a world-capable multiband width phone using a GSM system. This allows you to communicate in Peru, or Kenya, or Nepal. Once you have acquired these two things, call your provider before your trip and have "international roaming" activated. There is a downside to all of this technology—it isn't cheap. Roaming per minute can cost anywhere from $1 to $5 in some countries, so ask before you talk eight hours a day.

Another practical option, if you will be in Peru for an extended amount of time, is to buy a cheap cell phone. Local calls are relatively cheap, and incoming calls are free. You can choose a plan, or instead simply load your phone with minutes from a prepaid calling card (see below: Peru Calling Cards), and when they run out enter more minutes.

CALLING PERU

If you want to save money and the person you are calling has access to a computer, look into an Internet call via programs like Skype or iChat for very little cost or free.

From North America

If you have to call Peru from the U.S. or Canada, first dial the U.S./Canadian exit code (011), followed by Peru's country code (51), the appropriate city code, and lastly, the phone number itself.

Example: 011-51-54-526975

011 (U.S. exit code) + 51 (Peru country code) + city code (1-2 digits) + phone number (6-7 digits).

When calling a cell phone dial the following:

011 + 51 + area code + 9XX XXX XXX

From Europe

To call Peru from Europe, follow the instructions listed above, substituting the U.S. exit code with 00.

From Latin America

To call Peru from most Latin American Countries, follow the instructions listed above (Calling Peru from Europe). Brazil, however, is an exception. In this case, the exit code is followed by a two digit "carrier code." The following is a list of carrier codes:

- •   14 (Brasil Telecom)
- •   15 (Telefonica)
- •   21 (Embratel)
- •   23 (Intelig)
- •   31 (Telemar)

From Elsewhere

To dial Peru from most countries around the world, follow the following format:

00-51-XX-XXXXXX

Within Peru

In Peru, fijo (land line) phones generally have

six digits; people sometimes write them as XXXXXX, other times XX-XXXX and others XXX-XXX (you'll see the same number written all three ways at times). In Lima, fijos have seven digits. Phone codes begin with "o", Example: 074-044054

Calling Home
For international calls, dial 00 + country code + city code + telephone number.

Peru Calling Cards
Phone cards, called Tarjeta 147, can be purchased at newspaper kiosks and street vendors. To use the card, first rub off the secret code number. Dial the numbers 1-4-7 and then dial the 12-digit number on the card. A voice recording will tell you (in Spanish only) the value remaining on the card and instruct you to dial the desired telephone number. It will then tell you how many minutes you can expect to talk with the amount remaining. These cards can be made to make long distance calls.

Local Phone Codes

For local calls, you do not need to dial the area code (01 for Lima; three digits for all other cities—i.e. 054 for Arequipa); dial only the number. To make a long-distance call within Peru, dial the city code (including the zero) + telephone number. The following is a list of important city codes:

* **Arequipa:** 54
* **Cajamarca:** 76
* **Chiclayo:** 74
* **Cusco:** 84
* **Huancayo:** 64
* **Iquitos:** 65
* **Lima:** 1
* **Puno:** 51
* **Trujillo:** 44

Emergency Phone Numbers
To call information service, dial 103, for the operator 100, and international operator 108. In case of emergency, dial 105 for police, or in Lima, the tourist police at 225-8698.

NOTE: In the mid-1990s Spain's Telefónica privatized the national phone system, making it much more efficient. Many area codes in Peru were changed in 2003. Be wary of published telephone numbers, since many still contain old area codes. Updated: Sep 25, 2008.

Internet Access
Internet access is widely available in Peru, and even if you aren't traveling with your own laptop, you are bound to run in to Internet cafés, even in the smallest of towns. Computers with webcams and Skype capabilities are easy to find at internet cafés in bigger cities.

INTERNET CAFÉS IN PERU
Peru is well connected to the Internet with an abundance of inexpensive Internet kiosks, called *cabinas públicas*, available on just about every other street corner in most towns and every big city. Internet cafés, are also popular and easy to locate. Connection speeds are usually fast and reliable and fees to use Internet per hour usually run between $0.50 and $1. Youth hostels, hotels, barsand restaurants commonly have Internet for tourists and travelers to use for a small fee.

WIFI IN PERU
If you have WiFi or Blue Tooth in your laptop, you may be lucky enough to pick up a wireless signal from local networks if you are in a big city, or you can use your computer at an array of internet cafés or hotels that provide codes for WiFi surfing.

If you're traveling outside the reach of your ISP, the iPass network has dial-up numbers in most of the world's countries. You'll have to sign up with an iPass provider, who then tells you how to set up your computer for your destination. For a list of iPass providers, go to www.ipass.com and click on "Individual Purchase."

Although obvious, don't forget to back up all your work on your laptop. Thieves love to steal these electronics and if you take your eye off of your laptop for one moment in a public location, it is bound to be gone for good.

OTHER WAYS TO CONNECT
If you need to access files on your office computer while abroad, look into a service called GoToMyPC (www.gotomypc.com). It will allow you to get into all your files and programs on your desktop computer or laptop left behind at the office or at home. This allows you the comfort of working from abroad, without worrying about losing a laptop or having to make too many phone calls to the office.

Money and Costs
For the last several years Peruvian currency has stood at roughly three solés to one American dollar, making the cost of travel in this country

especially economical for budget-minded tourists. With this three-to-one ratio in mind, you can calculate costs accordingly, and frequently housing, food, and transportation costs are cheap; you can buy a decent lunch for $3 in cities such as Lima or Cusco.

Photo by: Whil.travel

Indeed, if your intention is to see as much of Peru on as low a budget possible, your daily costs can go for no more than $15 a day. But that means hostels with shared bathrooms and taking some of the cheaper (and riskier) buses between cities. If you are willing to spend at least twice that you can upgrade your comfort level and avail yourself to such activities as museums and guided tours.

Travelers with few budget restrictions will be able to glide through Peru; there are many top-quality hotels, restaurants, and tour operators that are relatively inexpensive by first-world standards.

The following banks have an agreement to exchange American Express travelers checks with no commission: Banco del Crédito del Perú (BCP), Interbank and Scotiabank Perú. Some branches of Interbank will also exchange other brands of travelers checks (Thomas Cook, MasterCard, Visa, Citibank, Citicorp). This differs from city to city, so check the local branch. In some cities Banco Azteca is open 365 days per year and into the evening. It exchanges U.S. dollars. (Though the rate

seems to differ from city to city, for example in Piura the rate could be bad, whereas Nasca and Tacna could have a much better exchange rate). A number of businesses handle Western Union transactions and the most convenient is Scotiabank. MoneyGram services are available at Banco de la Nación. Both banks fulfill money wires in solés or U.S. dollars. Updated: Sep 25, 2008.

Banks

ATMs are readily available in Lima, with many offering 24-hour service. Just approach them with caution, in particular at night, since many thieves target them. In general *casas de cambio*, or foreign-exchange bureaus, tend to give better rates than a bank for cash. They can be found throughout the city, with the highest concentrations being in touristy areas, such as Miraflores.

American Express

Lost or stolen travelers checks can be replaced here; however, they do not cash checks. They are open from 9:00 a.m. to 5:30 p.m. on Mondays through Fridays, and 9:00 a.m. to 1:00 p.m.on Saturdays. Santa Cruz 621, Miraflores. Tel: 51-1-221-8204, E-mail: amexcard@travex.com.pe.

Banco Continental

This bank chain in Lima is open from 9:00 a.m. to 6:00 p.m. on Monday through Friday, and 9:30 a.m. to 12:30 p.m. on Saturdays.

BCP

One of the more prevalent bank chains in Lima. All branches have 24-hour ATMs that make cash advances on Visa. Their bank also will change Amex, Citicorp and Visa travelers checks. They are open from 9:00 a.m. to 6:00 p.m. on Mondays through Fridays, and 9:30 a.m. to 12:30 p.m. on Saturdays.

Moneygram

If you need money wired to you, this is a good option. They are open from 10:00 a.m. to 6:30 p.m. Monday through Saturday. Alfredo Benavides 735, Miraflores. Tel: 51-1-241-2222, E-mail: moneyecpress@terra.com.pe.

Western Union

Western Union is another good choice if you need money wired to you in Peru. There are various locations all over the country, so you are sure to find one that is convenient for you. The best way to find the one that will work best for you is to visit their website at www.westernunion.

com, where you can find addresses, phone numbers and hours for the different stores. Updated: Jul 10, 2007.

Credit Cards

All international hotels and most higher-priced hotels and restaurants accept Visa and Mastercard. Many also accept Diners Club and American Express cards. Beware: an extra 10 percent is often added to your total bill if you pay with a credit card. Depending on the price, you may be better served withdrawing the cash from an ATM and stashing the credit cards. In general, most Peruvian shops do not accept credit cards. However, some exceptions are stores in larger malls as well as high-end gift and artesanía shops.

Etiquette and Dress

South Americans are usually polite, and Peruvians are no exception to this rule. When entering restaurants, a store, or even browsing goods at an outdoor market, its expected to greet the staff with a "*buenos dias*," "*buenas tardes*" or "*buenas noches*," depending on the time of day and to say "*gracias*" or "*hasta luego*" when you leave. Greetings involving women are a kiss on the right cheek and between two men, a handshake.

HOW TO DRESS

Peruvians are generally better dressed than most North Americans and Europeans, so if you're wearing old, tattered travel clothes and flip flops, you will invariably get some stares. That said, Peruvians are patient with the ways of the traveler and will treat you respectfully regardless of how raggedy your outfit—as long as you aren't trying to get into a nice restaurant, bar or club.

In the Andes, people tend to cover up a lot more than on the coast, partially because of the cooler climate and partially because the culture tends to be a bit more conservative. You will rarely see an Andino wearing shorts off the fútbol field, and flip flops are an oddity. Men should never plan to travel bare-chested in the Andes. Likewise, women should never wear just a sports bra or swimsuit around town. If blending in is important to you, wear pants more often than shorts, don't fly in a t-shirt and shorts and don't wear flip flops. When going out at night, men should wear collared shirts and women should wear clean, stylish clothes—pants are fine. On the coast and outside of the main cities, these rules are much more relaxed.

FOOD MANNERS

Like all countries, there is a certain way to eat all typical meals, like tossing popcorn and fried banana chips into ceviche soup, for example. Table manners are more relaxed, though, so don't worry too much about them. Tables at casual, crowded restaurants are often shared; so don't be surprised. When you get up to leave or join someone's table, it is appropriate to say "buen provecho"—bon appétit.

When visiting someone's home for a party or meal, it is polite to bring a small gift like a cake for dessert or a bottle of wine. Bigger gifts can be overwhelming and the host may feel like he or she needs to give you something in return, so stick with something small. Peruvians are generous by nature and will want to feel one ahead in gift exchanges, so try not to overwhelm your host with expensive presents.

If you are staying with your host for an extended period of time, offer to help out with groceries and bring fresh flowers. A memento from your hometown like a photo, post card or small book will be appreciated. Also remember that, unless you are staying with one of Peru's handful of insanely rich families, your visit will probably be something of a financial strain. You can make it less so by taking short showers—hot water is expensive—and minimizing electricity use—also extremely expensive. Phone calls to cell phones should never be made from land lines—they are expensive. Phone service and internet service in general tends to be very pricey, so try not to run up your host's bill. Updated: Jul 23, 2007

Responsible Tourism

Tourism is an extremely important source of income to Peru. Support this nation by encouraging local industries. Eat at local restaurants and stay at locally-owned hotels as opposed to international chains. There is a wide selection of comfortable, clean and reasonably priced hotels all over the country owned and operated by Peruvians. V!VA Travel Guides usually mentions if the owners are foreign, so choose wisely.

Use water and electricity carefully. When city officials cut down on the community's supply, travelers are usually given preference, so don't abuse the privilege.

BEGGARS

Don't give money or candy to children begging. You are just encouraging this destructive cycle by financing parents willing to send their little ones out onto the streets to work. Many disabled adults and senior citizens also beg; you can decide if you want to help them out or not, many Peruvians do.

PHOTOGRAPHY

ALWAYS ask before taking photographs or videos of people. Just because people look and dress differently doesn't mean you're in a zoo. Show your respect by talking to people before making them a souvenir of your vacation.

ENVIRONMENTAL AWARENESS

An ecotourism movement is slowly but surely making its way through Peru. The habits of throwing trash out bus windows and littering in general are deeply ingrained in Peruvian collective consciousness. Be responsible by not participating in these bad habits and make a point of leaving camping areas, nature walks, picnics, etc. cleaner than you left them. Peruvian cities have started putting up "Do Not Litter" signs, but there is a long way to go. Consider staying at an eco-lodge or volunteering for an organization working to educate the community and preserve the environment.

Photography

Peru provides amazing photographic opportunities, from the sweeping vistas at Machu Picchu to the still waters of Lake Titicaca.

High quality film can be found in most tourist locations and in all large cities. Fuji, Kodak, Konica, Polaroid and Forte film brands from 50 ASA to 400 ASA are commonly sold, but the higher speeds, especially 1600, are scarce. Color, black and white and slide film are widely available. The most common formats are 35 mm, 120 mm and Advantix (from Kodak). Professional formats like 6 x 6 are rare, but can be acquired at specialty stores. These stores also sell camera accessories such as batteries, cleaning kits, lenses, bags, tripods, flashes and filters and will perform technical services.

Pack an extra camera battery or camera charger (make sure you also pack and adapter for any electrical equipment: Peru uses 220 V, 60 Hz), as these accessories will be harder to come by. You will not want your camera to run out of battery life when you are in the middle of Colca Canyon or the Amazon jungle.

Camera equipment should be packed in airtight plastic bags when traveling to the rainforest to protect against the humid climate. When going through airport X-ray machines, ask to have your camera and film excluded from the screening process, as it can cause damage.

Film Development and Camera Repair

Laboratorio Color Profesional
Hours: Monday - Friday, 9 a.m. - 7 p.m., Saturday, 9:30 a.m. – 1 p.m. Av. Benavides 1171, Miraflores. Tel: 51-1-214-8430 or 51-1-242-7575.

Professional quality developing. One-day service available, highly recommended. Advantix, Color, B/W.

Foto Cristina Kodak Pro Center
Hours: Monday - Friday, 9 a.m. - 8:30 p.m., Saturday, 9 a.m. - 6 p.m. Calle Victor Maurtua 110, San Isidro. Tel: 51-1-440-4898, fotoscristina @infonegocio.net.pe

Kodak Express
Jr. De la Union 790, Lima. Tel. 51-1-428-6025.

There was no text here
Hours: Most stores open Monday - Saturday, 9 a.m. - 9 p.m. Av. Larco 1005, Miraflores Las Begonias 670, San Isidro
Tel: 51-1-441-2800

Taller de Fotografia Profesional
Hours: Monday - Friday, 9 a.m. - 7 p.m., Saturday, 9:30 a.m. - 1 p.m. Av. Benavides 1171, Miraflores. Tel: 51-1-241-1015 / 446-7421

Recommended for repairs.

If you are taking photographs of local people, always ask their permission beforehand. Do not take photographs of military installations or airports. There may be a charge to take pictures at museums or national tourist sights. Updated: Jul 23, 2007.

Travel Tips

WOMEN TRAVELERS
Female travelers, especially gringas,

should expect local men to call out to them and/or whistle. However, realize that this is as big of a part of Latin and Peruvian culture as the food or the art. Usually ignoring the comments or actions is sufficient, but occasionally words will need to be said.

Either way, keep walking. A good way to avoid this type of harassment is to cover up and avoid flirting. If the attention is really bothering, wearing a ring on your left hand may help. Traveling in groups and especially with males will also cut down on the unwanted attention. Use discretion when traveling alone; take cabs after dark, avoid deserted areas and always go with your gut instinct when it comes to safety. Tampons and other female care products are difficult to find outside of the big cities so women should stock up before heading out of an urban environment.

GAY AND LESBIAN TRAVELERS
Most of South America, including Peru has come a long way from the stereotypical male and female roles designated to each sex, especially with the younger generations. Lima, in particular, has an ever-growing gay scene including clubs, bars and gay-friendly travel agencies and hotels. Other cities like Cusco, Arequipa and Iquitos have small yet thriving gay scenes and are accepting of travelers from all walks of life. Be prepared though, as harassment of homosexual males still takes place. A common slang term for a male acting at all effeminate is "Maricón." It's best to avoid public affection of any kind, hetero- or homosexual, and keep a low profile while outside of a gay-friendly area.

Ambiente.com and gayperu.com are good Spanish resources for gay and lesbian travelers and http://lima.queercity.info/index.html is a good English source with gay or gay-friendly bars, restaurants, hotels and hostels in Lima.

SENIOR TRAVELERS
Energetic and enthusiastic seniors will find Peru extremely satisfying. Many travel agencies offer group tours of everything from the big cities to the ruins to hiking up mountains. Most health care providers do not cover travel, so seniors should check with their provider before traveling and buy special travel insurance if necessary. Generally, senior citizens are treated with respect and consideration by the locals. Retirement homes and senior care facilities—typical among gringos—are almost unheard of among South Americans. It is customary for older patrons to live with their children or other younger family members when they reach can no longer care for themselves.

Photo by: Whl.travel

DISABLED TRAVELERS
As in most Latin American countries, travel can be difficult for disabled persons in Peru. Uneven sidewalks, roads and a lack of wheelchair accessible hotels and restaurants can be frustrating. However, Peru is making strides to be more handicapped accessible through a nation-wide disability law. New hotels and restaurants often have wheelchair ramps, though few hotels will have specially-designed rooms. The best bet for travelers in wheelchairs is an upbeat attitude and travel with companions willing and able to lend a hand if need be. Call hotels and restaurants beforehand to ensure their accessibility. We suggest staying at more-expensive international chain hotels as they tend to be more accommodating.

TRAVELERS WITH KIDS
Take special care when traveling with children. In Peru very few central bus terminals exist. Kids can get very restless being dragged from one us office to another while you are looking for which bus to catch and at what price. In many cities it is difficult to board with a child and stroller. Because it can be difficult to get around with a stroller, travel costs increase, as you will be relegated to taking taxis to and from bus depots.

Once on the bus, children pay the full amount if they take up a seat, but sit them on your lap and they often ride for free on domestic buses. Generally, traveling families have few problems as locals tend to treat children with a lot of respect. Teach your child to say "Gracias" and "Por Favor" and the locals will get a real kick out of it. Bargaining is appropriate, if not encouraged, for family rates at hotels, and sharing food between children at a restaurant is fine. Discounts are often given for children on airplanes and make sure to ask your travel agent about special packages and itineraries for families. Updated: Aug 06, 2008.

)!)!)

Cusco

In addition to serving as a gateway to nearby attractions like Machu Picchu and the Inca Trail, Cusco offers travelers a host of culturally enticing museums, cathedrals and markets that make this city an excellent addition to any itinerary. For outdoor enthusiasts, the Cusco area presents a number of spectacular trekking opportunities. And for those who want to stretch their legs a bit but aren't up for a week-long adventure over mountainous terrain, the nearby Inca ruins of Sacsayhuamán, Q'enqo, Puca Pucara, Tambo Machay, Tipón, and Pikillacta and Rumicolca make excellent day trips.

In Quechua its name translates to "belly button of the world," and at its height Cusco truly was the center of the great Inca Empire, which stretched across parts of South America from Northern Chile to Colombia. In terms of architectural prowess and political importance, Cusco paralleled the well-known Aztec capital of Tenochtitlán as one of the great imperial capitals of America.

Today, Cusco is known for its inviting and intriguing blend of Spanish and Inca culture, most evident where Spanish churches and convents had been built squarely on top of perfectly laid Inca walls. While the Spanish did their best to pillage and plunder the city, they failed to completely destroy the massive network of Inca stonework, which continues to withstand both time and the elements, while the Spanish buildings crack and crumble. The Quechua people, the present-day ancestors of the Incas, are also a foundation for the city and bring the charm, humility and beauty that keep tourism booming in Cusco.

Because the city is a popular destination along the Gringo Trail, it has a variety of hotels and restaurants to accommodate any traveler's tastes, from five-star, world-class hotels to hostels the most miserly of backpackers will find affordable. It is an extremely visitor-friendly city, with tour agencies on every block and very helpful locals. Most of the major Cusco activities are within walking distance of one another and can be covered in about half a day, though you may want to devote a little more time to browse the various shops and markets you may encounter along the way. Some Cusco highlights include the Cusco Cathedral, Iglesia San Blas, San Blas, Qoricancha Templo del Sol and Santo Domingo, Museo Histórico Regional, Museo de Arte y Monasterio de Santa Catalina.Updated: Jul 17, 2007.

When to Go

The best season to hit Cusco is April through October, when the region is hot and dry during the day. However, temperatures drop drastically in the evening, and can approach freezing even in the dry season. November to April sees some rainfall and lower temperatures during the wet season; however, the advantage is that from September to May tourist numbers drop and as do prices. Cusco becomes packed with Peruvians and foreigners alike during all the major holidays, so book ahead. Travelers should also be forewarned that the Inca Trail closes for necessary maintenance for the entire month of February. Cusco is the center of much festival activity, so check the festival calendar before planning your route. Updated: Aug 09, 2007.

Safety in Cusco

Cusco has the highest rate of crime targeted at tourists in Peru. That said, there a few precautions that you can take to avoid being robbed. Taxis tend to be the biggest danger. As in the rest of Latin America, it is important to only take registered (radio) taxis. It is best never to walk alone late at night or early in the morning, as these times are the most common times for attacks. Word to the wise, as dehydration is a common effect of altitude sickness, caffeine, smoking and alcohol will only serve to intensify one's symptoms. Drink lots of water. Even though you're exhausted from just crossing the road at high altitude, don't even think about reaching for the tap, be sure to buy bottled water!

Chewing coca leaves or drinking coca tea is a good solution for symptoms of altitude sickness, or soroche. Also be cautious in bars, as drink-spiking is frequently reported. Be especially careful in trains and busy markets, where pickpockets and bag-slashers easily conceal themselves among the throngs of people. Updated: Jun 17, 2009.

Cusco History

CUSCO YESTERDAY

Cusco is best known for its Inca and colonial periods; however, those two epochs represent only about one-third of Cusco's settled history. The city's first settlements, located in the eastern part of the current city, date as far back as 3,000 years. As a result, some consider Cusco to be the longest continually settled city in the Americas. In the years since those first residents, various settlers have come and gone, including the Wari invaders around 750 AD—a period which preceded the construction of the buildings which today are called Pikillacta.

The Inca Civilization began around 1200 AD, and with it came the development of Cusco into a major political and religious center, one that could serve a relatively large population. A large expansion phase began around 1400 AD, when the Incas laid out the city in the shape of a puma, their sacred animal. The expansion was short-lived as the Spanish would arrive in the next century, on November 15, 1533. Thus began violent and ruthless attempts to conquer the city. In 1536 the Incas rebelled against the Spanish in an attempt to regain control of the city. The ensuing war lasted 36 years, finally ending when the head of Túpac Amaru, the Inca dynasty's last emperor, was lopped off in Cusco's main square.

Cusco experienced a large earthquake in 1650, after which nearly every colonial building needed to be rebuilt (further emphasizing the quality of the Inca architecture, much of which remains standing today). A valiant attempt at emancipation was attempted in 1780 by José Gabriel Thupa Amaro Inga. When he was betrayed by his followers, and he and his whole family were executed in Cusco's main square. Independence was finally achieved in 1821, following a long, bloody process that served as the template for Latin America. Updated: Jun 17,2009

CUSCO TODAY

Once a stunning Inca capital, Cusco today offers one of the finest mixes of pre-Columbian, colonial and modern mestizo culture of any South American city. Cusco is often referred to as the archeological capital of South America. The colonial history of the city is not completely untouched, but the central historical area has not undergone an overwhelming number of alternations despite the high concentration of stores, hotels, restaurants, tour operators and other tourist-driven enterprises. A quick walk through the city allows visitors to see the influence

of different periods of history with the naked eye. Inca ruins such as the Temple of the Sun contrast with Spanish churches and mansions, underscoring Cusco's various phases of development.

Cusco's unique mix of Amerindian and mestizo culture has persevered despite a massive influx of tourism. The best example is Inti Raymi, an Inca tradition that celebrates the winter solstice, according to the ancient Inca sundial. Locals and tourists alike are welcome to participate in the day-long event, in a show of how Cusco has reconciled its indigenous history with its recent tourism boom. Updated: Jun 17,2009

Lake Titicaca and the Founding of Cusco

Legend has it that when the ancient sun god made his two children, Manco Capac and Mama Ocllo, they emerged out of Lake Titicaca and on an island in the lake, he gave them a great golden staff to be used for a specific task. The task? Founding the Peruvian Incas and finding the most appropriate location by sticking the staff into the ground. Manco and his sister, Mama, searched Peru high and low for the right spot, but the staff would not stick into the ground. Finally, they came upon the most beautiful place they had seen yet. They stuck the staff in the ground and it stuck. They founded the city of Cusco, conquering the tribes already living there and ruling them under the Inca Empire. Manco married his sister and they ruled side-by-side.

So, for instance, to call the Guayaquil number 232-7100 from Quito, you would dial 04-232-7100. A mobile number must always be dialed with 08 or 09, then the seven-digit phone number.

Some legends say that in the spot where they stuck the golden staff, Manco and Mama also built a Temple of the Sun dedicated to their father. If the legends are correct Manco would have been ruling the Incas in about the 12th century. During the 17th century, the Santo Domingo Church and Qoricancha were built on the site of the Temple of the Sun; the spot remains one of the biggest and most impressive tourist attractions in Cusco. Updated: Jun 17, 2009

Getting To and Away

For the sake of convenience, most people get to Cusco via airplane; a bus from Lima can cost $35 but takes 26 hours. You can break up the trip by stopping over in Nasca, but you would still have to leave at night to resume your trip. By contrast, a plane trip costs $100 and only takes an hour. Except for chartered planes, there are no international flights to Aeropuerto Internacional Velasco Astete in Cusco, aside from flights to La Paz. The train stations, Estación de Huanchaq and Estación de San Pedro, connect to Aguas Calientes (Machu Picchu), Arequipa, Puno, and the Oriente (the Amazon jungle). There is also bus service between Cusco and those four regions.

BY AIR

If you plan on going to Cusco from an international city, be aware that all international flights that enter Peru enter through Jorge Chávez Airport in Lima, and you must make a connecting flight. To get to Cusco by air, you will need to book a connecting flight from Lima to Cusco's airport Teniente Alejandro Velasco Astete Airport (CUZ). Travel time is about one hour, but you will often find that international flights to Lima arrive late at night, and connecting flights to Cusco don't leave until the next morning. From Cusco, you can find flights to the other major cities and tourist destinations in Peru.

This often means a night in the airport, or at a hotel, so be careful when booking flights. People often choose to spend the night at the airport, and there is even a Ramada Hotel located inside the airport for the convenience of travelers. It is a busy airport, with many people there either waiting or in transit, all night long. It is relatively safe, but you should always guard your valuables. Regardless, it is recommended that you get to the airport at least an hour and a half before your scheduled departure time.

Air travel in Peru can be expensive, which is why tourists and locals alike often choose buses. But, because of the incredible distance between some of Peru's most alluring landmarks, it sometimes makes more sense to fly, especially if you are on a shorter vacation. Fare can vary wildly, so it is best to do some price shopping beforehand. For example, a flight between Lima and Cusco, one way, can vary in price from around $120 USD to $260. Most airlines have flights between Lima and Cusco five or six times per

day. You can find and compare fares for both international and domestic flights on websites such as www.airtickets-peru.com and www.peruvianairlines.com. Keep in mind that all domestic flights carry with them a tax of around 6 USD.

LAN: Avenida Jose Pardo Avenue # 513 Lima. Tel: 2138300, URL: Http://www.lan.com.

Aerolíneas Star Peru: Av. Comandante Espinar 331 Miraflores, Lima. E-mail: Atencionalcliente@starperu.com, URL: http://www.starperu.com.

Taca Airlines: Av. Irala # 616, Lima. URL: http://www.taca.com.Tel: 59-13-336-7400, E-mail: ventas@aerosur.com, http://www.aerosur.com.

Peruvian Airlines : Av. Santa Cruz 839 3er piso Oficina 4 Miraflores. Tel: 511-716-6000, http://www.peruvianairlines.pe. Updated: Jul 13,2010.

The airport is about three miles (5 kilometers) east-southeast of the city; a cab will take you there for 6 soles ($2), or you can take a bus for one sol. An ATM dispenses cash with most cards. A special feature of this airport is the domesticated and people-friendly alpacas that will greet you, and are open to both petting and pictures.

BY BUS

Traveling to Cusco by bus is the most common and most inexpensive way to reach one of Peru's most popular cities. In fact, due to economic hardships, buses are the only means of transport for most of the population, and this means there are a wide variety of options regarding both bus companies and departure times.

For most of the destinations along the Pan-American highway, you can expect smooth sailing. However, up in the mountains, or in less travelled areas, where nicely paved roads may be a luxury, expect delays due to inclement weather, landslides, mechanical trouble, and traffic. These may add hours to your trip, so be forewarned. The general travel times from Cusco to other destinations are as follows: Lima (24 hours), Puno (7 hours), Arequipa (10 hours), and Nazca (15 hours). Costs are around $1-2 per hour of travel, but the quality of buses can vary, as can the prices, so be careful when choosing a company. Buses traveling between Cusco and other major cities or tourist destinations can often sell out, so it's best to reserve tickets beforehand whenever possible. For longer trips, you may want to reserve a seat on one of the larger (and more expensive) buses that have toilets. Be warned, however, that these toilets are often out-of-order, and not necessarily sanitary. If you book a seat on a bus without a toilet, drivers will usually stop every couple hours for bathroom breaks and to allow passengers to stetch their legs and buy snacks. If all else fails, it's possible to talk to the driver, who may be willing to wait for you to use a bathroom at a stop. Regardless, it is a good idea to bring your own toilet paper and hand sanitizer.

Most bus companies offer two or three levels of service. If you want good quality, and don't mind paying a little more, ask for the "de lujo" (deluxe buses). The higher-quality option ususaly includes dinner served on the bus. The quality of the food can vary from company to company and by personal taste. The lower quality bus companies typically stop at restaurants for breakfast and dinner along the way. No matter the option you choose, bring snacks to tide you over on the long rides. In general, it is wise to be wary of budget service, as it can mean frequent stops and inconveniences. It can sometimes be better to pay a little more for comfort and security. In general, try to avoid certain bus companies that have a reputation among travelers of having safety problems and lacking quality. These companies include: Transportes Ronco Peru, Cueva, Molina Union, and Expreso Huamanga.

You will find that buses between major tourist destinations usually only leave in the afternoon or night. This is due to the incredible distances between places of interest in Peru. If you want to see the scenery, plan on taking the smaller regional buses, and hopping from town to town. In terms of price, both options are about equal, however, there is a difference between the national and regional bus companies. Regional bus companies are usually cheaper, leave much more frequently, are of lower quality, and obviously have shorter routes. The national companies deal with long distance travel, are usually more comfortable, but buses leave for destinations less frequently.

Regardless of the company you choose, try to get a seat on the first floor of the bus. It will be more expensive, but the drive will be more comfortable. Also, avoid seats above the wheels, as the bumps you'll feel will surely keep you awake. Bring a blanket, especially if you chose one of the higher-quality options with air-conditioning, as it gets really cold at night. If you are carrying a large bag, it is best to stow it under the bus, and bring a smaller carry-on with your valuables in it. If you really want to bring your luggage with you in the cabin, it may be a good idea to purchase an extra seat for it.

Some of the best companies to look for are Tespa, Civa, Cruz del Sur and Ormeno. These companies have a wide variety of routes, and high-quality buses. Cruz del Sur, typically the most expensive, offers two-story buses equipped with WiFi, air conditioning, sandwich bar, 180 degree reclining seats, after dinner bingo, and GPS tracking with their central headquarters. A ticket from Lima to Cusco (or the reverse) is around $60. On the newer Civa buses, seats have ample room, and some have personal televisions. Tespa has been rated by the newspaper El Commercio as having the safest and most secure buses in Peru. In addition, it is one of the cheaper high-quality options as tickets from Lima to Cusco are around $50 USD. Other quality bus companies include Línea, Oltursa, and Movil Tour.

There are several websites that offer an overview of bus companies and schedules, such as http://www.sabuses.com and http://www.cusco-peru.info/. The Terminal Terrestre in Cusco is located on Av. Sol, however unlike in some other cities in South America, many of the bus companies have private depots. It's a good idea to look up the address to the bus company you are planning on using, and buy your ticket in advance.

If you are traveling to Machu Pichu or the Sacred Valley, you will find several companies at the Terminal Terrestre that charge about $14 for the five-hour trip.

Company Contact Information:

Cruz Del Sur, 556 Av Pachacutec, Lima Tel: 51-84-221-909, URL: www.cruzdelsur. com.pe.

Ormeno, Located at the Terminal Terrestre, Tel: 51-84-227-501, URL: www. grupo-ormeno.com.

Civa also located at the terminal terrestre Tel: 51-84-249-961, URL: www.civa.com. pe. Updated: Jul 13, 2010.

BY TRAIN

The reason to take a train is because of the view and the experience from the journey. It's a great way to take in the beautiful and overwhelming landscape around Cusco in comfort. Trains leave from Poroy (20 min with taxi from Cusco) to Puno departing at 8 a.m. and arriving in Puno at 6 p.m., cost is $220, lunch is included. The train from Puno to Cusco also starts at 8am and prices are the same. The service run from November - March: Trains run Monday, Wednesday, Saturday and in April - October: Trains run on Monday, Wednesday, Friday and Saturday.

A train from Poroy to Machu Picchu takes about 3 hours and costs $48, $71 or $334 depending on the train. Note that different prices are for different trains, not different compartments in the same train. Don't forget to by an entrance ticket to Machu Picchu at Instituto Nacional de Cultura for 124 soles. Tickets can be booked at the train station or at http://www.perurail.com, a site in both English and Spanish. There are sometimes last minute offerings on the website, so it is worth a visit. Updated: Mar 22,2010

Getting Around

Most of what you will want to see in Cusco is within walking distance of the central Plaza de Armas, but if it is late and/or you are in a hurry and/or going to or from the outlying residential areas, there are plenty of cabs available. However, the tourist police advise to get in only in cabs that have the diamond-shaped sticker of official approval in their windshields. Apart from that, there are many combis, mini-vans, which can take you to the airport and other points around town. Updated: Aug 20, 2007.

Holidays and Festivals

Cusco plays host to several yearly festivals, some driven by Amerindian influences, others by post-Columbian traditions and some that blend both. The most well attended and most popular festival in Cusco is Inti Raymi, the yearly Inca festival celebrating the winter solstice on June 24, according to the Inca Sundial (modern science has since pinned the date to June 21).

Qoyllur Rit'i usually takes place on the Sunday before Corpus Christi. People make the pilgrimage from all over to pray to the Lord of Qoyllur Rit'i who they believe has powers to bring them success in love, school, etc. The festival is capped off by a procession

on the final night when hundreds of people climb the surrounding glaciers and lug down huge icicles. The icicles are melted to produce holy water which is thought to help the sick community members. As in pretty much all Latin American cities, Cusco lets loose for Carnival. The celebration peaks the Monday and Tuesday before Ash Wednesday and is a great time to visit Cusco if you want to party.

Likewise, Semana Santa, held during Easter, is celebrated all over Latin America. Cusco celebrates by holding numerous processions through the streets, including an Easter Monday procession led by El Señor de los Temblores (Lord of the Earthquakes). For the Santuranticuy festival, on December 24, hundreds of artisans head to Cusco's Plaza de Armas to spread their wares out on blankets. It is one of the largest craft fairs in Peru. Updated: Jun 17, 2009.

Gay Life in Cusco

The official flag of the city of Cusco is almost identical to the Rainbow Flag, universally adopted by the gay community as its banner. As globalization, via the information superhighway, has brought the rest of the world to Peru, including a nascent gay-rights movement, cusqueños themselves have become uneasy; some locals have proposed adopting a new flag without actually announcing why.

Cusco has a gay bar/discothèque by the name of "Queen," (at the intersection of the Lorena and Cementerio Streets). This is a small venue located in a poor and dangerous section of the city that would not appeal to most international visitors. However, it is at least a sign of an emerging, if fragile, tolerance for the community. Some gay cusqueños will let you know that at least in the tourist-heavy sections of Cusco, hand-holding and light-kissing is tolerated. Gay-owned cafés and restaurants, such as Macondo and Fallen Angel, have a stylishly camp sensibility. A gay visitor who is planning on an extended stay in Cusco might patronize these establishments and might even find fellow gay men to socialize with. Options for lesbian travelers are more circumscribed, since women have to fight against machismo as well as homophobia. Updated: Jun 17, 2009.

Cusco Services

Tourist Information Office
Monday - Friday 8 a.m. - 6:30 p.m, Saturday 8 a.m. - 2 p.m. Portal Mantas 117-A (next to the La Merced Church). Tel: 51-84-222-032.

Earthquakes

Earthquakes have plagued Cusco for at least the last 500 years. Three major quakes were recorded in the years 1650, 1950 and 1986, each one destroying large parts of the city. The quake of 1950 was responsible for destroying 63 percent of the city's homes, while the one in 1986 felled over 2000 houses. Older, less stable buildings, particularly from the colonial period, suffered the most damage. Following every quake there were concerns that the ancient Inca architecture, Cusco's heritage, would be lost, but the sturdy stonework has so far withstood all assaults from Mother Nature.

Some Cusqueños believe that further quakes can be avoided by paying their respects to the Lord of the Earthquakes, also known as Taytacha Temblores. During the Easter week, on the Monday, before good Friday, an idol resembling a dark-skinned Christ is carried through the city on a silver pedestal. The parade ends with a spectacular farewell to the Lord on Plaza de Armas, before he is returned to the cathedral, hopefully persuaded to prevent shattering natural disasters in the coming year.

Since Cusco is still affected by the occasional tremor, it is a good idea to keep a few safety tips in mind before making your trip:

Carry cash on you
Carry a First Aid Kit with water purification tablets
If the earthquake hits, be prepared to duck under a sturdy piece of furniture
In mountainous areas, watch for landslides, falling rocks and trees.
Expect aftershocks
Have your travel insurance information on hand Updated: Mar 23,2010

I-PERU / PROMPERU
For tourist information and assistance. Monday - Saturday 8.30am - 7.30pm. Av. El Sol 103, Office 102. Tel: 51-84-234-498. Also at Velasco Astete Airport Arrivals Hall. Tel: 51-84-247-364.

Tourist Police
The Tourist Police will provide information and will also investigate crimes that are committed against tourists, such as theft of property. More serious crimes are handled by other law enforcement organizations. Saphi 510. Tel: 51-84-249-654.

Immigration
Visas can be renewed for 30 days without leaving the country for $20. Monday - Friday 8 a.m. - 4 p.m. Av. el Sol 620 (1/2 block uphill from the post office). Tel: 51-84-222-741.

CIMA Hyperbaric Center
Cusco is often breathtaking...in more ways than one. Even the most athletic are not immune to high altitude sickness if they are not accustomed to high up climates. Altitude sickness is a condition which can affect people at over 2,400 meters (8,000 feet) over sea level. Cusco is 3,310 meters (10,859 feet), and such symptoms as dizziness and fatigue can develop into high altitude pulmonary edema (HAPE) or high altitude cerebral edema (HACE). The CIMA Hyperbaric Center, with its hyperbaric chamber, has become one of the most respected clinics in Cusco for treating high altitude sickness. They also provide any and all needed vaccinatio and medical assistance relating to o door sports. 978 Avenida Pardo. Tel: 84-255-550, E-mail: info@cimaperu.c URL: www.cimaperu.com.

Cusco Tourist Ticket / Boleto Turi Cusco
What is it? Even if you plan to few places in and around C purchase the Cusco Tourist Ticket (Boleto Turístico Cusco, or BTC). It's the only way to get into some of Cusco's main attractions. The sites that the Cusco Tourist Ticket covers include:

Museo de Arte y Monasterio de Santa Catalina
Museo Municipal de Arte Contemporaneo
Museo Historico Regional
Museo de Sitio del Qoricancha
Museo de Arte Popular

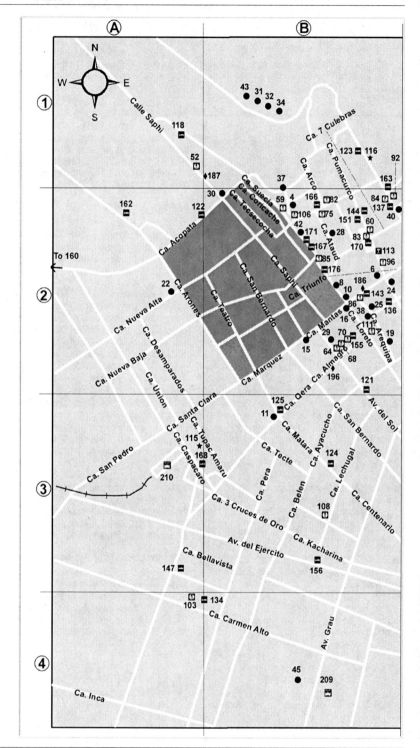

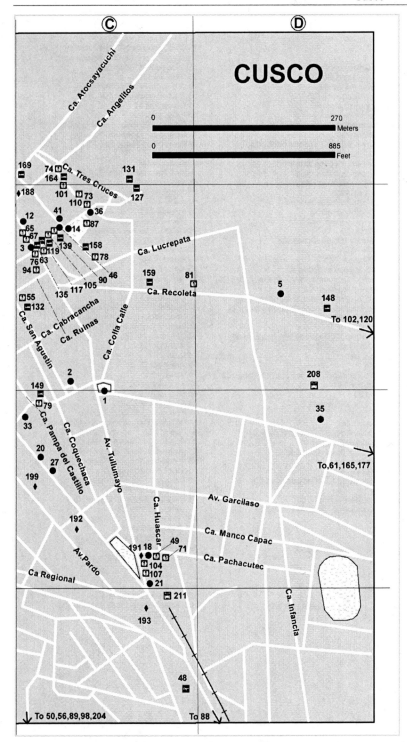

CUSCO

CUSCO INTRO

Activities ●

1 Academia Latinoamericana de Español C3
2 Acupari Language School C2
3 Aldea Yancay Project C2
4 Amauta Spanish School B2
5 Amigos Spanish School D2
6 Artesanías Pachucátec B2
7 Body Show Spa Cusco (See Inset Map, B1)
8 Cusco Cathedral B2
9 Cusco Spanish School (See Inset Map, A2)
10 El Triunfo Church B2
11 Excel Spanish Language Center B3
12 Fair Play Language School C2
13 Gringo Alley (See Inset Map, B2)
14 Iglesia San Blas C2
15 Iglesia y Convento de la Merced B2
16 La Compañía de Jesús B2
17 La Cholita (See Inset Map, B2)
18 Lingua Cusco C3
19 Macchu Picchu Spanish School B2
20 Maximo Nivel C3
21 Mercado Artesanal C3
22 Mundo Verde Spanish School A2
23 Museo de Arte Contemporáneo (See Inset Map, B2)
24 Museo de Arte Religioso B2
25 Museo de Arte y Monasterio Santa Catalina B2
26 Museo de Historia Regional (See Inset Map, A2)
27 Museo de Sitio Qoricancha C3
28 Museo Inka B2
29 Palacio Arzobispal / Museo de Arte Religioso B2
30 Proyecto Perú Language Center B2
31 Puca Pucará B1
32 Q'engo B1
33 Qoricancha Templo del Sol and Santo Domingo C3
34 Sacsayguamán B1
35 Salapunco D3
36 San Blas Spanish School C2
37 San Cristóbal B1
38 Santa Catalina B2
39 Seminario Ceramics A2 (See Inset Map, B2)
40 South American Explorers B2
41 South American Spanish School C2
42 Spanish in Perú B2
43 Tambo Machay B1
44 Tesoros del Andes A2 (See Inset Map, B2)
45 Tipón B4
46 Wiracocha Spanish School C2
47 Ying Yang Massage (See Inset Map, B2)

Airport ▣

48 Aeropuerto Velasco Astete C4

Eatings ⑪

49 7 Angelitos C3
50 A Mi Manera C4
51 Babieca Trattoria (See Inset Map, B1)
52 Bohème A1

53 Café Trotamundos (See Inset Map, B2)
54 Cappuccino Café (See Inset Map, B2)
55 Cava de San Rafael C2
56 Cicciolina C4
57 Drews (See Inset Map, B1)
58 El Cuate (See Inset Map, B1)
59 Encuentros B2
60 Fallen Angel B2
61 Gabriels D3
62 Govinda´s (See Inset Map, B2)
63 Granja Heidi Restaurant C2
64 Indigo B2
65 Inka….Fe C2
66 Inka Team (See Inset Map, B2)
67 Jack´s Café Bar C2
68 Juanito´s Café B2
69 Kachivache (See Inset Map, A2)
70 Kamikase B2
71 Khipus Restaurant C3
72 Kintaro Japanese Restaurant
   (See Inset Map, A2)
73 Km0 C2
74 Korma Sutra C1
75 Kukuli B2
76 Le Nomade C2
77 Los Perros (See Inset Map, B1)
78 Macondo C2
79 Maikhana The Indian Restaurant C3
80 Mama Afrika (See Inset Map, B2)
81 Mama´s Grill-Pizzeria Restaurant C2
82 Mandela´s Bar B2
83 Map Café B2
84 Moloko B2
85 Mhytology B2
86 Norton´s B2
87 Pacha-Papa C2
88 Pachacútec D4
89 Paddy Flaherty´s C4
90 Panadería El Buen Pastor C2
91 PepeZeta Bistro Lounge (See Inset Map, B1)
92 Prasada B2
93 Real McCoy (See Inset Map, B2)
94 Restaurant Aldea Yanapay C2
95 Restaurant Narguila (See Inset Map, B1)
96 Sweet Temptations B2
97 The Bagel Café (See Inset Map, B2)
98 The Cross Key Pub C4
99 The Film Lounge and Danish Café
   (See Inset Map, B1)
100 The Lek (See Inset Map, B2)
101 The Muse Too C2
102 Tika Bistro Gourmet D2
103 Tokoqachi A4
104 Truco Restaurant C3
105 Tupana Wasi C2
106 Two Nations B2
107 Ukuku´s C3
108 Vegeterian Restuarant B3
109 Victor Victoria (See Inset Map, B1)
110 Vuelto C2

111 Witche´s Garden B2
112 Yahuu   (See Inset Map, B2)

Nightlife 🎵

113 Mandelas Bar B2
114 Up Town (See Inset Map, B2)

Services ★

115 Mercado Central A3
116 Mercado Molina B1

Sleeping 🛏

117 Amaru Hostal C2
118 Andenes De Saphy A1
119 Arrieros C2
120 Casa San Blas Boutique Hotel D2
121 Cristina Hostal A1
122 El Balcón Hostal A2
123 Flying Dog B1
124 Gloria Pareja Guest House B3
125 Hatuchay Tower B3
126 Hatun Tuni (See Inset Map, A1)
127 Hospedaje El Artesano de San Blas C2
128 Hospedaje Emanuel (See Inset Map, A1)
129 Hospedaje Felix (See Inset Map, B1)
130 Hospedaje Granada (See Inset Map, A1)
131 Hospedaje Inka C1
132 Hospedaje Posada del Viajero C2
133 Hospedaje Q'una Wasi (See Inset Map, B1)
134 Hospedaje Sambleño A4
135 Hospedaj Turístico San Blas C2
136 Hostal Casa Grande B2
137 Hostal Choquacha B2
138 Hostal Corihuasi (See Inset Map, B1)
139 Hostal Hatun Wasi C2
140 Hostal Posada del Corregidor (See Inset Map, B2)
141 Hostal Procurador (See Inset Map, B1)
142 Hostal Rojas (See Inset Map, B1)
143 Hostal Santa Maria B2
144 Hotel Arqueólogo Exclusive Selection B2
145 Hotel Cáceres (See Inset Map, B1)
146 Hotel Carlos V (See Inset Map, B1)
147 Hotel El Grial A3
148 Hotel Emperador Plaza D2
149 Hotel Libertador C3
150 Hotel Marqueses (See Inset Map, A2)
151 Hotel Monasterio B2
152 Hotel Oblitas (Hotel Sol Plaza Inn) (See Inset Map, B2)
153 Hotel Royal Inka I (See Inset Map, A1)
154 Hotel Royal Inka II (See Inset Map, A2)
155 Imperial Palace B2
156 Inkayra Hotel B3
157 Intiq Samana (See Inset Map, A1)
158 Koyllur Hostal C2
159 Koyllur Hotel C2
160 La Casa de Kishkashta A2
161 La Casona Real (See Inset Map, B2)
162 Loki Hostel A2
163 Los Apus Hotel and Mirador B1
164 Mirador de la Ñusta C1

165 Mirador Hanon Qosco D3
166 Munay Wasi B2
167 Pirwa Hostel Bed and Breakfast B2
168 Rey Antares Mystic Hotel A3
169 Second Home Cusco C1
170 The Small Luxury Guest House B2
171 Sol Innka Plaza B2
172 Sonesta Posada del Inka
     (See Inset Map, B2)
173 Sumac Wasi (See Inset Map, B1)
174 Teatro Inka Bed and Breakfast
     (See Inset Map, A1)
175 Teqsiqocha Hostal (See Inset Map, B1)
176 The Chaksi Inn Hostal B2
177 The Garden House D3
178 The Niños Hotel (See Inset Map, A1)
179 The Point (See Map on pg. A2)
180 Villa Mayor (See Inset Map, B2)

Tours ◆

181 Action Valley (See Inset Map, A2)
182 All Trek Cusco Tours (See Inset Map, B1)
183 Andean Life Adventure (See Inset Map, B1)
184 Andes Nature Tours (See Inset Map, A2)
185 Apumayo (See Inset Map, A2)
186 Big Foot B2
187 Cóndor B1
188 Eko Trek Perú C2
189 Eric Adventures (See Inset Map, A2)
190 Explorandes (See Inset Map, A2)
191 Inka Express C3
192 Manu Expeditions C3
193 Manu Nature Tours C4
194 Mayuc (See Inset Map, B2)
195 Mounting Biking and Trekking
     (See Inset Map, B1)
196 Perú Inkas Adventures-Mountain Biking B2
197 Perú Travel Sustainable Tourism
     (See Inset Map, B2)
198 Perú Treks and Adventure
     (See Inset Map, A2)
199 Peruvian Andean Treks C3
200 Quad Bike Tours (See Inset Map, B2)
201 Sacred Land Adventure
     (See Inset Map, B2)
202 SAS Travel (See Inset Map, B2)
203 Sun Gate Tours (See Inset Map, B1)
204 Sun Good Expeditions Tours C4
205 Turismo Inkaiko (See Inset Map, A2)
206 United Mice (See Inset Map, B2)
207 Vilcabamba Expediciones
     (See Inset Map, B2)

Transportations 🚌

208 Bus To Pisac D2
209 Bus To Urubamba B4
210 Estación San Pedro A3
211 Estación Wachac C4

CUSCO INTRO

Centro Qosqo de Arte Nativo (folkloric dances)
Monumento a Pachacuteq
Saqsaywaman
Qenqo
Pukapukara
Tambomachay
Tipon
Pikillacta
Mirador de Pachacuteq
Pisac
Ollantaytambo
Chinchero

Places that are not included in the ticket are:

Catedral de Cusco
Templo del Qoricancha
Museo Inca
Templo de La Merced

The cost of the Cusco Tourist Ticket is 70 soles, with discounts for students. Note: The ticket only lasts ten days but can be renewed at any one of the two offices below. You can get them at all the sites on the ticket, theoretically, but it is better to buy it from one of the following two tour offices in Cusco: Monday - Friday 8 a.m. - 5 p.m. OFEC Avenida El Sol 103, #106. Tel: 51-84-227-037. Monday - Friday 7:45 a.m. - 6 p.m., Saturday 8 a.m. - 4 p.m., Sunday 8 a.m. - noon. Casa Garcilaso corner of Garcilaso and Heladeros Tel: 51-84-226-919. Updated: Jul 16, 2010.

Cusco Tours

Tours in Cusco vary from trips to local archaeological ruins to multi-day visits at sites outside the city. It is very possible to plan your trip from your home country, which is a good idea if you have limited time in Peru and want to see and do specific things. You can find also find a plethora of Peruvian tour operators just by taking a brief walk through the streets of Cusco. Chances are, upon landing in the small airport in Cusco, you'll be bombarded by solicitous tour operators. Most of them offer similar services, but here's one bit of advice: when planning a visit to the Inca Trail tour, pick carefully, as some provide much better tours than others. Updated: Sep 08, 2009.

Peru Treks

Based in Cusco, Peru Treks and Adventure is a licensed tour operator offering a variety of packages for different budgets. The company can not only take you on the classic four-day Inca Trail trek to Machu Picchu but also one-day tours of Cusco or the Sacred Valley; or white rafting and mountain biking excursions. All packages are offered on a group or private basis.

Peru Treks and Adventures prides itself on being an agency that practices socially and environmentally responsible tourism. It pays particular attention to the wages and work conditions of its cooks, porters and other staff, yet provides competitive prices and quality service. This company also supports a number of education projects in small villages. In 2006 Peru Treks and Adventures was awarded Best Cusco Travel Agency by the Ministry of Tourism. Calle Garcilaso 265, Office 11, 2nd Floor, Tel: 51-84-505-863, Fax: 51-84-221-032, E-mail: info@perutreks.com, URL: www.perutreks.com. Avenida Pardo 540, Cusco, Peru Tel: 51-84-222-722 Fax: 51-84-222-722 Email: info@perutreks.com URL: www.perutreks.com. Updated: Jun 19, 2009.

Turismo Inkaiko

Turismo Inkaiko is a well-established tour operator that offers trips to Cusco, Puno, Nasca, Paracas, Iquitos and Puerto Maldonado. The agency has a friendly and helpful staff who can offer an array of advice on expeditions as well as cultural and conventional trips throughout Peru. The agency is also partnered with hotels in a number of cities. Main Lima Office: Av. Jose Pardo 610, Office 4. Tel: 51-1-446-7500 / 4247 / 495-1283, Fax: 51-1-445-2532, E-mail: postmaster@turismoinkaiko.net, URL: www.turismoinkaiko.net. Updated: Jun 18, 2009.

United Mice

A company specializing in guided tours of the Inca Trail, United Mice offers reasonable prices, good food, quality camping equipment and English-speaking guides. Due to their popularity, however, their tour groups during the high season are often large. Calle Plateros 351 or Calle Triunfo 392, #218. Tel: 51-84-221-139, E-mail: unitedmi@terra.com.pe. Updated: Jun 18, 2009.

Trekperu

Trekperu has been one of Peru's leading tour agencies since 1986. Their mission is to create the perfect trip that doesn't negatively impact the environment or adversely affect local communities. They offer custom trips featuring horseback riding, city tours, visits to archaeological ruins, climbing, cultural tours, and adventure trips. Tours are available in Spanish, English, German, and French. Av. Republica de Chile B-15. Tel: 51-84-261-501, Fax: 51-84-238-591, E-mail: info@trekperu.com, URL: www.trekperu.com. Updated: Jun 18, 2009.

Llama Path

With only a few years under its belt, Llama Path has quickly become one of the principal Inca Trail and alternative trekking operators. With a real interest in porter welfare, fair working conditions and social and ecological responsibility, Llama Path offers a strong, responsible tourism option for treks in the Cusco area. Treks are reasonably- priced, with good, bilingual guides and high-quality service. The company can also book mountain biking, rafting and adventure sports trips, though trekking is their speciality. San Juan de Dios 250. Tel: 51-84-240-822, URL: www.llamapath.com. Updated: Jul 30, 2009.

Wayki Trek

Run by a guide from a mountain community, Wayki trek has become one of the most popular operators for the Inca Trail and alternative treks. It offers the exclusive "Wayki option" on Inca Trail treks, in which participants have the chance to spend the night in the local community of the porters who will be accompanying them. The company is also an advocate of responsible tourism initiatives and often seeks volunteers for community projects. Procuradores 351 and Av. Pardo. Tel: 51-84-224-092, E-mail: info@waykitrek.net, URL: www.waykitrek.net. Updated: Jul 30, 2009.

Enigma

Pioneers in the concept of "luxury trekking," Enigma offers the option of going on guided treks of a different standard, as well as the usual adventure treks offered by many Cusco-based tour operators. The company provides specialized programs designed for family travel or special interest programs such as photography or weaving tours. Their regular treks boast a high level of service; all their guides are well-trained professionals who are always bilingual and sometimes trilingual. Clorinda Matto de Turner 100. Tel: 51-84-222-155, E-mail: info@enigmaperu.com, URL: www.enigmaperu.com. Updated: Jul 30, 2009.

Apus Peru

Apus Peru Adventure Travel Specialists is a small, Australian-Peruvian company that focuses on alternative and sustainable tourism. The company has 15 years of tourism experience, and offers private or group tours to a range of spectacular destinations around Cusco and Peru, with affordable prices and a focus on understanding Peruvian culture. 366 Cuichipunco, Centro Historico. Tel: 51-84-232-691, E-mail: apusperu@westnet.com.au, URL: www.apus-peru.com. Updated: Jun 22, 2009.

Terra Andina

Tour operator in Lima and Cusco. Customised trips all around Peru. Off the beaten track adventure or traditional sightseeing tours, 4x4 expeditions, trekking, climbing. Calle Tandapata 296, San Blas. Tel: 51-1-243-0010, URL: www.terra-andina.com. Updated: Jul 10, 2008.

Peru Trek 4 Good

This travel agency was launched by Yure Chavez, a Peruvian travel agent/guide, and other tourism professionals. This agency organizes custom itineraries for anyone interested in: adventure, ecotourism, birdwatching conventional and off-the-beaten-track tours. Peru Trek 4 Good is for travelers who want more authentic holidays that also benefits the environment and local people. The company's mission is to act as a conduit and open a window into the little known aspects and insights in the region. Also note that every Peru Trek 4 Good trip has a volunteer component built in to raise funds. It is another way to support the community-based partners around the country and educate people through a direct, personal experience. URL: www.yurechavez.blogspot.com. Updated: Oct 21, 2008.

Sun Gate Tours

Sun Gate Tours offers nearly every hike imaginable in the Sacred Valley region. The company can also arrange trips outside the region, in Arequipa or other major tourist destinations throughout Peru. Some of Sun Gate's most unique excursions are those which head to the jungle for up to eight days. Saphy Street 476. Tel: 51-84-232-046, E-mail: davidlx@hotmail.com, URL: www.sungatetours.com. Updated: Jul 28, 2009.

Inca Land Adventures

Inca Land Adventures offers tours of all types, from the "Gringo Trail" to high-altitude adventure tours. Inca Land Adventures has several seasoned, bilingual Peruvian guides who can explain the natural and cultural history of Peru. Inca Land Adventures can also arrange multi-day adventure tours. Urbanización Flor de la Cantuta, B-2. Tel: 51-84-275-973, Fax: 51-84-275-973. URL: www.incalandadventures.com. Updated: Jan 22, 2010.

V!VA ONLINE REVIEW

INCA LAND ADVENTURES

Their level of service went above and beyond our expectations, and we are fickle Americans, after all!

Jun 09,2010

Eric Adventures

Eric Adventures offers experiences in rock climbing, canyoning, rappeling, kayaking, white water rafting, horseback riding, mountain biking and paragliding. Whatever suits your adrenaline-rush needs, it's likely that Eric Adventures will help you find that rush. Owner Eric Arenas, an international kayaking and rafting champ, has been operating tours in Cusco since 1993. The company has an array of half as well as full-day activities to three or four day trekking trips. City and cultural tours and, of course, tours to Machu Picchu are also available. Eric Adventures can also arrange for private group tours. While it may be on the more expensive side, you'll be paying for first-rate guides and a knowledgable, experienced company. Plateros 324. Tel: 51-84-228-475 / 234-764, E-mail: cusco@ericadventures.com, URL: www.ericadventures.com. Updated: Jul 28, 2009.

Peru Inkas Adventures

Peru Inkas Adventures offers great mountain biking, trekking, rafting and historic activities. The company is owned by passionate mountain bikers with many years of experience leading groups through the best trails in Peru. Wayo, one of the guides, is not only a nice guy to ride with, but also the winner of multiple National Champion titles. Diego de Almagro 535, Lima. E-mail: wayo@inkasadventures.com, URL: www.inkasadventures.com. Updated: Jul 30, 2009.

Quad Bike Tours

Quad Bike Tours offers more than its name suggests. Besides quad bike tours, you can also choose mountain bike, horseback riding, white rafting or rock climbing excursions. It also can take you trekking to Machu Picchu or other archaeological gems in the Cusco region. Daily 9 a.m. - 5 p.m. Plateros 324. Tel: 51-84-252-762, E-mail: reservas@atv-adventureperu.com, URL: www.atv-adventureperu.com. Updated: Nov 25, 2009.

Manu Expeditions

Manu Expeditions is one of the longest running operators in the Manu Biosphere Reserve and has been guiding tours since 1983. Owned and run by a husband and wife team this company relies on a trustworthy team of boat-crews for rainforest trips, wranglers for the mountains and trained camp cooks for remote areas. Leaders are fluent in English and Spanish, as well as experts in their fields. Manu Expeditions offers more than just trips to the Manu Biosphere Reserve; it also provides a variety of activities, including horseback riding and birdwatching. Custom itineraries can be arranged. Calle Humberto Vidal Unda G-5, Segunda Etapa. Tel: 51-84-226-671, E-mail: manuexpeditions@terra.com.pe, URL: www.manuexpeditions.com. Updated: Jul 28, 2009.

Horseback Riding with Perol Chico

Perol Chico specializes in exclusive, multiday equestrian tours that are off the beaten track. Founded in 1996, the riding center is located in the Sacred Valley of the Incas, between Cusco and Machu Picchu. It is surrounded by dramatic scenery; snowcapped mountains, deep blue lakes and lush flora and fauna. These make this a gorgeous base for your tour. The rides include stunning vistas, exciting trails and fascinating ruins. Perol Chico is dedicated to promoting ecological awareness while sustaining the local cultures and traditions. All horses are Peruvian Pasos trained through traditional Peruvian horsemanship and are kept in immaculate condition. Prices range from $720 for a three day ride to over $3,000 for a 12 day ride. Custom itineraries are available. Tel: 51-84-213-386, E-mail: info@perolchico.com, URL: www.perolchico.com. Updated: Jul 28, 2009.

Best of Cusco

BEST PLACES TO SEE SPORTS

The best place to see sports on a large screen with a crowd are Paddy's Irish Pub, Cross Keys, Norton's and Mushroom. Paddys is a bit more low-key, with many bar stools, while Cross Keys is bigger with nicer furnishings and some comfortable couches out the back. These two are the most popular for big sport matches with a lively atmosphere. You can also watch the big screen from bean bags in Mushroom, but they are only open at night. Norton's is another good option, with plenty of space and good food. Cross Keys has the best atmosphere.

BEST PLACES TO PEOPLE-WATCH

The Plaza de Armas serves as a prime people-watching spot. Being the central part of Cusco, most tourists will pass it daily, but it also gets high traffic from locals. Another good spot is the San Francisco plaza, where many locals relax. To watch people on the main street where you'll see many locals busy coming and going from work, visit Qoricancha, the Temple of the Sun. Another good spot is to sit outside the San Pedro market, which gets very busy with locals and tourists alike, and you'll see many coming to this spot for the outdoor trinket market on Sundays.

BEST PLACES TO MEET THE LOCALS

Cusco is pleasant as most people are fairly friendly. In restaurants, most barmen and waiters will happily start up a conversation with you. The locals are always interested in where you come from. You can also sit in the plaza and within a few minutes you will have locals coming up to talk to you, whether it's trying to sell you postcards or paintings, to shine your shoes, or just to chat. In the markets you will find the Quechua ladies very talkative, at the fruit stand in particular. If you go out at night to bars and clubs, you'll find a mix of locals and tourists mingling and these can be a good place to meet people. But do be aware of bricheros and bricheras, who romantically pursue gringas and gringos, either as a hobby or profession.

CUSCO INTRO

Photo by: Boring Lovechild

BEST PLACES TO MEET OTHER TRAVELERS

OR FELLOW EXPATS

Cusco is a very sociable place, but like anywhere you will need to make the effort to meet people. It will also help where you stay. You will meet more people if you stay in a sociable hostel. You will also make friends if you live in a Spanish school, a common option for many while studying, where people are often staying for longer periods of time than in hostels. You can meet other travelers by getting involved in the nightlife, or by taking part in the mountain activities that tourists enjoy, such as rafting and hiking, or salsa and yoga. Doing a trek with a group of people is a great way to meet others, as is going on a rafting trip or doing a salsa or yoga class. The South American Explorers Club is another great place to meet travelers or expats in Cusco.

Best Places to Volunteer

Volunteering is a very popular activity and there are many companies in Peru offering it. Spanish schools usually have a wide variety of charity projects, particularly the larger schools. Then there are independent companies focusing on specific projects. An excellent group is Bruce Peru, which makes special schools for street children who haven't been to school before. They care for them, provide medical attention and nutrition, and educate them to a level where the children are able to get into a real school. If you are strapped for cash, you can go to Loki hostel, which takes volunteers to help locals re-build the homes they lost after the floods – there is no charge for these services and no minimum time commitment.

BEST PLACES TO BUY SOUVENIRS/GIFTS

There are lots of small souvenir shops but all offer the same range of products. You'll find some a few circling the plaza, and some good ones on the way up the hill towards San Blas. In San Blas, you'll find a small but cute handicrafts market on Saturdays, times can vary but try the middle of the day. On Av. El Sol you'll find the artisans markets with many beautiful materials and textiles on offer. Another great place to find trinkets and souvenirs is the Pisac market, which runs all day on Thursdays and Sundays.

BEST PLACES TO LEARN SALSA

Although it only has a handful of options, Cusco offers the traveler and indeed the long term resident, with a great opportunity to lean salsa. Every night of the week from 9.30–11 p.m. in bars on the corner of the main square (including Mythology and Inka Team) various salsa schools gather and teach some basic salsa steps free of charge to all who are interested to learn. In this relaxed environment, you can choose the teachers you like the most and make contact with the schools directly to take private or group classes during the day.

The main schools include the Cusco Salsa S'cool (four local cusquenan guys with their own style and flavor), who favor Inka Team as their place to dance, and Mythology where Charlie, Raquel and Joseph offer private and group classes. Rico Ritmo (Holland/Peruvian couple), who teach up in San Blas have set up a school that aims to help the under-privileged youth in the Cusco area. If nothing else the hip shaking dance is a great way to meet locals and travelers while doing some exercise!

Mythology
Portal de Carnes 298, 2nd Floor
Plaza de Armas
Tel: 51-84-255-770
Charlie, Raquel and Joseph

CCS (Cusco Salsa Scool)
Zaguan Del Cielo N-3
Tel:-9-84-367-944/316-236

Coco, Hector, Franchesco and Carlos
Rico Ritmo - Salsa Academy
Asociacion Pukllasunchis
Siete Diablitos 222 - San Blas
Cusco, Peru
Tel: 9-84-262-103/ 262-103
  Renato Valdivia & Anke Brokerhof

BEST PLACES TO CATCH A LIVE BAND

The best place to see a live band is definitely 7 Angelito's, with Thursday through to Saturday being the best nights. Bands are usually supported by an enthusiastic, dancing crowd. For a more casual live band experience, Kmo is very popular with live music most nights. It's a little poky, but this means you get to be closer to the band. Opposite Jack's Café you'll also find a spot that has live music a couple of times a week, but usually between 9 and 11 p.m., whereas the band in 7 Angelitos will start around 11 p.m. and can go until early morning, and in Kmo the band goes from around 10 p.m. to 1 a.m.

BEST PLACE TO GET LATE NIGHT FOOD

The very best place to get late night food is at Los Perros, at the bottom of Calle Suecia near the main clubs on the plaza. They have a window in the wall, and offer their full menu that they offer in their restaurant around the corner. They are open until 6 a.m. most nights–sometimes on quiet nights they close early, however this is definitely the best spot to find tasty late night food. McDonald's is open till 3 a.m., otherwise you can also find good burgers on Plateros, just a few doors down from the corner of the plaza.

BEST PLACES TO GET BRUNCH

The best place for brunch is definitely Jack's café, a favorite of many tourists in Cusco. At Jack's you'll find huge portions of large breakfasts, great for hangovers. At times there might be a line on the weekends but the food is definitely worth it. The Bagel Café is also a great option for fresh bagels with tasty toppings. For a quick, fresh breakfast, try Yahuu for a triple sandwich and fresh juice.

BEST PLACES TO SPEND A RAINY DAY

There are some lovely cafes dotted around the center of Cusco where you can have a hot cup of coffee on a rainy day. These places include Encuentros on Calle Suecia, where you can see movies and Gabriel's on Santa Teresa, which also has a large screen with cable. You can also visit The Film Lounge on Procuradores, which offers a large lounge with comfortable sofas and plenty of games and books, as well as a separate movie room and DVD collection to choose from. The lounge serves good soup, sandwiches, cookies and hot chocolate.

!)))

CUSCO INTRO

Cusco Guide

With Cusco's numerous attractions, dozens of hotels and hundreds of restaurants, visitors to town are spoiled for choice. Here are the city's highlights.

Things to See and Do

A Walking Tour of Cusco

With a commanding spot at the center of the city, the Plaza de Armas is perhaps the best point to start exploring Cusco. From here you can access all of the Cusco's major attractions, which spread out across the city along all four points of the compass. Within the Plaza de Armas you will find the Portal de Panes, Cusco Cathedral, Chapel of the Immaculate Conception, Chapel of El Señor de los Temblores, Museo Inka, and Iglesia de la Compañía de Jesús.

Following Callejón Loreto to the west of the Plaza de Armas will bring you to the spectacular stone walls of ancient Acclahuasi, or Temple of the Sun Virgins, where the Spanish built the Convent of Santa Catalina in 1610. Today about thirty sisters continue to live and worship here. Inside you will find the Museo de Arte y Monasterio de Santa Catalina.

Southeast from the convent, at the intersection of Avenida El Sol and Calle Santa Domingo is the complex of Qoricancha Templo del Sol and Santo Domingo, a wonderful example of the city's characteristic mix of Spanish and Inca cultures. Within three minutes walk of this architectural amalgamation is the Museo de Sitio Qoricancha, which offers an interesting display of various archeological artifacts.

In the southwest corner of the plaza stands the Museo Histórico Regional, the residence of a prolific half-Inca, half-Spanish poet and author, and now the home to pre-Inca ceramics, Inca artifacts and numerous examples of Cusco's historic art. To the southwest of the Plaza de Armas are the Iglesia y Convento de la Merced and the Plaza de San Francisco, where you will find the Museo y Convento de San Francisco. Further to the south is the Central Market, which is known for its quality alpaca goods and antique textiles. Another area of interest lies near the Plaza Regocijo, just a block southwest of the Plaza de Armas.

If you're in need of a drink but don't want to stray too far, then follow Calle Santa Teresa from Plaza Regocijo to the House of the Pumas, a small café whose entrance sports six pumas carved by the Spanish during the rebuilding of Cusco. Not far from the café is the Iglesia de Santa Teresa, which features beautiful paintings of St. Teresa, usually illuminated by candlelight.

Wander northeast of the Plaza de Armas, along Calle Córdoba del Tucmán, and you'll stumble across Plaza Nazarenas, a small and quiet section of town that boasts the Chapel of San Antonio Abad, Museo de Cerámica, and Museo Taller Hilario Mendivil. This area also has four other important attractions: the Museo de Arte Religioso, Hathun Rumiyoq, the most famous Inca passageway in the city; and Iglesia San Blas and San Blas, a bustling artisan neighborhood whose steep cobblestone streets offer fantastic views of the city.

Whether or not you plan to visit all the attractions in Cusco, it is worth purchasing the Cusco Tourist Ticket (Boleto Turístico General, BTG), which covers many of the historic museums, cathedrals, and ruins in the Cusco area. Updated: Jul 01, 2010.

ARCHITECTURE & RUINS

Qoricancha, Templo del Sol and Santo Domingo

Of the numerous attractions in Cusco, this should be on the top of your list. Once home to nearly 4,000 of the Empire's highest ranking priests and their attendants, Qoricancha was once an extraordinary display of Inca masonry and wealth. Dedicated to the worship of the sun, the Temple of the Sun was the main astronomical observatory for the Inca. The complex also included smaller temples and shrines dedicated to the worship of less important deities of the moon, Venus, thunder, lightning and rainbows. In Quechua its name means Golden Courtyard, which is an appropriate title for a temple once adorned with gold panels, life-size gold figures, solid gold altars and a gigantic golden sun disc all intended to reflect sunlight and drench the entire temple in golden light. During the summer, light enters a strategically placed niche, where only the Inca Chieftan was allowed to sit.

When the Spanish ransacked the city during their conquests, this glorious shrine to the sun was stripped of its golden accoutrements and most of its aesthetic glory. The Temple of the Sun was awarded to Juan Pizarro, younger brother of Francisco, who willed it to the Dominicans after he was wounded during the siege of Sacsayhuamán. Eventually the temple's carefully constructed stones were used as the foundation for the Convent of Santo Domingo, a baroque church built in the 17th century.

Today the site of Qoricancha and Santo Domingo is a magnificent testament to the cultural collision that occurred when the Spanish descended upon the Inca Empire. Recent excavations have uncovered five chambers once belonging to the temple, in addition to some of the best stonework visible in Cusco. The 6-meter (20 ft.) curved wall beneath the west end of the church, which has withstood repeated earthquakes, is perhaps the best example of Inca masonry this site offers. Excavations below this wall have uncovered a garden of gold and silver animals, as well as maize and other plants.

Another remarkable stretch of Inca masonry extends from Calle Ahuacpinta, located outside the temple to the east of the entrance. Monday-Saturday, 8 a.m.-5 p.m., Sunday, 2 p.m.-4 p.m. Plazoleta Santo Domingo, Tel: 51-84-222-071. Updated: Nov 25, 2009.

Q'enqo

(ADMISSION: $10 or tourist ticket) The temple and amphitheater ruins of Q'enqo are located east of the giant white statue of Christ, perched on the hill next to Sacsayhuamán, and are only about a 20-minute walk from the famous fortress ruins.

The Q'engo ruins derive their name from the Quechua word meaning "zig-zag," a reference to the series of perfectly carved channels adorning the upper western edge of the temple's stone. In ancient times these channels probably flowed with "chichi," sacrificial llama blood used by priests during annual fertility festivals and solstice and equinox celebrations.

In addition to the channels, Q'enqo sports a series of intricately carved designs, including steps, seats, geometric reliefs, pumas and condors. The hollowed-out limestone outcropping which comprises the main altar emphasizes the importance of the Rock Cult in Inca cosmological beliefs, and similar rock carvings can be found throughout the surrounding foothills. The complex also offers visitors the opportunity to explore a series of caves and tunnels beneath the rock. If you're up for a walk, you can also access the ruins of Puca Pucara and Tambo Machay from here. Near Sacsayhuamán ruins, to get there follow the signs posted on the main road from Sacsayhuamán. 7 a.m. - 5:30 p.m. Updated: Jul 18, 2007.

Puca Pucara

(ADMISSION: $7 or with tourist ticket) Though perhaps the least impressive of the ruins around Cusco, Puca Pucara offers stunning views of the Cusco Valley and glaciers to the south. Located about 11 kilometers (7 mi.) outside the city, right beside the main Cusco-Pisac road, the ruins can also be reached via a one to two hour crosscountry walk uphill from Sacsayhuamán and Q'enqo. In Quechua its name means Red Fort, and the complex was probably used by Emperor Pachacútec as a tambo, or out-of-town lodge. It's likely that the Emperor's court was stationed here when the Emperor came to visit the nearby baths of Tambo Machay. Beneath the complex there are several chambers to explore; the platform on top offers spectacular views. To get there go 11 kilometers from Cusco down the Cusco-Pisac road. 7 a.m. - 5:30 p.m. Updated: Jul 18, 2007.

Pikillacta and Rumicolca

(ADMISSION: $7 or tourist ticket) Much of the ancient Inca's organizational expertise and city planning abilities originated from the pre-Inca Huari Empire, which dominated the lands of Peru from 500 to 1000 A.D. An interesting example of Huari engineering is Rumicolca, an ancient aqueduct poised on a valley along the side of the highway, about 32 kilometers (22 mi.) from Cusco. After their rise to power, the Inca converted this ancient water channel into a massive gateway to Cusco. Not far from Rumicolca is Pikillacta, the largest provincial outpost ever built by the Ayacucho-based Huari and one of the only pre-Inca sites of importance near Cusco. Were it not included on the Cusco Tourist Ticket, this 47-hectare (116-acre), adobe-walled compound might go unnoticed, yet it affords visitors a great opportunity to check out pre-Inca architecture. Though little is known about the site's history, we can tell you that the little turquoise figurines displayed in Cusco's Museo Inka were discovered here. 7 a.m. - 5:30 p.m. Updated: Jul 18, 2007 .

Tipón

(ADMISSION: Tourist ticket) Located 23 kilometers (14 mi.) southeast of Cusco, these ruins are not particularly popular among travelers eager to visit some of the bigger-name ruins around the Sacred Valley area. However, despite its position off the beaten tourist trail, this extensive temple complex is one of the best examples of Inca stonemasonry, and some might say it is equal to the more celebrated ruins of Pisac, Ollantaytambo, and Chinchero. The temple includes well-preserved agricultural terraces, baths, irrigation canals and aqueducts that emphasize the Inca's skillful building technique. The ruins can be reached via a steep one-hour climb up a lovely path, or up a dirt road by car. If you're feeling especially agile, you can check out the ruins located about a 2-hour climb above Tipón. Note: It's virtually impossible to visit the ruins during the rainy season. 7 a.m.-5:30 p.m., daily. Updated: Jul 18, 2007.

Tambo Machay

(ADMISSION: Tourist ticket) Located just a 15-meter (50-ft.) walk along a sign-posted path from the main road past Puca Pucara, Tambo Machay ruins are one of the more impressive examples of Inca baths, which can be found at nearly every important Inca temple, including Pisac, Ollantaytambo, and Machu Picchu. Water was worshipped by the Inca as a vital life element, and the painstakingly carved network of aqueducts and canals that comprise these baths echo the importance of and fascination with water. The complex consists of three tiered platforms which ingeniously channel spring water into three impressive waterfalls that continue to work today. The quality of stonework indicates that the site was probably restricted to higher nobility, who might have used the baths only on ceremonial occasions. The site also has an impressive Inca wall that rises above the ceremonial niches. 7 a.m.-5:30 p.m., daily. Updated: Jul 18, 2007.

Sacsayhuamán

(ADMISSION: Tourist ticket) Perched forebodingly in the hillsides rising above Cusco, the fortress ruins of Sacsayhuamán are some of the most impressive and closest ruins in the area. Though few structures now remain inside, the massive 20-meter-high outer walls that zigzag together like razor-sharp teeth have stood stalwartly against past battles, earthquakes and time. Emperor Pachacútec began building the hillside citadel in the 1440s, but the massive complex wasn't completed for almost another 100 years. Every Inca citizen was required to spend at least a few months a year on the public works, which involved dragging the massive stone blocks (one block is estimated to weigh an astounding 300 tons) via a system of log sleds and levers from as far as 32 kilometers (20 mi.) away. Legend has it that 3,000 lives were lost while dragging a single stone. During Manco Inca's great rebellion, the fortress witnessed the massacre of an estimated 1,500 Inca soldiers trapped inside the three stone towers. Rather than face death by the Spaniards, many Incas leapt to their deaths from the high towers. The next morning, condors feasted on the pile of corpses, an image captured forever on Cusco's coat-of-arms.

Even today, engineers marvel at the scope and scale of the ruin's stonework, which fits together perfectly without mortar. Like other ruins in the Cusco area, Sacsayhuamán exemplifies the Inca's extraordinary architectural prowess. A huge trapezoidal door leads into the ruins from the walkway. From here you can explore inside the ruins, which once consisted of an intricate network of small streets and buildings overshadowed by three main towers.

Today, adjacent to the grassy esplanade in front of the main defensive walls is Rodadero (Sliding Place), an intricately carved volcanic outcrop where the Inca throne once sat. In ancient times, this area was probably used for ceremonial gatherings. Even today you may be lucky enough to catch one of the many sun ceremonies still held throughout the year. If you can, plan to visit the ruins around the Inti Raymi festival held in June, during the summer solstice. From Sacsayhuamán you can also reach the Inca ruins of Q'enqo, Puca Pucara, and Tambo Machay. 7 a.m.-5:30 p.m., daily. Night tours available 8-10 p.m., but bring a flashlight and some friends. Getting there: From the Plaza de Armas, it's a 45-minute steep climb 2 kilometers (3 mi.) uphill. Follow Calle Suecia to Calle Huaynapata, to Calle Pumacuro, which winds its way uphill past a small café. From the café it's about a 10-minute signposted walk. Updated: Jul 18, 2007.

Salapunco

Salapunco is a group of small caves that housed the mummies of Inca priests and other Inca elite. Inside the caves, the walls and altars are decorated with pumas, snakes and other important cultural symbols. This hauca is dedicated to worshipping the moon, and the position of the entrance allows the interior to be lit up once a month by the light of the moon. 7 a.m. - 5:30 p.m. Km. 5, Highway to Pisac. Updated: Jun 17, 2009.

The Stone Puma

North of Cusco's Plaza de Armas towards Cuesta San Blas, you will come upon one of the most haunting tokens of a civilization: the foundation for the one-time palace of 14th century Inca ruler Inca Roca. Throughout Cusco, the Spanish attempted to establish their hegemony by demolishing a century's worth of physically impressive architecture from the Inca and pre-Inca civilization. But they couldn't quite destroy it all. The stone blocks were too large, too heavy and, above all, too tightly fit.

The wall on Calle Hatun Rumiyoc is particularly fascinating; locals will approach you and point out how the Inca were able to so tightly fit irregular blocks of stone, is a mystery yet to be solved by archaeologists and architects. The stones have the distinct outline of a puma, an animal considered sacred in Inca religion. The original city of Cusco itself is also supposed to resemble this animal. At the wall, the animal is seen in a crouching position. The smaller stones at the base of the wall serve as a reminder of Inca ingenuity, in that they functioned as shock absorbers for the wall itself, which accounts for how it endured though all the earthquakes in the region's history. Updated: Nov 04, 2009.

Monumento y Mirador Pachacuteq

(ADMISSION: Tourist ticket) The ninth leader of the Inca empire, and the man who spread its borders beyond the Cusco area, is honored with this striking modern monument. Pachacuteq's image is reproduced here in a massive bronze statue set atop a stone column. The stones were supplied by the surrounding villages, whose quarries provided the materials for the buildings of Pachacuteq's reign. There is a staircase winding up the tower, and the scenic lookout spot at the top has fantastic views of the city. The climb up is only recommended for those who can handle a few flights of narrow stairs and some claustrophobic spaces. Av. Pachacutec. Daily 10 a.m.-8 p.m. Updated: Jul 24, 2010.

Qeswachaca Bridge

An interesting day trip can be made by visiting the only bridge in South America made of grass. Andean grass, q'oya, is what the Inca used to build their handwoven bridges and this is the only remaining example. The bridge is 33 meters (108 ft.) long and hangs precariously over the Apurimac river, in the Canas province. While the bridge is located 3 hours south of Cusco by bus, there are some pretty lakes and typical villages to view along the way. Updated: Jun 30, 2010.

CHURCHES & CONVENTS

Iglesia y Convento de la Merced

The Church and Convent of Mercy was originally built in 1535, making it one of the oldest religious institutions in South America. It was rebuilt after an earthquake destroyed it in 1654, and is still host to the white-robed Order of Mercy priesthood. The impressively designed courtyard and select rooms, all filled with centuries-old religious art (including a 16th century menorah), are open to the general public. The wall murals were originally reproductions of Catholic iconography from the order's home in Seville, Spain, and they include what may be considered a very controversial depiction of the Virgin Mary. This is essential touring for those who want to understand Cusco's colonial past. Manta 121. Tel: 51-84-231-821. Updated: Oct 30, 2009.

Iglesia San Blas

(ADMISSION: $5.50) Iglesia San Blas is just one of the attractions located in the bustling artisan neighborhood of San Blas. Built in 1563, Iglesia San Blas is thought to be one of the oldest parishes in Cusco. Although unremarkable from the outside, this small, white-washed adobe church houses one of the most exquisite examples of woodcarving in the world. Carved in a churrigueresque style from a single tree trunk, the famous cedar pulpit features intricately carved images of the Virgin Mary, apostles, cherubs, a sun-disc and bunches of grapes. Perhaps as interesting as the pulpit is the story that accompanies it. According to legend (you'll have to decide for yourself if it's true), the carpenter who created the pulpit's skull was placed inside the masterpiece, at the top beneath St. Paul's feet. While you're looking for the skull (let us know if you find it!) be sure to check out the baroque gold-leaf main altar. Manta 121. Updated: Nov 25, 2009.

Cusco Cathedral

(ADMISSION: $9) Located in the center of Cusco on the Plaza de Armas, Cusco's massive stone cathedral is well worth a visit. Construction began in 1560; much of the stone used to build the cathedral was brought from Sachsayhuamán and other Inca sites. Time and earthquakes took their toll on the cathedral, but an ambitious resotration project took place between 1997 and 2002. Much of the stonework has been shored up and the magnificent paintings have been delicately wiped clean of centuries of grime. Be sure to check out the Matia Angola bell in the bell tower, made with more than fifty pounds of gold. The entrance is no longer included as part of the Cusco Tourist Ticket. You now have to buy a ticket separately.   Updated: Nov 25, 2009.

MUSEUMS

Palacio Arzobispal / Museo de Arte Religioso

For art aficionados and architecture fiends alike, the Museo de Arte Religioso is one of the most interesting spots in the city. Like many other attractions in Cusco, the museum sports a rich cultural history that appears in both the architecture outside and artwork inside. The museum itself is located inside the Palacio Arzobispal, which sits adjacent to Hatunrumiyoc, a magnificent pedestrian alleyway lined with Inca stone masonry. The name Hatun Rumiyoc means "Street with the Big Stone," which is a reference to the massive 12-sided stone situated perfectly in the center of the wall. Originally the site of Inca Roca palace, the building has also served as the residence of the former Spanish marquis and the Archbishop of Cusco. Today, this building houses a collection of colonial religious paintings. One room in particular is filled with paintings by Marcos Zapata, an 18th century mestizo artist whose work often mixed indigenous elements with religious themes. In addition to the artwork, you're

sure to admire the Moorish-style doors, ornately carved cedar ceilings and spectacular stained-glass windows. For a breath of fresh air, step out into the courtyard, adorned with blue and white tiles from Seville. Monday - Saturday 8a.m. - 11:30 a.m. and 3p.m. - 5:30 p.m.. Corner of Hatun Rumiyoc and Palacio. Tel: 51-84-225-211. Updated: Nov 25, 2009.

Museo Histórico Regional

(ADMISSION: Tourist ticket) Formerly the residence of one of Peru's most famous writers and Inca historians, Garcilaso de la Vega, the Museo Histórico Regional now offers an excellent review of Peruvian history, from pre-Inca civilizations to the Inca and colonial periods. Though the museum is not particularly well labeled, it does have interesting displays of Inca agricultural tools, colonial furniture and paintings, including a mummy with braids 1.5 meters (5 ft.) long and photos of the damage incurred after the 1951 earthquake. In terms of Cusco attractions, this is an excellent place to start, as it provides a thorough archeological overview of the Chavín, Moche, Chimú, and Chancay cultures, in addition to exhibits that trace the evolution of the Cusqueña School of painting. Whether you're an avid historian, or just want to learn more about Peruvian culture, plan to spend a couple of hours exploring the exhibits. Monday-Saturday, 8 a.m.-5 p.m. Plaza Regocijo (corner of Garcilaso and Helalderos). Tel: 51-84-223-245. Updated: Jun 17, 2009.

Museo de Sitio Qoricancha

(ADMISSION: Tourist ticket) Located under the garden below Santo Domingo, the Museo de Sitio Qoricancha consists of three small rooms, which contain a pre-Columbian collection, Spanish paintings from the 18th century and photos of the excavation of Qoricancha. Although it is one of the smaller attractions in Cusco, this museum also has a decent collection of ceramics, metalwork and textile weavings dating back to Inca and pre-Inca civilizations. Monday-Friday, 8 a.m.-5 p.m., Saturday 9 a.m-5 p.m. Avenida El Sol (across from Qoricancha). Updated: Jun 17, 2009.

Museo Taller Hilario Mendivil

(ADMISSION: Free) This quirky museum is housed within two beautiful courtyards decorated with interesting murals, statues and poems by the renowned Cusqueño artist Hilario Mendivil, his family and friends. The actual museum consists of just one room

CUSCO GUIDE

filled with Mendivil's colorful statues of religious figures and saints, with their signature long necks. Information boards (in Spanish) tell the life history of the artist, and provide anecdotes of his time spent with fellow artists (including Pablo Neruda) writing and drinking in the Plazoleta San Blas. Entrance to the museum is free and original artworks by the artist and his family can be bought at the attached shop. Looking out over the city from the Plaza San Blas, the museum is located in the plaza, on the left. 10 a.m. - 2:30 p.m. and 12:30 p.m. - 6:30 p.m., Closed Sunday. Updated: Mar 25,2010

Museo de Arte y Monasterio de Santa Catalina

(ADMISSION: Tourist ticket) Built by the Spanish between 1601 and 1610 on top of Acllahuasi, where the Inca emperor once housed his chosen Virgins of the Sun, this convent and museum houses an interesting collection of colonial and religious art. Like other attractions in Cusco, the museum has a number of pieces from the Cusqueña School, an art movement emphasizing the union of both Inca and Spanish culture. In addition to baroque frescoes depicting Inca vegetation, the chapel also houses macabre statues of Jesus, beautifully painted arches and 17th century tapestries. Perhaps the highlight of this site is a series of 3-D figurines which recount the life of Christ. Objects such as this were popular devices used by the Catholic Church's "traveling salesmen," who were responsible for converting many of the indigenous people throughout Peru. Santa Catalina Angosta, Tel: 51-84-226-032. Monday-Friday, 9 a.m.-5 p.m., Saturday, 9 a.m.-4 p.m. Updated: Jun 17, 2009.

Museo Inka

For a look at some spectacular Inca artifacts head over to Museo Inka. This recently renovated colonial home, run by the Universidad San Antonio de Abad, is located down an alley to the left of the Cusco Cathedral. Focused on the development of pre-Inca and Inca culture, the museum contains an intriguing collection of jewelry, ceramics, textiles, mummies, trepanned skulls, and a number of metal and gold pieces. Explanations are in English. Be sure to check out the stunning collection of miniature turquoise figures, among other examples of offerings to the gods. You may also have a chance to partake in the weaving demonstrations that take place in the courtyard. Among the attractions in Cusco, this museum is famous

for housing the world's largest collection of wooden queros, which the Inca once used for drinking. Allow 1.5 to 2 hours to see the whole collection. Open Hours From: Monday-Friday, 8 a.m.-5 p.m., Saturday, 9 a.m.-4 p.m. Cuesta del Almirante 103. Tel: 51-84-237-380. Updated: Jun 17, 2009.

Museo Municipal de Arte Contemporaneo

(ADMISSION: Tourist ticket) Housed in Cusco's city hall, the Municipal de Arte Contemporaneo is one of the few public modern art collections in the country. The museum is spread across three galleries, and displays a rotation of local, Peruvian and international paintings, photos and sculptures from its 300-piece collection. The museum is a great place to see how traditional themes in Andean art are treated today. Open Mon.-Fri., 9 a.m.- 5 p.m. Plaza Regocijo (City Hall). Updated: Jul 24, 2010.

Museo de Arte Popular

(ADMISSION: Tourist ticket) For a quick look at the traditional handicrafts and folk art of the Cusco area, check out the Museo de Arte Popular. The small museum is located in the basement of the tourist ticket office (OFEC). There are sculptures made from mud and rice, historical photos of Cusco, ceramics, carvings, gold-leaf work and paintings. Open Mon.-Sat., 9 a.m.-6 p.m. Avenida El Sol 103. Updated: Jul 24, 2010.

Photo by: Bernardo Carbajal

Center for Traditional Textiles of Cusco

No visitor to Cusco can fail to admire the vivid traditional textiles adorned by the local mountain communities. This free exhibit offers an insight into how these products are intricately made using wool from indigenous animals and colored with natural dyes. Practical usage is well explained, as is the significance of the textiles' elaborate designs. The adjoining store gives visitors a chance to witness a demonstration of the weaving process and the opportunity to purchase beautiful (yet pricey) examples. Av. El Sol 603. Updated: Feb 04, 2010.

Cusco Coca Museum

(ADMISSION: $1.75) Recently opened, this small, but informative, museum tells a fascinating account of the now infamous coca leaf. Your journey through time begins with the pre-Inca cultures to whom the leaf was considered sacred (there was even a coca God). Medicinal values and benefits are well explained before moving through to the modern day and the dramatic impact of the cocaine industry. Guided tours are available to Spanish speakers, while the museum's store stocks a wide range of coca-themed souvenirs. Guided tours are conducted in Spanish only, but a written explanation of exhibits is given in English. Suytuqatu 705. Updated: Feb 04, 2010.

Qosqo Center Of Native Art

(ADMISSION: Tourist ticket) For original folkloric dance from all over Peru accompanied by traditional live Andean music, the Qosqo Center of Native Art is where you want to be. The daily performance begins at 6:45 p.m., lasts an hour and gives an honest, lively and colorful representation of the many dances of the region. There is no escaping the fact that this is a tourist attraction but the dancers look as if they are having fun and their energy is contagious. The costumes are great and all in all it's an entertaining way to pass an hour before going out for dinner one evening. The entry is included on the Cusco Tourist Ticket or otherwise entry costs $5. 6.30p.m. - 8p.m., daily. Avenida El Sol 604. Tel: 51-84-227-901, Fax: 51-84-227-901. Updated: Jun 09, 2010.

SHOPPING

Mercado Mollina

Mercado Mollina is a shoppers Valhalla. Forget Machu Picchu logo t-shirts, watercolor paintings and llama postcards because you won't find a single souvenir or craftsy trinket in any of the mercado's several hundred stalls. Instead, you'll find nearly anything you may ever want to buy. Underwear, socks, jeans, shoes, sandals, belts, electronics, shirts, winter coats, plates, appliances, make up, toiletries...and of course, heaps and heaps of obscenely underpriced DVDs and CDs. Sprawled over the space of several city blocks and densely inhabited by temptations for all consumers, Mollina is the kind of shopping experience that dares to suggest that if you can't buy it at Mollina, then it can't be bought. Collectivos run from Choquechaca ($0.25) and taxis from the city center cost less than $1. Updated: Jul 18, 2007.

San Pedro Market

Be sure not to miss San Pedro, the interesting and cultural central market. Both locals and expats alike shop here for fruit and veggies, while textiles, herbs and the local San Pedro drug, can also be found. Toward the back you'll find the raw meat aisles. While strolling the stalls here, see little old men struggling with pig carcasses strung across their backs. If you feel adventurous, the ceviche and trout here are pretty good. Try a mixed fruit shake, or a freshly boiled choclo (corn) with cheese – a Cusco favorite!

SPAS & MASSAGE PARLORS

Body Show Spa Cusco

Body Shop Spa Cusco is a modern relaxation center where you can relieve your fatigue and reenergize after visiting the tourist attractions. It offers massages, sauna, Jacuzzi, skin cleansing and foot therapy by reflexology. Calle Procuradores #50. Tel: 51-84-236-647, URL: www.perucuzco.com/hotel_alquiler/sauna_real_state.htm. Updated: Jun 17, 2009.

Yin Yang Massage

Yin Yang Massage offers deep tissue massage, reiki, shiatsu or reflexology to help reduce stress, altitude sickness, sore muscles, twisted neck or backache. Music and Aromatherapy is included in the massages. Yin Yang has a staff of ten professional massage therapists on hand to take care of you. 9 a.m. - 10 p.m. Portal Comercio 121 (upstairs). Tel: 51-84-258-201, E-mail: info@yinyangtherapeuticmassage.com, URL: www.yinyangtherapeutic massage.com. Updated: Jun 17, 2009.

SPORTS & RECREATION

Action Valley

Action Valley is located just outside of Cusco. The company will provide transportation to and from Action Valley for $2 roundtrip. Videography and photo services are also available. Activities include bungee jumping ($64), slingshot ($59), swing ($20), free rappel ($20), flying fox ($10), climbing wall ($10) and the acrobatic bungee ($10). Monday - Saturday 9a.m. - 8p.m. Calle Santa

Teresa 325, Plaza Regocijo. Tel: 51-84-240-835, E-mail: info@actionvalley.com, URL: www.actionvalleycusco.com. Updated: Jul 28, 2009.

Bungee Jumping with The Inka Adventure

If you are looking for the ultimate bungee jump over the verdant jungle, or to see the Sacred Valley from a different viewpoint, The Inka Adventure can help you. It offers what is considered to be the highest bungee jump leaping point in the Americas. On its website, the company explains the security measures it uses to ensure a safe adventure for its clients. The actual jump takes about 10 to 15 minutes: three minutes to go up the 122 meters to the take-off point, and the rest spent on having the time of your life. Pasaje Sinchiroca 110. Tel: 51-84-233-742 / 967-0918. E-mail: info@theinkaadventure.com URL: www.theinkaadventure.com. Updated: Jun 22, 2009.

Trek in the Chicón Valley

Haku Trek is a new development in the Chicón Valley and is a collaborative project between NGO ProPeru and the local community. The traditional village of Chicón is situated deep in the Chaquihuayjo valley, just outside Urubamba in the Sacred Valley. All hikes are led by Chicón natives, ensuring that tourists have the opportunity to learn about native culture and language, as well as learning about the regional wildlife. The Chicón eco-tourism project aims to educate tourists about the natural environment while providing an alternative form of employment and income for the inhabitants of Chicón. The funds generated from the project are used toward the reforestation of the Chicón Valley and queuñal forest. As such, every trek contributes to the conservation of endangered plant and animal species in the area. Tel: 51-84-961-3001, E-mail: hakutrek@hotmail.com. URL: www.hakutrek.com. Updated: Jun 18, 2009.

Tours

Inka Express - Sightseeing Bus Tour

The First Class tourist bus runs between Cusco and Puno and vice versa, a distance of 388 km (242 mi). The bus service offers an English speaking guide, tourist stops and lunch. The trip takes approximately nine hours. Discover little treasures along a well-trodden journey. The first stop is the church of San Pedro in Andahuaylillas,

otherwise known as the Sistine Chapel of the Andes. The next stop is in Raqchi, site of some impressive Inca ruins.

After Raqchi, the bus enters the town of Sicuani and makes its way through the narrow streets in time for lunch. The tour stops for photo opportunities at La Raya, where a view of the glacier capped Andes beckons to be photographed. The last destination before you reach Puno is the Pucara stone museum. The first class bus service is a longer ride between Cusco and Puno compared to the direct bus or train route. However, the sights along the way are well worth the extra time. The tour runs daily departing Cusco at 7:30 a.m. and arriving in Puno at 5:00 p.m. Cusco office: Urb. El Ovalo Av. La Paz C-23. Puno office: Jiron Tacna 346. Tel: 51-84-255-770. Lima office: Av. Cantuarias 140 Oficina 215 Miraflores. Tel. 51-1-369-0771, E-mail: reservas@inkaexpress.com.pe, URL: www.inkaexpress.com. Updated: Jun 22, 2009.

Globos de los Andes

Globos de los Andes offers hot air balloon excursions around Cusco and the surrounding Andes. You can also use their services in other areas, such as to fly over the Nasca Lines or experience Huaca de la Luna and Salkantay. Globos can also organize excursions for photographic or journalistic special events, promotional hot air balloon tether flights and Cusco Land Rover 4x4 transportation. Contact the company for prices. Avenida de la Cultura 220, Suite 36. Tel: 51-84-232-352, E-mail: info@globosperu.com, URL: www.globosperu.com. Updated: Jun 22,2009.

Train Cusco to Puno

Treat yourself to a train ride through spectacular Andean landscape as a pleasant, more stylish alternative to the bus. The train runs in both directions from either Cusco to Puno via Juliaca or vice versa, a journey that takes nine and a half hours. When you arrive at the station, your attendant is already outside your carriage, waiting to welcome you aboard (regardless of carriage class). As you begin your journey, the attendant becomes your waiter and you can select between a wide selection of beverages (for which you have to pay). At the same time you can order lunch if you wish, choosing between a set lunch of $15, various entrees, and burgers or sandwiches for $6 or so. The journey passes through landscapes that are stunningly beautiful. At La Raya, the highest point of the journey, you may alight for a few moments to buy souvenirs from the locals, anxious to make a buck. Passing through the altiplano you can observe campesinos herding sheep, camelids and cattle, as they have for decades. Beats a cramped bus any day. Most agents can arrange the tickets for you in Puno or Cusco. Closed Tuesday, Thursday, Friday, Sunday. URL: www.perurail.com. Updated: Dec 19, 2007.

Cusco Lodging

The variety of Cusco hotels is amazing. The range of places to stay in the city runs from $4 youth hostels to internationally renowned hotels that charge several hundred dollars per night. In general, the quality of the Cusco hotels is very good. Youth hostels tend to be clean and friendly, the mid-range hotels are charming and comfortable, and the luxury hotels offer some of the best facilities and services in the world.

Higher-end hotels, are often located in beautiful old colonial buildings. If you stay in a lower-budget place, beware that it can get pretty chilly at nights in Cusco, so check that there are sufficient blankets for your needs. Whatever your budget, you'll find the right place in Cusco. Reservations are always recommended, as the best Cusco hotels tend to fill up fast, especially in high tourist seasons, such as May to November. Out of season, prices tend to be a bit lower. If you're in Cusco and looking around for a quiet spot, try a place off one of the main roads, as parts of the city can get very noisy. Updated: Jun 29, 2010

BUDGET

Hospedaje Granada

(ROOMS: $3) There is little to recommend the Hospedaje Granada beyond its extremely low price: three dollars. There are 27 rooms and four bathrooms, but each room is outfitted with a basinilla, a small pot to urinate in. It has wooden floors, a common-area kitchen, and within its limited plumbing facilities, hot water. The Hospedaje Granada is by-and-large a bracing reminder of the limited options for many of the poor of Peru and Latin America. The rooms do at least look like they are clean, and it is within a few blocks walking distance from the Plaza de Armas neighborhood. Siete Cuartones 290. Tel: 51-84-223-281. Updated: Jul 23, 2007.

Hospedaje Félix

(ROOMS: $4-9) The old building, with two-foot-thick walls, that houses the Hospedaje Félix looks like it was built at least 110 years ago and served as lodging for wandering gauchos and wayward vaqueros. It also does not look like it has been very aggressively looked after since the 19th century. For many the rough appearance of the building, along with the cheap price might be part of its appeal. It does have its own Internet cabinas, with what looks like fairly new computers. The location, near to the Plaza de Armas and the San Blas neighborhood, is another plus. Tecsecocha 171. Tel: 51-84-241-949. Updated: Jul 28, 2009.

Mirador Hanan Qosco

(ROOMS: $4-12) This simple and inexpensive, but well-maintained, hostel along the cobblestone Coricalle has the same attraction as its competitors: cheap rooms within walking distance to both the Plaza de Armas and San Blas. The rooms and beds are slightly more stylish than what you would expect at this price, though you may not get used to the old and uneven wooden floors. If you are taller than the average Peruvian, you should also watch for the Mirador's low-entrances. A newly renovated and modern common-area kitchen is currently under construction. Coricalle N445, Tel: 51-84-437-618. Updated: Jul 28, 2009.

Hostal Procurador

(ROOMS: $5-9) Hostal Procurador is one of several inexpensive hostels along the narrow and cobblestone Coricalle. The rooms have a spare, and even stale, quality, but they are clean and secure. Hostal Procurador also features a small common kitchen and a roof terrace complete with outdoor furniture, which provides an opportunity to relax and enjoy a nice view of the Cusco skyline and a wide sea of red-tiled roofs. The staff is warm and considerate of guests needs and the location is convenient. Corricalle 425. Tel: 51-84-243-559. Updated: Apr 23, 2010.

Hospedaje Q'ani Wasi

(ROOMS: $6-12) On the very short Calle Tigre, in the Plaza de Armas neighborhood, you will find the Hospedaje Q'ani Wasi. The rooms are aligned along a single main corridor. The place is a bit run down but the rooms are clean, and most importantly, to budget travelers, very cheap, complete with hot running water. The proximity to all the attractions of the Plaza de Armas and the surrounding neighborhood is also an advantage. The management also points out that the rooms all come with color televisions --but who manufactures black and white sets these days? Calle Tigre 124. Tel: 51-84-240-273, 51-84-242-659, E-mail: eliseoadventures3@hotmail.com. Updated: Jul 28,2009

La Casa de Kishkashta

(ROOMS: $6-8) A small, peaceful house with 12 beds, La Casa de Kishkashta provides guests with free WiFi Internet access, a fully-equipped kitchen and a small TV room with a DVD player and Playstation 2. The water is always hot and the breakfasts are tasty. La Casa de Kishkashta is located in the center of Cusco, a block and a half from the main plaza. The owners can also help you arrange everything that Cusco has to offer, rafting, bungee, trekking, trips to Machu Picchu and more. Marquez 259 patio int.3. Tel: 51-84-224-0465 E-mail: avi-tili@hotmail.com. Updated: Jul 28, 2009.

Munay Wasi

(ROOMS $6-9)If your main priorities for a hotel are cheap and secure rooms, you might want to go to for the Munay Wasi. Apart from its proximity to the best of Cusco, the cost and security are its main assets. It boasts of being in an "old colonial building," but some might be put off by the flies inside the entrance way. This is a family-run business; the staff treat you with courtesy and kindness. The rooms are clean, but if you are over 5'10" (1.78 meters) you would do well to remember to duck when entering. Munay Wasi is a few blocks further than the other hostels from downtown, and thus the rooms are quieter with less nighttime noise. Ca. Waynapata N 253. Tel: 51-84-223-661.

Hostal Rojas

(ROOMS: $6-30) The Hostal Rojas has been in business for 15 years, and you can tell the Rojas family takes its work seriously: the rooms are not only clean and comfortable, but belie their low-cost with high-quality furniture and bedspreads. The hostel has a cafeteria and a safe, and laundry service is also available. Calle Tigre N 129. Tel: 51-84-228-184, E-mail: hostalrojas@hotmail.com. Updated: Jul 28, 2009.

The Point

(DORMS: $7.50) The Point is a perfect place for the young, sociable backpacker. It combines a casual daytime atmosphere with a happening vibe at night, two blocks from the main Plaza. You'll find large, open areas with couches and DVDs, a large outdoor area with plenty of sun, a table tennis and pool table, a bustling bar, a BBQ area and cooking facilities. Decks overlook the garden, and they offer free Internet, WiFi and a book exchange. Communal bathrooms are clean with hot showers and beds are comfy with real duvets. Meson de la Estrella 172, www.thepointhostels.com/cusco. Updated: Jun 30, 2010.

MID-RANGE

Pirwa Hostel Bed and Breakfast

(ROOMS: $7-20) Falling within the mid-range price for Cusco, the Pirwa Bed and Breakfast is one of the best hostels in the Plaza de Armas area, and one of four hostels owned by Pirwa throughout Cusco. Owner Fernando Pilares deserves credit for both the creativity and care he has invested in the B&B in terms of the high-quality of its rooms and common areas. Guests are treated to a welcome drink and breakfast, served in a pleasant common area, included in the price. Some rooms are quieter than others in terms of distance from street noise, so you may want to ask about a room that fits your needs. In room facilities include free Internet access, WiFi and TVs. Check their website for more information on other Cusco Pirwa hostels. Calle Suecia 300 Tel: 51-84-244-315, 970-6148 E-mail: reservas2fpc@hotmail.com, URL: www.pirwahostelscusco.com. Updated: Jul 28, 2009.

Hostal Casa Grande

(ROOMS: $8) Many hostels use "family-managed" as a selling point, but Hostal Casa Grande is one of the few in which it has some real meaning. In a 19th century building constructed over what once was the Palace of Inca Yupanqui and featuring actual Inca-era blocks in its courtyard, the Casa Grande is managed by owner Sonia Mercado and her family. In terms of low-cost hostels, the rooms here are cleaner and have a more personal touch, though a few could use a fresh coat of paint. Additionally, there is a charming on-site museum, showcasing family lore, religious art, and Peruvian and cusqueño history, such as a display on the history of the sol, with actual bills and coins from the 19th century onward. Santa Catalina Ancha

353. Tel: 51-84-264-156.

Loki Hostel

(DORMS: $8) Loki Hostel is one of the most popular hostels in Peru and offers a fun, happening environment for sociable travelers. The hostel is set up in a restored 450-year-old house and is huge, with plenty of rooms and communal spaces, free Internet and WiFi, a large, busy bar that holds parties and themed events, an outdoor area to relax in the sun, and great food. This hostel offers excellent value. Cuesta Santa Ana 601, URL: www.lokihostel.com/cusco. Updated: Jun 30, 2010.

Hatun Tumi

(ROOMS: $8-10) This inexpensive but likeable lodge makes good use of its old colonial structure and offers attractive, clean, freshly painted rooms, and, most notably for its low price, electric heaters for coping with Cusco's notoriously brisk nights. There is a common area kitchen and television, the latter set up on a patio, along with sofas for lounging and relaxing. Breakfast is available. Even though Hospedaje Tumi is within walking distance of the Plaza de Armas, it is also sufficiently distant by several blocks from nighttime noise. Internet, phone and money exchange services are also available. The hotel also serves as a travel agency, and sells bus tickets to as far away as Puno and La Paz. Calle 7 Cuartones N° 245. Tel: 51-84-253-937, URL: www.hatuntumi.com. Updated: Jan 19, 2010.

Hotel Cáceres

(ROOMS: $8-12) The fancy-lettered sign for this place is sure to catch your gaze, but the entrance might be the most promising feature of this low-cost facility. Hotel Cáceres promises "comfortable rooms," with or without private bathrooms, and many of the same amenities that you will find in competing hotels, but this hotel is recommended only if 1) you are short on cash, 2) better, but similarly priced, facilities are rented out and 3) you want to stay near the Plaza de Armas. The rooms are stale and small, and at the high end of the price scale. There are better options during most of the year. Plateros Street 368. Tel: 51-84-232-616, E-mail: hotelcaceres@hotmail.com. Updated: Jul 28, 2009.

Hospedaje Posada del Viajero

(ROOMS: $8-12) A new facility, the Hospedaje Posada del Viajero has an edge over its competitors in the eight-dollar-a-room market due to the freshness of its rooms and the newly constructed lounge and dining areas. Located within a building complex the Santa Catalina Ancha neighborhood, this inn also benefits from being at a quiet, distant and safe remove from the street. Both breakfast and cable TV are available for an additional price. All the other expected amenities, such as laundry service, safety boxes and access to medical services, come as part of the regular room rate. There are also clean, common-use kitchen, dining and lounge spaces. Santa Catalina Ancha 366-J. Tel: 51-84-261-643, E-mail: laposadadelviajerocusco@hotmail.com. Updated: Jul 28, 2009.

Hostal Santa María

(ROOMS: $8-20) This hostel's most attractive selling point is its location right next door to the historic Compañía Catholic Church on the Plaza de Armas. Particularly pleasant is Hostal Santa María's second floor, where you can sit on the terrace and marvel at the church from a closer and more elevated angle than from the street. Continental breakfast is included. The hostel also has its own on-site massage clinic. Each room has a wooden cross displayed. Hostal Santa María has been in business for 18 years, and has a good reputation. Santa Catalina Angosta 158. Tel: 51-84-252-746, E-mail: hostalsantamaria@hotmail.com. Updated: Jul 28, 2009.

Flying Dog

(DORMS: $10; ROOMS: $25-50) Flying Dog offers a comfortable environment to relax and meet other backpackers. Located in a quiet area three blocks from the Plaza, Flying Dog provides clean rooms, a TV and DVD lounge, free Internet and WiFi, a cheap bar, free breakfast, hot showers, lockers and a fun bar with cheap drinks. Calle Choquechaca 469. www.flyingdogperu.com. Updated: Jun 30, 2010.

Teqsiqocha Hostal

(ROOMS: $10-25) As that old song goes, "you gotta have a gimmick," and for Tecsecocha it is that each room is outfitted with Castilian-Rococo furniture, which may or may not be authentic. There are fancy bed-spreads, too, which might lead you to overlook the threadbare quality of the rooms themselves. The manager admits that the hostel is still very much a work-in-progress. This hostel might appeal to travelers wanting to save a few dollars, and it is within walking distance of the Plaza de Armas, San Blas, and many restaurants and shops. The hostel also offers an on-site medical service, breakfast, a safety deposit box, and free movies in the coffee lounge, every day, from 5 to 7 p.m. Calle Teqsicocha N 474. Tel: 51-84-248-720, E-mail: teqhostal@yahoo.com. Updated: Jul 28, 2009.

Gloria Pareja Guest House !

(ROOMS: $11-15) Gloria Pareja Guest House is a clean and safe inn located in downtown Cusco. With personalized attention, the hotel is intimate and has double rooms with private or shared bathrooms, and a triple with a private bath. Ca. 250 Matará, 3rd floor. E-mail: vilcanotatour@yahoo.es. Updated: Jun 30, 2010.

Intiq Samana

(ROOMS: $15-25) Intiq Samana is one of the best buys in Cusco, with its attractive, clean, stylish and comfortable rooms belying its mid-range (though cheap by first-world standards) price of $15 for a single room and $25 for a double. Besides the expected storage space, hot water, private bathrooms, safety boxes, breakfast, a clean and spacious common-area kitchen, laundry service and cable TV, this hostel also features free Internet access for its guests. The owner, Richard Flores, has done a great job in not just relying on the natural charm of an old building, but remodeling it so it looks both fresh and traditional. Calle Meloc 422-2. Tel: 51-84-232-101. Updated: Jul 28, 2009.

V!VA ONLINE REVIEW

INTIQ SAMANA

Extremely friendly and helpful owner and staff. Only a few blocks from main Plaza de Armas. Guest kitchen.

Jun 13, 2010

Hostal Posada del Corrigedor

(ROOMS: $15-30) If the price is within your budget you will not be disappointed. The management of Hostal Posada del Corrigedor has invested more creativity and care in this hostel than at most of the other hostels you will find in this price level. The rooms are clean, comfortable and attractive. The hostel also has its own restaurant, the Plus Café, with a balcony view of the Plaza de Armas. Portal de Panes 151. Tel: 51-84-502-362, E-mail: 2fcp@hotmail.com. Updated: Jul 28, 2009.

Imperial Palace

(ROOMS: $15-40) This high-quality, but affordable, hostel has clean, carpeted rooms, hot running water, safe-deposit boxes, laundry service and a restaurant that serves a variety of breakfasts, which are included in the price. Single rooms start at $15, double rooms at $25. The location is a short walking distance from the Plaza de Armas, and within the same neighborhood, in which you will find many colorful shops, taverns and restaurants. The owner proudly boasts of 30 years in the travel industry, and is one of the more informed sources of travel and touring in Cusco, the Sacred Valley and Machu Picchu. Calle Tecsecocha N 490-B. Tel: 51-84-223-324, E-mail: imperialpalacehostal@hotmail.com. Updated: Jan 14, 2010.

Hotel Carlos V

(ROOMS: $20-50) Rooms are fresher, cleaner and simply better than what you get at most cheaper hotels and hostels in the area, and they come with all the expected niceties, such as hot running water, cable TV, a continental breakfast, security boxes, and most importantly for Cusco's chilly evenings, heated rooms. Hotel Carlos V also has its own restaurant, La Gruta. Strangely enough, it does not accept credit cards, only cash. Calle Tecsecocha 490. Tel: 51-84-223-091, Fax: 51-84-228-447, E-mail: reservas@carlosvcusco.com, URL: www.carlosvcusco.com. Updated: Jul 28, 2009.

Sol Innka Plaza

(ROOMS: $20-35) A bit pricier than the other hotels in this area, the Sol Innka should appeal to older travelers or those looking for an alternative to the standard backpacker lodging. The quality of the facility is first-rate in terms of comfort, cleanliness, security and design. There are additional niceties (beyond the cable TV, private bathrooms and continental breakfasts) such as a fax machine and WiFi. Calle Suecia 420-B. Tel: 51-84-431-350, E-mail: solinnkaplazahotel@hotmail.com, URL: www.solinnkaplazahotel.com. Updated: Jul 28, 2009.

Sumac Wasi

(ROOMS: $25-30) Sumac Wasi (Beautiful House) is in a large, 400-year-old colonial house located 50 meters from the main square, in the heart of the Cusco city. It has comfortable and pleasant rooms with private bathrooms, 24-hour hot water, heaters and televisions. Continental breakfast is part of the price for a night's stay here. Procuradores 366. Tel: 51-84-240-664, Fax: 51-84-20664, E-mail: informes@sumacwasi.com, URL: www.sumacwasi.com URL: www.sumacwasi.com. Updated: Jul 28, 2009.

The Chaksi Inn Hostal

(ROOMS: $25-50) An affiliate of Hostelling International (HI), this hostel is a little more expensive than the norm, although HI members do get a $5 discount. A breakfast is included in the cost, and all credit cards are accepted, but with a 10 percent add on. For those who want comfort right in the heart of everything in Cusco, the Chaksi Inn Hostal is an attractive option. The hostel claims to be both clean and quiet, though considering some rooms overlook the Plaza de Armas, the latter might be disputed. Portal Confiturias N 257. Tel: 51-84-245-230, E-mail: perutravel@hotmail.com, URL: www.vientosdelperu.com. Updated: Jul 28, 2009.

Inkayra Hotel

(ROOMS: $25-55) Inkayra Hotel, new on Cusco hotel scene, offers modern rooms with private bathrooms and hot water 24 hours a day. It also has Internet access. The price includes breakfast. Av. ejercito 270. Tel: 51-84-244-876, Fax: 51-84-244-876, E-mail: inkayrahotel_cusco@hotmail.com, URL: www.inkayrahotel.com. Updated: Apr 21, 2009.

Villa Mayor

(ROOMS: $30) It is hard not to like this very attractive and upscale hotel which faces the peaceful Plaza Regocijo. If you are planning to spend a little more money during your stay in Cusco, then this is one of the more appealing options. In addition to everything you expect from a hotel at this price, which includes heated rooms, the Villa Mayor has its own restaurant and spa, with the latter offering services that range from waxing to pedicures. It is still close enough to the rest of old Cusco, but at an enough of a distance to be fairly tranquil. Portal Nuevo 246, Plaza del Regocijo. Tel: 51-84-263-932, Fax: 51-84-252-688, E-mail: villamayorcusco@terra.com.pe, URL: www.villamayorhostal.com. Updated: Jul 28, 2009.

Hotel Oblitas (Hotel Sol Plaza Inn)

(ROOMS: $30-50) One of several hotels on Calle Plateros at the south end of the Plaza de Armas, Hotel Oblitas offers money exchange services, tourist information, airline ticket reservations and purchases, faxing and free Internet access. The rooms start at $15 during the low-season and go as high as $42 during the high season. The rooms, complete with private bathrooms, are clean, fresh and pleasantly designed. Safety boxes, a cafeteria and on-site security guard are part of the package. Proximity to everything that the neighborhood has to offer is, of course, an advantage. Calle Plateros 358. Fax: 51-84-223-871/249-031, E-mail: info@solplazainn.com, solplazainn@hotmail.com, URL: www.solplazainn.com. Updated: Jul 28, 2009.

Rey Antares Mystic Hotel

(ROOMS: $35-55) The more expensive room prices at the Rey Antares Mystic Hotel means a little bit extra, spiritually speaking. For interested guests, manager Yarly la Torre offers access to local shamans who will facilitate Earth ceremonies, and on its top floor the hotel has a salon for meditation and yoga. The Rey Antares' lobbies and rooms are painted in a calming light blue and green, congruent with the stated tranquil and spiritual intentions of the facility. The Hotel also has great rooftop views of Cusco and the valley, as well as a café and restaurant. Even though all single rooms are priced the same, they are not all the same size, so one might want to take this into consideration. The location, in a non-tourist area, is more distant than other similar-range hotels from the Plaza de Armas, but taxis in Cusco are very inexpensive. Calle Cascaparo 172, Tel: 51-84-225-420, E-mail: info@reyantareshotel.com, URL: www.reyantareshotel.com. Updated: Jul 28, 2009.

Hostal Corihuasi

(ROOMS: $38-66) Hostal Corihuasi is a charming mid-range hotel in a good location. The building is in a converted 17th century home. The view of the city from some of the rooms and terraces is great. Each room is unique, though some are better than others, so ask to see yours beforehand. The hotel also has an elegant lounge with fireplace. If you pay in cash, Hostal Corihuasi offers a $10 discount. Breakfast, taxes, and transport to and from the airport are included in the cost. Calle Suecia 561. Tel: 51-84-232-233 / 260-502, E-mail: hostal@corihuasi.com, URL: www.corihuasi.com. Updated: Jul 28, 2009.

HIGH-END

The Niños Hotel

(ROOMS: $40) The Niños Hotel has large, comfortable rooms, inside an old and neatly refurbished colonial property, attractively stylish and heated. The hostel accepts payment in cash only, though exceptions can be made for groups booking through travel agencies. The rooms are not numbered, but named after children, accompanied by childhood photos provided by owner Jolanda van den Berg. There is a reason for this. The Niños Hotel (and its restaurant), donates all its profits to help a foundation, which provides daily hot meals and assistance to 500 of Cusco's poorest. The overall quality of the facility justifies the price, and the knowledge that you are contributing to the humanitarian work should enhance the quality of your visit to Cusco. Calle Meloc 442. Tel: 51-84-231-424, E-mail: ninoshostel@terra.com.pe, URL: www.ninoshotel.com. Updated: Jul 28, 2009.

Andenes De Saphy

(ROOMS: $40-60) The Andenes de Saphy Hostel, is a beautiful and comfortable place in Cuzco, located at the foot of the Sacred Mountain of Sacsayhuaman in the Valley of the Saphy River. Being surrounded by a gorgeous scenery and far from the noise of the city gives the place an unbeatable location. Andenes de Saphi Hotel allows you to enjoy the countryside just 3 blocks from the Plaza de Armas, with its three flower- filled terraces where you will be able to receive the energy of the Sun God, Inti Tayta, and Mother Earth, Pacha Mama. This hostel has more than 10 years of giving its guests a wonderful service and has three times being awarded the best hostel of Cusco by the Dirección Regional de Comercio Exterior y Turismo (Dircetur) with the Qente Prize, award that its given to businesses which have excel in services and good practices to improve the tourism and ecotourism in Cusco. St. Saphi 848, Cusco, Cusco Tel: 51-84-227-561, E-mail: hotel@andenesdesaphi.com, URL: www.andenesdesaphi.com.

Teatro Inka Bed and Breakfast

(ROOMS $40-62) Located in the neighborhood just south of the Plaza de Armas, the Teatro Inka--named after Teatro Street, rather than an actual theater--offers the luxury and quality you'd expect for a place whose rooms start at $40. Amenities include heat, cable TV, breakfast, medical assistance (in case of high altitude sickness), airport pick-up and drop-off and Internet access. For a little bit extra, you also get laundry service and a massage. Both the common areas and the rooms themselves are old west-style with a modern deco twist, and have won prizes for their design. Calle Teatro 391. Tel: 51-84-255-077 / 228-104, E-mail: info@teatroinka.com. URL: www.teatroinka.com. Updated: Jul 28, 2009

El Balcón Hostal

(ROOMS: $40-90) Located in the colonial center of Cusco, only three blocks from the Plaza de Armas, El Balcón overlooks the city and the surrounding mountains. This hostel was originally constructed in 1630 atop Inca agricultural terraces, and was meticulously restored in 1998 to the beautiful condition it is in today. El Balcón has 16 rooms, each with a private bathroom. Bathrooms are spacious, with showers and hot water 24 hours a day. The beds are custom made (extra long!), with 100% cotton linen sheets, 100% alpaca and wool blankets and feather pillows. The hostel also features space heaters, cable TV, local, national and international phone service, free WiFi Internet access and room service. It has suites, matrimonial, single, double and triple rooms. In addition, El Balcón also offers airport pickup service, storage room, terraced garden, restaurant, laundry service and tourism information. Tambo de Montero. Tel: 51-84-236-738, E-mail: info@balconcusco.com, URL: www.balconcusco.com. Updated: Jul 28, 2009.

Hotel Marqueses

(ROOMS: $45-$125) Hotel Marqueses is only a block and a half from the Plaza de Armas, the perfect distance from many day and evening activities. A charming, safe and spotlessly clean place to stay, the hotel is adorned with a colonial motif that suits the building's 400-year-old history. The open-air courtyard is a real gem. The hotel offers two types of rooms: standard and deluxe. The deluxe rooms have more sunlight and are more spacious because of their positioning near the courtyard. All rooms include hot water, heat, cable TV and a private bath. The friendly staff will accommodate most needs, including airport pick-up and drop-off service. Internet is available, free of charge, and so is a full breakfast buffet. Hotel Marqueses is one of the only hotels in Cusco that has suites, for a more spacious stay. Calle Garcilaso N° 256. Tel: 51-84-264-249, Fax: 51-84-257-819, E-mail: info@hotelmarqueses.com, URL: www.hotelmarqueses.com. Updated: Jul 28, 2009.

La Casona Real

(ROOMS: $50-80) La Casona Real is perhaps one of the best hotels in Cusco. Located only a stone's throw from the Plaza de Armas, La Casona Real is on Calle Procuradores ("Gringo Alley") and is probably the best bang for your buck. Tastefully decorated with a modern Peruvian motif, the rooms are spacious, elegant and impeccably clean which may make you feel like you are truly at a home away from home. All rooms have comfy beds, private modern baths, 24-hour hot water, heat, phones, cable TV and room service. Also included in the price is continental breakfast in the courtyard and free airport pick-up.

The breezeway opens into a large airy and bright indoor courtyard with a fantastic bar for sipping wine or an ice cold cerveza. La Casona Real is exceptionally safe (the large outside double doors close early and you have to ring the bell to get in); the staff at La Casona Real are attentive, friendly and efficient, and will help you arrange anything you may need, including medical assistance. Calle Procuradores N 354. Tel: 51-84-224-670, E-mail: reservations@casonarealcusco.com, URL: www.casonarealcusco.com. Updated: Jul 28, 2009.

Cristina Hostal

(ROOMS: $55-65) Rustic, indigenous décor creates a true Peruvian ambience at Cristina Hostal. While the rooms are basic, they have such amenities as comfortable beds with private baths, 24-hour hot water, telephones, carpeting, cable TV and comes with continental breakfast. For a bit more money, the hostel also rents apartment-styled rooms with a kitchenette, refrigerator, dining table, ample closet space and a sofa. Avenida El Sol 341, two blocks from Plaza de Armas. Tel: 51-84-227-233, Fax: 51-84-227-251, E-mail: info@hcristina.com, URL: www.hcristina.com. Updated: Jul 28, 2009.

Hotel Royal Inka I

(ROOMS: $60-120) Hotel Royal Inka I is located in a Cusco landmark: the building was originally built by Inca Pachacútec and later became the home of Francisca Zubiaga de Gamarra, a heroine of Peruvian independence struggle and wife of Peru's first president. There are a variety of comfortable rooms and suites to choose from. The hotel bar and restaurant are full of colonial character. The rates are competitive for a hotel of this class: check it out if you're ready for a little splurge. Plaza Regocijo 299. Tel: 51-84-222-284/ 231-067, Fax: 51-84-234-221, E-mail: royalinka@aol.com, URL: www.royalinkahotel.com/hotels.htm. Updated: Jul 28, 2009.

Hotel Royal Inka II

(ROOMS: $60-120) Like its sister, the Royal Inka I, Hotel Royal Inka II occupies a converted colonial home. This hotel is a little more formal and expensive, and the rooms are more uniform. The entire establishment is more modern, which will appeal to some. The hotel is very conveniently located to all of Cusco's main attractions. The restaurant and bar on the top floor are pleasant and worth a visit even for those who do not stay there. 335 Santa Teresa. Tel: 51-84-222-284 Fax: 51-84-234-221 E-mail: royalinka@aol.com URL: www.royalinkahotel.com/hotels.htm. Updated: Jul 28, 2009.

Hostal Rumi Punku

(ROOMS: $70-140) Hotel Rumi Punku is an attractive hotel in old Cusco. Rumi Punku means "stone door" in Quechua: the entrance to the hotel leads through an ancient stone door, obviously of Inca design. The doorway is all that has survived of an Inca palace; today the door is considered a historic relic by the city of Cusco. The hotel itself is quite charming and the rooms are airy and neat. The restaurant is friendly; there is a small courtyard and chapel on the premises. Breakfast is included, as is airport pick-up if you call ahead. Calle Choquechaca #339. Tel: 51-84-221-102, E-mail: info@rumipunku.com, URL: www.rumipunku.com. Updated: Jul 28, 2009.

Hotel Arqueólogo Exclusive Selection

(ROOMS: $70-120) Arqueólogo Exclusive Selection Hotel is in a restored colonial house located in the historical heart of Cusco. The hotel's original Inca walls, exceptional vistas of Cusco and wood-beam ceilings make it very cozy. The rooms have private bathrooms with 24-hour hot water, telephone, cable TV, heating, WiFi, balconies and private security boxes. Rates include buffet breakfast, served in its cafeteria with a lovely panoramic view of Cusco. Pumacurco 408. Tel: 51-84-232-522, E-mail: reservation@hotelarqueologo.com, URL: www.hotelarqueologo.com.

Sonesta Posada del Inca

(ROOMS: $83-118) Owned and operated by the international Sonesta chain, Posada del Inca is strategically located right in the center of old Cusco. The rooms are bright and airy, there is a relaxing lounge with a fireplace, and the service is very good. The hotel has a tour desk which can help with trips and arrangements in Cusco (there is even an on-line "virtual concierge" so that you can book tours before you arrive). The Posada del Inca is fairly expensive; it falls somewhere around the upper mid-range or lower upper range in terms of costs, but the location is perfect and the value is good for the money. Portal Espinar 108. Tel: 51-84-227-061, Fax: 51-84-248-484, E-mail: salescusco@sonestaperu.com, URL: www.sonesta.com/peru_cusco. Updated: Jul 28, 2009.

The Garden House

(ROOMS: $89-249) The Garden House is a haven located only ten minutes from the center of Cusco. The balconies and garden terraces have commanding views over the former Inca capital and the mountainsides. The rooms are large and well furnished, all with private, hot-water bathroom and extra-long beds. Interconnecting suites are available, for families. There's a beautiful cloistered patio, garden and orchards. The Garden House also has a library, spa facilities, dining room with extensive wine list and two sitting rooms with fireplaces. Other amenities include babysitting, Internet, WiFi, cable TV, luggage storage, secure parking and airport pick-up. Larapa Grande B-6. Tel: 51-84-271-117, E-mail: info@cuscohouse.com. URL: www.cuscohouse.com. Updated: Jan 16, 2010.

Hatuchay Tower

(ROOMS: $235-335) Hatuchay Tower has 42 spacious rooms, all equipped with modern amenities such as satellite TV, telephone, in-room safe, 24-hour room service, and hot and cold water 24-hours. Smoking rooms are available. The on-site restaurant serves specialty Peruvian dishes and international cuisine. The restuarant is open 5 a.m. to 10 p.m. Ycou can enjoy a relaxing cocktail with friends in the Hatuchay Tower Bar, open 2-10 p.m. Av. Hermanos Ayar M-24. Tel: 51-84-211-201, E-mail: reservas@hatuchaytower.com URL: www.hatuchaytower.com. Updated: Jul 23, 2007.

Hotel Libertador

(ROOMS: $240-350) Hoteles Libertador is a small chain of ultra-luxury hotels operating in Peru. The Cusco branch of its chain is the Hotel Libertador (Cusco), and according to the Peruvian Ministry of Industry and Tourism, it is the best five-star hotel in the city.It is located in the former home of Francisco Pizarro, conquistador of Peru. The building is the well-known "Casa de los Cuatro Bustos" and it's right next door to the old Inca temple of the sun. Pizarro's home was built on the foundation of another Inca temple, and some of the stonework is still visible--you can admire it in the "Rumi" bar while enjoying a pisco sour. The well-furnished rooms are comfortable and the service is top-notch. The restaurant, "Inti Raymi," occasionally brings in traditional dancers. Ask if they'll have them while you're there. Plazoleta Santo Domingo 259. Tel: 51-84-231-961, Fax: 51-84-233-152, E-mail: 51-84-233-152, URL: www.libertador.com.pe/eng/cusco.php. Updated: Jan 15,2010

"The" Small Luxury Guest House

(ROOMS: $280-330) With just four, unique rooms, this incredible boutique guest house will attract a very particular clientele. Decadent and distinctive, each room contains its own magic—whether it is the personal sound system, fireplace, dining area, curtain covered bath tub, multi gym, original Inca stone wall or open plan design. With astonishing attention to detail, every furnishing is a creative work of art. All rooms are situated on the first floor surrounding the disco ball filled courtyard of the Fallen Angel Restaurant. With loud music and diners below from early evening until midnight; this is not the place to be if you want peace and tranquility. The owner and designer of the restaurant and Guest House, Andres Zuniga, has done a successful job of enticing the client into his flamboyant world. It has to be seen to be believed. Plazoleta Nazarenas 221 Tel: 51-84-258-184 E-mail: theguesthouse@fallenangelincusco.com, URL: www.fallenangelincusco.com. Updated: Jul 01, 2010.

Hotel Monasterio

(ROOMS: $470-1240) Owned and operated by the prestigious Orient Express Hotels group, the Monasterio is the most luxurious hotel in Cusco. The hotel complex was formerly the San Antonio Abad seminary, which was built over 300 years ago and served as an actual monastery and seminary until recently. The seminary foundations themselves were constructed on Inca stonework.

The monk's cells have been converted into elegant, comfortable rooms, and the courtyards still have ancient trees and much of the colonial art and paintings still adorn the walls and hallways. You can live like the monks did, except much, much better. The Hotel Monasterio has even installed a system to pump more oxygen into the rooms to counteract the effects of altitude sickness on its guests. The hotel is huge; it has over 100 rooms in addition to several suites. There are two restaurants and a bar on the premises as well as an original chapel that is still considered to be consecrated ground. There is an on-site travel agency which can arrange all sorts of tours. Ca. Palacios 136, Plazoleta Nazarenas. Tel: 51-84-241-777, Fax: 51-84-246-983, E-mail: info@peruorientexpress.com.pe, URL: www.monasterio.orient-express.com/web/ocus/ocus_a2a_home.jsp. Updated: Apr 23, 2010.

Cusco Restaurants

Cusco is a good place to eat. This is a city steeped in tradition, with fine Peruvian restaurants on almost every corner. The growth of tourism as an industry has also created a market for everything from international fine cuisine to fast food. Updated: Jul 30,2009.

ASIAN

Indigo

As Cusco's only Thai restaurant, Indigo definitely delivers. Spicy, tasty Thai dishes are offered, including all your favorites from home. Enjoy your meal within a lovely atmosphere including different types of tables including a swinging chair. Meals are around 30 soles, but worth it. Also a nice place to have a coffee or a fruit juice in the afternoon, and sit down to a game of chess or Connect4! Tecsecocha, 2nd floor, just one block from the plaza. Updated: Jun 30, 2010.

Kintaro Japanese Restaurant

Kintaro is the only Japanese restaurant in Cusco, and one of the few that can be found in Peru overall. Moriya Daisuke, a native of Japan, offers his customers as authentic an experience as possible, complete with a second floor where you sit barefoot in order to enjoy such specialties as anjonjoli and tofu, vegetable noodle soup, tempura, trout sashimi and white fish cake. Open every day from 2 to 10 p.m., it takes cash only and can seat up to forty. This restaurant also sells authentic, traditional, hand-dyed Japanese fabrics. Heladeros 149. Tel: 51-84-226-181, URL: www.kintaro-cusco.com. Updated: Jul 30, 2009.

CAFÉS

Jack's Café Bar

Manager Jane Berthelsen said she wanted "the sort of food from back home that you miss" when she came up with the idea of Jack's. Her vision included hearty pea and ham soup, and a big, juicy cheeseburger," not to mention Jack's antipasto which she calls, "a mixed plate of yummy things." And, Tex-Mex nachos. Located in the Plaza de Armas neighborhood, Jack's offers large, well-made platefuls of North American favorites, and that includes hummus with crispy ciabatta and a roasted pumpkin soup with fresh herbs. The restaurant is open every day from 6:30 a.m. to 11:00 p.m. and also has a bar. Choquechaka and Cuesta. Tel: 51-84-254-606/ 506-960, E-mail: janeb34@hotmail.com. Updated: Jul 30, 2009.

Encuentros

Encuentros was recently redecorated and offers superb coffee and good snacks such as sandwiches and cakes. There are tables on the first floor and more comfortable chairs upstairs with space to rest your laptop when working. Encuentros provides consistent WiFi and friendly service. Just off the plaza at the bottom of Calle Suecia. Updated: Jun 30, 2010.

Gabriels

You'll be amazed as soon as you walk in at how modern, clean and comfortable Gabriels is. This cafe would be better placed in New York or Sydney. You can easily spend an entire morning relaxing in the ridiculously large couches and taking advantage of their solid WiFi while sipping real coffee and good food. While slightly higher priced than regular cafes, it's worth it. Two blocks from the plaza on Santa Teresa. Updated: Jun 30, 2010.

Prasada

Prasada is a tiny little café that is literally a hole in the wall. But don't be fooled – this cute little café has charm, and friendly service invites you to pull up a stool while you wait for your sandwich and fruit juice and watch the passersby. It costs only five soles $1.80 for a great chicken sandwich. Conveniently located two blocks from the plaza on Choquechaca, just a few doors down from Jack's Café. Updated: Jun 30, 2010.

Moloko

A very chill café with free Internet downstairs and a movie room with comfy couches upstairs, Moloko is an easy place to socialize or to hunker down and enjoy a movie. Films show twice daily (pick up a monthly schedule at the café or have a look at the day's movies posted outside the front door), and admission is free, although movie watchers are expected to buy food or drink. The dinner menu is an unimpressive collection of sandwich and pizza selections; at lunch, the set menu is a basic but very economical and has tasty choices. The staff is young and friendly (and prone to periodically throwing great parties in lieu of a weekend film), and if the crowd is thin and the scheduled movie isn't a popular choice, it's possible to persuade the movie manager to change the selection. 216 Choquechaca, Tel: 51-84-240-109, 51-84-967-8241, E-mail: molokoperu@hotmail.com. Updated: Jul 30, 2009.

Cappuccino Café !

Cappuccino Café is a made-for-tourists specialty, with 22 varieties of coffee and a simple menu specializing in hamburgers, sandwiches and omelets. Located on the upper floor of the Portal Comercio, this eatery benefits from a spectacular view of the Plaza de Armas and the Catedral, particularly at sunset. Its apple pie has a soft and fluffy pancake-like crust with a light filling. Cappuccino Café also has computers: with Internet access, costing around $0.50 cents per hour. This is a popular place with tourists and expatriates who come to hang out, commiserate and/or to write home. Portal Comercio 141. Updated: Jul 30, 2009.

The Film Lounge and Danish Café

Part movie salon, part cafeteria and part crash pad, the Film Lounge and Danish Café at the far end of Gringo Alley (a.k.a. Calle Procuradores) is an opportunity to relax and hang with travelers as well as locals. Owner Dorthe Sandbeck cooks up favorites from her native Denmark, such as meatball sandwiches, baguettes and home-made soups. She also offers screenings from her selection of more than 450 film titles in the movie salon, complete with surround sound. You can also keep it simple by just hanging out in the lounge area and sharing travel stories with friends, old and new. Procadores 389, 2nd floor. Tel: 51-84-123-236, Open Hours: Noon to: 10:00 p.m. Closed Sundays. Updated: Nov 04, 2009.

Café Trotamundos

The name translates into "world trekker" and this eatery has its own trekker icon, a stick figure with a backpack. As much a tavern as a café, Trotamundos has a great view of the Catedral on the Plaza de Armas, along with a large fireplace to keep the place warm. It has a large selection of sandwiches, rolls and juices, along with drinks and coffee, and also makes and sells its own leather handbags and polo shirts featuring the Trotamundo mascot. A fine selection of wine can be purchased by the bottle. Portal de Comercio N 177. Tel: 51-84-239-590. Updated: Jul 30, 2009.

V!VA ONLINE REVIEW

CAFE TROTAMUNDOS

"Good food and excellent location for a good price. This is a nice place to have lunch, and pretty cheap considering it's in Plaza de Armas and has a great view.

Jul 28, 2009

The Bagel Café

The Bagel Café might well be the only place in Peru where you will find bagels. At the Bagel Café, large puffy bagels are served with all sorts of tasty toppings, from cream cheese and jam to avocado, hummus, olives and eggs. Fresh orange juice and other fruit juices are also on offer. The Bagel Café is located in a comfortable, cove-like setting with both indoor and outdoor seating, just off the plaza on Procuradores. Updated: Jun 30, 2010.

FRENCH

Le Nomade

Le Nomade offers a relaxed Bohemian ambience of couches and narguile pipes, the latter with a variety of tobaccos. The menu has more of an emphasis on French cuisine, with such plates as *bistec con roquefort* and *boeuf bourguignon*, but there are a number of sandwiches as well. There are no standard chairs, except for two that face windows with mini-balconies. The restaurant is open from 8 a.m. to 2 p.m., with happy hour from 3:30 to 7 p.m. Choqechaka 207 and Cuesta San Blas. Tel: 51-84-438-369. Updated: Jul 30, 2009.

INDIAN

Maikhana The Indian Restaurant

Maikhana Namaskar is a well-kept secret in Cusco. So well kept, in fact, that even locals who profess a love of Indian food don't know that this purveyor of samosas and hot chai tea even exists in Cusco. Coyly hidden in the Galería de Arte Señor Mérida, it's easy to pass right on by the restaurant, even if you know exactly what you're looking for. However, a well-honed sense of direction and a little persistence will be handsomely rewarded with spicy curries and homemade chutneys, hot rice, soft naan and a menu thick with options for vegetarians. The service requires some patience, and tandoori fans may be disappointed at the absence of tandoori-cooked options on the menu, but the food (prepared by Indian chefs) is some of Cusco's best ethnic fare. Av. El Sol 106 Int. 207 Galeria La Merced. Tel: 51-84-232-727, E-mail: maikhana@gmail.com, URL: www.maikhana.net. Updated: Jan 15,2010.

Govinda's

Govinda's has what is most likely the healthiest food in all of Cusco. Managed by local affiliates of Hare Krishna, and with a slant towards Indian-style cooking, the all-vegetarian, heavy on soy, menu offers such items as *apana de cusqueño*, that is, soy steak with fried bananas, cheese, and rice, or *palta rellena*, avocado stuffed with vegetables and yogurt sauce. Portraits of traditional Hindu religious figures, most notably Krishna, are prominently featured. Religious music plays on the sound system and a low-key smell of incense all contribute to a unique dining experience. Calle Espaderos 128. Tel: 51-84-504-864, E-mail: raghuraram@hotmail.com. Updated: Jul 30, 2009.

INTERNATIONAL

Two Nations

Two Nations offers travelers huge plates of great food. Try the massive Australian cheeseburgers, the tender cusqueñean alpaca, or the pork, salads and tasty desserts. The restaurant is small and cosy, with a separate lounge area with plenty of DVDs to watch while relaxing on the large comfortable couches. Being Australian-run, the staff speaks perfect English and offers service similar to what you'd expect back home. Closed on Sundays, prices range from 15 – 30 soles. One block from the plaza on Huaynapata. Updated: Jun 30, 2010.

Cava de San Rafael

Cava de San Rafael serves up a modern Andean menu that includes local trout and grilled alpaca (for the daring). But it offers more than just fine cuisine to its clientele; it has a panoramic view of Cusco's

Plaza de Armas, and has an ancestral and folk dance show. The restaurant is on the itinerary of most first-class tours. Santa Catalina Ancha 370. Tel: 51-84-261-691, E-mail: cavadesanrafael@infonegocio.net.pe. Updated: Jul 30, 2009.

Fallen Angel

A funky, artsy restaurant featuring tables made out of bathtubs (full of live fish!) and barbed wire on the toilets (it's tasteful), Fallen Angel is popular among visitors. They have a varied menu—their steaks are excellent. Fallen Angel occasionally has parties and other special events—check in if you're in town. Plazoleta Nazarenas 221, Tel: 51-84-258-184, URL: www.fallenangelincusco.com. Updated: Jul 30,2009.

Truco Restaurant

You will definitely not soon forget dining at the Truco Restaurant on the south end of the charming Plaza Regocijo, the latter a smaller and more tranquil compliment to the Plaza de Armas. El Truco is in a capacious and elegant building whose origin goes back to the 18th century, when it served as home to the Viceroy La Serna. It was later a coin plant, manufacturing gold and silver currency, then a gambling house. El Truco's limited, but choice, menu offers expert versions of continental favorites such as fillet mignon, trout menier and Napolitan spaghetti. Live music is common. The facility can easily accommodate over a 150 people, and is recommended for large groups. Plaza Regocio 261, Tel: 51-84-235-295, Fax: 51-84-262-441, E-mail: eltruco95@hotmail.com, URL: www.cuscuperu.com/eltruco. Updated: Jul 30, 2009.

El Cuate

Located halfway along Gringo Alley, you will find Cusco's longest established Mexican restaurant. With over 20 years of experience, this family-run eatery serves up a fine selection of traditional Mexican cuisine, including classic favorites such as tacos, burritos, fajitas and enchiladas. El

Cuate offers a cozy, friendly atmosphere and good value for money, El Cuate has always been a popular backpacker haunt, so if Mexican food is your thing, hang up your sombrero, kick back and enjoy another shot of tequila. Updated: Feb 03, 2010.

Restaurant Aldea Yanapay

As you walk up the flight of stairs to the Restaurant Aldea Yanapay, you are greeted by the colorful crayon impressions of children's artwork. The Restaurant Aldea Yanapay itself could be mistaken for a kindergarten, with cushions tossed on the floor as an indicator of its relaxed atmosphere. This is indeed a real restaurant, open from morning until night, offering up everything from huevos rancheros and Greek bread with tzatziki sauce, to pasta with bacon, mushrooms and tomatoes, Irish coffee and sangria. The Restaurant Aldea Yanapay raises funds for the non-profit Aldea Yanapay Project, an alternative school for disadvantaged children. Local musicians, clowns, and, not infrequently, tourists inspired to show off their guitar-picking aptitude also tend to perform there. Ruinas 415. Tel: 51-84-245-779, E-mail: mariellaaldave@hotmail.com, URL: www.aldeayanapay.org. Updated: Jul 30, 2009.

V!VA ONLINE REVIEW

RESTAURANT ALDEA YANAPAY

Delicious and for a good cause. Wide selection of food, and all the food is of a very high quality. The prices are very reasonable.

Oct 18, 2009

Restaurant Narguila

Head to Narguila if you want to try shakshuka, a spiced egg and tomato specialty; served with jahnun, the pride of Yemen's bakeries. Or perhaps with a malawach puffed pastry. The eatery also serves meorav, a mixed grill serving of chicken giblets with onions. After eating you can relax by smoking cured tobacco in a long-stemmed narguile pipe, a time-honored Israeli tradition. Narguila offers a taste of the land of milk and honey in the South American Andes. L'chaim! Tecsecocha 405. Tel: 51-84-931-3107, E-mail: wilfred783@hotmail.com. Updated: Jul 30, 2009.

Victor Victoria

Victor Victoria has made itself into a Cusco institution, winning the hearts and stomachs of young travelers with its cheap, tasty and filling breakfasts, including pancakes, French toast and special-order omelets. The restuarant is also open for lunch and dinner; the menu features native cuisine as well as old standards like hamburgers and fried chicken. There is also offers a salad and pasta bar. Owner Rosa Victoria graciously welcomes all customers with maternal kindness. And, no, the name of the restaurant has nothing to do with the 1983 movie. Calle Teqsaqocha N 466, Tel: 51-84-252-284, E-mail: cleocardenas@yahoo.com. Updated: Jul 30, 2009.

V!VA ONLINE REVIEW

VICTOR VICTORIA

WOW! Fresh french fries and the free salad bar! Excellent, quality homemade food for a very cheap price.

Jun 06, 2009

PIZZA

Babieca Tratoria

One of the most popular pizzerias in town, the Babieca boasts the table-sized pizza kilometrica, which can feed up to eight people. A good selection of toppings is available, as is the homemade pasta. Although the ground floor dining room is quite large, it can feel cramped as tables and chairs have been squashed in to make room for all the hungry pizza eaters fresh off the various trails in the area. Babieca also offers set lunch menus, but they do not usually include pizza. Tecsecocha 418. Tel: 51-84-221-122. Updated: Jul 30, 2009.

Bohème

Just a few blocks from the Plaza de Armas, the Bohème Bar, Restaurant and Pizzeria is both an informal pizzería and a slightly more formal but still convivial dining area. There is also a bar you can sit at and order drinks. The pizzería includes pizza with alpaca, white corn or frijoles toppings. The Bohème itself, having opened in 2006, still conveys a fresh, clean, upbeat air. It is large enough to accommodate parties of up to 60 diners. Calle Saphy 476. Tel: 51-84-247-381. Updated: Jul 30, 2009.

PUBS & BARS

Cicciolina

Spanning a long room split between the bar and tapas area, and the elegant dining area, Cicciolina offers a top class dining experience and the atmosphere to match. Walk in and immediately enjoy the ambience and fine design. The plush red colors provide a subtle romantic feel. Unwind with a drink at the bar, taste tapas in a corner window, or take a table in the dining area to enjoy the exquisite meals and fine wine. Definitely place to spoil yourself. Two blocks from the plaza on Calle Triunfo 393, 2nd floor. Updated: Jun 30, 2010.

Mama Africa

A well-established bar and dance club, Mama Africa is like stepping onto a Caribbean island, with its reggae-funk music and sweet, smooth cocktails. The club is located on the second story along the Plaza de Armas; the restaurant-cum-nightclub turns out some of the best dance music in town, playing everything from reggae, funk and electrónica to Latin pop, salsa and samba. The DJs here know how to spin it up and, if you like to dance, you won't be disappointed. While traditional Peruvian and international cuisine is served up during the day, most people come to Mama Africa in the daylight hours to watch one of the 3:30 p.m. movies (daily), nibble food and sip happy hour specialties - the perfect way to rest before the dancing begins. The club hosts special African and Brazilian dance performances throughout the year. Portal Harinas 191, Second Floor, Plaza de Armas. Tel: 51-84-246-544, E-mail: mamafrica@mamaafrica.com. URL: www.mamafricaclub.com. Updated: Jul 30,2009.

The Cross Keys Pub

A Cusco nightlife institution, the Cross Keys recently moved from its old location in the Plaza de Armas to Calle Triunfo around the corner. Still the most authentic English Pub in Cusco, it is packed with memorabilia and has pool tables and darts. Cross Keys offers bar snacks and a small selection of pub classics, including giant juicy burgers, home-made lasagne and a huge choice of drinks. Look out for happy hour specials on cocktails and wine. Calle Triunfo 350, 2nd Floor. URL: www.cross-keys-pub-cusco-peru.com.Updated: Jul 30, 2009.

Los Perros

A funky and popular hangout for travelers, Los Perros is Australian-run and has a great vibe. Designed with modern effects, Los Perros is a comfortable place to have a few drinks and snacks with friends while listening to good music. They serve excellent food, including tasty tapas and sandwiches. The spring rolls are perhaps the best item on the menu. Los Perros is a great place to hang out with a group of people before hitting the town later on. Conveniently located just one block from the plaza on Tecsecocha, next door to Zazu's night club. Updated: Jun 30, 2010.

Real McCoy

Although not officially a pub, The Real McCoy is an English restaurant which hosts regular pub quizzes and offers traditional pub fare – pie and mashed potato with gravy, big greasy breakfasts, baguettes and baked potatoes with a choice of fillings. With lots of genuine ingredients imported from the UK (including PG tips tea-bags), they have a devoted following among resident ex-pats in Cusco. The Real McCoy also has a four-hour happy hour every night with cheap cocktails, live sports on their giant TV, magazines and board games. Calle Plateros 326; 2nd Floor. Tel: 51-84-261-111. Updated: Jul 30, 2009.

Paddy Flaherty's

Paddy Flaherty's calls itself "the highest Irish pub in the world." And at Cusco's altitude, who wouldn't want to treat themselves to the only place in town where you down a Guinness or English draft beer? At Paddy Flaherty's you can also sample authentic shepherd's pie, not to mention bread and butter pudding and other Celtic cuisine. Open every day from 11:00 a.m. to 2:00 a.m., including lunch, which features salads and roast chicken specialties. The main fun is hanging with the crowd every night for rousing revelry. Calle Triunfo 124. Tel: 51-84-247-719, 51-84-225-361. Updated: Jul 30, 2009.

Pepe Zeta Bistro Lounge

Take a bit of pub atmosphere, mix it with a touch of lounge and you might get an idea of Pepe Zeta's flavor. Its menu is varied and unpretentious, offering many appetizers and a wide selection of cocktails. Cozy sofa areas, a beautiful fireplace to keep you warm, a huge screen by the bar area to watch sports or movies, and soft house or bossa nova music makes it a relaxing option. Every weekend the bar has live music until the wee hours of the night. Teqsecocha 415, 2nd floor. Tel: 51-84-223-082, Fax: 51-84-223-082, E-mail: pepezeta@gmail.com, URL: www.pepezeta.com. Updated: Jul 30, 2009.

Mandela's Bar 🔔

Mandela's Bar is a fantastic bar/restaurant hidden behind the cathedral, serving a mixture of Peruvian, contemporary and traditional South African food (spicy chicken, etc.) and a full bar (juices and cocktails). This bar has the best views in Cusco at night, by far, over the main Plaza and beyond. Mandela's also has regular live music on weekends and weeknights (local tribal groups, jazz, rock and blues) from 10 p.m. The atmosphere is homey, with candles in the main area, sofas in the lounge area and a chill-out section with cushions. Average costs: $3+ for a main course. Calle Palacio No 121, 3rd Floor. Updated: Jul 30, 2009.

SANDWICHES

Yahuu

A very clean and American-looking juice bar, Yahuu serves fresh fruit juices and excellent sándwiches. Very reasonably priced and with a colorful and bright décor, Yahuu makes a nice afternoon stop. Try their signature thick fruit smoothies for 9 soles. Just off the plaza on Procuradores. Updated: Jun 30, 2010.

Sweet Temptations

For those seeking a cozier and quieter corner of Cusco to relax and reflect, Sweet Temptations is a peaceful place in which to enjoy a light bite, like a salad or sandwich. The specialty, as the name suggests, are pastries, such as alfor de ponca, layers of thin cake with a caramel-like filling in between, courtesy of Argentine-trained chef Jimmy Flores. Jimmy also makes cheesecake, chocolate and carrot cake. Sweet Temptations has select gift items, all at very affordable prices. Herrajes 138-A, Tel: 51-84-244-129 / 227-510 E-mail: swetemptation-cafe@yahoo.com Price description: No credit cards accepted. Updated: Jul 30, 2009.

TRADITIONAL / PERUVIAN

Drews

(ENTREES $9) Drews serves fantastic, authentic Peruvian cuisine prepared by a chef trained in France. The restaurant is very reasonably priced, its location one block off of the Plaza means prices are lower than elsewhere. Drews has an intimate, comfortable atmosphere. Plateros 327. Tel: 51-84-224-203. Updated: Jul 30, 2009.

Kukuly

Kukuly is a cosy, local restaurant. Food is simple and cheap, but good. For both lunch and dinner you can choose to have the set menu for only $2, including a wholesome vegetable soup, followed by a main plate of chicken or meat with rice. Slightly more expensive dishes offer fresh fried trout, tasty soups, vegetarian options and juicy steaks with veggies for only$4-6. Freshly chopped fruits and yogurt along with alchoholic coffees and hot chocolates make perfect desserts to top off a filling meal. Service can be slow, but friendly, however is Spanish-speaking only. One block from the plaza on Huaynapata. Updated: Jun 30, 2010.

A Mi Manera

A good choice for those thinking of trying Peruvian food, this restaurant caters to all tastes. The menu offers freshly prepared soups and sandwiches, fish and meat choices, simple vegetarian options and local dishes such as ceviche, lomo saltado and cuy. Just one block northeast of the Plaza de Armas, go through the pretty courtyard of La Casa de las Arpias and climb the stairs to the restaurant. Make sure to get a window seat with a view of the happenings in the plaza below. With Peruvian music and great service, you can "experience Peruvian gastronomy with all your senses," their way. Triunfo 393, Cusco. Tel: 51-84-222-219, E-mail: info@amimaneraperu.com, URL: www.amimaneraperu.com. Updated: Mar 23, 2010.

Pachacútec

Pachacútec, on the Plaza de Armas is a first-class restaurant with an appealing ambience that could be described as "Inca deco." A large portrait of legendary warrior Pachacútec hangs on the wall along with other samples of local art that incorporates indigenous motifs. Its menu, offered not only in Spanish and English, but French as well, is a mix of continental and native dishes, including asparagus rolls with ham, marinated mackerel ceviche and a "warm salad" that includes grilled peaches and roasted onions served over a cool bed of greens. Surprisingly, this high-quality eatery is quite inexpensive, with a three-course meal going for as little as $3. Portal de Pones 115. Fax: 51-84-245-041, E-mail: reservas@pachacutecrestaurant.com, URL: www.cuscoperu.com/pachacutec. Updated: Jul 30, 2009.

VEGETARIAN

Vegetarian Restaurant

This little place offers healthy vegetarian fare, and a wide range of it, too. Large salads come with a variety of ingredients and veggie burgers are served with substitute meat and fries. Try the enchilada for a taste of heaven. With a relaxed atmosphere, you can eat at the veggie restaurant for just $3.50 for a filling meal, for both lunch and dinner. Even boys enjoy this place. Located on Tigre, one block from the Plaza, just opposite Zazu's night club. Updated: Jun 30, 2010.

WINE

Los Perros Wine and Couch Bar

This is a very popular and extremely trendy hangout where you'll find travelers lounging about with snacks and drinks. In addition to fabulous food, the restaurant also has a variety of board games, books and magazines. The artsy décor and funky music add to the laid-back atmosphere. On the weekends there is usually jazz music. Tecsecocha 426 Tel: 51-84-241-447. Updated: Jul 30, 2009.

San Blas

Characterized by steep cobblestone alleys that offer spectacular views of the city, San Blas is one of the oldest and most picturesque neighborhoods in Cusco. A thriving artistic community lives here—some families have been operating in San Blas for decades—and it is reputed for producing fine traditional and contemporary artwork. As many streets are pedestrian-only, San Blas is an excellent place to explore on foot. A relaxed stroll through the streets lined with studios and workshops is a great way to soak in the artistic atmosphere and perfect the fine art of window-shopping. While you're in the neighborhood, you may want to head over to Iglesia San Blas, home to one of the New World's most famous woodcarvings. As you wander, be sure to look out for your belongings, as tourists aren't the only people scoping out the area. Updated: Jul 17, 2007.

Lodging

This charming neighborhood, full of art and artesanía, is a fun place to stay within Cusco. With options for all types of travelers, it's worth staying a night or two to explore San Blas' zigzagging streets and artist's workshops. Updated: Jul 28, 2009.

Hospedaje El Artesano de San Blas ⚐

(ROOMS: $5-7) If you stroll up Cuesta San Blas and keep heading north, the name changes to Suytucato, and on your left you will see the sign for the Hospedaje El Artesano de San Blas, one of the best little secrets for those really wanting a bargain without giving up a decent night's comfort. This is a first-rate backpacker's hostel, located in a clean and well-maintained Spanish colonial facility, with hot water, spacious rooms and a well-kept common kitchen area. Suytucato 790, Tel: 51-84-263-968, E-mail: manosandinas@yahoo.com. Updated: Jul 31, 2009.

V!VA ONLINE REVIEW

HOSPEDAJE EL ARTESANO DE SAN BLAS

A lovely hostel! Friendly staff, big rooms, a pretty patio, good location in San Blas.

Jul 30, 2009

Hospedaje Sambleño

(ROOMS $6-18) Around the corner from the Plazoleta San Blas, Hospedaje Sambleño offers a cheap price--single rooms at $6--in a great location. You can buy breakfast for a little extra at its own in-house Niña Niña restaurant. The rooms are spare and even a bit stale, with bare wooden floors. When we visited it, the receptionist was smoking a cigarette behind his desk in the lobby, an indication of what you can expect here. If none of this is an issue for you, and you are on a tight budget, you might not mind. Otherwise, as the Romans used to say, caveat emptor. Carmen Alto 114, Tel: 51-84-262-979, E-mail: sambleno@hotmail.com, URL: www.barnmed.com/hostalsambleno/index.htm. Updated: Feb 17, 2010.

Hospedaje Inka

(ROOMS: $6-20) This inn is located at the very summit of Suytucato on the path leading north from San Blas. Owner Américo Pacheco will welcome you into his rustic Hospedaje Inka, a former ranch home now serving as a backpacker palace, complete with an outdoor grill and, spare wooden floors (as well as private bathrooms). Américo is proud of what he calls his "orthopedic" beds and his breakfast featuring real cusqueño chocolate and barley bread. Take a deep breath of the fresh, mountain air and enjoy the spectacular views of Cusco and the mountain ranges surrounding it. This is one of the few hostels that offers parking and is a good way to sample both Cusco's urban and rural charms. Suytuccato 848, Tel: 51-84-231-995, E-mail: americopacheco@hotmail.com, URL: www.hospedajeinka.weebly.com. Updated: Jan 18, 2010.

Arrieros

(ROOMS: $8.50-12) Blink and you might miss this charming little hostel a little to the right, off the Cuesta San Blas, on a street called Kurkurpata. The owner himself does not go out of his way to advertise his facility too well, using a paper sign to announce rooms over a more conventional sign calling attention to his café and gift shop. Perhaps with reason, since he only has five rooms; but consider yourself lucky if you can rent one. Rooms have private bathrooms, hot water, and great views of the Cusco valley and city. As advertised Arrieros has its own in-house restaurant and gift shop. Calle Kurkupata 122, Tel: 51-84-237-386. Updated: Jul 28, 2009.

V!VA ONLINE REVIEW

ARRIEROS

The hike up to small, family-run Arrieros Hostel is worth it for the wonderful views of Cusco and its surrounding hillsides.

May 05, 2010

Mirador de la Ñusta

(ROOMS: $10-20) This hostel is blessed with one of the best spots in Cusco: at the head of the fountain of Plazoleta de San Blas. There is a nice garden patio inside, and the rooms are clean, comfortable and attractive. The very colorful owner, Daríos Segovia, provides local tours, starting at $100, to the Sacred Valley and other noteworthy archaeological sites, with himself as the guide. Breakfast is offered by request, and laundry as well as taxi service--at any hour, says Darios--is also include in the price. Calle Tandapata 682, Tel: 51-84-248-039. Updated: Jul 30, 2009.

Hostal Hatun Wasi

(ROOMS: $15-20) This hostel is managed by the Mendivil family, whose religious and indigenous-themed folk art has gained recognition beyond Peru. This hotel has a great location and offer rooms designed with an artistic flair commensurate with the talent that made them famous. If you are fortunate to reserve a room on the terrace, there will be a great view of Cusco. Heating is available for an extra $3. There is also an attractive bar and cafeteria on the first floor. The owner, Francisco Mendivil, is often willing to personally show his art to you. Cuesta San Blas 619-B. Tel: 51-84-242-626, 51-84-233-247, E-mail: hostalhatunwas@hotmail.com. Updated: Jul 30, 2009.

Hospedaje Turístico San Blas

(ROOMS: $20-25) Located in the trendy, bohemian San Blas neighborhood north of the Plaza de Armas, Hospedaje Turístico San Blas is slightly more than mid-range in its price (a single room starts at $20 during the low-season and goes to $25 during the high season), but its high quality rooms in an area full of stylish shops and restaurants should appeal to many tourists. The interiors are a model of moderated elegance. Free Internet access comes with the usual amenities, such as heated rooms and a continental breakfast, and their terrace offers pleasant views of the beautiful city of Cusco. Cuesta San Blas 526. Tel: 51-84-225-781/ 244-481, E-mail: sanblascusco@yahoo.com, URL: www.san-blashostal.com. Updated: Jul 30, 2009.

Amaru Hostal

(ROOMS: $20-25) Many hostels just north of the Plaza de Armas in the "artist community" of San Blas are a little bit more expensive, but the Amaru Hostel is the only one that includes "American breakfast," featuring eggs and fruit salad, rather than the standard continental breakfast, that is included in the price. The hotel is a very pleasant place to stay, with large-windows in its rooms and a garden in the back. For colder nights, heating is available for an additional $3, negotiable for groups. There is a book exchange, and an overall friendly atmosphere. Cuesta San Blas 541. Tel: 51-84-225-933. Updated: Jul 30, 2009.

Hostal Choquachaca

Hostal Choquachaca is a small and quiet hostel located in a quiet area of Cusco, but still within convenient distance to tourist attractions and Plaza de Armas. It is good value for the money and has clean rooms with balconies for views over Cusco. The walls are thin, but it's not a party hostel, so noise isn't an issue. They have a lounge with a TV, free luggage storage, but they do not have Internet. The family running the hostel also lives there, giving it a different atmosphere compared to a chain. Prices may be negotiated during low season. The hostel is easy to miss, so look out for it. It's located opposite to Flying Dog, which has big signs on the wall. Calle Choquechaca 436-B, San Blas Tel: 51-9-743-8790, E-mail: hostal_choquechaca@hotmail.com. Updated: Mar 22, 2010.

Hotel El Grial

(ROOMS: $30-$64) Situated on a quiet corner of Cusco's San Blas artisan district, this mid-range hotel is a clean and comfortable accommodation. The rooms are set on the second floor, around a covered colonial courtyard, in which a free continental breakfast is served each morning. Rooms are spacious and tastefully decorated, all with private bathrooms and cable TV. The hotel has free Internet, WiFi, laundry services, and the building also hosts the South American Spanish School (for which hotel guests receive a discount). Carmen Alto 112, San Blas. Updated: Feb 04, 2010.

Casa San Blas Boutique Hotel

(ROOMS: $65-140) Casa San Blas Boutique Hotel offers superior service and hospitality. A warm atmosphere and clean, comfortable rooms are not even the hotel's main bent: this meticulously restored 18th century colonial-style house is also located in the historic artisan's quarter of San Blas. Spend the day browsing local wares, from woodcarvings and jewelry to weavings and paintings, and pass the night sampling gourmet dishes at the hotel's Cava de San Blas restaurant. Service, style and a spectacular location make Casa San Blas a traveler's gem. Tocuyeros 566. Tel: 51-84-251-563, 1-888-569-1769 (US), 1-303-539-9300 (US), Fax: 51-84-237-900, E-mail: info@casasanblas.com, URL: www.casasanblas.com. Updated: Jul 30, 2009.

Los Apus Hotel and Mirador

(ROOMS: $89-109) The independent Swiss Los Apus Hotel and Mirador opened in December 1999. It is nestled in the foothills of the unspoiled historical site of San Blas, three blocks from the Plaza de Armas. Los Apus' 20 rooms, some with balconies, have wooden floors, double-paned windows, extra long beds, cable TV, smoke detectors, telephones and private baths. Non-smoking and rooms for the disabled

are available. Other services include: free airport pickup, WiFi and an Internet cabin down at the patio, mail service, fax, money exchange, laundry and flight and train reservations. Hair dryers and safes are available upon request, as are oxygen and a doctor. The El Mirador Restaurant and Bar is on the roof terrace and has magnificent panoramic views. El Patio Restaurant is surrounded by stone columns and features international and regional cuisine. Atocsaycuchi 515 and Choquechaca. Tel: 51-84-264-243, Fax: 51-84-264-211, E-mail: info@losapushotel.com, URL: www.losapushotel.com. Updated: Jan 18, 2010.

Second Home Cusco

(ROOMS: $110-$120) Second Home Cusco is a bed and breakfast located in the historic district of San Blas. Offering 21st century comfort in a colonial house, Second Home Cusco features three juniors suites, furnished in an eclectic style. Each suite has a private bathroom, queen-size bed, cable TV, telephone and other amenities to ensure an enjoyable stay. A continental breakfast is served each morning. Atocsaycuchi 616, San Blas. Tel: 51-84-235-873, Fax: 51-84-242-200, E-mail: info@secondhomecusco.com, URL: www.secondhomecusco.com. Updated: Feb 11, 2009.

Restaurants

ASIAN

Tika Bistro Gourmet

Tika Bistro Gourmet is a unique restaurant in Cusco. The cuisine you'll find at Tika is probably unlike anything you've ever tasted, combining Thai and Vietnamese flavors and techniques with traditional Peruvian ingredients. Tel: 51-84-251-563, E-mail: recepcion@casasanblas.com, URL: www.casasanblas.com/tikabistro Updated: Jul 30, 2009.

CAFÉS

Juanitos Café

This San Blas café offers tasty sandwiches served hot on fresh ciabatta rolls. Fillings include local specialties such as alpaca and lechon (suckling pig) as well as international favorites such as hamburgers and vegetarian options. All sandwiches can be served with fries, while a choice from the extensive juice and smoothie list is sure to quench the thirst. Reasonably priced at $3 - 5, Juanitos opens daily for lunch and dinner, whereas late-night service on Fridays and Saturdays makes for an ideal post-party snack. Updated: Feb 03, 2010.

Panadería El Buen Pastor

Truly, the best way to find El Buen Pastor is to follow your nose. Each morning, Monday through Saturday, the aroma of freshly baked bread and pastries wafts from the walk-in oven at El Buen Pastor through the streets of San Blas and drives tastebuds to distraction in anticipation of pan con crema and buttery empanadas. Personal pizzas, cream-filled cakes, caramel churros, fluffy empanadas, dozens of varieties of bread and goodies of all shapes and sizes can be promptly wrapped up to go or quickly served with a cup of coffee in the upstairs dining area. Because it's a non-profit organization benefiting a home for orphan girls, pastry lovers can feel slightly less guilty about making multiple trips in a single day. 575 Cuesta. Updated: Jul 30, 2009.

Vuelto

Among party-loving travelers, Cusco has a reputation for hosting daily fiestas, for the traveler with a mean sweet tooth, Velluto is the best place to be during happy hour, with two-for-one crepes from 3 to 6 p.m. The happy hour selection has slightly slimmer pickings than the proper menu's long list of the sweet and the savory crepes, fresh salads and a variety of sandwiches; but the prices are a bargain for such rich food. Satisfy your sweet side with toppings like Nutella, fruit, ice cream or caramel, or make the nutritionally responsible decision with Velluto's oh-so-simple yet oh-so-delicious tomato, basil and mozzarella on ciabatta. Fine espresso and a nice selection of wine round out the café's European flavor. Plazoleta San Blas Tandapata. Updated: Mar 26, 2007.

The Muse Too

This is the new, cleverly named smaller sister to The Muse restaurant on Calle Plateros. Sitting on top of the Plaza San Blas, this funky café bar is a popular hangout for travelers wanting to chill out with a book on a comfy couch. Take the stairs to the second floor for a pleasant view over the plaza and city. The restaurant serves a variety of delicious appetizers, sandwiches and meals, including vegetarian options, along with fresh fruit juices served in giant goblets. Breakfast is served all day. Happy Hour is from 6 to 8 p.m., and there is often live music or a DJ after 9 p.m. A great

aspect of this establishment is that it will fill your water bottle (at $0.20 a liter) as part of its boycotting plastic campaign. Tandapata, San Blas. Tel: 51-84-984-762. E-mail: themusecusco@yahoo.com. Updated: Mar 25, 2010.

INTERNATIONAL

Granja Heidi Restaurant

Owner Karl Heinz-Horner grew up in Germany, but proudly considers himself Peruvian because he settled here and started his own dairy farm, where he sells his own milk, yogurt and cheese. He is also the proprietor of Granja Heidi, one of the best restaurants in Cusco, midway between the Plaza de Armas and Cuesta San Blas. Karl's level of consideration for his customers extends to providing menus in up to six languages, with an expertly prepared variety of Peruvian and Central European dishes, along with a good wine list. And of course, don't forget to try the desserts, which are made with fresh milk and cheese from Karl's dairy farm. Cuesta San Blas 525. Tel: 51-84-238-383. Updated: Apr 27, 2010.

Pacha-Papa

Pacha-Papa offers an intimate setting filled with modern art and candlelit tables. For more informal dining, there is also a fireplace area with comfy sofas. Like the restaurant's art and music selection, the dishes are funky and flavorful with a distinct Peruvian and international flair. In fact, owner Tanya Miller previously worked in several London restaurants.

On the menu you'll find roasted guinea pig and alpaca anticucho, in addition to other Peruvian specialties like tamales and quinoa soup. Also recommended are the beef tenderloin in red-wine-and-onion sauce, and the tropical chicken curry with bananas, peaches and strawberries. The hip, laidback atmosphere and reasonable prices appeal to a young crowd who come for the food and popular happy hour (daily 6:30 p.m.-7:30 p.m.). The Sunday roast (by reservation only) has become famous among locals and features a roast chicken, potatoes, veggies and homemade apple pie. Plaza San Blas 120. Tel: 51-84-241-318 E-mail: pachapapa@cuscorestaurants.com, URL: www.cuscorestaurants.com. Updated: Jan 15, 2010.

Tupana Wasi

Restaurants that claim to offer meals as varied as Italian, Mexican and Peruvian often arouse suspicion that none of those options will really be very good. This is not true in the case of Tupana Wasi Grill Bar. This intimate little restaurant, with capacity for 25 diners, offers an excellent variety of entrees and provides great service too. The restaurant is close to the heart of the San Blas district and is colorfully, but tastefully decorated in a Peruvian / Mexican style. Cuesta de San Blas 575. Tel: 51-9-358-920. Updated: Jul 30, 2009.

Korma Sutra

The newest addition to the Indian scene is Korma Sutra, now considered by many as the best of just three Indian restaurants in Cusco. Korma Sutra serves excellent curries, just like your favorite Indian from home, but a bit spicier. Set in a dim, plush setting, and with good service, Korma Sutra sets the scene and won't leave you disappointed. Indian curry lovers shouldn't miss this one. Up in the artistic area of San Blas, five blocks from the Plaza on Tandapata, and just next to the funky San Blas bars for an after dinner drink. Updated: Jun 30, 2010.

ITALIAN

Mana's Grill - Pizzeria Resturant

(ENTREES: $2.50-9) This small Italian restaurant is full of charm. It feels like going into a family home. The food is good, and the set menu is recommended $3.50-5. Prices for individual dishes are between $2.50-9 and a glass of wine cost $1.50-2, good value for the money. The menu has pizzas, pasta, lasagna and many other Italian dishes. It is located within walking distance from the Plaza de Armas, on a narrow street. Ca. Recoleta 555 Tel: 51-84-221-860. Updated: Mar 23, 2010.

Toqokachi

(SET MENU: $5-9) This small restaurant is a two-minute walk from San Blas. The table décor consists of wine bottles arranged on the table with cotton napkins.

The food is good here, especailly the Pasta Alfredo. The prices are midrange and a good value for the money. In the $5 set menu, a Pisco Sour is included, and in the $9 set menu you get either wine or beer. There are also non-alcoholic drinks available for those who prefer that. Ca. Carmen Alto 244, San Blas. Tel: 51-84-221-857. Updated: Mar 23, 2010.

TRADITIONAL / PERUVIAN

Macondo

(ENTREES: $4-10) This bar and restaurant provides a chic, art-gallery ambience, with contemporary artwork displayed on its walls and candles on each table providing a mellow glow. The menu items include chicken with mango and orange sauce, trout salmon with curry sauce, or a local specialty, papas locas, which consist of potatoes in a creamy mint sauce and pickles. There is also a selection of fancy coffees to complement your dinner, and an extensive wine and spirits list. Macondo is open for breakfast, lunch and dinner, with prices ranging from $4 to $10. 571 Cuesta San Blas, Tel: 51-84-229-415, E-mail: macondo@telsar.com, URL: www.macondoincusco.com. Updated: Jul 30, 2009.

Khipus Restaurant

One of the main reasons people may want to visit Khipus is that it is the restaurant of choice of Edilberto Mérida, one of Peru's most famous painters and sculptors. Merida first created the now-common image of the poor Latin American with outstretched and massive hands. A new and very large Mérida sculpture of an Andean folk musician greets visitors to Khipus, along with other displays of his work. This is also an excellent restaurant with three stories and multiple rooms, each with its own theme. Expert preparations of traditional and continental cooking are also offered at reasonable prices. Carmen Alto 133. Tel: 51-84-241-283, E-mail: khipusfood@hotmail.com, URL: www.khipusfood.com. Updated: Jul 30,2009.

Witches' Garden

Owned and run by a hospitable French Canadian expat who gladly chats with her clientele and doles out loads of free traveling advice, Witches' Garden might be one of Cusco's best all-around culinary experiences. The candle-lit dining room is very mod and yet cozy and relaxing. The menu is almost too big and too tempting. And the cocktail list—like the bar stocked with imports not found in any other Cusco watering hole—has one of the best selections of concoctions in town. The menu is heavy on favorites borrowed from all over the world (for example, the starter menu offers stuffed baked potatoes, Greek spanikopita, and oriental spring rolls), but also offers an alpaca option on most entrées, lending the restaurant a decidedly Peruvian theme. Lamb and vegetarian options make a appearance for diners less enthusiastic about the Andean meat. Be sure to save room for dessert (or be daring and start your meal with it) because the Black Hole Cake (Oreo cookie, vanilla ice cream, hot fudge and hot whiskey butterscotch) deserves its rumored "world-famous" reputation. Loreto 125. Tel: 84-244-077, 984-741569, 984-733068, E-mail: witchesgardencusco@post.com, URL: www.witchesgarden.net. Updated: Jul 30, 2009.

Kachivache
While the owners call it a coffee shop, Kachivache is much more. This restaurant has a clean, artistically rustic atmosphere—with local art on the walls— and is perfect for a break from the city. Chefs at Kachivache use fresh seasoning and spices to create bold, rich, flavorful entrées. Mediterranean overtones dominate the eclectic menu which includes a variety of international dishes. Especially tasty are the kabobs plates with a choice of marinated chicken, beef or seafood and fresh grilled vegetables. The Spanish omelet is another excellent option, as are the assortment of gourmet sandwiches, which are a deal at only $1.25 each. If you are in search of a good cup of joe, there is a reason Kachivache is called a coffee shop, it has some of the strongest, boldest beans in town and will satisfy almost any craving. It is open Monday-Saturday, 9 a.m. - 11 p.m. but sometimes they do close randomly. San Juan de Dios 260 Tel: 51-84-974-6638/ 256-143, E-mail: Kachivache_peru@yahoo.es. Updated: Jul 30, 2009.

Inca....Fe
Set in the artsy San Blas neighborhood, Inka... Fe Café is a find. Step off the cobblestone streets into this welcoming little restaurant and for between 15 to 25 soles ($5-8) you can have your choice of a wide variety of international and Peruvian cuisine. From pasta and sandwiches to chicken, beef, pork and vegetarian options, this menu is sure to keep even the pickiest eater happy. Dishes are of a very generous size. The restaurant is small, intimate and homey, and the service impeccable. Calle Choquechaca

131-A. Tel: 51-84-254-073, E-mail: reservas@inkafe.com.pe. Updated: Jul 30, 2009.

VEGETARIAN

Prasada
This small vegetarian restaurant/café has a lot of character. Guests sit outside on bar chairs, under a roof and order food through an opening in the wall. The reasons to go here include good food, the opportunity to talk to other guests and the friendly staff. The menu contains pizzas, veggie burgers, sandwiches and vegetarian lasagna, all for around $1 - 2, which is good value for the money. Soup of the day is available during lunchtime as well. The Hindu gods and signs add to the vibe of the restaurant. It is a popular place for travelers who stay a little bit longer in Cusco, but, it's easy to miss, so look out for it. Calle Choquechaca. Nearest cross-street: Choquechaca, Hathunrumlyok and Cuesta San Blas. Updated: Mar 23, 2010.

Nightlife
Cusco has a great nightlife scene. In particular there is a pumping club vibe, with five main clubs holding the majority of the partying travelers (Inca Team, Mythology, The Lek, Mama Africa and Zazu). Outside these clubs, around the plaza, prepare to be hounded by young guys handing out free drink tickets and trying to pull you into the club they work for. The free drinks will always be rum and coke and are fine, but do be wary that they are made with the cheapest type of rum. Outside of the main clubs are some lovely pubs and bars overlooking the plaza, and a block or two from the main plaza you will find a few Latin clubs, and the lovely neighborhood of San Blas is where you can find relaxed bars hosting live music. Updated: Jun 30, 2010.

Inca Team
Inca Team is probably the most popular club in Cusco. Every night of the week, it pumps popular Western tunes and is absolutely packed from midnight through until five in the morning. Due to its popularity, it can get very packed and difficult to move. There are two bars on the ground floor, while the second floor offers a nice viewing point overlooking the dance floor, as well as plenty of seats to relax in. The new third floor also has a small, quiet bar. Free salsa lessons from 9–11 p.m. plus free coat check. Free drink tickets 11-12 p.m. On the plaza, at the bottom of Calle Suecia. Updated: Jun 30, 2010.

Mythology

Next door to Inca Team, Mythology is also popular and plays the usual Western tunes. Similar to Inca Team but slightly less packed, Mythology has one main floor including surrounding seating, a further adjoining room with more couches, as well as a quiet bar downstairs with seating. Mythology also offers free salsa lessons from 9-11 p.m. and free coat check. Free drink tickets 11 p.m.-12 a.m. Updated: Jun 30, 2010.

The Lek

The Lek is also on the same corner of the plaza as Inca Team and Mythology but offers a larger space and a pool table. Also plays popular Western music and is generally fairly busy. Very comfortable couches can be found in the corner couch area, plus there are tables and stools in the opposite corner and a large dance floor in the middle. No coat check is available. Also offers free drink tickets 11 p.m.-12 a.m. Updated: Jun 30, 2010.

Zazu

Zazu has a very nice feel upon walking inside, set in a very large, plush room, with a bar spanning the length of the room. Both Western tunes and Latin music are played here. Sometimes they have salsa lessons between 9 and 11 p.m, but not always. Zazu is normally very busy on Friday and Saturday nights, but often quiet early week. Zazu is a nice place to have a quiet drink on the comfortable couches, or indulge in a game of pool. Coat check is available here and they also offer free drinks before midnight. Updated: Jun 30, 2010.

KmO

Kmo is a very popular and casual bar which often has live music between 10 p.m. and 1 a.m. Great cocktails are served, and you can either sit downstairs, very close to the band, or upstairs if you prefer to talk among friends. This small, cosy bar has a loyal following and is a great place to check out some live local music. Located at the top of Cuesta San Blas, five blocks from the plaza. Updated: Jun 30, 2010.

7 Angelitos

Small but popular, 7 Angelitos has live music every weekend and some weeknights, till the early hours of the morning and is usually pumping with a happy, dancing crowd. Small yet alive with a great vibe, 7 Angelitos has two main rooms, one with the band and the dance floor, the other with a small corner bar and seating. This is a superb little bar if you enjoy live music and they serve the best Mojitos in town! It is fairly hidden away in the quiet, upper streets of San Blas (Calle Siete Angelitos 638) and is easy to miss, so be sure to take a taxi. Updated: Jun 30, 2010.

Mushroom

Mushroom is a suave, funky bar. As you walk into the large open space, you are greeted with a large mushroom-shaped bar in the center of the room, decorated with fruit. Mushroom provides a quality pool table and plenty of seating including tables as well as couches. In addition, there's a special corner area with bean bags and a large TV screen. This bar serves excellent cocktails for good prices, and overlooks the plaza, which is very pretty at night. Located directly on the plaza and downstairs from Mama Africa. Updated: Jun 30, 2010.

Bullfrog

Bullfrog is a comfortable and inviting bar. It has many bean bags scattered around small tables on the ground level where the bar is located, and usually have a live band on Wednesdays and Saturdays. The upper level includes multiple rooms including a dance room with a DJ station, open on weekends, a pool room with a separate bar, and various other corner rooms with couches where you can sit quietly. Situated on Warankallqui 185, three blocks from the plaza. Updated: Jun 30, 2010.

Norton's

Norton's is a very large English-style pub, just opposite Paddy's Irish bar. It offers a pool table and darts boards, and cheap beer. Due to its large size, it can often seem empty but the customers are usually just spread out around the bar. The food is reasonably priced and pretty good for pub grub. There are some nice outdoor seats overlooking the plaza. Updated: Jun 30, 2010.

Ukuku's

Ukuku's is an interesting bar, with an alternative live band performing on Tuesdays and Thursdays. On other nights they play mainly Latin music. The bar has a good atmosphere and a mix of clientele, both locals and tourists. Easy to miss, you'll find it upstairs a few doors down from the Real McCoy on Plateros. Updated: Jun 30, 2010.

Kamikase

Hidden away yet only one block from the plaza, Kamikase is a great little relaxed bar with live local bands on weekends and good drink specials. Popular with the locals, Kamikase is a good place to see some live music and party with the locals. On Plaza Cusipata. Updated: Jun 30, 2010.

Galabato's

Galabato's is very popular with the locals for live salsa music. The bar is very wide, spanning the whole floor of a building and has a dance floor and stage for the band, with many funky tables and chairs for watching the action. Galabato's offers reasonably priced drinks and is a great place to see some live salsa. Located just off the main plaza between Plateros and Plaza Cusipata – take the stairs above the burger restaurant. Updated: Jun 30, 2010.

CULTURAL NIGHTLIFE

Municipal Theater

The Municipal Theater hosts a variety of events throughout the year including, comedy, ballet, local entertainers, dance and some international artists. Posters publishing events are scattered around the town, so look out for something that grabs your interest. Alternatively visit the tourist information center or just make your way directly there to enquire about the current showings. The actual theatre has a cozy and relaxed atmosphere with comfortable seating and decent visibility from all angles. A block from the Main Plaza, this is a great place to watch local acts among locals at local prices. Mesón de la Estrella 149. Updated: Jul 13, 2010.

Pre-Columbian Art Museum

(ADMISSION: $7) A short walk from the main square up in Plaza Nazarenas, MAP Café and the Pre-Columbian Art Museum provides one with an evening of combined fine dining and culture. Housed in a striking colonial mansion (Casa Cabrera), this stylish museum, exhibits a select number of artifacts, jewelry, ceramics, and handicrafts in gold and silver from eras including Nasca, Moche, Chancay, and Inca. After meandering through the beautifully yet simply displays of this mansion, why not move into the courtyard and treat yourself to a meal at the elegant restaurant enclosed in a glass box that offers a mix of traditional and international cuisine. 9 a.m.-10 p.m. Casa Cabrera, Plaza Nazarenas. Tel: 84-233-210. Updated: Jul 13, 2010.

ANDAHUAYLILLAS AND SAN PEDRO

This small colonial village, located 37 kilometers (23 mi.) south of Cusco, is home to one of Peru's most beautiful churches. Whether or not San Pedro is the "Sistine Chapel of the Americas," as some have claimed, is a hotly debated subject (and one which we'll let you make up your own mind about). Built in 1631 in accordance with Spanish tradition, on top of ancient Inca foundations, the church bombards visitors with an explosion of Baroque art and religious imagery. In contrast to its rather dull looking exterior, the church's interior is lavishly decorated with wall-to-wall colonial paintings from the Cusqueña School, frescos and painted ceilings.

To maintain the decadent theme, the altars and wood carvings are accented in leaf gold. Also worth a look is the mural by Luis de Riaño, which flamboyantly depicts the road to heaven and road to hell, each paved with its own respective set of alarming images. The town itself is also visually appealing, with a charming plaza draped in blossoming red-flowered pisonay trees.

Most excursions to Andahuaylillas can be combined with trips to the ruins of Rumilcolca and Pikillacta. If your visit to San Pedro wasn't spiritual enough, you can always head to the Centro de Medicina Integral (Garcilaso 514, Tel. 51-84-251-999, 9 a.m.-7 p.m., medintegral@hotmail.com) where you can relax in the aesthetically pleasing stone courtyard or spend the night in one of the center's plain rooms. Travelers from around the world come here for massages, meditation, harmonizing energy therapy and other treatments. Updated: Jul 28, 2009.

)))))

The Sacred Valley

SACRED VALLEY

Stretching west of Cusco and linking together some of the finest countryside, ruins and villages in the region, The Sacred Valley is one of the most beloved destinations in Peru. The valley's most famous draw is its collection of Inca ruins, including the legendary Machu Picchu, as well as other Inca ruins at Pisac, Ollantaytambo, Vilcabamba and Choquequirao. Carefully sculpted by the Incas, the valley and its major attractions constantly echo the importance of lunar and solar movements in Inca culture. The temple fortresses of Pisac and Ollantaytambo both exemplify the Inca's ability to integrate nature with magnificent feats of human engineering.

Due to its lower elevation, the Sacred Valley area is also an ideal place for travelers to acclimatize to altitude, before tackling any of the major mountains around Cusco. Adventure travelers will especially love this section of Peru. Some of the most spectacular hikes in the world are found here. The Inca Trail, leading to Machu Picchu, is the most popular, but there are many other, lesser known trekking opportunities in the Sacred Valley that are equally breathtaking.

With spectacular Inca ruins and countless colonial churches and modern markets, this area has plenty to see and do while you prepare to surmount the area's higher-altitude attractions. The best time to visit is from April to May or October to November, when you can avoid the flocks of tourist that arrive during the high season from June to September. Even if you don't plan to see all the attractions in the Sacred Valley area, it is recommended that you purchase the Cusco Tourist Ticket, which covers many of the main ruins' entrance fees. If you make your arrangements through a tour operator, the entrance fees are usually included. Updated: Aug 06, 2007.

History of the Sacred Valley

In Quechua, the Sacred Valley is known as Vilcamayo, and in Spanish El Valle Sagrado de los Incas. This fertile valley, irrigated by the Urubamba River that stretches from Pisac to Ollantaytambo, has a settlement history going at least as far back as 800 B.C. to the Chanapata civilization. The valley provided some of the best agrarian opportunities in the region, and as the early tribes of Peru shifted from nomadic hunters to a settled society of farmers it became a popular place to live.

The Sacred Valley was central to pre-Columbian Peru's development. Other pre-Inca civilizations that lived in the valley included the Qotacalla, who were there from 500 to 900 A.D., and the Killke, who continued to reside in the valley until Inca domination of the region in 1420. The Incas, in turn, lasted until the arrival of the Spaniards one hundred years later. The valley itself was regarded as sacred by the Incas as the terrestrial partner of the Milky Way. Their mythology had the founding fathers of the region, the Ayar Brothers, emerging from the Ollantaytambo pyramid.

Ollantaytambo also served as the battleground for one of the last successful defeats of the Spanish army, when the Manco Inca withdrew from Cusco and his forces redirected the Río Patacancha to keep Pizarro's soldiers at bay, while at the same time enlisting the support of jungle tribes. Pizarro retreated, but eventually returned with reinforcements. Ironically, despite the subsequent attempt to remake the region and its people under Spain, much of the culture has remained unchanged throughout the centuries. People still speak Quechua, and farming methods are still very basic. Updated: Jul 28, 2009.

When to Go

The best time to visit the Sacred Valley is during the dry season, which lasts from mid-April until November. The Sacred Valley is no different from the rest of Peru, and the dry season coincides with high tourist season. June through September is especially busy; if you plan on hiking the Inca Trail, be sure to book well in advance as spots are very hard, if not impossible, to come by. During the wet season, from November to April, there are significantly fewer tourists but, hiking can be tougher. The Inca Trail is closed during February for maintenance, but other treks in the region remain open. Updated: Jul 28, 2009.

Sacred Valley Acclimatization

While neighboring Cusco sits at approximately 3,300 meters (10,825 ft.) above sea level, the Sacred Valley's elevation is about 2,500 meters (8,200 ft.), making acclimatization easier. If you are arriving by air from sea level it is generally recommended to give yourself at least two days to get used to the altitude.

The best advice to beat potential altitude sickness, or soroche, is to drink lots of water and lay off the alcohol. Your appetite may be affected, and eating smaller meals may also help your body adjust. If you plan on doing any trekking or climbing while you are in the area, you will want to give your body at least a few days to adjust. Strenuous physical activity may exacerbate symptoms of altitude sickness. Updated: Jul 28, 2009.

The Sacred Valley Activities

The Sacred Valley offers much to see and do, and a few days spent checking out the sights is recommended. Base yourself in one of the little towns, such as Pisac, Urubamba or Ollantaytambo, and explore the surrounding area from there. Pisac, in particular, makes a great kick-off point. The town features the famous and not-to-be missed Pisac Market. Aside from the market, the ruins of the Pisac fortress should be visited. The Sacred Valley also boasts a few interesting museums, such as El Museo Catcco in Ollantaytambo, which provides information about the fascinating local history. But the main reason for visiting this region is the seemingly limitless number of scenic hikes and treks through the Sacred Valley. Many of the hikes combine walking through beautiful countryside on your way to various ruins. Updated: Jul 28, 2009.

Sacred Valley Hiking Safety

The main safety consideration for most trekkers in the Sacred Valley is proper acclimatization and physical fitness. Pushing yourself into a trek without being fit enough or giving you enough time to get used to the altitude can be dangerous. Many of the guides speak several languages, and it is important to get a guide that can speak the language you're most comfortable with in case there is an emergency. With regard to safety, the guides have the final say on all treks if they feel that something is unsafe or if the group should take a break. Respect your guide's decision and understand that they have superior experience and knowledge of the area, and considering the safety of the group as a whole. Updated: Jul 28, 2009.

Sacred Valley: What to Bring Trekking

Most of the treks in the Sacred Valley are done with a guide and an outfitting company that provide all the necessary camping gear (tents, sleeping bags, stoves and cooking equipment).

You will be responsible for your own clothing, and the most important items are broken-in hiking boots, comfortable pants (many people use quick-dry pants although they are by no means a necessity), a mixture of short and long-sleeve shirts suitable for layering, an insulating layer (preferably fleece or wool as both keep you warm even when wet), and an outer shell to block the wind and to protect you from precipitation.

A warm hat to wear at night is a good idea, as well as one to protect your face from the sun during the day. A second pair of shoes to wear around camp at night will be appreciated after a long day in hiking boots. Two common items that are prohibited on the Inca Trail are plastic water bottles and trekking poles with exposed metal tips. To avoid the water bottle issue, bring along refillable containers or hydration systems. If you are bringing trekking poles, plastic tips are preferable but metal tips with duct tape on them are allowed.

Other Items To Bring Along:
• Camera
• Flashlight (and spare batteries)
• Bugspray
• Sunscreen
• Pocket knife
• Roll of toilet paper
• Personal toiletries
• Some large garbage bags to keep your things dry in the rain. Updated: Dec 03, 2008.

Sacred Valley Trekking

The cost of trekking in the Sacred Valley has risen sharply in recent years (especially on the Inca Trail), mostly due to the enforcement of minimum pay standards for guides and porters. However, there is still quite a bit of variation for the prices of similar tours. The higher-priced options generally offer better tents, sleeping bags and meals.

By far the most popular trek in the Sacred Valley (and in all of Peru) is the Inca Trail. The 2007 fee for four days on the Trail is $73, over four times what it was in 2000. For the shorter, two-day version, the fees are $25 for adults and $15 for students. Porters also now have to pay to enter as well, but this fee will be included in your overall tour price. More information is available in our Inca Trail section (p. 137). The fee to enter Machu Picchu is $40 for

SACRED VALLEY

foreign adults and $20 for foreign students with a valid International Student Identification Card (ISIC) card. The ISIC card is the only accepted form of student identification.

The Lares Valley Trek is a popular alternative to the Inca Trail because it also finishes at Machu Picchu. Depending on your group size, the four-day trek costs between $260 and $420. There is no trail fee for the Lares Valley Trek, but your entrance to Machu Picchu at the end is included.

There is also a 6-day Salcantay trek leading into the Inca Trail that costs about $450-650 depending on group size. Included in this are the fees for both the Inca Trail and Machu Picchu.

In order to save money, book a tour with a local operator. Although booking through an agency in your home country may seem easier, many of the local operators have extensive websites and booking through an agency in Cusco can sometimes cost half the price of foreign agencies.

Nearly all tours include the train ride back to Cusco from Aguas Calientes. There are two prices: one is about $46 while the cheaper option costs $15. Most companies include the train ride back and if your company has you booked for the $46 ticket you can save a few bucks by asking them to remove it from your package. The catch is that the cheaper ticket can only be bought in person, in Aguas Calientes, one day in advance. The train will take you to Ollantaytambo where you can catch a bus (about $3) to Cusco. Be warned, however, that this option is a bit risky in the high season, as tickets are sold on a first-come, first-serve basis.

The 'fees' associated with Sacred Valley treks are mostly in relation to the Inca Trail. Aside from outfitter costs, there are no trail fees for the other Sacred Valley treks. Guided hikes of the other major trails in the Sacred Valley cost approximately the same per day as the Inca Trail. The majority of tours offer discounts to those carrying valid ISIC cards and some give discounts to members of South American Explorers, so ask around.

The following are approximate prices for some of the more popular hikes in the Sacred Valley. The price variations are due to changes in price between low and high season. Vilcabamba–$700 for 7 days

Choquequirao–$545 for 3 days, 4 nights
Salcantay–$450-650 for 5 days
Lares Valley–$260-450 for 4 days
Updated: Dec 03, 2008.

Choquequirao

Among trekking opportunities in the Sacred Valley this trail entices trekkers with the chance to view magnificent, albeit less well-known, Inca ruins. The Inca Choquequirao complex sitting precariously on a ridge-top in the Vilcabamba area consists of magnificent Inca walls and double recessed doorways. Most likely, it was built as a winter palace for Inca Túpac Yupanqui, in the same fashion that his father, Pachacútec, built Machu Picchu. Since Hiram Bingham discovered the ruin in 1911 it has remained the relatively less-traveled sibling of Machu Picchu.

The trek to Choquequirao starts at Cachora, which you can reach by taking a bus to Abancay and getting off at a dirt road past Saywite Stone. If you're keen, you can hitchhike the final stretch to Cachora, where you can rent guides and mules. The first day involves a hike down to Río Apurímac, and on the second day you'll embark on an arduous six-hour climb straight up the other side to the cloud forest ridge where the city sits. Some Cusco tour agencies offer a combined ten-day trek from Choquequirao to Machu Picchu. Another approach to Choquequirao is to start at Huancacalle and make the eight-day trek across the Cordillera Vilcabamba via the Vitcos ruins. Updated: Dec 03, 2008

Photo by: Bernardo Carbajal

Lares Valley Trek

If you're looking to get off the beaten path but don't want to miss out on stellar scenery, then the Lares Valley Trek is an excellent option. In contrast to the popular Inca Trail Trek, the Lares Valley Trek has yet to fully appear on the tourist radar. Trekkers traverse high mountain passes, plunge into sub-tropical valleys rich in intriguing flora and fauna, and weave past tranquil lagoons, natural hot springs and Inca remains.

This less-traveled trek passes through the remarkable pastoral regions of the Cordillera Urubamba, and presents travelers with a unique opportunity to experience the enchanting Andean landscape and its Quechua culture. Due to the area's relative remoteness, its inhabitants have maintained their traditional ways of life, holding steadfastly to age-old practices of llama and alpaca herding, potato cultivation and colorful weaving. The area has changed very little over the last 500 years, and provides travelers remarkable insight into the lives of Andean farmers. Trekking through the Lares Valley, past thatched stone houses, herds of llamas and farmers dressed in their traditional brightly colored ponchos, is like traveling back in time.

On this trek tradition and scenic splendor collide, leaving those lucky enough to experience the combination wondering why the Lares Valley is still just a whisper among the traveling community. Or perhaps those who do complete the Lares Valley Trek leave with pursed lips, in an attempt to preserve the pristine culture and landscape that make this area so inspiring. Although the trek is rated as moderate, it does include high passes over 4,000 meters (13,125 ft.) so pre-trail acclimatization is essential. If arriving from sea level, it is recommended that you spend at least 3 days in Cusco before attempting the trek.

Peru Treks and Adventure has put together a series of special non-profit trek packages aimed at spreading the financial benefits of tourism to the local people. Trekkers on these tours have the opportunity to distribute warm clothes and school equipment to the mountain communities located along the trail—a great way to meet and interact with the people of this remarkably beautiful region. Updated: Dec 03, 2008.

Vilcabamba

For a true adventure, make the knee-buckling climb up to Espíritu Pampa, believed by some to be the true Lost City of the Inca. Here you'll discover the captivating ruins of Vitcos, where the Inca launched their 35-year rebellion against the Spanish. The trail offers some of the most diverse and intriguing scenery you'll encounter while trekking in the Sacred Valley. The journey through time and up mountains begins in Huancacalle, which can be reached by taking a bus or truck from Cusco over the Abra Málaga to Quillabamba and getting off at the Huancacalle turnoff.

From Huancacalle a path will bring you to where the Inca emperor was originally exiled and to the resting place of the sacred rock of Chuquipalta. From here the trail heads to New Vilcabamba, a colonial-era mining town, and ascends towards a 3,800-meter (12,500 ft.) pass before dropping into the jungle below. The ascent to the ruins involves a steep climb up ancient Inca staircases and offers magnificent views of the valley below. Instead of walking back to Huancacalle, you can trek another one to two days along the river to a small town called Kiteni and take a bus back to Quillabamba. The entire trip takes between seven to ten days, depending on your fitness level. Updated: Dec 03, 2008.

Ausangate and Cordillera Vilcanota

The trail that winds its way through the Cordillera Vilcanota and up to the sacred Nevado Ausangate (6,384 meters / 20,945 ft.) goes through one of the more pristine, untouched areas in Peru. For those seeking to avoid the tourist trails this is a good choice among the trekking opportunities in the Sacred Valley. You can choose from a number of trekking routes through this range, but the classic seven-day trek offered by most Cusco tour agencies begins in Tinki, a small town situated high in the puna grasslands, and gradually loops around Ausangate. The trail traverses up and across four very high mountain passes (two over 5000 m. / 16,400 ft.), and offers magnificent views of the glacial faces of all the mountains in the range, including Colquecruz and Jampa. Passing through some of the more remote areas in Peru, the trail also affords trekkers glimpses of Andean llama herders and weavers. Updated: Dec 03, 2008

Salcantay

In terms of trekking opportunities in the Sacred Valley, this one requires a bit more physical and logistical preparation. The crowning jewel of the Salcantay trek is Nevado Salcantay (6,271 meters), the massive mountain that looms above the Inca Trail and plunges into the magnificent city of Machu Picchu. Most Cusco tours offer a four-day trek from Mollepata, located in the Limatambo Valley about 3.5 hours from Cusco. You can reach Mollepata by hopping onto a bus heading from Cusco to Abancay. From Mollepata it's a three-kilometer walk to Parobambo, where you can hire mules and guides. The route itself stretches across Cordillera Vilcabamba and includes a steep ascent up to the Incachillasca Pass (5,000 meters) followed by a sharp descent along the glaciers of Salcantay. Though physically demanding, the trail offers rewarding views of snow-covered peaks and glacial valleys. On the last day you'll depart your campsite at Acobamba and head towards the Inca ruins of Patallacta, near the popular tourist gateway to the Inca trail, Km. 88. From here you can catch a train to Machu Picchu or Cusco.

Alternatives to the Salcantay Trek are also possible for those who would like something more off-the-beaten-path. Updated: Dec 03,2008

Salcantay alternative route
The alternative trek takes in three more unusual, quieter campsites along the route, largely away from other tourists. On the alternative Salcantay trek, many choose to take transport further along the road than Mollepata. After drop off on the first day, the hike heads as far as the laguna, which is about 30 minutes after the uphill crossbacks section, and 45 minutes before the main pass. Be prepared, it can get very chilly here at night and has been known to snow.

On the second day, the trek continues on past the other campgrounds in the cloud forest, and to an area where there is a tiny hotsprings. There is not much space here to camp, so you need to try to arrive early, ahead of other campers. The hotsprings are very welcome after a tough hike that is primarily downhill all day.

On the afternoon of the third day, instead of taking the route from Playa to Santa Teresa, the trail follows an old, recently discovered Inca Trail to Llactapata. After hiking for two to three hours (depending on fitness), hikers are rewarded with a small Inca ruins site from which you have a spectacular view of Machu Picchu. It is thought that in the past, this was a watchtower, to protect the city. Hiking down a little from the ruins, the campsite also overlooks Machu Picchu.

On the final day, the hike descends down for a couple of hours to the town of Hidroelectrico, from where you can take the train to Aguas Calientes. The train leaves at around 3 p.m. and you need to buy tickets early, to secure passage.

This hike can be fairly tough, especially the stretch from Playa up to the Llactapata ruins, and it is advisable to have porters or horsemen, at least to help out with this section of the route.

Companies that offer this hike include Sun Gate Tours. Ask for guide Domingo Atao. Updated: Dec 03,2008

Jungle Trek
The four day jungle trek is a very popular alternative to the Inca Trail. A little bit easier than the challenging Salkantay due to the lower altitude, this trek also includes mountain biking, and trekkers stay in basic hostels along the way, rather than camping. The jungle trek begins with a few hours driving into the Sacred Valley, stopping for coffee in a small village, before driving up a mountain where you'll see the snowy peak. You'll spend the afternoon cruising down the mountainside with a great view and peaceful surroundings.

The second and third days are spent trekking up and over the mountains, with some parts overlooking the river. It's hot and hard work, but enjoyable with a group of people and there are a few little huts along the way to stop for water and snacks. You'll be rewarded with a dip in the hot springs as well. At the end of each day you'll arrive at small villages along the way and stay the night in a simple hostel. It sure is handy not to have to carry your sleeping bag, and showers are available, but they are likely to be cold.

On the third day you'll arrive to Aguas Calientes where you'll be treated to a nicer hotel, and a hot shower. The fourth day is spent exploring Machu Picchu. You can choose to wake up at 4 a.m. to walk up to the town, in order to get in line for the 7am opening. Your group will be given a very interesting two hour tour and discussion where you'll learn about the lives of the Inca and their culture, as well as finding out which places of the city they used for various purposes. The rest of the day will be yours to explore the city, and if you wish you can also climb Huayna Picchu. Updated: Aug 09, 2010.

Uchuy Qosqo
If you are short on time and looking for a route much less traveled, Uchuy Qosqo offers a good option as an alternative to the two day Inca Trail. Uchuy Qosqo is a two day hike through the Urubamba valley to Machu Picchu, passing lagoons, valleys and mountains

before arriving in the lost city of Machu Picchu. The trek begins at the ruins of Sacsayhuaman and passes through some small villages and the Llaulliqocha lagoon, which is at an altitude of 4,000 meters (13,123 ft). The trek passes the mountain of Veronica, of which you can see the snowy peak, as well as the lakes of Piuray and Llanaqocha. In the late afternoon you'll reach the town of Huchuyqosqo, or Small Cusco, in the Urubamba Valley, followed by the village of Lamay. From Lamay a short bus is taken to Ollantaytambo, where the group usually stops for dinner, before boarding a train to Aguas Calientes to spend the night. The second day is all about exploring the lost city, including the option to walk or bus up to the city, a guided tour of Machu Picchu, followed by the rest of the day to explore, before catching the train back to Cusco. Updated: Aug 09, 2010.

Huayoccari

For the adventurous solitude-seeker, this hike is a sure win. In contrast to other trekking opportunities in the Sacred Valley, this one offers slightly less tourist-trodden trails. Along this two-day hike one way from Yucay to the small Andean village of Huayoccari, you'll encounter some of the most enchanting mountain scenery, from Inca terraces overlooking the San Juan River ravine to Sakrachayac and ancient rock paintings. After one night of camping you'll make the arduous ascent to Tuqsana Pass (4,000 meters) and then descend to Yanacocha Lake. From here you'll follow the trail to Huayoccari. Updated: Dec 03,2008

Pinculluna

If you are not up for a full-day's journey, Mt. Pinculluna, rising up behind Ollantaytambo, is an excellent choice among short trekking opportunities in the Sacred Valley. The trail offers a pretty two-hour walk up past agricultural terracing. Because the trail is not well marked in some spots, you may be better off hiring a guide in town to avoid getting lost. Updated: Dec 03,2008

Pumamarca Ruins

Among trekking opportunities in the Sacred Valley, this one rewards trekkers with spectacular views of Andean mountains and remote villages. The trail follows the banks of the Río Patacancha, where you will eventually encounter the small but well-preserved Inca ruins of Pumamarca. Completing the loop from Ollantaytambo requires about five hours. To begin, take the road north of Ollanta along the Patacancha. When the road crosses the river it becomes a footpath and you'll follow this past Munaypata village. Take a left and follow the path towards the valley and terracing and then make a sharp left towards the agricultural terraces in front of you. Updated: Jul 25,2007.

The Sacred Valley Tours

Making arrangements to see the Sacred Valley through a tour operator, either in Peru or your home country, can be an excellent way to get to know this spectacular valley rich in Inca ruins, agriculture and magnificent views. In particular, there are several tour agencies in Cusco that will gladly help you plan an itinerary.

SACRED VALLEY

Photo by: Bernardo Carbajal

Hiking tours are especially popular in this area. The Sacred Valley offers some of South America's most beautiful and historic hikes.

Another extremely popular option are archaeological tours in the Sacred Valley. These are best for travelers who want to see as many of the incredibly preserved Inca ruins throughout the valley as possible. Aside from purchasing Sacred Valley tours in Cusco, for those who are a little more adventurous and perhaps have a decent smattering of Spanish, it is possible to base yourself in any of the smaller towns, such as Pisac, Urubamba or Ollantaytambo and get local advice and information about the best trips offered.

Biking tours can also be arranged. This mountainous region has excellent rides and gives travelers a chance to experience the exhilaration of cliff-side roads up close. Updated: Dec 03,2008.

The Sacred Valley Lodging

Sacred Valley hotels are by and large a good value, with friendly hospitable staff and low ceilings. Take care if you're tall! It is worth checking what the hotel rates include, as most don't include breakfast, but you can usually get it for a reasonable fee. Many Sacred Valley hotels can arrange local tours, often at a good rate.There are a range of hotels in Pisac to suit all budgets. Some of the best Sacred Valley accommodations have a great view of either the surrounding spectacular countryside or of the ruins. There are places conveniently close to the Pisac Market and local transportation. Just a bit further up the valley, Urubamba accomodations are limited to just a few lodgings. This is a great place for budget travelers to pick up cheap hostels with easy access to the ruins. Ollantaytambo hotels are, on the whole, a good bet with cheap bed and breakfast options, through to more expensive places set around pretty courtyards or in well-kept gardens. Several places here offer a scenic vista over the ruins or a backdrop of the mountains. Shop around for a good deal. Updated: Jun 29,2010

CHINCHERO

Located 28 kilometers (17 mi.) northwest of Cusco, the sleepy Andean town of Chinchero is one of the best places in the valley for Andean textiles and basic goods like hats, gloves, and shawls. Commanding sweeping views of the Salcantay and Vilcabamba mountain ranges, this traditional Andean village will captivate visitors with its natural beauty and cultural integrity. In the main square, which is dominated by a formidable Inca wall composed of huge stones and 10 trapezoidal niches, you'll find the famous Chinchero markets. Here you'll be greeted by bustling artisan sellers, dressed in traditional clothing, and eager to win your attention (and secure a purchase). The market is divided into two sections, one focusing on handicrafts and the other on produce. Even on Sunday, the busiest day, Chinchero's markets seem more authentic than the Pisac markets. For the best bargaining chances, visit the markets on Tuesday or Thursday, when there are fewer crowds. If you're looking for a lively atmosphere, you may want to check out Pisac market, which is bigger and more flamboyant. Updated: Jul 28, 2009.

PISAC

Pisac (32 km. / 20 mi. northeast of Cusco) is popular both for its ancient and modern attractions. The ancient ruins at the top of the mountainside featuring a small Inca village with temples, palaces, solstice markers, baths and water channels draw archaeologists from around the world. Its modern attraction is the weekly market on Sundays, drawing travelers looking for bargains on indigenous weavings, souvenirs and knit clothing. Updated: Dec 03,2008.

Getting To and Away

To get to Pisac from Cusco, most travelers take either combis or colectivos, vans or minibuses that depart from the corners of Puputi and La Cultura in Cusco, or Tullumayo and Garcelazo, when they have enough passengers, which is usually every 15 minutes. The cost is about two soles, or $0.70. The trip itself takes about 45 minutes. To return to Cusco, or head on to Urubamba and other cities, the colectivos and combis arrive and depart continuously from near the town market. Cabs can take you back and forth for about $5. There are also chartered bus tours which can be arranged through any travel agency. Updated: Dec 03,2008.

Pisac Market

The Pisac market is a must-see for those visiting the Cusco region. Every Tuesday, Thursday and Sunday, the streets fill to overflowing with artisans selling their goods and tourists of every stripe buying them. Even if you must go to Pisac on another, non-market day, you'll find a lot of the same stuff for sale in little shops around town. Sunday is the best day to visit by far, as there is also a smaller market for local

SACRED VALLEY

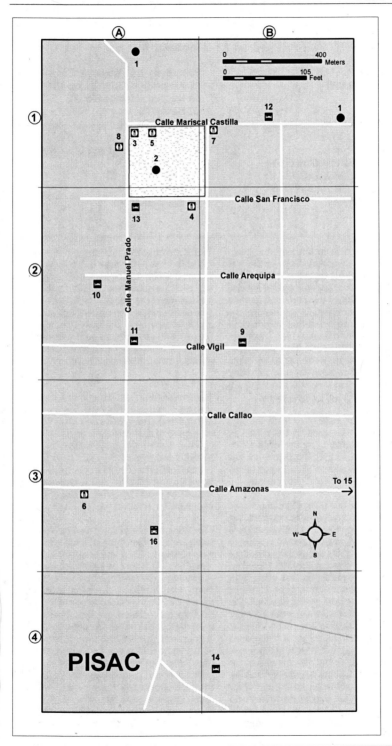

Activities ●

1 Pisca Ruins A1 B1
2 Pisac Market A1

Eatings ⑪

3 Miski Mijuna Wasi A1
4 Mullu A2
5 Restaurant Doña Clorinda A1
6 Restaurant Valle Sagrado A3
7 Restaurant Samana Wasi B1
8 Ulrike´s Café A1

Sleeping ▣

9 Hospedaje El Artesano B2
10 Hospedaje Kinsa Cocha A2
11 Hospedaje Linda Flor A2
12 Hostal Varayoq B1
13 Hotel Pisac A2
14 Hotel Royal Inka Pisac B4
15 Paz y Luna Bed and Breakfast B3

Transportation ▣

16 Bus Station A3

villagers who come from miles around packing up their llamas and donkeys in the wee hours of the morning in order to arrive and set up stalls where they sell vegetables and other produce. Often, the preferred method of commerce is bartering, as opposed to buying and selling, a tradition that goes back to before the Inca. Even if you're not a shopper, the market is worth a visit. It's a great place to take photos and people-watch. Many of the cafés around the market have second-story balconies with good views of visitors from around the world haggling with locals.

The quality of the goods is a little sketchy. If you're looking to spend a lot of money on any one item, you're better off in a fine gallery in Cusco or Lima. But prices are low and the market is a great place to buy memorable souvenirs for friends back home.

Most of the goods sold at the Pisac market are textiles, jewelry, carved gourds, ceramics, felt hats, antiques (buyer beware) and sweaters, to name a few. Bargaining is standard practice in the Pisac market. There are no price tags since you pay the price you agree to with the seller. Some tips: Never make the first offer. Wait until the seller starts with a price. Don't be afraid to walk away from a price you don't like. Chances are you'll see the same thing further on. Another good tip is to buy a lot of things at the same stall, even if they're not of the same type (for example, gourds, sweaters, tapestries, etc.). Vendors will often discount prices for those buying in bulk. Be aware of your location; stalls tucked into back regions of the market far away from where the tour buses from Cusco stop, will often have better prices than stalls nearer the bus stops and on strategic corners.

The Pisac market ends around five o'clock when the last of the tour buses goes back to Cusco. If you're staying in town, the end of the day is also a good time to look for bargains, since some of the sellers may be a little more willing to make a deal rather than pack their goods for next time. Shopping at markets like the one in Pisac can be a lot of fun if you lighten up and allow yourself to wheel and deal in a friendly way. Updated: Dec 03,2008.

Pisac Ruins

The ruins of the fortress at Pisac are among the most interesting in Peru. Today, historians and archaeologists believe that Pisac was a compound that mainly served as a line of defense against the Anti Indians. These implacable enemies of the Inca held lands to the east of Cusco. The Pisac complex is made up of several different areas. Outside of the walled complex is Qanchisracay, a small compound of rough stone buildings.

This area probably served as a military garrison and may have housed local villagers in case of attack. There are also some ruins of aqueducts. The area might have been home to farmers who worked the lower terraces. From Qanchisracay, the Inca trail heads up the hill to a crossroads of sorts, known as Antachaka. There are four baths at the crossroads, with water brought in by duct. To the west, you'll see the cemetery known as Tankanamarka, an important pre-conquest site that has been largely looted by grave robbers. According to Inca belief, the dead could carry their possessions with them into the next life. For that reason, there were often treasures left in grave sites, a fact that the conquering Spanish soon

Activities ●

1 Pisca Ruins A1 B1
2 Pisac Market A1

Eatings 🍽

3 Miski Mijuna Wasi A1
4 Mullu A2
5 Restaurant Doña Clorinda A1
6 Restaurant Valle Sagrado A3
7 Restaurant Samana Wasi B1
8 Ulrike´s Café A1

Sleeping 🛏

9 Hospedaje El Artesano B2
10 Hospedaje Kinsa Cocha A2
11 Hospedaje Linda Flor A2
12 Hostal Varayoq B1
13 Hotel Pisac A2
14 Hotel Royal Inka Pisac B4
15 Paz y Luna Bed and Breakfast B3

Transportation 🚌

16 Bus Station A3

villagers who come from miles around packing up their llamas and donkeys in the wee hours of the morning in order to arrive and et up stalls where they sell vegetables and ther produce. Often, the preferred method f commerce is bartering, as opposed to buying and selling, a tradition that goes back to efore the Inca. Even if you're not a shopper, e market is worth a visit. It's a great place take photos and people-watch. Many of the fés around the market have second-story lconies with good views of visitors from ound the world haggling with locals.

e quality of the goods is a little sketchy. you're looking to spend a lot of money any one item, you're better off in a fine llery in Cusco or Lima. But prices are low d the market is a great place to buy memble souvenirs for friends back home.

st of the goods sold at the Pisac market are tiles, jewelry, carved gourds, ceramics, felt s, antiques (buyer beware) and sweaters, to ne a few. Bargaining is standard practice in Pisac market. There are no price tags since pay the price you agree to with the seller. me tips: Never make the first offer. Wait l the seller starts with a price. Don't be id to walk away from a price you don't like. nces are you'll see the same thing further Another good tip is to buy a lot of things at same stall, even if they're not of the same (for example, gourds, sweaters, tapestries, . Vendors will often discount prices for e buying in bulk. Be aware of your location; s tucked into back regions of the market far from where the tour buses from Cusco will often have better prices than stalls er the bus stops and on strategic corners.

The Pisac market ends around five o'clock when the last of the tour buses goes back to Cusco. If you're staying in town, the end of the day is also a good time to look for bargains, since some of the sellers may be a little more willing to make a deal rather than pack their goods for next time. Shopping at markets like the one in Pisac can be a lot of fun if you lighten up and allow yourself to wheel and deal in a friendly way. Updated: Dec 03,2008.

Pisac Ruins

The ruins of the fortress at Pisac are among the most interesting in Peru. Today, historians and archaeologists believe that Pisac was a compound that mainly served as a line of defense against the Anti Indians. These implacable enemies of the Inca held lands to the east of Cusco. The Pisac complex is made up of several different areas. Outside of the walled complex is Qanchisracay, a small compound of rough stone buildings.

This area probably served as a military garrison and may have housed local villagers in case of attack. There are also some ruins of aqueducts. The area might have been home to farmers who worked the lower terraces. From Qanchisracay, the Inca trail heads up the hill to a crossroads of sorts, known as Antachaka. There are four baths at the crossroads, with water brought in by duct. To the west, you'll see the cemetery known as Tankanamarka, an important pre-conquest site that has been largely looted by grave robbers. According to Inca belief, the dead could carry their possessions with them into the next life. For that reason, there were often treasures left in grave sites, a fact that the conquering Spanish soon

before arriving in the lost city of Machu Picchu. The trek begins at the ruins of Sacsayhuaman and passes through some small villages and the Llaulliqocha lagoon, which is at an altitude of 4,000 meters (13,123 ft). The trek passes the mountain of Veronica, of which you can see the snowy peak, as well as the lakes of Piuray and Llanaqocha. In the late afternoon you'll reach the town of Huchuyqosqo, or Small Cusco, in the Urubamba Valley, followed by the village of Lamay. From Lamay a short bus is taken to Ollantaytambo, where the group usually stops for dinner, before boarding a train to Aguas Calientes to spend the night. The second day is all about exploring the lost city, including the option to walk or bus up to the city, a guided tour of Machu Picchu, followed by the rest of the day to explore, before catching the train back to Cusco. Updated: Aug 09, 2010.

Huayoccari

For the adventurous solitude-seeker, this hike is a sure win. In contrast to other trekking opportunities in the Sacred Valley, this one offers slightly less tourist-trodden trails. Along this two-day hike one way from Yucay to the small Andean village of Huayoccari, you'll encounter some of the most enchanting mountain scenery, from Inca terraces overlooking the San Juan River ravine to Sakrachayac and ancient rock paintings. After one night of camping you'll make the arduous ascent to Tuqsana Pass (4,000 meters) and then descend to Yanacocha Lake. From here you'll follow the trail to Huayoccari. Updated: Dec 03,2008

Pinculluna

If you are not up for a full-day's journey, Mt. Pinculluna, rising up behind Ollantaytambo, is an excellent choice among short trekking opportunities in the Sacred Valley. The trail offers a pretty two-hour walk up past agricultural terracing. Because the trail is not well marked in some spots, you may be better off hiring a guide in town to avoid getting lost. Updated: Dec 03,2008

Pumamarca Ruins

Among trekking opportunities in the Sacred Valley, this one rewards trekkers with spectacular views of Andean mountains and remote villages. The trail follows the banks of the Río Patacancha, where you will eventually encounter the small but well-preserved Inca ruins of Pumamarca. Completing the loop from Ollantaytambo requires about five hours. To begin, take the road north of Ollanta along the Patacancha. When the road crosses the river it becomes a footpath and you'll follow this past Munaypata village. Take a left and follow the path towards the valley and terracing and then make a sharp left towards the agricultural terraces in front of you. Updated: Jul 25,2007.

The Sacred Valley Tours

Making arrangements to see the Sacred Valley through a tour operator, either in Peru or your home country, can be an excellent way to get to know this spectacular valley rich in Inca ruins, agriculture and magnificent views. In particular, there are several tour agencies in Cusco that will gladly help you plan an itinerary.

SACRED VALLEY

Photo by: Bernardo Carbajal

Hiking tours are especially popular in this area. The Sacred Valley offers some of South America's most beautiful and historic hikes.

Another extremely popular option are archaeological tours in the Sacred Valley. These are best for travelers who want to see as many of the incredibly preserved Inca ruins throughout the valley as possible. Aside from purchasing Sacred Valley tours in Cusco, for those who are a little more adventurous and perhaps have a decent smattering of Spanish, it is possible to base yourself in any of the smaller towns, such as Pisac, Urubamba or Ollantaytambo and get local advice and information about the best trips offered.

Biking tours can also be arranged. This mountainous region has excellent rides and gives travelers a chance to experience the exhilaration of cliff-side roads up close. Updated: Dec 03,2008.

The Sacred Valley Lodging

Sacred Valley hotels are by and large a good value, with friendly hospitable staff and low ceilings. Take care if you're tall! It is worth checking what the hotel rates include, as most don't include breakfast, but you can usually get it for a reasonable fee. Many Sacred Valley hotels can arrange local tours, often at a good rate.There are a range of hotels in Pisac to suit all budgets. Some of the best Sacred Valley accommodations have a great view of either the surrounding spectacular countryside or of the ruins. There are places conveniently close to the Pisac Market and local transportation. Just a bit further up the valley, Urubamba accomodations are limited to just a few lodgings. This is a great place for budget travelers to pick up cheap hostels with easy access to the ruins. Ollantaytambo hotels are, on the whole, a good bet with cheap bed and breakfast options, through to more expensive places set around pretty courtyards or in well-kept gardens. Several places here offer a scenic vista over the ruins or a backdrop of the mountains. Shop around for a good deal. Updated: Jun 29,2010

CHINCHERO

Located 28 kilometers (17 mi.) northwest of Cusco, the sleepy Andean town of Chinchero is one of the best places in the valley for Andean textiles and basic goods like hats, gloves, and shawls. Commanding sweeping views of the Salcantay and Vilcabamba mountain ranges, this traditional Andean village will captivate visitors with its natural beauty and cultural

integrity. In the main square, which is dominated by a formidable Inca wall composed of huge stones and 10 trapezoidal niches, you'll find the famous Chinchero markets. Here you'll be greeted by bustling artisan sellers, dressed in traditional clothing, and eager to win your attention (and secure a purchase). The market is divided into two sections, one focusing on handicrafts and the other on produce. Even on Sunday, the busiest day, Chinchero's markets seem more authentic than the Pisac markets. For the best bargaining chances, visit the markets on Tuesday or Thursday, when there are fewer crowds. If you're looking for a lively atmosphere, you may want to check out Pisac market, which is bigger and more flamboyant. Updated: Jul 28, 2009.

PISAC

Pisac (32 km. / 20 mi. northeast of Cusco) is popular both for its ancient and modern attractions. The ancient ruins at the top of the mountainside featuring a small Inca village with temples, palaces, solstice markers, baths and water channels draw archaeologists from around the world. Its modern attraction is the weekly market on Sundays, drawing travelers looking for bargains on indigenous weavings, souvenirs and knit clothing. Updated: Dec 03,2008.

Getting To and Away

To get to Pisac from Cusco, most travelers take either combis or colectivos, vans or minibuses that depart from the corners of Puputi and La Cultura in Cusco, or Tullumayo and Garcelazo, when they have enough passengers, which is usually every 15 minutes. The cost is about two soles, or $0.70. The trip itself takes about 45 minutes. To return to Cusco, or head on to Urubamba and other cities, the colectivos and combis arrive and depart continuously from near the town market. Cabs can take you back and forth for about $5. There are also chartered bus tours which can be arranged through any travel agency. Updated: Dec 03,2008.

Pisac Market

The Pisac market is a must-see for those visiting the Cusco region. Every Tuesday, Thursday and Sunday, the streets fill to overflowing with artisans selling their goods and tourists of every stripe buying them. Even if you must go to Pisac on another, non-market day, you'll find a lot of the same stuff for sale in little shops around town. Sunday is the best day to visit by far, as there is also a smaller market for local

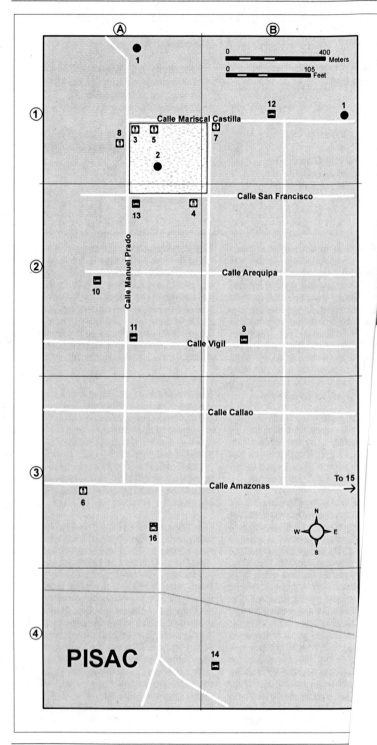

realized and exploited. By some estimates, there may have been as many as 10,000 graves at the site at one time. The looters took everything and left only holes.

Continuing the hike, you'll pass through the wall through Amarupunku, the Door of the Serpent, and into Upper Pisac. The Incas' amazing skills with stonework are on display here. Note how they cut this path through the rock and remember that they did not have iron tools or explosives to help them tunnel. Upper Pisac, with most of the ceremonial and religious structures in the complex, is the most important and impressive section of the ruins. The stonework is incredible. There are several temples in Upper Pisac. Unfortunately, it is not known today which temples corresponded to which deity. One exception is the impressive Temple of the Sun, an oval building built directly into the rock. From the top of the building, Inca astronomers could track the movements of the sun, moon, and stars. There is also an altar that may have been used to sacrifice animals for purposes of divination. Sadly, some of the decorative stonework on the temple of the Sun was recently chipped off by thieves. There are also a series of restored baths in Upper Pisac.

The last area of the Pisac ruins is the residential area known as P'isaca, from which the ruin complex gets its name. It is a series of terraces and stone buildings. Some archeaologists believe that these were homes for the elite. From here, there is a trail you can take back to the town of Pisac. Most visitors to the ruins take a taxi from Pisac. You can hike it, but it is very steep and at high altitude; you need to be in great shape and accustomed to altitude. 7 a.m.-3 p.m. Updated: Nov 04,2009.

Pisac Lodging

If you're planning on visiting either the Pisac ruins or markets you may want to spend the night in town. Pisac has a variety of accommodation types, which range from backpacker havens to modern luxury hotels. The only time you may have trouble finding a place to stay is in September, when pilgrims heading towards nearby Huanca descend on the town. Updated: Jul 24, 2007.

Hospedaje Kinsa Cocha

(ROOMS: $5-9) Run by the friendly Familia Chalco, the inviting Hospedaje Kinsa Cocha offers simple, clean dorm-style rooms. The shared bathrooms have wood-heated hot water, so be sure to throw some logs on before showering! Calle Arequipa 307 Tel: 51-84-203-101. Updated: Jul 24, 2007.

Hospedaje El Artesano

(ROOMS: $6-12) Hospedaje El Artesano is probably the most minimal of hostels in Pisac. You have to walk through a soiled corridor with exposed wiring coming out the walls to access the reception. It has only five rooms, none of them with private bathrooms. They all go for about $6. The rooms themselves are fresh and clean, and the bathrooms do have hot water. Apart from that there are no other amenities, though laundry and such is easily available elsewhere. The hostel has neither a phone nor an e-mail address. If you are thinking of your stay strictly in terms of just crashing for a night, and nothing better at a similar price is available, this is at least serviceable, and the staff is friendly. Calle Vigil 244. Updated: Dec 04, 2008.

Hospedaje Linda Flor

(ROOMS: $6-12) Hospedaje Linda Flor offers good clean and inexpensive rooms, some without bathrooms, some with, and little else. Single rooms without bathrooms are priced at $6, while private, double, matrimonial (with queen-sized beds) rooms go for $12. The rooms themselves have spare wooden floors and are freshly painted, and the bathrooms are newly remodeled. You register through the convenience store that owns it, and walk up a dirty stairway to access the rooms. Some of the ceilings are low, so if you are tall, be mindful. It is only a few blocks walk to the center of Pisac and its markets, buses and restaurants. Pardo Esquinal and Vigil Tel: 51-84-203-035. Updated: Dec 04, 2008.

Hotel Pisaq

(ROOMS: $10-16) Hotel Pisaq is a bright, friendly bed and breakfast located on the plaza in Pisac. The owners, a Peruvian-American couple, go out of their way to make their guests feel at home. There are a number of features that lower mid-range hotels don't usually offer, such as a sauna, well water and a café. The interior of the hotel is painted in a native American theme, which "reflects the spirit of the indigenous nations of the Americas" according to their web site. They are very knowledgeable about the surrounding areas, and can arrange tours and visits to sites of interest. Tel/Fax: 51-8-420-3062, E-mail: hotelpisaq@terra.com.pe, URL: www.aart.com/aart/HOTELPISAQ.html. Updated: Dec 04, 2008.

Hostal Varayoq

(ROOMS: $14-28) Hostal Varayoq calls itself a two-star hostel but this brand-new facility, right in the heart of the village of Pisac, has the look and feel of three-star hotel. Yet the prices are indeed hostel prices: single rooms start at $14, doubles and matrimoniales go for $28, with an American breakfast (with eggs, milk and fruit) included. This is probably the best bargain in this beautiful village. Hostal Varayoq also has its own in-house restaurant, El Helecho, with excellent $5-7 prices for well-made local and continental cuisine. Mariscal Castilla 380. Tel: 51-8-420-3263, E-mail: manudiaz@hotmail.com. Updated: Dec 03, 2008.

Paz y Luz Bed and Breakfast

(ROOMS: $20-35)For a rustic retreat, this gorgeous bed and breakfast next to the sacred Urubamba River is an excellent choice. With spectacular views of the enchanting Andean mountains and the nearby Pisac ruins, Paz y Luz offers visitors a relaxing atmosphere to contemplate the surrounding beauty. For active travelers, there are a number of trails nearby to explore the countryside. Rooms are comfortable, tastefully decorated and include brand new bathrooms. In the central area you'll find a dining table, woodstove and an immaculately polished wood staircase. In a separate building in the rear is a one-bedroom apartment with its own kitchen. One kilometer from Pisac Bridge to the right, following the river along a dirt road. There are signs. Tel: 51-8-420-3204, E-mail: diane@pazyluzperu.com, URL: www.pazyluzperu.com. Updated: Mar 12, 2008.

Hotel Royal Inka Pisac

(ROOMS: $55-115) Hotel Royal Inka Pisac is a converted hacienda and chapel on the road out of Pisac on the way to the ruins. The hotel is attractive and offers a view of the ruins, and the rooms are large if a little bit dull. It is definitely the place to stay in Pisac if you're looking for a little bit of luxury. It has an indoor swimming pool, jacuzzi and spa. They also offer classes taught by local artisans, such as woodworking. Carretera Pisac Ruinas s/n. Tel: 51-8-420-3064, Fax: 51-8-420-3064, E-mail: royalinka@aol.com, URL: www.royalinkahotel.com/hotels.htm. Getting there: Easily located just outside of Pisac on the way to the ruins. Updated: Dec 04, 2008.

Pisac Restaurants

Pisac offers an array of restaurants that are sure to suit any traveler's taste or budget. Even vegetarians can find some good eats in this small city. A number of restaurants serve up tasty Peruvian fare, and a particular treat in this region is fresh trout. For those on a quest for something quick to eat, take a short stroll to the bakery on Mariscal Castilla 372, just across from the plaza. Here you can grab vegetarian empanadas and hot breads straight from adobe ovens. The bakery treats are particularly popular on market days. Updated: Jul 24, 2007.

Mullu

This little corner of bohemia in Pisac is a hangout lounge and art gallery/craft shop downstairs and a café/restaurant upstairs. The lounge part has rows of black bean bag cushions along the wall facing a large-screen television. On the second floor, you can order yourself an alpaca cheeseburger, trout tartar or a plate of Andino-Thai sushi. Another Thai-influenced item, tomka, is a chicken dish cooked with coconut milk and lemon grass. Carrot juice and various mixes with other extracts are also available, like a banana-honey-nutmeg smoothie or té piseño, made from the local muña herb. Plaza de Armas 352. Tel: 51-8-420-3073, URL: www.mullu.com.pe. Updated: Jul 24, 2007.

Miski Mijuna Wasi

Facing Pisac's famous pisonay tree in the central plaza and, three days a week, the colorful market fair that takes over the town, Miski Mijuna Wasi restaurant offers traditional Peruvian and more standard cooking in a pleasant Andean setting, complete with native folk music complementing the tranquil environment. Treat yourself to the indigenous tarwi soup made of broth, local vegetables and legumes, cheese, and local herbs and spices. Miski Mijuna Wasi can accommodate up to 96, one of the larger options for groups in this small village, and its

SACRED VALLEY

in-house pastry chef will whip up any number of flavorful desserts. Plaza de Armas 345. Tel: 51-84-203-266, E-mail: michell776@hotmail.com. Updated: Dec 04, 2008.

Restaurant Samana Wasi

(ENTREES: $2) For tasty and inexpensive dishes, check out Restaurant Samana Wasi. Among the restaurants in Pisac, this is one of the best. Enjoy the popular trout, salad and fried potatoes plate while relaxing in the cozy little courtyard situated towards the back. With great service and a pleasant atmosphere, complete with majestic mountains looming in the background, this restaurant is an excellent option for almost any hungry traveler. It is priced very reasonably, with appetizers starting at $1 and entrées at $2. The restaurant also has a couple of basic rooms for rent. Calle Mariscal Castilla and Plaza Constitución 509. Tel: 51-84-203-018. Updated: Dec 04, 2008.

Restaurant Doña Clorinda

(ENTREES: $2-5) To try some excellent and safe traditional Peruvian food, make your way to Restaurant Doña Clorinda. Despite its rather humble looking façade, the restaurant serves up some delicious dishes, such as lomo saltado and rocoto relleno. If you ask for a table upstairs, owner doña Clorinda will take you on a little tour of her house to a spacious dining room that overlooks the plaza. Try the basic lunch menu for $2, or splurge and get the slightly more extravagant version for $5. Plaza de Armas 350 Tel: 51-84-203-051. Updated: Dec 04, 2008

Restaurant Valle Sagrado

If you're in the mood to try some of the best trout in the Cusco area, then head over to Restaurant Valle Sagrado. At lunch this place is packed with locals, who flock to the restaurant for owner Carmen Luz' tasty soups and sandwiches, as well as the trout, chicken and lamb rib dishes. The building's faux-Inca walls distinguish it from the numerous other restaurants situated nearby. Avenida Amazonas 116. Tel: 51-84-203-009. Updated: Jul 24, 2007.

Ulrike's Café

This classy new café promises some of the most creative menus in town. Even vegetarians can find something delectable to eat here. If you're in the mood for something sweet, try one of the delicious homemade cheesecakes. With art-adorned walls and a relaxed music-filled atmosphere, the café is a great place to take a break and grab a bite to eat. Plaza Constitución. Tel: 51-84-203-195, E-mail: ulrikescafe@terra.com.pe. Updated: Jul 24, 2007.

URUBAMBA

Located in the middle of the Sacred Valley, Urubamba is an attractive little town, making it a good base for traveling around the area, exploring the countryside and visiting the Inca ruins. Urubamba tends to be passed over more than other towns in the region, making it a quieter place to kick back for a few days. The pleasant palm-fringed Plaza de Armas has a small fountain at the center. The town boasts a decent array of services, hotels and restaurants and is close to Cusco, within about an hour's drive. There are excellent hiking opportunities surrounding the town, especially in the area of Moray, a town close-by with Inca terraces that have been sculpted into the hillsides. Alternatively, nearby Salinas makes for an interesting stop with its Inca salt pans, still in production, following an ancient tradition. Updated: Jul 25, 2007.

Getting To and Away from Urubamba

The same buses that depart from Cusco to Pisac will also take you to Urubamba, as well as to the next town heading north, Ollantaytambo. The point of departure is at Avenida Ferrocarril, several blocks away from the Urubamba Plaza de Armas. There are plenty of inexpensive mototaxis that can take you to your hotel or hostel. Departures and arrivals are continuous from morning until night. Cabs, of course, are also an option, and if you have enough fellow riders the split cost is roughly equal to what you would pay on a bus. Updated: Dec 04,2008.

Urubamba Services

Pl@net.Com

Whatever your communication needs while visiting Urubamba—writing or talking to your loved ones, catching up on news from home or anywhere else, or downloading and sending photos from your Peru journey—Pl@net.Com is by far the best Internet station in town. Not just by default, in that most of the others here have older-model computers with barely functioning keyboards in cramped spaces. Pl@net.Com features twelve fresh-model computers with high-speed access. Each is in a large, spacious, private cubicle, complete with headphones and a microphone. It is open everyday from 9 a.m. to 10 p.m., and costs only one sol an hour. It also has telephone cabins that allow you to make inexpensive international and local calls. 9 a.m.-10 p.m., daily. 449 Jirón Grau. Tel: 51-84-201-420, E-mail: rvvlap@hotmail. com. Updated: Dec 04, 2008.

Things to See and Do

Viento Sur

Adventure Club Viento-Sur offers a unique combination of eco-tourism, adventure, sport and culture through a variety of outdoor activities: horseback riding, mountain biking, paragliding, walking, treks and cultural trips. It also provides exclusive, customized, multi-adventure travel programs. Pricing ranges from $100 to $500 depending on the activity. Tel: 51-84--201-620 E-mail: info@aventurasvientosur.com URL: www.aventurasvientosur. com. Updated: Jul 19, 2007.

Sacred Valley Mountain Bike Tours

It is one thing to visit the Sacred Valley, but how about mountain biking across it, pushing up and across its slopes for the tour of a lifetime? The Sacred Valley Mountain Bike tour guides rent bicycles and gear for half-day, one-day and two-day trips through some of the world's best scenery, stopping now and then to appreciate sites such as the Inca Fortress of Ollantaytambo, or better yet, riding along some of the very same downhill trails used by the Inca in competitive events used to train young warriors for battle. The tour guides are as knowledgeable about local geography as they are about bicycles, and all bikes are thoroughly inspected before usage. Jirón Convención N° 459. Tel: 51-8-420-1331 / 1884, E-mail: tourjardin@hotmail.com. URL: www.machawasi.com. Updated: Jul 25, 2007.

Urubamba Lodging

Hotel Urubamba

(ROOMS: $3-10) The Hotel Urubamba is recommended for those traveling on the cheap with a general indifference to where they are crashing for the night. It offers not only shared bathrooms, but shared rooms, as in more traditional hostels, at $3 a night, with private rooms going for $10. The rooms featured ragged, old, green carpet. The owners will fix a breakfast for $2, and they are considerate and friendly. The hotel also has its own convenience store. Bolognesi 605 Tel: 51-8-420-1400 / 1062. Updated: Dec 04, 2008.

Hospedaje Mach'a Wasi

(ROOMS: $10-36) Mach'a Wasi is a small, standard guesthouse. The accommodation can house 13 people in five rooms featuring comfortable mattresses. Three of the rooms have their own shower, with another shower and a bath available for the remaining rooms. Hot showers are available at any time. Besides accommodation, the services of the hostel also include mountain bike tours using quality Trek and GT mountain bikes. Jirón Padre-Barre. Tel: 51-84-201-612, URL: www. machawasi.com. Updated: Dec 04, 2008.

Hospedaje los Jardines

(ROOMS: $12-27) A little bit away from the Plaza de Armas in Urubamba, up in the hills, the Hospedaje los Jardines has increasingly become one of the hostels of choice in town. As befits its name, the hostel has a great, big, beautiful garden and a manicured lawn you can unwind on and contemplate the view of the aforementioned valley—if you are not distracted by the in-house jungle monkey, Juanito. A private room with a bathroom goes for $14, and a room for two is priced at $20. Breakfast is available for an additional $2. Hospedaje los Jardines rents bicycles and offers tours. Jirón de Convención N° 459. Tel: 51-8-420-1331, 51-8-420-1884, E-mail: info@machawasi.com, URL: www. machawasi.com/English/English.html. Updated: Dec 04,2008.

Urubamba Restaurants

The Muse

The Muse opens at either 10 or 10:30 a.m., depending on the season, but still serves breakfast, probably because it rightly assumes that its mostly young and mostly fun-loving foreign customers were up late the night before. You can order your eggs or pancakes any time throughout its work day. The Muse has a hip vibe, with its throw pillows and lounging chairs, bohemian art, and variety of vegetarian and non-vegetarian options like thai-style vegetables. Live music, pub quizzes and movies are all part of the experience. Calle Comercio and Jirón Grau. Tel: 51-8-424-6332, E-mail: claritadean@hotmail. com. Updated: Dec. 04, 2008.

V!VA ONLINE REVIEW

THE MUSE

Had a great time at Muse, the atmosphere's friendly.

Apr 05,2009

Cusco Café and Bar

(ENTREES: $3-8) Located in one corner of the city of Urubamba's Plaza de Armas, the Cusco Café and Bar shows off a flashy sense of design and décor, from its ornately-carved banister to gallery displays of modern art on its walls. It features continental and Peruvian cooking, the latter with a more creative edge than you will find in local restaurants, such as a wheat risotto with Andean curry and banana chips. The prices rise slightly during peak tourist season. It is one of the few restaurants you will find that accepts credit cards. Calle Comercio 515. Tel: 51-84-201-681. Updated: Dec 04, 2008.

Café Plaza

This charming little restaurant on the Plaza de Armas in Urubamba offers a variety of filling but inexpensive Peruvian and continental favorites. It also has a large selection of coffees, including a variety of liquor-spiced cafés, not to mention liquor-spiced hot chocolates. Chocolate pancakes are also on the menu as a dessert. Café Plaza also features a long selection of fruit smoothies, cocktails and sandwiches. There is a magazine rack with a diverse selection of foreign and local publications, and an attractive selection of framed black-and-white photo portraits of locals adorning the walls. 440 Jirón Bolívar. Tel: 51-84-201-118. Updated: Dec 04, 2008.

YUCAY

Located a few kilometers east of Urubamba, Yucay is a peaceful town with a few interesting colonial homes and the restored colonial church of Santiago Apóstol. Inside the church, you'll find exquisite oil paintings and fine altars. The main square is divided by a large, grassy plaza where futból games are held. Facing the Plaza Manco II is the adobe palace of Sayri Túpac, who settled here after arriving from Vilcabamba in 1588.

In the hillsides near the town there are extensive Inca terraces, perfect for an afternoon excursion. Aside from the hotels clustered around the main square, there are few services in Yucay. One of Cusco's best-kept secrets is also located near Yucay. Huayoccari Hacienda Restaurant is an elegant, converted country manor perched on a ridge overlooking the Sacred Valley, about two kilometers outside of Yucay. In addition to walls decorated with colonial paintings and ceramics, and a rustic courtyard, the hacienda has some of the best cuisine in all of Cusco. Updated: Dec 04, 2008

Huayoccari Hacienda Restaurant

($35 per person) Located high above the Sacred Valley, about two kilometers (1.2 mi.)outside of Yucay, Huayoccari Hacienda Restaurant is one of the best places to grab a bite to eat and relax. The cooking is completely organic and based on the hacienda's original recipes. The menu includes homemade soups, fresh cheeses, steamed river trout and mouthwatering chicken. Save room for dessert, as the sweets are as delectable as the main meals. Though a bit out of the way, this place is definitely worth the trek. Who can say no to spectacular food and a to-die-for atmosphere? Be sure to make reservations in advance, as there are only a few tables. Kilometer 64 off the Pisac-Ollantaytambo highway. Call for directions beforehand. Tel: 51-84-962-2224 / 226-241, E-mail: hsilabrador@latinmail.com. Updated: Dec 04, 2008.

OLLANTAYTAMBO

Poised in the northeastern end of the Sacred Valley, about 97 km from Cusco, this little town is a cultural haven well worth the visit. Surrounded by snow-capped peaks on both sides, Ollantaytambo boasts spectacular views of both Andean scenery and ancient Inca ruins. The town itself offers a number of hotels and restaurants, and it is recommended that you spend the night in town to ensure that you get to the ruins early, before the crowds. For a truly unique experience, rise early and watch the sun rise over the mountains. Because the scenery around Ollantaytambo is some of the most remarkable in the region, it's a great place to wander while you explore nearby ruins and other landmarks of the Inca Empire. Of the marks left by the Incas, some of the most intriguing are the Inca andenes, or agricultural terraces, that adorn either side of the massive gorge surrounding the town.

The town itself, with its adobe brick walls draped in blooming bougainvillea and perfectly carved canals that continue to carry water down from the mountains, is testament to the Inca engineering and architectural genius. Take a stroll through the characteristic grid of streets and you'll be astounded by the sight of locals lingering in the doorways of ancient Inca residential cachas, once inhabited by several families during the 15th century.

As you meander through town you may want to stop by El Museo Catcco, which has displays of textiles and archeological objects recovered from the local ruins, in addition to

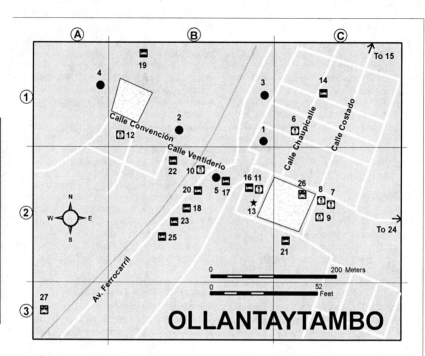

SACRED VALLEY

Activities ●

1 El Museo Catco B1
2 Iglesia de Ollantaytambo B1
3 Ollantaytambo Adventure Center B1
4 Ollantaytambo Heritage Trail A1
5 Talleres Los Andenes B2

Eatings 🏠

6 Alcázar C1
7 Cactus C2
8 Hearts Café C2
9 Kusicoyllor Café-Bar C2
10 Mayupata B2
11 Ollantay Bar and Restaurant B2
12 Restaurant Miranda B1

Services ★

13 Police B2

Sleeping ▣

14 Andean Moon C1
15 Apu Lodge C1
16 El Albergue B2
17 Hospedaje
   Los Andenes B2
18 Hospedaje
   Pumamarka B2
19 Hostal La Ñusta B1
20 Hostal Las
   Orquídeas B2
21 Hostal Ollanta C2
22 Hotel Pakaritampu B2
23 K'antuyoc B2
24 Las Portadas C2
25 Munay Tika B2

Transportation ▦

26 Bus Station C2
27 Train Station A3

a plethora of ethnographic and archaeological information. If you get lost, just follow the Ollantaytambo Heritage Trail, denoted by blue plaques, which highlights the most important historical sites around town.

Onwards from the main plaza, towards the outskirts of town, are a number of enchanting Inca ruins. Perhaps the biggest attraction is the massive "fortress", perched among steep stone terraces carved into the hillside. One of the Inca Empire's most impressive architectural examples, the structure successfully held the Spanish at bay during an attack in 1537. Despite its forbidding façade, however, the edifice was probably originally intended as temple for worship and astronomical observation rather than military purposes.

Between the temple and town, adjacent to the Patacancha River, you will encounter another interesting site: Baño de la Nusta (Bath of the Princess). This ancient ruin composed of grey granite was once used for ceremonial bathing, and offers excellent views of ancient granaries built by the Inca. If you've got a keen eye you may also make out the face of an Inca carved into the cliffs rising high above the valley.

Ollantaytambo can be reached from Cusco by train. You can also leave from here for Machu Picchu: the train has seven daily departures. Updated: Dec 04,2008.

History of Ollantaytambo

As the only standing fully preserved Inca Town in all of Perú, the town of Ollantaytambo is an important national heritage site. The word Ollantay has its roots in the Aymara (ulla nta wi) for "place that looks downwards," while tambo comes from the Quechua tampu, meaning "lodging and rest-stop for weary travelers." In one popular myth, Ollantaytambo is held to be the birthplace of the Inca people.

However, most hold that Ollantaytambo was named after Ollantay, the Inca General whose military prowess helped to extend the borders of the Inca empire northwards and southwards. He is famous for having asked Inca Pachacutec for his daughter's hand in marriage. Being summarily denied the honor of marrying his love, Cusi Coyllor, due to his lower social origins, the indignant Ollantay rebelled against his ruler and was thrown in prison. A play written in the 16th century dramatized their tale of tragic love.

Militarily, Ollantaytambo is celebrated as the outpost of the most victorious defeat of the Spanish conquista. Manco Inca retreated with his troops here from Sascsayhuamán in 1537.

The fortress of Ollantaytambo was important to the Inca defense against the conquistadores. It was originally constructed as a fortification against the Amazonian Antis (generic term used for the indigenous Peruvians of the jungle). However, following the discovery of remains of ritual baths and a Sun temple, archaeologists are questioning the defense theory. Historians also believe that Ollantaytambo may have held even more significance than Machu Picchu to the Inca Empire.

Today, Ollantaytambo serves as a popular transportation hub for getting to and from Aguas Calientes (at the base of Machu Picchu) by train. Updated: Aug 16,2007.

Getting To and Away from Ollantaytambo

The most popular way to visit Ollantaytambo is with a tour agency on a day trip from Cusco. Usually tour operators combine a stop in Ollantaytambo with several other surrounding villages like Chinchero or Piscac, and prices start at $10. The most economic, and arguably the most enjoyable, way to explore Ollantaytambo is at your own leisure and on your own time by going it alone without a guided tour.

BY BUS

Though rumors abound of buses running directly between Cusco and Ollantaytambo, the easiest thing to do is to catch a bus from Cusco to Urubamba from one of two Cusco stations that service Urubamba, and then to change buses. The terminal on Grau runs via Chinchero (1.5 hours) while the terminal on Avenida Tullumayo takes the Pisac route (2 hours). Fares to Urubamba are $1-$1.50. Once at the Urubamba bus terminal, there's no shortage of collectivos running to Ollantaytambo or any question about where to find them. Collectivo operators bound for Ollantaytambo greet passengers from Cusco the moment they step off the bus and usher them into a waiting mini-van. From Urubamba, the ride into Ollantaytambo takes about 30 minutes in a collectivo ($0.30) or, for those with

SACRED VALLEY

deep pockets, taxis make the trip slightly quicker for about $3.

TRAIN

Ollantaytambo is the mid-point for trains running between Cusco and Aguas Calientes (the point of disembarkation for Machu Picchu and the last stop on the train). Though it's tempting to stop in Ollantaytambo en route or returning from Aguas Calientes, it can be an expensive endeavor if done solely by train, as fares to and from Ollantaytambo to Aguas Calientes are the same as from Cusco. Keep in mind that while it's possible to get to Ollantaytambo by road, Aguas Calientes can only be reached by train, and therefore travel between Aguas Calientes and Ollantaytambo requires train travel. The rail station in Ollantaytambo is about 1200 meters from the town proper, and the road is currently under serious construction, so be prepared to walk most of the distance.

Nine trains, offering a variety of classes and rates, stop in Ollantaytambo from Cusco every morning before continuing on to Aguas Calientes. It's possible to disembark in Ollantaytambo from a morning train, as well as embark on any of the trains en route to Aguas Calientes. Though a number of trains return to Cusco from Aguas Calientes everyday, only three trains returning to Cusco stop in Ollantaytambo, so be sure to correctly book your ticket if you plan to alight at Ollantaytambo from Aguas Calientes. Trains leave Ollantaytambo bound for Cusco everyday between 5 p.m. and 6:45 p.m. Schedules and exact times are subject to change, so check with the train station directly or visit www.perurail.com for information. Updated: Dec 04,2008.

Things to See and Do

Ollantaytambo Fortress

Ollantaytambo's "fortress" may not actually have been built with defense in mind, but it is still a captivating sight that attracts armies of visitors. The massive religious complex was built shortly after Emperor Pachacuteq's conquest of the region. Today, most of it is spread on the face of a mountain, divided over 16 terraces. The terraces and accompanying temples were built using some of the finest stonework in the Inca empire. The most impressive structures are actually at the foot of the mountain, where there are also some wonderful examples of Inca irrigation and waterworks. If you can climb

all the way to the top of the complex, however, you will be rewarded with excellent views of the town and surrounding ruins.

The fortress is one of the most-visited sites in the Sacred Valley, so during peak hours of high season, it can be swamped with tour groups. If you can, it is best to visit the ruins first thing in the morning, which means staying somewhere nearby the night before.

Ollantaytambo Heritage Trail

The Ollantaytambo Heritage Trail is a collection of about a dozen sites of importance throughout town. If you're visiting on a day trip, most guided tour groups from Cusco, as well as city walking tours booked in Ollantaytambo, stroll through the small town, pointing out various stops along the trail, including Manay Raqay, the CATCCO Museum and the Temple of Santiago Apóstol. If you're self-guiding, blue plaques mark some of the sites, but the most complete list of trails stops, as well as a map, can be found just inside the entrance to the fortress on the wall outside the INC (Instituto Nacional de Cultura) office building. It's a giant mural map of the town and surrounding area, marked with the Rutas Ancestrales, the Heritage Trail and main parts of the fortress. Updated: Jul 25, 2007.

El Museo CATCCO

Despite its relatively small size, El Museo CATCCO (Centro Andino de Tecnología Tradicional y Cultural de las Comunidades de Ollantaytambo) is an excellent source for historical and cultural information on Ollantaytambo. The museum has interesting displays of textiles from local ruins, and ethnographic and archaeological information. All exhibits are in English and Spanish. The museum also has a ceramic workshop where you can buy some quality pottery pieces. One block from plaza in Casa Horno. Tel: 51-84-204-034, 10 a.m-3 p.m. Tuesday-Sunday. Updated: Jul 25, 2007.

SHOPPING

Shopping at Manay Raqay (Square of the Request)

Nearly all visitors to Ollantaytambo pass through Manay Raqay as it's the only entrance to the fortress and in addition, it's a designated stop on the Heritage Trail. The Inca square's most unique feature (aside from the looming fortress obviously) is the water element, a forceful channel of water flowing openly through the square from the ruins just up the valley.

With so many tourists taking the walk through Manay Raqay to enter the fortress, tourism officials have, of course, taken full advantage of the wide open space to erect several rows of market stalls. From afar, it looks like there's more shopping to be had than you'll actually find, as the stalls are sparsely occupied and those that are open for business hawk the same collection of books, jewelry, bags and walking sticks. However, the square is the most shopping you'll find in one place, and it is a great place to buy a book to self-guide you on your way in to the fortress. Updated: Dec 04, 2008.

The Fair Trade Association in Ollantaytambo

For cultural and conscientious collectors, the Fair Trade Association outlet in Ollantaytambo on the Jirón de la Convención is a must-visit in their Peru journey. It is the retail outlet for the Patacancha Women's Cooperative, created with the intention of preserving and reviving the art of weaving done with traditional methods and natural dyes, a practice going back centuries. Lliqllas (a sort of very wide and long scarf), chullos (caps), handbags, ponchos, blankets and other hand-woven products are all produced with an authenticity that is priceless. As regards the Fair Trade Association's practice, the women employed earn a living wage for their work. In cooperation with the Casa Ecológica, this store also sells organic honey, soy, and sesame oil, among other products, not to mention pottery and ceramics. Jirón de la Convención. E-mail: ollantaytextiles@gmail.com. Updated: Jul 25, 2007.

Talleres Los Andenes

A veteran weaver Félix Calla, proprietor of Hospedaje Los Andenes, also sells a creative assortment of alpaca wool, handmade ponchos, handbags, shawls, vests, belts, wallets and hats, all at reasonable prices. In terms of stone and clay, his gift shop also features goods, animals, deities, Inca symbols and other features central to Andean culture, which are also represented in Felix's colorful collection of expressive wooden masks. Old-fashioned irons—actually made from iron—should appeal to antique collectors. Calle Ventiderio. Tel: 51-84-204-095. Updated: Jul 25, 2007.

Tours

Ollantaytambo Adventure Center (OAC)

Tour agencies in Cusco would have you believe that trekking or riding the train between Cusco and Aguas Calientes are your only two options to get to the lost city. Do something a little different with Ollantaytambo Adventure Center. OAC offers a two-day trip starting in Ollantaytambo, that's heavy on the trekking with a stint in a car. It's $240 for two people, and $230 with three or more.Rutas Ancestrales Follow the trails the Inca used to trek. For a map, more information or to hire a guide, visit the INC office located in the fortress monument. To Yanacocha via Rumira: 18 kilometers (11.3 miles); via Inka: 15 kilometers (9.4 miles); via Chaquebamba: 23 kilometers (14.4 miles). To Pumamarca via Cahaquebamba: 14 kilometers (8.8 miles); via Pallata: 13 kilometers (8.2 miles) To Cachicata via Choquekillca and Inca Bridge (Puente Inka): 9 kilometers (5.7miles); via Rumira and Tired Stones (Piedras Cansadas): 10 kilometers (6.3miles) To Pinkuylluna via Muñaypata: 5 kilometers (3.2 miles) To Willoc via Marcacocha: 19 kilometers (11.9 miles) To Pachar via Choqana: 8 kilometers (5 miles); via Inca Pintayoc: 8 kilometers (5 miles). Updated: Dec 04, 2008.

KB Tours

What to do in Ollantaytambo—apart from ascending the monumental Inca Pueblo steps? How about rafting, horseback riding, mountain-biking, and even simple hiking? KB Tours will organize any of the above, with excursions offered at beginning, intermediate and advanced levels, both for individuals and groups. KB Tours can take you for a ride through the Class II and Class III rapids of the Urubamba River, or on bicycle to the famous Inca quarries above the Sacred Valley or the salt mines of Maras. Tours range from a half-day price of $25 to a four-day price of $189. Plaza de Armas. Tel: 51-84-204-133, 51-84-994-7608, E-mail: kbtours_2@hotmail.com. Updated: Jul 24, 2007.

Ollantaytambo Lodging

Despite its relatively small size, Ollantaytambo boasts a variety of accommodation options. In particular, the city has plenty of good budget options for backpackers taking the train to Machu Picchu. Ollantaytambo hostels are also a good option, and many exist in the area, however make sure you ask to see the room before you buy it. If you're really

SACRED VALLEY

penny-pinching, then head towards the San Isidro neighborhood, where many families have turned their homes into hostel rooms ($3-5 per person). You can reach this hostel haven by following the main road through town and heading left towards the ruins. Hotels in Ollantaytambo are going to be pricier, but offer relaxing river-side locations after the stresses of a hike up to Machu Picchu or a stint in Cusco. Hotel Pakaritampu (starting around US$100.00) is probably the swankiest option, but it makes up for it in convenient location and alpacas! Updated: Jul 01, 2010.

Hostal El Bosque

This hostel is about a two-minute walk from the train station. It has small and comfortable rooms with private bathrooms and hot water. The inviting courtyard and gardens are a great place to relax. Av.Ferrocarril s/n (two minutes from the train station). Tel/Fax: 51-84-204-148, E-mail: reservas@elbosqueollantaytambo.com, URL: www.elbosqueollantaytambo.com. Updated: Jun 17, 2009.

Hospedaje Pumamarka

(ROOMS: $3-5) With only four rooms in an old rustic building, the Hospedaje Pumamarka evokes a pioneer spirit of a romantic past. In terms of budget accommodation, if you are looking for cheap but quality, this is one of the better deals in Ollantaytambo. Prices for a single room vary from $3-5 depending on the season, and the rooms are top-notch: spacious, comfortable and artfully fashioned, with great window views of the looming green Sacred Valley mountains. One caution: this really is an old building, and the second floor hallway and entrance have low-ceiling. The hotel has Internet service, a telephone boxes for making international calls, and a small bookstore. The owners also rent horses, arrange tours and offer money exchange services. Patecalle and Plaza de Armas. Tel: 51-84-204-128. Updated: Jan 19, 2010.

Las Portadas

(ROOMS: $3.50-14) Don't panic when you step through the gate at Las Portadas and find yourself in an ultra cozy courtyard surrounded by only a handful of rooms. The path winds through the flowered courtyard and opens up into a second, much more spacious communal outdoor area and another two-story building with plenty of rooms. The rooms differ in character, some with squeaky wooden floors and others with smooth tile,

so check out a few to find one that suits your needs. Electric showers provide hot water. There is also a garage and camping facilities on the premises. Calle Principal s/n. Tel: 51-84-204-008. Updated: Jul 24, 2007.

Hostal La Ñusta

(ROOMS: $4.50-9) At Hostal La Ñusta dark, basic rooms give way to spectacular views of nearby mountains and ruins. Among the hotels in Ollantaytambo, this is one of the friendliest. Always ready to extend a hospitable hand to guests, owner Rubén Ponce is also a fountain of knowledge about the town's ruins. For those prepared to explore the area on horseback, you can also rent horses here for $10 per day. Carretera Ocobamba. Tel: 51-84-204-035. Updated: May 18, 2009.

Hostal Ollanta

(ROOMS $4.50-9) Offering simple, clean rooms with wood floors, Hostel Ollanta is great for anyone on a budget. The shared bathrooms are brand new, and have hot water. Plaza de Armas. Tel: 51-84-204-116. Updated: May 18, 2009.

K'antuyoc

(ROOMS: $7-20) Perched on a very slender piece of land between the road and the river, K'antuyoc may be as close to sleeping in a grove of eucalyptus as it gets without actually swinging from a hammock. From the café downstairs (which boasts a menu with seven different flavors of pancakes, typical plates like saltado de lomo, chicken and trout, and a healthy list of soups, salads and pastas), you can nearly reach out and touch the river as it slides narrowly between tree trunks. The rooms are few, but well kept by the friendly proprietor, and all have hot water. Avenida Ferrocarril s/n. Tel: 51-84-204-147 / 994-7005. Updated: Jul 24, 2007.

Hotel Munay Tika

(ROOMS $9.25-38) From the front courtyard of Hotel Munay Tika you can hear the hum of the river as it tumbles down from Inca ruins and makes its way into the Río Urubamba. If the lull of babbling brook doesn't suit your fancy, weave around the bright yellow and red buildings and cozy up with your book among the flowers and silence in the back courtyard. It is run by a family who has taken great care to manicure the inside of the accommodation as well as the outside. The rooms are tidy, colorful and each has a private bath with hot water. The hotel also offers Internet service, national and international calling, and room service.

And because it's located on the road connecting the rail station and town, the only noise you're likely to contend with is that of the river. Avenida Ferrocarril 118. Tel: 51-84-204-111, E-mail: reserves@munaytika.com, URL: www. munaytika.com. Updated: Dec 04, 2008.

Hostal Las Orquídeas

(ROOMS $10-20) Small, but comfortable rooms with a private bath and hot water ensure that any visit to Hostal Las Orquídeas will be a restful one. Of the hotels in Ollantaytambo, this is definitely one of the coziest. The inviting courtyard and gardens are a great place to relax, and if you're hungry individual meals can be ordered. Estación s/n. Tel: 51-84-204-032 . Updated: Jul 24, 2007.

Hospedaje Los Andenes

(ROOMS: $10-20) This minor hostel offers inexpensive but pleasant rooms that start at $10 for an individual, $20 for two. All rooms come with bathrooms and hot running water. The rooms themselves are spacious, clean, comfortable and attractive for this price range, with colorful, heavy wool blankets for warmth once night falls. The owners, Félix Calla and María Palomino, will also fix you breakfast for an additional $3. They are also proprietors of a folk art and wool product shop. As with so many old frontier buildings now serving as hostels, even though ceilings in individual rooms are high, hallways and entrances are low, so the vertically advantaged should be careful. Calle Ventiderio. Tel: 51-84-204-095. Updated: Dec 04, 2008.

Andean Moon

(ROOMS: $20-40) Set back from the main square, up one of Ollantaytambo's pretty cobblestone streets, the Andean Moon is a pleasant place to crash for a day or two. The owner is friendly and accommodating, and you can bargain with her during the low season for a reduced rate. Rooms are a generous size and have beamed ceilings, bare wooden floors and are tastefully adorned with the works of local artists. Head up the spiral staircase to the roof, from where you have a first class view of the fortress. Later, take a dip in the Jacuzzi—though it will set you back a bit at $25 for a group of four people. This place has 24-hour hot water and the prices include a simple continental breakfast. Calle del Medio s/n. Tel: 51-84-246-398, Cel: 51-84-960-5360, E-mail: info@andeanmoonhostal.com, URL: www.andeanmoonhostal.com. Updated: Feb 17, 2010.

Apu Lodge

(ROOMS: $20-40) This hotel has amazing views of the peaceful old Inca town and of the fortress, the main ruins in Ollantaytambo, and great service, provided by its British owner and her local husband and staff. Apu Lodge is very quiet and clean, and has spacious gardens. It is a great place to relax before and after visiting Machu Picchu, and is a good base for visits to the Sacred Valley. Lari Calle s/n. Tel: 51-84-797-162. URL: www.apulodge.com. Updated: Jan 18, 2010.

V!VA ONLINE REVIEW
APU LODGE

Watching either the sunrise or sunset from this location is a treat indeed. The couple, Arturo and Louise, are gems and are very very hospitable
May 10, 2009

El Albergue

(ROOMS: $38-94) This peaceful establishment is perfect for travelers seeking a place to kick back and relax. Owned by Wendy Weeks, a painter from Seattle, the hotel has spacious whitewashed rooms tastefully adorned with wooden tables and beds. The inviting rooms are accented by a tranquil atmosphere and graceful decorations that include local weavings, Wendy's paintings and vases blossoming with flowers. Grab a seat on the wood balcony overlooking the lively garden and thumb through your favorite book, or try a wood-fired, eucalyptus steam sauna. In the morning, enjoy homemade French toast and coffee, and afterwards head to the hotel's shop where you can browse through an interesting collection of books, weavings, Ekeko dolls and Waq'ullu dance masks. Tel: 51-84-204-014 /049, E-mail: albergue@rumbosperu.com, reservations@elalbergue.com, URL: www.elalbergue.com. Updated: Dec 04, 2008.

Hostal Sauce

(ROOMS: $69-105) An upscale establishment offering cozy, sun-filled rooms overlooking the Ollantaytambo ruins, Hostal Sauce invites visitors to relax in its tranquil atmosphere. Of the places to stay in Ollantaytambo, this one offers some of the most spectacular views of Inca ruins. On cold nights, snuggle into the comfy couches and warm yourself in front of the central fireplace. When your tummy starts to grumble, head over to the hotel's restaurant and choose from a menu of delicious salads, meats and pastas. Calle Ventiderio 248. Tel: 51-84-204-044, E-mail: hostalsauce@viabcp.com, URL: www.hostalsauce.com.pe. Updated: Jul 24, 2007.

Hotel Pakaritampu

(ROOMS $100-135) Life in Ollantaytambo doesn't get much swankier or much more relaxing than Hotel Pakaritampu. Located on Avenida Ferrocarril, which links the railroad station with the city center, the country grounds at Hotel Pakaritampu quickly whisk away any residual city stress after a stint in Cusco. The hotel campus itself is a rambling ranch-style hotel that captures only the most scenic views of the valley below and ruins above.

In addition to plenty of green space to wander, Hotel Pakaritampu has indoor and outdoor dining areas, a TV room, a library and reading room, and alpacas on site. The rooms are clustered in pairs throughout several buildings, and both inside and out, accommodations better resemble comfortable homes rather than temporary lodgings. All rooms include private baths with hot water, and the hotel provides telephones for international calls, safety deposit boxes, laundry services and Internet access. Avenida Ferrocarril s/n. Tel: 51-84-204-020, 204-104. URL: www.pakaritampu.com. Updated: Dec 04, 2008.

Ollantaytambo Restaurants

Ollantaytambo has a number of great eateries, each catering to a variety of budgets, palates and styles. From sophisticated modern cafés to popular gringo dives and Peruvian-style restaurants, Ollantaytambo has it all. The majority of cafés are centered near the main plaza, which is also a great place to scout out for vegetarian options. For the truly adventurous, drop by any one of the private houses displaying a red plastic bag on a pole outside the door. Here you can try the local chicha maize beer, and mingle with the lively and ever-hospitable local hosts. Updated: Dec 04, 2008.

Tayta Pizzeria-Trattoria

Tayta Pizzeria-Trattoria has a stunning view of the Ollantaytambo fortress. This artsy dive specializes in homemade wood-oven pizzas and Italian pasta. Cheap and good, the menu also includes an array of appetizers and a wide wine selection, including a tasty pisco

sour among many other cocktails, and of course beers are on hand as well. The right place for a perfect cup of Italian espresso.

Jazz and local music . 10:00 a.m.-9:00 p.m Av. Ferrocarril s/n, Ollantaytambo. Tel: 51-84-204-114. E-mail: reservas-tayta@hotmail.com. Updated: Dec 04,2008.

Sonccollay Restaurante Café Bar Pizzeria

(ENTREES: $4-12) Thanks to its giant heart-shaped sign, Sonccollay attracts a fair amount of attention from visitors, despite its faraway corner location in the Plaza Mayor. A smattering of outdoor tables creates a modest patio, which unfortunately sits in the street proper and forces diners to contend with the noise and pollution of large tour buses as they pass within inches. Inside service may not allow for the same fantastic views of the surrounding ruins, as the atmosphere is severely no frills, but the family who runs the café is eager to chat up the clientele. The menu is well priced and offers the standard fare from Peruvian typical dishes to gringo favorites pizza, pasta, burgers, and sandwiches, in addition to breakfast choices like omelets and pancakes. If you have your backpack in tow, Sonccollay offers free backpack storage while you gallivant on a day's excursion, which you can book through the restaurant as well. Updated: Jul 24, 2007.

Mayupata

(ENTREES: $3-8) For a taste of home, make your way to restaurant Mayupata, which specializes in international treats like thin-crust pizzas and massive burgers smothered in cheese. On cold nights the inviting central fireplace is a popular spot to gather for drinks, and on any night you can chill out and enjoy the relaxing atmosphere paired with spectacular river views and great food. Jirón Convención s/n (across from bridge, on the way towards the ruins). Tel: 51-84-204-009. Updated: Dec 04, 2008.

Alcázar

A popular joint for breakfast and lunch, Alcázar is praised for its simple, cheap breakfasts and mouth-watering vegetarian lunch options. Try the French toast or honey-and-banana-pancakes, which can be washed down with one of their delicious fresh juices. This is a great place to grab a snack or midday meal if you're in a rush to head off and explore the city. Or,

SACRED VALLEY

if you've got some time to sit and relax, savor a glass of wine while you contemplate a menu of vegetarian dishes, spaghetti, steak fillet, chicken, ham, sausages and dessert. Calle del Medio (one block from main square). Tel: 51-84-204-034. Updated: Jul 24, 2007.

Restaurant Miranda

(ENTREES: $2-3) Compared to the number of touristy restaurants in Ollantaytambo, Restaurant Miranda has a refreshingly local feel. Early risers can enjoy a $2 breakfast of fresh juice, eggs, tamal and coffee, and those who prefer a little more sleep a bit later can head here for a cheap but filling $3 lunch. Even vegetarians can find something to munch on here, and owner Alicia Miranda is always eager to please. Near Patacancha bridge, between the plazas. Tel: 51-84-204-097. Updated: Dec 04, 2008.

Il Capuccino

For a little more sophistication, Il Capuccino is the ideal place to relax, sip on a drink and sink into a pleasant conversation. In addition to excellent coffee, the café also has a selection of fine wines, tempting desserts and a book exchange. Stop by in the morning and prepare for a day of Andean adventure by fueling up with a good American-style breakfast. Ventiderio s/n. Updated: Jul 24, 2007.

Kusicoyllor Café-Bar

(ENTREES $5-8) International treats and Peruvian delicacies collide at Kusicoyllor Café-Bar, where you can choose from a diverse menu of novo-Andean dishes, homemade croissants, real espresso and homemade ice cream (the only in Ollantaytambo). The restaurant also has a fairly extensive selection of fine wines. With great food, friendly service and a full bar, this place has all the ingredients for a fantastic night out. Plaza Araccama s/n. Tel: 51-84-204-114. Updated: Dec 04, 2008.

Inka Traveler

The Inka Traveler bar has a narrow winding staircase, decked out in stained wood bark, which you carefully walk up in order to access the restaurant itself, an efficient provider of well-made and inexpensive items from spaghetti and pancakes, to fried chicken and alpaca cutlets. Owner John Walter Serrano opens his restaurant at 6:00 a.m., one of the few to do so in Ollantaytambo,

making pancakes and other carb-rich items for visiting early risers eager to get a head start on their climb up Machu Picchu. You can enjoy your meals with a view of the world-famous Ollantaytambo Fortress. Calle Ventidiero 2nd floor. Tel: 51-84-967-5995. Updated: Jul 24, 2007.

Ollantay Bar and Restaurant

(ENTREES: $3-6) It calls itself a pizzeria, café, and restaurant, and what it claims is pretty much what you get. The menu includes pasta, soup, salad, steak, chicken, wines, lots of trout dishes, sandwiches, fruit juices, coffees and wines. Meals are generally in the $3-6 price range, and the locals of Ollantaytambo prove they can prepare such items as well as anyone else. It deserves kudos for the Old Spanish West atmosphere, especially in the brighter second floor. The restaurant itself is open from 7 a.m. to 10 p.m. every day. With a capacity for 70, groups are welcome. Discounts are available for members of the South American Explorers club. Plaza de Armas (east side). Tel: 51-84-204-001, E-mail: ollantay@ollantaytambo.org, URL: www.ollantaytambo.org. Updated: Dec 04, 2008.

Quechua Blues Bar Cafe

More of a bar than a restaurant (though you can get international food here), the Blues Bar Cafe is great for sinking a beer early evening after most of the tourists have left town. Their marketing materials boast, "the best view in Ollantaytambo," and they're probably right—the bar looks out over the fortress and has a pleasant, chilled out atmosphere. It is quiet early on, but livens up later with a mixed crowd. Food offered includes burgers and standard international fare. It's a bit on the pricey side, but with the best view in town, what do you expect? Tel: 51-84-204-130, E-mail: ketsaleoat@hotmail.com. Updated: Dec 19, 2007.

Hearts Cafe

Hearts Cafe is becoming something of a backpacker favorite. Set right on the Plaza de Armas, Hearts offers wholefoods in well-sized portions to its patrons. Try the delicious chicken casserole, complete with mashed potatoes and veggies, or stop by to pick up a take-out breakfast before heading to the ruins. What's great about this place is that they donate profits to childrens' projects in the region—while you wait for your food, check out the walls that are adorned with the pictures of the help that the owner has provided to the local region. You can eat well here, knowing that your cash is going to a good cause. 7 a.m.-9 p.m., daily. Plaza de Armas. Tel: 84-204-013, E-mail: hearts.cafe@hotmail.com. URL: www.heartscafe.org. Updated: Dec 04, 2008.

Cactus

This bar has cool decor, great music and atmosphere, friendly service and tasty, good value food including a fixed menu for $3.50 with chicken or veggie option. Pizzas excellent too. Happy Hour prices unbeatable. Open from late afternoon. Great place to hang out. Calle Principal s/n, just off the Plaza de Armas on the way into town (behind Hearts Cafe), Ollantaytambo. Tel: 51-84-797-162, E-mail: cactus at leaplocal.org. Updated: Feb 24, 2009.

V!VA ONLINE REVIEW

CACTUS

Great find...
It is hard to find a place to eat and drink with atmosphere and good prices so close to Machu Picchu but this places fits the bill.
Feb 21,2009

AGUAS CALIENTES

The town below Machu Picchu, Aguas Calientes is the last stop on the train from Cusco. From here, just a few blocks from the train station, you can catch a 20-minute bus up a winding mountain road to the park entrance. To avoid crowds at Machu Picchu, it is recommended to stay one night at Aguas Calientes and taking the bus up to Machu Picchu before the first train arrives in the morning. Aguas Calientes is an unremarkable town, and you won't want to spend more than one night there, but there are a number of international restaurants and tourist-friendly hotels that live off the Machu Picchu crowds. There are some nice hikes in the area with decent bird and butterfly watching. Updated: Sep 29, 2006.

Getting To and Away from Aguas Calientes

There are no buses or roads that go to Aguas Calientes, the stopping-off point to access Machu Picchu—at least not all the way. The closest you can get via bus or taxi is Ollantaytambo, and from there, like everyone

else you have to board a train. For those wanting to board a train directly from-Cusco, there are two options. At the San Pedro Station in Cusco, at the intersection of Cascapara and Santa Clara, PeruRail has two daily departures, a "Vistadome" which leaves at 6:00 am and arrives at Aguas Calientes three-and-a-half hours later, and a "Backpacker" which leaves at 6:15 am and arrives in four hours. The Vistadome at $110 is the luxury trip, includes snacks, beverages, and a sky dome (ergo the name).

The Backpacker, at $75 is the budget trip, but still comfortable. The return trips leave at 3:30 p.m. and 3:55 p.m. respectively. There are also morning departures from Aguas Calientes, beginning at 5:45 am. Schedules are subject to change, however, so one is best advised to purchase ahead. And be prepared to bring cash, credits cards of any sort are not accepted.

Those who can afford it and want four star luxury and convenience can take the new Hiram Bingham Deluxe Train, which departs from the city of Poroy, about 20 minutes north of Cusco. This train leaves at 9:00 a.m. and gets to Aguas Calientes at 12:30 p.m. The train, complete with a bar car, is modeled on the classic Orient Express train of its eponymous owner. The $470 price includes exclusive buses to the ruins of Machu Picchu and guided tours. The trip back includes cocktails and a four-course supper.

Once you are in Aguas Calientes you must head over to the Tourist Information office at their Plaza de Armas, and purchase two things: 1) a three-day access pass to the ruins, priced at $43, and 2) a round-trip bus pass for $12. The bus itself leaves from the Plaza. Updated: Dec 04,2008.

Aguas Calientes Services

The Discovery Internet Café and Snack Bar Communication Company

There are plenty of Internet cafés throughout Aguas Calientes, and this one is slightly more expensive by charging you four solés rather than three an hour, but you more than get your extra $0.33 back. This is the only cybercafé in the area with genuine high-speed access. The computers are all latest models, connected to large flat screen monitors. Furthermore, this is located in a terrific spot, in a corner of the Manco Capac

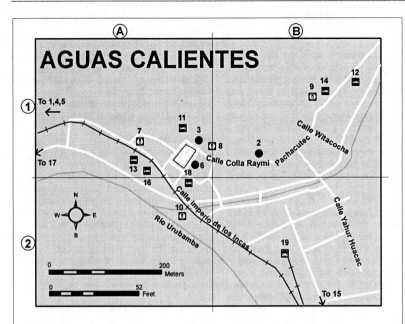

AGUAS CALIENTES

To 1,4,5

To 17

Calle Colla Raymi

Calle Witacocha

Pachacutec

Calle Imperio de los Incas

Río Urubamba

Calle Yahur Huacac

To 15

0   200
Meters

0   52
Feet

Activities ●

1 Aguas Calientes Campgrounds A1
2 Angela´s Laundry B1
3 Iglesia de Aguas Calientes A1
4 Manuel Chávez Ballón
   Site Museum A1
5 Putcusi A1
6 The Discovery Internet
   Café and Snack Bar A1
   ⊕

Eating

7 Aiko Restaurant A1
8 Indi Feliz Restaurant Bistro A1
9 La Cabaña B1
10 Toto´s House A2

Sleeping ▄

11 Gringo Bill´s A1
12 Hostal Ima Sumac B1
13 Hostal Machu Picchu A1
14 Hotel La Cabaña B1
15 Machu Picchu Pueblo
   Hotel B2
16 Presidente Hotel A1
17 Sumaq Machu Picchu
   Hotel A1
18 Viajeros A2

Transportation ▄

19 Train Station B2

plaza, and the cybercafe's wide, spacious windows offer a great view of such. And they actually do serve coffee and snacks besides. International phone call service is also available. 8-11, daily. Manco Capac Plaza, Aguas Calientes Tel: 51-84-211-355 / 040. Updated: Dec 04, 2008.

Angela's Laundry

The little things you don't take into account when you set off to conquer the Inca Trail...such as your dirty laundry. Dubious tourist rates apply here in a popular destination spot like Aguas Calientes as anywhere else, so here is the scoop: Angela's is the cheapest and the best, washing your smelly clothes for $2 a kilo. Down coats are washed for $3, sleeping bags and sneakers for $4, and all guaranteed washed, dried, and returned in four hours or less. Avenida Pachaqutec 150, Aguas Calientes. Tel: 51-84-211-105. Updated: Jul 20, 2007.

SACRED VALLEY

Things To See and Do

Putucusi

This is an excellent walk up the mountain opposite to Machu Picchu that offers breathtaking views of Machu Picchu and the surrounding area. It can be steep and part of it requires going up wooden ladder rungs that get slippery in the wet season and tends to deter many hikers. The scenery is worth the hike though. Getting there: Follow the railroad tracks 250 meters (820 ft.) west of the station and look for the sign identifying the trail. Updated: Jul 17, 2007.

The Thermal Baths of Aguas Calientes

The town of Aguas Calientes derives its name, Hot Waters, from the natural, sulfur-heated waters here, near the base of the world's most famous lost city. They have long been considered to have medicinal properties, and in consideration of their popularity, the local government has set up changing rooms and even a cafeteria so you can enjoy as much leisure time as you need to unwind and relax, especially if you have just completed the Inca Trail as well as explored Machu Picchu. Swimwear, towels and sandals are mandatory (the latter can be rented). The cost is $3 for foreigners. Plaza Marco Capac 110. Tel: 51-84-211-099, E-mail: machupicchuperu@hotmail.com, URL: www.machupicchuperu.net. Updated: Jul 17, 2007.

The Mandor Gardens and Waterfalls

(ADMISSION: $1.20) Machu Picchu is the main attraction in the area, but many visitors, while they are here, stop over and visit the Mandor gardens and waterfalls. Your options for accessing it are: 1) take a cab; 2) walk for two-hours; or 3) take the train that leaves at 12:30 p.m. Entrance to the gardens comes to $1.20, and there are places to eat while you are there. In addition to the waterfall, there is much exotic flora and fauna, including rare birds. Updated: Jul 17, 2007.

Manuel Chávez Ballón Site Museum / Museo de Sitio Manuel Chávez Ballón

Anyone interested in a more thorough appreciation of Machu Picchu should pay a visit to this museum outside Aguas Calientes and named after Peruvian archeologist Manuel Chávez Ballón. Most of Machu Picchu's artifacts were removed by American explorer Hiram Bingham and kept at Yale University. As a result, the focus of the museum is on the discovery of Machu Picchu and the findings therein. There are some remaining artifacts, as well as maps and video presentations. The botanical garden across the way showcases some of Peru's most impressive orchids and other flora. By Puente Ruinas at the base of the footpath to the Machu Picchu Citadel. 1.7 km from Machu Picchu town (Aguas Calientes). 10-4, Monday-Saturday. Getting there: A 25-minute walk from Aguas Calientes, towards Puente Ruinas, the entrance to Machu Picchu. Updated: Nov 04, 2009.

Artesanal Market

In the last hour or two, when you've done Machu Picchu and you're waiting for your train to leave Aguas Calientes, the artesanal market is worth a wander. This covered market is right next to the train station and offers a wide selection of goods, including intricate weavings, jewelry, sweaters, bags and all the other trinkets you'd expect. In addition to souvenirs and gifts, you can pick up snacky foods ahead of your train journey to Ollantaytambo or Cusco. Next to the train station. Updated: Dec 19, 2007.

Aguas Calientes Lodging

Aguas Calientes is the closest stopover to Machu Picchu. Staying the night at one of many Aguas Calientes hostels or hotels will allow you to catch the first bus to the ruins and the last one to return home, thus avoiding the crowds headed back to Cusco hotels. The close proximity to Macchu Picchu has encouraged an onslaught of accommodation options to pop up in Aguas Calientes. Hostels and hotels exist for every budget, but prices are higher in the high season and can be negotiated down in the low season. A night at a budget hostel in Aguas Calientes, such as the Pirwa Hostel Bed and Breakfast, will cost between $7-20 depending on the amount of privacy you request. Camping in Aguas Calientes is also an option. Updated: Jun 29, 2010.

Camping

(CAMP SITE: $5) Aguas Calientes is one of the few towns in Peru that offers its own campgrounds. It is a walk of about 2 kilometers (1.2 mi.) north of Aguas Calientes, on the road leading to the winding trail towards Machu Picchu. The entrance fee is $5 per night and per tent. It features the roaring river, lots of lush green grass, a bathroom and---when the shop is staffed—snacks and drinks for sale. Updated: Dec 04, 2008.

Cusi Q'oyllor Hostal

(ROOMS: $5-30) This simple, efficient hostel offers breakfast, hot water, telephone and fax service, a safety box, luggage storage, a row of computers in the lobby with Internet access, an in-house massage therapist, free tourist information and even pool. Not the swimming variety, but billiards. The rooms start at the low-rate of only $5 for single unit without bathroom during the low-season, and go only as high as $30 for a double-bed unit with a private bathroom during the high season, and when you consider that breakfast comes with the package, it makes this one of the best deals in town. Las Orquídeas Mz 23 Lote 10. Tel: 51-84–211-113, E-mail: rjarc@hotmail.com. Updated: Dec 04, 2008.

Hostal Mandor

(ROOMS: $6-15) This is another small, efficient, clean hostel on the popular and touristy Avenida Pachacútec, perfect for travelers just wanting to be close to everything before and/or after their Machu Picchu ascent. The rooms and bathrooms are small; indeed, it seems that the shower stalls are right over the toilet for those who want an all-in-one experience, but the prices range from a mere $6-$15 depending on season. Towels are an additional $2. Each room features an empty beer bottle amusingly outfitted in miniature folk dress garb. Avenida Pachacútec. Tel: 51-84-435-804, E-mail: hostalmandor_2005@hotmail.com. Updated: Dec 04, 2008.

Hotel Restaurant La Cabaña

Hotel Restaurant La Cabaña is a friendly hotel and restaurant not far from the center of town. It offers a variety of services not always found in a mid-range hotel, such as travel desk, Internet, guides for the ruins and a TV with DVD library. They will also pick you up at the train station if you let them know in advance. The rooms are cozy and tastefully decorated, and the restaurant is quite pleasant and neat. Avenida Pachacútec M-20 - L3. Tel: 51-84-211-048, E-mail: lacabana_mapi@latinmail.com. URL: www.cabanahostal.com. Updated: Jul 17, 2007.

Hostal Varayoc

(ROOMS: $20) Just a stone's throw from the train station and buses to Machu Picchu, the Varayoc has a prime location. Blink and you'll miss it—it can be found right above the Internet cafe. This place is simple and lacks any real character, but is good nonetheless. There is 24-hr hot water, much appreciated after a long hike. It is a bit noisy early evening, but soon quietens down as everyone gets to bed early, ready to hit Machu Picchu before the crowds. Imperio de los Incas av 114. Tel: 51-84-211-334,

Fax: 51-84-211-334, E-mail: hostal.varayoc@hotmail.com, Updated: Dec 19, 2007.

Hostal Ima Sumac

(ROOMS: $20-30) This is one of the mid-range hostels you will find along the tavern-and-tourist filled Avenida Pachacútec, with prices fluctuating between $20 and $30 for single rooms with bathrooms, depending on the season. There are only 14 rooms, all of them spacious, clean and nice to look at, and they are the main raison d'etre for the higher price. If you are looking for a more comfortable stay but don't want to pay four-star hotel rates, this could be an attractive option. However, they don't take credit cards, so a stop at the local ATM is recommended. Breakfast, of course, is included. Avenida Pachacútec. Tel: 51-84-211-021, E-mail: reservas@hostalintiwasi.com URL: www.hostalintiwasi.com. Updated: May 15, 2009.

Viajeros

(ROOMS: $25-45) Cozy, comfortable and safe, Viajeros calls its self a "bed and breakfast" hostel. It is run with the same efficiency as its sister agency, SAS Travel in Cusco. While it provides twin and doubled-sized beds, it's a great place to meet other hikers without feeling like you are at a youth hostel. Perhaps the best part is the helpful staff, who can offer advice and tips about the area. They are used to tired trekkers from Machu Picchu, so they are prepared to serve your hot shower needs (24 hours) and provide some great, hearty cuisine at their on-site café and restaurant. A full breakfast is also included in an overnight stay. Calle Sinchi Roca N 4. Tel: 51-84-211-237, E-mail: info@sastravel.com. Updated: Jul 16, 2007.

Hostal Machu Picchu

(ROOMS $30-35) This hostel, right next door to the Presidente Hotel is managed by the same company, and very much resembles it except that by defining itself as a hostel rather than hotel, and virtually functions as the no-frills version of its more expensive neighbor. The prices—single rooms go for $30 and doubles go for $35—are fixed, regardless of season, and there is no cable television and no bathtubs with Jacuzzi jets, but rather standard shower stalls. Otherwise you are treated to the same breakfast buffet, in the same in-house restaurant, as guests at the Presidente Hotel, and the Hostal Machu Picchu has a back terrace that offers a great opportunity to sit and watch the river roll on. Imperio de los Incas 135. Tel: 51-84-211-212, E-mail: sierrandina@gmail. Updated: May 15, 2009.

Presidente Hotel

(ROOMS: $45-50) The Presidente Hotel has earned two-star expectations, but charges a rate more in common with three-star facilities. Single rooms start at $45 in low-season and $50 in high. However, it justifies its higher price with niceties such as Jacuzzi bathtubs in the rooms. This hotel sits between railroad tracks and the roaring Urubamba River, and offers great views of the steep, moss-covered mountains surrounding Aguas Calientes. Other services such as cable TV and a buffet breakfast are included in the price. This is a popular place to stay for international tourists who want the reassurance of quality that paying more money entails. Imperio de los Incas 135. Tel: 51-84-211-212, E-mail: sierrandina@gmail.com. Updated: May 15, 2009.

Gringo Bill's

(ROOMS: $45-105) Something of an Aguas Calientes institution, Gringo Bill's has been around for at least 20 years. Although it calls itself a hostel, it is actually a bit more upscale and expensive than your typical hostel. The rooms are bright and airy, and some of them feature balconies. The restaurant is spacious. They offer trip packages and bag lunches for those visiting the ruins. Calle Colla Raymi 104. Tel/Fax: 51-84-211-046, E-mail: gringobills@yahoo.com, reservas@gringobills.com, URL: www.gringobills.com. Updated: Aug 04, 2008.

Hotel Apu Majestic

(ROOOMS $70) Hotel Apu Majestic is within a short walking distance from the Peru Rail Station in Aguas Calientes, though so is pretty much everything else. Its other listed amenities include heating, cable TV, room service, laundry (at an extra price), and ecological tours (ditto). And a hairdryer in every bathroom. You can hear the roaring Urubamba River outside your room, which is good or bad depending on your taste, and there is a pervasive smell of mildew throughout the whole facility. Both a modest buffet breakfast and lunch come with the price, which is $70 per person per night. Alameda Hermanos Ayar. Tel: 51-84-211-127, E-mail: reservas@go2machupicchu.com, URL: www.go2machupicchu.com. Updated: Jul 16, 2007.

Machu Picchu Pueblo Hotel

(ROOMS: $187-480) Probably the best luxury option in Aguas Calientes, the expensive but beautiful Machu Picchu Pueblo Hotel is located just on the outskirts of town, about a five-minute walk from the station. The hotel is a complex of guest bungalow cabins and finely tended gardens. A nature lover's paradise, the gardens boast several hundred species of orchids, ferns and other cloud forest foliage. More than 150 species of birds and hummingbirds have been identified on the hotel grounds. The cabins are spacious and comfortable. The Machu Picchu Pueblo Hotel has won numerous awards, including being named one of Travel and Leisure Magazine's top 25 hotels in Latin America. All in all, a very special place; if you can afford it, you won't be disappointed. Machu Picchu Km. 110 Tel: 51-84-211-122, USA: 1-800-442-5042, E-mail: central@inkaterra.com. Updated: Jun 30, 2010.

Sumaq Machu Picchu Hotel

(ROOMS $451-876) Sumaq Machu Picchu Hotel is an exclusive luxury hotel at the base of Machu Picchu. This four-star hotel blends in well with its location: everything from the architecture to the cuisine borrowed from Andean influences. The exterior design aims to blend with the landscape, while interior decorations reflect Inca culture and Peruvian craftsmanship. The resort has 60 ample and luxurious rooms, equipped with alarms, WiFi, mini-bar, mp3 radios, and cable TV.

The Qunuq Restaurant and Suquy Café-Bar, serves exquisite and varied gourmet, novo-Andean, regional and international gastronomy. Menus are elaborated by well-recognized Peruvian Chef Rafael Piqueras. After trekking to Machu Picchu guests can relax in the andquot; Natural Spa Axllaandquot; which employs ancient Inca therapeutic techniques, including saunas, thermal baths, reflexology and massages that use essential oils and local herbs to heal your weary soles. Av. Hermanos Ayar mz 1 lote 3. Tel: 51-1-447-0579 / 628-1082, Fax: 51-1-445-7828, E-mail: reservas@sumaqhotelperu.com, URL: www.sumaqhotelperu.com. Updated: Jan 23, 2009.

Aguas Calientes Restaurants

Just as hotels sprung up to cater to the tourists, so have restaurants. Little cafés serving cheap Peruvian fare dot the railroad tracks, and vegetarian options, meat dishes, buffets and pizza joints line Pachacútec on the way to the hot springs. Again, prices tend to be a little higher due to the town's popularity with tourists traveling to Machu Picchu, so be prepared to pay a little more in some restaurants. Updated: Dec 04, 2008.

Aiko Restaurant

One of several restaurants alongside the railroad tracks on Imperios de los Incas, the advantages of this eatery are: 1) its attractive location; 2) its small seating capacity--36--ensuring relatively quick service; and 3) its low prices, particularly in Aguas Calientes. The selection offered is fairly standard: varieties of spaghetti, roasted chicken, steak and potatoes and trout, along with the expected fruit juices and alcoholic beverages, but the restaurant has a pleasant look, and the cooking is more than competent. Imperio de los Incas 153 Tel: 51-84-211-001. Updated: Dec 04, 2008.

El Charro

This restaurant has style to spare, from the stained and varnished logs holding up its roof to the combination of dyed cotton and black leather tablecloths on its tables to the sheepskins on it its benches, El Charro is fun simply to look at. It offers Peruvian, Mexican and Italian dishes, with fixed-item menús. A three-course meal goes for $5. The à la carte items, such as roast chicken, are a bit more expensive, $8, and the house specialty, roast guinea pig, goes for $15. The restaurant also has three computers set up with high-speed Internet access. El Charro opens at 9 a.m. and serve breakfast as well as lunch and dinner. Imperio de los Incas Tel: 51-84-211-286 E-mail: elcharrosrestaurantmapi@hotmail.com. Updated: Dec 04, 2008.

Toto's House

Toto's House Restaurant is one of the largest restaurants in all of Peru, with a seating capacity for 400. Its main feature is a huge buffet featuring an all-you-can eat cornucopia of just about everything Toto's can prepare. And the price is big too: $18, though they also feature smaller à la carte items, such as sandwiches that go for $3. It sits alongside railroad tracks on the banks of the loud, churning Urubamba River, viewable from all windows, both of which necessitate raising your voice, but such is congruent with the outsized charm of the place. Imperios de los Incas. Tel: 51-84-224-179, Fax: 51-84-234-312, E-mail: reservas@grupointi.com. URL: www.grupointi.com. Updated: Dec 04, 2008.

Indi Feliz Restaurant Bistro

Indi Feliz has acquired a reputation--not just in Aguas Calientes, but in all of Peru--that is nothing less than legendary. In ten years, the restaurant has won eight prizes, including, in two consecutive years, top honors in a national contest as Peruvian Business of the Year. It is the restaurant of choice for dignitaries and celebrities on their way to Machu Picchu. What is all the buzz about? It might be its unique mix of French and native cuisine, courtesy of its French chef, Patrick Vogin, and his Peruvian wife, Cannie Pacheco. Ginger chicken with Caribbean mustard and rum sauce or garlic sauce trout are among the many creative selections offered up for a surprisingly affordable $12. Great coffees, great drinks and great desserts complement the friendly atmosphere and overall good time you will have there. Calle Lloque Yupanqui Lote 4M–12. Tel: 51-84-211-090, E-mail: patvog@caramaic.com. Updated: Dec 04, 2008.

Yakumama II Restaurant

This standard but very decent restaurant on Manco Capac Plaza offers standard Peruvian food along with, of course, the universal favourite, pizza. There is an amusing touch in terms of its look: sitting on every table there are folk-art dolls representing classical stereotypes of rural Peruvians, playing harmonica, resting, et cetera. They are open from 8 a.m. until the last customer goes home and they do accept credit cards. Lunch and dinner items go for about $8, which is about average for Aguas Calientes. Calderón Quispe Saturnino. Tel: 51-84-211-185. Updated: Dec 04, 2008.

El Tunqui

El Tunqui calls itself a tourist restaurant, and fittingly it offers international and Peruvian cuisine, American and continental breakfast, beef, trout and chicken dishes, pizzas, pastas and Mexican food. Dinner and lunch items go for about $9 and along with the free garlic bread, there is a free glass of wine, pisco sour or sangria. El Tunqui also sells paintings, folk art and jewelery. This is a serviceable restaurant, good for those who are hungry and want something that is mid-range in both price and quality. Calle Antisuyo 101. Tel: 51-84-211-030, E-mail: shellny15@hotmail.com. Updated: Dec 04,2008.

Apu Salkantay

This is a cheap and cheerful restaurant offering a three course meal for around $5. Pick between starters such as stuffed avacado, garlic tomatoes and various soups. Then move onto your main where options such as traditional beef or chicken with rice, or your own mini-pizza await you. Save space for dessert - top of the list will surely be the chocolate pancake. The food here is not gourmet, but is filling and tasty enough. Imperio de los Incas Av. (opposite the police station). Updated: Dec 04, 2008.

MACHU PICCHU AND THE INCA TRAIL

Framed by spectacular Andean peaks and surrounded by verdant jungle, Machu Picchu is an one of the world's great examples of the harmony between man and nature. Located high above the clouds, the city's streets, temples and staircases spread across a jungle ridge that eventually plunges more than 300 meters (1,000 ft.) into the treacherous waters of the Río Urubamba below. Everything within this city, from the intricate terraces and delicate gardens to the complex system of aqueducts, was designed to both promote and preserve the sacred relationship between man and nature.

Natural phenomena, like the sun, moon, water and earth, were sacred to the Inca and were the inspiration for much of the city's layout. Besides its awe-inspiring architecture and spiritual atmosphere, perhaps the most enchanting aspect of Machu Picchu is its relative historical ambiguity. Since it was first introduced to the modern world in 1911 by Yale archeologist Hiram Bingham, this mountain city has yet to reveal the purpose of its origins. A number of theories have circulated throughout intellectual circles, including one suggesting that it was a boarding school where the children of those conquered by the Inca were brainwashed.

Despite, or perhaps due to its enigmatic character, Machu Picchu has become one of the single most popular destiniations in South America, drawing nearly 2,000 people per day to its ancient grounds, high above the Sacred Valley. Tours of Machu Picchu can be arranged in Cusco. The ticket office is located next to the entrance to the ruins, where you will also find a left-luggage office, toilets, a shop and a place to hire guides. During the dry season, the ruins are a popular area for sandflies, so take insect repellent and wear long clothes. Updated: Jun 30, 2010.

Inca Trail and Machu Picchu

Environmental Issues

The principle environmental issue facing the Inca Trail and Machu Picchu is the increasingly demanding presence of tourism on the fragile natural environment. Prior to implementation of restrictions on tourism by the Peruvian government in 2001, the Inca Trail and Machu Picchu were getting run-down to a point many feared would soon be beyond repair. The trampling of the shallow dirt, the trail-side deforestation for firewood, human waste and other garbage left on the side of the Inca Trail were major environmental threats facing the famous 'lost city.' It was deteriorating to such a degree that UNESCO repeatedly threatened to add Machu Picchu to the World Heritage in Danger sites.

In 2001 Peru responded by creating a series of restrictions to protect the Inca Trail and began seriously enforcing them in 2003. There is now a limit of about 500 people per day on the trail, including all tourists, guides and porters. This works out to approximately 200 tourists per day. Additionally, all trekkers must be accompanied by a certified guide. The idea is that having guides present with all visitors not only provides employment for many local residents, but also that environmental standards and regulations will be enforced.

All reputable tour agencies promote a 'pack-in, pack-out' policy, meaning that anything taken on the trek will be taken out. Open-fires are prohibited on the trail (deforestation for firewood was out of control), so make sure your company uses gas stoves. Permanent toilets have also been installed to combat the human waste problem.

Before the implementation of the regulations visitors could find bargain-basement tour prices, most often through operators that were skimping on protecting the natural environment that was paying their bills. Prices have increased significantly, but the porters now have a guaranteed daily wage and other standards (maximum carrying weight, sleeping pads, acceptable meals, accident insurance). As the prices have gone up, companies are cutting fewer corners and are able to invest in the preservation and protection of the Inca Trail and Machu Picchu. Many of the critical environmental issues the Trail and Machu Picchu were facing—litter, human waste, literal pounding of the trail—have been curbed or eliminated.

So don't sigh and lament about the good ole days when hiking the Inca Trail could be done for under $200. Instead, relish the fact you are contributing to environmentally responsible, sustainable tourism in Peru and helping provide a decent, living wage for those who guide you on your trek. Updated: Jul 17, 2007.

The Inca Trail

Characterized by rugged ascents boasting magnificent views of Andean scenery and trails that wind their way through the cloud forest and past ancient archaeological sites, the Inca Trail is perhaps the most eminent of South American experiences.

While other trails in the Sacred Valley area and around Cusco offer the same spectacular scenery, this is the only Inca trail that leads to the awesome gates of Machu Picchu, the ultimate climax to any trekking experience. This world-famous trail is part of the Sanctuario Histórico de Machu Picchu, an area of over 32,000 hectares set aside by the Peruvian state to protect the host of flora and fauna that flourish here. In 2001, in an attempt to restrict the number of hikers and damage to the trail, the Peruvian government established new regulations requiring all Inca Trail hikers to be accompanied by a licensed guide.

Currently, a maximum of 500 hikers are allowed on the trail per day. Recently, regulations involved in obtaining an Inca Trail trekking permit have changed. Please note: In order to secure your permit you must now provide your passport information no later than 90 days before your departure. So plan ahead, book early and avoid added stress.

Tours can be arranged through a number of tour companies in Cusco, and most cost between $200 and $300, which includes the entrance fee ($50 for adults, $25 for students and free for children under 11), transportation to and from the trail, an English-speaking guide, tents, mattress, three daily meals and porters who carry group gear.

For about $50 extra/trip a personal porter can be hired to carry your gear. If you'e inclined (and it's recommended) you can tip your porters and guides. Independent travelers will generally be placed with a mixed group of travelers, and groups tend to be between 12 and 16 people. For premium-class service, groups are generally smaller and an upgrade on the return train is included. Prices for these treks range from $275 to $650 per person.

Be cautious if the price is under $180, as the company may be cutting corners, or not adhering to the strict environmental regulations recently imposed. Only purchase your ticket from officially licensed agencies, and be sure to make your payments at the physical tour agency office. Direct any questions you may have regarding a tour company to the main tourism office in Cusco. You can save a little money by arranging your own transport back to Ollantaytambo, either for the last day of your tour, or by staying an extra night in Aguas Calientes and taking the early morning train, then catching a bus back to Cusco.

If you do take the train back to Cusco after your tour, make sure your return ticket has your name on it for the tourist train, or you will have to pay for any changes. Be sure to inquire if the guide for the Inca Trail and Machu Picchu will be the same, as some companies save money by sending a less experienced guide on the trail and hiring a new, certified guide at Machu Picchu. Also, if you have any concerns regarding the working conditions of the porters, contact Porteadores Inka Nan, Dept. 4 Choquechaca 188, Cusco, Telephone: 246829.

When To Go

The single most important factor in planning your Inca Trail experience is making sure you give yourself plenty of time to acclimatize to the high altitude before attempting the physically demanding trail. The best way to avoid soroche, or altitude sickness, is to spend a few days in the Sacred Valley area, which is slightly lower in elevation. The first two days of the climb involve arduous ascents, so do not attempt them if you're feeling unwell.

In most cases, four days will ensure a comfortable journey, and you should allow an extra day to see Machu Picchu after recovering from the hike. Usually the best month for trekking the Inca trail is May, when the weather is fine and skies are clear. From June to September, the trail is a busy stretch of mountainside, with people from all over the world flocking to its rugged peaks and lush valleys. During the rainy season, from October to April, it is less busy but for obvious reasons, slightly wetter. Note: the trail is closed every February for cleaning and repair.

For a truly unique experience on the Inca Trail, try to depart two to three days before a full moon. According to the locals, the weather is best at this time and at night the Andean skyline is fully illuminated by the moonlight.

What to Bring

The trail involves rugged ascents and unpredictable mountain weather, so it is imperative that you be prepared with the proper equipment. Be sure to pack strong footwear, rain gear and warm clothing, in addition to food, water (no plastic water bottles are allowed, canteens only), water purification, insect repellent, plastic bags, a flashlight, durable sleeping bag, tent and stove.

What to Expect

The popular four day trek will take you along the ancient stone Inca highway, past dozens of archaeological sights, rushing rivers and uncountable views of the cloud forest and eye-captivating mountain scenery. Along this 43-kilometer (27 mi.) trek, you will tackle three formidable mountain passes and cruise to a maximum altitude of 4,200 meters (13,800 ft.). The trek begins at Qorihuayrachina near Ollantaytambo, often referred to as Km. 88 of the Cusco railway.

Another, slightly less intense version of the classic four-day trek is also growing in popularity. The two-day version, referred to as the Camino Sagrado del Inca, or "Sacred Trail," is a good alternative for time-pressed or fitness-deficient individuals. Along this journey you'll reach a maximum altitude of only 2,750 meters (9,000 ft.), which involve less arduous ascents, yet still leads to the wondrous mountain-mecca, Machu Picchu.

This mini-trek begins at Km. 104, just 14 kilometers (9 mi.) away from the ruins, and groups spend the night near the ruins of Wiñay Wayna before departing at sunrise for the gates of Machu Picchu. However, if you're looking for divine mountain scenery, then the four-day trek is your best bet, as most of the best views and ruins are not included in the

two-day tour. Updated: Jul 17, 2007.

4-Day Inca Trail Trek

To give you a better sense of what the four-day trek involves, we've put together a brief day-by-day summary of the trip.

DAY 1

Total Distance: 10 to 11 kilometers (6-7 mi.)
Arrive by train from Cusco, getting off at Km. 88, or by bus at Km. 82. From the station, cross the footbridge spanning the Río Urubamba and begin the gentle ascent up to the Inca ruins of Llactapata, where Bingham and his team first camped on their way to Machu Picchu. The trail then slopes upwards, following the Río Cusichaca, until it reaches Huayllabamba. To reach this small village, the only one along the trail that is still inhabited, it's about a two to three-hour climb. This is a good place to hire horses or mules, if you're so inclined. Most groups spend the night here, in preparation for the arduous journey up to the aptly named Dead Woman's Pass.

DAY 2

Total Distance: 11 kilometers (7 mi.)
Although equal to the first day in terms of distance, Day 2 is perhaps the most difficult day of the trip. From Huayllabamba, you're in for a steep, one-hour climb to the ruins of Llullucharoc (3,800 meters / 12,500 feet). Catch your breath and prepare for another 90-minute to 2-hour steep climb through the cloud forest to Llulluchapampa, an isolated village situated in a flat mountain meadow. Spectacular views of the valley below will keep your mind off the steep ascent. From Llulluchapampa make your way up the quad-killing climb towards Abra de Huarmihuañusca (Dead Woman's Pass), the first pass and highest point of the trek (4,200 meters / 13,800 feet). The 2 ½ hour climb is a mental and physical challenge, subjecting trekkers to a killer sun on the way up, and thin air and bitterly cold winds at the summit. Don't be surprised if snow or freezing rain greets you at the summit. Inevitably, however, the mind-blowing views will distract you from the body-numbing cold and physically demanding ascent. Do make sure that you shelter yourself from the wind while you check out the valley below.

Between Huayllamba and Huarmihuañusca there are three places to camp, if you're in need of a rest. The most popular among these is Three White Stones. From the summit the trail descends sharply via stone steps into Pacamayo Valley (3,600 meters). This area also offers excellent camping, and if you're lucky, you can catch a glimpse of the ever-playful spectacled bears.

DAY 3

Total Distance: 15 kilometers (9 mi.)
About an hour's trek towards the next pass, Abra de Runkuracay, you'll come across the intriguing ruins of Runcuracay. The name means "basket shaped" and is an appropriate title for the circular ruins unique among those on the trail. From the ruins it's about a 45-minute to one-hour steep climb to the second pass (3,900 meters / 12,800 feet). Just over the summit is another camp site, where you'll encounter magnificent views of the Vilcabamba mountain range. Follow the trail through a naturally formed tunnel and up a spectacular stone staircase to the ruins of Sayacmarca (3,500 meters / 11,500 feet). These beautiful ruins include ritual baths and terrace viewpoints overlooking the Aobamba Valley. It is believed that this tranquil area was once a resting spot for ancient travelers traversing the Inca Trail. You can camp near the remains of an aqueduct that once supplied water to the ancient settlement.

From Sayacmarca the trail descends via a remarkably well-preserved Inca footpath into thick cloud forest where you'll be astounded by exotic flora like orchids and bromeliads, and unique bird species. The trail winds its way towards Conchamarca, another rest stop for the weary. Pass through another Inca tunnel and follow the path up a gentle two-hour climb towards the third pass and the ruins of Phuyupatamarca (3,800 meters / 12,500 feet). This section of trail, whose name translates to "Town Above the Clouds," offers spectacular views of the Urubamba valley in one direction and in the other a grand view of the snow-covered peaks of Salcantay (Wild Mountain). The ruins include six small baths that, during the wet season, are teeming with constantly running fresh water.

There is an excellent place to camp here, where you may even catch a glimpse of wild deer feeding. Also, keep an eye out for the fantastic view of Machu Picchu peak. From the ruins the trail forks and you have two options. Follow the knee-buckling 2,250 step stone staircase to the terraces of Intipata, or head towards the stunning ruins of Wiñay Wayna. Only discovered in 1941, the ruins of this ancient citadel, named "Forever Young,"

for the perpetually blossoming orchids that flourish here, include spectacular stone agricultural terraces and ritual baths. A nearby hostel offers weary wanderers hot showers, food and well deserved beer. Be aware, however, that during peak season this hostel area can appear more like a tourist circus than peaceful mountain retreat.

DAY 4

Total Distance: 7 kilometers (4 mi.)
The final leg of this journey is all about getting to Intipunku (Sun Gate) and Machu Picchu. Be prepared for an early rise, as most groups depart camp at 4 a.m. to arrive at the ruins by 6:30 a.m. This climatic journey involves a 60 to 90-minute trek along narrow Inca stone paths, and a final push up a 50-step, nearly vertical climb to the ruins of Intipunku. The descent to Machu Picchu takes about 45 minutes. Upon reaching the ruins, trekkers must deposit their packs at the entrance gate and get their entrance passes stamped. From here you can bask in the glory of having completed the rugged journey to one of the world's greatest attractions. Updated: Aug 07, 2007

Getting There

There are only two ways to reach Machu Picchu: train and the Inca Trail. If hiking isn't your style, you can grab a train from Cusco (four hours), Urubamba (two hours and ten minutes) or Ollantaytambo (one hour and 15 minutes). The train will take you to Machu Picchu Pueblo station (located in Aguas Calientes), where you can then catch a bus to the ruins.

If you are taking the train directly from Cusco, go to the San Pedro Station at the intersection of Cascapara and Santa Clara. PeruRail has two daily departures, a Vistadome, which leaves at 6:00 a.m. and arrives at Aguas Calientes three-and-a-half hours later, and a Backpacker, which leaves at 6:15 a.m. and arrives in four hours. The Vistadome at $110 is the luxury trip, and includes snacks, beverages and a sky dome (ergo the name). The Backpacker, at $75 is the budget trip, but still comfortable. The return trips leave at 3:30 p.m. and 3:55 p.m. respectively. There are also morning departures from Aguas Calientes, beginning at 5:45 a.m. Schedules are subject to change, however, so you are best advised to purchase ahead. And be prepared to bring cash--credits cards of any sort are not accepted.
Those who can afford it and want four-star

Inca Trail Porters

You've waited so long to trek these rugged 43 kilometers (27 mi) to that Inca Holy Grail, Machu Picchu. But after two days, your feel muscles you never knew existed, another blister is welling up. As you momentarily rest on a rock, gasping for breath in this rarefied air, you see one of the porters striding smoothly by you, on his way to set up this night's camp for you and the others. Almost like The Motorcycle Diaries.

The lot of the porter changed with new regulations instituted in 2002. Before, it was not uncommon for one to carry 45 kilos (100 lbs.), sleep under mere plastic and a blanket, receive the trekkers' leftovers or cook for himself and be paid only four dollars per day. Frequently porters would have to cut firewood to keep warm and eat, thus aumenting deforestation.

Now the load limit is 25 kilograms (50 lbs.) and the minimum wage is $12.50 per day. Unfortunately, some tour companies are still getting around the new regulations by paying 5.30 per day (to be able to offer travelers a bargain price), and making trekkers carry their own packs across the weigh-in spot, then shifting the weight to the porters or denying porters their personal allowance.

Porters are the work horses of the trek—but they should not be treated that way. As consumers, we have the responsibility to ensure porters' fair treatment. How can you help to make sure the regulations are followed?

• Familiarize yourself with the regulations of the Inka Trail; see http://www.andeantravelweb.com/peru/treks/incatrail_regulations.html
• Ask the tour company how much porters are paid, and if they are provided with food

and proper camping equipment. Make clear your concern for the porters' welfare.
• If don't like the answers, look for a different company or hire your own porter. You'll be supporting the local economy by providing employment.
• Ask the company precisely what equipment you are expected to take (sleeping bag, etc.—and, of course, warm clothing, canteen, etc.). Leave all unnecessary items stowed at your hostel. Don't unnecessarily weigh down the porter.
• During the trip, remember common courtesies. Learn a little Quechua. Thank them. Share your coca leaves.
• Talk with them about their lives and culture. Ask them to sing. Share photos of your family or homeland with them.
• Pool tips for the porters with other travellers; $7-9 total per porter is fair. If you feel like giving a higher tip, donate money to projects supporting porters rights or their communities.

Mistreatment of porters should not be shrugged off with "Well, that is the way things are in these countries."
• File complaints with MINCETUR (Ministerio de Comercio Exterior y Turismo), Avenida de la Cultura 734, 3rd floor; Tel: 51-84-241-508, Fax: 51-84-223-761, E-mail: webmaster@mincetur.gob.pe, URL: www.direcetur-cusco.gob.pe; 7:30 a.m.-12:45 p.m., 2:15-4:30 p.m.
• If you are a member, inform the South American Explorers Club.
• Drop line to us here at Viva Travel Guides, or make a posting on our site to share your experience with others.

To learn more about the porters' life, read the BBC's Inca Trail Porter Photo Journal (americas_inca_trail_porter). The Inka Porter Project (http://www.peruweb.org/porters) has information about porters' rights. Updated: Aug 08, 2007.

luxury and convenience can take the new Hiram Bingham Deluxe Train, which departs from the city of Poroy, about 20 minutes north of Cusco. This train leaves at 9 a.m. and gets to Aguas Calientes at 12:30 p.m. The train, complete with a bar car,

is modeled on the classic Orient Express train. The $470 price includes exclusive buses to the ruins of Machu Picchu and guided tours. The trip back includes cocktails and a four-course supper.

Once you are in Aguas Calientes you must head over to the Tourist Information Office at their Plaza de Armas, and purchase two things: 1) a three-day access pass to the ruins, priced at $43, and 2) a round-trip bus pass for $12. The bus itself leaves from the Plaza. Again, no credit cards are accepted, but there are ATMs in the area.

It is possible to walk to the ruins from the train station, but it takes about one to one and a half hours depending on your fitness level, and whether you choose to take the steeper, more direct path, or the roundabout paved road.

Recently, Cusco regional president Hugo Gonzalez proposed raising the entrance fee to $100 for foreigners, a measure which has been opposed by Peru's tourism minister, Mercedes Araoz. Meanwhile, Araoz is investigating the possibility of working with the private sector in constructing cable cars to provide more expedient access to Machu Picchu, while recently the mayor of a neighbor pueblo, Santa Teresa, approved the construction of a small bridge crossing over the Vilcanota River, as a means of increasing tourism to the village by providing alternative access to Machu Picchu. Critics have complained that the bridge will make regulation of access more difficult, increasing the possibility of environmental damage, as well as facilitating drug trafficking. Updated: Aug 09, 2007.

Machu Picchu History

In July, 1911, Yale archaeologist Hiram Bingham was exploring the area near Cusco, searching for the lost city of Vilcabamba, the final stronghold of the Inca before they were defeated by the Spanish. Acting on a tip from local guides, he climbed a misty, rainy hill and made a marvelous discovery: Machu Picchu, which means Old Mountain, the ancient retreat of the royal Incas.

Following several years of exploration and excavation (and the borrowing of countless Inca artifacts by Bingham on behalf of Yale University), the mysteries surrounding Machu Picchu were cleared up. It is believed that Machu Picchu was a small city that served as an observatory, religious center and sort of vacation home for the royal Inca, who governed their empire from relatively nearby Cusco. Archaeologists believe the site was built about 1440, and was sparsely inhabited until the Spanish conquest in the

1530s, when it was abandoned and forgotten by all except a few locals.

In 1913, the National Geographic Society published a special edition about Machu Picchu, bringing it worldwide renown. It captured the imagination of people around the globe, and has since been one of the most sought-after visitor destinations in the world. Recently, Machu Picchu has been in the news, as Peru has been pressuring Yale University to return hundreds of artifacts taken from the site during Bingham's initial excavations. Updated: Oct 21, 2009.

Photo by: Anthea Okereke

Machu Picchu Activities

Despite the peace and tranquility conjured up by its astounding natural beauty, Machu Picchu is a fervently protected place, inhabited by numerous whistle-blowing guards who noisily herd unsuspecting travelers who have strayed from the main path. To explore the ruins in peace, the best option is to hire a guide or to buy a map and stick to the specified routes. Guides are available on the site, and often prove to be extremely knowledgeable.

For a spectacular experience, obtain permission from the Instituto Nacional de Cultura in Cusco to enter the ruins before 6 a.m. and watch the sunrise over the Andes. From the ticket booth, you'll enter the south side of Machu Picchu through the Guard's Quarters, now the modern-day entrance. From here, there are a number of ways to explore the ruins, all of which offer striking views of intricate Inca architecture, Andean mountains and terraced staircases. A few of the can't-miss Machu Picchu attractions include the Temple of the Sun, Royal Tomb, Three-Windowed Temple, Chamber of the Princess, Principal Temple, Intihuatana, Huayna Picchu, Temple of the Moon and Intipunku. Updated: Jun 30, 2010.

Intihuatana

A brief walk uphill from the Principal Temple

will bring you to one of the most important shrines at Machu Picchu. Intihuatana, or Hitching Post of the Sun, is an intriguing carved rock whose shape mimics that of Huayna Picchu, the sacred peak rising beyond the ruins. Though the Incas created rocks like this for all their important ritual centers, Intihuatana is one of the few not destroyed by the Spanish conquistadores. Overlooking the Sacred Plaza, this sundial-like rock served as an astronomical device used to track constellation movements and to calculate the passing of seasons. Given its shape and strategic alignment with four important mountains, many scholars have conjectured that Intihuatana is symbolically linked to the spirit of the mountains on which Machu Picchu was built. If you follow the steps down from here, past the Sacred Plaza and towards the northern terraces you'll arrive at the Sacred Rock, gateway to Huayna Picchu Updated: Jul 17, 2007.

Temple of the Sun

Upon entering the main ruins you'll cross over a dry moat and come across the first site of major interest, the Temple of the Sun. Once used as a solar observatory, this unique complex is the only round building at Machu Picchu. At sunrise during the summer solstice, the sun's rays flood through the window and illuminate the tower with a precision only the Incas could have executed. Also known as the Torreón, the temple presents a spectacular, semicircular wall and carved steps that fit seamlessly into the existing surface of a natural boulder, forming some sort of altar. Although access inside the temple is not permitted, the outside architecture is spectacular in and of itself. The temple displays some of Machu Picchu's most superb stonework, and has a window from which the June solstice sunrise and constellation of Pleides can be observed. In Andean culture the Pleiades continues to be an important astronomical symbol, and the locals use the constellation to calculate the arrival of the rains and to determine the best time of year to plant crops. Next to the Temple of the Sun is the Chamber of the Princess, and below the temple is The Royal Tomb. Updated: Jul 17, 2007.

Royal Tomb

The Royal Tomb is a bit of a misnomer due to the fact that neither graves nor human remains have ever been encountered here. Though it may lack the macabre history that some travelers may expect, this cave-like structure is an excellent example of the Inca's stonemasonry genius. Located inside is a magnificent stepped altar and a series of tall niches, once used to present offerings, which capture the sun's rays to produce brilliant patterns of morning shadows. Just down the stairs leading from the Royal Tomb is a series of interconnected fountains and a still-functioning water canal. Updated: Jul 17, 2007.

Chamber of the Princess

The two-story structure sitting adjacent to the Temple of the Sun is the Chamber of the Princess. The building was most likely used for Inca nobility, which may explain why Yale archaeologist Hiram Bingham chose its name. A three-walled house standing next to the chamber has been restored with a thatched roof and provides a good illustration of how Inca buildings might have once looked. From here you can follow a staircase that leads upwards past the Royal Area (denoted by characteristic imperial Inca architecture) and to the two most impressive buildings in the city: the Three-Windowed Temple and the Principal Temple. Updated: Dec 09, 2009.

Three-Windowed Temple

Not far from the Chamber of the Princess is the spectacular Three-Windowed Temple. It is part of a complex situated around the Sacred Plaza, a ceremonial center that some argue is the most captivating section of the city. The temple's unusually large, trapezoidal windows perfectly frame the mountains unfolding beyond the Urubamba River valley. To your left as you face the Three-Windowed Temple is another popular Machu Picchu attraction, the Principal Temple. Updated: Dec 09, 2009.

Principal Temple

Situated next to the Three-Windowed Temple, this magnificent three-walled building derives its name from the immense foundation stones and fine stonework that comprise its three high main walls. The wall facing furthest east looks onto the Sacred Plaza. In contrast to most ancient temples in the Americas, whose entrances face east, the Principal Temple's entrance faces south. White sand found on the temple floor suggests that the temple may have been tied symbolically to the Río Urubamba, a theory that is not too farfetched considering the importance of water in the ancient Inca culture. The kite-shaped sacred stone sitting in the small square around the temple is thought to represent the Southern Cross constellation. A short stroll uphill from here brings you to one of the most spectacular sites of Machu Picchu, the Intihuatana, or Hitching Post of the Sun. Updated: Dec 09, 2009.

Huayna Picchu

Just down the steps from Intihuatana and across the Sacred Plaza is the Sacred Rock, a massive piece of granite curiously shaped like the Inca's sacred mountain of Putukusi, which looms on the eastern horizon. Little is known about this rock, except that it serves as the gateway to Huayna Picchu. Access to the sacred summit is controlled by a guardian from a kiosk behind the Sacred Rock. The trail is open daily 7 a.m.-1 p.m., with the last exit by 3 p.m. The steep walk up to the summit takes about one to two hours and includes a 20-meter climb up a steep rock slab using a ladder and rope. (Those afraid of heights may want to pass on this climb.) Your physical labors will be rewarded, however, with a spectacular panoramic view of the entire Machu Picchu complex and the Andean mountains and forests which cradle it. About two-thirds of the way down the trail behind the summit, another trail leads to the right and down to the exquisitely situated Temple of the Moon. Updated: Dec 09, 2009.

Temple of the Moon

Situated about 400 meters (1,300 ft.) beneath the pinnacle of Huayna Picchu (about a 45-minute walk each way from the summit) is The Temple of the Moon, another spectacular example of Inca stonemasonry. The temple consists of a large natural cave with five niches carved into a massive white granite stone wall. Towards the cave's center is a rock carved like a throne, next to which are five carved steps that lead towards darker recesses where even more carved rocks and stone walls are visible. The temple's name originates from the way it radiates with moonlight at night, but many archaeologists believe that it was also symbolically aligned with the surrounding mountains. Steps on either side of the small plaza in front of the temple lead to more buildings and some interesting stone sanctuaries below. For equally incredible views of Machu Picchu and Huayna Picchu you can take the other trail leading down from the guardian's kiosk behind Sacred Rock. The thirty minute climb to Intipunku, the main entrance to Machu Picchu from the Inca Trail, is a good option for anyone

lacking in time or energy. Updated: Dec 09, 2009.

Intipunku

If you don't have the time or energy to make the climb up to Huayna Picchu and Temple of the Moon, then you may prefer to take the trail leading from the guardian's kiosk behind the Sacred Stone to Intipunku, the main entrance to Machu Picchu from the Inca Trail. Intipunku, also known as the Sun Gate, consists of two large stones that correspond to the winter and summer solstices, and on these dates the gates are illuminated by laser-like beams of light. In addition to their symbolic importance, the gates also provide remarkable views of Machu Picchu and Huayna Picchu. Updated: Dec 09, 2009.

Wiñay Wayna

A rough two or three-hour descent from the ruins of Puyupatamarca, located on the Inca Trail, will bring you to the spectacular ruins of Wiñay Wayna. Here you will find a hotel and restaurant where you can grab a cold drink and hot shower. Originally a companion site for Machu Picchu, these ruins nestled high above the Río Urubamba probably served as a ceremonial and agricultural center. Like today, they may also have served as a rest stop for weary travelers on their way to the grand gates of Machu Picchu. The complex is divided into two architectural sections, with temples at the top and more rustic structures below. As many as 19 different springs carry water to various stone baths located at different levels throughout the characteristic Inca terracing. If you're up for a bit more walking (about 2 hours), you can take the well-marked trail from the ruins to Intipunku, the gateway to Machu Picchu. Updated: Dec 09, 2009.

Machu Picchu Tours

Some people wait years to be able to get a chance to see the majestic Inca ruins at Machu Picchu, so if you get a chance to reach the spectacular cloud-enshrouded green peaks that are home to the ancient and incredibly well-preserved UNESCO World Heritage site, you want to be sure to do the trip right.

It is entirely possible to travel to Machu Picchu independently. However, because of its popularity and the limited number of visitors allowed on the site each day, it pays to plan ahead; tour operators can be an invaluable help. If you book with a tour operator in your home country, you will have the advantage of planning well in advance; however,

SACRED VALLEY

you may pay more than if you plan the trip when you are in Peru. Peruvian tour operators based out of Lima, Cusco or any other major Peruvian city can also help you book your tour--usually at a slightly lower price than international operators.

During the day, there are always guides available at the entrance to Machu Picchu. More expensive guides can be hired at the nearby Sanctuary Lodge. Most local operators offer a one-day excursion from Cusco to Machu Picchu, which includes all transport and a professional guide. (It's usually a good idea to make sure the guide speaks English.) From Cusco, you'll have to take a train to Aguas Calientes, the nearest town to Machu Picchu. From Aguas Calientes it's a 20-minute bus ride up to the ruins.

If you're visiting Machu Picchu as part of a day tour, you'll usually spend about four hours at the ruins. Two of these hours are spent as part of the guided tour. If you want to stay longer, or see the ruins at sunrise (highly recommended), spend the night in nearby Aguas Calientes or in the expensive Machu Picchu Sanctuary Lodge--the only hotel adjacent to Machu Picchu. Some tour companies offer tours spread over two days, but you may have to pay for the additional costs of accommodation. In addition to Machu Picchu tours, treks of the Inca Trail can also be arranged at one of the many Cusco tour agencies. Updated: Jun 26, 2008.

Machu Picchu Lodging

Machu Picchu hostels and hotels that are directly on-site are few and far between—one option is the Machu Picchu Sanctuary Lodge, but since the low-end price is $715 per night, you might want to explore other options in towns nearby to the ruins. Hostel goers tend to head back to Cusco, one of the cheapest places to find hotels near Machu Picchu. In Cusco, you can stay the night in a youth hostel for as little as $4 a night. In Cusco, hotels are also abundant in the mid-range and there are a handful of luxury hotels as well.Other visitors look to the town of Aguas Calientes for hotels near Machu Picchu.

Aguas Calientes offers an array of different lodging options, ranging from extremely cheap and basic to considerable luxury. The cheapest Aguas Calientes hotels are to be found along the railroad tracks. These don't consist of much more than a place to lay

your head. If you're prepared to spend a bit more, there are a number of places along the river, some with balcony views. A number of the better hotels have adjoining restaurants. There are also a couple of decent lodges, one extremely close to the ruins, but be prepared to pay a premium. Updated: Jun 29, 2010.

Machu Picchu Sanctuary Lodge

(ROOMS $715-1,165) For the jet-setting traveler who has no interest in staying in dusty, rabble-filled Aguas Calientes, there is the Machu Picchu Sanctuary Lodge. The Sanctuary is the only hotel right up on the top of the hill next to the ruins; the entrance is a short walk away (about fifty feet). The hotel has two suites and 29 rooms, some of which have an incredible mountain view (be prepared to pay more if you want a scenic room). The hotel is run by the internationally renowned Orient Express hotel group where you'll get luxurious comfort and great service. The Sanctuary Lodge offers all of the expected amenities for a hotel in its class: Internet, room service, etc. For those who really want to keep their exposure to riff-raff to a minimum, the hotel can help you book a helicopter flight from Cusco. If you cough up several hundred dollars to spend the night, be sure to be first in line to visit the ruins in the morning before the train arrives, bringing hordes of tourists with it. There is an excellent restaurant on the premises as well. Check their web site for special rates and promotions. Machu Picchu—right next to the ruins. Tel: 51-1-610-8303, Fax: Fax: 51-84-211-053, E-mail: info@peruorientexpress.com.pe, URL: machupicchu.orient-express.com/web/omac/omac_a2a_home.jsp. Updated: Oct 21, 2009.

Machu Picchu Restaurants

Machu Picchu doesn't offer much in the way of memorable meals. In fact, there's only one restaurant near the ancient city. The rest are down slope in Aguas Calientes, the village at the foot of Machu Picchu's peak. Even there, much of the food is typical cheap traveler's fare. Still, it's not as if people flock to Machu Picchu for the great meals. Updated: Jun 23, 2008.

Tinkuy Buffet Restaurant

Tinkuy Buffet Restaurant is a part of Machu Picchu Sanctuary Lodge, the only hotel within walking distance of Machu Picchu. The buffet is pricey if you're only looking for a light meal, though the price does include salad, main course, dessert and nonalcoholic beverages. Tinkuy fills quickly with day trippers, and the noisy, crowded room can make it easy to forget this restaurant is part of a high-end hotel. Machu Picchu Tel: 51-1-610-8300, E-mail: reservas@peruorientexpress.com.pe, URL: www.orient-express.com/web/omac/omac_dining_tinkuy.jsp. Updated: Jul 30, 2009.

Tampu Restaurant Bar

Tampu Restaurant Bar is an à la carte restaurant a short stroll away from Machu Picchu's entrance, within the Machu Picchu Sanctuary Lodge. The restaurant serves international and Peruvian food for breakfast, lunch and dinner, along with high tea in the afternoon. Prices are high but with Tampu's prime location, well-known reputation and lack of competition, the restaurant can get away with charging more. Machu Picchu Sanctuary Lodge has two dining choices — Tampu and Tinkuy Buffet Restaurant, a fixed-price buffet only open for lunch. Of the two, Tampu is the better choice. The restaurant is less crowded, entrée prices are generally cheaper than the buffet and you get a great view of the Andes. Machu Picchu Tel: 51-1-610-8300, E-mail: reservas@peruorientexpress.com.pe, URL: www.orient-express.com/web/omac/omac_dining_tampu.jsp. Updated: Jul 30, 2009.

!!!!!

Lima

A culturally rich yet modern city on the rise, Lima has an edge worth exploring. Its raw vibe mixed with its new sense of pride is sure to bring this once-Spanish capital back into the spotlight. Lima is home to Peru's best museums, most notably the Larco Museum and the Museo de la Nación (The National Museum), one of the largest museums in South America. Other highlights include colonial architecture at Iglesia de San Francisco, pre-Inca pyramids at Pachacámac and catacombs in Central Lima.

The recently renovated Plaza de Armas (or Plaza Mayor) has been Peru's governmental center since 1535, with the Palacio de Gobierno (Presidential Palace) and the Archbishop's Palace at its center. Recently, upscale restaurants and cafés have sprung up in the area right around the plaza. The coastal suburbs of Miraflores, San Isidro and Barranco are popular places to stay to avoid Central Lima's smog and chaos. Barranco is especially popular for its nightlife and performing arts center.

While high unemployment rates in the 1980s and 90s contributed to the deterioration of the city and rise in crime, Lima also suffered from intense pollution, mostly emitted by the large number of cars and emerging industry. The smog, combined with a heavy fog, called garua, blankets the city from June to December, making Lima seem dark, gloomy and scary. But under it all, Lima is a colorful city, and in recent years the government has cracked down on crime and made many tourist areas safer. As a result, the city as a whole, with its renowned gastronomic scene, musical talents, lively historic and contemporary art scene, terrific performing arts and cosmopolitan shopping venues, has become a great place to explore.

In 2003, under the mayor's orders, the old city got clean. For years, the historic center, El Centro, had been considered an unsafe area not worthy of any attention. But like in so many South American cities that hold exquisite architecture and rich history, all that was needed was a bit of money and a whole lot of loving. Today, the Plaza de Armas, located in the historic center, shows off its beauty. Lima declared its independence from Spain here in 1821. The renovation of this area has also made it easier and safer to visit some of the center's most unique treasures, such as the Iglesia de San Francisco, which houses catacombs whose tunnels reportedly hold bones from 75,000 people, or the Museo de Arte de Lima, a Peruvian art museum.

If you are just using Lima as a portal to Cusco, your flight will most likely arrive late at night and leave for Cusco early in the morning. You can either tough out the layover in the airport or go to a hotel for a few hours until your flight leaves. The Miraflores district is your best bet for a reasonable rate on a room and you won't have to travel too far. Central Lima is about 30-45 minutes from the airport. Be sure to get to the airport early, as the flights to Cusco are usually packed and often delayed due to cloudy weather in this mountainous city.

History of Lima

Lima has long bee one of the most important cities on the South American continent. The area now covered by Lima hosted many pre-Columbian civilizations, several of which erected pyramids that still stand. In the 15th century, the Inca civilization conquered the region and settled in areas around Lima.

In 1535, Lima was founded by Francisco Pizarro as the capital of Spain's South American empire. The site was selected for its access to the ocean and the fresh waters of the Río Rimac. Lima was one of two viceregal capitals in Spain's New World empire (the other was Mexico City), and was the administrative center for all colonial activity running from Colombia to Tierra del Fuego.

As the mines in Peru and Bolivia yielded riches, Lima grew wealthy on trade, which was required by law to pass through the nearby port of Callao. In the late 17th century, however, pirate raids, earthquakes and competition from a new viceregal capital in Buenos Aires dimmed Lima's fortunes.

After independence, Lima lost much of its influence, and it became a rather stagnant city. Just as the economy was turning around in the 1870s, the War of the Pacific broke out and the Chilean army captured the city, damaging large parts of it. By the end of the 19th century, the city expanded beyond the borders of the historical center. A 1940 earthquake damaged large parts of the city, but it did not stop the city's steady growth.

Six Things to See in Lima

Parque de la Exposición

The Parque de la Exposición (A.K.A. Cultura) downtown is a tribute to Lima's urban planners from the 19th century. It was conceived and built in 1868 as the Parque de la Exposición, and is still referred to this way by many locals. Its mix of fountains, Victorian houses and modern art make this a popular favorite. Av. Wilson and 28 de Julio, Central Lima.

National Museum

The largest museum in Peru features four floors of history and exhibits in a sprawling building in the San Borja neighborhood. The museum provides a fairly complete overview of Peruvian history and culture. Of particular interest are the sections on pre-Spanish life in the area and the reproductions of Peru's major archaeological sites. Av. Javier Prado Este 2465, Lima, 41 Tel: 51-1-476-9875.

Parque de la Muralla

This new park, complete with a pedestrian walkway, sits on the banks of the Rio Rimac. During its construction diggers unearthed the remains of 500 year old city walls that were once meant to repel both the rising river and Dutch pirates. A small museum on the site explains some of the history of the wall. Av. Abancay and Jiron Amazonas Central Lima, Peru.

The San Francisco Catacombs

This Franciscan church and monastery is one of the most haunting (almost literally) and memorable sites in all of Lima. Originally constructed in 1546, it is the oldest church in South America. It also served as the first official Catholic cemetery in Lima, at a time when the dead were laid to rest in catacombs beneath the church.

You will get to visit the catacombs and view the hundreds of centuries old bones and scores of skulls as part of the guided tour. The church also has one of the oldest and most historically significant libraries in the Americas and dramatic collections of religious and secular art, including renaissance era tiles imported from Spain. Plaza San Francisco, Lima; Jiron Ancash and Lampa, Central Lima, Tel: 51-1-426-7377/427-1381, ext 111, URL: www.museocatacumbas.com.

Gold Museum

(ENTRANCE: $10) The Gold Museum features gold figures, jewelry, masks, knives and artifacts from the Inca and colonial periods. It also contains mummies, headdresses and other ancient relics. In 2001, a huge scandal broke: it was proven that many of the pieces in the museum were fakes. The museum now only houses genuine pieces, though there is still a cloud of skepticism that hangs over the exhibits. Upstairs from the Gold Museum is the equally fascinating Arms museum, which houses weapons and armor from many cultures. Artifacts from Peru's history are also on display. Alonso de Molina 1100, Lima, Peru, Tel: 51-1-345-1271.

Plaza de Armas

Throughout Lima's history, the Plaza de Armas has been the city's focal point, with its cathedrals, ornate buildings and government palace. Created in 1650, the Plaza de Armas spans four large blocks, with a park in the center. A bronze fountain with an angel perched on top blowing a trumpet is its centerpiece. The Plaza is surrounded by such landmarks as the Governor's Palace, the Catedral de Lima, and the stylish post office. There is a ceremonial changing of the guard six days a week, as well as regular marching band performances. Updated: Aug 13, 2007.

LIMA INTRO

In the 1980s and 1990s, Lima was transformed by an influx of migrants, mostly arriving from the poverty-stricken and war-town Andean cordillera. Rings of *pueblos jóvenes*, shanty-towns, spread around the city. In the early 1990s, Shining Path was active in Lima, carrying out several attacks in Miraflores and elsewhere.

By the late 1990s, however, the war was over, the crime rate had fallen significantly, and the city began to flourish once more. Updated: Jun 15, 2009.

Getting To and Away

Lima's airport, Aeropuerto Internacional Jorge Chávez, is located 16 kilometers (10 mi.) northwest of Lima, about 30 minutes away from the Miraflores area. It is recommended that for domestic flights you arrive at least two hours in advance, and for international flights at least three hours in advance.

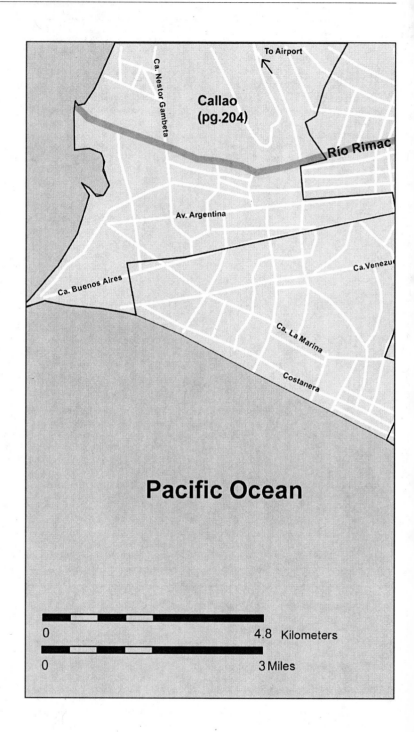

To Airport

Ca. Nestor Gambeta

**Callao
(pg.204)**

Río Rimac

Av. Argentina

Ca.Venezu

Ca. Buenos Aires

Ca. La Marina

Costanera

Pacific Ocean

0   4.8 Kilometers

0   3 Miles

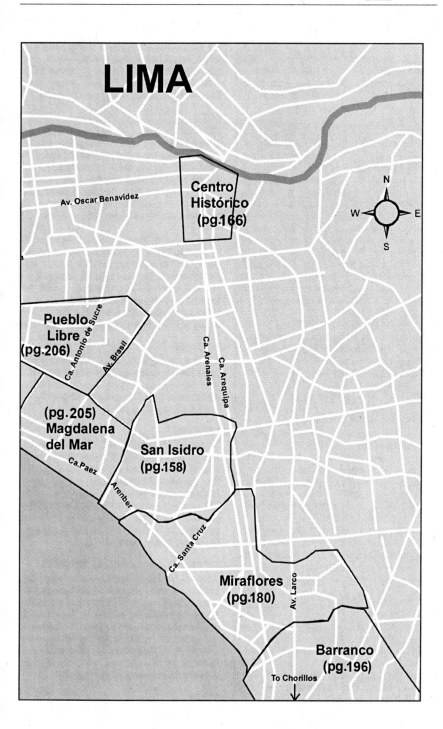

LIMA

Av. Oscar Benavidez

Centro
Histórico
(pg.166)

N
W   E
S

Pueblo
Libre
(pg.206)

Ca. Antonio de Sucre

Av. Brasil

Ca. Arenales

Ca. Arequipa

(pg.205)
Magdalena
del Mar

San Isidro
(pg.158)

Ca.Paez

Arenber

Ca. Santa Cruz

Miraflores
(pg.180)

Av. Larco

Barranco
(pg.196)

To Chorillos

Traveling with Kids in Lima

As with most travel, there seldom is anything more helpful than tips from an on-site parent about where to take kids. Here are a few suggestions for the little ones:

Cieneguilla

At 30-40 minutes from Lima, Cieneguilla is a short drive by local standards. Typically the weather is much nicer than downtown. There are a variety of restaurants that have good food, large kid-friendly play areas and reasonably good service. These play areas have playgrounds complete with trampolines and sometimes even horse rides. Avoid more crime-prone parks downtown and be selective, there are some parks in Miraflores that are ok. Ask desk clerks or locals for their assessments of local green spaces before hanging out with your tot. URL: www.cieneguilla.com.

The Museo de la Nacion

The museum is home to a children's theatre. It also features a variety of exhibits of native Peruvian artwork and hosts different art-related events, including an evening of art called Noche de Arte. URL: www.nochedearte.com.

Restaurant Rosa Náutica

Enjoy the sweeping view of Miraflores from your table. You will feel as if you are right over the surf as it comes to shore at sunset. If you or your small companion insist on sand between your toes, park near the restaurant and walk the beach looking for shells, rocks or observing the local surfers catching a wave. Tips on ordering in a restaurant: Stick with the appetizers and skip the main courses. The appetizers are simply more varied, making for a great shared dining experience. URL: www.larosanautica.com/rn_homeing.html.

San Francisco Church and Catacombs

The church and its design are grandiose and magnificent especially from the perspective of a seven-year-old. The catacombs are chilling and fascinating for parent and child. You can go to the underside of the church building and look at all of the bones of the people interred there. Updated: Jun 15,2009

At the time of press, the airport fee, or TUUA, was $6.05 for domestic flights and $30.25 for international flights. It tends to change often, so you may have to pay a bit more. You pay the fee at the airport payment teller windows, which are located across from the Mini Market on the second floor.

TAXIS

Although taxis are a bit more expensive than other modes of transportation from the airport, they are by far the easiest. This way, there is no lugging your luggage to the bus station, plus you will get dropped off at exactly where you need to be. The taxi ride from the Lima Airport to the center of Lima will take anywhere between 30 minutes and an hour, depending on traffic.

Upon arrival in Lima it is best to book a taxi in the reception area, rather than catching one of the taxis waiting outside, which will surely overcharge you. Ask for information at the Customer Care counters, which are located in the international and domestic arrivals area before the terminal exits. Expect to pay between $10 and $20 for the taxi ride.

LOCKERS

If you are going to be in the airport for a long period of time and would rather not deal with your luggage, the airport does have lockers available for rent. The suitcase storage service is located in the domestic arrivals area.

PARKING

There is both hourly and long-term parking available at the airport. The hourly rate is 3.50 nuevos soles (around $1.25). The payment teller windows can be found in front of the terminal. Long-term parking costs 17.50 nuevos soles (around $5) per day. The long-term parking lot is the parking lot located on the right, directly following police control.

INTERNET AND TELEPHONE SERVICES

Recently the Lima airport became WiFi compatible. However, there is a charge to use this service. You can buy Wi-Fi cards at the coffee shops located in Peru Plaza, in the domestic and international terminals and in the public call center of the Telefónica, which is on the second level. Telephone booths are located throughout the airport, with the highest concentration being in the Telefónica.

BUSES

There are no actual bus stations on the airport premises, so if you have a lot of stuff it is probably best not to venture outside looking for a bus. Updated: Jun 15,2009

Banks in Lima

ATMs are readily available in Lima, with many offering 24-hour service. Just approach them with caution, in particular at night, since many thieves target them. In general, casas de cambio (foreign-exchange bureaus) tend to give better rates than a bank for cash. They can be found throughout the city, with the highest concentrations being in touristy areas, such as Miraflores.

American Express
Lost or stolen travelers checks can be replaced here; however, they do not cash checks. They are open from 9 a.m. to 5:30 p.m. on Monday-Friday, and 9 a.m. to 1 p.m. on Saturdays. Santa Cruz 621, Miraflores, Tel: 51-1-221-8204, E-mail: amexcard@travex.com.pe.

Banco Continental
One of the more prevalent bank chains in Lima. All branches have 24-hour ATMs that make cash advances on Visa. Their bank also will change Amex, Citicorp and Visa travelers checks. They are open from 9 a.m. to 6 p.m. Monday-Friday, and 9:30 a.m. to 12:30 p.m. on Saturdays.

Moneygram
If you need money wired to you, this is a good option. They are open from 10 a.m. to 6:30 p.m. Monday-Saturday. Alfredo Benavides 735, Miraflores, Tel: 51-1-241-2222, E-mail: moneyecpress@terra.com.pe.

Western Union
Another strong choice if you need money wired to you in Peru. There are various locations in all of the country, so you are sure to find one that is convenient for you. The best way to find the one that will work best for you is to visit their website at www.westernunion.com where you can find addresses, phone numbers and hours for the different stores. Updated: Jul 10,2007

Emergency Medical Care in Lima

The U.S. Embassy maintains a list of medical providers in Lima; although they do not officially recommend any, the list is of places used by embassy staff. Generally, the places listed will have someone on duty who speaks English. A couple of clinics they list:

Clínica San Borga
Av. Guardia Civil 333, San Borja, Tel: 51-1-475-3141

Clínica el Golf
Av. Aureliano Miro Quesada, San Isidro, Tel: 51-1-264-3300

The complete list includes specialists, including cardiologists, dentists and more. You can find the complete, up-to-date list here: URL: http://lima.usembassy.gov/medical.html Updated: Jul 10, 2007.

Lima Services

Gold's Gym Peru
With 11 locations in and around the city, Gold's Gym Peru is far more than a weight training center and suits most workout needs. Catering to all ability and exercise levels, the facilities are fully equipped, clean and modern. Equipment is in excellent and new condition, and feature Stair masters, Elliptical machines, treadmills and stationary bikes. There are also large studios for aerobic, dance and strength training classes. A sample of classes include Pilates, yoga, step aerobics, spinning, strength training, cardio kickboxing, among others. Gold's Gym Peru also has extensive weight-training equipment for both males and females. Most locations also have nutritionists, personal trainers, daycare, small cafeteria, massage services and on-site sauna. It also provides a running club and outdoor athletic excursions. Prices vary among clubs and member sign-up discounts are frequent. Miraflores, San Miguel, Camacho, San Isidro, Lima Norte, Las Begonias, Ovalo Higuereta, Minka-Callao, San Borja, Jesús María, Chorrillos E-mail: miraflores@goldsgymperu.com.pe, URL: www.goldsgymperu.com. Updated: Jun 15, 2009.

Ibero Librerías
With some of the most helpful staff around, Ibero Librerías is a great bookstore to hunt down that hard-to-find souvenir or to simply browse around. While most titles are in Spanish, they do carry some English-language books. Stocked with a variety of literature, the store also offers exceptional travel, art, history and reference selections. If you are on the hunt for a Peruvian cookbook, you won't want to miss the collection of traditional and modern cuisine. Cookbooks always make great souvenirs,

and many of these are translated in Spanish and in English within the same book. There are several locations around Lima proper, three within Miraflores. Tuesday-Saturday 9:15 a.m. - 5 p.m., Sunday 10 a.m.-5 p.m. Closed Mondays. Plaza Bolívar, Tel: 51-1-463-5070, Updated: Jun 15, 2009.

Lima Lodging

With approximately 50 distinct districts, each neighborhood in Lima offers varying accommodations to suit individual travelers. Depending on the atmosphere and price range you are looking for, there are multiple hotels in Lima that will enhance your experience.

For history-loving travelers who want to devote their time to exploring colonial buildings and historic plazas, the Lima Centro neighborhood has everything from cheap, clean hostels to high-end hotels overlooking all of Lima.

Hotels in San Isidro are best for business travelers interested in a quiet, luxurious stay. The area has many restaurants and bars to enjoy late into the evening and accommodations tend to cater to the middle and upper class.

For cultured travelers interested in delicious restaurants, happening clubs and excellent shopping, consider staying in the Miraflores neighborhood, which has some of the best hotels in Lima. Miraflores sits atop cliffs overlooking the beach. The area is residential and packed with great restaurants, clubs and shops. For someone looking to go out at night and then return to some of the most fun-loving and easy-going hotels in Lima, Miraflores is the perfect option.

For artistic, fun-loving night owls, head straight to the hip neighborhood of Barranco. The architecture and sights in this area appeal to the world's traveling artists. Inspiring by day and wild by night, Barranco is up-and-coming with some of the most friendly and colorful, chic hostels and budget hotels in Lima.

Scattered amongst the more well-known districts are the smaller neighborhoods of Chorrillos and Pueblo Libre. These neighborhoods tend to be a little less touristy. Both have lodging options that range from inexpensive to high end.

Outside of Lima, camping is also an option. Plenty of travel agencies and adventure shops can point you to the best camping sites and even help you rent gear so you don't have to drag huge packs around Lima. Camping in the wild outside of Lima should be done with caution: make sure you ask permission from the police or nearest landowner before pitching a tent. Never camp alone in Peru, especially on beaches, because if thieves don't get you the sandflies will. Updated: Jul 01, 2010

Lima Tours

As a huge, thriving metropolis, Lima can be overwhelming when it comes to planning the day. There are enough museums, churches and colonial buildings to exhaust even the most ambitious tourist in town. There are many parks and plazas to explore and most are within walking distance of each other. For the history buffs, there are a handful of Inca ruins scattered around the city that oddly contrast with the more modern additions. Athletic travelers can combine their love for exercise with their love of exploration and experience any of the biking, swimming, surfing or paragliding tours in town. For the traveler that would like to sample a little of everything, careful planning will make the best of their time.

There are quite a few companies that offer tours in Lima as well as trips around Peru and it's worth it to do a little research to compare operators and individual tours that are offered. Tours outside of Lima tend to be cheaper if organized in cities closest to tour destinations. Additionally, there are travel agencies in Lima that can assist with your plans and offer advice. Updated Jul 07, 2007.

Fertur Peru

Fertur Peru has a well-established reputation as one of the best travel agencies and tour operators in the country. A four-day excursion to Machu Picchu can be easily arranged through them for as low as $230. A three-day trip from Iquitos to the Amazon rainforest can go as low as $185, and two nights in Lake Titicaca from Puno, in a room with a private bath, as low as $94. Siduith Ferrer, owner and founder, is devoted to eco-friendly and sustainable travel in Latin America, with a belief that conscientious tourism is essential for progress in developing countries. Monday - Saturday 9 a.m. - 7 p.m. Jirón Junín 211. Tel: 51-1-427-2626 / 1958, Fax: 51-1-428-3247, E-mail: receptivo@ferturperu.com, URL: www.fertur-travel.com. Updated: Dec 03, 2008.

Info Peru

They are officially a travel agency, capable of booking travel via bus or plane, as well as stays in any variety of hotels, hostels, lodges

LIMA INTRO

and cabins, but they also serve, completely free of charge, as an information outlet for anyone who comes by to seek out virtually any information having to do with travel in Peru, where to go, what to do, and whom to contact. They boast fifteen years experience in the business and a fluency in both English and French. URL: www.infoperu.com. Updated: Dec 03, 2008.

Mirabus

The only one of its kind so far in Lima, the Mirabus tour bus is highly recommended for newcomers to Lima, especially upon arriving. They offer a variety of urban tours on their open air double-decker bus, some for one hour around the historical district and some for a more inclusive three hours, going as far as the beach neighborhoods of Miraflores and Chorillos. The guide explains the history and background of many Lima landmarks, letting you know which monument, for example, was built by Gustave Eiffel, of Eiffel tower fame, or that the Palace of Justice is almost an exact duplicate of the one in Brussels. Private excursions are also available. However, they only offer tours in Spanish. Tel: 51-1-476-4213 / 242-6699 / 243-7629, E-mail: reservas@mirabusperu.com. Updated: Dec 03, 2008.

Class Adventure Travel

Class Adventure Travel has tour options in many cities all across Peru. Its owners operate tour companies all across Latin America, and are very knowledgeable and helpful. All tours are fully customizable, and can range from three days to weeks. Grimaldo del Solar 463, Miraflores. Tel: 51-1-444-2220, URL: www.cat-travel.com. Updated: Dec 03, 2008.

Enjoy Peru

Enjoy Peru offers Lima tours; in fact, they can provide a two-day "Archaeological Tour of Lima," which takes in the historical central part of the city, most of the historically important churches and religious buildings and a few museums, including the Government Palace and City Hall, the Church of Santa Domingo and the tomb of Santa Rosa, the Convent and Church of San Francisco and the Larco Herrera Museum. It also takes a trip around the areas of Miraflores and San Isidro. On the second day, the tour goes to Pachacamac, the important ancient pre-Columbian archaeological site.

Tel: 1-888-317-3383 (USA), URL: www.enjoyperu.com. Updated: Jul 11, 2007.

Lima Visión

Lima Visión has a decent tour offering, taking three hours to look around all of Lima, both modern and old. The tour includes the Plaza Mayor, the City Hall, the Government Palace, the Cathedral and the San Francisco church. Following the old town stint, the tour heads over to the new town, to San Isidro, visiting the Huaca Huallamarca, which is of an adobe pre-Inca style. The tour finishes up in Miraflores, in the Parque del Amor. As with many of the other tour companies, Lima Visión offers tours all over Peru. Jr. Chiclayo 444. Tel: 51-1-447-7710, Fax: 51-1-446-9969, E-mail: peruvisi@this.peruvision.com, URL: www.peruvision.com. Updated: Jul 11, 2007.

Things to See and Do

There are enough activities in Lima to entertain even the most determined sightseer. A tentative itinerary may begin with a morning stroll to one of Lima's many plazas or parks. These quiet refuges in a bustling city will ease you into a busy day, rich with Peruvian history. Surrounding these areas are landmark buildings and beautiful testaments to colonial architecture. Next, wander into a church or monastery that highlights the dominating role of religion throughout Peru's history. If religious anecdotes inspire your appetite, you will want to step into a Peruvian café to sample authentic foods from the country. Next, be sure to make time to visit one or two of the country's most extensive and fascinating museums followed by a traipse through various Inca ruins that are set against Lima's modern backdrop. Exhausted, take a quick nap and refresh yourself for an exciting evening. Enjoy a dinner of the freshest seafood available overlooking the ocean and dance the night away to the lively rhythms that define South America.

Spend a day or a week in Lima, and you will undoubtedly find yourself awed, inspired, enlightened and thoroughly entertained at every moment. Try not to miss a single activity in Lima, with its rich history, bold culture and warm people. Updated: Jun 15, 2009.

Lima Museums

Perhaps due to its unpleasant climate, Lima is home to numerous excellent museums. Although some of them are clustered in the old town near the cathedral, many of the other good ones are spread out throughout the city, making them sometimes difficult to find. If you're in Lima for a few days, chances are you'll find a museum that will interest you. Some museums—such as the Archaeology Museum or the Larco Museum—are worth spending time in Lima for. Updated: Jun 30, 2010.

National Archaeology Museum / Museo Nacional de Arqueología

This museum, whose full name is El Museo Nacional de Arqueología, Antropología y Historia, is a must-see for history buffs visiting Lima. Like the National Museum, it provides an overview of the history of the region, mostly before the arrival of the Spanish. It is easier to navigate than the National Museum, however, and most visitors prefer it to its larger cousin. The museum oversees one of the largest collections of pre-Hispanic art and relics in the world. Some of the highlights include exceptionally well-preserved mummies from the Nasca region and the Estela Raimondi, an enormous carved stone that once resided at Chavín de Huántar, a major pre-Columbian site. It is carved with snakes, animals and gods. The building that houses the museum is also beautiful and historic and is included on the tour. As not all of the exhibits are labeled in English, a guide is suggested if your Spanish is not very good. Tuesday-Saturday, 9.15 a.m.-5 p.m., Sunday 10 a.m.-5 p.m., Closed Mondays. Plaza Bolívar, Tel: 51-1-463-5070. Updated: Apr 27, 2010.

Larco Museum / Museo Larco

The Museo Arqueológico Rafael Larco Herrera, commonly known as the Museo Larco or Larco Museum, is one of the most popular in Lima. Set in a gorgeous old hacienda, the museum is the private collection of Rafael Larco Herrera. It is considered by many to be the largest and most complete collection of pre-Columbian artifacts and relics in the world. It is comprised of more than 40,000 pieces of pottery and 5,000 pieces of gold and textiles. Of particular interest is the section on erotic art and ceramics, politely set off from the rest of the exhibits by a garden. The pieces show that the early inhabitants of South America were quite uninhibited. The artifacts on display are quite interesting and occasionally humorous. Monday to Sunday (incl. holidays) 9 a.m.-6 p.m. Av. Bolívar 1515, Pueblo Libre, Lima, Peru Zip: Lima 21, Tel: 51-1-461-1312, Fax: 51-1-164-5640, E-mail: webmaster@museolarco.org, URL: www.museolarco.org, Updated: Jul 01, 2010.

Photo by: Nejiros

National Museum / Museo de la Nación

The largest museum in Peru, the National Museum features four floors of history and exhibits in a large, sprawling building in the San Borja neighborhood of Lima. Of particular interest are the sections on pre-Spanish life in the area and the reproductions of Peru's major archaeological sites. The galleries often feature temporary exhibits as well. The museum provides a fairly complete overview of Peruvian history and culture. Tuesday-Sunday, 9 a.m.-5 p.m., Av. Javier Prado Este 2465, Tel: 51-1-476-9875. Updated: Jul 01, 2010.

Gold Museum / Museo de Oro

The Gold Museum is considered one of Lima's premier attractions. It houses the private collection of Miguel Mujica Gallo, who spent years amassing it, often by purchasing relics from grave robbers. It features gold figures, jewelry, masks, knives and artifacts from the Inca and colonial periods. It also contains mummies, headdresses and other ancient relics. In 2001, a huge scandal broke out. It was proven that many of the pieces in the museum were fakes. Experts had been suspicious of many of the pieces for years. The Mujica Gallo family claimed that the fakes had been purchased by mistake and that the museum now only houses genuine pieces. However, there is still a cloud of skepticism that hangs over the exhibits. Upstairs from the Gold Museum is the equally fascinating Arms Museum, which houses weapons and armor from many cultures. Artifacts from Peru's history, such as items owned by the Pizarro brothers and Simón Bolívar, are also on display. You may want to do both museums as part of a tour, since the displays are not always clearly marked. Daily, 11.30 a.m.-7 p.m. Alonso de Molina 1100, Tel: 51-1-345-1271. Updated: Jun 30, 2010.

Bullfighting Museum / Museo Taurino

The Museo Taurino, or Bullfighting Museum, has information on everything you could ever want to know about the art of bullfighting, comprising displays, photos, weapons, relics and more. Hualgayoc 332, Rímac Tel: 481 1467 E-mail: museotaurino@hotmail.com, Updated: Nov 25, 2009.

Museo de los Descalzos

El Museo de los Descalzos, (literally, "The Museum of the Shoeless Ones") is housed in a convent that formerly was a spiritual sanctuary for the Franciscan order. Today it contains lots of religious and colonial art, as well as a restored chapel with gold-covered altars, an old wine-making area and a pharmacy. The museum is quite interesting, particularly for those who wish to know more about the colonial era or the art of Peru's early history. English-speaking guides are often available. Mass is still celebrated, typically before the museum opens in the morning and after it closes at night. Tuesday-Sunday, 10 a.m.-1 p.m. and 3-6 p.m., northern end of the Alameda de los Descalzos, Tel: 51-1-481-0441.

Lima Art Museum / Museo de Arte de Lima

The Lima Art Museum has the best collection of Peruvian art in the country. The paintings cover the colonial era to the present, and there is also a selection of woodcarvings, furniture, etc. There is also a coffee shop, gift shop and movie theater. Check with the museum before you visit, as they often arrange interesting temporary exhibits. 10 a.m. - 3 p.m.(Closed Wednesdays), Paseo Colón 125, Lima, 1 Peru, Tel: 51-1-423-4732, URL: www.museoarte.perucultural.org.pe. Updated: Jun 15, 2009.

Photo by: Jorge Enrique Aguayo

Central Bank Museum / Museo del Banco Central

The Central Bank Museum has three sections: archaeology, numismatic (coins and money) and art. The archaeology section is located in the basement and has an interesting pottery collection. The currency exhibit is on the first floor and features colonial-era coins. The art exhibit on the top floor features paintings from the 19th and 20th centuries, many by Peruvian artists. 9 a.m.-5 p.m. Plaza Bolívar. Updated: Jun 15, 2009.

Museum of the Inquisition / Museo de la Inquisición

Located on the Plaza Bolívar, which is also home to the Peruvian Congress building, the Inquisition Museum is one of Lima's most-popular and most-visited museums. Housed in the building that was home to the Inquisition from 1570 to 1820, the museum has exhibits that explain the impact and importance of the Inquisition in Peru's history. Imported from Spain in the late 16th century, the Inquisition was responsible for eliminating heresy and blasphemy in the New World. Some of their targets included Spanish Jews and their descendents, who were often accused of maintaining their practices in secret. In this museum, you can visit the lightless dungeon cells where those accused awaited judgement or punishment. It was also from this location that the public burning of heretics was ordered. Plaza Bolívar. Updated: Jun 30, 2010.

Parque de la Muralla

This new park, complete with a pedestrian walkway, sits on the banks of the Rio Rimac. During its construction diggers unearthed the remains of 500 year old city walls that were once meant to repel both the rising river and Dutch pirates. A small museum on the site explains some of the history of the wall. Av. Abancay and Jiron Amazonas Central Lima, Peru.

The San Francisco Catacombs

This Franciscan church and monastery is one of the most haunting (almost literally) and memorable sites in all of Lima. Originally constructed in 1546, it is the oldest church in South America. It also served as the first official Catholic cemetery in Lima, at a time when the dead were laid to rest in catacombs beneath the church. You will get to visit the catacombs and view the hundreds of centuries old bones and scores of skulls as part of the guided tour. The church also has one of the oldest and most historically significant libraries in the Americas and dramatic collections of religious and secular art, including renaissance era tiles imported from Spain. Plaza San Francisco, Lima; Jiron Ancash and Lampa, Central Lima, Tel: 51-1-426-7377/427-1381, ext 111, URL: www.museocatacumbas.com.

!!!!!

LIMA INTRO

San Isidro

The San Isidro district of Lima is one of the city's most affluent. It is known for green areas, nice residential zones, fine hotels and dining, and decent nightlife. It is a favorite of visitors who come for the hotels and good food. Updated: Jul 12, 2007

History of San Isidro

Originally the site of an extensive olive grove outside of Lima, San Isidro wasn't founded until 1931, so it does not possess as much history as other neighborhoods. San Isidro is a moneyed zone, home to upscale shopping, a financial district and many of Lima's finest hotels. Most of the foreign embassies also take up residence in San Isidro, adding to its debonair atmosphere. San Isidro is intellectual, too—the San Isidro Municipal Library is considered the most complete and extensive in Lima. Visitors and residents come to San Isidro for its green areas. The swank Lima Golf Club is located right in the heart of the district. For those with no clubs in tow, more green patches can be found in the famous El Olivar park, named for its groves of olive trees, some of which were planted centuries ago. The park was established as a national monument in 1959. Updated: Apr 15, 2009.

Activities ●
1 Huaca Huallamarca B2
2 Museo de Historia Natural UNMSM B3
3 Parque El Olivar B3

Eating ⓘ
4 Alfresco A3
5 Antica Pizzaría A3
6 Como Agua Para Chocolate B3
7 El Cartujo B3
8 Matseui A3
9 News Café A3
10 Punta Sal C3
11 Punto Italiano A3
12 Tai Lounge B3
13 Trattoria San Ceferino A3

Services ★
14 Camino Real Shopping B3
15 DHL B1
16 Dr. Astor Aste B3
17 Ilaria A2
18 Segunda Vuelta D3

Sleeping 🛏
19 Casa Bella B2
20 Country Club Lima Hotel B1
21 Hotel Libertador San Isidro Golf B1
22 Hotel Los Delfines B2
23 Sonesta Lima Hotel El Olivar B3
24 Suites Antique A2
25 Suites del Bosque B3
26 Swisshotel B3
27 Youth Hostel Malka A4

San Isidro Services

TOURISM

iPeru

iPeru offers tourist information and an assistance service where visitors can ask about information on Peru, as well as assistance if the tourist feels the service paid for was not provided as advertised. Please note that iPeru does not give recommendations for travel agencies, lodgings or transport services, nor does it make reservations or file applications for customs or immigration. Monday-Friday 8:30 a.m.-6 p.m. Jorge Basadre 610. Tel: 51-1-421-1627, E-mail: iperulima@promperugob.pe. Updated: Apr 15, 2009.

KEEPING IN TOUCH

DHL

DHL is easily accessible for all of your mailing and shipping needs. Monday – Friday last drop at 5 p.m., Saturday / Sunday closed. Ausejo Salas 153, floor 3. Tel: 51-1-232-1976.

MEDICAL

Dr. Victor Aste

Should you need to see a doctor while visiting San Isidro, Dr. Victor Aste speaks English and will be able to assist with most non-emergency needs. In the event of an emergency, please visit an area hospital. Antero Aspillaga 415, Oficina 101. Tel: 51-1-441-7502.

SHOPPING

Camino Real

This is a large mall with a collection of smaller, less pretentious shops than in shopping areas in Miraflores. Belaunde 147.

Ilaria

Browse this stylish jewelry and silverware shop for unique and beautiful creations by master jewelers. Silver and gold are intricately combined with precious materials such as amethyst, pearl, sapphire, and ruby to create stunning necklaces, bracelets, rings, and more. Additionally, contemporary and traditional silverware sets including wood and silver home accessories are available. Prices tend to be high in this shop. Av. 2 de Mayo 308. Tel: 51-1-441-7703.

El Virrey

Following their recent move to a much bigger and nicer store, El Virrey now offers three times their original selection of books. Founded 30 years ago by the Sanseviero family, this store offers a large selection of local and imported books on nearly every subject you could possibly be interested in.

With the additional space, you'll find plenty of room to sit down and enjoy a good book in one of their comfortable reading rooms. Plan on browsing for awhile. Miguel Dasso 147. Tel: 51-1-440-0607.

Segunda Vuelta

For the fashionable traveler with a weakness for unique designs, this tiny shop features clothes by young Peruvian designers. If you don't find anything to suit your taste from this selection, don't miss the excellent assortment of second-hand and vintage garments. The shop is small and partly hidden from view, so be careful not to miss it. There is no sign out front, just a big number 330. Av. Conquistadores 330. Tel: 51-1-421-7163. Updated: Apr 15, 2009.

Things to See and Do

As one of Lima's residential districts, San Isidro has fewer activities than surrounding areas, but it is still a diverting neighborhood. There are a handful of museums boasting highly recommended private collections of pottery, jewelry, textiles and ceramics, fascinating archaeological and anthropological artifacts and interesting tidbits of Peruvian history. Be sure not to overlook San Isidro activities in favor of other neighborhoods in Lima. Finish the day with a visit to the area's Inca ruins and a nice view of modern San Isidro. Updated: May 14, 2007.

Huaca Huallamarca

This ancient Maranga monument seems out of place, sandwiched between neighboring hotels and apartment buildings. Constructed with adobe bricks dating from 200 to 500 AD, this landmark has been lovingly restored and now offers interesting views of San Isidro. 9 a.m. - 5 p.m, Closed Monday.Nicolás de Rivera 201. Tel: 51-1-222-4124. Updated: Apr 15, 2009.

Museo de Historia Natural UNMSM

The Museum of Natural History, founded on February 28, 1918, consists of four main divisions: botany, zoology, ecology and geoscience. Visitors can browse Peruvian landscapes and a modest taxidermy collection that highlights the region's mammals, primates, invertebrates, birds, botany, fossils, dinosaurs, fish and minerals. Open from Monday–Friday, 9 a.m.-3 p.m., Saturday 9 a.m.-5 p.m. and Sunday 9 a.m. - 1 p.m. Av. Arenales 1256, Jesús Maria. Tel: 51-1-471-0117, E-mail: museohn@unmsm.edu.pe. Updated: Apr 15, 2009.

El Olivar

A park and historical monument, El Olviar is covered with 500-year old olive trees planted by Dominican monks. The monks once cultivated olives on a huge expanse of land, though El Olivar is the only part that survived

the sprawl of San Isidro. Today, the park provides a romantic setting for a stroll. Jirón Choquehuanca s/n. Updated: Apr 15, 2009

Parque Combate de Altao

San Isidro is Peru's premier business district: men in black suits with silk ties, cell phones in the left and briefcases in the right, scurry by in droves. Movement and chaos abound. But calmly sleeping amid all the energy and the endless commotion is the Parque Combate de Altao. The park is large and square, filled with the lush vegetation, broad overhanging trees and the moist fragrance of grass. The fresh air, the roaming dogs, the feasting pigeons and the desolate jungle gym all contribute to a feeling of peace. If you're in the area and need to relax, check it out. Corner of Av. Las Orquídeas and Andréas Reyes, only a few blocks away from Avs. Arequipa and Javier Prado. Updated: Apr 15, 2009

San Isidro Lodging

The affluent San Isidro district is known for some of the best upscale hotels in Lima. This residential and quiet area caters to the mid to high-end visitor, and you will find many business travelers in the area. There are a few exceptions, however, and the tourist with a lower budget can find places to stay as well. The area is safe and recommended for travelers who plan to stay for an extended period of time. Updated: Jul 12, 2007

BUDGET

Youth Hostel Malka

(ROOMS: $8 - 20) One of the few low-budget options in San Isidro, Youth Hostel Malka is clean and pleasant, with a garden, climbing wall and ping-pong tables. It is very popular among budget travelers and backpackers, and word-of-mouth in South America has it as one of the best low-cost options in all of Peru. They are particularly proud of their comfortable mattresses. Prices include tax, breakfast is $2 extra. Los Lirios 165. Tel: 51-1-442-0162, Fax: 51-1-222-5589, URL: www.youthhostelperu.com Updated: Apr 15, 2009.

Hostal Collacocha

(ROOMS: $26 - 49) Located on a tranquil tree-laden street, Collacocha is pleasantly small and unassuming. Easily one of the best deals in San Isidro. The atmosphere inside is even better and it will be hard to find a lobby that rivals

Collacocha's in character and taste: The décor is rustic, eclectic and even eccentric. One finds delft tiles and gold-framed orthodox reliefs on the walls, stained-glass lamps, a fireplace and a pool table. The rooms though basic, are cozy and nice with beds, carpet, cable TV, private bathrooms, hot water and linens. One room is newly remodeled for handicap accessibility with a private bathroom. Although simple, all rooms have a really cozy feel to them. It's definitely a place you should check out (and into). Price includes tax for foreign tourists. Andrés Reyes 100, Zip: 27. Tel: 51-1-442-3900, Fax: 51-1-442-4160, E-mail: collacocha@viabcp.com, URL: www.hostalcollacocha.com. Updated: Apr 15, 2009.

Casa Bella

(ROOMS: $35 and up) Casa Bella is a pleasant, quiet spot in San Isidro. It's not too far from the action, however: Miraflores is only 10 minutes away. A converted private home, Casa Bella does not have a lot of rooms, so best to book ahead. Free Internet access, breakfast and airport pick-up for those staying three or more nights. Ask for one of the rooms that has a garden view. Taxes are included. Las Flores 459. Tel: 51-1-421-7354, URL: www.casabellaperu.net. Updated: Apr 15, 2009.

MID-RANGE

El Marqués Hotel

(ROOMS: $70-150) An excellent option if you want to treat yourself, but not spend a fortune. The hotel is beautiful--inside and out. The red brick building, with its surrounding foliage and broad shutters, resembles something of a chalet in the Swiss Alps. The interior–the lobby, bar and restaurant--is very quaint and provides for a relaxing stay. The rooms are clean, comfortable and individually decorated. A good, solid economic choice. Av. Chinchon 461, near the intersection of Av. Petit Thouars and Paseo Parodi. Tel: 51-1-442-0046, Fax: 51-1- 442-0043, E-mail: reservas@hotelelmarques.com, URL: www.hotelmarques.com. Updated: Apr 15, 2009.

Suites Antique

(ROOMS: $85-100) Suite Antique hotel is located in central San Isidro, so it's near restaurants, embassies, banks, parks, supermarkets, shopping malls, museums, markets and evening entertainment centers. All are just close enough to be convenient but far enough away to provide a quiet, restful stay. Rooms are comfortable and spacious with warm décor. Biarritz, the on-site restaurant-café, serves Peruvian and international dishes. The staff is friendly and the service is good. The property also features a business center, free parking, 24-hr front desk service and garden or city views. Av. 2 de Mayo 954. Tel: 51-1-222-1094, URL: www.suitesantique.com. Updated: Apr 15, 2009.

HIGH-END

Hotel Libertador San Isidro Golf, Lima

(ROOMS: $105-210) The Hotel Libertador faces the Golf Club. The 53 rooms have been decorated to provide the highest levels of comfort and quality. The Ostrich House Restaurant will dazzle you with the diversity of dishes and the Bar El Balcón will delight you with his special Pisco Sour. Wireless Internet access, fitness center, sauna and jacuzzi are offered. Rates do not include taxes but do include buffet breakfast. Los Eucaliptos 550. Tel: 51-1-421-6666, Fax: 51-1-442-3011, E-mail: reservaslima@libertador.com.pe, URL: www.libertador.com.pe. Updated: Apr 15, 2009.

Basadre Suites Hotel

(ROOMS: $130-177) Located in the San Isidro district of Lima, the Hotel Basadre Suites offers quick access to the best tourist spots and shopping centers. A great hotel for business as well as vacationing travelers, the hotel is 15 minutes from the international airport. Four room types are available: Single Room, Double Room, Junior Suite or Senior Suite. The inviting restaurant, with garden and swimming pool view, is a special place to start your day with a hearty breakfast, or enjoy a delicious lunch or dinner with a select variety of dishes of traditional Peruvian cuisine or international specialities. There is a shuttle from the airport to the hotel for $22-80. Taxes are included, as is breakfast. Av. Jorge Basadre 1310 Zip: 27. Tel: 51-1-442-2423, Fax: 51-1-222-5581, E-mail: reservas@hotelbasadre.com, URL: www.hotelbasadre.com. Updated: Apr 15, 2009.

Suites del Bosque

(ROOMS: $140-200) These upscale suites boast a cozy and pleasant atmosphere designed for the most aristocratic of travelers. With 54 contemporary suites that include all the latest in gadgets and luxuries including among others Internet, kitchenette, and air conditioning, the Suites del Bosque will accommodate almost any need. Dine on-site at the Crystals Restaurant that serves a variety of pastas and salads in addition to their buffet. There is also a business center with fax, phones, photocopier, computer access and laundry service available. Paz Soldan 165. Tel: 51-1-221-1108, URL: www.suites-delbosque.com. Updated: Apr 15, 2009.

Swissôtel !

(ROOMS: $240-1,500) Swissôtel's mission is to make your stay a memorable one, and with their luxury offerings--including sophisticated royal rooms, some of the most comfortable beds ever, top-of-the-line staff, and let's not forget to mention every amenity you'd ever want. It doesn't get much better than this. From their state-of-the-art spa services, fitness facilities (even a tennis court) to spotlessly clean quality, the hotel is a great place to indulge. Well-equipped for business people who want space for work (all rooms have desks and Internet), it's also great if you have lots of people in your party.

The 18-floor hotel with 244 rooms has ample space, but of course, it will cost you a few hundred a night. But even the most ragged traveler who wants serious luxury won't be disappointed. Three fabulous restaurants serving Swiss, Italian and Peruvian fare are also on the premises. Vía Central 150, Centro Empresarial Real Zip: 27. Tel: 51-1-611-4400, Fax: 51-1-611-4401, E-mail: reservations.lima@swissotel.com, URL: www.swissotel.com/lima. Updated: Apr 15, 2009.

Sonesta Lima Hotel El Olivar

Smack in the middle of the business district, Sonesta Lima Hotel El Olivar is perfect for business folks, along with families and travelers looking to stay in a safe nice area away from Miraflores. The large rooms have comfortable beds, cable TV, phones, carpet, air conditioning, minibar and a safe. The décor is bright and cheery, with colorful Incan fabrics. If you choose your hotel on the basis of bathrooms, look no further; the large, beautiful, marble bathrooms are perhaps this hotel's best feature. Well, that and the fact that the seven-story hotel overlooks Parque El Olivar, this is one of the best bangs for your bucks in all of Lima. Prices include taxes and breakfast. Childen under 8 stay free. Pancho Fierro 194. Tel: 1-800-SONESTA (US and Canada) / 51-1-222-4273 (locally), E-mail: reservations@sonesta.com, URL: www.sonesta.com. Updated: Apr 15, 2009.

Hotel los Delfines

Another luxury hotel in the swanky San Isidro district, Los Delfines is in an attractive, modern building. It sets itself apart by actually having two dolphins in residence there, Yaku and Wayra, who are quite popular with the guests. The rooms are pleasant and spacious, and there are a variety of suites and special rooms to choose from. The hotel features a cafe, bar and restaurant. The restaurant specializes in international cuisine. According to the web site, it has "an extraordinary view of the Dolphinarium," which is presumably a fancy name for the dolphin tank. The hotel also features a gym, spa and bakery that offers delivery. Los Eucaliptos 555. Tel: 51-1-215-7000 Fax: 51-1-215-7073 / 215-7071 E-mail: reservas@losdelfineshotel.com.pe, URL: www.losdelfineshotel.com.pe/ingles/default.asp. Updated: Apr 15, 2009.

Country Club Lima Hotel

The Country Club Lima Hotel was built in 1927 and refurbished in 1998. Today it stands as one of Lima's finer hotels. Popular with business and pleasure travelers, the hotel has everything you would expect from a five-star hotel: good service, a good restaurant, a travel desk and huge decadent and well-decorated rooms. Included are luxuries such as Internet, cable TV, a safe box, air conditioning, and more. No-smoking and handicap accessible rooms are available.Price description: There are no rates listed on their web site; however, the hotel falls into the luxury class. Los Eucaliptos 590. Tel: 51-1-611-9000, Fax: 51-1-611-9002, E-mail: country@hotelcountry.com, URL: www.hotelcountry.com. Updated: Apr 15, 2009.

V!VA ONLINE REVIEW
COUNTRY CLUB LIMA HOTEL

"The people who work here really know how to keep up a room. Also a great place if you like antiques."

Feb 27, 2010

San Isidro Restaurants

Like nearby Miraflores, the upscale San Isidro district of Lima is home to many excellent restaurants. Some of the best San Isidro restaurants them can be found in the international hotels that dot San Isidro, but many of the best restaurants are independent. If you're hungry for some local flavor, try lunch at a cevichería restaurant.

ASIAN

Matseui !

(ENTREES: $12-17) Often described as the best sushi bar in Lima, Nobuyuki Matsuhisa (founder of world-renowned Nobu Restaurants) co-founded this popular and classy sushi bar. Even the most critical sushi lovers will approve of the sashimi and maki rolls, and delight in the tempura and yakitori dishes. Manuel Bañon 260 Tel: 51-1-422-4323. Updated: Jul 12, 2007.

Tai Lounge

This exclusive restaurant and bar tends to attract the swankiest of Limeños who don't mind paying the elevated prices for drinks. Enjoy the lavish surroundings and lush lounging areas, watch the sophisticated patrons. and even if you're just stopping in for a drink, don't rule out sampling the tasty Thai food. Conquistadores 325. Tel: 51-1-422-7351. Updated: Apr 15, 2009.

CAFÉS

News Café

This delightful coffeehouse/café serves up excellent, strong coffee and a light menu of sandwiches and tasty gourmet salads. Anyone looking for international newspapers will be in heaven here with an array of daily and weekly papers from around the world to choose from. Intellectual sorts tend to hang out here and so if you're looking for conversation, you're likely to find it at News Café. Av. Conquistadores and Santa Luisa. Tel: 51-1-421-6278. Updated: Apr 15, 2009.

V!VA ONLINE REVIEW
NEWS CAFE

" The club sandwich is delicious and big enough to feed an elephant, if elephants ate bacon. "

Oct 23, 2010

INTERNATIONAL

El Cartujo

Removed from the activity of the city, El Cartujo enjoys a quiet location near a park. Stop in for a drink at the long wooden bar, a light salad, or order a delicious lunch from a menu that features anything from pasta, to sole-stuffed lobster or Argentine beef. The food is complimented by an excellent wine list. Reservations are recommended. Calle Los Libertadores 108. Tel: 51-1-221-4962. Updated: Apr 15, 2009.

V!VA ONLINE REVIEW
EL CARTUJO

" Their Pisco Sour will please anyone. It's true!!! "

Jun 01, 2010

Los Delfines

Join the posh clientele for pricey (and refreshing!) cocktails at this upper class hotel and casino. The Oceanus Lounge. is the perfect place to relax and enjoy good company in a marvelous setting. Should there be a lull in the conversation, let the resident dolphins entertain you with their antics in the surrounding tanks. Los Delfines Hotel, Los Eucaliptos 555 Tel: 51-1-215-7000. Updated: Apr 15, 2009.

ITALIAN

Punto Italiano

(ENTREES: $10-16) This traditional trattoria-style restaurant features Italian dishes that are sure to satisfy the hungriest of travelers. Dine on handmade ravioli stuffed with tasty ingredients. Don't miss the pizza unless, of course, it is to try one of the rich pasta dishes with the meat of your choice. Av. 2 de Mayo 647. Tel: 51-1-221-3167. Updated: Nov 14, 2008.

Alfresco

(ENTREES: $10-18) This popular oceanfront restaurant is part of a well-known chain and offers diners a delightful meal overlooking the water. With excellent seafood selections such as reasonably priced ceviche, a delicious charcoal fillet of sea bream, a tasty pulpo a la brasa (grilled octopus) or fetuccini negro con camarones (squid ink pasta with shrimp), you'll experience a dish you've never tasted before. Complement your meal with a South American wine from the extensive list and you'll leave with a full tummy. Santa Luisa 295. Tel: 51-1-422-8915. Updated: Apr 15, 2009.

Trattoria San Ceferino

(ENTREES: $11-19) Centrally located in the heart of San Isidro's comercial centre, this Italian restaurant serves traditional Italian dishes, such as pasta, pizza, lasagna, ravioli and spaghetti. Frequent diners of the Trattoria San Ceferino often request the famous shrimp dish timbal de camarones, the bife de chorizo (a large strip steak) or the unique potted duck and green risotto dish. Av. 2 de Mayo 793. Tel: 51-1-422-8242. Updated: Jul 12, 2007.

MEXICAN

Como Agua Para Chocolate

This colorful little cantina offers deliciously traditional Mexican entrées in a vibrant atmosphere. Enjoy specials like barbacoa de cordero (lamb steamed in avocado leaves) or albóndigas al chipotle (spicy meatballs and yellow rice). A creative lunch menu has many choices and the dessert menu includes tasty sweets doused in chocolate. Pancho Fierro 108. Tel: 51-1-222-0297. Updated: Feb 22, 2010.

PERUVIAN / TRADITIONAL FOOD

La Casa Verde

(ENTREES: $2-4.50) Located on Avenida Arequipa, merely a block away from the intersecting Javier Prado, La Casa Verde is in a central, convenient location. On the surface, it seems that it would be an excellent choice for the price, between $2-4.50 a plate. The exterior is quite impressive, almost café-like, with its broad green and white-striped awning. The seating area is spacious and you can enjoy an abundance of natural light pouring through the many windows. Unfortunately, the inattentive service can be a turn-off, and the food is nothing to write home about, but it does fill you up and keeps the budget low. Open Mon-Sun 7a.m.-11p.m. Av. Arequipa 2795. Tel: 51-1-222-1672. Updated: Apr 15, 2009.

El Buen Sabor

(ENTREES: $2-5) If you're looking to sample cheap, classic Peruvian dishes as well as to try Peru's most renowned dish, ceviche, this is it. Well-lit, clean and spacious, the service is professional and efficient. Only a block away from Avenida Arequipa, you shouldn't have too much trouble finding it. Av. Petit Thouars 3320. Tel: 51-1-422-9737. Updated: Apr 15, 2009.

Lalo's

(ENTREES: $3-5) Lalo's is in Lima's modern San Isidro financial district, on the corner of Augusto Tamayo. They serve traditional Peruvian food like ceviche, mixto, lomo saltado, papa a la huancaína, aguadito de pollo, chupe de camarones and escabeche de pescado. Daily specials also feature international dishes from other South American cuisines. The food is fresh. Eduardo Garland Barón, the executive chef and owner, was born in Peru and has operated restaurants in Cancun, Costa Rica and Houston. The restaurant modern decor is brightly colored. It is a great setting to enjoy a wonderful meal. Drop by for a frozen margarita or pisco sour. Augusto Tamayo 196. Tel: 51-1-421-4471. Updated: Apr 15, 2009.

T'anta

(ENTREES: $5 - 9) For quick eats in the café or for takeout, T'anta makes tasty salads, paninis, Peruvian sandwiches, homemade pastas and excellent desserts. This chic café is comfortably stylish and there is bound to be something on the menu that will hit the spot. Stop in for a coffee and to sample the exceptional passionfruit tart. Pancho Fierro 117. Tel: 51-1-421-9708. Updated: Apr 15, 2009.

PIZZA

Antica Pizzería

Antica Pizzería is one of Lima's most popular Italian restaurants, specializing in wood-burning oven-style pizzas and standard but well-done Italian meals. The long, wooden tables can be awkward, but the pizza is first-rate. Av. 2 de Mayo 728-744. Tel: 51-1-422-7939 / 222-9404. Updated: Jul 12, 2007.

SAN ISIDRO

SEAFOOD

Punta Sal

(ENTREES: $9-15) Serving the freshest in seafood, Punta Sal offers top-notch ceviche, scallops and other gourmet nationally and internationally famous dishes at reasonable prices. With excellent service and a well-rounded South American wine list, Punta Sal delivers a satisfying dining experience. Conquistadores 958. Tel: 51-1-441-7431. Price description: Updated: Jul 12, 2007.

STEAK

La Carreta

La Carreta is a steak house favored by Lima locals. It attracts an interesting power-lunch crowd of bankers, lawyers and politicians. The décor is colonial hacienda and quite pleasant. A carnivore's delight, La Carreta offers various cuts of meat prepared in different ways. It is expensive by Lima standards, but still one of the best steak houses in town. Rivera Navarrete 740. Tel: 51-1-442-2690. Updated: Apr 15, 2009.

)))))

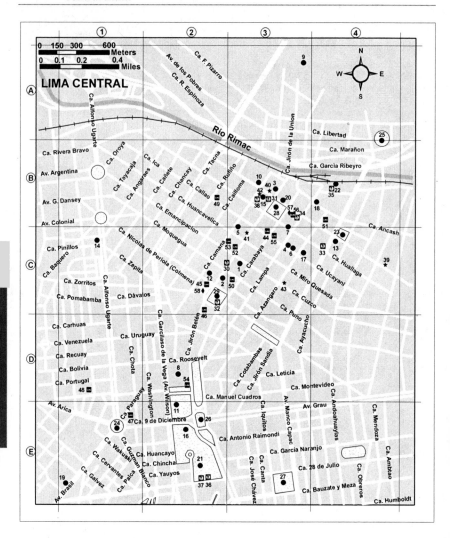

Central Lima

Centro Historico is the heart of Lima. Once an important Incan city, Lima became major port under Spanish rule. Although their first efforts at building a city on the site were destroyed in a 1746 earthquake, the city was rebuilt and today is home to some of the most impressive architecture in the Americas.

Any visitor to Lima should visit the historical center at some point. All of the important churches, monasteries, and plazas are located there, as well as many of the most interesting museums. There are also a number of hotels and hostels, the most interesting of which are stately colonial homes that have been converted to hotels. Backpackers and those on a budget will find Central Lima's hotels affordable and unique. Updated: Jul 10,2007

History of Central Lima

Lima's central colonial district is one of the most historic in all of Latin America. The center has seen a great deal of history. since established by Francisco Pizarro in 1535.

Pizarro founded Lima as the "City of Kings."

Activities ●
1 Almacén Metro C3
2 Arte en Cuero Sánchez C2
3 Casa de Aliaga B3
4 Casa Goyeneche C3
5 Casa Riva-Agüero B3
6 Casa Torre Tagle C3
7 Catedral de Lima B3
8 Centro Cívico D2
9 Cerro de San Cristóbal A3
10 Convento de Santo Domingo B3
11 Italian Art Museum E2
12 Iglesia de Jesús C2
13 Iglesia de San Pedro C3
14 Iglesia San Francisco B4
15 Libería El Virrey B3
16 Museo de Arte de Lima E2
17 Museo de la Inquisición C3
18 Museo de la Nación B4
19 Museo Larco E1
20 Palacio de Gobierno B3
21 Parque de la Exposición E2
22 Parque de la Muralla B4
23 Plaza Bolívar B4
24 Plaza Bolognesi D1
25 Plaza de Acho A4
26 Plaza Grau E2
27 Plaza Manco Cápac E3
28 Plaza Mayor B3
29 Plaza San Martín C2

Eating 🍴
30 Aero Club del Peru C2
31 Consentino Gourmet B3
32 El Estadio Fútbol Club C2
33 Jimmy's Baguetería C4
34 La Catedral Restaurant and Bar B3
35 La Muralla B4
36 Laguna Dorada E2
37 Palacio de Sancochado E2
38 Pardo's Chicken B3

Services ★
39 Belmundo en Línea C4
40 Correa Central de Lima B3
41 Diana Net and Tattoo Parlour B3
42 Lima Municipal Tourism Information Office B3
43 Teleperu Telephone C3

Sleeping 🛏
44 El Balcón Dorado B3
45 Gran Hotel Bolívar C2
46 Hostal Belén C2
47 Hostal de las Artes D1
48 Hostal Iquique D1
49 Hostal Roma B2
50 Hotel Continental C3
51 Hotel España B4
52 Hotel Inka Path C3
53 Hotel Kamana B3
54 Hotel Lima Sheraton and Casino D2
55 Hotel Maury B3
56 The Wiracocha Hotel B3

Tours ♦
57 Fertur Peru Travel B3
58 Mirabus C2

himself, with the cathedral on one side, the Cabildo (town hall) on another side and Pizarro's own house on another. Pizarro lived in what is now known as the presidential palace until his death in 1541; he was hacked down in the street by rival conquistadores. His remains are in the cathedral.

After Pizarro, Lima continued to be very important historically. Lima became the seat of one of only two Spanish viceroyalties in the New World; the other was in Mexico City. A third was added in Buenos Aires later. As such, it was the political and spiritual hub of Spanish South America for centuries.

Spanish civil and religious authorities set up shop in Lima, ruling the part of the Spanish Empire that stretched from Quito to Chile. The discovery of rich mineral deposits in parts of Bolivia and Peru meant that a great deal of wealth flowed into Lima, and some of the old colonial homes still reflect this.

The Holy Office of the Inquisition was established in Lima, and began looking for heretics to prosecute. Under the Inquisition, there was a great deal of paranoia and witch-hunting. The Inquisition was charged with destroying idolatry, but they were forbidden to persecute indigenous Andeans. The idea was that the natives, recently pacified and brought to Catholicism, needed time to adapt to Christianity. Therefore, they were given a "free pass" of sorts. They were punished when they were found to be continuing to practice their traditional rituals, but they were not executed or burned at the stake (not always, anyway).

Since the natives were off limits, the Inquisition went after crypto-Jews (Jews who had "converted" but who continued to practice Judaism in secret) and Protestants. Lima's central square was often the site of *Auto de Fé's*, which were public penances for those tried and convicted. Some, but not all, of those convicted were later executed by burning at the stake.

In 1746, a devastating earthquake hit the city, killing thousands and toppling many buildings. The city was rebuilt, although a great deal of historic architecture was lost.

In 1988, Lima's Historic Center was named a UNESCO World Heritage site. One of the architectural features of colonial Lima is its balconies. By some estimates, there are

CENTRAL LIMA

Although no kings ever visited during its early history, it was home to 40 viceroys during the colonial era. The central square (Plaza de Armas) was laid out by Pizarro still more than 1,600 balconies that have survived since Lima's earliest days.

In the late 1990s, local efforts were made in Lima to significantly clean up downtown Lima. Street vendors were kicked out, more police were sent in on patrol and street crime diminished significantly. Updated: Jul 10, 2007.

Central Lima Services

TOURISM OFFICE

Lima Municipal Tourism Information Office

Most visitors to the historical center of Lima will be pleased to take advantage of Lima's Tourism Municipal Information Office, located on the Plaza de Armas and in between some of the best restaurants in the area. With a concierge who can communicate in English as well as Spanish, this is one of the best first places to go before you start taking advantage of Lima's urban and coastal niceties. The office provides any number of brochures, maps and references about where to go and what to see-not only in Lima, but throughout Peru. 10:00 a.m. - 6:00 p.m. Jr. de la Union 300 / Jr. Conde de Superunda 177. Tel: 51-1-315-1300, URL: www.munlima.gob.pe. Updated: Nov 25, 2009.

KEEPING IN TOUCH

Teleperu Telephone

The telephone cabinas at Teleperu Telephone provide an inexpensive and expedient manner to call outside the country: the USA and Canada are only 25 céntimos a minute, or nine cents US. Spain, Italy, and Japan are 12 cents a minute, and the rest of the world 20 cents. Calling within South American and within Peru is also available. These cabinas can be found throughout most tourist-trafficked areas of Peru, and usually operate from 8 a.m.-10 p.m. Updated: Nov 04, 2009.

Correo Central de Lima

Not just a post office, this very big and ornate edifice behind the Palace of the Governor in the historical center is worth visiting simply for its architecture. The building also serves as a historical museum, complete with displays of notable stamps. The displays detail the importance of the Peruvian postal service as a hub of communications technology from its founding in the 19th century, when it provided the first telegraph, and later radio, services to the country. The interior is divided by a walkway under elegant metal arches. Be prepared for merchants who will very aggressively try to get you to purchase the postcards that they have for sale. Monday - Saturday 8 a.m. - 8:45 p.m., Sunday 8 a.m. - 4 p.m. Pasaje Piura, next to the Palacio de Gobierno. Tel: 51-1-533-2005 / 5152. Updated: Nov 04, 2009.

Belmundo en Línea

This particular Internet station is clean, cool and well-ventilated, with modern computers, large monitors, webcams and headsets with microphones for calls via Skype and other software programs possible. It also offers scanning and other copying services, as well as printing. The cost is about 45 cents an hour, and there is a minor offering of juice, snacks and stationary supplies. The only drawback is that their well-used keyboards wear out frequently, so you might find yourself having to type with extra-tactical tenacity. Av. Petit Tours 3006 and Javier Prado. Updated: Dec 03, 2008.

Diana Net and Tattoo Parlor

Diana Net could be considered an attractive option for travelers considering two different purchases: an hour's worth of surfing the net and a tattoo. That is, this Internet cabina on the mercantile Jirón de la Reunión offers both, though the owner, Augusta, said she would prefer not to work on you while you are instant messaging. All the computers come with webcams and microphones. International long-distance calling services are also available. The cost of time on the computer is only one sol per hour. Jiron de la Union 518, Suites 203 and 204. Tel: 51-1-428-2793, E-mail: blackline_tatto@hotmail.com. Updated: Apr 15, 2009.

SHOPPING

Almacén Metro

There are any numbers of stores along Jirón de la Reunión selling clothes, food and office supplies, but you might prefer to cut to the chase and simply stop at the massive Metro, occupying an entire block of Avenida Cuzco between Calles Carabaya and Lampa. Part of the Almacenes Metro chain, one of the most extensive in Latin America, this superstore is your Wal-Mart south of the equator. There is a large supermarket downstairs, a food court upstairs, and everywhere else all you need for just about everything. Av. Cusco, between Lampa and Carabaya. Updated: Jul 13, 2007.

Arte en Cuero Sánchez
Another great bargain for tourists, this is your chance to get custom-made, personally designed leather goods at cheap prices. A top-notch leather jacket can be tailored for less than $60. Owner Lourdes Sánchez and her expert staff can also fashion such suede and/or leather items as hats, pants, skirts, belts, wallets, handbags, ties and even undergarments, in a variety of tones, shades, cuts and zippers—in three days or less. Jirón de la Unión N835, 506. Tel: 51-1-427-3951 / 520-8352. Updated: Dec 03, 2008.

Librería El Virrey
This handsome bookshop in the historical center has a larger and more cosmopolitan selection than most in Lima. It is one of the few that stocks both foreign language books and magazines. El Virrey also offers a variety of useful maps and guides. It is open every day, early to late, and takes all credit cards. Pasaje los Escribanos 107-115. Tel: 51-1-427-5080, E-mail: libreria@elvirrey.com, URL: www.elvirrey.com. Updated: Dec 03, 2008.

Palacio de las Maletas
This store, with a name that translates literally as "The Palace of Suitcases", offers exactly what it promises: total luggage lunacy. Leather, canvas, plastic? Briefcases, suitcases? With wheels, without? Portfolio, travel bag? Backpack, rucksack, knapsack? Duffel bag, satchel, wallet, handbag, purse? Got it, got it, got it. The staff also promises to reconstruct and repair all suitcases in accordance with the highest standards of quality. They are the exclusive representatives in Peru of the Airliner, Pagani, and Arena Milano brands. 9 a.m. - 9 p.m. Jirón Junín 405. Tel: 51-1-427-9671 / 3278. Updated: Jul 12, 2007.

Palacio de la Esmeralda
At Palacio de la Esmeralda you can pick out an exquisitely polished and mounted emerald, presented on rings, amulets, bracelets, necklaces and earrings, and shaped in a variety of forms: heart, tear, oval, square or simply round. The creative designs include incorporations of Incan motifs. Palacio de la Esmeralda also sells other high quality folk art. Plaza de Armas, Pasaje Santa Rosa 119. Tel: 51-1-426-7432, URL: www.emeraldsandgems.com. Updated: Apr 15, 2009.

Feria Manos Artesanas
Just outside the north entrance to the Parque de la Exposición is your opportunity to sample a tradition that pre-dates Peru itself; the folk bazaar. Under a bright yellow and red tent, this event sponsored by a variety of indigenous retail and cultural associations is a colorful, sometimes gaudy spectacle of folk art and services. Which is to say, beyond the crafts, you can also have your future divined or your back massaged. There are also a number of food vendors selling shish kabobs and ice cream, and even one restaurant, the Plazuela de los Artesanos, with indoor and outdoor seating. 9 a.m. - 11 p.m. Plaza de los Artesanos, Avenida 28 de Julio. Tel: 51-1-424-1937. Updated: Jul 12, 2007.

DJ Tattoo Machines
Leave Peru as a new you—literally. With the exchange rate favoring the dollar over the sol, nearly one to three, go ahead and put that Chinese dragon on your thigh or the Sun God Viracocha on your chest, or simply your mom's name on your arm, at an exceptionally low cost but very skillfully and professionally done by owner and tattoo pro David Manuel Fernández. The process is sterile and hygienic, and David is committed to a solid rapport with his all clients, ensuring a harmony between what you want and what the artist can provide. The staff will work on literally any requested area. Cuadra 5 Jirón de la Unión, Galería Espadero, Sótano #103. Tel: 51-1-9-729-3218, E-mail: dmfc8@hotmail.com. Updated: Jul 12, 2007.

Things to See and Do
The colonial center is the heart of Lima, and a can't-miss for any visitor. It is where you'll find the best museums, restored homes and city parks, as well as numerous good hotels and restaurants. There are many churches and other religious buildings, plus good shopping. Updated: Jul 11, 2007.

CULTURAL TOURS

Casa Torre Tagle
One of the oldest and most accomplished expressions of Spanish colonialism, the Casa Torre Tagle merits a visit. It is named after the Marquis Torre Tagle, a former treasurer of the Spanish Armada. Built in 1735, this is one of the last examples of Baroque design found in the Americas, with imperial staircases, ballrooms and tiling that alludes to the influence of the earlier Moroccan conquest of Spain. A gilded, 16th-century carriage is

also on display. The coat of arms itself was designed by the Marquis. Its very ornate balconies and stone carvings on the outside evoke all the grandiose presumption of the Spanish empire. As headquarters for the Ministry of Foreign Affairs, public access is limited to the courtyards. Tel: 51-1-424-9066 / 7560. Updated: Apr 15, 2009.

Casa Goyeneche

Across the street from the Casa Torre Tagle is the Casa Goyeneche, also known as the Casa Rada, constructed 40 years later. These side-by-side buildings provide a striking opportunity to observe the shift from early 18th-century Baroque to the late-18th century, somewhat sparer, style of Rococo. By any standard, however, its carefully carved balconies are models of elegance. The building is now under the auspices of Peru's Banco de Crédito. From the Plaza de Armas go west from Jirón Wiese to Jirón Ucayali. Turn left and walk two blocks. Jirón Ucayali 358. Tel: 51-1-349-0606. Updated: Nov 04, 2009.

PARKS

Parque de la Cultura

Featuring some of the most exquisite architecture in Lima, the Parque de la Cultura is a tribute to Lima's urban planners in the 19th century, when it was conceived and built in 1868 as the Parque de la Exposición, as it is still referred to by many locals. Its mix of fountains, Victorian houses and modern art make this a popular favorite for Lima families and lovers. It is also home to two theatre companies that showcase cutting-edge work for both children and adults. Currently, and perhaps as a way of reducing crime and litter, only one or two of its high-iron gates are open at any time Avenida Wilson and 28 de Julio. Updated: Jul 13, 2007.

Parque de la Muralla

This new park, complete with a track for children to cycle and a pedestrian walkway, sits on the banks of the Río Rímac. During its construction, diggers unearthed the remains of 300-year-old city walls that were once meant to repel both the rising river and Dutch pirates. A small museum on the site explains some of the history of the wall and the city of Lima. There are also modern restaurants and tourist shops. It is clearly designed for families with children, but even on your own, it is a surprisingly pleasant

experience. Av. Abancay and Jirón Amazonas. URL: www.serpar.munlima.gob.pe. Updated: Apr 15, 2009.

PLAZAS

Plaza de Acho

The Plaza de Acho was founded in 1766 by the Viceroy Amat and stands proudly as the primary bullring of Lima. It is also considered the oldest in South America. Various celebrations are held here, such as the Señor de los Milagros Fair. The Museo Taurino is nearby. The bullring is made of adobe and wood and has survived earthquakes for centuries. 10 a.m. - 6 p.m. Closed Monday. Jirón Hualgayoc 332. Tel: 51-1-481-1467. Updated: Apr 15, 2009.

Plaza de Armas

Inca temples once stood here. Spanish conquistador Francisco Pizarro was assassinated here. Accused sorcerers were brutally punished around the square in the 17th century. Throughout history, the Plaza de Armas, or Plaza Mayor, has been a focal point of Lima, with its cathedrals, ornate buildings and government palace. Now, it is a UNESCO World Heritage Site. The Plaza de Armas spans four large blocks, with a park in the center. A bronze fountain with an angel perched on top blowing a trumpet is its centerpiece. It's also the oldest remaining structure, created in 1650. On the north end of Plaza de Armas is the Palacio de Gobierno (governor's palace), which is now home to Peru's president and is open for tours. Visitors can see a traditional changing of the guard (Monday through Saturday, at 11:30 a.m.), but guards are always on duty here if you just want a dose of presidential (and military) ambiance. Catedral de Lima is home to a religious museum and what are believed to be Pizarro's remains, which are encased in a casket.

The Iglesia de Merced dominates another block and the main post office is right off the plaza. Several other historic buildings and churches are within a few blocks, including the San Francisco monastery and church. Catacombs are its claim to fame and open for tours. At night, hundreds of people stroll the park and sit on the church steps to experience the culture. There's also an information office here to get tips on the next sightseeing stop. Located about two blocks south of the Río Rímac. Monday

- Friday 9 a.m.-4:30 p.m., Saturday 10 a.m.
-4:30 p.m, Closed Sunday. Tel: 51-1-427-
9647 . Updated: Apr 15, 2009.

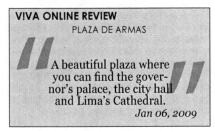
Plaza San Martín

Plaza de San Martín is one of the largest
and most impressive city squares in Lima.
Built in 1921 and named for José de San
Martín, a hero of South American independence, the plaza is paved with stones and
decorated with antique-looking lights and
benches. There is an impressive statue of
San Martín in the center of the park. On
one side of the plaza is the seen-better-
days Gran Hotel Bolívar. The Teatro Colón
and El Club Nacional are also located on
the plaza at the end of Jiron Bolognesi,
near La Punta in the Callao neighborhood.
Updated: Apr 14, 2009.

MUSEUMS

San Francisco

(ADMISSION: $1.60) San Francisco is a
sixteenth-century church and convent located in central Lima. Visitors can stroll
around the gorgeous courtyards and marvel at the woodwork, tiles and paintings
that adorn the inside of the convent. One
highlight is the catacombs, a public cemetery where bodies were stacked like wood
and allowed to decompose before being
stored elsewhere. Also, look for the painting of the last supper in which the disciples
are eating cuy, or guinea pig, a traditional
Andean dish. Part of the San Francisco
convent has been set aside as a museum
(admission: $1.60, open 10 a.m.-5:45 p.m.
daily). It houses an impressive collection of
colonial and republican era paintings and
religious art, such as carved crosses, urns,
etc. The museum prides itself on its collection of paintings by Francisco Zurbarán, a
well known artist. Aficionados of colonial
or relígous art will enjoy the museum. San
Francisco is located in central Lima, only
about two blocks away from the Plaza Mayor
and the Cathedral. Updated: Apr 15, 2009.

Casa de Aliaga

Casa de Aliaga, or the Aliaga Home, is a fascinating home and museum. Jerónimo de
Aliaga was one of Francisco Pizarro's most
trusted lieutenants during the exploration
and conquest of Peru, and he was rewarded
in 1535 with a huaca, or Indian temple, which
he converted into a home. In some places the
original stonework is still visible. The home
has since remained in the Aliaga family for an
astonishing 17 generations. Today it is a restored colonial home, and features a series of
rooms that represent life in Lima in the 16th,
17th, and 18th centuries. Casa de Aliaga is not
open to the public; all visits must be arranged
beforehand through Lima tours. Jirón de la
Unión 224. Tel: 51-1-424-7560, URL: www.
casadealiaga.com. Updated: Nov 25, 2009.

Photo by: José Manuel Azcona

Italian Art Museum / Museo de Arte Italiano

Only a short distance from the Parque de la
Exposición, the Museo de Arte Italiano (Italian
Art Museum) is a pleasant detour into Renaissance culture, complete with a neo-classical
building and well-manicured front yard that
evokes 16th-century Rome. Designed by Mila-
nese architect Gaetano Moretti and donated by
Peru's Italian community to commemorate the
centennial of Peru's independence, it features a
combination of contemporary and classical art,
sculptures, paintings and furniture, as well as
works by local artists. 9 a.m.-2:30 p.m. Paseo de
la República 250. Updated: Apr 15, 2009.

The San Francisco Catacombs

This Franciscan church and monastery is one of the most haunting and memorable sites in all of Lima. Originally constructed in 1546, it is one of the oldest churches in South America. It also served as the first official Catholic cemetery in Lima, at a time when the dead were laid to rest in catacombs beneath the church—an echo of an old Roman custom. You will get to visit the catacombs and view the hundreds of centuries-old bones and scores of skulls as part of the guided tour. The church also has one of the oldest and most historically significant libraries in the Americas and dramatic collections of religious and secular art, including renaissance-era tiles imported from Spain. Plaza San Francisco, Jirón Ancash and Lampa. Tel: 51-1-426-7377 / 427-1381, ext. 111, Fax: 51-427-4831, E-mail: informes@museocatacumbas.com, URL: www.museocatacumbas.com. Updated: Apr 15, 2009.

Casa Riva-Agüero

The twenty-seven rooms in Casa Riva-Agüero provide yet another echo of a distant past in which the rich and powerful built large homes as tributes to their own importance. The last owner, Don José de la Riva-Agüero, at least had the good sense to donate the building to Peru's Pontifica Catholic University. It is now home to both a folk-themed Museum of Popular Art and a historical library, and at any given moment features some interesting scientific or cultural exhibit. Its colonial balconies and courtyard are worth looking at themselves. 8 a.m.-1 p.m. and 2 p.m.-7:30 p.m. Tel: 51-1-626-2000, E-mail: matp@pucp.edu.pe URL: www.pucp.edu.pe/ira, Updated: Apr 15,2009

HISTORICAL BUILDINGS

Lima Cathedral / Catedral de Lima

The Lima Cathedral, known simply as "La Catedral," is a highlight of any visit. The first stone of the cathedral was laid by Francisco Pizarro, the Spanish conquistador who defeated the Inca. Ironically, Pizarro would be laid to rest in the same cathedral less than ten years later, when he was murdered in the streets during the brutal warring among Spanish factions that followed the fall of the Inca. There are 15 smaller chapels within the larger cathedral structure, each of which is dedicated to a different saint or religious figure. The cathedral is famous for the ornately carved choir stalls and several impressive paintings. There is a museum which contains sacred items and relics as well as a collection of religious paintings, mostly from the colonial era. Updated: Apr 15, 2009.

Iglesia de San Pedro

A stunning church built by the Jesuits starting in the 16th century, St. Peter's Church is one of Lima's most popular landmarks. It is now a major visitor destination, as it features an impressive collection of fascinating colonial art. This church was built over the course of 200 years and as such contains a mish-mash of techniques and styles making it of particular interest to architecture students. Monday - Saturday 7 a.m.-12:30 p.m and 5-8 p.m., Closed Sunday. Jr. Ucayali at Jr. Azángaro. Updated: Oct 21, 2009.

Iglesia de Jesús, María y José

This small church doesn't look like much from the outside, but the baroque interior—considered the best baroque church interior in Lima, is worth a look if you're nearby. Monday -Saturday 9 a.m.-12 p.m. and 3-5 p.m. Jr. Camaná and Jr. Moquegua. Updated: Oct 21, 2009.

Convento de Santo Domingo

Two saints for the price of one! The remains of Lima's two saints, Santa Rosa de Lima and San Martín de Porres, rest forever at the Convento de Santo Domingo. Like other religious buildings in Lima, the convent was built over a long period of time and reflects varying architectural styles and movements. A very popular place to visit for limeños and travelers alike, it is well worth checking out. 9 a.m.-1 p.m. and 5 p.m.-8 p.m. Updated: Oct 21, 2009.

Palacio de Gobierno

On the northeast side of the Plaza de Armas, the Government Palace is one of the city's architectural delights. The home of the president was built in the 1920s and 30s in several phases by several architects, and was once the home of Marquis Francisco Pizarro, founder of the city of Lima. The mostly baroque style is reminiscent of Peruvian colonial art. There is a ceremonial changing of the guard every day at noon worth seeing, and a free guided tour of the palace that must be arranged 48 hours in advance at the Office of Public Relations around the corner. 10 a.m.-5:45 p.m. Updated: Apr 15, 2009.

ENTERTAINMENT

Concert Disco

The past and present meet at Concert Disco, a dance club in an antique building with imperially high ceilings, columns and rococo trim for what was most likely an old-money dynasty. Located on the Calle de Baquijano, near Cuzco and Jirón de la Reunión, it is now where local limeños take their sweethearts and even children to dance to a mixture of salsa, merengue, reggaeton, electronic rock and much more. Sunday through Thursday admission is free, on Fridays and Saturdays the DJ has a special mix of '80s and '90s hits. The bar serves beer, sangria and everything in between. Calle de Baquijano and Cuzco. Updated: Dec 09, 2008.

Palace Concert

Fast, loud and new, the Palace Concert dance club and bar will keep you on your feet from when doors open 6 p.m. until it closes the next morning at 9 a.m. You will find it right on the corner of Calle de Baquijano and the Jirón de la Reunión; admission is free, but the only requirement to get in, besides being over 18, is that you are a party of at least two. The DJ plays a mix of Latin genre favorites such as reggaeton, meringue and salsa, along with international pop hits and '80s and '90s favorites. Jirón de la Reunión 700. Updated: Apr 14, 2009.

Central Lima Lodging

Before staying in the historic city center of Lima, you should weigh the advantages and disadvantages. The disadvantages include much more noise than other parts of the city, smog and pollution, lack of parking and the general chaos that characterizes the downtown centers of many of Latin America's largest cities. On the plus side, you'll be close to historical structures and places as well as some of Lima's best museums. There is an assortment of restaurants in the area, for every taste and budget. There are a variety of hotels to choose from, the most interesting of which are the converted colonial mansions. These vary greatly in quality, cleanliness, comfort, and cost, so if you're interested in staying at one, shop around. They tend to have a lot of character: crooked, creaky floorboards, maze-like floor plans, and no two rooms exactly alike. The only general rule in the area is that you'll pay more for a room with a private bathroom. Updated: Jul 12, 2007.

BUDGET

Hotel España

(DORMS: $3.50, ROOMS: $17) Located on the same block as the San Francisco church and only a couple of blocks from the main city plaza, Hotel España is a boisterous, fun hostel favored by many international backpackers. Check out the rooftop garden

and café: they keep interesting birds and other animals there. The dorm-style rooms are among the cheapest in Lima. Bring your own lock to use one of their small lockers to store your things. Jirón Azángaro 105. Tel: 51-1-428-5546, E-mail: info@hostelespanaperu.com, URL: www.hotelespanaperu.com. Updated: Aug 03, 2009.

Hostal de las Artes

(ROOMS: $5-24) The Hostal de las Artes is located in Lima's historical center, not far from Paseo Colón and Plaza Bolognesi. The hostel itself is in a nicely restored 19th-century home, most of which is relatively original (their website points out that their plumbing and hot water system have been modernized). They offer an array of lodging options in different rooms, such as single with bath, single without bath, double with bath, double without, etc. Whatever option you need, their rates are among the lowest in Lima. Rates are tax-free for foreigners. Jirón Chota 1460. Tel: 51-1-332-1868, E-mail: artes@terra.com.pe. Updated: Apr 13, 2009.

The Wiracocha Hotel

(ROOMS: $9) For very undiscriminating travelers, the Wiracocha Hotel has one advantage; its proximity to the Plaza de Armas and all the other attractions in the Historical Center. Apart from that, Wiracocha is about as minimalist as a low-cost lodge in Peru can offer; rooms with or without bathrooms, lacking shower curtains. There is no electric fan and no television (though few people would miss the latter), and the rooms, while not filthy, could be described charitably as "institutional." Jirón Junín 284. Tel: 51-1-427-1178. Updated: Apr 13, 2009.

MID-RANGE

Hostal Iquique

(ROOMS: $11-32) Fernando and Nelly opened Hostal Iquique in 1991 and take pride in being a positive part of travelers' experiences. The hostel is known to be clean and friendly, but a little drafty. There is warm water, a shared kitchen and storage facilities. It's recommended you try to get a room on the top floor, in the back. Jirón Iquique 758. Tel: 51-1-433-4724 / 423-3699, E-mail: iquique@hostaliquique.com, URL: www.hostaliquique.com. Updated: Jan 17, 2010.

Hotel Inka Path

(ROOMS: $14-39) Very conveniently located on Jr. de la Reunión, the long and

CENTRAL LIMA

very mercantile walkway linking the Plaza San Martín with the Plaza de Gobierno, Hotel Inka Path offers high quality but low-cost rooms inside a refurbished old building. The rooms have ample space and very high ceilings. They all come equipped with cable TV and hot running water. Continental breakfast and free internet access come as part of the package. Jirón de la Unión 654. Tel: 51-1-426-1919 / 9302, Fax: 51-1-426-8967, URL: www. inkapath.com. Updated: Jan 15, 2010.

Hostal Belén

If you can book a room in this former military officers' club-turned-hostel and restaurant, consider yourself lucky. There are only ten rooms, and each comes with private bathrooms, hot running water and cable TV. The hotel is elegant and classy, and is located in one of Peru's most attractive areas (in front of Plaza San Martín on Av. Nicolás Piérola) Guests have access to theatres, taverns and a generally exciting nightlife—plus the hotel has its own cafeteria. Laundry, banking and internet services are ubiquitous throughout the neighborhood. Av. Nicolás de Piérola 953. Tel: 51-1-427-7391, E-mail: ryexport2000@ yahoo.es. Updated: Apr 13, 2009.

Hostal Roma

(ROOMS: $10-40) Having been in business for 35 years, the well-regarded Hostal Roma is something of a Lima institution. Travelers can say they slept in a converted mansion that dates from 1892, located mere blocks away from the central square, cathedral and other points of interest. Hostal Roma has 36 rooms, all of which are singles, doubles or triples. During high season rates may go up, and they suggest you make reservations ahead of time through their website. Located two blocks away from the main square and cathedral. Jirón Ica 326. Tel: 51-1-427-7572, URL: www.hostalroma.8m. com, Updated: Apr 13, 2009.

V!VA ONLINE REVIEW

HOSTAL ROMA

What is important in Lima? A clean room and a safe haven from the streets. This place has both.

Oct 03, 2010

Mami Panchita

(ROOMS: $20-40) Hostal Mami Panchita, located in the San Miguel district, is highly rated by past visitors. With only about 15 rooms, Mami Panchita is small, neat and comfortable. The owners speak Spanish, English and Dutch. Airport transfers available for an additional cost. Av. Federico Gallesi 198. Tel: 51-1-263-7203, E-mail: info@ mamipanchita.com, URL: www.mamipanchita.com. Updated: Apr 13, 2009.

Hotel Kamana

(ROOMS: $28-60) Hotel Kamana is located one block from the pedestrian street Jr. de la Unión, which is packed with restaurants, cafes, internet, shops and more. Important tourist sites can be visited by a short walking tour and the airport is just 30 minutes from the hotel. The hotel offers pleasant simple, double, triple and matrimonial rooms that come with cable TV, security box, telephone with national and international long distance access, a private bathroom and 24-hour hot water. Other services include the Mr. Koala Restaurant (serving traditional Creole cuisine and international dishes), the Koala Bar, WiFi internet service, foreign currency exchange, tourist information, laundry service, taxi service and free luggage storage. English and French are spoken. Jirón Camaná 547. Tel: 51-1-426-7204, E-mail: reservas@hotelkamana.com, URL: www. hotelkamana.com. Updated: Apr 13, 2009.

El Balcón Dorado

(ROOMS: $35-75)This bright little hotel offers a range of accommodations for backpackers, students and budget travelers. Rooms are furnished with cable TV, private bathrooms and hot water 24 hours a day. The hotel also has a travel desk, telephon and fax facilities, smoking rooms, restaurant, laundry, Internet access, 24-hour reception and luggage storage. Breakfast and linens are included. Credit cards are accepted and airport pickup is available. You can check in any time of the day. Jr. Ucayali N°170-180-194. Tel: 51-1-427-6028, URL: www.balcondorado.com. Updated: Apr 23, 2010.

Hotel Continental

(ROOMS: $40-75) Travelers willing to pay a little extra for North American standards of upscale comfort might be tempted to park their dollars at the Hotel Continental, but they'll be sorry. Despite the presence of a large lobby and a restaurant, the hotel and its rooms could be described as threadbare at best. In both the corridors and units, the carpeting is old and dirty, and you can see rust and grime along the metal trims in the windows. Worst of all, the rooms come neither with air conditioning nor electric fans. The hotel does offer fax, internet, laundry service, parking and a continental breakfast, but all are easily available elsewhere in the area. Jirón Puno 196. Tel: 51-1-427-5898 / 715-8749, E-mail: reservas@hotelcontinentallima.com, URL: www.hotelcontinentallima.com. Updated: Dec 03, 2008.

V!VA ONLINE REVIEW
HOTEL CONTINENTAL

If I was made to go back to Lima, I would stay here. It's old, but it has a charm. My grandkids might complain, but I rarely hear their cries.

Sep 31, 2010

HIGH-END

Gran Hotel Bolívar

(ROOMS: $50-150) Conveniently located on the Plaza de San Martín, the Gran Hotel Bolívar is a stately, elegant white building that was first built in 1924. It was specifically constructed to accommodate visiting heads of state and dignitaries who were coming to Lima to celebrate the 100-year anniversary of the pivotal battle of Ayacucho, and it shows. Arched doorways, crystal chandeliers and tasteful rooms and corridors abound. There are several large salons for special events such as meetings and weddings. Their list of previous guests includes many presidents and leaders of Latin American countries, as well as Ernest Hemingway, Orson Welles and even the Rolling Stones. Although expensive by old town standards, the room rates are surprisingly reasonable for such a historic and well-located building. Mid-range travelers may want to consider upgrading for a night. Breakfast is included in the rates. Jirón de la Unión 958. Tel: 51-1-619-7171, Fax: 51-1-619-7170, E-mail: reservas@granhotelbolivarperu.com, URL: granhotelbolivarperu.com. Updated: Apr 13, 2009.

V!VA ONLINE REVIEW
GRAN HOTEL BOLIVAR

¡Viva el Presidente! That's what people will say to you if you stay in the presidential suite, unless you're the type of leader that inspires coups.

Jan 26, 2010

El Lava

Near the historic Plaza San Martin is one of the best deals in Lima. It offers nearly first class-hotel rooms at hostel rates, and provides views of the historic plaza nearby. Once upon a time, this was one of Lima's premier hotels. It is still well-maintained and, for the price, you not only get your own room, but a private bath, electric fan, cable TV and a continental breakfast. The rooms themselves are clean and fresh. The El Lava hotel also comes with its own bar and restaurant. Av. Nicolás de Piérola 850. Tel: 51-1-242-5860 / 339-0545, E-mail: hplazareservas@terra.com.pe. Updated: May 18, 2009.

Hotel Maury

(ROOMS: $70-130) Hotel Maury was one of the best-known hotels in Peru for most of the second half of the 20th century. They closed their doors during the 90s, but re-opened in 2000 with a completely redone interior. The hotel offers all the services of an upscale hotel such as internet, air conditioning, room service and private parking. Jirón Ucayali 201, corner of Jirón Carabaya. Tel: 51-1-428-8188. Updated: Apr 13, 2009.

Hotel Lima Sheraton and Casino

(ROOMS: $72-275) The Sheraton Lima is one of the finest hotels in the city and almost certainly the best luxury hotel in the historic district. It is in a modern, stately building with 431 rooms and features all of the amenities you would expect from a five-star hotel; comfortable rooms, good service, fine dining, a spa and more. The price is competitive with other hotels in the city in the same class. A good option for those who want to be close to the old town without sacrificing any comfort or luxury. As the name implies, there is also a casino on the premises. Av. Paseo de la República 170. Tel: 51-1-315-5000 / 619-3300. E-mail: reservas@sheraton.com.pe, URL: www.sheraton.com.pe.Updated: Apr 13, 2009.

V!VA ONLINE REVIEW
HOTEL LIMA SHERATON AND CASINO

We like a good deal and we also like popcorn. With this we got the best of both worlds, minus the popcorn.

Aug 03, 2010

Central Lima Restaurants

As in the rest of Lima, there are plenty of diverse and great tasting options for every

CENTRAL LIMA

meal in Central Lima. The streets that are most populated with restaurants happen to be Pasaje Olaya on the Plaza de Armas and between Jirón de la Unión and Jirón Carabaya. Jirón Carabaya is a small pedestrian walkway that sees a lot of businessman during the lunch hour. Prices are a little higher in this area. Updated: Jul 11, 2007.

AMERICAN

R.H. Atlantic

R.H. Atlantic is the closest you will get to an American diner in Lima. Indeed, one of their offerings is "American-style steak," complete with an order of fries and a coke. The checkered red and black tablecloths help contribute to a pop-1950s ambience. However, the local cuisine is not forgotten, so you can sample fried yucca with cheese sauce, as well as pasta dishes. They also have many sandwich items and an extensive coffee list. Jirón Huallaga 146. Tel: 51-1-426-9627. Updated: Jul 11, 2007.

De César Restaurant

The style of this small restaurant points to an affection for Amerian pop culture, decorated as it is with posters of Elvis and Marilyn (as well as Chaplin, and Laurel and Hardy), race cars, and other iconic evocations of the United States of America. Here is where you will also find 18 selections of coffee and 13 alcohol-spiked options, such as espresso with vodka, gin, amaretto, and that Peruvian favorite, Pisco. There are also approximately 200 main course selections on the menu. Jirón de Ancash 300. Tel: 51-1-428-8740. Updated: Apr 13, 2009.

ASIAN

Chifa Fuc Seng

One of the brighter Chinese restaurants that you will find near the Historical Center, Chifa Fuc Seng's offerings include chicken chijaukay, tempura-fried chicken breast served with soy dipping sauce, lobsters with

mushrooms, pork with peach, and of course, Beijing duck. Hungry already? It is open every day from 11:30 a.m. onwards. Sorry, no credit cards accepted. Also, the staff speak very limited Spanish and absolutely no English. Jirón de Carabaya 612. Tel: 51-1-427-3223. Updated: Apr 13, 2009.

CHILEAN

Rincón Chileno

Now in its 42nd year, Rincón Chileno qualifies as an institution around the Plaza de Armas, serving as a goodwill ambassador of Chilean cuisine and culture since 1965. Here, if nowhere else in Lima, you will be introduced to popular Chilean favorites such as loco mayo, a seafood platter with mayonnaise; empanadas caldúas, a juicier version of the traditional meat pastry; pastel choclo, a fondue in a clay pot with chicken and beef; and poroto granado, a stew with squash and white corn. The restaurant, with its multiple rooms, is a lively tribute to Chilean culture, especially its music. Monday-Saturday, 10 a.m.-7 p.m., and Sundays and holidays until 4 p.m. Jirón Camaná N 228, Tel: 51-1-428-8640, E-mail: rinconchileno@yahoo.com, URL: www.rinconchileno.com.pe. Updated: Apr 14, 2009.

INTERNATIONAL

España Restaurant

Nothing like some fettuccine, a salad, steak with fries or even a vegetarian soyburger for lunch while a pair of large turtles walk between the restaurant's tables. All in a day for the Restaurant España, on the top floor of the popular, idiosyncratic Hotel España. You don't have to be a guest to enjoy this place and its laid-back bohemian vibe. Just be open to the unexpected. Jirón de Azángaro 105. Tel: 51-1-427-9196, E-mail: cmundo@hotmail.com, Updated: Apr 13, 2009.

Cosentino Gourmet

Inside the Palacio de la Unión and facing the Palacio del Gobierno, Cosentino Gourmet has a look that could be described as "classy" and a specialized, limited item menu, but you still pay no more than at any other restaurant in the area. The menu changes every day, but a typical offering is a choice between grilled chicken with oriental sauce or spaghetti with marinara. All items come with salad, bread and dessert. The facility is large and can seat upwards of 120, ideal for groups. Jirón de la Union 364. Plaza de Armas, Tel: 51-1-426-2279/2418, E-mail: cosentinogourmet@hotmail.com, URL: www.cosentinogourmet.com. Updated: Apr 13, 2009.

ITALIAN

Los Escribanos

This fashionable restaurant has a graceful and creative design (the internal harp of a piano is incorporated into a stairwell), along with high-quality preparations of Italian and Peruvian cuisine, sandwiches, vegetarian selections and European coffees. The prices here are slightly higher than average for Lima, though falling into mid-range for people accustomed to dollars and euros. It is open every day and accepts all credit cards. Nicolás de Ribera El Viejo N°106-112. Tel: 51-1-428-1005, E-mail: miraf@free.com.pe. Updated: Jan 18, 2010.

San Paolo

One of the few restaurants with a distinctly European atmosphere in the historical center, San Paolo features 13 selections of tea and 14 of coffee, including "banana café," made with actual bananas. This could be described as an Italian restaurant (many lasagna and ravioli items, and pizza) with a large selection of traditional Peruvian offerings. The wall display across the entire facility is original and appealing; glass panel exhibits of vintage wine bottles. No credit cards accepted. Jirón de Ancash 454. Tel: 51-1-427-5981.Updated: Apr 14, 2009.

MEXICAN

Hotel Continental Restaurant

The Hotel Continental Restaurant provides a more professional and cosmopolitan ambience than most in the area, though the menu items are mostly provincial. This is not to say that they aren't tasty. That includes items such as the *pescado a la chorrillana*, a Mexican-style plate with tomatoes, fish and vegetables, variations which include sliced beef. In Peru's winter season, the restaurant is open for breakfast, lunch and dinner, and during the summer only lunch and dinner. All credit cards are accepted. Jirón Puno 196. Tel: 51-1-427-5890, E-mail: hotelcontinental_04@yahoo.es. Updated: Dec 09, 2008.

PUBS / BARS

Rincón Cervecero

With life-size models of jolly guys in lederhosen and buxom barmaids, the spirit of an eternal Oktoberfest reigns supreme at Rincón Cervecero (literally, "beer corner"), a veritable Disneyland of drinking holes. The pub does serve food, and proudly boasts quality meals "guaranteed by a graduate of Le Cordon Bleu," Peru's most prestigious culinary school. It also serves beer fresh out of a barrel, and honor not only Oktoberfest (in September), but the Peruvian Beer Festival in January. Rincón Cervecero has an ample dance floor, too, making this one a lively place to spend an evening drinking, dancing and cheering on the favored soccer teams. Av. Nicolás de Piérola 926. Tel: 51-1-428-8866, E-mail: eliasumber@estadio.com.pe.Updated: Apr 14, 2009.

Rusti Bar

You walk up a flight of stairs that features logs as banisters. Then you step inside to find a pile of logs bound together to form a bar, logs and sticks forming chairs, and a general jungle atmosphere worthy of the backlot of an old Tarzan movie. You are in the Rusti Bar, near the main square of the Plaza de Armas. Open everyday and generally filling up later in the day, the Rusti Bar offers live music in addition to beer and pizza. They have an on-site wood stove where the chef tosses and bakes the pizza right before your eyes. 11 a.m. - 3 a.m. Jirón Callao 177, Tel: 51-1-439-9620. Updated: Oct 17, 2008.

TRADITIONAL / PERUVIAN

Raulito's

(ENTREES: $1.25-4) From its corrugated tin ceiling and artificial foliage decorating its spare white walls to its simple name, "Raulito's," after its owner Raúl, this eatery is pure working class Peruvian. However, the place is clean, the staff treats like you like a member of the family, the food is decent and the price is cheap. Hamburgers with frijoles, ceviche, steak and potatoes and fresh fruit juices are some of the menu items that are handwritten by the staff on a whiteboard. Jirón Lampa 148. Updated: Oct 17, 2008.

Pardo's Chicken

One of a great many competing restaurant chains in Peru, Pardo's Chicken boasts a more professional and less manufactured environment than most. Their location on the Plaza de Armas is a bonus for those who want to eat a traditional but well-made dinner in a pleasantly stylish setting, without having to pay the higher charges of other restaurants in the vicinity. Chicken is their specialty and they feature a variety of different preparations. Monday through Sunday, their Happy Hour includes two-for-one Pisco Sours, Cuba Libres and Piña Coladas. All credit cards are accepted. Pasaje Santa Rosa 153. Tel: 51-1-427-2301, URL: www.pardoschicken.com.pe. Updated: Oct 17, 2008.

Palacio de Sancochado ♪

(ENTREES: $6) The Palacio de Sancochado is not just a restaurant. A uniquely limeña local legend for 25 years, the Palacio de Sancochado relies on word of mouth and little else. Owner Juan Ruggiero's creative coup offers up more than lunch on its menu; it has to, since only lunch is served, from noon to 5 p.m., and only one plate offered, with no coffee or desert, either. He has converted his elegant 70-year-old childhood home into a virtual temple of time past. His home features everything from first–model jukeboxes to tintypes and just about anything uniquely obsolete. The total effect is intoxicating. The food? The one-entrée-only special is a proudly Peruvian platter of potatoes, yams, yucca, carrots, cabbage, garbanzos, rice, creole sauce and a half-kilo of beef—all for $6. You can forget about eating anything else the day you dine there. Av. 28 de Julio N 990, in front of the Parque de la Exposición. Tel: 51-1-331-0789. Updated: Oct 17, 2008.

Laguna Dorada

While visiting the Parque de la Cultura, the Food Rotunda is a fast, pleasant and convenient stop for your group. This food court is located beneath the stands of the outdoor Teatro de Exposición, and its climate, no matter how hot and humid the park may be on a given day, is always cool and dry. The food itself is inexpensive by foreign standards, and very filling. The restaurant offers what Peruvians like most; ceviche, arroz con pollo, batter-fried seafood and other local plates. Av. 28 de Julio, inside the Parque de la Exposición. Tel: 51-1-424-6015, E-mail: francon@yahoo.com. Updated: Apr 14, 2009.

Belén Restaurant

If you are hosting a special group event, or simple want to impress your friends while staying within your budget, you will have a hard time doing better than the Belén restaurant. Once a former military officers' club, it still retains an imperial ambience, complete with high ceilings, ornate trim, columns, marble floors and, most of all, a bust of former military president, Marshall Óscar Raymundo Benavides Larrea, whose imposing façade accompanies your dining experience. The focus is on native cuisine, with such exotic-sounding plates as sancochado (soup with chicken, beef, rice, potatoes and herbs), and mid-range prices starting at four dollars. Av. Nicolás de Piérola 953. Tel: 51-1-427-7391, E-mail: ryexport2000@yahoo.es. Updated: Jul 11, 2007.

Jimmy's Baguetería and Pastelería

Local bakeries are a mainstay of the Latin American economy, as much in Peru as anywhere else. It is hard to walk by most streets without being tempted by any number of carbo-rich items. Jimmy's Baguetería and Pastelería, specializing in breads and pastries, is no exception. It also features a large assortment of chicken, beef and pizza empanadas, along with the fresh baked bread and stylish wedding cakes. You will have a hard time saying no to anything once you step inside. Av. Abancay 296 Central. Tel: 51-1-428-8942. Updated: Dec 09, 2008.

La Posada del Márquez

Facing the Palacio de Gobierno, La Posada del Márquez offers high-quality local favorites such as beef cooked with beer and grilled chicken breasts that come with a side order of cheese-filled potatoes. The red and green-designed interior also comes with both an upper and lower floor, and seats 100. They accept all credit cards and are open everyday for breakfast, lunch and dinner. Jirón Huallaga 140. Updated: Dec 09, 2008.

La Muralla

The newly constructed riverside Parque la Muralla, along the Jirón de Amazonas in Lima, includes a slick, modern-style restaurant, La Muralla, complete with glass walls. It features seafood, sandwiches and salads, as well as a variety of pies, custards and other deserts. The prices are about average for Lima, inexpensive for most tourists. They can seat up to 150; a group wanting to enjoy the park and other nearby attractions could book space here. Jirón de Amazonas, Parque la Muralla. E-mail: restaurantelamuralla@hotmail.com. Updated: Oct 17, 2008.

El Estadio Fútbol Club

"Our motto is good food, good times and soccer," claims El Estadio Fútbol Club. And, with a large stained-glass soccer ball in the window and life-size models of some of Latin America's most famous soccer players sitting at the tables, what else could you expect? This sports-pub-to-end-all-sports-pubs is a Latino Bubba's dream, with a native menu that includes milanesa de pollo a la pobre (fried breaded chicken), French fries, fried banana, fried egg, white rice and salad- a "very light" offering we are assured. At three-stories high El Estadio Fútbol Club can accommodate up to 300 people, which makes it an ideal location for groups. Nicolás de Piérola 926 (Plaza San Martín). Tel: 51-1-428-8866. Updated: Mar 10, 2008.

V!VA ONLINE REVIEW

EL ESTADIO FUTBOL CLUB

Peruvian dishes laid out buffet style. You can eat till you develop a condition that will need surgery to correct. But it's worth it.

Mar 10, 2010

T'anta

In opening T'anta, famed restaurateur Gastón Acurio promised dishes that range from "light to forceful." T'anta features exotic dishes like chicharroncito, sliced pork with creamed sweet potato, orange sauce and Peruvian criolla, and Cheeses of the World, which as it promises is just that, with as many varied cheeses you can put on a plate. The restaurant can serve up to 100 people and accept all major credit cards. Monday - Saturday 9 a.m. - 10 p.m., Sundays 9 a.m. - 6 p.m. Pasaje Nicolás de Rivera El Viejo 142. Tel: 51-1-428-3115, E-mail: lima@tanta.com.pe, URL: www.tanta.com.pe. Updated: Dec 09, 2008.

Los Vitrales de Gemma

(ENTREES: $7-10) A former colonial mansion converted into a slick, classy restaurant, the Vitrales de Gemma is a great place for groups; it can seat up to 210. This restaurant is definitely more upscale; its appetizers start at around $5 and main courses go for $7 to $10. The menu

offers variations of traditional Peruvian favorites, such as ceviche, steak, and shrimp-filled crepes. It accepts all credit cards and is open for breakfast, lunch and dinner. Jirón Ucayali 332. Tel: 51-1-426-7796, E-mail: losvitralesdegemma@hotmail.com. Updated: Jan 19, 2010.

La Catedral Restaurant and Bar

(ENTREES: $12) If you are walking around the Plaza de Gobierno and in the mood for a more professional and modern environment in which to dine, La Catedral should satisfy you, from its checkered maroon and beige marble tiles to its carefully designed wooden chairs meant to echo the twin spirals of the Catedral de Lima. This restaurant offers appetizers that start at $4 and main courses, such as a Hawaiian steak, priced at $12. There are eight varieties of the perennial Peruvian favorite, ceviche, as well as a bar and a large selection of drinks. Jirón Junín 288. Tel: 51-1-856-4465, E-mail: Lacatedral_carowa@viabcp.com. Updated: Apr 14, 2009.

VEGETARIAN

Villa Natura

This is a very popular vegetarian restaurant; if you come alone you might have to share a table. They offer varieties of meatless cuisine, with or without eggs and dairy, fruit juices, carrot and other vegetable extracts, and such specialties as maca punch and quinoa drink. The service is somewhat sloppy, but the food is good. This restaurant also serves as a natural health store, with many organic herbs and remedies for sale. Monday - Saturday 7 a.m.-9 p.m. Jirón Ucayali 3200. Tel: 51-1-426-3944.Updated: Dec 09, 2008.

Miski Wasi

This vegetarian restaurant on Jr. de Ucayali has a very funky design, with East Indian, Cambodian and Tibetan folk art on display. The food is a competent offering of tempeh, soy and other vegetarian favorites, along with meatless South American offerings, such as choclo. The service is so-so, but the prices are very reasonable. It also has its own gift shop, selling many of the same folk crafts as in the restaurant, as well as some Peruvian work. Jirón de Ucayali 212. Tel: 51-1-247-0877. Updated: Apr 14, 2009.

)))))

CENTRAL LIMA

MIRAFLORES

Miraflores is one of Lima's most upscale districts. The area is full of fancy hotels, good shopping, elegant restaurants, bookstores, banks and more. Better nightlife can be found in the Barranco neighborhood, but that's not to say there's none in Miraflores. There is an archaeological site in Miraflores called Huaca Pucllana which is open daily and has a small but interesting museum. Updated: Apr 21, 2009.

History of Miraflores

This attractive area, with its ocean views and cliffs, was one of the first areas to be settled by the Spanish after Lima was founded. It was named San Miguel de Miraflores in 1535. From 1879 to 1884, Peru and Bolivia united to fight Chile in South America's bloodiest war, the War of the Pacific. One of the most famous battles was fought in Miraflores, in January 1881, during which 2,000 dedicated Peruvians fought the invading Chileans in Miraflores. They were Lima's last line of defense. The

Peruvians, short on munitions and outnumbered, were defeated and Lima was sacked. Nevertheless, the bravery of the Miraflores defenders is remembered today: Miraflores' official nickname is "the heroic city." One famous resident of the Miraflores district during this time period was Ricardo Palma (1833-1919), one of Peru's most celebrated writers.

In the 19th century, the area became known as a beach resort of sorts and its popularity grew. By the 1950s, it was one of Lima's most important districts. In 1992, the infamous Sendero Luminoso ("the Shining Path") detonated a car bomb in Miraflores; weeks later, terrorist leader Abimael Guzmán was captured in nearby Surquillo, only blocks away from Miraflores.

Today, Miraflores is one of the most affluent and attractive sectors of Lima. The streets are lined with trees, the buildings are well-kept and street crime is closely controlled

Activities ●
1 Costa Verde Beaches C3
2 El Faro de la Marina C3
3 Huaca Juliana A2
4 Larcomar Mall D3
5 Organic Market (Bioferia) C4
6 Parque Del Amor C3
7 Parque Kennedy C3
8 Redondo D3
9 South American Explorers SAE B3
Eating 🍽
10 Astrid y Gastón C3
11 Balthazar D3
12 Café Haiti B3
13 Café Café D3
14 Chifa "Jin" B1
15 Murphy's Irish Pub C3
16 Pescados Capitales B1
17 Scena C2
18 Shehadi NYC C3
19 The Old Pub C3
Nightlife 🍸
20 Aura D3
21 Pub Cubano 443 C3
Services ⚒
22 Correo B3
23 Dragón Internet C3
24 Jedi Travel Service-Internet Café C3
Sleeping 🛏
25 Albergue Miraflores B2
26 Casa Andina Miraflores San Antonio D4
27 Casa del Mochilero D2
28 El Condado Hotel and Suites C3
29 Flying Dog Backpackers C3
30 Home Peru C2
31 Hostal Buena Vista 31
32 Hostal Torreblanca B1
33 Hotel Antigua Miraflores C3
34 Hotel Colonial Inn B2
35 Inka Lodge Hostel B2
36 JW Marriot Lima D3
37 Loki Hostel Lima B3
38 Mirafolores Park Hotel D3
39 Soul Mate Inn Hotel B1
40 Wasijaus B3
41 Wayuro's Backpackers B2

"Lover's Park" is a step in the right direction. The central square, Parque Kennedy, is great for strolling and hosts occasional art shows and flea markets. Updated: Apr 21, 2009.

Miraflores Services

COMMUNICATION

Dragón Internet

This little internet café is located along a tiny boulevard adjoining the busy Avenida José Larco. It's a quiet, friendly place offering both internet access and international calling stations, but the internet cabins lack partitions. It's a good choice if you want to avoid the crowds and congestion of central Miraflores. Open 24 hours a day, seven days a week. Calle Tarata 230. Tel: 51-1-446-6814. Updated: Jul 13, 2007

MacPlanet Internet Café

This cozy little internet café is comfortable, with 11 private terminals, multimedia equipment, and services including E-mail, FTP, international calls, chat, printing capabilities, document scanning and web-hosting. Monday - Saturday 9 a.m.-11 p.m., Sunday 10 a.m.-3 p.m. Av. Aviacion 3380. Updated: Apr 21, 2009.

Jedi Travel Service - Internet Cafe

Located in the dead-center of Miraflores, across from Parque Kennedy, this café is a convenient option to check your E-mail and make international phone calls. The environment is clean and orderly, and the cabins are spacious and private. Monday - Sunday 8 a.m. - 2 a.m. Av. Diagonal 218 (second floor). Miraflores, Tel: 51-1-445-4227. Updated: Apr 21, 2009.

RadioShack

It's not uncommon to leave home without bringing all the necessary gadgets and adapters. Without these essentials, say goodbye to your cell phone, MP3 player and hairdryer. But in foreign countries like Peru, RadioShack with a large offering of electronics and products of the sort can be a godsend. Monday-Friday, 9 a.m. - 6p.m., Saturday and Sunday, 10 a.m. - 3p.m. Av. Salaverry 3310. Tel: 51-1-264-2600, URL: www.radioshack.com. Updated: Apr 21, 2009.

TRANSPORT

Manchego Turismo

Airport transfers, museums and city tours, and everything else you need. 9 a.m.-8 p.m. 7 days a week. Conjunto habitacional Elias Aguirre Modulo C, Dpto A, Callao. Tel:

(although not nonexistent). An effort has been made to preserve green space in Miraflores, and the dedication of the famous

51-1-420-1289, E-mail: manchego@terra.com.pe, URL: http://manchegoturismo.com. Updated: Apr 17, 2009.

SHOPPING

Organic Market (Bioferia)

Every Saturday morning locals flock to Parque Reducto in Miraflores to buy fresh organic produce and to taste an assortment of organic breads, jams and coffee as part of the weekly Bioferia, or organic market. With a wide selection of fruits and vegetables, the Bioferia is cheap, delicious, unique and is definitely worth a visit. Nearly a block long, the market is largely made up of a local organic farmers and environmental, education and natural health organizations, along with NGOs. It is a child-friendly zone, as there are many hands-on education activities for the young ones and many presentations on ecology and organic food production. Aside from fresh organic fruits and vegetables, you can pick up items such as chicken, eggs and a number of cow and goat milk products, including cheese. The organic baked-goods and jams are perhaps the best choice and don't forget to wash it down with a fresh organic guanábana juice or a sip of organic coffee. Saturdays only 8 a.m.-2 p.m. Behind Parque Reducto, Avenida Benavides and the Vía Express. Updated: Apr 21, 2009.

Larcomar

From the street, Larcomar looks like a nice cliffside park with fountains, a few palm trees and a crowd of people hanging along the railing looking out to sea. Walk a few steps closer and discover a three-story mall packed with restaurants, fast-food joints, shops, discos, a 12-screen movie theater and a 24-lane underground bowling alley.

Visitors gather topside for nightly sunset shows or to take take a breather from the fanfare below. On clear, calm days, a paraglider may drift by on their way to the beaches below. On the first level, which is open-air, shoppers can browse under the sun and watch daredevils get strapped to bungee cords and bounce around in a metal frame near the edge of the cliff.

Stores vary from mainstream jean and T-shirt shops to bookstores and boutiques that specialize in Peruvian handicrafts. American staples like RadioShack, KFC and Burger King make an appearance here. People who forgot to pack guidebooks and film can find it at Larcomar, as well as sleeping bags and other outdoor gear at Tatoo Outdoors. There's also a Western Union. People looking for more obscure things, like Che Guevara shirts, should head to the small trendy stores on Av. José Larco.

If you're shopping for crafts sold by the artists themselves or a bargain on crafts, Mercado de los Indios (Petit Thouars 5245) has a massive collection of artists and sellers under one roof. Larcomar's draw is its dramatic location with views of the Pacific. Larcomar is at Avenida Malecón de la Reserva 610, Miraflores, at the southern tip of Avenida José Larco. It's about 12 blocks south of Parque Kennedy. Buses run the strip; a taxi from Parque Kennedy runs about a dollar each way. Avenida Malecón de la Reserva 610. URL: www.larcomar.com. Updated: Apr 21, 2009.

Tatoo Adventure Gear

Tatoo Adventure Gear is a top source for brand-name sportswear, trekking and camping equipment, biking accessories and more. Located in Miraflores, Tatoo Larcomar stocks guidebooks and maps, and the knowledgeable staff provides information on mountaineering courses and seminars, and offers tips on everything from the best routes to climb to buying the perfect hiking boot. Monday to Sunday 11 a.m. - 10 p.m. Locales 123-126. Malecón de la Reserva and Av. Larco. Tel: 51-1-242-1938, E-mail: larcomar@tatoo.ws, URL: http://cl.tatoo.ws/store?id=15, Updated: Oct 16, 2009.

Things to See and Do

With interesting daytime sites to complement the exciting nightime antics, activities in Miraflores abound. During the day, you can visit a number of museums, Inca ruins or landmarks. Relax in the shade of a local park and peruse the markets that sell handicrafts, jewelry, artwork and food. Try your hand at surfing or wade through one of the more sandy beaches in Lima. Take a Spanish class to brush up on the language or hit a local club to taste the dance scene. Updated: Jul 13, 2007

SURFING

Costa Verde Beaches

There are four main surfable beaches along the Costa Verde beach road in Miraflores. All are within a 15-minute walk of each other. South of the pier at Rosa Náutica Restaurant is Redondo, and from there head north of the pier to find the breaks of Makaha, Waikiki and La Pampilla. All breaks are fairly consistent year round but best with a swell from the southwest. The shore and beach area of all four beaches consists primarily of large and small pebbles, making walking and entering/exiting the water difficult.

The water can be very polluted. When you think you've just paddled through a jellyfish, it's more likely a just plastic bag or some other form of trash. All breaks handle up to a maybe a little overhead wave, but consistently see waist-high to head-high surf. At Waikiki parking is tight, but the other three beaches have plenty of parking. You can find the beaches along Costa Verde Beach Rooad near the pier near Rosa Náutica Restaurant Updated: Apr 21, 2009.

Redondo

Picturesque Redondo is the only Costa Verde beach located south of the pier at Rosa Náutica Restaurant. The waves here break closer to the beach, providing an easier paddle. It is also less damning on the feet, as Redondo has less rock and more sand than the other Costa Verde beaches. The breaks here tend to be better with a more southerly swell. Costa Verde Beach Road—head south of the pier at Rosa Náutica Restaurant in Miraflores. Updated: Apr 21, 2009.

Makaha

Makaha is the most popular for beginner surfers, with both good inside and outside left and right breaks from an exposed reef. Schools and newbies occupy the inner break, and be warned, it can get fairly crowded on weekends. This beach, north of Rosa Náutica Restaurant's pier, has several kiosks along the sidewalk which rent boards and wetsuits for about $6.60 per hour or less, and offer lessons for about about $13.30 per hour. Go to Miraflores and head to the beach near Rosa Náutica Restaurant's pier—north of the pier you'll come upon Playa Makaha. Updated: Nov 25, 2009.

Waikiki

Not to be confused with Hawaii's famous Waikiki, Lima's Waikiki may not have crystal clear, warm waters, but when the surfs breaks it's a Lima favorite. With consistently good waves, Waikiki is made of an exposed reef break and has a more northerly swell than the other Costa Verde Beaches. It's not typically crowded, but when the waters get moving, the people come running. The beach is located along the Costa Verde Beach Road in Miraflores. Go north of the pier at Rosa Náutica Restaurant and you'll hit Waikiki, near La Pampilla Beach. Updated: Apr 21, 2009.

Photo by: Anaïs Marshall

La Pampilla

Of all the Costa Verde beaches, La Pampilla is by far the most popular break for intermediate and advanced surfers—and it should only be surfed by those who are skilled and know what they are doing. All breaks can see very good outer break wave formation, especially as the swell passes head-high. La Pampilla is along the beach road in Miraflores. Go north of the pier at Rosa Náutica Restaurant. It's near Makhaand Waikiki. Updated: Jul 16, 2007.

PARKS

Parque del Amor

Finish your cup of coffee or glass of wine at Larcomar and head north along Malecón de la Reserva. Walk along the scenic path for ten minutes and you'll see a little yellow bridge; behind the bridge is an imposing red sandstone sculpture of a man embracing his love sitting atop a black marble pedestal. This is Parque del Amor. The park's charm and character compensate for its small size. Beds of crimson roses, daffodils and violets have been carved in various shapes and stud the green grass. A white concrete bench, decorated with colorful mosaic tiles, presses against the cliffs' edges. Various couples, young and old, cuddle in the little enclaves and savor the sunset. The park truly embodies its name and is as safe as a hug. Av. Malecón Cisneros and Av. Diagonal. Updated: Apr 21, 2009.

El Faro de la Marina

El Faro de la Marina is a blue and white candy cane-striped lighthouse that faces the ocean. El Faro de la Marina doesn't have the cutting originality of Parque del Amor, but it affords beautiful, expansive views of the ocean and the softly eroded cliffs. On the broad patches of grass families picnic, dogs sprint back and forth and couples lay teasing one another. Like Parque del Amor, it has a distinct magnetism and is best accented by the pastel strokes of peach and purple at sunset. Av. Malecón Cisneros and Avenida Diagonal. Updated: Apr 21, 2009.

Huaca Pucllana

Machu Picchu may get all the glory, but ruins even older than the Cusco giant can be explored without ever leaving downtown Lima. Indigenous Peruvians started building Huaca Pucllana in 400 A.D.—nine centuries before the Incas started setting stones at mighty Machu Picchu. Those earliest residents gathered, traded, made community decisions, worshiped and sacrificed women and children at Huaca Pucllana for 300 years. They abandoned the site when the Wari empire conquered the area in 700 A.D., and built a cemetery for its elite on top of the pyramid. The Incas moved in some three centuries later.

Although Huaca Pucllana is ancient, it's a relatively new attraction. Grounds opened for tours in 1984 and excavation is ongoing. At the top, take in a panoramic view of downtown Lima and a bird's eye view of just how intricate the ruins are. Huaca Pucllana once stretched nearly eight square miles. Development whittled it to less than two and a half. There's a small flora and fauna park on the grounds, and a gift shop with a small selection of native crafts. Staff have built pens for animals that were used (or eaten) through the centuries, including guinea pigs. Even though the tour is guided, don't expect to be hurried. Guides are committed to Huaca Pucllana's preservation and welcome questions. If you want to grab a coffee or snack and savor the sight after the tour, the mid-range Restaurant Huaca Pucllana is right beside the ruins. The ruins are lit at night and nearly every table has a view. 9 a.m.-5 p.m. Closed Tuesday. The archeological site is at the end of Calle General Borgoño block 8, between block 4 of Avenida Angamos Oeste and block 45 of Avenida Arequipa. Updated: Apr 21, 2009.

V!VA ONLINE REVIEW

HUACA PUCLLANA

"This is expensive but interesting. I recommend it if you have the time."

Apr 23, 2010

Parque Kennedy

Smack dab in the middle of Lima's upscale Miraflores neighborhood is Parque Kennedy, flanked by two major thoroughfares— Avenida José Larco and Diagonal. The park is a small oasis among tall buildings and the congested traffic for which Lima is famous. A paved walkway runs through the center of Parque Kennedy, which draws a good number of people at all times of day. Young couples snuggle on benches, men in business suits read the paper while they get their shoes shined, and vendors sell salty popcorn from red and white carts. The southern end of the park is home to a children's playground, and there's a good view of the very ornate Iglesia de la Virgen Milagrosa on the north end.

Parque Kennedy is across the street from Restaurant Row, famous for its dozens of restaurants and bars that range from Italian and wood-oven pizzerias to Brazilian barbecue and Cuban dance floors. Get ready to make a run for it—crossing Diagonal is like dodging speeding bullets. Restaurant Row is pedestrian only and hopping at night, even during the work week. Competition is fierce: Nearly every eatery or bar has a tout outside, shouting out drink specials and personally beckoning you in. It's difficult to decide if a place is packed because it's got great food or because they offer the cheapest pisco sour. In the evening, Parque Kennedy takes on the atmosphere of a little fiesta. Some nights, the elevated cement circle in the park center plays host to artists selling woodwork, jewelry and other handiwork or vendors selling antiques. Outside cafés are usually full and decorated with white outdoor lights and table canopies. A meal at the parkside cafés will run you about 22 nuevo sols ($7) and up. Between Diagonal and Avenida José Larco to the west and east and Schell to the south. Parque Central is adjacent directly to the north. Updated: Apr 21, 2009.

Miraflores Tours

KTM Peru Adventure Tours

KTM Peru Adventure Tours has been around officially since 1997, though their guides have been riding motorcycles and dirt bikes since the 1970s. Do the math: that is more than 30 years of experience. KTM caters to the most adventurous traveler and guarantees an exciting tour. There are one, two and three-day tours through the dunes of Ica. Prices are roughly $200 per day. They have every kind of bike for whichever adventure you would like: sport, racing, off-roading, adventure or minicycles. Safety is a primary concern of KTM Peru, and their expert guides are very careful to supply all the knowledge and advice a rider may need. Av. Benavides 2854. Tel: 51-1-260-8854, E-mail: informes@ktmperu.com, URL: www.ktmperu.com, Updated: Apr 21, 2009.

Bike Tours of Lima

Biking in Lima is an unforgettable experience. The tours cover the best neighborhoods and spots of this big city, mainly using bicycle lanes and less-traffic roads and streets. The bikes are also comfortable and safe, and you can rent a bike if you want to tour on your own. It's a great way to see the city with a very cool and friendly staff. Calle Bolivar 150. Tel: 51-1-445-3172, E-mail: info@biketoursoflima.com, URL: www.biketoursoflima.com. Updated: Nov 04, 2009

Southamerican Quality

This travel agency in Peru offers all kind of programs, but specializes in mystical and adventure tours. Calle Enrique Palacios 585. Tel: 51-1-446-4659, E-mail: info@southamerican-quality.com, URL: http://www.southamerican-quality.com. Updated: Oct 07, 2008.

Miraflores Lodging

Miraflores is one of Lima's swankier neighborhoods with fancy hotels and chic hostels. Accommodations for the budget traveler include many clean, cheap hostels. Miraflores tends to be laid back and sociable with youthful staff excited to offer advice about the city. There is also a variety of mid-range to high-end hostels and hotels in Miraflores that offer many luxuries and great views overlooking the ocean. Miraflores is generally safe; however, like all cities, it is recommended that you be aware of your surroundings, as things do happen all across Lima. Miraflores attracts many young travelers and weekends can get pretty noisy. As long as you stay aware of your surroundings, staying at one of many hotels in Miraflores is a good bed. Updated: Jul 01, 2010.

BUDGET

Casa del Mochilero

(DORMS: $4) Casa del Mochilero ("House of the Backpacker") is a clean, efficient hostel just a few blocks from Kennedy Park. It has bunk rooms and visitors must share a bathroom, but at about $4 per night, the price is right. Chacaltana 130-A. Tel: 51-1-444-9089. Updated: Apr 21, 2009.

Home Peru

(DORMS: $7-13) Home Peru, located in the swank Miraflores district, is a restored colonial mansion popular with the backpacker crowd. Although it's a little bit more expensive than your typical dorm-style hostel, the comfortable rooms and new bathrooms make up for it. Avenida Arequipa 4501. Tel: 51-1-241-9898, E-mail: reservations@homeperu.com, URL: www.homeperu.com. Updated: Apr 21, 2009.

The Shark Hostel

(ROOMS: $8) The Shark is a traveler's haven in Miraflores. The hostel was built by ex-backpackers who love Peru and it's people, and it offers all a traveler needs. The hostel, an old house, was completely renovated and now includes luxuries like super-clean showers with 24/7 steaming hot water, free Internet and free breakfast, as well as a big plasma screen with loads of movies, PS2 and in-house bar and restaurant. Within a five-minute walk from the hostel you can find local markets, open gardens and all the tourist services you may need, such as banks, restaurants, shops, malls, travelling agencies and the like. Also within a few minutes walk are large and beautiful public gardens and the coast of the Pacific Ocean. Coronel Inclan 399. Tel: 51-1-715-3137, E-mail: info@thesharkhostel.com, URL: thesharkhostel.com. Updated: Jul 01, 2010.

Wasijaus

(ROOMS: $8-25) Wasijaus is a clean, comfortable and secure B&B. Conveniently located in the Miraflores district, it is close to restaurants, travel agencies, supermarkets, banks and other services. Coronel Inclan 494. Tel/Fax: 51-1-445-8025, E-mail: reservas@wasijaus.com, URL: www.wasijaus.com. Updated: May 14, 2009.

Flying Dog Backpackers

(DORMS/ROOMS: $8-22) Flying Dog Backpackers is a clean, airy hostel located very close to Kennedy Park, which puts it near most of the sites of interest in the Miraflores district. It has a variety of options ranging from dorm-style rooms with shared bath to more private double rooms. The staff is very knowledgable about the surrounding areas: where to eat, good bars, etc. They speak English and Spanish and understand Portuguese and Italian. There are discounts for longer stays. Diez Canseco 117. Tel: 51-1-445-6745 / 0940, Fax: 51-1-445-2376, E-mail: flyingdog@mixmail.com, URL: flyingdog.esmartweb.com. Updated: Apr 21, 2009.

Wayruro's Backpackers

(DORMS: $9) Wayruro's Backpackers is a small, clean backpacker's hostel in Miraflores. Rooms are dormitory style. There is a game room with ping-pong, a pool table and sapó (a local game in which the object is to throw coins

into the mouth of a brass frog). Enrique Palacios 900. Tel: 51-1-444-1564, E-mail: wayruros@wayruros.com. Updated: Apr 21, 2009.

Loki Hostel Lima

(DORMS: $9-12, ROOMS: $32) Formerly called Incahaus, this hostel is the new little brother of the stunning Loki Hostel in Cusco. Built in the 1920s, this house was used until 2000 as an office building. In 2005, it was beautifully transformed into the place to stop and party in the heart of Miraflores. The friendly, outgoing staff will point you in the right direction to all the best bars, clubs, restaurants and markets. The hostel also has all the services that a backpacker could possibly want: free internet, free continental breakfast, comfy beds, excellent showers, a movie room with a DVD collection and Loki's famous barbecue nights. The in-house bar offers great views of Miraflores Park and surrounding areas. Jose Galvez 576. Tel: 51-1-651-2966, Fax: 51-1-241-3701, URL: www.lokihostel.com. Updated: Jan 19, 2010.

Stop and Drop Lima Backpacker Hotel and Guest House

(ROOMS: $9-30) Part surf haven, part hotel, Stop and Drop might feel a bit like crashing at a friend's house. Rooms and common areas are basic, but the service is friendly and knowledgeable. Stop and Drop offers a number of services, including Spanish and/or surf lessons, personal lockers in each room, cable TV, movies, music, internet and kitchen. The reception is open 24 hours. Berlin 168. Tel: 51-1-243-3101, E-mail: info@stopandrop.com, URL: www.stopandrop. Updated: Apr 21, 2009.

MIRAFLORES & BARRANCO

Kkinacoperu-Lodge

(DORMS: $10-28) This hostel is located a close to the intersection of the avenues Larco and 28 de Julio, near the Larcomar shopping center, cinemas, bars, restaurants, shopping malls, discos, and so on. A variety of room types are offered. Calle Manco Capac N° 517. Tel: 51-1 654-3214, E-mail: kkinacoperu-lodge@kkinacoperu-lodge.com, URL: www.kkinacoperu-lodge.com. Updated: Apr 17, 2009.

Albergue Miraflores House

(ROOMS: $11-32) If you're looking for a clean, secure and comfortable place to stay after an exhausting trip, the friendly staff at Miraflores House will welcome you. They offer travel advice on local sights, as well as planning tips and assistance with purchasing tickets for your next destination. Enjoy the lounge room, watching DVDs or cable TV, using the free internet, playing board games, or jamming on the musical instruments provided. Airport pickups can be arranged. Albergue Miraflores House has a late check in/out, offers free lockers for your valuables, free luggage storage, free kitchen and laundry service. Avenida Comandante Espinar 611. Tel: 51-1-447-7748, Cel: 51-998-231-953, E-mail: fchauvel@terra.com.pe, URL: www.alberguemiraflореshouse.com. Updated: Apr 21, 2009.

Inka Frog Hostel

(ROOMS: $13-46) The hostel has brand new equipment and pleasant decorations. Rooms are equipped with cable TV, safe deposit box, radio-alarm clock and walk-in closets. Inka Frog also has a deluxe floor with double rooms (ensuite), triples and group rooms, all with private bathrooms and TVs. There is also the backpacker floor with shared rooms, but separate dressing rooms and bathrooms for each gender. The hostel is located one block away from two main avenues (Pardo and Comandante Espinar) where there are restaurants, coffee shops, travel agencies and movie theaters, among other services. Calle General Iglesias 271. Tel: 51-1-445-8979, E-mail: info@inkafrog.com, URL: www.inkafrog.com. Updated: Apr 21, 2009.

Lima Lodging

(ROOMS: $15-40) Traveler's lodging run by an ex-backpacker, this is an ideal place if you don't want to spend much money, yet want a pleasurable stay in a private and homely inn. Avenida Roca and Boloña. Tel: 51-1-9-117-8801, E-mail: limalodging@aim.com, URL: www.limalodging.blogspot.com. Updated: Feb 19, 2009.

Inka Lodge Hostel

(DORMS/ROOMS: $10-25) The Inka Lodge is a modern, friendly hostel. All of the facilities are new and well-maintained. There is a pleasant patio and space to relax on the roof. The decor is an interesting mix of modern with ancient Inca themes. The hostal has space for 30 in a variety of dorm rooms and doubles. Breakfast included in price. Elias Aguirre 278, Tel: 51-1-242-6989, URL: www.inkalodge.com/home.htm. Updated: Apr 21, 2009.

V!VA ONLINE REVIEW

INKA LODGE HOSTEL

"Had a wonderful stay. Very friendly staff and good value. I will come back."

Jul 14, 2010

MID-RANGE

JC Guesthouse

(ROOMS: $25-40) This is a nice apartament with a great view. The hosts are very nice people.The price includes taxes and cleaning service once a week, if you ask for it.The rate is negotiable if you stay longer. It doesn't include laundry, but laundry service is available nearby. Malecon Balta 810-Miraflores. Tel: 51-1-993-994-602, E-mail: mirafloresforrent@hotmail.com. Updated: Apr 21, 2009.

Residencial el Faro

(ROOMS: $30-80) More along the lines of a U.S. beach motel than hostel, the rooms at the Faro Inn Hostel are loaded with simple features and have a bland decor. All 20 of the hostel's rooms come with a TV and queen-sized bed, and features such as a small refrigerator and larger closets come as you move from standard to suite and executive-level rooms. The senior suite, at the top end, comes with a Jacuzzi tub in the bathroom. There is a sea view from the building's terrace. Calle Francia 857. Tel: 51-1-242-0339, Fax: 51-1-243-2651, E-mail: residencialelfaro@hotmail.com, URL: www.elfaroinn.com. Updated: May 18, 2009.

Hostal Eiffel

(ROOMS: $30-80) Only 15 minutes from downtown Lima and 30 minutes from Jorge Chávez International Airport, Hostal Eiffel, in the middle of Miraflores, enjoys a central location near banks, shopping centers and entertainment. The hostel is comfortable, secure and quiet. Each room is equipped with cable TV, private bathroom and hot water. Juan Fanning 550. Tel: 51-1-9-961-1737, Fax: 51-1-565-0016, E-mail: hotelsperu@yahoo.es. Updated: Apr 21, 2009.

Hostal Buena Vista

(ROOMS: $35-65) Hostal Buena Vista is well-located in the Miraflores district: It is close to old town as well as the hip Miraflores nightlife. The streets immediately surrounding the Buena Vista are, however, relatively quiet and tranquil. The common areas have a bit more pizzaz. Avenida Grimaldo del Solar 202. Tel: 51-1-447-3178, E-mail: hostalbuenav@bonus.com.pe, URL: www.hostalbuenavista.com. Updated: May 04, 2009.

V!VA ONLINE REVIEW

HOSTAL BUENA VISTA

The people are warm and friendly. I love it here. Will be back when I head back through town.

May 13, 2010

Hostal El Patio

(ROOMS: $35-65) Hostal El Patio is a small, cozy mid-range hotel in Miraflores. A bit chic by design, it looks more like a B&B than a hostel, with wonderfully decorated common areas and a relaxing patio. If you need a break from the more raucous hostels, this place is worth checking first. The hostel is very charming but has limited space, so reservations are suggested. Diez Canseco 341a. Tel: 51-1-444-2107, Fax: 51-1-444-1663, E-mail: hostalelpatio@qnet.com.pe, URL: www.hostalelpatio.net. Updated: Apr 21, 2009.

V!VA ONLINE REVIEW

HOSTAL EL PATIO

If you want to spend a few days in Lima, I recommend this place.

Sep 06, 2010

Hotel Colonial Inn

(ROOMS: $50-80) Hotel Colonial Inn is an attractive mid-range hotel, with elegant and comfortable rooms; two have a jacuzzi. There is a pleasant lobby and a bar for relaxing, and a restaurant and terrace. The Colonial Inn welcomes all visitors but particularly caters to business travelers, providing a business center and conference room. The hotel also boasts a restored vintage automobile; city tours in the car are available. Avenida Comandante Espinar 310. Tel: 51-1-241-7471, Fax: 51-1-445-7587, E-mail: hotel@hotelcolonialinn.com, URL: www.hotelcolonialinn.com. Updated: May 05, 2009.

Soul Mate Inn Hotel

(ROOMS: $50-90) The Soul Mate Inn Hotel offers comfortable rooms, a cafeteria, a bar, facilities for social activities and special events (for up to 50 people) and room service 24 hours per day. Additionally, suites have free internet. The hotel's Sky Bar, on a wide terrace with a view to the sea, serves up barbecue. The hotel is located just 20 minutes from the airport. Toribio Pacheco 350. Tel: 51-1-221-5046 / 421-4167, Fax: 51-1-421-5134, E-mail: reservas@soulmate-inn.com, URL: www.soulmate-inn.com. Updated: Jan 15, 2010.

Hostal Torreblanca

(ROOMS: $53-77) Hostal Torreblanca is a pleasant mid-range hotel which offers a wide variety of services, including cable TV in every room, taxis, business services (copies, internet, etc.) and more. They also arrange tours and excursions, such as visits to the Nasca Lines and Lima city tours. The attached restaurant specializes in steaks and pasta. Breakfast is included in the price. Avenida José Pardo 1453. Tel: 51-1-447-3363, Fax: 51-1-447-3363, E-mail: hostal@torreblancaperu.com, URL: www.torreblancaperu.com. Updated: May 05, 2009.

Best Western Embajadores

(ROOMS: $65-80) Unlike the U.S. chain, Best Western South America is not just a motel on the side of the highway. While not over-the-top luxury, Best Westerns in Latin America tend to be more upscale than their northern counterparts. Best Western Embajadores is no exception. The hotel is a good, safe choice without too many frills. Comfortable beds, cable TV, a mini-bar, telephones and clean bathrooms are what you get for a reasonable price, and the swimming pool and mini gym don't hurt either. Juan Fanning 320. Tel: 51-1-242-9127, 1-800-780-7234 (US & Canada), Fax: 51-1-242-9131, E-mail: htelembajadores@mixmail.com, URL: www.bestwestern.com. Updated: May 05, 2009.

HIGH-END

Hotel Antigua Miraflores

(ROOMS: $64-119) A charming turn-of-the-century mansion that has since been converted to a hotel, Hotel Antigua Miraflores has the homey feel of a bed and breakfast with fully modern facilities. The staff provides excellent service. The hotel is expensive, but good value for the money. Prices include service and breakfast. Avenida Grau 350. Tel: 51-1-241-6116, Fax: 51-1-241-6115, E-mail: info@peru-hotels-inns.com, URL: www.peru-hotels-inns.com. Updated: May 05, 2009.

Casa Andina Miraflores Hotel

(ROOMS: $85-118) Upscale but not over the top is the best way to describe Casa Andina's Miraflores location. A small hotel chain in Peru, Casa Andina is decorated in colorfully bright Incan décor with super comfortable beds and clean, carpeted rooms. The Miraflores location has all the standard American and European amenities, including: cable TVs, air conditioning, phones and modern, marble baths with 24-hour hot water. The hotel is expanding from 42 rooms to 58, which are scheduled to include new deep bathtubs. The super friendly staff and a suburb location--smack in the middle of bustling Miraflores-make this a great hotel to call home. Av. Petit Thouars 5444. Tel: 51-1-447-0263 / 241-3160, Fax: 51-1-447-0336, URL: www.casa-andina.com. Updated: May 15, 2009.

Casa Andina Miraflores San Antonio

(ROOMS: $85-118) Although not in the heart of Miraflores like its sister hotel, Casa Andina Miraflores, Casa Andina Miraflores San Antonio is perfect for the traveler who wants to be out of the hustle of Miraflores, but within walking distance of the major attractions and amenities. Unlike the Miraflores-proper hotel, San Antonio includes an on-site restaurant, Waykuna Andean. The hotel has cable TV, phones, clean rooms, modern bathrooms and firm beds; local and international companies often hold conferences and meetings at this location, which also has a 25-person conference room, free wireless internet, parking and, of course, food. As with all Casa Andina hotels, if you're traveling the tourist circuit you're likely to see many of the same foreigners at one Casa Andina and then at another, as the company makes it super easy to book all hotels (which are scattered throughout tourist areas of Peru) from just one location.

Av. 28 de Julio 1088. Tel: 51-1-241-4050, Fax: 51-1-241-4051, E-mail: Direct email through website URL: www.casa-andina.com. Updated: May 05, 2009.

El Condado Hotel and Suites

(ROOMS: $110-190) A tranquil boulevard lined with various quaint bars and restaurants separates El Condado from the chaotic, casino-lined Avenida Larco. The hotel is close to the action, but the narrow one-way street contributes to a detached, relaxed vibe. Individual rooms and common areas are all decorated with class and subtlety. All rooms are equipped with a standard minibar and wireless connection, not to mention private baths, hot water, comfy beds, cable and phones. With a gym, hot-tub, classy bar and restaurant, El Condado is a definite contender for those willing to spend the cash. Alcanfores 465. Tel: 51-1-444-0306, E-mail: ventas@condado.com.pe, URL: www.condado.com.pe. Updated: May 05, 2009.

Miraflores Park Hotel

(ROOMS: $350-1650) The Miraflores Park Hotel is one of Lima's finest. Owned by the prestigious international Orient Express group, the hotel offers everything you would expect from a $350 per night hotel: impeccable service and facilities, comfortable rooms, swimming pool, squash court, etc. The Miraflores Park Hotel caters to well-heeled tourists and international business travelers. It features business facilities, a five-star restaurant and even an English pub. Miraflores Park is a great place to stay if you can afford it. Avenida Malecón de la Reserva 1035. Tel: 51-1-242-3000, Fax: 51-1-242-3393, E-mail: mirapark@peruorientexpress.com.pe, URL: www.mira-park.com. Updated: May 05, 2009.

V!VA ONLINE REVIEW

MIRAFLORES PARK HOTEL

The service here is outstanding! Spectacular views from the top floor.

Sep 08, 2010

JW Marriott Lima

The Marriott hotel chain is well-known for luxury lodgings, and their Lima branch is no different. JW Marriot offers everything you would expect from a five-star hotel. Malecón de la Reserva 615. Tel: 51-1-217-7000, Fax: 51-1 217-7100, URL: www.marriott.com/property/ propertypage/LIMDT. Updated: May 05, 2009.

Miraflores Restaurants

The Miraflores district of Lima is home to some of the best food in the city. There is a variety of options, from five-star restaurants to street vendors. If you love fish and other dishes from the sea, you'll want to splurge for a fine meal at one of Miraflores' many seafood restaurants. Updated: May 05,2009

ARGENTINE

Patagonia Art-Bar

(ENTREES: $12) Owned by a couple of Argentine artists, this art bar's ambience feels like Buenos Aires and its cultural life. The bar is divided into three main areas: a comfy bar lounge at the entrance, a European-style dining area and an open-air terrace. They also have a room for alternative events like theatre, poetry or dance. Photos and paintings adorn the walls. Not surprisingly, the kitchen serves a variety of Argentinean cuisine, like matambre and their famous steaks. Tango workshops are held twice a week. Calle Bolívar 164, Updated: May 05, 2009.

V!VA ONLINE REVIEW
PATAGONIA ART-BAR

Great atmosphere. Try the steak. Ask the server about a good wine to go with your meal - they are very knowledgeable.

Sep 06, 2010

ASIAN

Chifa "Jin"

(ENTREES: $2-4) While in Lima you have to try the Chifa "Jin." The Chinese food here, however, is distinct from western countries: it's more flavorful and fresh, and the ingredients, especially the spices, are far more eclectic. Chifa "Jin" is an excellent place to sample this unique Asian food; the atmosphere is relaxed and the food is high quality. Try the sopa wantan, wantan frito or pollo chi jau kay, some of the local favorites. Head away from Parque Kennedy on Av. José Pardo and get off at the first circle you see, about a mile away. Right on Ca. Moore, only a few shop fronts from the circle. Calle Moore 152. Tel: 51-1-445-0122. Updated: May 05, 2009.

Fluid

(SET LUNCH: $5) For great Thai food right in the heart of the Miraflores district, head to Fluid. This new, British-run venue serves Asian cuisine amid a relaxed ambience and funky décor. It is popular with the backpacker set and trendy Limeños alike. The food is carefully prepared, tastefully presented and exquisite. Try the red chicken curry for an authentic Thai experience, or go at lunchtime (midday-4 p.m.) for the generous set "Thai Combo" menu for 15 soles. Owners Kia and Richard Haylett go out of their way to ensure that your experience is a good one. In case you're not sold already, this place also has a happy hour everday 6-9 p.m., WiFi internet, a book exchange and a pool table to boot. Ca. Berlín 333, Tel: 51-1-242-9885 , URL: www. fluidperu.com, Updated: Jun 30, 2010.

V!VA ONLINE REVIEW
FLUID

The food was great, the service was great, the atmosphere was great. Nothing I would change about this place .

Jun 30, 2010

Fuji

Fuji is a great Japanese restaurant; the prices are reasonable and you can choose from among many different dishes, such as sushi, sashimi, chicken teriyaki, tempura, etc. The food is authentic and if you're looking for a pleasant dinner, this place comes highly recommended. Av. Paseo de la Republica 4090 (between Av. Aranburú and the Domingo Orué bridge). Tel: 51-1-440-8531, E-mail: restaurant_fuji@ yahoo.co.jp. Updated: Feb 03, 2009.

BARS & PUBS

Tasca Bar

(DRINKS: $1.50) Under the same ownership as the Flying Dog, and located conveniently underneath the Diez Canseco branch of the hostel, Tasca Bar is a popular hangout. It is all too easy to drop in from the hostel above, joining the trendy Limeños. Bar stools are arranged around a long, narrow bar, from which patrons can (and do) purchase all manner of alcoholic drinks and cocktails. A local brew, Cusqueña, is on tap. 117 Diez Canseco. Updated: May 12, 2009.

The Old Pub

(DRINKS: $1.50) Oddly enough, the most authentic English pub in Lima, The Old Pub, is centrally located in Lima's "Little Italy" or as some call it "Pizza Street." But don't let a whiff of Italy deter you; after all, it's an English pub, owned by a proper Brit—and it's in Peru—so you've probably come searching for that refreshing taste of home and comfort. Quickly upon entering, you know you've got the real deal with the large display of beers on tap, the colorful mosaic of old drink coasters pinned to the wall, and of course, the dart board, one of only a few in town. The super friendly crowd (not surprisingly many ex-pats and travelers) and the nostalgic environs of the The Old Pub will fill you with a sense of place and some jolly good cheer. Sadly, you won't be able to satisfy those hunger pangs with a plate of old fashioned English fish and chips—the pub doesn't serve food. But let it be known that seafood in Lima is plentiful and delicious, and you can always find a place for some fresh fish after a few good beers and merrymaking. San Ramn 295. Updated: May 12, 2009.

Murphy's Irish Pub

Directly across the street from Parque Kennedy, in the center of the tourist mecca of Miraflores, you will find this excellent café/restaurant. Decked out with soft orange lighting, a chic bar, tasteful wooden décor and a nice sidewalk vista, you would expect the place to be more expensive. For a reasonable price you can

enjoy classic Peruvian cuisine, pizza or a broad array of salads. One of the best bets in central Miraflores. Calle Schell 619. Tel: 51-1-447-1082. Updated: Jan 11, 2010.

CAFÉS

Café Haití

(ENTREES: $7-12) The bamboo chairs and plastic cream-colored tables exude a pungent air of 1960s Havana. Along the sidewalk, you see a broad, maroon awning with golden rails and dozens of full tables that emit a hum of excited, amicable conversation. Discussions are on all sides: political corruption, literature, fútbol. Whether you're sipping on a coffee or sampling one of their three most popular dishes—ceviche, lomo saltado (marinated strips of steak over rice and potatoes) or sopa criolla (Creole soup), you'll appreciate the ambiance of this 45-year-old Miraflores relic. Diagonal 150. Tel: 51-1-445-0539, E-mail: fafg@infonegocio.net. Updated: May 05, 2009.

Shehadi NYC

(ENTREES: $7-14) Directly across the street from Parque Kennedy, in the center of the tourist mecca of Miraflores, you will find this excellent café/restaurant. Decked out with soft orange lighting, a chic bar, tasteful wooden décor and a nice sidewalk vista, you would expect the place to be more expensive. For a reasonable price you can enjoy classic Peruvian cuisine, pizza or a broad array of salads. One of the best bets in central Miraflores. Diagonal 220. Tel: 51-1-444-0630, Updated: May 05, 2009.

Balthazar

This modern café/restaurant is a tasty, affordable option if you want to eat in the popular Larcomar shopping complex. With comfortable, stylish sofas, a beautiful ocean view and a comprehensive menu of gourmet sandwiches, salads and desserts, Balthazar is not a bad place for a pit stop. Larcomar shopping complex. Tel: 51-1-242-0140. Updated: May 05, 2009.

La Dalmacia

This is a place where people from Miraflores go for coffee, for a drink or to eat, and, of course, to look and be seen. The daily special is chalked on a board and the food is displayed around their horseshoe-styled bar. Tapas are popular, and great for a light lunch or supper. La Dalmacia is candlelit. It is full by about 10 p.m.—so if you want a table, get there early. Slices of home-baked bread served with seasoned olive oil for dipping greets you as you decide what to order. La Dalmacia has a good selection of wines and a bar. Quiches are very popular as well as soufflés of spinach and artichoke. If you are a vegetarian, try the outstanding veggie lasagna. When La Dalmacia is full, the noise level is high. It is within walking distance from Larcomar and the center of Miraflores. San Fernando 401. Tel: 51-1-445-7917. Updated: May 05, 2009.

Café Café

As the name suggests, this is the place for coffee, twice-over-good coffee. However, you can also enjoy large breakfasts, lunches and dinners with generous servings of well-cooked, down-to-earth food at reasonable prices, plus a well-stocked bar. The dessert trolley is frighteningly sumptuous. But really the main reason for making this a must is the suspended-over-the-ocean view that you have. You can sit outside on the balcony and be nicely blown away as you watch airplane wings swoop past at eye level, and watch the tiny cars below you, with the ocean stretching away to the horizon. At night, it is equally impressive, as you can see the lights of the neighboring coastal districts strung like a diamond necklace around the bay. They do have a large cozy indoor area for those who prefer creature comforts. Inside Larcomar Mall. Tel: 51-1-445-1165. Updated: May 05, 2009.

INTERNATIONAL

Super Rueda

(ENTREES: $3-4) Super Rueda is a nice joint with tasty, greasy fast food. Popular on the weekends, it's a pit stop for revelers after a night of partying at local bars. The outdoor patio creates a pleasant atmosphere for chatting and drinking some more beers. The food selection is varied—Peruvian-style tacos, empanadas (beef-and chicken-filled pastries) and hamburgers are typical fare. If you want to indulge yourself a bit and chill out in a relaxed ambience, you've got to check out Super Rueda. Av. José Pardo 1224, Tel: 51-1-445-6919, Updated: May 05, 2009.

Coco de Mer

(ENTREES: $10-15) This is an excellent home-away-from-home when you're feeling lost in Lima's hectic core. The place has a lovely atmosphere and the British owners have given it a classy yet casual feel. One of the interesting aspects is that they have local art on the walls and it isn't the usual artesany, poncho-style stuff! The other great thing is that the restaurant serves food and drinks all day long, unlike most places, and the prices are very reasonable. Coco de Mer is highly recommended if you are passing through Lima. Av. Grau 400. Tel: 51-1-243-0278, E-mail: cocodemerlima@gmail.com. Updated: May 05, 2009.

MIDDLE EASTERN

Scena

If you don't feel like you're in a swanky New York City bar when you walk into Scena, it is solely because of the lack of New Yorkers. Like a Big Apple bar, Scena is a place to see and be seen. A more upscale restaurant and bar with bright colors and bright lights, Scena takes its name literally from "The Scene," as in theatre. Don't be surprised to see champagne on multiple tables here. As for the food, the menu is influenced by the Middle East and combined superbly with fresh Peruvian ingredients. More fun arrives at 10 o'clock when a surpise 20-minute performance begins. The lights lower and the entertainment begins—a trapeze show, a tight rope walker or perhaps a harlequin flirting with the audience. The decoration is nicely bizarre. A surprising touch is a man's voice dictating yoga lessons in the ladies' restroom, which can be quite a shock for the unprepared. Francisco de Paula Camino 280. Tel: 51-1-445-9688/241-8184, URL: www.scena.com.pe. Updated: May 12, 2009.

V!VA ONLINE REVIEW

SCENA

"Very entertaining and a great time was had by all."

Mar 03, 2010

SEAFOOD

El Kapallaq

El Kapallaq is an upscale cevichería, considered one of Lima's best by locals. Try a ceviche or one of the traditional stews, made in clay pots. Open only for lunch. Av. Petit Thouars 4844. Tel: 51-1-444-4149. Updated: May 12,2009

Pescados Capitales

Pescados Capitales is a very highly recommended seafood and ceviche restaurant hidden away in a corner of the Miraflores district. The restaurant's name is a play on the seven deadly sins or pecados capitales in Spanish, therefore the menu is designed around the seven deadly sins of fish - raw fish that is. Pescados Capitales is one of the premier ceviche restaurants in the premier ceviche capital of the world. The restaurant devilshly mixes raw fish, lemon juice, onions, sweet potato and hot peppers like lucifer himself. Pescados Capitales is open only for lunch and reservations are recommended. Pescados Capitales is pricey, but it's so good, and so unique, it's well worth it. La Mar 1337. Tel: 51-1-421-8808 / 222-5731. Updated: Feb 22, 2010.

La Rosa Náutica

La Rosa Náutica is not only a top-of-the-line, first-class restaurant with elegant décor, but its cuisine includes some of the freshest, most creative gourmet dishes in all of Lima. Perched out on Pier 4 along Lima's beachfront in Miraflores, the restaurant is literally on the water, allowing patrons to overlook the waves and out into the horizon. La Rosa serves everything from unique seafood combos like the ceviche norteño (a mix of sole, scallops and flounder in a large sea scallop with corn, chili pepper and fried yucca) to grilled meats, poultry, pastas and outstanding salads like the warm goat cheese salad (tossed with mixed greens, sun-dried tomatoes and caramelized figs).

Although La Rosa Náutica serves up a serious selection of seafood, the restaurant is sure to please even the vegetarian in your party, as iy also has many vegetarian options, including the mushroom ceviche: a savory mix of mushrooms, peppers, garlic, ginger and hot chilis. If you can't afford the prices, go for just for a drink at the restaurant's bar, El Espigón Bar. You can watch the sunset while drinking a Pisco sour overlooking the ocean—it's a surreal, romantic experience that is difficult to be had anywhere else in town. Espigón 4 (Pier 4) Circuito de Playas. Tel: 51-1-445-0149 / 447-0057 / 447-5450, E-mail: reservas@larosanautica.com, URL: www.larosanautica.com. Updated: Jan 18, 2010.

La Isla del Mono

La Isla del Mono offers Lima's seafood at its best. Menu items include their mouth-watering "Ceviche de Lenguado" and "Sole Ceviche"—raw sole served dripping in a delicious lemony-chili sauce. You can also partake in a variety of other fishy treats. If you're lucky, they may offer you a free pisco sour or two. The decor is modern and chic but minimal, located in one of the few remaining older buildings in Miraflores. Calle San Martín 835. Tel: 51-1-243-3080, Fax: 51-1-243-3080, Email: laisladelmono@terra.com.pe, URL: www.laisladelmono.com.pe. Updated: May 05, 2009.

TRADITIONAL / PERUVIAN

Fuente de Soda "Amy's"

(ENTREES: $1-1.75, SET LUNCH: $1.50, SNACKS: $0.40-1) This small family-owned restaurant is run by the same three señoras day-in and day-out. It is a great alternative to the more expensive, tourist-hungry establishments in Miraflores. Located in the Lince district, only a ten-minute taxi or bus ride from Miraflores, the restaurant offers an excellent meal at unbeatable prices. The restaurant's decorum is austere and simple, but the workers' calm and friendly personalities, along with the tranquil pace at which locals dine, makes you feel right at home. Amy's joint offers a fine menú del día, where one can delve into classic Peruvian dishes. For only $1.50 you can have a two-course meal, consisting of a hearty, vegetable and pasta-filled soup or a portion of the fresh and zesty ceviche, along with a chicken, meat or fish main platter. Bartolomé Herrera 149. Updated: 15 Apr, 2009.

Restaurant Aries

(ENTREES $2-6) If you want to save some money and taste some excellent, typical Peruvian cuisine, be adventurous and head to Restaurant Aries. Across from Ripley's Department store, only four storefronts from the corner of Ca. Lima and Ca. Schell, family-run Aries forms part of the pulse of Miraflores downtown. The frank simplicity—faded mustard-yellow walls, worn tile floors—nicely complements the authenticity of the food. Two dollars will get you the two-course menú del día. Try ceviche or papa rellena (a fried potato stuffed with ground beef, onions and olives) for the entrada, and for the main dish, you can't go wrong with cabrito (goat meat) or picante de mariscos (shrimp, octopus and squid covered in a creamy garlic sauce). Calle Lima 110. Tel: 51-1-446-5708. Updated: May 05, 2009.

El Parquetito Café

(ENTREES: $7-12) Hip Parque Kennedy attracts bar-goers, sightseers and park strollers to central Miraflores, and diners at El Parquetito Café have a ringside seat to the daily parade. Candles light individual tables, which stretch from the restaurant front to the park. The tiny white lights illuminate the eating area in a soft glow. The menu offers traditional Peruvian dishes such as cebiche, which is raw shrimp or fish marinated in lemon juice and served chilled, as well as beef dishes such as grilled steak served with

an egg, rice and fried plantains. Fresh juices, Pilsener and other beers, and mixed drinks are served, as well as a fairly extensive list of desserts, including cakes and flan. Patrons who order breakfast can relax with a cup of coffee and juice, eat toast and eggs and watch other people hurry off to work. Ambiance is the draw here. Jirón Diez Canseco 117. Tel: 51-1-444-0490. Updated: May 05, 2009.

Astrid y Gastón

(ENTREES: $11-26) Consistently rated as one of Lima's best restaurants, Astrid y Gastón is located on a little side street not far from Parque Miraflores. The food is outstanding. Don't forget to save room for dessert. Be sure to call ahead for reservations, as Gastón Acurio's growing fame has made this a tough table to get. Cantuarias 175. Tel: 51-1-444-1496. Updated: May 12, 2009.

V!VA ONLINE REVIEW

ASTRID Y GASTON

" Ate here after two-week trip to the area. Food was outstanding and service was unmatched. "

Jan 27, 2009

Arúgula

(ENTREES: $20-25) Arúgula is a quiet restaurant a few blocks from Larcomar and the centre of Miraflores that makes for a great stop after a movie or show. The décor is quiet and unassuming with a played-down elegance. Arúgula is one of the favorite hangouts for Peru's best writers and artists, who usually are found conversing in the corner tables over the excellent wines. Dishes of the day are written on a blackboard and include such delicacies as tuna tartare, rabbit ravioli and osobucco with saffron, among other wonders. The three-mushroom pizza is wonderful. Salads are delicious and include items such as squash flowers filled with prosciutto, fresh dates with blue cheese or grilled chicken breast rolled in sesame, all served over a bed of arugula. Calle San Fernando 320. Tel: 51-1-444-0132. Updated: May 05, 2009.

Las Brujas de Cachiche

You'll find this impressive restaurant tucked away in the tranquil backstreets of Miraflores. A fusion of international techniques with classic Peruvian recipes, you can't find Peruvian food much better than Brujas. The menu is broad and features an excellent three-course buffet as well as a long list of individual entrees. Located in a large, wooden chalet-like mansion—high wooden ceilings with basic, yet tasteful interior design—Brujas has a very relaxed, unpretentious ambience. If you're going to spend the bucks, Brujas is something you shouldn't miss. Bolognesi 460. Tel: 51-1-444-5310 / 447-1883, E-mail: alcorta@brujasdecachiche.com.pe. Updated: May 12, 2009.

Miraflores Nightlife

Murphy's Irish Pub

A great bar close to the centre of Miraflores, only a few blocks away from Parque Kennedy. Free pool table and darts. Open 6pm till late Monday to Friday. Just come and have fun. Live music Thursday, Friday and Saturday. Closed Sunday. Schell 627. Tel: 51-1-242-1212 Updated: Nov 04, 2009.

V!VA ONLINE REVIEW
MURPHY'S IRISH PUB

This is an expat hangout in the best way. Stay for a while and have a beer; you'll hear great stories.

Aug 27, 2010

Pub Cubano 443

Always packed on the weekends, this club is the hotspot for Cuban salsa. Though the club isn't too big, it packs in a lot of energy and movement. Hidden down an inconspicuous side street, it attracts a more local, less touristy crowd, but the drinks can be steep. It's a good option if you feel like dancing and absorbing the local vibe. Monday-Thursday 10 p.m.-2 a.m., Friday-Sunday: 10 p.m.-Sunrise. San Martin 443. Tel: 51-1-242-2038 / 9-921-8684, E-mail: pubcubano@443pubcubano.com,URL:www.443pubcubano.com. Updated:May 12, 2009.

Tumbao VIP

Near Parque Kennedy, at the end of the touristy Calle de los Pizzas ("Pizza Street"), this salsa club is a good option for those who want to get down, get dancing and get to know the locals. Of the many clubs on Calle de las Pizzas, Tumbao VIP is one of the largest and most impressive. It also features renowned salsa artists monthly. Monday - Sunday 10 p.m.

til late. Calle Bellavista 237. Tel: 51-1-446-5530, Updated: May 12, 2009.

El Latino

Head to El Latino if you feel like dancing but aren't in the mood for a club that is too overwhelming. One of the many dance clubs on Calle de las Pizzas, El Latino is a small club, with a medium-sized dance floor, dark lighting and a big screen TV. If you're looking to chill out and relax to some music, you probably won't find that here: salsa, samba and reggaeton always hold sway. So, if you want the fast upbeat music and have your dancing shoes on, this is where it's at. Monday-Thursday until 2 a.m., Friday and Saturday until til 4 a.m., Closed Sundays. Pasaje San Ramón 234, better known as Calle de Las Pizzas or "Little Italy." Tel: 51-1-242-7176, Updated: May 12, 2009.

Aura

Located in Larcomar, Aura is the premier upscale dance club in Miraflores, and for that matter, in all of Lima. A huge dance floor, several bars and lots of lounge areas turn it up with a mix of pop (Latin, US and Brit), electrónica and techno. It's the place for posh, youthful 20-something Limeños to be seen. Sophisticated, classy dress is typically the attire, men should plan to wear collared shirts; oddly enough, jeans are okay. Reminiscent of the Buenos Aires nightlife scene with a little LA and Manhattan spice thrown in, neon lights and modern decor keep it fresh.

Aura is open until sunrise on the weekends and doesn't really pick up speed until 2 a.m., giving party-goers three to four hours of non-stop dancing. Any traveler who wants to keep the party going past the typical 3 a.m. closing hour will have to fork over a pricey 40 soles (or $12.50) to get in, but won't be dissapointed. As long as you dress nicely and pay the cover, you can get in. The drinks are cheap and the club is very safe. 11 p.m. - 5 a.m. Larcomar Local 236. Tel: 51-1-242-5516, E-mail: informes@aura.com.pe, URL: www.aura.com.pe, Updated: May 12, 2009.

V!VA ONLINE REVIEW
AURA

Awesome! Liked everything: music, atmosphere, drinks, people!

May 13, 2009

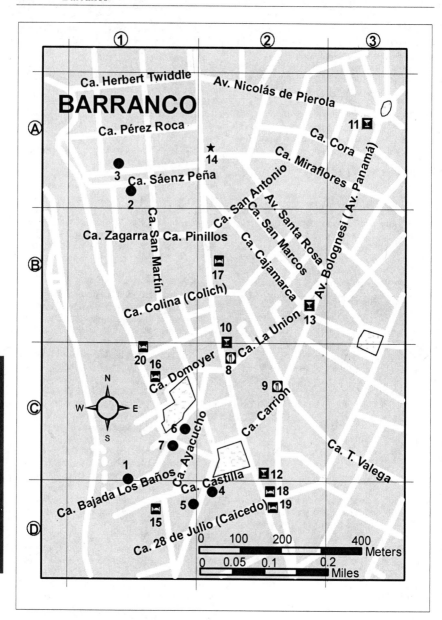

BARRANCO

Like Miraflores, Barranco is an upscale district of Lima. Barranco is located on the waterfront, south of the city center, San Isidro and Miraflores. Formerly a rather posh beach resort, today the district is known for a thriving arts and music scene, as well as good restaurants, bars and nightclubs. Updated: May 12, 2009.

History of Barranco

The village of Barranco was founded by early Spanish settlers and soon became known as a popular seaside resort. By the time Peru became independent, it was a thriving retreat for Lima's wealthiest families. Barranco was also a favorite for international

Activities ●

1 Bajada a los Baños C1
2 Dédalo A1
3 Galería Lucía de la Puente A1
4 Museo de la Electricidad D2
5 Museo Galería Arte Popular de Ayacucho D1
6 Parque Principal
7 Puente de los Supiros C1

Eating ①

8 El Mortal C2
9 La Noche C2

Services ★

14 Lavanderia Neptuno A2

Nightlife 🖾

10 Bodega Bar Juanito's B2
11 El Dragón A3
12 El Ekeko Café Bar C2
13 Kitsch B2

Sleeping 🛏

15 Barranco's Backpackers Inn D1
16 Domeyer Hostel C1
17 Hostal Gémina B2
18 Mochilero's Backpackers D2
19 Quinto de Allison D2
20 The Point C1

families. Now it is an upscale district of Lima. Barranco has a great deal of history. According to local legend, a group of fishermen were lost at sea at night, enshrouded in Lima's famous dense fog. They prayed for salvation, and a luminous cross appeared, guiding them back to shore. The Ermita Church was constructed on the site where the cross allegedly appeared, and since has become the preferred church for fishermen. Although the church was sacked by invading Chilean troops in 1881, is has been rebuilt and is an interesting site to visit. Barranco was once known as "the city of windmills," as early settlers often used windmills to draw water from their wells.

In 1870, the famous "Bajada a los Baños," a series of stairways that leads to the ocean, was constructed, and has since become an important Barranco landmark. Nearby, lovers meet on the Puente de Los Suspiros, "the Bridge of Sighs." In 1940, a strong earthquake hit the region and did a great deal of damage to Barranco. The town recovered, however, and was rebuilt. There are many architectural wonders in Barranco, most of which date from the Republican era. Check out the Casa Nash or the Casa Checa Eguren, both of which are fantastic examples of older architecture. Today, Barranco is a romantic, bohemian, artistic district, known for lively nightlife. Updated: May 12, 2009.

Barranco Services

LAUNDRY

Lavanderia Neptuno: For your clothes laundering needs, visit Lavanderia Neptuno. Av. Grau Cda4.

SUPERMARKETS

There are two large supermarkets in Barranco. Plaza Vea is located on Av. Republica de Panama and Metro in Chorrillos. Updated: May 12, 2009.

SHOPPING

Dédalo 🎵

Dédalo is a must see. Even if you don't plan to spend any money, it is well worth the visit. Staged in an old refurbished house in Barranco, a block away from the sea, it offers Peruvian non-traditional workmanship at its best. You will find beautiful handmade ceramics, blown glass, design-winning woodwork, stone carvings and the latest in textile design, among other works of art on a world-class level. They have a nice coffee shop on the inside patio, a children's toy area, handmade jewelry and a permanent exhibition of unique objects made out of recycled materials. There is no pressure to buy, so you can just wander at your leisure through the treasure-filled rooms. 10 a.m. - 9 p.m., closed Sunday. Paseo Sáenz Peña 295. Tel: 51-1-477-0562. Updated: May 12,2009

VIVA ONLINE REVIEW

DEDALO

Pleasant atmosphere with great finds. Just disappointed we had only a short time to browse, we would have bought much more if time had permitted.
Nov 26, 2009

Things to See and Do

Barranco's activities are not of the tree-swinging, white-water variety. Instead they highlight the art and culture of one of Lima's nicest neighborhoods. If you find yourself in Barranco, make sure you check out the galleries and art shops, because even if you're not buying, looking is worth the effort. This cliff-top town also showcases beautiful colonial architecture and a bridge that has inspired thousands of artists and poets the world over. Updated: May 12,2009

MUSEUMS

Museo Galería Arte Popular de Ayacucho

The Museo Galería Arte Popular de Ayacucho in Barranco, Lima, displays an excellent collection of art from the Ayacucho region, known for its painted religious panels. The anonymous murals found in the churches and basilicas of Ayacucho since the colonial period afford great insight into the social customs of bygone areas. Pieces range from pre-hispanic to contemporary. Check out artifacts from the conquista such as El Cajón de San Marcos and several examples of Cruces de Camino. For a lesson in recent history, check out the Retablo Cayara, a representation of the 1998 standoff between the military and the Sendero Luminoso in which around 30 people were assassinated and another 45 "disappeared." Monday - Saturday 9 a.m.-5 p.m., Closed: Sunday 116 Av. Pedro de Osma. Tel: 51-1-247-0599, E-mail: info@mugapa.com, URL: www.mugapa.com. Updated: Jun 15, 2009.

Galería Lucía de la Puente

This famous commercial gallery is known as "the" art center in Lima. Housed in an old, fully refurbished Barranco mansion, its huge rooms illuminated by natural light offer a great opportunity to appreciate works of art. Paseo Sáenz Peña 206. Tel: 51-1-477-9740, Fax: 51-1-247-4940, E-mail: idelapuente@gluciadelapuente.com, URL: www.gluciadelapuente.com. Updated: Oct 29, 2009.

Museo de la Electricidad

Directly adjacent to Parque Principal, this miniature museum—better said, exhibit—may be a 15-minute visit, but worth it. Posted to the walls are some charming old photos of Peru, and there's a room dedicated to antique, outdated electrical devices: telephones, record players, jukeboxes. Spanish speakers interested in Peru's history of electrical technology will also get something out of this simple, unassuming museum. This museum also has resources in Braille for the visually impaired and guides are available upon request. 9 a.m.-5 p.m. Av. Pedro D'Osma 105. Tel: 51-1-477-6577, E-mail: museoelectri@speedy.com.pe, URL: museoelectri.perucultural.org.pe. Updated: May 12, 2009.

PARKS

Parque Principal

This is one of Lima's most beautiful and unique parks, planted in one of Lima's most charming and rustic areas. This little park serves as a plaza—and surrounded on four sides by beautiful Spanish architecture, tasteful restaurants and bars, and an imposing crimson catholic church. The originality of the ambience is refreshing and invigorating. You can simply sit on the bench and consume all the energy and color. In the distance a green marble stage, reminiscent of a Greek amphitheatre, rests below the prominent, white marble neoclassical columns. Statues of Cupid and figures of Roman Goddesses spring from the vibrant, decorative patches of flowers. Above, large trees spread outwards, serving as umbrellas against Lima's piercing summer sun. Av. Grau (José María Eguren) and Av. Carrión. Updated: May 12, 2009.

Puente de los Suspiros

The Puente de los Suspiros (Bridge of Sighs) was built in the late 1800s, and to this day remains a romantic landmark for couples and a place for families to enjoy the company of loved ones. Overlooking the waters that gently run down to the beach, the Puente de los Suspiros has inspired musicians and artists with its antique planks and quaint cobblestone road that lead to a great ocean view atop a cliff. The old bridge connects the streets of Ayacucho and La Ermita and is surrounded by little eateries and sidewalk vendors selling local foods at good prices. Calle Ayacucho and Bajada a Los Baños. Updated: May 12, 2009.

Barranco Lodging

Barranco's demographic has changed over the years and is now known as one of Lima's most lively districts. Beautiful colonial architecture combined with a vivacious nightlife tends to draw the younger, more transient crowds, and this is exactly who accommodation is geared toward. There are several top-notch hostels that will meet any backpacker's needs. There are also plenty of good mid- to high-end accommodations for the wealthier traveler wanting a piece of the nightlife. Updated: May 12, 2009.

The Point !

(DORMS: $7-18) The Point Backpacker's Hostel considers itself Lima's "original party hostel," a joint immensely popular among the international backpacker set. It is relatively new but becoming well known due to its lively, welcoming atmosphere. There are a number of entertaining extras here, such as a bar, ping-pong table, Nintendo, and more, that you don't find at every youth hostel. The nightly organized events and convenient location near some of Lima's best nightlife guarantee an enjoyable stay. Malecón Junín 300. Tel: 51-1-247-7997. Updated: May 12, 2009.

La Casa Barranco

(DORMS: $8-13) La Casa Barranco is a small, home-style hostel in Lima's Barranco district. Friendly, neat and clean, it's popular among the backpacker crowd. There are only ten beds, plus a kitchen and cable TV for the use of the guests. If you contact them, they'll pick you up at the airport for $14. Avenida Grau 982. Tel: 51-1-477-0984 / 9-6727-449. Updated: May 12, 2009.

V!VA ONLINE REVIEW

LA CASA BARRANCO

I like this place, it's a hostel very close to all in the Barranco district, with big rooms, and very clean, prices are good.

Apr 17, 2009

Barranco's Backpackers Inn

(DORMS: $10-11, ROOMS: $30) Located in a quiet and scenic area, Backpacker's Inn is a short walk from surfing, a plaza, bars, live music, restaurants and shows just down the street. Ocean views from this renovated mansion are stunning, and rooms for two, four or six people are clean and comfortable. There is 24-hour hot water and showers, complimentary cable TV and internet access, laundry service, housekeeping and airport pick-up at below average rates. Tours, trips and surfing can be organized by the hostel. The staff also speaks both Spanish and English. Mariscal Castilla 260. Tel: 51-1-247-1326, URL: www.barrancobackpackers.com. Updated: May 12, 2009.

La Quinta de Allison

(ROOMS: $10-20)The La Quinta de Allison resides on a quiet side street in Barranco. Inconspicuous and modest, this is one of the cheaper hotels in the area. Rooms tend to be smaller but are very comfortable. The bathrooms are decent, and some of the more expensive rooms have whirlpool tubs. Interior rooms tend to be a little darker and rooms with windows onto the street can be noisy at times. There is also an on-site restaurant, room service and bar. Jr. 28 de Julio 281. Tel: 51-1-247-1515. Updated: May 12,2009

Domeyer Hostel

(DORMS: $12, ROOMS: $25-35) Stroll down this placid side street in Barranco you'll be greeted by a friendly labrador retriever who calls the funky, colonial Domeyer Hostel home. With boldly painted walls, bright bedspreads, vivid Peruvian tiles, local artwork decorating the walls and bronze statues setting about, this sophisticated hostel boasts comfortable rooms with high ceilings, tall windows and shutters that open to a fresh ocean breeze. Domeyer Hostel also has a guest kitchen with barbecue area, a small bar and lounge and the rates include free internet access and continental breakfast. Airport pickups can be arranged. Jiron Domeyer 296. Tel: 51-1-247-1413, URL: www.domeyerhostel.net. Updated: May 12, 2009.

Safe in Lima

(DORMS: $16-22) Travelers will indeed feel safe in this wonderfully cozy hostel with a warm family atmosphere, located in a quiet, green just 20 meters (65 feet) from ocean view. The main square in Barranco is a ten minute stroll away and surrounding neighborhoods can be easily accessed. All rooms have a private bathroom and double rooms have a queen-sized bed. Rooms are clean, comfortable and spacious and guests can use the kitchen for free. Safe in Lima also offers a pick up service from the airport or bus terminal, offers free information and maps about Lima and will help organize tours of the city. Alfredo Silva 150. Tel: 51-1-252-7330, E-mail: info@safeinlima.com, URL: www.safeinlima.com. Updated: May 12, 2009.

Hostal Aquisito

(ROOMS: $17-20) Hostal Aquisito is a cheap and comfortable hostel in Lima. Jr. Centenario Nr. 114. Tel: 51-1-247-0712, URL: www.aquisito.com.pe, Updated: Jan 19, 2010.

Hostal Gemina

(ROOMS: $30-50)This modern hotel, located above a shopping center, houses 31 small but comfortable rooms that have cable TV, decent bathrooms (with endless hot water!) and friendly service. Rates are negotiable, there is an on-site cafeteria, and room service serves meals 24-hours. Av. Grau 620. Tel: 51-1-477-0712, E-mail: gemina@tsi.com.pe. Updated: May 12, 2009.

Casa De Leeuw

(ROOMS: $50-100) Casa de Leeuw is a unique fairytale Mansion (1911) situated in the heart of bohemian Barranco with pretty apartments and rooms. All are fully equipped, stylishly decorated and have comfortable beds. Rental period is a minimum 7 days – 6 nights. Sometimes last minute bookings are accepted for shorter stays. The Mansion can also be booked for weddings and events. The owner also has nice and spacious apartments in Miraflores near Kennedy Park. Av. Saenz Peña 103 - Barranco Zip: L4, Tel: (+51) (1) 247 5011, E-mail: info@casadeleeuw.com, URL: http://www.casadeleeuw.com, Updated: Jul 01, 2010.

Second Home Peru

(ROOMS: $75-95)Second Home Peru embodies the spirit of the Peruvian culture combined with the tranquility of the Pacific. This majestic Bandamp;B with five private rooms is conveniently anchored in central Barranco. To enter the once the home of Peruvian sculptor Victor Delfín, is to enter an artist's imaginative world replete with its creative works. You do not need to search far to find seedlings of inspiration; they abound in the gardens, terrace and Pacific view of this historic Tudor mansion. Taxes are included in their rates. Domeyer 366, Barranco Zip: 04, Tel: 51-1-247-5522, Fax: 51-1-995-679-704, E-mail: liliandelfin@gmail.com, URL: www.secondhomeperu.com. Updated: May 12, 2009.

Barranco Restaurants

Barranco's gastronomic scene reflects Lima's diverse and colorful food culture and has many options for a satisfying dining experience. If you aren't quite hungry enough for a big meal, meander through the passageway under El Puente de los Suspiros and pick up a quick treat from one of the various vendors along the way. If you do happen to be hungry enough for a large meal or want to make dinner a memorable experience, you'll find options for every pocketbook and may want to consider a big bowl of ceviche on the beachfront. Updated: Jul 10, 2007.

El Delfín

(ENTREES: $4-8) A soft ocean breeze filtered through the ravine below softly brushes against the plants that hang from the wooden rafters. You stand up, approach the deck's railing and gaze in both directions—to the left, a calm moonlit ocean; to the right, a quaint lamp-lit path ascending towards Puente de Los Suspiros. You return to your seat, pick up your fork and delve into your papa a la huancaína (sliced potatoes topped with a creamy, slightly spicy sauce) and anticucho (grilled cow heart), which taste better than you ever thought possible. Scattered about the restaurant sit whispering couples and boisterous groups of friends. With everything from ceviche to burgers, El Delfin if perfect if you're looking for a relaxed restaurant with tasty food. Monday - Sunday, 11 a.m. - 3 a.m. Bajada de Baños 403. Tel: 51-1-477-6465. Updated: Jul 10, 2007.

Punto Blanco

(BUFFET LUNCH: $16) Along a new promenade by the sea, you will find Punto Blanco, a circular white building of glass windows overlooking Lima's bay. It offers an extensive and creative buffet, a large selection of ceviches, sushi and traditional creole Peruvian dishes. The staff is helpful and service is excellent. You can choose to sit on the terrace overlooking the beach, or have a bit more formal meal inside the main building. Prices are set for the main lunch buffet at 49 soles ($16), including desserts and an optional drink. Circuito de Playas Costa Verde, Barranco. Tel: 51-1-252-8454 / 8423. Updated: Jul 10, 2007.

El Mortal

Stumble out from the bars, walk a few steps and you're there. An excellent place to indulge that drunken appetite of yours—grease, grease and more grease. But you can't deny the tastiness and the price. Fried chicken and heavy-duty sandwiches. We're talking cheeseburgers, eggs, bacon, ham and french fries. It's an easy sell for food and alcohol-lovers. It's got a cool atmosphere, too, in a rustic-dive-charming sort of way. Go eat and forget the consequences. 9 a.m. - 3 a.m. Av. Grau 230. Tel: 51-1-255-9730. Updated: Jul 10, 2007.

Las Hamacas

Las Hamacas is a typical beach restaurant, but quite charming. You can sit in the open dining area or have your food and drink taken to your beach umbrella and lounge chairs. The food is very tasty, since the restaurant is owned solely by a man named Carlos who buys everything himself and also looks after every detail in the kitchen. You may want to try a jalea, an assortment of deep fried seafood on top of a delicious piece of fish, served with crispy golden yams and a salad. One plate is enough to feed about four people, but of course you've got to have a ceviche, either before or after the jalea, to complete the meal. There is private parking and this spot might be a good lunch choice if you want to explore the ruins at Pachacamac in the morning. Km 42 Panamerican Highway, Playa Punta Rocas. Updated: Jul 13, 2007.

La Posada del Ángel

If you like angels you'll find them here, hanging from the roof, peeking at you around corners, staring from the walls. This dark, cozy, rustic setting is blessed. Another enchanting, old "Barranco-style" house with many small rooms leading on and on through a maze of antiques, collected found objects and cuckoo clocks that make you forget time. Tables and chairs are scattered around in a storybook atmosphere. Mainly beer and wine are served, spirits abound. Pizza is a good choice, freshly made and not very expensive, among other starters. Music is performed live every night, mainly Latin American "nueva trova" with songs from well-known Cuban socialist Silvio Rodríguez, often described as the Latin American Bob Dylan. Open until 3 a.m.! Three locations: Av. Prolongación San Martín, Pedro de Osma 164 Tel: 51-1-247-5544 (Av. Prolongación San Martín) / 51-1-247-0341 (Pedro de Osma 164). Updated: Dec 15, 2008.

Restaurante Vida

Fantastic bar and restaurante located under The Bridge of Sighs arguably the most romantic place in Lima. Features haute Peruvian cuisine, but not haut prices. Bajada de baños 340. Tel:

51-1-252-8034, Fax: 51-1-252-8035, E-mail: info@restaurantevida.com, URL: www.restaurantevida.com. Updated: Dec 19, 2007.

Chala

(ENTREES: $15-20) One of the newest upscale restaurants to hit Barranco is Chala, located in an old colonial-style house converted into a very hip, minimalistic restaurant and bar. Videos of photographs taken of Lima at the beginning of the last century are shown, from which you can get an idea of the changes that have taken place. The veranda where lunch and dinner are also served is the same as it was 100 years ago, overlooking a tree-lined, cobbled pathway going down to the sea.

From there you can see the two main features of Barranco, Puente de Los Suspiros and the old La Ermita church. The food at Chala is spectacular and inventive. Many of Peru's exotic fruits are used in its preparation. As a starter try the shrimp, which includes three extra-large shrimp stuffed with seasoned yam, and served with a thick sauce of passion fruit. Among the entrees, the fresh tuna fish steak with a Peruvian berry topping really stands out. The complimentary, homemade nut-herb bread is delicious.

The wine list is extensive, and the service is excellent. Reservations are still a good idea. Bajada de Baños 343. Tel: 51-1-252-8515, URL: www.chala.com.pe. Updated: Dec 15, 2008.

Barranco Nightlife

La Noche 🎵

One of the most famous venues in this bohemian district, La Noche is a widely known cultural stage for music, film, photography and performing arts. It is located in a traditional wooden building with two floors, each one with its own bar and vibe. One has daily live performances and the other an art gallery. The club has jazz every Monday night from 11 p.m., with no cover. This is definitely a place that's alive any night of the week. Beer is mostly served in pitchers at a good price, and there are plenty of traditional Peruvian cocktails made out of pisco. Tapas dishes are available. Av. Bolognesi 307 (El Boulevard). Tel: 51-1-477-5829. Updated: Jul 10, 2007.

Bar Mochileros

Near the main square park of Barranco, Bar Mochileros is a former backpacker hostel now transformed into a series of bars and a cultural center where you can enjoy live circus-like performances, dance, music and emerging local concerts. A young hip crowd gathers around the porch and the different terraces of this museum-like house. Concerts mainly take place in the basement bar which has a Liverpool "Cavern" feeling. All kinds of drinks are served at a moderate to inexpensive rate. Av. Pedro de Osma 135. Tel: 51-1-477-0302 / 247-1225. Updated: Dec 15, 2008.

Bodega Bar Juanito's

Popular and well-established, this bar has called Barranco home for more than 70 years. Founded by Juan Casual Villacorta and still run by Juan's family, Juanito's is loved by locals and its not out of the ordinary to see writers scribbling thoughts and lyrics on napkins. Cozy and friendly, Juanito's is a great place to share a pitcher of beers with friends. Does not accept credit cards. Monday – Saturday 11 a.m. - 3 a.m. and Sunday 11 a.m. - 1 a.m. Av. Grau 274. Tel: 51-1-9-949-6176. Updated: Dec 15, 2008.

Kitsch

For travelers who packed their dancing shoes, the main dancing drag in Barranco is Av. Grau, with a variety of discos and raucous clubs. One of Lima's hottest bars is Kitsch, boasting flamboyant décor and tunes that range from 70s and 80s pop to Latin and techno. This bar is gay and straight friendly, and you'll most likely see a variety of people from all backgrounds. 7 p.m. to late. Bolognesi 743. Tel: 51-1-242-3325. Updated: Dec 15, 2008.

El Ekeko Café Bar

(COVER: $2.85 - $5.70) Not quite as wild as other popular joints in Barranco, this artsy locale boasts two levels with live music Wednesday through Saturday. Most acts tend to be Latin, including Cuban, tango, musica folklorica and cha-cha-chas. There are free poetry readings on Monday evenings and El Ekeko also offers a range of hors d'oeuvres. Monday - Wednesday 10 a.m. - midnight and Thursday- Saturday 10 a.m. - 3 a.m. Av. Grau 266. Tel: 51-1-247-3148. Updated: Jul 20, 2007.

El Dragón

(COVER: $3.50-6) A typical barranquino-styled house is the home of this well-established cultural bar, one of the first to promote bands with a special kick on fusing funk and Latin rhythms with local jazz elements. Inside El Dragón you can see a collection of wall paintings done by young local artists. The week starts on Tuesdays with blends of Afro jazz, funk and reggae; Wednesdays they turn electronic; Thursdays is a mix of local, well-known bands; and Fridays

and Saturdays DJs perform to a lively, buzzing, but fun crowd. All events are performed live so you may have to pay an entrance fee of generally 10 soles ($3.50), depending on which band is playing; this usually includes a free drink. They have a large dragon-tailed bar fully stocked to satisfy your thirst for exotic or classic drinks. Av. Nicolas de Pierola 168. URL: www.eldragon.com.pe. Updated: Dec 15, 2008.

CHORRILLOS

Chorrillos, which means a "constant trickle of water," is a lesser-known neighborhood in Lima. Once a beach resort town, it was the scene of heavy fighting during the war between Peru and Chile in 1880-1881, and much of it was destroyed. Today, Chorrillos is tucked up against the Pacific Ocean and offers stunning panoramic views of the bay of Lima and the island of San Lorenzo in El Callao. With an atmosphere that resembles a fish market and décor to match, the mood is very relaxed in Chorrillos. Famous for its beach resorts at La Herradura and restaurants specializing in spicy dishes, this neighborhood is not without its attractions. The astronomical observatory El Planetario is located here and built on the historical Morro Solar. El Malecón is the area's boardwalk and a great place to spend a lazy afternoon. Updated: Jun 15,2009

Chorrillos Services

SHOPPING

Centro Comercial Plaza Lima Sur

This massive and modern shopping complex is a consumer heaven. Featuring Peru's largest retailer, Metro, and a glossy array of local and North American corporate franchises, including Ace Hardware and the Canadian Scotiabank. Lima Sur has outlets for every need or want, including health facilities and electronics. Bring your credit card. Av. Paseo de la República (and Matellini). Updated: Jun 15, 2009.

Things to See and Do

PARKS

Pantanos de Villa

The only protected area in metropolitan Lima, the Villa Swamps is an Ecological park just 30 minutes from downtown Lima. The swamps, or humedales (humid lands), cover more than 2,000 hectares (4,940 acres) and are home to many migrating birds. Updated: Jun 15, 2009.

HISTORICAL BUILDING

El Planetario

This astronomical observatory was erected on the historical Morro Solar, a landmark location of important events during the war with Chile (1879-1883). From this spot, spectacular views of the Lima coast and San Lorenzo Island can be enjoyed. Eima del Morro Solar, Tel: 51-1-431-3084, Updated: Jun 15, 2009.

CITY WALK

El Malecón

Once considered the soul of Chorrillos, this boardwalk is where generations of locals have spent lazy afternoons and moonlit evenings. El Malecón has undergone two transformations, the first after the war with Chile, and the second at the beginning of the 20th century. Now, the once wooden planks have been replaced with bright tiled mosaics and the lighting system is electric instead of gas. With panoramic views of the bay of Lima, El Malecón proudly remains on the map and indestructible. Updated: Jun 15, 2009.

Chorrillos Lodging

As a less touristy area of Lima, Chorrillos enjoys a quieter and less raucous environment. After a crazy night out in Miraflores or Barranco, plan on coming back to Chorrillos for a deep, peaceful sleep. Updated: Jun 15,2009

Hotel Olaya

(ROOMS: $20-30) The Olaya has 38 basic but comfortable rooms with hot and cold water, telephone, cable TV and 24-hour room service. Hotel services include airport pickups, travel agency, cafeteria-bar and E-mail access. Av. Huaylas 710. Tel: 51-1-467-3047, E-mail: holayareservas@infonegocio.net.pe, URL: www.hotelolaya.com.pe. Updated: Jun 15, 2009.

Chorrillos Restaurants

The dining scene in Chorrillos, formerly a bustling fishing village, is reminiscent of its seaside history. There are many good cevicherías and small restaurants along the fish market that offer excellent samples of fresh fish. Also popular here is the chorrillana style of cooking that uses tomatoes and chilis. Careful, it's very spicy. Updated: Jun 15,2009

Puntarenas Restaurant

(ENTREES: $9-12)Staying true to Chorrillos's fishing roots, this restaurant serves up fresh seafood at a reasonable price. Calle Santa Teresa 455. Tel: 51-1-467-0053, URL: www.restaurante-puntarenas.com. Updated: Dec 15, 2008.

El Hornero

If you want meat, if you really, really want meat, like a nice, big, juicy steak served with golden, crisp fries, a freshly tossed salad topped with an impeccable dressing, and all served with warm rolls and a fine red wine, head to El Hornero, a family-owned and-managed restaurant. The beauty is of it is that you can indulge in all this while under an open window terrace, letting in a soft sea breeze and a view that stretches to the horizon. Of course, instead of a single meal, you could order an individual BBQ to be brought to your table, which easily feeds three or four hungry people. The BBQ comes with sausages, chicken, pork and steak. The meal is perfected when you throw in the great pisco dours, sublime desserts, damask napkins, large goblets, friendly service and reasonable prices—yes, you've got it all at El Hornero. Open for lunch and dinner, but more popular at lunchtime. Try to get a table on the second floor. Malecón Almirante Miguel Grau 983. Tel: 51-1-251-8109. Updated: Jun 15, 2009.

El Suizo

(ENTREES: $7) When asked if they know "El Suizo," most limeños will respond, "Is that still there?" And yes, after 50 years it is still churning out the same wonderful dishes—mussels a la suisse, fresh sea bass and their most famous recipe (which isn't even on the menu), Corvina al Pardo, a delicious sea bass wrapped in a spinach sauce. Cooked however you'd like, the fish can also be steamed and served with burnt butter and capers over a perfectly boiled potato; this delicacy has a savory, delicate flavor. For dessert, try the apple pancakes with caramel.

While catering to Lima's intelligentsia and academic crowds, the restaurant is situated on a small bay surrounded by impressive cliffs. It's easy to watch surfers from here, and when the sea is high it has some of the best waves in all of the Pacific, fit only for professional surfers. Prices are average and the wine list limited, but you can bring your own bottle. The pisco sours are classic and the strawberry cocktails are unique. Arrange for a taxi to pick you up. Located on Playa La Herradura. Tel: 51-1-467-0163 Updated: Jul 10, 2007.

!!!!!

Elsewhere in Lima

Lima Airport

Lima's airport, Aeropuerto Internacional Jorge Chávez, is located 16 km northwest of Lima, about 30 minutes away from the Miraflores area. If you want to know more about Lima airport visit: www.lap.com.pe. Updated: Jun 15,2009

Lodging

There are a few accommodations close to the airport that are worth checking out, as it takes at least 20 minutes by taxi to get into Central Lima from the airport, and even more to San Isidro, Miraflores, etc. If you need to stop over for just a night, or wish to stay close to the airport for an early morning flight, it's definitely a good idea to stay in a hostel or hotel near Jorge Chávez International. Updated: Feb 02,2010

Hostal Victor

(ROOMS: $35-55) Hostal Victor is a small hotel near Lima's Airport, which is very convenient due to the early departure of the flights going to Cusco. The hostel is very quiet and clean and the service is generally good. Calle Manuel Mattos 325 Zip: Lima 31 Tel: 51-1-5694662 Fax: 51-1-567-5107 E-mail: hostalvictor@terra.com.pe URL: geocities.com/htlvictor Getting there: call for a free pick up from the airport. Updated: Jun 30,2010

Lima Travel Lodge

(ROOMS: $8-32) This hostel is close to Lima airport. The house owners are an English/Spanish-speaking couple willing to embrace foreigners in their cozy house that is located in a classic neighborhood in Lima and is cheap and safe. They have comfortable and clean rooms with a pleasant atmosphere and decent services. They also arrange interesting tours of the un-touristy side of Lima. Calle San Juan Carlos 163 - San Miguel Altura de la cuadra 12 de la Avenida La Marina. Tel: 51-1-997-283-336. E-mail: info@limatravelodge.com URL: limatravelodge.com Updated: Feb 03, 2009

Pay Purix Backpackers Hostel

(ROOMS: $10-36) Located just three minutes from the airport, Pay Purix Backpackers Hostel is a friendly and comfortable place. Service is warm and welcoming. Advice can be given on trips that can be taken in the highlands and the jungle. Airport pickup can be arranged upon request for an extra charge. Av. Paseo Japon, Mz. F, Lote 5, Urb. Los Jazmines, 1ra Etapa - Callao Lima - Perú Zip: 51 Tel: 51-1-484-9118, URL: paypurix.com. Updated: Jan 14,2010.

Machu Picchu Suites

(ROOM $25-50) Machu Picchu Suites is a comfortable, affordable apartment/hotel located in a quiet, residential neighborhood near Jorge Chávez International Airport. The combination of furnished apartments and a warm atmosphere with hotel services makes the Machu Picchu Suites an excellent choice for a stay in Lima. The "homey" feeling and inclusion of a kitchenette make it a good option for business travelers who require an overnight stay. However, it's also very suitable for tourists. Jr. Machu Picchu 128, Maranga, San Miguel Zip: Lima 32. Tel: 51-1-452-5379 Fax: 51-1-452-6042, E-mail: machupicchusuites@gmail.com, URL: machupicchusuites.com. Updated: Jan 18, 2010

Manhattan Inn

(ROOMS: $40) Perhaps the closest hotel to the airport, Manhattan Inn provides safe lodging on a quiet street in northern Lima. Nothing resembles upscale Manhattan New York here, but the beds are comfy, the cable TV is extensive and this place is perfect if you have a lay-over that extends overnight, have a super early flight out or a late night flight in. For $40, you get a comfortable double bed, clean bathroom, cable TV and a breakfast of bread, jam and coffee. Although a bit on the older side, the hotel is quite comfortable. What is even better is that they do not charge extra to pick you up from the airport or to drop you off; it's all included. They have a safe and a you can even get a wake-up call. If you need a hotel near the airport, check it out. Jr. Javier Luna Pizarro N-168, Urb. La Colonial, Callao. Tel: 51-1-464-5811 Fax: 51-1-464-5820 E-mail: hotel@hmanhattan.com URL: hmanhattan.com. Updated: May 18, 2009.

Neighborhoods

Callao

Approximately 14 km from downtown Lima, Callao still possesses some of the best examples of colonial mansions and plazas (Plaza Gálvez and Plaza Grau chief among them) in Lima. Visitors here can also check out the Real Felipe fortress, which dates back to 1747, when it was built to defend Lima's primary the port from pirates. Also worth a visit is La Punta, a traditional district that once was the home Lima's aristocracy. Of particular interest is the sea-side promenade, beaches and homes. Off the coast of Callao are a set of islands that can be visited by tours leaving from Plaza Grau square, near the Real Felipe fortress. Updated: Nov 05, 2007

La Punta

At La Punta you'll find the Maritime Museum where you can explore the inside of a submarine, visit the Fort of San Felipe, and if you can fit it in, take a boat trip around the bay of Callao. Tickets can be bought from the museum, and all are within easy walking distance. La Punta is a narrow peninsula which separates the bays of Miraflores and Callao. It was once joined to the islands San Lorenzo and El Frontón, which you can see close by, until a tidal wave drowned half of the town many years ago. The Naval Officers' School is based here, as well as the Peruvian Yacht Club. It is an older area with a markedly Italian flavor due to the immigrants who arrived after the last war. Many of the houses have now been catalogued as National Historical Treasures by the government, which means that they can not be altered in any way or sold. You can walk all around the peninsula following the promenades on both sides. Many migratory birds can be found on the south side as well. At the tip of the peninsula there are a few economical restaurants, the best being Brisas Marinas. Port of Lima and Callao. Getting there: From Miraflores hop on a bus headed for Callao. It's a short ride. Updated: Jun 15,2009

Restaurants

Restaurante La Rana Verde

La Rana Verde (The Green Frog) has made a name for itself over the last 30 years and should be on your agenda, as it serves some of the best seafood in town. The restaurant is built on stilts over the water, and although it is a little on the expensive side, the cuisine is superb and is served in generous quantities. Of course, being on the ocean and all, the specialty is fish—flounder, sea bass and scallops are all caught daily. You can even watch your lunch being delivered, freshly caught, to the restaurant's pier by fishing boats. Served a variety of ways, it is up to you to decide how you would like your fish cooked. Since the restaurant is over the sea and is built of wood, it is kind of creaky and damp, and you may get splashed when the sea is high, but with the open windows all around, you can watch the

coming and going of the boats and ships of one of the largest ports in South America. Plan carefully, it is only open for lunch. Parque Gálvez, La Punta, Callao. Updated: Jul 11, 2007.

Magdalena del Mar

Lodging

Magdalen House Tourist Hostel

(ROOMS: $6 per person) Magdalen House opened its doors in January 2006 in the district of Magdalena of the Sea. The beauty and nostalgia of old Lima has been lovingly preserved here. At Magdalen House you will enjoy the hospitality and kindness of the owners. All rooms have a private bathroom; reservations include breakfast. Jr. Ayacucho 778 Magdalena del Mar, Lima, Perú Zip: 511. Tel: 51-1-461-6768 E-mail: magdalenhouse@magdalenhouse.com, URL: magdalenhouse.com. Updated: Aug 14, 2007.

Restaurants

Chifa Fon Wa

Chifa Fon Wa is a Cantonese-style, family-run restaurant that reflects the original Chinese-Peruvian cuisine created during 150 years of cultural exchange between Chinese immigrants and locals. You cannot leave Peru without having sampled the Fon Wa and Chicken Tay Pa, and to top it off a cup of Jazmine tea or an Inka Kola. Av. Javier Prado Oeste 564, Magdalena del Mar, Lima, Peru. Tel: 51-1-461-9733 URL: chifa-fonwa.com. Updated: Feb 26, 2010

Monterrico

Most famous for its horse racing, Monterrico is one of Lima's less touristy neighborhoods. Monterrico's Hippodrome gets packed four days a week, hosting both national and international races, Tuesdays and Thursdays at 7 p.m. and Saturdays and Sundays at 1 p.m. There's also a Gold Museum, Textile Museum, and Arms Museum all housed within one building. Here clothing samples over a thousand years old can be found, as well as feather capes hailing from Western Peru. Gun enthusiasts won't want to miss the Spanish colonial firearms that are on display here. Updated: Jun 15,2009

Lodging

El Polo Hotel

(ROOMS: $425-495) El Polo is mostly frequented by business travelers who like to be comfortable, if not spoiled. Opened in 1997, this seven-story luxury building is close to one of the most modern shopping centers in Lima. The Centro Comercial El Polo has cinemas, cafés, bars, restaurants and any other kind of shop you might need. There are 38 rooms in total and each has a living room, dining room and fully furnished kitchen. The hotel also has laundry service, an on-site restaurant, 24-hour room service, business facilities and a fitness club. Av. La Encalada 1515 Tel: 51-1-434-2050 E-mail: reservas@hotelelpolo.com URL: hotelelpolo.com. Updated: Jun 15, 2009.

Restaurants

Sushi Ito

Don't let the small size of this restaurant deter you from enjoying the delicious sushi creations that Sushi Ito is reputed to serve. Start with light appetizers and move on to the sushi and sashimi. Share a traditional spicy tuna roll with your dining companion or enjoy a Ninja roll all to yourself. For customers who prefer their fish cooked, there is an extensive menu of yummy entrees to choose from. Finish the meal with a brulée or fruit sorbet. Av. El Polo 740. Tel: 51-1-435-5817, URL: sushi-ito.com. Updated: Jun 15, 2009.

Pueblo Libre

Pueblo Libre is a quiet residential district located not far from the historic center of Lima. Originally founded in 1557 as Magdalena Vieja, this section of town was given a new name in 1821 by none other than José de San Martín, one of the Great Liberators of South America. The town was renamed for the great patriotism and desire for freedom that San Martín saw in the inhabitants. In 1881, during the disastrous War of the Pacific, the government of Peru briefly used Pueblo Libre as the seat of government. Pueblo Libre is also sometimes called "Villa de los Libertadores" because different leaders of the independence movement, such as Bolívar, Sucre, Córdova and others, maintained official residences there. Well known for its museums, including two of Lima's best, the Rafael Larco Herrera Archaeological Museum and the National Anthropology Museum, this part of town is also good for shopping. Updated: Jun 15, 2009.

Pueblo Libre History

Originally founded in 1557 as Magdalena Vieja, this section of town was given a new name in 1821 by none other than José de San Martín, one of the Great Liberators of South America. The town was renamed for the great patriotism and desire for freedom that San Martín saw in the inhabitants. In 1881, during the disastrous War of the Pacific, the government of Peru briefly used Pueblo Libre as the seat of government. Pueblo Libre is also sometimes called "Villa de los Libertadores" because different leaders of the independence movement, such as Bolívar, Sucre, Córdova and others, maintained official residences there. Updated: May 08, 2007.

Things to See and Do

Plaza Bolívar

Away from the bustle of Lima's downtown lies the green park of Plaza Bolívar, flanked by three of Lima's more interesting museums. Travel back 8,000 years as you peruse the pre-Columbian artifacts at the yellow painted monolith, the Museo Nacional de Antropología, Arqueología e Historia del Perú. The museum is home to two 2,500 year old mummies recovered near the Nazca Lines and other national gems not to be missed. The private Museo Arqueológico Rafael Larco Herrera, just across the plaza, equally warrants a visit. Larco's museum has one of the largest collections of Peruvian cultural artifacts as well as an exhibit of ancient erotic art that never ceases to amaze visitors. Don't forget the Museum of National History, which displays art and artifacts from the colonial and republican eras. Av Abancay and Jr. Ayacucho. Getting there: Getting to Pueblo Libre on public transportation is a little tricky but can still be done. Hop on the bus marked Todo Brasil and ask the driver to drop you on Av General Vivanco, a short walk away. A taxi from Miraflores will set you back about $2. Updated: Aug 30, 2007.

Bodega Santiago Queirolo

There are two huge wooden wine barrels on the right, and an antique model car on the left, which is how you'll know you are in the Santiago Queirolo Winery, one of the largest manufacturers of Peruvian wine in the area. Their selection includes dry, semi-dry, sangria, champagne and, of course, the Peruvian favorite, pisco. A bottle of wine is $5-7—a great bargain for an exceptionally high-quality product. Av. San Martín 1062, Pueblo Libre, Lima. Tel: 51-1-463-1008 / 6503, E-mail: vtas_sq@millicom.com.pe, URL: www.santiagoqueirolo.com. Updated: Jun 15, 2009.

Photo by: Al Tuttle

Shopping

Sidrik's Peruvian Handicraft

Sidrik's is one of the leading alpaca wool retail outlets in Peru, and it is worth going out to Pueblo Libre in order to take advantage of dazzling array of native clothing items, including but not limited to the world famous chullo, the somewhat pointed wool cap designed to keep ears warm in high and cold attitudes—perfect for your hike to Machu Picchu. There is also the accompanying floor-length scarf, as well as alpaca trousers, skirts, vests and ties--with many colorful varieties of indigenous designs and patterns. With exchange rates favoring the dollar over the sol, the prices are a fraction of what you would pay for these clothes as exported items. Avenida la Marina 612 (and Sucre), Pueblo Libre Tel: 51-1-461-6095 Fax: www.sidriks.com.pe E-mail: sidriks@hotmail.com URL: www. sidriks.com.pe. Updated: Jun 15, 2009.

Lodging

A quiet, less popular area for tourists, Pueblo Libre doesn't have as many colorful or varied accommodations options as nearby Miraflores or other sections of Lima. However, there are still options available with all the basic amenities and the area is conveniently located close to surrounding landmarks, tourist spots, restaurants and activities. Updated: Jun 15, 2009.

Casa Marfil

(ROOMS: $7) This is an option for travelers who are looking for a quiet, more personal experience. This eco-friendly guest house provides a comfortable stay with a local family in their home. Enjoy cable TV, laundry facilities, kitchen, Internet, free luggage storage, hot water all day and travel information. Parque Ayacucho 126 Tel: 51-1-463-3161 / 628-3791 E-mail: casamarfil@yahoo.com URL: casamarfil.com.   Updated: Jun 15, 2009.

Hospedaje Residencial Santa Fé

This is a family-run guest house/hostel located in the residential area of Pueblo Libre, 15 minutes from the Jorge Chávez International Airport. All rooms have private toilets and bathrooms, hot water and cable TV. The hostel is near popular museums, churches, markets, restaurants and services such as banks, exchange money offices, travel agencies and supermarkets. Private airport pickup or transport into the city can be easily arranged. Jiron Santa Fe 328. Tel: 51-1-461-8263, E-mail: lima@hotelmamatila.com, URL: santafehostel.com. Updated: Jun 15, 2009.

Hotel Mamatila

Hotel Mamatila is a simple, comfortable option with 20 single, double and triple rooms. All rooms have hot and cold water 24-hours a day, television with cable, telephone and 24-hour room service. The hotel also provides internet, continental breakfast, an on-site restaurant, safe-deposit box, fax, laundry and open areas to relax. Additionally, tourist information and airport pick up can be arranged. Antonio Arrieta 110 Esq. Cdra 16 Av. Brasil. Tel: 51-1-463-1573, URL: www.hotelmamatila.com. Updated: Jun 15, 2009.

Bait Sababa Lodge

The Bait Sababa Lodge prides itself on making you feel at home. Unlike most other hotels in the area, they speak Hebrew. Their rooms have hot water, and breakfast is included. Bait Sababa is centrally located, close to Internet, laundry, banks, museums, hospitals, restaurants and the bus terminal. Av. San Martin 743. Tel: 51-1-261-4990, URL: geocities.com/sababalodgelimaperu. Updated: Jun 15,2009.

Restaurants

Though not as large as nearby neighborhoods, Pueblo Libre offers some nice, quiet places to dine on authentic, Peruvian fare and other popular favorites. Prices are decent, and the experience will be memorable. Updated: Jun 15,2009

Antigua Taberna Queirolo

(ENTREES: $5-6) This large, attractive and stylish restaurant, with its swinging wood doors, is modeled on what a 16th-century European tavern would have looked like. There are also displays of nostalgic photos of old Peru on its walls. The taberna's 14-item menu includes such choice offerings as chorolitos a la chalaca (mussels on the shell) with generous helpings of corn, tomato and spices. As an extension of the Santiago Queirolo Winery next door, it offers a naturally great selection of beverages. No credit cards are accepted. Avenida San Martín 1062, Pueblo Libre Tel: 51-1-460-0441, E-mail: tabernaqueirolo@yahoo.com, URL: www.antiguatabernaqueirolo.com. Updated: Jun 15, 2009.

Curry Treat

(ENTREES $10-20) Catering and delivery of vegetarian and non-vegetarian Indian food. Tel: 99-555-5457 / 994-2929, E-mail: currytreat@gmail.com, URL: www.currytreat.tk. Updated: Jul 01, 2008.

El Bolivariano

Step into one of the many rooms at El Bolivariano and enjoy a unique dining experience. Choose between a more formal meal in the Comedor Manuelita or enjoy a cocktail in the Boli-Bar and catch up with friends. If you are looking for an intimate, romantic experience, dine in La Pergola. If you happen to come in on a Sunday afternoon, be sure to try a little bit of everything on the Creole Buffet. El Bolivariano serves a wide variety of seafood, Creole food, salads, desserts and creative drinks. Pasaje Santa Rosa Tel: 51-1-261-9565, E-mail: reservas@elbolivariano.com, URL: www.elbolivarano.com. Updated: Jun 15, 2009

San Borja

San Borja is primarily a residential neighborhood of Lima, though it is also home to one of the city's most important museums, the Museo de La Nación. Upon entering the Banco de la Nación building, one will find a plethora of cultural offerings. The Museo Peruano de Ciencias de la Salud is also located here, with an extensive collection of mummies and models of all the Inca ruins to be found in the country accompanied by both Spanish and English explanations. Toward the basement you'll find the Instituto Nacional de Cultura's bookshop. There's a café next door where you can sit down, mull over your purchases and relax after a full day of museum-hopping. Updated: Aug 08, 2007.

Things to See and Do

Huaca San Borja

This archaeological zone was constructed by the Ichma culture and resembles pyramid foundations made of mud. Inside there are enclosures, passages and uneven floors to explore. Guided visits are offered. Av. Canada y de la Arqueologia (on the corner). Updated: Aug 08, 2007.

The National Library

This expansive library was established in 1821 and originally located in Central Lima. Despite having most of the library's works stolen during the war with Chile, the library has been able to build up its offering and moved to a new building in 2006. The new building boasts a theater, cafeteria, exhibition halls, 12 reading rooms, storage areas and administrative offices. The library also contains the largest selection of newspapers and magazines in the country. Avenida de la Poesia 160. Tel: 51-1-513-6900, URL: www.bnp. gob.pe/portalbnp. Updated: Aug 08,2007

Lodging

Hotel Britania

(ROOMS: $40-80) Located in a quiet area and just minutes from important places of business, the Hotel Britania tends to target business travelers. There are single, double and triple executive suites all offering a modern environment with air conditioning, jacuzzi and sauna and a comfortable living room. There is also an on-site restaurant with a varied menu featuring national and international cuisine and a bar that hosts happy hour. There is a basic gym with cardio machines and weights. The staff is helpful and room service is prompt. Av. San Borja Sur 653 Tel: 51-1-224-2006 ,E-mail: hotelbritania@hbritania.com, URL: www.hbritania.com. Updated: Dec 15, 2008.

Prince Hotel Suites Spa

(ROOMS: $147-236) This higher end property offers a choice of either the Prince Suite or the Executive Suite. Both have a king-size bed, sauna, Jacuzzi and WiFi; airport pickup is included as well. The Executive Suite also has an adjacent living room with guest bathroom. This property is somewhat removed from restaurants, shopping and the business district, but it's only a short cab ride away. Av. Guardia Civil 727. Tel: 51-1-225-3025, E-mail: reservas@princehotel.com.pe, URL: www.princehotel.com.pe. Updated: Dec 15, 2008.

Restaurants

Edo Sushi Bar

This Japanese restaurant offers amazing flavors, the freshest in seafood ingredients and is reasonably priced. Although it has only been around for a while, Edo Sushi Bar has already won over a devoted following. San Borja Sur 663, Tel: 51-1-225-0881. Updated: Aug 08, 2007.

AROUND LIMA

Things to See and Do

PACHACÁMAC RUINS

Roughly 40 kilometers south of Lima you will find the ancient city of Pachacámac. The city was originally constructed by a pre-Incan culture, but has been occupied by other civilizations. This causes the site to have a very interesting mix of architecture styles. There is a gift shop, if you want to take something home to remember it by, and café located in the ancient city, if you need a snack after admiring the ruins. Antigua Panamericana Sur Km. 31.5 / Distrito de Lurín. Tel: 51-1-430-0168, E-mail: museopachacamac@perucultural.org.pe. 9 a.m.-5 p.m., daily. Updated: Jun 15, 2009.

HORSEBACK RIDING

Cabalgatas Horseback Riding

Visitors to Lima who want to explore ancient ruins, sandy beaches and the Peruvian countryside can do so in a traditional way riding a Peruvian paso horse. Pasos are pure descendants of the steeds Spanish conquistadors brought to the Americas 400 years ago and are a great source of national pride today. Known for their unique gait, pasos seem to kick their feet to the side instead of to the front. It's an uncommon sight in the horse world, and purely Peruvian. Cabalgatas, in the Mamacona stable complex outside Lima, will suit everyone up, from novices to experienced riders, for a trail ride through the Pachacámac ruins. Begun in 200 A.D., Pachacámac was expanded by the Wari tribe and then incorporated into the Inca empire. It's the closest major archeological site to Lima. Riders tour the Templo del Sol (Temple of the Sun) and Palacio de Mamacuña (House of the Chosen Women) and other sun-drenched remains before heading along tree-lined dirt roads. Riders pass several small ranches where foals and horses graze. A long stretch of deserted beach is the final destination. Seagulls soar overhead as the horses wade through the surf, ankle-to knee-deep. Beginners may want to hang on because more frisky horses may break into gallop. Before the bump becomes too breathtaking, the guides will easily rein the horses back to a walk. Except for the occasional rumble of a truck passing on the highway behind, riders are alone. The entire trail ride is about three hours long, but the time on the beach seems endless because the sand goes on and on.

Trail riding at Cabalgatas is an authentic paso experience. Watching the Cabalgatas guides prepare the horses and cool them down after the tour is a glimpse into the real cowboy life. Cabalgatas riders compete in the National Paso Horse tournament, which is conveniently held right on Mamacona grounds every April. Go at the right time and you've got a front-row seat to the country's most heralded paso competition. Breeders from all over Peru strut their stuff, decked out in traditional white pants and shirts, hats and serapes. You can hang out right where the competitors warm up, watch the action in the tournament ring and hobnob with owners and spectators alike.

Getting there: The easiest way to reach Cabalgatas stable is by taxi, to Mamacona, 15 miles (24 kilometers) south of Lima. The Mamacona entrance is before the entrance to Pachacámac ruins. Look for the shield that says Asociación del Caballo Peruano de Paso. Tel: 51-1-9-837-5813 / 507-8444, Fax: 51-1-221-4591, E-mail: informes@cabalgatas.com.pe, URL: www.cabalgatas.com.pe. Updated: Jun 15, 2009.

PARAGLIDING

Aeroxtreme

Paragliding instructor Michael Fernández has more than 15 years of experience. He offers tandem flights year-round that fly over the beautiful Costa Verde in Miraflores. Flights are around 10 minutes long and no experience is necessary. Be sure to bring your camera. Mike also offers one-day courses allowing you to fly solo close to the ground with proper instruction. This includes five solo glides on a small dune in Lurín, one tandem flight over Costa Verde or Pachacámac and transportation to the flying sites from Miraflores. A beginner pilot course is offered during which you will learn the basic techniques of flight in eight classes and includes the use of paragliding equipment, flight manual and transportation to the flying sites. Contact Mike for more information. Trípoli 345 Apt. 503. Tel: 51-1-242-5125 / 999-480-954, URL: www.aeroxtreme.com, Updated: Mar 25, 2010.

SURFING

Surfers come from around the world to board the waves of Peru, and Lima's coast is no different. For the beaches near Lima

you will need a 3mm full wetsuit pretty much year round, but come Peru's summer months, January and February, you can just trunk it. Most folks ride their short boards year round, so much so, that they vastly outnumber the long boards, even when the waves are small. Updated: Jun 15, 2009.

Punta Hermosa Beaches

At the town of Punta Hermosa, not only will you find larger resorts and good restaurants along the beach, but you'll have two great surf beaches to choose between. The board-breaking shore-break of Playa Norte is north of the headland, and the large rollers of La Isla, is to the south. La Isla breaks from the left and right and can get a big hold-up to double overhead. A beach paddle can take 20 minutes or more if a good swell exists, but you also make similar time if you enter the water over the rocks near the headland. The beaches are located 40 kilometers south of Lima, along a beach access road easily reached off the Pan-American Highway.

The area around the coastal town of Punta Hermosa is lined with numerous world-class breaks. It is no coincidence that Peruvian champ Sofía Milanovich owns a prime location beach house here. Heading south from Lima to around the 40 km. mark, it is best to take the side road beach access highway from the Pan-American Highway. In addition to numerous decent and cheap restaurants along the road, well-marked signs mark off each major beach from there, starting with Caballeros. A few of the many other notable breaks within a few kilometers south include Señoritas, La Isla and Punta Rocas. Updated: Jun 15, 2009.

Caballeros

Caballeros is a right point break and one of the few tubing options in Peru, as the wave becomes perfectly hollow at about a head-high swell. It can hold up to about a meter overhead. This place is good for the skilled surfer. It is 40 kilometers south of Lima. Near Punta Hermosa, take the beach access road from the Pan-American Highway towards the ocean. Near Punta Hermosa Getting there: About 40 kilometers south of Lima. Take the beach access road from the Pan-American Highway towards the ocean. Updated: Jun 15, 2009.

Señoritas

Just south of Caballeros, Señoritas beach is just around the headland south. It's is a nice left point break. The reef here can be fairly well-exposed in low tides, and can handle a swell of up to about a meter overhead. South of Punta Hermosa 40 kilometers south of Lima, near Punta Hermosa. Take the Pan-American Highway and then the beach access road towards Punta Hermosa. Follow the beach road south of Punta Hermosa and you'll find Señoritas Beach. Updated: Jun 15, 2009.

Punta Negra and Punta Rocas

Three kilometers south of Punta Hermosa you'll find Punta Negra, home of the world-famous Punta Rocas break. Located in the northern part beach, this area is usually full of families and is lined with umbrellas and restaurants. Punta Rocas is one of the most consistent waves in Peru. It has good shape from all directions of a swell. Waves here are typically a half-meter larger or more than other breaks, and it can hold up well, with up to a double overhead swell. It has good left and right breaks over a reef, but Punta Rocas can quickly get blown out if there is wind of any kind. Getting there: This beach is 3 kilometers south of Punta Hermosa Route, located 43 kilometers south of Lima, along the beach access road off the Pan-American Highway. Updated: Jun 15, 2009.

Cerro Azul

Famously listed, just after "Laguna" in the Beach Boy's song "Surfin' Safari," Cerro Azul is a consistent left point break located about 130 kilometers (80 mi.) south of Lima. It sees the best waves with a swell from the southwest that will wrap nicely around the headland, and can take you 150 meters (1,490 ft.)or more all the way to the pier. Another left and right closer to the pier the typical surf is chest-high, and can tube up. It occasionally sees waves up to a meter overhead. The outer breaks stay fairly light with surfers on the weekends, but the take-off zone can be jam-packed when the waves are really good. The inner breaks are often crowded with kids and body boarders. The beach is very family-friendly and attracts most of the town on the nicer weekends. There are numerous hostels, all with easy beach access and a big plate of fresh ceviche can be had for 20 soles (around $6.60)at the numerous restaurants. Updated: Jun 15, 2009.

))))]

Living in Peru

With such attractions as Machu Picchu, Lake Titicaca, the Amazon and the Nasca Lines, Peru is the most visited country in all of South America. It is only natural that many travelers would take the extra step and move here. The strength of the dollar and the euro against the Peruvian sol is an additional incentive.

Check out LivinginPeru.com, a great resource for information on extended stays in Peru, including all of the latest Peruvian news, job classifieds, and events calendars. The website also has excellent features on everything from local travel destinations to food. Updated: Dec 08,2009

HOUSING AND REAL ESTATE

Where to Live in Cusco

Be careful with the areas that you choose to live in. It is safest for travelers to live in central Cusco, and most do, for outside the center, there is more crime and poverty. The better areas where the middle and higher class families live, are in the suburbs of Magisterio and Marcavalle, both near Avenida la Cultura and the largest supermarket in Cusco.

In the center, the areas of San Blas and around the hills here are known as good, safe areas. Anywhere that is within three blocks of the Plaza de Armas should be reasonably safe. In addition, the nicer apartments and homes are also found in the central radius as well, and in the upper class neighborhoods. Naturally, the closer you are to the center and the Plaza de Armas, the nicer the neighborhoods are, the nicer the restaurants, and the nicer the apartments as well. Of course these elements also affect the price.

Prices vary by how close you are to the Plaza de Armas, how many rooms in the building, how new it is, the security of the building, and whether you have views of Cusco. Given the shape of Cusco and the fact that it is surrounded by mountains, you will find that many of the good apartments advertised do actually come with nice views. You just might have to hike up a steep hill each time to get to your new pad. If you are looking at a place with other travelers, chances are the landlord has increased the prices to cater for tourists, and you will probably pay more than what you might pay living with locals.

The average price to pay for a room in an apartment around the center of Cusco is $100 per month. This can vary from $80 - $150 depending on how nice the apartment is and who you are living with. If you want to rent a one bedroom apartment alone, you will be looking at around $200 - $400 per month, while a three bedroom apartment will cost between $300 - $500 depending on how nice it is and the size.

Houses are much are harder to come by in the center, and are only really found in the suburbs of Cusco, where the locals live, and these areas can be particularly dangerous for tourists given the poverty that is prevalent in these areas. Houses will be cheaper for this reason, around $200 a month for a three bedroom house in the suburbs of San Sebas, or around Mulino market, or around the airport. Houses around the nice, upper-class areas of Magisterio and Marcavalle are more expensive, around $300 - $400 per month, however this is a safer and a nicer place to live.

Most of the apartments in the center of Cusco come furnished, as they cater for tourists. Cusco tends to have a transient population and is very much set up for tourists who live there while volunteering, studying or working temporarily. Having a furnished apartment is easiest, however, furniture shops can be found further out, along Avendia la Cultura. Houses in the suburbs tend not to be furnished.

Renting and Buying in Cusco

Suitable accommodation in Cusco can be hard to find. First, be sure to check things such as hot water availability, water pressure and rubbish disposal when viewing a home. Most accommodation in central Cusco and close to the Plaza is in apartments. Slightly out of the center, you will find many terraced houses and larger apartment buildings. Further out again, you will find standalone houses.

If you want to live with other travelers, the best places to look for an available room are on the public notice-boards found within local tourist hangouts. Check the notice-boards found in the Real McCoy restaurant on Plateros, at the top of the stairs of the Indigo bar on Tecsecocha, just outside the Muse bar on Plateros, within Kusikuy restaurant on Suecia, inside Nortons pub on Santa Catalina Angosta, and in Paddys Irish bar on Calle Triunfo. You can also visit the South American Explorers Club on

Atoqsaycuchi 670, in San Blas—they have a large notice-board with accommodation listings and other offerings. SAE often rents rooms within their clubhouse, but in most cases you have to be a member.

Other than noticeboards, the main publication for rooms and apartments for rent is the local trade newspaper, Rueda de Negocias. This comes out every Thursday and can be found at all the small newsstands that sit on street corners selling papers and magazines. At just 50 centavos, this is full of all the apartments available in Cusco.

If you are looking to purchase in Cusco, there are some real estate offices at the very bottom of Avenida El Sol where you can browse their current listings and discuss your desires with an agent. Be wary of overpriced buildings and drainage systems. Be aware that many buildings in Cusco are very old and this may have repercussions.

Another very popular option for accommodation in Cusco is living with a host family. These are local, middle-class families that work with organizations to have foreigners come and live with them temporarily. This can be a pleasant experience to meet locals, a good way to experience the local culture within the family home and also a way to improve your Spanish. You will also be privy to the local cuisine and cooking methods. Good organizations that can arrange your stay with a host family are: www.hostfamilyincusco.com and www.hostfamilyinperu.com. Updated: Jul 13,2010.

Where To Live in Lima

Lima is a large city and the neighborhoods vary wildly due to the disparity of wealth. Therefore, be careful where you choose to live and don't rent an apartment without visiting it and the surrounding neighborhoods first. Most permanent expatriates with families live in San Isidro, one of the wealthiest residential districts in the city with gated communities, watchmen, and ample street lighting. San Isidro is also popular with young professionals and business people because of the excellent shops, hotels, and proximity to the most established golf course. Other residential areas for families or retirees are Monterrico, and La Planicie in the La Molina district. La Molina is home to many Peruvian politicians and businessmen, and has large sprawling homes, country clubs and private schools.

Young professionals, travelers, and students tend to prefer leafy and safe Miraflores with its modern cafes, restaurants and shopping, or the colorful bohemian district of Barranco with its colonial architecture, galleries, and lively nightlife. In Miraflores, the nicest places are near Parque Kennedy with its sleek cafes and restaurants, and near Larcomar and Avenida Larcos where travelers can shop in the Cliffside mall or in the boutiques along the avenue. Barranco has popular jazz and salsa clubs and more of an accepting atmosphere, but it can be noisy at night in certain areas. If you need to wake up early be aware of bars close to your apartment.

Photo by: En Peru

Short-term guests or students looking to rent a room in a shared house can expect to pay between $200 and $350 per month in Miraflores, San Isidro, Barranco, and La Molina. This price varies from small rooms with shared bathrooms to master bedrooms in new apartments. In the middle class areas of Lima you can expect to pay between $150 and $250 for a room.

To rent a studio or one bedroom in a coveted neighborhood expect to pay between $450 to $750 depending on the age of the building, and whether or not there are modern appliances, whether utilities are included, and if there are views. If you are looking for a modern, sleek, spacious apartment with views and a balcony expect to pay at least $1,000. In neighborhoods like Jesus Maria on the other hand you can find three bedroom two bath apartments for under $500 per month.

There are some neighborhoods outside the coveted tourist areas that are still relatively safe and nice for those on a budget who can't quite afford Miraflores or San Isidro, but want to be nearby. These neighborhoods are more for middle class Peruvian families, however, they are cheaper and more affordable for long-term housing. Jesus

Maria, Lince, Pueblo Libre, San Miguel, Chorrillos, Surco, and Surquillo are near San Isidro, Miraflores, and Barranco and are considered fairly safe for foreigners, though be certain to view the neighborhood at night before renting anything.

Tourists should avoid San Juan de Lurigancho, Villa El Salvador, Huaycan and La Victoria as they are over-populated nighborhoods with inhabitants that are mostly struggling economically.

Downtown Lima, or the historic center of Lima, is full of churches, museums, and many of the other treasures of the city, but the endless traffic and subsequent pollution mean that almost all expatriates prefer to live elsewhere, if they can afford to. With that being said, if you are a history or architecture buff and want to live near these gems, downtown Lima is much safer and cleaner than it used to be and apartment rentals are cheaper than the other tourist districts previously mentioned. However, most people are happiest visiting downtown Lima in the day and staying in the more upscale neighborhoods.

One of the best options for foreigners who are looking for an apartment is to stay at the South American Explorers for two weeks to a month while you get a feel for the different neighborhoods and check out the local market. Rooms range from $200 to $400 per month and their clubhouse is near Parque Kennedy in Miraflores.

Renting and Buying in Lima

Finding affordable and comfortable housing in Lima can be difficult. To get a handle on the local Peruvian market check out their Commercio online search engine: http://clasificados.elcomercio.pe/macro/in-home.asp?id=4. Here you can enter whether you want a room, an apartment, or a house and enter the district as well. Most locals will tell you to check the El Commercio newspaper on Sunday mornings for great deals on apartments. Rental contracts are pretty informal here but expect to pay a deposit of two months if you are renting your own place. For a room, you will normally be asked to pay a deposit of one month's rent. The terms of lease can vary from month-to-month to a year. El Commercio is also a great place to see apartments and houses for sale.

In the more sought after neighborhoods, WI-FI, furnished housing, hot water, etc. are the

norm. However many of the older buildings, as spacious and full of rustic charm as they may be, will need to be carefully inspected for electric wiring and access to hot water, and you may need to furnish them yourself.

If you are looking to buy, be sure to check with SUNARP, the public registry. You can check the status of the property, whether or not there is a mortgage on the property, or if there are any other legal issues. It costs only a few soles to check, and it could save you money in the long run. You can either go in person to the office, located in the Jesus Maria neighborhood, or go to their online website: https://enlinea.sunarp.gob.pe/interconexion/webapp/extranet/Ingreso.do. There are a few legal steps that must be taken to buy a property, and you must make sure that you have the correct legal status and documentation. Visit a notary when you've found something you like to get specifics on what you'll need.

Here is a list of helpful websites to get you started on your search for housing in Lima:

http://www.kotear.pe/categoria/209-inmuebles
http://clasificados.elcomercio.com.pe/macro/In-Home.asp
http://www.expatperu.com/rhousing.php
http://www.livinginperu.com/classifieds/housing
http://lima.en.craigslist.org/hhh/
http://urbania.pe/

MOVING

Moving House

Some families with children who move to Peru use one of the relocation services that can help with customs, shipping, finding housing, schools for children, help with immigration issues, as well as give you the names of reliable doctors, lawyers, and other professionals in your new city. If you choose to use one of these services, make sure they come with great references and research the company thoroughly. If, like most people, you are making the move without the assistance of a relocating company, there are excellent websites that can help you make many of the important decisions regarding packing, and help prepare you for what to expect. Try www.expatperu.com to get you started. One of the main questions people usually want answered is whether it is best to ship their possessions or sell them back at home and buy all new items. In general, shipping can be a huge hassle and it's almost always better to sell your things at home and purchase new ones in Peru. Don't ship your car unless it is a 4X4 and you know for a fact you will be driving all the time, and unless the move is completely permanent or you have family heirlooms you can't part with, don't ship your furniture either. Custom duties are high and unless you have a strong sentimental attachment to a certain piece it will almost always be cheaper and easier to replace the item in Peru rather than pay all the fees and cost of shipping. Take a look at our section about things that are cheaper or more expensive to help you decide what to pack. Updated: Jul 13, 2010

Moving Pets

Bringing pets with you to Peru is relatively easy as long as you get all the proper paperwork ready well in advance. You must get a veterinarian in your home country to fill out an International Health Certificate for each of your pets within ten days of your travel date. Your pets must be internationally microchipped, current on all vaccines, have no communicable diseases, and have a blood test verifying they are healthy enough to travel. If traveling from the USA, the International Health Certificates need to be approved by your local USDA, and many European countries require an EU Pet Passport.

If you have pets that are too large to fit under your seat on the airplane, your veterinarian must feel they will have no problems being stored down in cargo. It's best to first check with the airline you are using for regulations, fees, and information about climate control, then calling your veterinarian at least a month before you plan on leaving to discuss the process. Although the health certificates need to be completed in the last 10 days before travel, it's advisable to see your vet one time prior to this last examination. If your pet has even a minor problem like worms or fleas, your veterinarian may not feel comfortable signing the paperwork and you might miss your flight. Pets do not need to be quarantined and are not held at customs in Peru as long as you provide the proper paperwork.

Animals held in cargo sometimes require a small customs fee, usually under 150 soles ($53). If you are incredibly busy, or found out that you need to travel on short notice, there are international pet shipping companies that can take care of all the logistics and paperwork for you, but often it is cheaper for you, and easier on the pet, to travel together. If you prefer to have your pet shipped, check out pettravelcenter.com.

SERVICES

Laundry

Getting your laundry done isn't difficult in the center of Cusco, or in any of the Lima neighborhoods, as there are laundromats on nearly every corner. The cheapest rate is 3 soles (about $1) per kilo, however many also charge 4 or sometimes 5 soles per kilo. Most of the laundromats will also do dry cleaning, which is more expensive, running at around 5 soles per garment. In Cusco you might sometimes find that you lose a garment or two each time, however once you start going to a place regularly and they know you, you might find they take better care of your things. Updated: Jul 13, 2010.

Tailors

Tailors are easy to find in Cusco. Just pop into the San Pedro market and behind the fruit stalls you'll find many ladies lined up with their sewing machines who will fix your clothes for a pittance. There is another slightly larger tailor shop on Calle Trinitarias, where you can also get clothes altered to a high quality, or even made, but take a design and your material for this. In addition, you can also find shoe-fixing shops, along Calle Tecte, Concevidayoc and Matara, all near the San Pedro market. In Lima, tailors and shoe-fixers can be found easily in all neighborhoods. Updated: Jul 13, 2010.

Maid Services

It is fairly common for people to have maids in Peru, even throughout the middle class, families, singles and couples alike hire maid services. Maid services are relatively cheap and easy to find. Many families have maids that live in the house with them, in order for them to be available the majority of the time, but wages are slightly higher in these situations. With those that travel to work, some are also paid transportation costs.

As a benchmark, in Lima, total costs range from 400-500 soles a month for an apartment, and 500-700 soles for a house, for a full time maid working five days a week. If the maid lives in the house she will work six days and be paid a bit more.

You can also arrange for a maid to come once a week, clean the house and cook a few meals for the week as well. This will cost you around 50 soles per visit and is usually 4-5 hours each time. This option is popular with singles and young couples.

Services include everything you might want, from cooking and shopping, to cleaning, washing and deep cleaning. As far as reliability goes, maids can be known to steal sometimes or leave without notice, however if you go through an agency it's safer as the maids come with recommendations and references. Another option is to take a personal recommendation from someone who has been employing a maid for a long time and who can vouch for reliability and trustworthiness. Updated: Jul 27,2010.

Cable TV Providers

There are three cable TV providers in Peru - Direct TV, Telmex and Cable Magico. You don't need a local bank account to set up cable. You can easily pay your bill with cash in the Mega supermarket or at a local bank. The easiest way to set up an account is to organize a technician to install your cable via the provider's website, as the call centers often have a long waiting period when you call through, and can be known to cut you off without warning. Updated: Jul 13,2010.

Cable Magico

(MONTHLY RATE: $42) Cable Magico are the largest and most popular provider and offer up to 512 channels. Their cheapest package is 128 channels for $42, up to 256 channels for $58, and the maximum capacity with 512 channels for $83. You can pay extra for your favorite channels to be shown in HD. Or you can select their HD plan, which offers 12 cable channels in HD, as well as a further 16 premium cable channels, for $40 per month. URL: www.cablemagico.com.pe.

Direct TV

(MONTHLY RATE: $32 and up) Direct TV is more expensive yet smaller, offering between 105-160 channels. Their cheapest package is $32 a month with 105 channels. Prices increase up to $63 and depend on how many channels you choose and how many you choose to have in HD. URL: www.directv.com.pe.

Telmex

(MONTHLY RATE: $35 and up) Telmex offers a range of packages from between 138 and 161 channels. The cheapest package is $35 per month for 138 channels and goes up to $52 a month for 161 channels. Prices depend on how many TVs you have, and how many HD channels you want. URL: www.telmex.com/pe.

Internet Providers

There are just four Internet providers in Peru and these are Telefonica, Claro, Nextel and Telmex. However, the largest and most popular providers are Telefonica and Claro, both are cell phone companies as well.

The cheapest plans start from around $35, but you do need a home phone in order to get broadband. You can get a WiFi plan, which you don't need a home phone for, however these are more expensive—plans start from around $40 a month, and you also have to purchase a small antenna for the WiFi to operate from, a one-off cost of about $45.

One of the cheapest and most popular plans is with Telefonica, who offers a plan on broadband including WiFi for 140 soles a month, which also includes a phone line and a free phone.

To get Internet you will need some identification such as your passport, and often they will ask you for a credit card number for emergencies. Although you can pay your bill directly from your bank account, you don't need to have a bank account set up in order to pay for this. You can have your bills sent to your home and then pay these with cash at a local bank, or in a supermarket such as Mega. Updated: Jul 13,2010.

Hair Salons

CUSCO

In Cusco you get what you pay for. The best hairdressers are found around the main plaza. Be careful with small, pokey places that offer cheap prices—these hairdressers are usually not qualified. That said, they are likely to have experience and if you just want to get a cheap cut you can try them. Easy cuts such as trims will be fine in these smaller shops, however for anything more in-depth, or if you have a unique type of hair, it is safer to pay a bit more and go to a good hairdresser such as Kap Salon, on Avenida El Sol, in Cusco Sol Plaza. This cozy little plaza is just next to the post office and also has a few other quality salons to choose from. Updated: Jul 13,2010.

LIMA

Just like any other large, international city Lima has a variety of hair salons with a range of prices. However, the higher-end salons in Lima are still only a fraction of what you would pay in a high-end salon in Europe or the USA, so if you have the money, it can be fun to splurge. If you don't have money for this, you can still find a great hairdresser and pay under $10 for a good cut. The most popular salons frequented by expats are in Miraflores, San Isidro, Barranco, and the malls. Amarige Salón & Urban Spa gets great reviews and is a full-service spa known for their great cuts and color for both men and women. Some of the hairdressers speak English. Av. Juan Pezet 1630, San Isidro Av. Primavera 609, Chacarilla del Estanque. Tel: 51-1-264-2047 / 3108 / 51-1-319-0090 / 0091 URL: www.amarige.com.pe, E-mail: epozo@amarige.com.pe. Updated: Jul 13,2010.

MONEY AND COSTS

Money

The local currency in Peru is the nuevo sol, which has been hovering at an exchange rate between approximately s/2.80 and s/3.00 to the US dollar in the few years.

Lima and Cusco are among the most expensive cities in Peru. In the whole country credit cards including Visa, Mastercard, Maestro and American Express are accepted. In most mid-range hotels and restaurants and some shops, cards will be directly accepted, but double check the percentage charged as it is normally easier and cheaper to pay in cash.

ATMs are easily accessed in most well-sized cities and exchange bureaus (casa de cambio) are found without difficulty in most places. It is not advisable to change money on the street. Most ATM machines give the option of US dollar or soles. The US dollar is widely accepted but be aware that in Peru the notes have to be perfect with no rips or tears in order to be accepted, especially in Cusco.Updated: Jul 13,2010.

Costs

Comparatively cheap compared to Europe and the US, but more expensive than Bolivia you can travel Peru easily on any budget. With a mix of basic dorm accommodation, cheap set menus and local public transport expect a daily budget of about $20. For a more mid-range travel experience, staying in a small hotel with private bathroom and hot water and eating a la carte in average priced restaurants, you are looking at a realistic outlay of about $50-80 a day. For the luxury

traveler residing in 4 or 5 star accommodations, eating in mid-high end restaurants and traveling with the occasional flight, you would need to plan for over $200 day.

For those looking to stay a little longer, renting a room or apartment per month is a very realistic option with rooms in a house available for $100-150 and one to two bedroom apartments offered fully furnished for $250-300 per month depending on the area. Food can be bought very inexpensively from local markets and supermarkets for those that have kitchen access and do not want to eat out in restaurants all the time, however lunch menus can sometimes work out cheaper. Updated: Jul 13,2010.

LIVING ABROAD

Registering With Your Embassy

When traveling or living in Peru, it's a good idea to register with your embassy so that you can be contacted and assisted in the event of an emergency in Peru, such as civil unrest, terrorism or a natural disaster, or informed of a family emergency in your home country. Registering with your embassy is free and can be done online before you arrive in Peru or at your embassy once you arrive. All you need to do is provide certain travel information and personal details, including your passport number, and address and contact info in Peru, as well as emergency contact details in your home country. If you choose not to register with your embassy, it is recommended that you leave a detailed travel itinerary and contact details with family or friends at home, and provide them with the Peru-based embassy's contact information. Updated: May 18, 2010.

Voting Abroad

For long-term foreign residents of Peru, and even some short-term visitors, the issue of voting from overseas is an important one. Most visitors who would like to have a say in their country's elections have a number of options for voting, but it does vary from country to country.

VOTING OVERSEAS IN U.K. ELECTIONS

Citizens of the United Kingdom living abroad can vote in national elections, but not local ones. To do so, they must register as overseas voters. In theory, overseas voters can vote by mail, but ballots are usually not sent out until a week before elections, and must be returned by election day.

In most cases, this turn-around time will be too short for Britons living in Peru. As an alternative, you can appoint a proxy to vote on your behalf back in the UK. Check the site www.aboutmyvote.co.uk for more details.

VOTING OVERSEAS IN U.S. ELECTIONS

American voters in Peru will have to check with their local municipal or county clerks' offices, as voting rules vary from jurisdiction to jurisdiction. As a general rule, however, citizens can register to vote, request an absentee ballot and vote in absentia by mail.

VOTING OVERSEAS IN CANADIAN ELECTIONS

Canadians' eligibility to vote is determined by a number of factors, including the amount of time they have spent abroad, whether they plan to return to Canada and why you are abroad. Check with www.elections.ca to learn more. If you are eligible to vote, you can receive an absentee ballot to vote in national elections. Most provinces will also let you vote in provincial elections.

VOTING OVERSEAS IN AUSTRALIAN ELECTIONS

For Australians who are abroad on election day, voting is not obligatory, but they can enroll for overseas voting. Mail ballots can be requested, and voters can also visit the polls at Australia's diplomatic missions—in Peru's case, the nearest one is in Santiago, Chile. If you are leaving Australia shortly before election day, you may be able to vote at one of the early voting centers set up at airports.

VOTING OVERSEAS IN NEW ZEALAND ELECTIONS

Citizens can vote in New Zealand's elections by requesting a ballot by mail, downloading a ballot or picking one up at a diplomatic mission (again, the nearest one to Peru is in Santiago, Chile).

VOTING OVERSEAS IN ISRAELI ELECTIONS

At the moment, the only Israelis allowed to vote from outside Israel are diplomatic staff members. The issue is being debated in the Knesset at the time of writing, however, so this law might change. Updated: Jul 13,2010.

WORK AND BUSINESS

Finding a job while in Peru can be both challenging or surprisingly easy. If you plan to teach English, know that you ususally won't be able to find a job before you arrive. Although you should research and contact schools before your trip, it is unusual to be offered a job before you're in the country. Peruvians are big on face-to-face contact, and that coupled with the lack of technology saturation means that you'll need to put your feet to the street in order to secure a job. In addition, many jobs in Peru go unadvertised, and are often filled through word of mouth. If you are going to get a good job in Peru, you are going to have to network too. A good place to start is one of the many expat social clubs that exist, especially in Lima.

Those looking for a long commitment (two years or more) can apply to the international schools, which pay similar salaries to what you would expect back home in the U.S. These schools may hire you from your home country, and may even pay part of the cost of moving.

For other types of work, it is best to check the newspaper, El Comercio. They have a classified section that lists many of the jobs. The website www.computrabajo.com.pe is another good place to look. Expatperu.com's forums, and livinginperu.com also host classified ads that may be helpful. New jobs are posted daily, so check back often. It is usually advisable to follow up your email containing your resume with a phone call, due to the emphasis on face-to-face communication.

Native English speakers are at a special advantage in an economy that is both growing more international and heavily reliant on tourism. Being a native English speaker can get you a job at many of the companies, both small and large, throughout Peru doing work related to translation. Being bilingual and sociable can help you to get jobs in many of the tourism agencies, especially in Lima and Cusco. Peru for Less, for example, is a growing tourism company that is continually seeking workers that have a variety of skill sets from language to design. Their website (www.peruforless.com) lists the currently available jobs. Another option is online writing as there are many travel sites that are always looking for new writers. You may have to work free at first, until you build a portfolio and rapport with the company, but paid positions or contract work could soon follow. Updated: Jul 20,2010.

Volunteering

Volunteering in Latin America has become very popular in the last decade and Peru is a particularly busy location, full of volunteer

The Cost of Living in Peru

Range, Food, Accommodation
Budget $2-5, $5-10
Mid-range $5-15, $10-50
Top End $15 plus, $50 plus

In general, the cost of human labor here is considerably cheaper than in many other countries. Wages are less, which means paying for a nanny, maid, cook, employees for your new business, or construction labor is much cheaper than in the United States, Europe, or Australia and many foreigners find they can hire household help that they could never afford in their home countries.

However, anything imported, which includes cars, large appliances, electronic items, televisions, high-quality cookware, pre-fabricated furniture, high-quality sheets, area rugs, etc are often much more expensive. Imported specialty foods like olives, jalepenos, California wine, sausage, lunch meats, and sauces can be found, but for a higher price than at home, whereas fresh fruit, vegetables, fish, and other local foods are significantly cheaper.

Spa treatments, beauty procedures, and medical care cost less, but high-end beauty products like expensive creams, lotions, and hair products fetch a higher price than you might be used to.

Housing and the cost of property is cheaper in Peru than in many other countries unless you are in the upper class neighborhoods around Lima.

PC laptops can be found in Lima for not too much more than at home, but Macintosh computers, computer accessories, and external hard drives are much more expensive. Likewise, if you use a professional quality camera, bring it from home along with any accessories—these things cost more in Peru and stores have smaller selections.

If you do extensive outdoor sports such as mountain climbing, bring your own gear. High-quality outdoor gear fetches high prices and may be difficult to find.

Magazines and books in English are very expensive and are mostly found only in the large cities. Some products are both more and less expensive at the same time depending on whether you go the illegal or legal route to acquire them. For example legitimate dvds and computer programs are often double, and sometimes triple, what you'd pay at home, but down the street at the pirated dvd store you can purchase dvds for 2 soles and computer programs for 5. Updated: Jul 13,2010.

projects and charity organizations helping those in need. Volunteering has also grown during 2010, when in January, floods caused devastation to many families in the surrounding regions of Cusco and the Sacred Valley, taking lives and destroying crops and infrastructure. There is still a lot of work involved in the rebuilding and reconstructing of people's homes and small villages. Many organizations charge you a fee to give your time for volunteering, but mostly these costs cover supplies and go toward purchasing goods for the project, such as food, materials and infrastructure. Many projects work with underprivileged children, however others work with adults, single mothers, the elderly, and poor, isolated communities. Volunteering can be a very rewarding experience and a great way to feel involved in the community and bridge the gap between foreigners and locals.

VOLUNTEERING IN LIMA

Volunteers for Peace

This Burlington, Vermont based organization sends volunteers to various work-camps in Lima as well as Ayacucho, Peru. Trips average a length of three weeks. 1034 Tiffany Road, Burlington, VT, USA Zip: 05730, Tel: 1-802-259-2759 Fax: 1-802-259-2922, E-mail: vfp@vfp.org, URL: www.vfp.org, Updated: Jun 16,2009

Global Volunteers

Global Volunteers provides volunteers with short-term placements working in orphanages in Lima. 375 East Little Canada Road, St. Paul, MN, USA Zip: 55117-1628, Tel: 1-800-487-1074 Fax: 1-651-482-0915, E-mail@globalvolunteers.org URL: www.globalvolunteers.com, Updated: Jun 16,2009

I to I

I-to-I (based in the UK) offers-short term

volunteer opportunities from one to twelve weeks. They also offer help in finding short-term teaching jobs abroad. Volunteer placements in Peru have included positions on archaeological digs in the past. Programs run between $1000 and $1500 average for three weeks. Woodside House, 261 Low Lane, Leeds Zip: LS18 5NY. Tel: 44-800-011-1156, E-mail: info@i-to-i.com, URL: www.i-to-i.com. Updated: Jun 16,2009.

VolunTourism

VolunTourism specializes in organizing short trips to volunteer in numerous countries. Their website lists about twelve different NGO's and organizations that operate internationally, connecting volunteers with opportunities to serve in local communities. 717 Third Avenue, Chula Vista, California, USA Zip: 91910. Tel: 1-619-434-6230 / 426-6664, E-mail: vt@voluntourism.org, URL: voluntourism.org, Updated: Jun 16,2009.

Cross Cultural Solutions

Cross Cultural Solutions offers listings of volunteer positions in education and social justice. The organization charges fees but provides in-country assistance to volunteers in exchange. 2 Clinton Place, New Rochelle, New York, USA Zip: 10801. Tel: 1-800-380-4777, 1-914-632-0022 / 8494, E-mail: info@crossculturalsolutions.org, URL: www.crossculturalsolutions.org. Updated: Jun 16,2009

Earthwatch Institute

Earthwatch Institute is an environmental organization that lets volunteers and students join archaeological and conservation projects for a fee. One to three-week programs run around $1700. 3 Clock Tower Place, Suite 100, Box 75, Maynard, MA, USA Zip: 01754. Tel: 1-800-776-0188, 978-461-0081, E-mail: info@earthwatch.org, URL: www.earthwatch.org. Updated: Jun 16,2009.

Bruce Peru

Bruce Peru is a nonprofit organization dedicated to educating poor children and mothers in Lima while improving their quality of life. This organization, which started in the coastal town of Trujillo, costs volunteers around $360 a month and is open to anyone who is interested. However, you should speak a fair amount of Spanish as the demographic you will be working with will most likely speak only Spanish. The type of volunteer work you can do varies from basic teaching and teaching assistant jobs to the office related jobs that keep nonprofits afloat. Accommodation is incuded, as is food (three meals a day, five days a week). Bruce Peru also has satellite projects in many other places in Peru. Tel: 51-94-992-4445, URL: bruceperu.org, E-mail: info@bruceorg.org, Updated: Jul 20,2010.

Geovisions

Geovisions in a worldwide nonprofit organization that has established several volunteer programs in Peru. In Lima, opportunities range from working with children to working at medical clinics. You can volunteer at a kindergarden/daycare, or be a teacher's assistant at a local school. At the community medical clinic in Lima, volunteers can get hands on experience working with nurses and doctors while working to provide preventative care and treatment to an impoverished community. All Geovisions volunteer opportunities include accommodations, most meals, training, preparation and support, and extensive insurance. Costs vary depending on the program. URL: www.geovisions.org. Updated: Jul 20,2010.

Cross Cultural Solutions

Cross Cultural Solutions is a nonprofit that works in many parts of the world and prides itself on its drive toward community development for which it received a Nobel Peace Prize nomination. The organization has a program assisting the poverty-stricken people of Lima that is mostly focused on the shantytown of Villa El Salvador. Depending on the current needs, and your skills, you may be involved with teaching, healthcare, or caregiving to the eldery or disabled. Programs range from 1-12 weeks, with costs differing as well. URL: www.crossculturalsolutions.org. Updated: Jul 20,2010.

Bunac

Bunac has programs in both Cusco and Lima. In Lima, volunteer programs can last anywhere between 8-12 weeks and volunteers work with underdeveloped communities on projects including teaching, caring for the disabled, and building construction. Participants must speak Spanish well and pass a placement test in orer to participate. The program costs around $1,500 and includes two meals a day, six days per week. You will most likely stay with a host family as part of your immersion. URL: www.bunac.org/usa. E-mail: volunteer@bunacusa.org. Updated: Jul 20,2010.

Green Heart Travel

Green Heart Travel is a program started by CCI exchange. They have many volunteer opportunities all around Peru that vary in time and cost. In Lima, you can work with school children from kindergarten to high school as a teacher's assistant, helping to educate impoverished youth. The school is in the south of Lima, in a neighborhood that only recently acquired running water. Volunteers stay with a host family and are provided two meals Monday-Saturday, and have access to the program's built in local support network. URL: www.cci-exchange.com. Updated: Jul 20,2010.

Experiential Learning International

Experiential Learning International offers a program working with the many impoverished people of Peru. Projects range from the education of street children and domestic workers, both of whom often face abuse and extreme poverty as part of their daily life, to construction projects in underdeveloped communities. Costs range from $900-1800 depending on the length of stay. Working with children requires the longest commitment to maintain a sense of continuity for the children. Costs include two meals a day, and accommodation with a local host family. URL: www.eliabroad.org. Updated: Jul 20,2010.

VOLUNTEERING IN CUSCO

Aldea Yanapay Project

The Aldea Yanapay website states "another way of living." For many of the children cared for by Aldea Yanapay, that means undoing the effects of abuse promulgated at home and even in schools, where a very casually applied corporal punishment has taught violence more than it has reading or math. Aldea Yanapay, an alternative school for children from the age of six to 14, is founded on the principles of love and acceptance. Aldea Yanapay is open to volunteers who want to help children with educational and development needs, as well as teaching English, or anything else related to the well-being of children. Volunteers are compensated with lodging and food, and of course, the smiles of children regaining their self-confidence. Calle Ruinas 415 Cuzco. Tel: 51-84-235-870, E-mail: aldeayanapay@yahoo.com, URL: www.aldeayanapay.org. Updated: Nov 05,2009.

Nexos Voluntarios

Nexos Voluntarios is a volunteer organization based in Peru and supported by the Inter-American Development Bank (IDB). It provides opportunities for caring individuals to make significant contributions to the development of Peru's poorest communities by offering their time as volunteers in the country. Apart from the regular full time volunteering programs, Nexos Voluntarios has organized comprehensive and personalized programs that combine tourism with volunteer work, in a wide variety of locations around the country and with high-impact, non-profit organizations. Av 28 de Julio 842, Casa H4, Miraflores. Tel: 51-1-440-0739, E-mail: coordinator@nexosvoluntarios.org, URL: www.nexosvoluntarios.org. Updated: May 12,2009.

South American Explorers Club

Internships in PR, travel research/writing, member services and volunteering resources are available year round at SAE Cusco. Positions run for a minimum of 12 weeks and are unpaid, though volunteers are provided with lunch as well as Spanish and yoga classes. Subsidized housing is also occasionally available. Mon-Fri 9:30am-5:00pm, Sat 9:30am-1:00pm. Atoqsaycuchi 670, in San Blas. E-mail: cuscoclub@saexplorers.org, URL: www.saexplorers.org. Updated: Jun 18,2009.

Global Crossroad

Global Crossroad offers social service volunteer projects and internships in health and education at local hospitals, schools, and orphanages. Opportunities to work on conservation projects in re-forestation and on indigenous rights campaigns in local communities are also available. Programs run from around $1,400-$1,600 for four weeks ($2,074-$2,174 for eight) and include food, accommodation, insurance and project placement. 11822 Justice Avenue, Suite A-5 Baton Rouge, LA, USA. Tel: 800-413-2008 (USA), 800-310-1821 (UK), E-mail: info@globalcrossroad.com, ukinfo@globalcrossroad.com. Updated: Jun 18,2009.

Volunteer Visions

Volunteer Visions places volunteers on health projects in understaffed medical clinics on the outskirts of Cusco. Projects run from two to 12 weeks. Food and accommodation is included. Volunteers in Cusco are expected to work 8:30 a.m.-1 p.m., Monday-Friday. Basic Spanish skills are recommended. The Program costs: $650/2 weeks, $1050/6 weeks, $1,340/8 weeks, $1,800/12 weeks. Tel: 1-330-871-4511, E-mail: info@volunteervisions.org, URL: www.volunteervisions.org. Updated: Jun 18,2009.

PERU LIVING

United Planet

United Planet runs unique programs working in orphanages, state hospitals, mental institutions and in rural villages. All volunteers live with host families. The program fee includes insurance, accommodation, food, a trip to Machu Picchu for 2 days with a guide, as well as 4 hours of Spanish instruction per week. There is a minimum of one week at $1,395 and the cost is $200 per week thereafter for up to twelve weeks. There are discounts for families of three or more. 11 Arlington Street, Boston, MA, USA. Tel: 1-800-292-2316, 617-267-7763, Fax: 001-617-2677764, E-mail: quest@ unitedplanet.org, URL: www.unitedplanet.org. Updated: Jun 18,2009.

Institute for Field Research Expeditions (IFRE)

Work as a volunteer in education (teaching English as a volunteer), health, conservation and development projects part-time, 20 hours a week, in Cusco, Peru. There is an application fee of $349. Placements can run for as little as four days or as long as 12 weeks. Program fee includes a donation to the project, insurance, room and board plus two hours of Spanish instruction per week. 8500 N Stemmons Frwy #4015 F, Dallas, Texas, USA. Tel: 1-800-675-2504 (USA), 1-800-310-1437 (UK), E-mail: info@ifrevolunteers.org, URL: www.ifrevolunteers.org. Updated: Jun 18,2009.

Q'ewar Project

Among the volunteer opportunities in Cusco is the Q'ewar Project, a non-profit that employs indigenous women to make high-quality, hand-made dolls for export to markets in Europe and North America. Attempting to redress issues of ethnocentrism, sexism and ignorance, the project pays a fair wage to women. Their dolls, made from alpaca and sheep wool, use ancient techniques for dying, incorporating indigenous foliage and even insects. Volunteers are needed for their social development and day care programs and knowledge of Spanish is a must. At the local chapter of the South American Explorers Club, former volunteers have written very favorably of their time with the Q'ewar Project. E-mail: juhebu@hotmail.com, URL: www.qewar.com. Updated: Jun 18,2009.

Amauta Spanish School Volunteer Program

Amauta Spanish offers a wide range of volunteer projects including working with street children in daycare centers, kindergartens and after school projects, working with the elderly, reading books to the blind, and working in orphanages and medical clinics. The most popular program is the eight week program including four weeks of Spanish classes and four weeks of volunteering for $1,567, or if you already have a reasonable level of Spanish, you can do just four weeks volunteering for $603. Both programs include all food and accommodation. Calle Suecia 480. Tel: 51-84-262-345, E-mail: info@amautaspanish.com, URL: www.amautaspanish.com. Updated: Jul 13,2010.

Loki Hostel

When the floods of January 2010 began, Loki Hostel took staff and guests to the Sacred Valley to help those affected by the disaster. Volunteers work on clearing sites of rubble, helping to build new homes, as well as repairing others. Loki also takes volunteers to a small children's home in the Sacred Valley, to play and spend time with the children. The best part of volunteering with Loki is that it's completely free, and that the minimum commitment is just one day. Cuesta Santa Ana 601. Tel: 51-84-243-705, info@lokihostel.com, www.lokihostel.com. Updated: Jul 13,2010.

Fairplay

Fairplay is primarily a Spanish school but also connects travelers with charity organizations that run various volunteer projects. Fairplay doesn't charge for finding you a volunteer placement but only wishes to help the charity organizations find workers. Some of the projects they work with take a fee, and others don't. Fairplay offers various placements for short term volunteers of up to one month, as well as placements for longer term volunteers. Pasaje Zavaleta C-5, Wanchaq, Tel: 51-84-984-789-252, E-mail: support.fairplay@gmail.com, URL: www.fairplay-peru.org. Updated: Jul 13,2010.

Internships

There are a variety of internships in Peru available for college students seeking academic credit and for those interested in doing social work, such as helping children in orphanages, or assisting rural communities to develop small businesses. Unfortunately, many of the internships are not only unpaid, but also quite expensive. Make sure if you are working for free, or paying to work, it is for a reputable organization that will give you the necessary skills to advance in your field and a letter of recommendation.

PERU LIVING

Travel writers, web content developers, and computer programmers can often find internships by contacting companies based in Peru that may or may not advertise open positions. Updated: Jul 20, 2010.

IFRE

The Institute for Field Research Expeditions (IFRE) has a photojournalism internship writing for a free magazine in Cusco aimed towards tourists and visitors. The internship provides some college credit so students should be working towards a degree in journalism, photography, or writing. IFRE provides housing, food, travel medical insurance, and supervises interns, but the program costs from $530 for 4 days to $2,413 for 12 weeks. Internships begin on the first and third Monday of each month. 8500 N Stemmons Frwy #5030 K Dallas, TX, USA. Tel: 1-214-390-7950, Fax: 1-214-666-3169, E-mail: info@ifrevolunteers.org, URL: www.ifrevolunteers.org. Updated: Jul 20, 2010.

South American Explorers Club

The South American Explorers Club in Lima and Cusco offer 3-month or longer internships at their clubhouses. Interns work 12 to 15 hours per week and can intern as an Events Coordinator, Clubhouse Assistant, Fundraising and Development Intern, Advertising and Marketing Intern, or a combination of these roles. Internships are unpaid, but the clubs provide free lunch, a free membership, weekly Spanish classes, and yoga. Interns also normally find friends and helpful contacts through the many events put on by the South American Explorers. Lima office: Calle Piura 135, Miraflores. Tel: 51-14-453306, E-mail: limaclub@saexplorers.org. Cusco Office: Atoqsaycuchi 670, San Blas. Tel: 51-84-245-484, E-mail: cuscoclub@saexplorers.org, URL: www.saexplorers.org. Updated: Jul 20, 2010.

Peru for Less

Peru For Less offers periodic six-month long internships in a variety of areas such as web development and office administration. Interns need to be native English speakers, be college-educated with exemplary grades, and have some past travel experience, preferably in South America. Most interns are paid around $500 per month, receive partial payment for medical insurance, and are allowed a two-week paid vacation after three months. However, interns must be prepared to work hard and commit to long hours. An average workweek is 40-48 hours spread across five days. Peru For Less has offices in Lima and Cusco. URL: www.peruforless.com, E-mail: hiring@latinamericaforless.com. Updated: Jul 20, 2010.

U.S. Embassy

The U.S. Embassy in Lima offers summer internships for students focusing on museum studies, art restoration, art conservation, and art history. Interns are usually provided with housing and meals, or given a living stipend of around $850. Internships take place at a variety of museums and focus on things like textile, metal, oil painting, mural, or ceramic conservation as well as cataloguing art, marketing museums, and learning how to manage the press. In order to apply, students must submit a CV, letter of reference from a professor, and a one-page essay of interest before March 31st of each year. E-mail: wagner@state.gob, URL: http://peru.usembassy.gov/internship.html. Updated: Jul 20, 2010.

Teaching

There are many opportunities for people wanting to teach English in Peru. Some schools do require you to have a TEFL/TESOL certificate and/or some teaching experience, but there are plenty of openings for first time teachers that have a degree and are native speakers. Most of the larger cities including Lima, Arequipa, and Cusco have a number of schools and colleges where English is taught. The easiest way to secure a job is to visit schools personally on your arrival with an up to date Curriculum Vitae, photograph and enthusiasm. The pay will depend on the school and the number of hours you work, but an average salary to be expected is $5-6 an hour. Updated: Jul 13, 2010.

PRIVATE LANGUAGE CLASSES

A good option for anyone wanting to teach English in Cusco or Lima is to offer private classes. There are always a large number of locals that are very interested and motivated to learn. Being the tourist capital of Peru, having a good grasp of the English language is hugely important for work and social opportunities. An average amount to charge per hour is about $15-20 and you can offer classes in any quiet restaurant or bar that you find. You will need to have some of your own materials or just be creative. Updated: Jul 13, 2010.

PRIVATE TEACHING ACADEMIES

Maximo Nivel

Maximo Nivel is a popular and internationally accredited school chain which after being founded in Cusco in 2003, now also has schools in Costa Rica and Guatemala. They offer TEFL courses, Spanish lessons, voluntary opportunities and housing as well as English teaching opportunities at all levels. Students range from children to adults and their classrooms are well equipped and professional. They also offer access to a teacher's lounge, free tea and coffee to teachers and students, salsa classes and an on-site snack bar. Located on the main street, Avenida el Sol, this school is and will always be a popular choice in Cusco. Avenida El Sol 612. Tel: 51-84-257-200, E-mail: info@maximonivel.com. Updated: Jul 13,2010.

ICPNA

The ICPNA (Instituto Cultural Peruano Norteamericano) is an Academy that concentrates on teaching American English in Lima and Cusco. They look for professional teachers and offer monthly lectures and development skills to their teaching staff. The institute is among the most recognized in Peru for teaching English and Spanish to high standards, with a very good success rate. The school offers an extensive cultural program and uses a specific teaching methodology. The school is a short 5 minute walk from the main square on Avenida Tullumayo. Av. Tullumayo 125. Tel: 51-84-224-112. Updated: Jul 13,2010.

Business Links

Business Links is a British owned company and is one of the better language institutes to work for as they pay a bit more and can accommodate a variety of teaching schedules. They teach business English to employees and executives of companies and organizations. Teachers need to be native English speakers, have teaching experience, and be professional and responsible. The classes vary from one-on-one, 8-hours per day immersion, to hour-long classes for groups of employees. Tel: 51-84-226-002, E-mail: informes@bl.com.pe, Fax: 51-84-216349 URL: www.bl.com.pe. Updated: Jul 20, 2010.

English Life

In Lima, English Life teaches small groups of students and concentrates on conversational skills like listening and speaking, though they also teach business English. Teachers must be native English speakers and have some experience teaching or tutoring in Peru or elsewhere. Courses are usually a month long, with two hour classes either twice or three times per week. Av. La Paz 434, (Edificio Ejecutivo) Oficina 602, Miraflores. E-mail: englishlifeperu@gmail.com, URL: www.englishlifeperu.com. Updated: Jul 20, 2010.

INTERNATIONAL SCHOOLS

There are a few international schools in Cusco that offer teaching opportunities to travelers willing to commit to an academic year and with teaching experience or qualifications from their home country. You will also need to provide references before any reputable school will hire you. With a decent expat community in the city, demand for good international schools is high. Lima is the best place to base yourself for this kind of work. The normal work-day is 8.30a.m.–2.15p.m.

The starting salary at most international schools is around $26,000 per year. Most offers include a round-trip international flight, some health insurance coverage, and an allowance for living expenses. However, applicants need to commit to two years, be native English speakers with teaching experience, and hold a relevant degree. In general, applicants receive a better package if they are hired in their home country than if they are hired in Peru. Updated: Jul 20,2010.

Cambridge College

Cambridge College is a British/Peruvian school located on almost 42,000 square meters in La Encantada de Villa, 20 minutes by car from the upper-class residential areas of Lima. They have a library, science and computer labs, art rooms, and emphasize the importance of athletics with sports teams and dance classes. Classes are taught in English, Spanish, and French. The curriculum complies to both Peruvian and bilingual British standards. Alameda de los Molinas 728-730, La Encantada de Villa, Chorrillos. Tel: 51-1-245-0107, URL: www.cambridge.edu.pe. Updated: Jul 20,2010.

Markham College

Markham College also follows the British/Peruvian education model and has roughly 2,000 students ages 4-18 and 280 staff members. The school is internationally recognized as being one of the best in Peru for students seeking a bilingual and international education. Augusto Angulo 291, San Antonio Miraflores, Lima Apartado 18-1048 Apartado 1918-1048. Tel: 51-1-315-6750, Fax: 51-1-315-6751, URL: www.markham.edu.pe. Updated: Jul 20,2010.

Starting Your Own Business

Many expatriates at one time or another decide to start their own company in Peru to generate an income and sometimes to get the necessary visa to stay longer in the country. To start the process, you only need to have a valid passport and a three month tourist visa, as well as special permission to sign contracts from the Peruvian General Directorate of Immigration and Naturalization, or DIGEMIN. Obtaining permission from DIGEMIN only takes a few minutes and grants you the right to sign legal documents in the country.

If you live abroad and want to own a company in Peru, you can set up a company through a power of attorney. The power of attorney must be registered at the Peruvian Public Register (Registros Públicos). If you plan on living in Peru and running the business yourself, keep in mind that while the tourist visa permits foreigners to own their own company, it does not allow foreigners to legally work in Peru. If you want to manage your own company, you must have a visa and a residence card (carné de extranjería). Alternately, you can get an investor visa (visa de inversionista). To obtain one of these you must invest $25,000 into the country, submit a business plan before the DIGEMIN, and promise to hire five employees within the next two years. It is important to note that Peru does not require a minimum share capital, which means you do not need to have a lot of money to invest in order to start your own company, but you do need a lot of money to get the investor visa required to run it.

There are a variety of business types in Peru and it's important to know in advance which type of company you want to open as the fees are often different depending on the size of the company. There are Limited Liability Commercial Companies or Sociedad Comercial de Reponsabilidad Limitada (SRL), and a Corporation or Sociedad Anónima. Among the latter type there are three subgroups: the Standard Corporation or Sociedad Anónima Ordinaria, the Open Corporation or Sociedad Anónima Abierta, and the Closed Corporation or Sociedad Anónima Cerrada. The Standard Corporation must have fewer than 750 shareholders and the corporate name must be followed by the abbreviations S.A. The Open Corporation must have more than 750 shareholders and is the type of company most often used by big corporations. The corporate name for this type of company must be followed by the abbreviations S.A.A. The Closed Corporation must have fewer than 29 shareholders and its name must be followed by the

abbreviations S.A.C. The Closed Corporation business model is by far the most popular because it is the easiest to work with. This business type does not require a Board of Directors and the organization can be very flexible.

Once you have decided whether it's best for you to run your own company or not, and what type of company you want to begin, you can get started on the legal formalities required. The first step if you are in Peru, as previously mentioned, is to obtain permission to sign contracts before the DIGEMIN which only takes a few minutes. If you want to live abroad but still own a company in Peru, you must grant power of attorney to someone who can set up the company before the Peruvian Consulate in your country and then legalize the signature of the Consulate at the Peruvian Ministry of Foreign Affairs. Your second step should be to make sure your company name is not already taken by doing a search at the Public Registry. Each search costs under $2 and to reserve the name for 30 days costs under $10. This step should take less than a day.

Next, a lawyer should prepare the by-laws and you, the lawyer, and all shareholders should sign them at a notary and then have them notarized. The notary fees are typically around $200. The notary will then register and file the deed with the Mercantile Registry. The deeds must include the company name, purpose and duration of the company, initial capital, number of shares, the names and information of all shareholders, names of employees, and the date of startup operations. This process normally takes around five days. You must also open a bank account in Peru under the name of the company and pay in 25% of the share capital and obtain proof of these proceedings. This usually just takes a few hours.

After these steps are finished you need to register the company with both the Registros Públicos (around $50) and with the National Superintendency of Tax Administration or SUNAT, to obtain a RUC or fiscal number (no charge). This process usually takes under a week. Next you must obtain a Certificate of Compatibility from the District Council stating that your business is compatible with the neighborhood where you will be located. The charge is normally under $50 and may take up to another week.

You must also pass an inspection and obtain a technical report of approval from the National Institute of Civil Defense or Instituto

Nacional de Defensa Civil (INDECI) stating that the premises where your business is held is safe for employees and customers. This charge is normally around $2 per square meter and can take up to two weeks. The last step is to get the business license or licencia de funcionamiento from the City Council. The City Council will want to see proof that all these other processes have been completed and may take up to two weeks to approve the license request. The cost is usually around $90. The entire process of starting your own business typically takes from four to eight weeks and costs between $1,000 and $3,000 depending on the size of your business and lawyer fees.

Some business tips are as follows: It pays off to conduct business in person as Peruvians are big on face-to-face contact as opposed to emails and phone calls. Peruvian business culture is more similar to European culture than American culture, so keep this in mind when trying to assimiliate. It also may be easier to open a company as a branch of a foreign company rather than a separate corporation as there are fewer fees and less paperwork involved. Updated: Jul 13,2010.

ENGLISH-SPEAKING LAWYERS

If you are looking for an English-speaking lawyer in Peru, check the US embassy's list of local lawyers lima.usembassy.gov. The lawyers are divided by specialty. The Embassy has only collected this list and is not endorsing any lawyer in particular. You will still need to do some research and pick one with which you are comfortable. It is best to talk to other expats and get references from them. Some may have had good experiences with certain lawyers, or know of one that is not on the embassy's list. The more research you do on your own, which will most likely involve talking to people, the better your choice will be. Keep in mind that you'll likely pay more than a native Peruvian would. It is a good idea to research the laws yourself as many of the basic legal tasks may not require a lawyer at all, and either way you'll be less likely to be fleeced if you know at least a little about the legal process beforehand. Most lawyers are located in Lima and Cusco, so you if you are further afield your options will be limited. Updated: Jul 20,2010.

DOING PERUVIAN TAXES

Taxes in Peru are collected by Superintendencia Nacional de Administración Tributaria, or SUNAT. Personal income is taxed on a progressive scale. If you earn any revenue in Peru, from real estate, commercial, or other services, you will have to pay taxes in Peru. Even if you work for a company that is not located in Peru, but did the work in Peru, you must pay taxes on the income you make. If you live in Peru, as opposed to just visiting, you must pay taxes on all income you make. The Peruvian government has ruled that, as an expatriate, you are "domiciled" in Peru, and therefore subject to taxes if you meet any of the following criteria: (1) you have lived in Peru for more than 2 years without leaving the country for more than 90 days in a calendar year, (2) you have lived in Peru for six months, and are in the Registry of Taxpayers, or (3) you have lived in Peru for 6 months, and have asked your employer in Peru to consider you to be domiciled in Peru.

There are five categories of income for SUNAT: (1) income produced through rentals, (2) capital gains such as royalties, interest, etc., (3) income through commercial and industrial activity, (4) income produced by independent professionals (entrepreneurs), and (5) income gained through employment. Entrepreneurial income is taxed at a flat 30%, while the other categories differ depending on the amount you make. That amount is measured in a unit called the Unidad Impositiva Tributaria, or UIT. This is a fixed amount set by the government, and about equal to a thousand US dollars. If your revenue was below 27 UIT (27,000 USD) you pay 15% of your income, if you are between 27 UIT and 54 UIT, that number increases to 21%. If you make more than 54 UIT, you pay 30% of your income. Updated: Jul 13,2010.

IMPORTING/EXPORTING

Before starting an import/export company in Peru, it is necessary to understand the huge potential in the country for this type of industry, as well as the bureaucratic complications you will face. So, let's start with the advantages: Peru's economy is expected to grow 5% in 2010 and a main reason for this is Peruvian exports. Peru is rich in a variety of natural resources like food, raw materials, and energy. The main trends in exporting right now are agriculture, energy, forestry, mining, and textiles.

Peru has more than 19,300 square miles of producing farmland and is currently the world's number one exporter of asparagus, organic coffee, and organic bananas. It is second place in paprika, and also they export artichokes, grapes, mangos, and avocados.

Famous Peruvians

Peru has a long history punctuated by some truly incredible people. From pre-Inca times all the way up to the present, Peru has been home to many artists, statesmen, sports figures, and scholars. The most famous Peruvian of them all, **Miguel Grau Seminario**, was voted by Peru's people as the "Peruvian of the Millennium." He was an admiral in the navy during the War of the Pacific, a war in which Peru fought the more powerful Chile. He was known as "El Caballero Del Mares," the knight of the sea for his daring strategies. The Chilean Navy was much stronger than was its Peruvian counterpart, and it was in large part due to the tactics of Miguel Grau that Peru was able to reverse the momentum and bring the fight in to Chile. So feared was his military acumen that the entire Chilean fleet took six months to finally corner him, and he was killed in the ensuing battle.

In pre-colonial times, no Peruvian was more famous than **Huayna Capa**, a ruler of the Inca empire known for his grand plans for conquering and development. He was able to expand the empire many times over, while encouraging public works projects like roads and infrastructure.

Javier Peréz de Cuéllar Guerra, born in Lima on January 19th, 1920 was a diplomat and politician for over 60 years who served as the Secretary General of the United Nations from 1982-1991.

Peru's greatest literary figure, Ricardo Palma, was a greatly admired scholar who lived in the 19th century. His works include the 10-volume Tradiciones Peruanas, a mix of history, historical fiction, proverbs, and folk knowledge that shows the way people lived at different times in the history of Peru. After the War of the Pacific, he was named director of the National Library, which had been all but destroyed during Chile's occupation, and he helped to rebuild and expand the facilities, which once again gained recognition for being one of South America's most important libraries.

Famous modern Peruvians include **Mario Vargas Llosa**, Peru's best known novelist and the first Latin American president of the international writer's organization PEN. He began publishing works of fiction in the 1960s with his book La Ciudad y Los Perros, and has continued to be an important literary figure ever since.

Famous sports stars include **Sofia Mulanovich**, the first South American to be crowned champion of the Association of Surfing Professionals Work Championship Tour in 2004, winning three of the six events held.

Teófilo Cubillas is the most famous and respected soccer player Peru has produced. In 1972, he was nominated South American footballer of the year, and helped Peru win their historic victory in the Copa America in 1975. A talented midfielder, he was named by Pelé as one of the greatest living footballers in 2004.

Cesar Vallejo, one of the most famous Spanish language poets in history, and one of the most important poets of the 20th century in any language, also hails from Peru. Strongly situated in the modernist school of poetry, he moved to Lima, and lived a bohemian lifestyle while writing his first and most famous work, Los heraldos negros.

Fernando de Szyszlo was a Peruvian artist who is considered a key player in bringing abstract art to Latin America, and remains one of Peru's leading artists. Working in both painting and plastic arts, he has had over 100 exhibitions since his first in 1947. Updated: Jul 20,2010.

The bilateral free trade agreement allows Peru to export Haas avocados to the US, the largest avocado market in the world. Peru is also the largest exporter of fishmeal and fish oil which is primarily purchased by China.

As far as energy is concerned, Peru produces 150,000 barrels of oil per day and plans to expand their hydrocarbon industry. Peru also has both hard and soft woods available for export which are currently primarily shipped to Mexico and the US. Peru is the world's top producer of silver and is a leader in tellurium, zinc, tin, lead, gold, and copper.

Peru definitely has an edge over the competition regarding clothing exports, as Peru produces some of the best natural fibers in the world like alpaca and cotton. Unfortunately, Peru is currently in direct competition with countries like China and Vietnam, which sell similar goods at an even lower cost. The future of Peruvian clothing exports will be in producing innovative designs and luxury goods to create a niche for themselves, a niche currently held by Italy and France.

The US is Peru's top buyer because of the preferential tariff agreement between the two countries. The US allows 99% of Peruvian products into the US duty-free, and Peru allows 90% of American products to be imported duty-free. However, Peru is expecting to reach preferential tariff agreements with Australia, India, and Russia that could greatly increase the potential for exporters breaking into the business.

Imports tend to be more on the manufacturing level in Peru. Many companies choose to manufacture their products here as the cost of labor is cheaper and Peru is generally friendly towards foreign business owners. If you read the "how to start a business in Peru" section, you will see that to own your own business in Peru, you need little more than a tourist visa and $1,000.

Now for the irritating bureaucracy. Before exporting goods from Peru you must present 7 different documents to customs: commercial invoice, certificate of origin, a standard custom declaration, packing list, bill of lading, technical or sanitary certificate, and document for cargo handling. Each paper needs to be issued by different authorities and the whole process takes 24 days. Steps are being taken to ease this process and Peru hopes to create a new system where all paperwork is handled in one office, and fewer days are needed for clearance. However, this is not yet the case.

There is much talk about "suitcase exporting" where people carry their merchandise home with them on the plane without going through the legal steps. Here is the official word on that. Travelers are allowed to leave Peru with $1,000 worth of merchandise at a time, and $3,000 per calendar year. When you carry more than $1000 worth of

merchandise with you at a time, you are subject to the full tariff duty that corresponds to the items. If the items are found to be for commercial use instead of personal use you will have to pay a fine of 30% of the C.I.F. value. Updated: Jul 20, 2010.

EDUCATION

Studying Abroad

Peru has a lot of study abroad options for college students, though, generally speaking, they tend to be pricey. However, they are perhaps not as pricy as a private school in the US. Most programs that provide college credit are reliable and get good reviews from past students. It's important to check with your home school's study abroad office to make sure the credits will be applicable towards your degree or general education requirements. This is especially true if your home school doesn't have a program already established with a Peruvian university. Students trying to fulfill a general education requirement and have an adventure at the same time can find numerous summer-long programs working with orphans, sustainable development, and wildlife conservation that typically count for one semester-long course. There are also Spanish immersion programs that can be applied towards foreign language requirements. The best source of information for a comprehensive overview of programs is on the web at sites such as www.studyabroad.com, and www.studyabroaddirectory.com.

Those wishing to do an academic semester or year abroad will find that the universities in the large cities are their best bet. Most schools require that students speak at least intermediate-level Spanish and students may have to pass a placement test before acceptance. There are many more programs than the ones listed below, but these are the most reputable.

The University of Lima

The University of Lima has a student exchange program, but students need to be fairly autonomous. You must cover your own housing arrangements (unless you want to live with a Peruvian family), flight, meals, etc., though they do arrange transportation from the airport when you first arrive. All classes are in Spanish, but you can take any course offered in all eight of their colleges and stay for up to one academic year. To apply you must submit a completed application form, a notarized copy of your passport, a copy of your home university registration and transcripts, a letter expressing personal and professional motivations, a presentation letter written by the Exchange Coordinator, proof of health insurance, two "passport size" (3.5 x 4.5 cm) color photographs on a white background, and your resume. Av. Javier Prado Este s/n, Monterrico, Lima. Tel: 51-1-437-6767, Fax: 51-1-437-8066, URL: www.ulima.edu.pe/webulima.nsf.

Universidad Antonio Ruiz de Montoya

Universidad Antonio Ruiz de Montoya has partnerships with four universities in the US and five in Europe. They have summer, semester, and yearlong programs and depending which school you receive your credits from you can take courses in English or Spanish, or both. If you don't speak Spanish there are still a variety of interesting courses you can take, but there are many more course options if you do. Most exchange students live with families, but you also have the option of finding your own accommodation. Av. Paso de los Andes 970, Pueblo Libre, Lima. Tel: 51-1-719-5990 / 424-5322, Fax: 51-1-423-1126, E-mail: informes@uarm.edu. pe, URL: www.uarm.edu.pe.

International Education Programs

International Education Programs (IEP) arranges credits through Jacksonville University in the US and has study abroad options for students wishing to take courses in Cusco. Most students do one academic semester for up to 16 academic credits. Content courses are taught in English, but students do take Spanish language classes as well as a variety of courses in the humanities such as art history and architecture of Peru, and special issues in development. The program costs about $13,000 per semester but includes full room and board with a Peruvian family and excursions to Machu Picchu and the Amazon. To apply send an IEP application form, $200, and an official transcript to Jacksonville University. 2800 University Blvd North Gooding 105 Jacksonville, Florida. URL: www.iepabroad.org. Updated: Jul 20,2010.

Spanish Schools

Studying Spanish is another productive way in which to spend your time in Peru. Below are some schools located in Cusco and Lima.

CUSCO

There are a great number of language schools within Cusco to choose from, whether you want to make part of your vacation a time to learn Spanish or if you realize your Spanish skills are less sharp than you thought upon arrival in Cusco. Classes vary in level and length, with both group settings and private instructions, so with a little research you are sure to find a program that is perfect for you.

Máximo Nivel

This school is internationally accredited by the Peruvian Ministry of Education, Máximo Nivel specializes in top-notch Spanish classes and TEFL/TESOL certification. Travelers choose from a variety of programs that blend travel, study and volunteer options. The TEFL/TESOL certification can be completed entirely on-site or through their hybrid program that blends on-site training with distance/online education. A variety of volunteer projects are available, from teaching English to orphanage assistance to environmental conservation. Máximo's Volunteer and Study program combines intensive Spanish lessons with organized excursions to Machu Picchu, the Sacred Valley and the Amazon Jungle. All programs include housing, meals and daily two-hour Spanish lessons. Most volunteers and students live at The Family House, which offers hot water, cozy yet modern bedrooms, a communal lounge and private courtyard to relax or intermingle. The local staff is extremely friendly, and the lovely chef, Paula, whips up a variety of fresh and piping hot meals three times a day. Other housing arrangements are available upon request, and include private/shared apartments, hostels and family homestays. Av. El Sol 612, Cusco. Tel: 51-84-257-200, E-mail: info@maximonivel.com, URL: www.maximonivel.com. Updated: Mar 18,2009.

Mundo Verde Spanish School

This non-profit school is located four blocks from the Plaza de Armas in Cusco. The school assists a conservation project in the rainforest and the Health Fund for the Needy and runs a school in Urubamba. The Standard Spanish Course includes 20 hours of lessons, four hours per day. Groups rates are $110: for individuals, $150. The Intensive Spanish Course includes 30 hours of lessons, six hours per day. Groups cost $150 and individuals, $225. The Total Immersion Spanish Course includes 40 hours of lessons, eight hours per day, lunch with the teacher, daily visits to local spots and transportation expenses. For groups, the cost is $300 and for individuals, the cost is $400. Family stays can be arranged for $100 per week, and additional activities such as cooking classes,

PERU LIVING

tai chi, salsa classes, workshops and city tours are offered. Calle Nueva Alta 432-A. Tel: 51-84-221-287, E-mail: pabmirj@hotmail.com, URL: www.mundoverdespanish.com. Updated: Jun 18,2009.

Excel Spanish Language Center

All programs at the Excel Spanish Language Center include optional activities in addition to the curriculum and are included in the tuition. The frequency and availability of activities depends on the time of year (and the season). Examples of prior activities are day hikes, tours of historical ruins and religious sites, cultural and historical lectures and dance lessons. Prices are based on 20 hours per week: individual lessons are $7 per hour; group lessons are $5 per hour (2-5 people); the homestay option is $120 for 7 days/nights and includes 3 meals a day. Calle Cruz Verde 336. Tel: 51-84-235-298, E-mail: info@excelinspanish.com, URL: www.excel-spanishlanguageprograms-peru.org. Updated: Jun 18,2009.

Cervantes Spanish School

The Spanish language study program at the Cervantes Spanish School includes salsa classes, cooking classes and walking city tours. Volunteer work can also be arranged. Individual lessons are $120 per week; group lessons, with a maximum of four persons, are $90 per week. Both options include 20 hours of classes. Urb. Fideranda, Calle Camino Real 10, Wanchaq. Tel: 51-84-507-051, E-mail: cervanteschool@yahoo.es. Updated: Jul 18,2007.

Amigos Spanish School

Amigos Spanish School is a non-profit language school. With every four hours of classes, you pay for one child's education and food at The Amigos Foundation, an organization that is commited to the futures of child workers. Individual lessons are $8 per hour. Group lessons (4-person maximum) are $108 for 20 hours per week and can be combined with a homestay for $215. The homestay includes private bedroom, laundry, all meals and airport pick-up. Additional activities include salsa, meringue, traditional Andean dancing classes, cooking classes and city tour. Zaguan del Cielo B-23, Tel: 51-84-242-292, E-mail: amigo@spanishcusco.com, URL: www.spanishcusco.com. Updated: Jun 18,2009.

Acupari Language School

Acupari Language School offers lessons in not only Spanish, but also Quechua. Lesson packages include conversational practice, salsa lessons, cooking lessons and excursions. Individual Spanish lessons for one week are $140, and small group lessons (two to five persons) for one week are $100. Both options encompass 20 hours of lessons. Additional Spanish lessons can be arranged for $6 per hour. Quechua lessons for those with existing Spanish skills can be arranged for an additional cost of $7.50 per hour. Homestays can be arranged for $12 per day, and include breakfast and either lunch or dinner. San Augustín 307, Tel: 51-84-242-970, E-mail: acupari@terra.com.pe, URL: www.acupari.com. Updated: Jul 18,2007.

FairPlay Spanish School

FairPlay is an NGO based out of Cusco that employs single Peruvian mothers to train and empower them to support themselves as capable Spanish teachers. You pay your teachers directly so they earn a fair income. All teachers have successfully finished an intense seven-month training course. The school also uses a unique learning method that combines grammar and real-world practice. Only private lessons are offered: 20 hours per week costs $120 and 30 hours per week costs $190. The price includes the grammar and practice books, as well as a set of flashcards for beginners. FairPlay also offers homestays with Peruvian middle class families. One week costs $72 for a private room with a shared bathroom and three meals a day. $82 will get you a room with a private bathroom and three meals a day. Individuals pay $15 a week to FairPlay and to the rest to the family. Choquechaca 188. Tel: 51-84-978-9252, E-mail: support.fairplay@gmail.com, URL: www.fairplay-peru.org. Updated: Nov 14,2008.

Academia Latinoamericana de Español

The key to learning and understanding a language lies in your experience and the degree that you are able to delve into the culture. At Academia Latinoamericana de Español, you will find yourself swiftly learning Spanish amidst the warm Peruvians and rich history that defines Peru. Regardless of your level of proficiency, students will find a program that suits their needs, goals and learning styles. Classes are 60 minutes in length for four hours per day. The maximum number of students per class is four. Students learn using the four language skills: listening, grammar, oral and written comprehension. Students homestay with native, middle-class families who live no further than a ten-minute bus ride from the school. Programs range from $275-$470 per week, depending on the course that is chosen. Additionally, there are volunteer programs, activities and other arrangements that can be made to enhance the students' stay. Plaza Limacpampa 565. Tel: 51-84-243-364, E-mail: info@latinoschools.com, URL: www.latinoschools.com. Updated: Jun 18,2009.

Machu Picchu Spanish School

Machu Picchu Spanish School has several activities to get students involved in the community and within the school. Each Monday there is a welcome dinner for that week's new students. Additionally, there are dancing and cooking classes available for interested students. Most of the activities are included in the course fees, but other more elaborate activities can be planned with extra costs. All of the teachers at Machu Picchu Spanish School are native speakers and are university graduates in either languages or literature. Calle Arequipa 251, Pasaje Q'aphchik'ijllu. Tel: 51-84-257-635, URL: www.machupicchuschool.org. Updated: Jul 18,2007.

Cusco Mania Spanish School

Cusco Mania Spanish has several long-term packages ranging from a few weeks to six months. All teachers are fully qualified. The school also has several other extensive programs such as cooking, dancing and volunteering in and around Cusco. Cusco Mania is not a school focused on intensive language programs like many of the others. But if you want to settle down in Cusco and do a variety of things besides Spanish school, it's a great option. Urb los Portales B-7. Tel: 51-84-966-694, E-mail: info@cuscomania.com, URL: www.cuscomania.com. Updated: Jul 04,2008.

South American Spanish School

South American Spanish School in Cusco has some uniquely blended programs. One is Spanish mixed with Inca culture and the other is Spanish mixed with modern Peruvian culture. Half of the day is spent learning Spanish and the other half is spent learning about culture. They can also set up students with volunteer activities. Carmen Alto Street 112, San Blas. Tel: 51-84-223-012, E-mail: info@sasschool.org, URL: www.sasschool.org. Updated: Jun 18,2009.

Proyecto Peru Language Centre

Proyecto Peru Language Centre offers a wide range of free activities, such as Peruvian cooking classes, quiz nights, Spanish movie nights, dance classes and Internet. It also has several different language school options. Traditional, 20-hour-a-week programs are most popular, but there are also half courses and special purpose courses catered to teach vocabulary for healthcare, business or technical fields. Proyecto Peru Language Centre also has a special program for children between the ages of 5 and 12. Ca.Tecsecocha 429. Tel: 51-984-683-016, 51-84-984-954-184, E-mail: info@proyectoperucentre.org, URL: www.proyectoperucentre.org. Updated: Jun 30,2010.

Cusco Spanish School

Cusco Spanish School is a small, personal, and flexible Spanish language school with more than ten years of experience. It is made up of professional Peruvians with a broad knowledge of the teaching of Spanish as a foreign language and certain expertises, such as history, literature, economics, and sociology. The professionals of Cusco Spanish School teach Spanish in an easygoing entertaining manner, without the stress typical of a conventional school, which allows students to develop their abilities and improve at their own pace. It also offers several volunteer opportunities that give students a chance to practice Spanish while helping out in the Cusco community. They offer lessons in Urubamba also. Cusco Spanish School teaches Spanish and Quechua. Urbanización Constancia A-11-2 Apartment N° 103, Fourth Floor. Tel: 51-84-226-928, E-mail: info@cuscospanishschool.com, URL: www.cuscospanishschool.com. Updated: Jun 18,2009.

Lingua Cusco

Lingua Cusco Spanish School is also part of the Asociacíon Pukllasunchis which works with the Cusco community to provide aid to under-privileged children. The project is well-regarded throughout Peru, and students can participate in the program. One-on-one lessons cost $9 per hour; two or three-person groups are $5 per hour, per person; and four or five-person groups are $4 per hour, per person. The homestay options are more flexible than those at many schools, as students can choose the number of meals they want each day. Siete Diablitos 222, San Blas. Fax: 51-84-237-918. Updated: Jul 18, 2007.

Inticahuarina Spanish School

Inticahuarina Spanish School offers a full range of language school options. More importantly, Inticahuarina can arrange volunteer opportunities in and around Cusco. This gives students a chance to give a little back to the community they are studying in but also to get out and practice Spanish. Inticahuarina Spanish School also arranges (and recommends) homestays for students. Zarumilla Bloque 5-A 103-105. Tel: 51-84-251-481 / 978-1844, E-mail: info@inticahuarinaspanishschool.com, URL: www.inticahuarinaspanishschool.com. Updated: Jul 18, 2007.

San Blas Spanish School

If brushing up on your Spanish skills is a priority in Cusco, San Blas Spanish School is one of the most visible tutoring outfits in town. It's located in the center of a cluster of popular cafés just above Plazoleta San Blas, and if the school's conspicuous sign doesn't catch your attention, the ever-present crowd of students lingering outside will. Full-immersion classes are offered in one-week blocks to students of all abilities, in four-hour morning or afternoon sessions. Placement exams are given to students with Spanish experience, and group, as well as individual lessons, are offered. At the conclusion of each week's sessions, classes close with a field trip that offers real world experience and a Friday night social gathering (usually salsa dancing or pisco sour making lessons) which offers students from all classes a chance to socialize together. Family stay opportunities are also available, as are sessions at a second campus in the small village of Cai Cay about an hour from Cusco. Tandapata 688, Plazoleta San Blas. Tel: 51-84-247898, E-mail: info@spanishschoolperu.com, URL: www.spanishschoolperu.com. Updated: Jul 18, 2007.

Amauta Spanish School

Amauta Spanish School offers the unique opportunity to study Spanish while immersed in Peruvian culture. Other activities that make Amauta Spanish School a distinct educational destination in Cusco include Quechua language courses, workshops on Latin American and Peruvian Culture, and free daily student activities, such as lectures, Latin American cinema and salsa dance classes. Amauta Spanish School offers different accommodation options and, for anyone interested, great volunteer work opportunities. It also has schools in the Sacred Valley and the Peruvian rainforest. Placement tests are given to all students, and university credit is available. Suecia 480. Tel: 51-84-241422, E-mail: info@amautaspanish.com, URL: www.amautaspanish.com. Updated: Jul 18, 2007.

Wiracocha Spanish School

If you're interested in brushing up your Spanish skills while in Peru, then you should check out Wiracocha Spanish School. Offering a fun, friendly and professional environment, the school has a variety of beginner, intermediate and advanced programs. With so many options to choose from, the programs are almost as diverse as the Peruvian culture itself. Depending on your needs and how much time you have, you can choose from part-time, intensive, super intensive, immersion and individual courses. A number of special courses combine learning Spanish with another facet of Peruvian culture. You can study Spanish while volunteering or learning about Latin American Culture. Preparation courses for the DELE exams and other advanced Spanish certifications are also available. Besides Spanish classes, you can enjoy free salsa and Latin American dance classes, arqueological visits to town with your teacher, cooking classes and walks around town. For a truly enriching experience, you can choose to live with a local family. All teachers have university degrees and share a genuine passion for teaching Spanish. Calle Inka Roca 110. Tel: 51-84-9670918, URL: www.wiracochaschool.org. Updated: Jul 18, 2007.

Amauta Spanish School Volunteer Program

Amauta Spanish School runs a combined program to learn Spanish and volunteer in Cusco. Eight weeks is the minimum commitment. Volunteers are placed on social service projects in: hospitals, orphanages, schools, centers for street children among others. The standard price of the program, including language instruction, a small volunteer fee, and accommodation, is

$1,379 (up to $2,200 if you choose a different option). Suecia 480. Tel: 51-8-4262345, Fax: 51-8-4241422, E-mail: info@amautaspanish.com, URL: ww.amautaspanishschool.org. Updated: Jun 18,2009.

Mijn Bestemming Peru

Mijn Bestemming Peru is a really good Dutch-Peruvian organization for Spanish lessons and also for volunteer work in Peru. Volunteering is free with this organization; you don't have to pay volunteer fees. Santa Ursula M-5, Wanchaq. E-mail: info@mijnbestemmingperu.nl, URL: english.mijnbestemmingperu.nl. Updated: Mar 01,2010.

LIMA

Academia Castellana Language School

Academia Castellana offers Spanish classes in Lima, including a variety of levels and business Spanish. Classes begin whenever the students want, and time and hours per day are flexible. Lodging is with host families or in student residences, and the academy offers organized trips and activities, such as cooking courses, volunteer opportunities, guided visits to the city center, etc. Ernesto Diez Canseco 497, Tel: 51-1-247-7054 / 51-1-444-2579 E-mail: acspanishclasses@gmail.com, URL: www.acspanishclasses.com. Updated: Jun 16,2009.

El Sol Spanish School

A quaint, friendly Spanish language school in the heart to Miraflores, El Sol Spanish School offers a range of courses, from beginner and advanced Spanish grammar to Peruvian cooking. Salsa classes are also offered in the late afternoon, along with a variety of weekly social activities. It has a great international mix of students from Europe, Canada, Australia, New Zealand and the United States. Homestays are available, as are apartment accommodations. 8:30 a.m.-5:30 p.m., Monday-Friday. Grimaldo del Solar 469, Tel: 51-1-2427763, 2413806; from US or Canada: 1-800-381-1806, E-mail: elsol@idiomasperu.com, URL: elsol.idiomasperu.com. Updated: Jun 16,2009.

Caminante School

The Caminante School has branches in several areas of Peru, including Arequipa, Ica, Cusco, Lima, Lambayeque, Puno and Trujillo. It intends to open another branch in Iquitos in the near future. They have a great variety of options for Spanish instruction and lodging—see their website for details.

The programs in Lima are more expensive than in the other cities. If you're on a budget, you may want to look into some of the different programs. Tel: 51-1-91563835, 51-8-425-2233, 51-84-254927. E-mail: info@caminanteschool.org, URL: www.caminanteschool.org. Updated: Jun 16,2009.

EEC Spanish School

The EEC Spanish School is a professional school with tailor-made courses for different needs. They offer professional Spanish courses that will train students to effectively interact and conduct business with Latin Americans and standard Spanish courses that will help students to learn about the local culture, habits and traditions. With a minimum age of 20 and no more than six students per class, EEC provides a fun atmosphere with a focus on personal attention for each student. Immersion activities such as Spanish films, presentations, speakers, discussions and outings are also offered. Classes help to prepare students to take the DELE. There is a $30 mandatory registration fee and prices range from $18/hr for private classes to $249 for 26-hr programs. Calle Mariano de los Santos 120, Tel: 51-1-442-1509, E-mail: administration@eec-spanish-school.com, URL: www.eec-spanishschool.com. Updated: Jun 16,2009.

Conexus Language Institute

Conexus is a small school in Lima offering courses in Spanish and English. Class size varies, but never more than five students, and individual classes are available. They accept walk-ins, and are very flexible with their scheduling. Conexus is best for travelers who just want to learn Spanish, but who don't want to be tied down to a rigid schedule and don't need college credit or a diploma. Students can be housed with Peruvian families and are encouraged to go on Conexus' regularly planned excursions. Av. Paseo de la República 3195 Oficina 1002, Tel: 51-1-421-5642, E-mail: info@conexusinstitute.com, URL: www.conexusinstitute.com/home.htm. Updated: Jun 16,2009.

Universidad del Pacífico Centro de Idiomas

The Spanish program at the Universidad del Pacífico is a serious, rigorous course of study designed for those who really need to learn the language, such as businessmen, diplomats, etc. Courses start regularly, but run on the university schedule, not that of students. Classes usually meet in the evening. The

PERU LIVING

center also offers classes in French, Portuguese, Italian, and Mandarin Chinese. Av. Prescott 333, San Isidro. Tel: 51-1-421-1628, 51-1-421-3483, 51-1-421-2969, E-mail: idiomas@up.edu.pe, URL: www.up.edu.pe/idiomas.

Pontíficia Universidad Católica del Peru Instituto de Idiomas

The Pontíficia Universidad Católica del Peru, recently celebrating its 90th birthday, is a fully accredited and prestigious Peruvian university. They offer Spanish classes to foreigners, but without the flexibility of smaller walk-in places. If you're planning on being in Lima for a while, or if you need a diploma or college credit, you may want to consider this option for learning Spanish. Camino Real 1037, San Isidro, Tel: 51-1-6266500 / 6266430, E-mail: idiomas@pucp.edu.pe, URL: idiomas.pucp. edu.pe, Updated: Dec 03,2008.

S.I.I.E School

S.I.I.E School offers a wide variety of Spanish programs and courses designed for each student's individual needs, from absolute beginners to advanced (DELE Certificate and credits awarded), Spanish for careers; professionals, one to one, academic rrograms for scholars, school group cultural tours, voluntary work/ experience and homestays with and without lessons. S.I.I.E will also coordinate housing with local bed and breakfasts or hotels with some meals provided. Tel: 56-2-5552909, E-mail: siieinfo@netline.cl, URL: www.studenttravel-siie-chile-peru.cl. Updated: Jun 16,2009.

ICPNA Spanish School

ICPNA is much more than a simple, garden-variety walk-in Spanish school for foreigners, the sort of which are found from Cuernavaca to Santiago. This large institution offers English classes for Peruvians, cultural programs, testing prep (SATs, etc.) and more. The Spanish program can be taken monthly, with classes meeting Monday through Friday in the morning from 8:45-10:15 a.m. A complete Spanish course can be taken in a year. A very serious school, ICPNA has been recognized by several international organizations, and has five branches throughout Lima. Av. Angamos Oeste 160, Miraflores. Tel: 51-1-706700, E-mail: postmaster@icpna.edu.pe, URL: www. icpna.edu.pe/ingles. Updated: Jun 16,2009.

Hispana Spanish Language School

This is an excellent school to study Spanish. There are extra-curricular activities such as excursions in Lima, salsa dancing and Peruvian cooking lessons and a great library with excellent bilingual books. Centrally located in the heart of Miraflores district. The school is centrally located just one block away from the the intersection of Larco Ave. and Benavides Ave or five blocks away from Larcomar shopping center. Calle San Martin 377 Miraflores. Tel: 51-1-446-3045 / 348-1737, E-mail: spanish.school@hispanaidiomas.com, URL: www. hispanaidiomas.com.Updated: Jun 16, 2009.

Spanish Rules

This is a Spanish language school aimed at helping foreign students start and/or improve their Spanish skills. Lessons are available for visitors traveling to or living in Peru. Located three blocks south of Central Park. Schell 635. Tel: 511-9-855-0335 E-mail: mauricio@spanishrules.com. Getting there: Updated: Dec 24, 2007.

Nurseries

With nurseries you will get what you pay for. If you pay for a good one, you will get a good quality of care and will be able to tell by the state of the place. You can leave your kids there full time, or part time, or by the hour; you can make your own schedule.

Prices range depending on the quality of care. For a part time schedule in Lima, you can pay $100 per month for a good quality place. Any that are cheaper than $80 per month will only offer care within a house, and kids won't be educated like at an actual nursery.

The main requirement for entry is that the children are healthy. Applications are basic – it is easier to get your child into a nursery than a school. If you wish, you can to take extra diapers and personal things for your children.

The standard of care is good and at the best ones they will give you a report of what the child did and ate. Nurseries will include education if you pay more. There is usually one carer per two children, similar to a nanny situation, however if you wish you can pay extra and make the arrangements to have one carer just for your child.

Activities include games, teaching, playing with the other children and art. You can also find nurseries with English speaking carers. Updated: Jul 27,2010.

Kindergartens

There is a reasonable standard of education in Peru, but you definitely get what you pay for. Better kindergartens have better education and include English classes. Some kindergartens will teach half the curriculum in Spanish and half in English. Or you can go to an all-English kindergarten. Classes will generally have 15-20 children, with one tutor and two assistants.

Entry requirements include an application with photos and copies of parents identification and birth certificates, name of relatives and all medical information including vaccinations records and allergies or diseases. The children must have medical insurance. Children won't have to take a Spanish test but will need to know some Spanish in order to get into a Spanish speaking kindergarten.

Costs range from $100 per month for an average kindergarten in Lima, or up to $200 for a good one. Religion is also taught in some kindergartens, and in these, children are taught to pray. Some kindergartens even have uniforms. One of the best kindergartens in Lima is Little Villa Kindergarden, which offers a curriculum in both Spanish and English. Updated: Jul 27,2010.

Schools in Peru

There are many public schools in Peru, however these are really only for the lower classes of society. In Peru, the divide in society by class is extreme and is seen at every level. Middle and upper class families all send their children to private schools. For the most expensive schools, monthly costs are around $1,000 per month – for this you will get a spot in a top quality school. You'll find very good quality schools for $800 per month then good schools for $500 per month. An average school would cost around $250 per month.

Entry requirements can be difficult. It is definitely harder to get into the better schools. You will need to show all your child's results from previous schools, as well as psychiatry, vision and medical tests. For the better schools, children must be able to show a good record from their previous school, as well as a clean record of health. Sometimes children may need to take exams depending on where they previously went to school.

There are approximately 25 students per class and classes are taught in Spanish, Chinese, English and French. You can also take your children to schools with full English or French curriculums.

There are quite a few differences between schools in Peru and those in the States or Europe. In the US, schools tend to be larger, with more space, have air conditioning, plus accommodation and cafeterias on-site. They play sports such as baseball, football and hockey. In Peru, schools do not generally have these types of luxuries, plus the types of sports are different – in Peru there is more soccer and volleyball and recess is often shorter. In Peru you don't pick the subjects you are interested in – you just do the curriculum provided. The curriculum tends to be more difficult in Peru, particularly with maths and science. Children are pushed harder and schools are generally more strict. Religion is taught in most Peruvian schools as well, and kids must always wear a uniform. They also give a fair amount of homework, however teachers can be more involved with the kids and more caring, due to the culture being different and more welcoming. The top schools in Lima are Markhan, Newton, San Silvestre and Russbelt school and are highly recommended. Updated: Jul 27,2010.

Schools in Cusco

Ausangate

Ausagate is a bilingual primary school with a good reputation in Cusco based in a suburb, 25 minutes drive from the center of the city. The school prides themselves on providing a safe environment where students can learn and grow and they use their own particular theory known as Multiple Intelligence. These eight different types of intelligence outlined in the theory allow the school to work and respect the individuality of the students. Classes are held in Spanish and in English allowing good development in both languages. There are a maximum of 20 students per class. To work at the school you need to be qualified or have experience working with children, to provide 3 written references and will need to have a phone or personal interview. Urb. Santa Maria S/N, San Sebastian. Tel: 51-84-275135 , URL: www.ausangate. edu.pe. Updated: Jul 13,2010.

Association Pukl.asunchis

The Association Puklasunchis holds a number of facets under its umbrella. With about 750 students between the age of 4 and 17, the Puklasunchis College in Cusco was founded in 1988. Over the years the association has developed a number of other programs including an intercultural bilingual program (Spanish and Quechua), a center of educational services, and a radio program with the boys and girls of Cusco participating. An average cost for students is $135 per month and Pukllasunchis is among the schools with the best reputation in the area for local and expat children. Siete Diablitos 222, San Blas. Tel: 51-84-237918, E-mail: contactenos@ pukllasunchis.org, URL: www.pukllasunchis.org/piloto. Updated: Jul 13,2010.

LONG-TERM HEALTH

Private clinics in Peru that cater to foreigners and have English-speaking doctors are your best bet for long-term healthcare in Peru. It is possible to buy health insurance directly from some of the clinics like Clinico Anglo-Americana in Lima for around $200 per month, or you can buy international health insurance from travel insurance companies for emergencies, or do a combination of both. The private clinics are generally of a much higher quality than the public hospitals and it's recommended that foreigners use them instead. However, remember that they do cost more than the public options, and may still not be quite up to par with the best hospitals and clinics in Europe or North America, though that is disputed. Still, most health issues can be resolved or monitored in Peru and will cost you less than they would in your home country if you were involved in a privatized health-care system. In fact, medical tourism has become quite popular in Peru and many people travel to the country for the purpose of having expensive medical procedures done for a fraction of the cost of back home. The most popular procedures are dental, cosmetic, and fertility treatments. Updated: Jul 13,2010.

Getting Vaccines

There are health risks to foreigners traveling and living in Peru, but taking a few precautions before traveling can minimize the dangers. One of the most important steps is to get the proper vaccines at least eight weeks before departure and keep your vaccination record with you. Yellow Fever vaccines are recommended, though not necessary if only traveling to Cusco, Machu Pichu, and Lima, but highly recommended for the jungle regions. The vaccine is good for ten years, but make sure you speak with your doctor about the risks involved before taking it. You may also want to get a typhoid vaccine, Hepatitis A and B vaccines, and get boosters for measles and tetanus before traveling to Peru. Updated: Jul 13,2010.

Women's Health

Getting oral contraceptives while in Peru is, in many cases, easier than in the United States or in other places. No prescription or gynocological consultation is necessary; you can simply walk into any pharmacy and ask for it. The more difficult part is finding the particular brand of birth control you are on, as not all brands are available in Peru and each pharmacy carries different kinds. It is possible to get either generic (like Microgynon) or brand name pills (like Yaz or Yasmin).

Accessing emergency contraception is sometimes a bit more complicated. It really depends on the pharmacy and pharmacist, as it differs from place to place. Some people in Peru believe the morning-after pill skews closer to an abortive measure than a contraceptive method, and sometimes these viewpoints affect the willingness of a pharmacist to give you the pill. A prescription may be necessary for emergency contraception and sometimes an entire gynocological exam is required before the doctor will give you a prescription.

Foreigners living in Peru should keep in mind that abortion is currently illegal and women who undergo the procedure can face up to 2 years in jail unless there is a threat to the health or life of the woman. So, if you are having sex, be careful - after all, contraceptives and birth control are widely available and the morning-after-pill is available at hospitals, pharmacies, and medical clinics, but it may be difficult to find in rural areas. Beginning March 10, 2010 the pill is free for Peruvians at all public clinics, but usually foreigners must have a prescription from a doctor and pay around $7. Updated: Jul 20,2010.

Parasitic Infections

One long-term health risk while traveling South America is the possibility of contracting a parasitic infection. This can happen as a result of consuming food (usually raw or undercooked) or water contaminated with parasites or their eggs, having contact with parasite-infected water or soil, or being bitten by an infected insect. Parasites are tiny organisms that live off of and feed off of larger hosts at the expense of the host. Both one-cell protozoa and worms infect humans, often seeking refuge in their intestinal tracts, causing digestive problems and abdominal pain. Other symptoms include fever, rashes, weight loss and muscle aches. Parasitic infections are more common in rural areas than in urban ones. Some preventive measures include not drinking tap water, only eating thoroughly cooked food, avoiding street food or unpeeled fruits and not wading in stagnant pools of water. Parasitic infections are treated with anti-parasitic drugs or through natural methods. If you suspect you may have a parasitic infection, contact your doctor immediately. Updated: Jul 13,2010.

Cytomegalovirus (CMV)

CMV is a common infection that belongs to the herpes virus group, and is much like Mono (Glandular Fever). CMV is transmitted through direct contact with saliva, semen, urine, blood and other bodily fluids, or can be passed on to a newborn baby through the mother. Most people are infected by CMV at some point in their lives, but often times the symptoms remain dormant and the infected person is unaware of even having had it. Symptoms closely resemble those to mononucleosis like swollen glands, fatigue, a sore throat and fever. Those traveling to Peru are more likely to contract CMV because it is more widespread in South American populations. There is no vaccine nor any official treatment available, though there are some drugs that can be prescribed to subdue the symptoms. Updated: Apr 21, 2010.

Health Insurance

Health insurance is widely available in Peru. Insurance costs are usually around 200 soles a month for an average plan, which works out to about $70. Most medicines can be bought over the counter, so health insurance is really for accidents or health emergencies.

Although Peru has a universal health care system, it is recommended to buy private insurance because Peru's state run hospitals lack funding, resources, and at times, hygiene. Being able to go to a private clinic can mean a world of difference for your health.

There are two types of companies that offer health insurance in Peru, clinics and insurance companies. Slightly different than the traditional insurance company, clinics offer access to a network of private clinics, and are usually smaller and cheaper. You'll have to go to a participating clinic to get care. Private clinics may not treat certain specific health concerns, so read carefully when looking for a good plan. There are typically two to three levels of service in health insurance plans, from the basic, which covers most everything except outpatient, dental, or any sort of routine maternity care. The midlevel plans include more preventative and routine care, and the top of the line plans often include such extras as prescription plans, home

nursing, and other needs. Costs ar.. do vary depending on the plan and co.. so there are many variables to consider. u such variable is the proximity of participating healthcare facilities to your home. As when buying insurance in your home country, read the fine print, and make sure you know what you are getting. Updated: Jul 20,2010.

Pacifico

Pacifico is one of the top health insurance companies in Peru and is highly recommended by many expats. They offer some of the best care, especially in dense urban areas like Lima. They are also on the costlier side, with plans priced above the market average. However, it may be worth the money as this company is rated highly both nationally and internationally. Av Juan de Arona 830, San Isidro. Telephone: 51-1-518-4000, URL: www.pacificoseguros.com. Updated: Jul 20,2010.

La Positiva

La Positiva has been around for almost 70 years. With nearly two million customers, they are also one of the largest insurers. They have a big network, but you may find care in the provinces (rural areas) limited. In big cities, it comes highly recommended. With a strong network of clinics, you should not have to travel very far to get help. Prices are about average for Peru. Tel: 211-0-211, URL: www.lapositiva.com.pe. Updated: Jul 20,2010.

RIMAC

RIMAC is Peru's largest insurance company, and prides itself on having the largest network of hospitals and clinics in the country. It offers a variety of health care plans, including some that give you coverage anywhere in the world, and include emergency travel assistance. The higher echelon of plans includes such amenities as a prescription plans, and homecare. Av. Las Begonias 475, 2do Piso, San Isidro. Av. Comandante Espinar 689, Miraflores, Lima. URL: www.rimac.com.pe. Updated: Jul 20,2010

CRP Clinica Ricardo Palma

Clinica Ricardo Palma, or CRP, is another network of clinics based in Lima. With around a quarter of a million patients a year, and a hundred locations, it is a solid bet for care. Clinics are open from 8:00am – 9:00 pm Monday through Friday, and have limited hours on Saturdays. CRP prides itself on flexibility and speed of service. Avenida Javier Prado Este 1066 San Isidro. Tel: 224-2224, 224-2226, URL: www.crp.com.pe. Updated: Jul 20,2010.

PERU LIVING

Good Hope

Good Hope is a network of clinics that provide their own health insurance plans. While more affordable than the larger companies, you are limited in that you must go to a Good Hope facility to receive care. However, while the availability of care may be less, the quality is on par with the other insurance companies. Malecón Balta 956, Miraflores. Tel: 610-7300, E-mail: garantia@goodhope.org.pe, URL: www. goodhope.org.pe. Updated: Jul 20,2010.

Hospitals

There are many private clinics and hospitals all around Peru, especially in the main cities. These private health care facilities are often a traveler's best bet should an emergency occur. While public hospitals exist in Peru, they service mostly the poor, and due to long wait periods and low standards, many middle and upper class Peruvians go to private hospitals and clinics. While some of the more rural clinics may not be a picture of modernity, you will find that most clinics are clean and contemporary. The US embassy lists recommended doctors on its website, so go there if you want to visit a private practice or specialist. In Lima, you can try Clinica Anglo Americana, located on Avenida Alfredo Salazar in San Isidro, or the chain of clinics called Clinica International. In Cusco, Clinica Pardo, located at Av. de la Cultura 710, treats a wide range of ailments, as does Clinica Panamericana, Av. Infancia 508. Updated: Jul 20,2010.

Pharmacies

There are several good pharmacy chains in Peru. Pharmacies have signs that read "botica." In Cusco or Lima, you should have no problem finding one, as they are on almost every block. A few good chains to consider are Boticas BTL, InkaFarma, and Boticas FASA. The private clinics and hospitals also have their own pharmacies, so if you need a prescription filled, you won't have to go to two places. Keep in mind that some medicines will be hard to find, and most will be sold under a different name than they are at home. For example, it would be a good idea to bring something like Sudafed from home, but aspirin (or something similar) would be easy to find. Pharmacies also sell personal hygiene products. The quality of a pharmacy varies from shop to shop, some offer home delivery, and some have been caught rebranding expired medicine and reselling it. While you still need a prescription for any sort of narcotic medication, the pharmacies do sell some pretty strong drugs over the counter. To save money

(and time), you can often describe your symptoms to the pharmacist and get something to take care of it without having to go to the doctor. Updated: Jul 20,2010.

Dentists

CUSCO

There are a several dentists in Cusco that you can consider. They include:

Centro Odontológico Americano
Av. Pardo 605 - D-2. Tel: 51-84-248124.

Odontocusco
Urb. La Florida K-4. Tel: 51-84-235003.

Centro Odontológico Haoc
Av. Diagonal Ramón Zavaleta 173, Wanchaq, Tel: 51(84) 229552

Centro Odontológico Personalizado
Av. Cultura 2122, Wanchaq. Tel: 51 (84) 227963 / 9745834

Centro de Odonlogía Integral
Av. Infancia 508-B 3er, Piso Clínica Americana, Wanchaq. Tel: 51-84-245052 / 9751101.

Centro Odontologico Prodental
Av. De la Cultura 2109 - Wanchaq, Tel: 51-84-233723 / 9621878. Updated: Jul 20,2010.

LIMA

The US Embassy offers a list of dentists in Lima on its website. However, one comes recommended by other expats: Travel and Smile. Travel and Smile is a dental practice with an English speaking staff. Headed by Dr. Enrique Yuen, this dental practice offers a wide range of services from regular checkups to cosmetic dentistry. They are clean, and use up-to-date equipment and techniques. They accept most insurance plans as well. 355 Monterrey St, 3rd and 4th floors Chacarilla, Lima. Tel: 999-44-5647, E-mail: info@travelandsmile.net, URL: http://www.travelandsmile.net. Updated: Jul 20,2010.

Eye Doctors

LIMA

When looking for an eye doctor in Lima, your first step should be to go to the US embassy's website, which lists doctors of every profession in the Lima area. Many eye doctors can also be found on Av. Arequipa near the intersection with Jose Pardo de Zela. There is a good selection of doctors, and prices are generally less than back home. Do some research and price shopping, and you should be able to get a good deal. Updated: Jul 20,2010.

CUSCO

Finding an eye doctor in Cusco is more difficult than it is in Lima as there are significantly fewer options. One place to start is a company called Ceprece, which offers computerized eye exams, perimetry, ocular microsurgery, and ultrasound. Urb Cachimayo F-32 - San Sebastian. Tel: 51-84-27-5765. Updated: Jul 20,2010.

Another option is Lima Optics, which despite its name has an office in Cusco. The clinic offers a full range of optic needs, from glasses to contacts and eye exams. Calle Matara 250. Tel: 51-84-248-040, URL: www.opticaslima.com. Updated: Jul 20,2010.

GPs

CUSCO

Dr. Maria Elena Farfan sees patients at her clinic, or does house and hotel calls. She charges around $20 for an evaluation at her clinic and around $30 for house calls. She speaks some English and is good for non-emergency calls. Procuradores 50 - 2nd Floor. Tel : 51-84-650-122 / 227-385. Updated: Jul 20,2010.

LIMA

Dr. Ernesto Casalino C is fluent in English and very friendly and professional. He treats all sorts of problems and patients of all ages. If you are staying long-term in Lima, he is recommended as a reliable GP. Clínica Ricardo Palma: Av. Javier Prado Este 1066 - San Isidro. Tel: 51-1-224-2224 Updated: Jul 20,2010.

Pediatricians

CUSCO

San Jose Clinica

Dr. Luis Gonzales, Dr. Fernando Quesada, and Dr. Jímmy Borja are three pediatricians who work at the San Jose Clinica. The full-service and private clinic also has gynecologists and a variety of specialists and they accept international travel health insurance. Av. Los Incas Nº 1408 - B Tel:

51-84-253-295 Cell: 51-84-98-470-8990, E-mail: info@sanjose.com.pe URL: www.sanjose.com.pe, Updated: Jul 20,2010.

LIMA

Erika Sturmann & Jamie Freundt

Genaro Castro Iglesias

Erika Sturmann & Jamie Freundt Genaro Castro Iglesias speak English and German in addition to Spanish and come highly recommended by expats in Lima. 245 Urb. Aurora Tel: 372-7127 / 372-7239. Other options include:

Javier Ferreyros Pediatras Asociados

Av. Santa Cruz 647, Miraflores. Tel: 51-1-441-8407 / 441-8333.

Dr. Carlos de la Piedra Encinas

141 Miraflores. Tel: 51-1-444-2285. Updated: Jul 20,2010.

Gynecologists

CUSCO

The Cusco Medical Assistance Clinic provides medical assistance to travelers and takes most of the international travel insurance companies. They provide 24-hour emergency care and do hotel and house calls as well as travel medicine, surgery, plastic surgery, cardiology, and general wellness. They also handle all paperwork related to your claims, which is a big bonus. If you don't have travel insurance, it is very expensive. Dr. Renan Ramírez Vargas is the internal medicine specialist and Dr. Giuliana Pinto Torres is the gynecologist. Urb. El Ovalo Av. La Paz B-1. Tel: 51-84-224-016, Fax : 51-84-224-178, E-mail: info@cuscomedicalassistance.com, URL: www.cuscomedicalassistance.com. Updated: Jul 20, 2010.

LIMA

Clinica Vitality

Dr. Alfredo Guzman at Clinica Vitality offers treatment such as obstetrics and gynecology, infertility, contraception, and menopausal treatment. He speaks English, attended John Hopkins in the US, and is a past president of the Peruvian Society of Obstetrics and Gynecology. Calle Monteflor 320, Chacarilla, Surco. Tel: 51-1-372-5500, Fax. 372-5500, E-mail: alfredoguz@gmail.com, URL: www.clinicavitality.com. Updated: Jul 20, 2010.

Cultural Differences Regarding Health

There are quite a few subtle differences relating to health and wellness in Peru, compared to North America, Australia and Europe. It is important for visitors and longer term residents to be aware of and sensitive to such issues. Some of the common issues that you may come across are:

NO BARE FEET

It is commonly thought that having bare feet walking about the house can lead to illness. Your Peruvian friends may be very surprised to see you walking about in this way. You will also find that Peruvian women wear flip flops less frequently, for similar reasons.

COLD DRINKS

Cold drinks are frequently thought to exacerbate colds. You may be asked in a restaurant when ordering a drink if you want "con hielo" (with ice) or "clima" (room temperature). If you have a cold and want to avoid a lengthy discussion about it with your Peruvian friends, you should opt for "clima".

SCARF AROUND YOUR NECK

Another widely believed myth is that keeping your neck warm will help you to get well. That is, if you have a cold, and go out in a tank top, you can expect this to be frowned upon by your Peruvian counterparts.

BABY'S HEAD COVERED WITH BLANKET

In the Andes, particularly at night, you'll notice that a baby's head will be covered with a blanket, to keep the cold from him/her. This is a common practice and it does not matter what the temperature is—baby will still be all covered up.

ANTIBIOTIC / PHARMACEUTICAL USE

Antibiotics are handed out like candy at the drug store. Many people self-medicate and are familiar with the names of the antibiotics that they believe will fix what is wrong with them. There is also a belief among some that cold and flu medication will make you well, rather than simply mask the symptoms of your illness.

ALLERGIC TO THE COLD

Some people, including some doctors, believe that it is possible for a person to be allergic to the cold. When faced with this attitude, it is better to seek out a doctor who does not share this belief, in order to get to the bottom of what is really wrong with you. Updated: Jun 2, 2010.

Montesur
Av. El Polo 505. Tel: 434-0559 / 435-2131 / 436-3630.

Jamie Velarde Instituto de Ginecología y Reproducción
Av. Monterrico 1045 - El Derby Monterrico. Tel: 434-2130 X 120. Updated: Jul 20, 2010.

Veterinarians

CUSCO

Lazzy Veterinary Clinic

Lazzy Veterinary Clinic, in Cusco, is a favorite among expats because it offers home-care in addition to 24-hour emergency service. They see dogs, cats, rodents, chickens, and turtles and offer a range of services from routine care to x-rays, surgery, and dentistry. In the attached pet store you can find your next family member, or purchase high-quality dog and cat food, toys, and accessories. They also do full-grooming. Av. de la Cultura No 748, Cusco. Tel: 51-84-249-452 / 765-805, URL: www.veterinarialazzy.com. Updated: Jul 13,2010.

LIMA

Animal Life

Animal Life, in Lima, is a full-service veterinary clinic offering everything a pet could need. Their staff does everything from routine vaccinations, annual check-ups and microchips, to lab work, x-rays, dental cleanings, dermatology, and surgery of all types. A few of their veterinarians speak English and they have a 24-hour emergency care clinic. They also treat exotic animals like snakes, turtles, iguanas, fish, and marsupials. They have three locations throughout Lima, but their main location is on Sol de la Molina Av. La Molina 799. Tel: 51-84-792-325, URL: www. vetanimallife.com. Updated: Jul 13, 2010.

Gyms and Yoga Studios

CUSCO

Gyms in Cusco are few and far between, however there is one very good, principal gym, followed by a couple of other smaller ones. The best gym in Cusco is called Empire Gym, just off the main plaza, where you can find services similar to what you'd expect from a gym back home, however you'll also find smaller, cheaper set-ups scattered around the city, usually just with weights and a few machines. Updated: Jul 13, 2010.

Empire Gym

Cusco's main gym is located within the small mall at the very top of Av. El Sol, by the plaza. Take the stairs to the bottom floor, underneath the Indian restaurant. Empire Gym offers a full room of modern machinery and weights, with an aerobics room and full schedule including step, dance, aerobic and boxing classes. There is also a separate spinning room with both morning and evening classes. Membership cost between 40-100 soles per month, depending on which aspects of the gym you choose to use. There is no minimum contract period—you can purchase just one month at a time. A casual, day pass is also available for 10 soles.Updated: Jul 13, 2010.

Gym on San Miguel

There is another small gym located on the corner of San Miguel and Cementerio streets. This small set-up has a couple of small rooms with machines and weights, as well as mats for stretching and sit-ups. Only 5 soles for a day pass, this offers a more relaxed alternative to the main gym listed above. Updated: Jul 13, 2010.

Free Spirit Peru

There are a few yoga places in Cusco. One of the best ones is Free Spirit Peru, who are registered by the Yoga Alliance. They have a comfortable studio just off San Blas plaza on 115/#1 Lucrepata. They provide mats and teach classes in English, using soothing music as well. Classes are given Monday through Friday, at 8 a.m. and 6 p.m. for 1.5 hours. Free yoga classes are sometimes offered on Saturday mornings. The price for a class is taken by way of donation between 10-20 soles. Updated: Jul 13, 2010.

Yoga Inbound

An excellent yoga option is Yoga Inbound, who have a very nice studio in San Blas and offer a range of yoga styles. Classes are scheduled at 9 a.m., 11 a.m. and 6 p.m. each day and cost 20 soles each, however you can purchase unlimited cards for one week, two weeks or a month (70, 120 and 180 soles respectively). Yoga Inbound also offers yoga retreats, teacher training, astrology and natural childbirth education. Calle Carmen Alto 111 San Blas. Updated: Jul 13,2010.

LIMA

Gold's Gym

Gold's Gym has ten locations in and around Lima and is one of the best options for serious fitness addicts as in addition to the usual aerobics and weight-lifting machines it offers daycare, massage, personal training, physical therapy, nutrition counseling, and a variety of group classes. Group classes include pilates, yoga, tai bo, and cardio kickboxing. They sometimes have promotions for 6-month or yearlong memberships, but by the month it is usually pricier than gyms in your home country. Mon-Fri they are open 6 a.m.-11 p.m. and have limited weekend hours. E-mail: miraflores@goldsgymperu.com, URL: www. goldsgymperu.com. Updated: Jul 20,2010.

Sportlife

Sportlife is slightly cheaper than Gold's Gym, but the equipment is a little older. Still, they have four locations in Lima and offer personal training, martial arts, pilates, nutrition advice, group classes, and a sauna. Their group classes include aerobics, step, dancing, and kickboxing. Some of the best features are their pool and squash courts, as well as the special programs and classes they offer for teens and kids. E-mail: gdiaz@sportlifeperu.com, URL: sportlifeperu.com. Updated: Jul 20, 2010.

Other Gyms

If you just want a couple of machines to use, there are plenty of local gyms with small membership fees that are perfectly adequate for a daily run on a treadmill or to lift a few weights. Updated: Jul 20, 2010.

SAFETY

Common Scams

When traveling through the cities of Peru, as with any major urban area, the first threat that you should be wary of is pickpocketing. In Peru, this is usually an organized team

PERU LIVING

effort. Once you are marked as a tourist, one of the team will come up to you and distract you, often by bumping or shoving you, while another fleeces you. Other times, you may be literally, and discreetly, marked with chalk as so that nearby accomplices will be able to recognize you. It is best not to keep anything valuable in your back pockets, and when bumped, to reach for your pockets. Be especially wary in Mercado de San Pedro in Cusco, as it is infamous for pickpockets.

A common scam often takes place in a park or outdoor café. Some bait, be it a little bit of money or some other trinket of value is put on the ground, and the tourist, leaving their valuables for only a moment, goes to retrieve the item, only to find their backpack gone when they turn back around. Never take your eyes off your luggage while in public, for any reason. In a similar vein, often times in a crowded bus for example, someone will slash the bottom of your bag while you are distracted by some other commotion. Then, either the same person or an accomplice will simply reach in and take out any valuables they find. For this reason, it is best to keep your backpack in plain sight and on your lap on the bus or in public areas.

On overnight buses, the scam is even simpler. The thief will wait until you are asleep, and then either rifle though your belongings, taking what they want, or take your bag and get off at the next stop. The best defense against this is to travel light and keep your bag on your lap at all times.

Peru has been known to be home to several fake police scams, some more malicious than others. While you should never argue with, yell at, or confront a police officer, you should be wary when dealing with them. There have been reported cases of fake police doing "random searches" at public places like bus stations, and under some pretense demanding that you come with them to (what will later be revealed to be) an isolated location where you will be relieved of your valuables. It is best to ignore a single officer by pretending you don't understand him, and not to follow any police officer unless there are multiple officers and vehicles, or it has otherwise become obvious that they are in fact real police.

Be wary when returning from the bars or clubs at night. Taxi drivers will often drive you around in hopes of disorienting you. In the least vicious form of this scam, they will simply overcharge you when they finally do reach your destination, but in more violent forms they will drive you to a secluded location where armed accomplices will rob you. Be wary, and aware, of your surroundings and always know the way home. Updated: Jul 13, 2010.

SHOPPING

Pirate DVD Stores

Throughout Peru, in cities big and small, in almost every neighborhood, you'll find a curious industry: pirated DVDs. Whereas in the states the purveyors of bootleg movies are relegated to the streets and need to worry about the police, here it is an accepted industry. Shops and store fronts will proudly display their selection of movies, which they sell as burned DVDs in plastic sleeves. The selection varies depending on the store, but you can usually find a large selection of foreign films (including some still in theaters), local feature length music DVDs, and Latin American movies. Most stores also sell compilation DVDs, where 5-8 movies linked by a theme are put together on one DVD (note: this type is always only in Spanish). The quality varies widely, even in the same store. Some movies are camcorder recordings taken in movie theaters, while others are perfect copies of commercial DVDs, with title, menu, and bonus features. Some DVDs have an English language track, but others do not. It can be hit or miss, because all of the movies are packaged the same but have different sources and features, and often the sellers won't be much help on specifics. Of course, a DVD only costs between 2-4 soles, (less than 2 USD) so the risk of wasted money is low. Updated: Jul 20, 2010.

CUSCO

As Cusco is a small city, you'll find that it has many small markets that you can visit, rather than large centers, but for the most part it will cater to all your shopping needs.

The main supermarket chain is Mega, and this can be found on Calle Matara, just 2 blocks from the main street—Avenida El Sol.

This is a safe place to buy meat and other goods. There is another supermarket located on Avenida Grau, 3 blocks off Avenida El Sol.

There are two small mini-markets closer by, just off the plaza Gatos, found underneath Paddys bar, and the other found just next to Avenida del Sol, where you can buy food, including imported products for tourists such as HP sauce and peanut butter. Do expect higher prices in these markets due to their close proximity to the Plaza.

Six blocks from the plaza, on the corner of Santa Clara and Ccascaparo, is San Pedro market, a popular place for locals and tourists alike. Here you can find plenty of fruit and vegetables, herbs, and excellent fresh fruit juices, as well as llama and alpaca clothing items and souvenirs. You can also have your clothes fixed by the local sewing ladies here.

Just off Avenida El Sol, about 12 blocks from the Plaza, you will find Centro Comercial Confraternidad (2.50 soles in a taxi). This is a large market selling many types of clothes, household items, shoes, bathroom products and all for very cheap prices. This is a popular market for locals.

A well-known market, set up for tourists, is Mulino. Also known as the Black Market, Mulino sells everything from clothes and shoes to jewellery and alcohol as well as electrical goods such as cameras, and many DVDs and CDs. Reasonably cheap prices can be found here but be sure to bargain.

If you are looking for quality shopping, visit Cusco Sol Plaza on Avenida El Sol, just next to the post office. Here you´ll find some nicer clothes shops, as well as quality beauty salons and hairdressers. Also on Av. El Sol you will find a couple of good photography stores, within the first two blocks from the main Plaza.

There are quite a few outdoors stores nearby the plaza selling and renting everything in outdoor sporting equipment. The best streets for these are Calle Suecia and Procuradores. There is also an authentic Northface store on Plazoleta Espinar, in front of the church, just one block from the Plaza where you can find quality sports gear.

For more of a unique shopping experience, take a walk up the hill to the artistic neighbourhood of San Blas, where you´ll find many jewelry and trinket stores offering unique pieces. Be sure to visit the market in the San Blas square on Saturdays, which offers delicate handcrafts and jewelry. Updated: Jul 13, 2010.

Tatoo Adventure Gear

Tatoo Adventure Gear is a top source for brand-name sportswear, trekking and camping equipment, biking accessories and more. There are two stores in Cusco near the Plaza de Armas. The adventure gear distributor also stocks guidebooks and maps. You will find that the knowledgeable staff provides information on mountaineering courses and seminars, and offers tips on everything from the best routes to climb to buying the perfect hiking boot.Monday-Sunday 9a.m-9:30p.m. Calle del Medio 130. Tel: 51-8-425-4211. Calle Triunfo 346. Tel: 51-8-422-4797 URL: http://cl.tatoo.ws. Updated: Nov 06, 2009.

San Pedro Market / Mercado Central

Located across from the San Pedro train station; a few blocks southwest of the Plaza de Armas, the central market offers one-stop shopping for the traveler with a grocery list and limited needs in the souvenir department. Though the Mercado Central is largely dedicated to sales of fruits, vegetables, meats and bread, there are a few vendors hawking souvenirs to those tourists who wander in. For practical goods, like socks or batteries, the Mercado Central gets the job done, although the range of goods is infinitesimal compared to Mercado Mollina. Like most markets in Peru, the Mercado Central has plenty of cheap local eats for the traveler with a sense of adventure and an iron stomach. Open daily. Updated: Jul 13,2010.

LIMA

Leafar

Leafar is an electronics and computer store in Lima. They have a good reputation for quality and service. They offer many brand name computers and peripheries, along with a host of other electronic equipment. Leafar tends to be more expensive than some of the other stores, but you may find that going with a sure thing is worth the extra cost. 8:30 a.m.-6:30 p.m., daily. Av. Larco 880, Miraflores. Tel: 51-1-700-5050, URL: www.leafar. com.pe. Updated: Jul 20, 2010.

Lima Malls

Lima has some of the best shopping in Peru, and like any large, international city there are a variety of shopping districts and malls spread throughout the city. Prices are a bit higher in Lima, particularly in the high-end malls and shoppers should be prepared to pay a little more than they may have hoped to for luxury clothing, fine leather goods, and outdoor equipment. However, if there is something you covet and can't find, the malls are the best place to look. Despite the cost, the malls are frequented by locals, are generally clean, and can be quite beautiful. Some of them are nice places to spend an afternoon or evening with friends as they all have food courts and entertainment options.

The enormous Jockey Plaza in Lima's Monterrico district on the Javier Prado is one of the most modern shopping centers in Peru with two stories of shops boasting small boutiques, specialty shops, department stores, and international designers like Benetton, Christian Dior, and Guess. Besides shopping, the mall also has extensive entertainment options like a bowling alley and twelve-screen movie theater. As far as dining goes, there are a few international restaurants like Chili's, and the popular Plaza del Chef is open every day until midnight. Parking spaces are usually available and free, which makes it a good meeting place for people with cars. Open 11 a.m.-9 p.m.

Perched atop a cliff in Miraflores, with spectacular views of the stretch of the Pacific known as the Green Coast, is Larcomar, a relatively new high-end shopping and entertainment center. Throughout the day, idlers browse the shops, enjoy the view, and watch brave people do the bungee jump ride on the bottom floor of the three-story mall. At sunset, they grab some dinner in the popular food court or dine at one of the more upscale restaurants with sweeping views like Balthazar. In the evening families, young people, and adults go to the underground 24-lane bowling alley, or the 12-screen movie theater, and at night, both locals and travelers flock to the ever-popular Aura, a late-night upscale dance club where you can party until sunrise on the weekends. Shoppers won't be disappointed either, as in addition to the mainstream clothing shops and specialty boutiques many of the hard-to-find items like electronics and adventure outdoor gear can be purchased here in the stores like Radio Shack and Tatoo Outdoors. If you have a car, it's good to know that there are over 400 free parking spots at Larcomar. Open 10 a.m. - 8 p.m.

In San Isidro on the Belaunde travelers can find the large, indoor Camino Real Mall. Compared to the malls in Miraflores this shopping center is a little less pretentious and full of smaller shops with slightly cheaper wares. It is near the Lima Golf Club and the iPeru tourist office. Belaunde 147. Updated: Jul 20, 2010.

Ace Peru

Ace Peru, like its American counterpart, is a well-stocked hardware store located in the Surquillo district. If you are looking for anything from nails to power tools, this is your one stop shop. The first floor is where you'll find the odds and ends, nails, light fixtures, paint and building materials, while the second floor houses the bigger items like power tools. They advertise a diverse stock and reasonable prices. 10a.m.-9p.m. Paseo de la República 3480, Lima. Tel: 51-1-221-0418. Updated: Jul 20, 2010.

Hiraoka

Hiraoka is a chain of electronic stores in Peru. They are large stores, and offer a decent selection of computers, peripheral devices, and other electronics. If you are looking for that cord you swore was in your bag or a new webcam for your laptop, you should be able to find what you need. Prices are higher than at home, so be prepared for a little sticker shock. Av. Petit Thouars 5273. Tel: 241-7474, URL: www. hiraoka.com.pe. Updated: Jul 20, 2010.

Alpamayo

In the Miraflores neighborhood, you'll find several shops that sell outdoor gear. Alpamayo is one such store that has everything the intrepid hiker needs. They sell tents, backpacks, sleeping mats, boots, climbing gear, water filters, stoves, and most other outdoor adventure gear. As an added bonus, the owner speaks English fluently. Monday - Friday 10 a.m. - 8 p.m., Saturday 10a.m. - 2p.m. Av Larco 345, Miraflores at Parque Kennedy. Tel: 51-1-445-1671. Updated: Jul 20, 2010.

Boticas BTL

Boticas BTL has locations all around Lima. What really makes this pharmacy stand out is that they offer 24-hour home delivery. You can call them yourself, tell them what you need, and have it delivered. They also deliver to hotels, so if you are sick and staying in a hotel, you can ask the front desk to order whatever you need. If you feel like making the trek yourself, their website hosts a list of all of their locations, so you can find one close to you. Tel: 51-1-612-5000, URL: www.btl.com. pe. Updated: Jul 20, 2010.

Ibero Larcomar

If you are looking for English language books, consider Ibero Larcomar. They have many locations throughout the city. This store has books on subjects of all kinds in both Spanish and English. Most English books tend to be novels, or history/travel related. They only sell new books, so used book lovers will have to look elsewhere. Most locations are open every day from around 10 a.m. to 10 p.m. Avenida Malecon de la Reserva 610, Store Number 127 (Miraflores), Tel: 242-6777, URL: www. iberolibros.com. Updated: Jul 20, 2010.

Metro Supermarkets

Metro supermarkets can be found all around Lima. They offer a good selection and tend to be cheaper than their competitors. Unfortunately, this means Metro locations are usually crowded and lines can be long. They sell fresh produce and meat, as well as many packaged foods, condiments, and miscellaneous food items that you may not be able to find elsewhere. Many locations offer a deli section that has pre-prepared food ranging from Peruvian roasted chicken to little Chinese treats. Updated: Jul 20, 2010.

Photo by: WhlTravel

Polvos Azules

Polvos Azules, "the blue powders" is a market located on Paseo del la Republica, close to Plaza Grau, and is in a large building housing literally hundreds of little stalls that sell almost anything you could want. Like any good South American market, you get can anything from kitchen appliances to pirated DVDs and CDs. Prices are generally cheaper than elsewhere in the city. It is a popular shopping center and is always packed and very loud. Ask any taxi driver, and he'll be able to take you there. Updated: Jul 20, 2010.

Maps

While finding maps can be easy, finding specific or detailed maps can be difficult especially outside of the major urban areas. In cities, many bookstores or similar businesses will offer maps for sale, and you can usually find trail maps, or other regional maps of tourist areas, in tourist information offices, but be prepared to pay more than a map should cost. If your time in Peru takes you to Cusco or Lima, the South American Explorer's Club has a wide variety of maps, trail guides, and other useful travel information for members. Updated: Jul 20,2010.

PACKING FOR PERU

Hard to Find Items

There are a number of items that it may be harder to find in Peru. For example, it may be difficult to find a variety of international spices and specialty foods outside of the huge supermarkets and the large cities. A really good adapter for plugs can be hard to find in the more rural areas so, unless you are flying into Lima, bring a good one with you. Any medicine you take regularly such as birth control should ideally be brought from home. Although you can get most medicines here, you may have to switch types or brands if you don't bring your own. High-quality electronics are more expensive and of lesser quality. Bring a laptop and spare parts from home if you plan on using one and the same goes for other electronic devices like ipods. If you are buildng your own home in Peru, you may want to bring some building supplies like nails that don't rust, and faucets for sinks. Updated: Jul 13, 2010.

Things to Leave at Home

Unless you are permanently settling in Peru, and even then we still wouldn't recommend bringing them, leave your expensive jewelry, watches, and sunglasses at home. Most people do not wear these things here, and unless your lifestyle depends on it, it's best not to wear them either. Don't bring your important documents and the full contents of your wallet like all your credit cards, social security cards, etc. If you are trying to get a residency visa, start your own business, or buy property, find out exactly what important documents you need and bring those, but nothing else. Household appliances like blenders and televisions, as well as furniture and cell phones are also readily available. Unfortunately, there is a wide-spread rumor that tampons are hard to find in Peru, and this is simply not true, so women, please don't pack a suitcase full of them. Updated: Jul 13, 2010.

Beauty Products

In Lima and Cusco and the other large cities it's possible to find every sort of beauty product imaginable, but you may not be able to find the specific brand that you use. The pharmacies and supermarkets carry lower-end beauty products similar to those at home and you can find higher-end products in the malls or in salons. If you are addicted to a certain eye cream, face wash, or high-quality sun block, bring it with you, but in general

you can find what you need though it may be more expensive than at home. In the smaller towns you may not be able to find the higher-end items anywhere, but the lower-end products will still be readily available. Updated: Jul 13, 2010.

Clothing

Before you pack, think very carefully about what you will really be doing in Peru and where you want to go. Peru is a large country and the different regions can vary dramatically in temperature depending on the season and altitude. If you are spending a lot of time on the beaches, especially in the north, you may only need sandals, a swimsuit, a few t-shirts and shorts, and a pair of linen pants with a light-weight button up shirt or a cute dress for going out to dinner. However, if you are planning on hiking in the Sacred Valley, you will need warm clothes, comfortable hiking shoes, and a rain poncho. In general, most clothing items are easy to find here, especially warm clothes like sweaters, scarves, and gloves made of alpaca. If you plan on buying these items anyway, leave some of the warm clothes out of your suitcase. Most people end up lamenting that they brought too many clothes and shoes, and not enough of the electronics, personal items, or outdoor gear like a first aid kit, mini speakers, ipod, or climbing gear which are extremely difficult to find in Peru at a good price. However, if you have feet over a size 10, or are exceptionally tall, keep in mind that large shoes and large clothes are tough to find and you should bring them from home. Women might also want to bring a few high-quality bras as stores with a range of sizes are scarce except in the expensive malls. Updated: Jul 13, 2010.

DRIVING / BUYING A CAR

In Peru, you can drive with a foreign driver's license or an international driver's permit (IDP) for six months. The better option is to use an IDP, which you should get in your home country, if you intend to use one. The best way to get an IDP or a driver's license in Peru, or to request the necessary extension is by going to the Touring and Automótiv club del Peru (known as El Touring to locals). They are at Ave Cesar Vallleo 699, Lince, in Lima (www.touringperu.com.pe). Tel. 51-1-211-9977. They are open from 9 a.m. to 4:45 p.m. They are authorized to give driving tests, and issue international licenses.

Getting a local license can be a relatively quick process. You need a psychological exam and a medical exam, a written test, and an actual driving test. To do this you must go to one of the clinics authorized by the Ministry of Transport and present two color carnet-sized photos, your passport, and a photocopy of it. The medical exam covers the basics, and the psychological test, which is different at each clinic, is made up of a series of questions that may seem random and unrelated. The written test covers local road rules and regulations, and you can get all the information you need to study from the Touring Club. The actual driving test may not be necessary if you've driven for more than three years. If you have, you need only take the medical and written tests.

Buying a car in Peru can be an expensive venture. One must consider the cost of customs and taxes, in addition to the value of the vehicle. Most people buy used cars, many of which have been imported from Japan. In years past, Japanese imports could be found for significantly cheaper because they were shipped as parts (thus subject to less tax) and reassembled in country. The Peruvian government has cracked down on this type of importation, but Japanese cars remain popular.

There are several things to consider when buying a car in Peru. First, there are some areas called reduced duty import zones, which will mean a cheaper sale price. One such place is in Tacna, and is called Ceticos. You must also consider that, like with so many other things, being a foreigner will mean that you will pay more than a Peruvian would for the same car.

Most people here buy used cars and as with buying a used car anywhere, it's a good idea to know something about cars, or bring someone with you who does. Depending on how well you speak Spanish, it may be a good idea to have a Peruvian friend negotiate the price for you. The better you know both subjects, the better a deal you will be able to get.

In terms of payment, dealers most often will require that you pay in cash. In such a situation, it is best to take the seller to the bank, and handle both the transfer of money and the paperwork there, rather than travel anywhere with large sums of money. In terms of paperwork, you will need to get the tarjeta de propiedad (Proof of Ownership).

Be aware that after this process, if there are any fines on the car from before you bought it, you will now be responsible for them. You will also need to visit a notary to get the paperwork finalized. Registration, once the paperwork has been filed, takes between one and two weeks, with the license plates following soon after.

Type of Car

Before you buy a car, consider the type of driving you intend to do. A four wheel drive, or *quarto por quarto*, is the best option for traveling long distances, or for those living in the country. Not surprisingly, because of the demand, these tend to be priced at a premium. The roads are often in disrepair, or rough, or both, and the four-wheel drive will help you get to where you are going. Generally, bigger is better due to the "the bigger car has the right of way" attitude of many Peruvian drivers. If you plan on staying in the city, it may be better to go with a smaller car, as the heavy traffic and tight spaces of the city will make it a better investment. If you intend on doing both, it may be worth your while to buy a small city car, and a larger, long distance car. Stay away from convertibles, as security is a big issue. For the same reason, you should never leave your car radio in plain view when you park your car, even for a few minutes - especially in urban places like Lima and Cusco. If you are considering driving in Peru, you should be aware that it can be very dangerous. Nearly 2000 people a year die on the roads here in Peru. The rules of the road are lax at best, and driving in Peru is often described using the word extreme, as in extreme sport and extremely dangerous. Road conditions are often poor, especially in more rural areas, and finding yourself in a game of chicken with a much larger vehicle is not at all uncommon. Traffic accidents, including those that result in death, are frequent here. Before deciding to buy a car it is worth considering whether another option might be better.

Getting Insurance

Each driver in Peru is required to buy liability insurance called SOAT, which is renewed yearly. In years past, few locals actually bought insurance, including many of the bus transport companies, so the government felt it necessary to implement a required insurance plan. In the event of a car accident resulting in injury or death, the SOAT provides immediate third party coverage. You are required to have both a SOAT sticker on your car, and a certificate in your car at all times. You can get these almost anywhere. You can purchase additional coverage through a variety of insurance companies and brokers. If you have international car insurance, through a recognized company, that includes third party liability, you may not need to buy SOAT separately.

Driving Rules

While many rules of the road remain the same, there are some aspects of driving in Peru that can be, well, foreign. Always drive defensively and be aware of other cars around you. In Peru, vehicles, not pedestrians have the right of way. Most importantly, there seems to be an unwritten rule that the bigger car has the right of way. Expect that the bigger car will attempt to shoehorn itself in front of other drivers. Expect to be passed at high speeds and from either side, sometimes both. Although the law says that slower cars should stay on the right, this is often ignored. Use your car horn, and expect others to use theirs. Cars, trucks, and buses often pass the median line in order to pass other cars, creating a safety hazard for oncoming traffic. Turn signals are usually eschewed for the arm out of the window approach to signaling. Sometimes, no signal is given at all. Stop signs, traffic lights, and similar guides on the road are often ignored by local drivers, who give a quick beep at intersections or sharp turns, and if no beep is heard in return, continue at full speed.

Always carry your documents with you when you travel between cities and towns because police checkpoints can be inconvenient and time-consuming at best, or dangerous and expensive at worst. If a policeman pulls you over, either by signal or whistle, you are not required to get out of your car, nor can the police take away your driver's license. You can pay traffic tickets at the Banco de la Nación. If you pay the traffic ticket in the same week it is issued, you may be eligible for a discount. Updated: Jul 13, 2010.

LEISURE TIME

Sports

Sports are very popular in Peru, and you will find that Peruvians are enthusiastic about them. The most popular sport by far in Peru

is soccer and if you don't personally enjoy it you might want to pretend you do anyway. Volleyball is also a popular sport, as are bull fighting and racing, but none of these can hold a candle to *futbol*, which is the national pastime. In fact, soccer is important in many ways to the modern history of Peru, helping to forge a national identity during the 1960s and 1970s by defeating many favored teams on their way to the 1970 Mexico Cup. In fact, during the 1990s, when many of the other cultural institutions of Peru seemed on the brink of disaster it was the football clubs, and their "barras" or street promoters, that seemed to fill the gap left by the other failing institutions. Perhaps this is why Peruvians love soccer so much.

The three most popular teams in Peru are Sporting Cristal, Alianza Lima, and Universitario de Deportes, and all three are based in Lima. Alianza Lima and Universitario de Deportes are archrivals, and any match between these two is sure to be exciting and entertaining. Every year they play a game known as the Clasico that is watched throughout Peru. There are many nationally and internationally famous Peruvian soccer players, such as Teofilo Cubillas, and Hugo Sotil.

If you want to catch a soccer match, Lima is your best bet as the top three teams in Peru all hail from here. You can attend games at the Estadio Monumental, home of the Universitario de Deportes, which opened in 2000. Despite being Peru's largest stadium, the second largest in all of South America, and being the home of one of the country's most famous teams, the stadium has never hosted any of the international sporting events that have been in Peru. In addition, due to concerns over security, the Classico was not held here for almost five years, but returned in 2008.

The Alianza Lima Club plays their home games at Alejandro Villanueva Stadium. Sporting Cristal plays home games at either Estadio San Martin De Porres, or the Estadio National. Estadio National is also the home of the Peru National Football team, which is part of FIFA's CONMEBOL conference. They last made it to the World Cup in 1982. The national football team was briefly suspended from FIFA play in 2008 due to charges of corruption between government authorities and the Peruvian Football Federation, which manages the national team.

Cusco Nightlife

As well as being a beautiful, colonial city, Cusco has a diverse and hip nightlife seven days a week with something for every type of traveler. Conveniently, the action is located around or near the Main Plaza or up in the San Blas neighborhood. Cheap drinks and extended happy hours are offered almost everywhere and touts will entice you into bars and clubs with free drink vouchers. Options include low key lounge bars, restaurants and cafes, to pubs, crowded dance clubs, theatre and live music venues.

LIVE MUSIC
Every night of the week, groups play live music including reggae, rock, 80's, salsa, creole, son cubano and traditional Andean music. Ukuku's nightclub normally has some great local bands playing (especially at weekends) and has a buzzing atmosphere with a good local crowd. San Blas hosts bands in a cluster of bars including Siete Angelitos, La Taberna de San Blas and KMo. Oshito Cub has a live salsa band every Saturday night and The Lek normally has live music at least four times a week. Most restaurants will be frequented by pan-pipe playing local artists too.

BARS AND CLUBS
You can dance salsa from Monday to Sunday from 9.30-11 p.m. and then from 11 p.m. onward most clubs have DJ's that play a mix of dance, hip hop, reggaton, electro, rock, reggae and Latin music. Popular clubs include Mythology, Inka Team, Mama Africa, Zazu's and Ukuku's.

Bull Frogs is a bar a few blocks from the plaza that offers regular theme parties, live music, cinema room, games room and food. Other bars also show films early evening.

PUBS AND RESTAURANTS
You can play darts at Norton's Rats or Cross Keys Pub, The Real McCoy's restaurant holds Pub Quizzes every Wednesday evening and you may even find Texas Hold'em poker evenings! Updated: Jul 13, 2010.

Club Cienciano, based in Cusco, is a play on the word science, as the first members of the team were the faculty of the science department at the University of Cusco. Their stadium, Estadio Garcilaso de la Vega, is said to be one of South America's most beautiful stadiums because of its resistance to the often variable climate in Cusco. The team takes a similar spirit of resilience when playing.

In Arequipa, Arequipa Stadium hosts games as well as other events. Updated: Jul 13, 2010.

Expat Clubs and Communities

South American Explorer's Club
The South American Explorer's Club has a lot to offer any traveler. For a small annual fee ($60 per person or $90 for a couple), you get access to a wealth of information, a lending library, discounts at restaurants, hostels, travel agencies, and many other businesses all over Peru, and a chance to meet fellow travelers. There are two clubhouses in Peru, one in Lima and one in Cusco. Both organize social events such as quiz nights on a regular basis. URL: www.saexplorers.org. Updated: Jul 20, 2010.

The American & Canadian Association of Peru
This Lima-based organization of long time expats began as a club for those from the US and Canada, but has grown to accept members from any English-speaking country. Founded in 1917, this club attempts to offer a social network and support for members now living in Peru. Members can share the customs of their native country, while learning about and embracing those customs of Peru. They also host a range of cultural and social activities, and do charity work. E-mail: acap@infonegocio.net.pe, URL: www.acap-peru.org. Updated: Jul 20, 2010.

ExpatPeru
ExpatPeru is a club for expatriates of any country who are now living in Peru. It is an

PERU LIVING

online organization, and their website has a wealth of information on moving to and living in Peru, from questions on basics like health insurance and paying taxes to traveling and sightseeing. They host a popular forum where you can ask questions on any subject and get information from more experienced expats. They also have a popular Expatriate Newsletter mailing list. E-mail: contact@expatperu.com, URL: www.expatperu.com. Updated: Jul 20, 2010.

American Women's Literacy Club of Peru

Founded in 1922, this literary club has had a long history in Lima. They host social gatherings and trips. Membership includes people from many nationalities, ages, and professions. Both native Peruvians and expatriates make this club their own with English as their common language. They meet the first Monday of every month in Miraflores. They have several active literary discussion groups, publish a popular bilingual cookbook, and have an extensive lending library. URL: www.awlc.webs.com, E-mail: awlcinperu@gmail.com, Updated: Jul 20, 2010.

The Lima Hash House Harriers

There are Hash House Harrier groups, known as HHH or H3, across the globe. If running is your thing, or even just walking, Hash House Harrier is the place for you. They arrange outings that usually include between 20 and 60 people. You don't have to run either, as they usually have a walking route for the people who want to take it slow. Afterward, everyone eats, drinks, and socializes. Expatriates as well as locals participate, so it's a good place to meet people. URL: http://groups.yahoo.com/group/LimaHHH, E-mail: LimaHHH-subscribe@yahoogroups.com, Updated: Jul 20, 2010.

Rotary Lima Sunrise

The ever-expanding Rotary Lima Sunrise is the only English-speaking Rotary club in Latin America. They meet every Thursday morning at 7:30 a.m. at the Marriot Hotel in the Miraflores district. It is a good way to meet other professionals from all over the world who are doing business in Lima, network with them, and make friends. Activities include guest speakers and community service projects directed at improving the health of the less fortunate people in the area. Tel: 9-817-6151,

E-mail: betz.01@t-online.de, URL: www.rotary-limasunrise.com. Updated: Jul 20, 2010.

Club Regatas

Club Regatas is a beachside member-only club with four locations (two on the beach) a variety of water sports like sailing, swimming, surfing, parasailing, beach volleyball, crew, and other sports like fencing. They have special three-month memberships for tourists who won't be staying for the full year. They also have a full Turkish bath, gymnasium, salons, and theater as well as a few restaurants. The Chifa, or Chinese food restaurant, and the bar on the seventh floor get good reviews. It costs around $25,000 to join, and charges a $65 monthly fee. URL: www.clubregatas.org.pe. Updated: Jul 20, 2010.

Club Tennis Las Terrazas

Club Tennis Las Terrazas is primarily for members and guests of members, though they do allow the public to use their courts for an hourly fee. The main attraction and focus is definitely on tennis and their ten red-clay courts, but they do offer squash, swimming, surfing, chess, and soccer too. Memberships are hefty and similar to the other clubs in Lima. Open from 7 a.m. to 6 p.m. Malecón 390 July 28, Miralfores. Tel: 51-1-512-3200, URL: www.clubterrazas.com.pe. Updated: Jul 20, 2010.

Golf

The golf clubs in Lima are typically the most exclusive country clubs and are for members and guests of members only. If you are traveling through Peru and want to play, your best bet is to stay at one of the hotels that offer golf packages to guests such as Country Club Lima Hotel and Sonesta Hotel Olivar. If you would like to become a member, fees are around $30,000 and monthly dues are around $150.

Country Club de Villa

Country Club de Villa has an 18-hole golf course, pools, tennis courts, squash, a soccer field, and a gym. Av. Hernando de Lavalle Chorrillos. Tel: 51-1-254-0032, URL: www.countryclubvilla.org.pe.

Lima Golf Club

Lima Golf Club has a scenic 18-hole course with a par of 72, and a clubhouse including a pool and tennis courts. Avenida Camino Real 770, San Isidro. Tel: 51-1-442-6006.

PERU LIVING

Country Club La Planicie

Country Club La Planicie in La Molina has an 18-hole course and other facilities like tennis, and squash. Av. José León Barandiarán 457 La Planicie, La Molina. Tel: 51-1-479-0045, E-mail: oficinagolf@cclaplanicie.org, URL: www.clublaplanicie.org. Updated: Jul 20, 2010.

))))!

PERU LIVING

Index

A
Academia Castellana, 233
Academia Latinoamericana de Español, 230-231
Action Valley, 84-85
Acupari Language School, 230
Aeroxtreme, 208
Aguas Calientes, 64, 110, 112, 123, 130-136
Aguas Calientes Activities, 132
Aguas Calientes Lodging, 132-134
Aguas Calientes Restaurants, 134-136
Aiko Restaurant, 131, 135
Airport transportation, 147, 150
Albergue Miraflores House, 187
Alcázar, 122, 128-129
Aldea Yanapay Project, 97, 221
Alejandro Velasco Astete International Airport, 64
Alfresco, 161
Almacén Metro, 168-169
Amaru Hostal, 101
Amauta Spanish School, 232
Amauta Spanish School Volunteer Program, 222
Amigos Spanish School, 230
Andahuaylillas and San Pedro, 107
Andean Moon, 122, 127
Andenes De Saphy, 91
Andex Adventure, 35
Angela's Laundry, 131
Antica Pizzería, 165
Antigua Taberna Queirolo, 208
Apu Lodge, 122, 127
Apu Salkantay, 136
Apus Peru Adventure Travel Specialists, 74
Arrieros, 101
Arte en Cuero Sánchez, 169
Artesanal Market, 132
Artesanías Pachacútec
Arúgula, 194
Astrid y Gastón, 194
Aura, 195
Ausangate and Cordillera Vilcanota, 111

B
Babieca Tratoria, 97
Back Roads Cusco to Quito, 33
Bait Sababa Lodge, 208
Balthazar, 198
Banks in Lima, 151
Bar Mochileros, 199-200

Barranco, 152
Barranco Lodging, 189-200
Barranco Restaurants, 200-201
Barranco's Backpackers Inn, 197
Basadre Suites Hotel, 159
Belén Restauran, 178
Belmundo en Línea, 168
Best Western Embajadores, 188
Bike Tours of Lima, 185
Birdwatching in Peru, 35-36
Bodega Bar Juanito's, 202
Bodega Santiago Queirolo, 206
Body Show Spa Cusco, 84
Bohème, 97
Bullfighting Museum / Museo Taurino, 155
Bungee Jumping with The Inka Adventure, 85

C
Cabalgatas Horseback Riding, 207
Caballeros, 208
Cactus, 130
Café Café, 192
Café Haití, 191
Café Plaza, 121
Café Trotamundos, 95
Callao, 204-205
Callao Restaurants, 205
Caminante School, 233
Cappuccino Café, 95
Casa Andina Miraflores San Antonio, 189
Casa Bella, 161
Casa de Aliaga, 171
Casa De Leeuw, 200
Casa del Mochilero, 185
Casa Goyeneche, 170
Casa Riva-Agüero, 172
Casa San Blas Boutique Hotel, 102
Casa Torre Tagle, 169-170
Cava de San Rafael, 96
Center for Traditional Textiles of Cusco, 83
Central Bank Museum / Museo del Banco Central, 156
Central Lima, 166-179
Central Lima Activities, 169-173
Central Lima History, 166-168
Central Lima Lodging, 173-175
Central Lima Restaurants, 175-179
Central Lima Services, 168-169
Centro Comercial Plaza Lima Sur, 202
Cerro Azul, 211
Cervantes Spanish School, 230

Chala, 201
Chamber of the Princess, 141
Chifa "Jin", 191
Chifa Fon Wa, 205
Chifa Fuc Seng, 176
Chinchero, 114
Chincheros Activities, 114
Choquequirao, 110
Chorrillos, 202-203
Chorrillos Activities, 202-203
Chorrillos Lodging, 203
Chorrillos Restaurants, 203
Chorrillos Services, 202
CIMA Hyperbaric Center, 67
Class Adventure Travel, 153
Coco de Mer, 192
Como Agua Para Chocolate, 164
Concert Disco, 172
Conexus Language Institute, 233
Convento de Santo Domingo, 172
Correo Central de Lima, 166
Cosentino Gourmet, 176
Costa Verde Beaches, 183
Country Club Lima Hotel, 162
Cristina Hostal, 92
Cross Cultural Solutions, 218
Culinary Vocab in Peru, 47
Curry Treat, 208
Cusco, 62-107
Cusco Activities, 78-85
Cusco Airport, 64
Cusco Cathedral, 82
Cusco Coca Museum, 84
Cusco Lodging, 86
Cusco Overview, 62
Cusco Restaurants, 94-100
Cusco Services, 67-72
Cusco Spanish School, 230
Cusco Spanish Schools, 229-233
Cusco Today, 63
Cusco Tourist Ticket / Boleto Turístico General, 68-72
Cusco Tours, 72-75
Cusco Yesterday, 62-63
Cusco--Holidays and Festivals, 66
Cusco, Machu Picchu and the Sacred Valley, 108-145
Cusco, Machu Picchu and the Sacred Valley Overview, 108
Cusco, Machu Picchu and the Sacred Valley: When to Go, 108
Cusco Mania Spanish School, 231
Cusi Q'oyllor Hostal, 132-133

D

De César Restaurant, 176
Dédalo, 197
Diana Net and Tattoo Parlour, 168
DJ Tattoo Machines, 169
Domeyer Hostel, 199
Dragón Internet, 181
Drews, 99

E
Earthquakes – Cusco, 67
Earthwatch Institute, 220
Edo Sushi Bar, 207
EEC Spanish School, 233
El Albergue, 127
El Balcón Dorado, 174
El Balcón Hostal, 91
El Bolivariano, 208
El Buen Sabor, 164
El Cartujo, 163
El Charro, 135
El Condado Hotel and Suites, 189
El Cuate, 96
El Delfín, 200
El Dragón, 202
El Ekeko Café Bar, 202
El Estadio Fútbol Club, 179
El Faro de la Marina, 184
El Hornero, 203
El Kapallaq, 192
El Latino, 195
El Lava, 175
El Malecón, 203
El Marqués Hotel, 161
El Mortal, 200
El Museo Catcco, 109
El Olivar, 160
El Parquetito Café, 194
El Planetario, 203
El Polo Hotel, 205-206
El Sol Spanish School, 233
El Suizo, 203
El Tunqui, 135
Emergency Medical Care in Lima, 151
Enigma, 74
Enjoy Peru, 153-154
Eric Adventures, 74
España Restaurant, 176
Etiquette in Peru, 58
Excel Spanish Language Center, 230

F
FairPlay Spanish School, 230
Fallen Angel, 96
Feria Manos Artesanas, 169
Fertur Peru Travel, 152
Fluid, 190

INDEX

Flying Dog – Cusco, 88
Flying Dog Backpackers, 186
Flying to Peru, 31
Fuente de Soda "Amy's", 194
Fuji, 190

G
Galería Lucía de la Puente, 198
Gay life in Cusco, 66
Gay Peru, 24
Getting around Cusco, 66
Getting There, 31-33
Getting to and Away, 29-30
Getting To And Away – Cusco, 64
Getting to and from Aguas Calientes, 130
Getting to and from Ollantaytambo, 123
Getting to and from Pisac, 114
Getting to and from Urubamba, 119
Getting to Cusco, 64
Global Crossroad, 221
Global Volunteers, 219
Globos de los Andes, 85
Gloria Pareja Guest House, 89
Gold Museum / Museo de Oro, 155
Gold's Gym Peru, 151
Govinda's, 96
Gran Hotel Bolívar, 175
Granja Heidi Restaurant, 103
Gringo Alley, 92, 95, 96
Gringo Bill's, 134

H
Hatuchay Tower, 93
Hatun Tumi, 88.
Health and Safety, 52-53
Hearts Cafe, 122, 129-130
Hispana Spanish Language School, 234
History of Lima, 146-147
History of Ollantaytambo, 123
History of San Isidro, 158
History of the Sacred Valley, 108
Holidays and Fiestas, 18-19
Home Peru, 183
Homestay, 229, 230, 231, 232, 233, 234
Horseback Riding with Perol Chico, 75
Hospedaje El Artesano, 116, 117
Hospedaje El Artesano de San Blas, 100
Hospedaje Félix, 86
Hospedaje Granada, 87
Hospedaje Inka, 101-102

Hospedaje Kinsa Cocha, 116, 117
Hospedaje Linda Flor, 116, 117
Hospedaje Los Andenes, 125, 126
Hospedaje los Jardines, 120
Hospedaje Mach'a Wasi, 120
Hospedaje Posada del Viajero, 88
Hospedaje Pumamarka, 126
Hospedaje Q'ani Wasi, 86-87
Hospedaje Residencial Santa Fé, 208
Hospedaje Sambleño, 100
Hospedaje Turístico San Blas, 101
Hostal Aquisito, 199
Hostal Belén, 172
Hostal Buena Vista, 188, 189
Hostal Casa Grande, 87-88
Hostal Choquachaca, 101-102
Hostal Collacocha, 160-161
Hostal Corihuasi, 90
Hostal de las Artes, 173
Hostal Eiffel, 187-188
Hostal El Bosque, 126
Hostal El Patio, 188
Hostal Gemina, 197, 199-200
Hostal Hatun Was, 101
Hostal Ima Sumac, 131, 133
Hostal Iquique, 173
Hostal La Nusta, 122, 126
Hostal Las Orquídeas, 127
Hostal Machu Picchu, 131, 133-134
Hostal Mandor, 133
Hostal Ollanta, 122, 126
Hostal Posada del Corrigedor, 89
Hostal Procurador, 86
Hostal Rojas, 88
Hostal Roma, 174
Hostal Rumi Punku, 92
Hostal Santa María, 88
Hostal Sauce, 127-128
Hostal Torreblanca, 188
Hostal Varayoc, 133
Hostal Varayoq, 116, 118
Hostal Victor, 204
Hotel Apu Majestic, 134
Hotel Arqueólogo Exclusive Selection, 92
Hotel Britania, 209
Hotel Cáceres, 88
Hotel Carlos V, 89
Hotel Colonial Inn, 188
Hotel Continental, 174-175
Hotel Continental Restaurant, 177
Hotel El Grial, 102
Hotel España, 171, 174

Hotel Inka Path, 173-174
Hotel Kamana, 174
Hotel Libertador (Cusco), 93
Hotel Libertador San Isidro Golf, Lima, 161
Hotel Lima Sheraton and Casino, 175
Hotel Los Delfines, 162
Hotel Mamatila, 208
Hotel Marqueses, 91
Hotel Maury, 175
Hotel Monasterio, 93-94
Hotel Munay Tika, 126-127
Hotel Oblitas (Hotel Sol Plaza Inn), 90
Hotel Olaya, 203
Hotel Pakaritampu, 122, 126, 128
Hotel Pisaq, 117-118
Hotel Restaurant La Cabaña, 133
Hotel Royal Inka I, 92
Hotel Royal Inka II, 92
Hotel Royal Inka Pisac, 38, 116, 118
Hotel Urubamba, 120
Huaca Huallamarca, 154, 160
Huaca Pucllana, 180, 184, 185
Huaca San Borja, 208
Huayna Picchu, 1, 2, 112, 141, 142, 143
Huayoccari, 113
Huayoccari Hacienda Restaurant, 121

I
Ibero Librerías, 151-152
ICPNA Spanish School, 234
Iglesia de Jesús, Maria y José, 172
Iglesia de San Pedro, 172
Iglesia San Blas, 78, 81
Iglesia y Convento de la Merced, 81
Il Capuccino, 129
Imperial Palace, 89
Inca, 14
Inca Kola, 48
Inca Land Adventures, 74
Inca Trail Porters, 140
Inca....Fe, 105
Incan Mythology, 108
Indi Feliz Restaurant Bistro, 132, 135
Indigo, 94
Info Peru, 152-153
Inka Express, 185
Inka Frog Hostel, 187
Inka Traveler, 129
Inkayra Hotel, 90
Institute for Field Research Expe-

ditions (IFRE), 222, 223
Inti Raymi, 18, 19, 22, 63
Inticahuarina Spanish School, 232
Intihuatana, 1, 141-142
Intipunku, 2, 143
Intiq Samana, 89
Is It the Real Thing?, 51
Italian Art Museum / Museo de Arte Italiano, 171

J
JC Guesthouse, 187
Jimmy's Bagueteria and Pasteleria, 178
Juanitos Café, 102
JW Marriott Lima, 189-190

K
K'antuyoc, 126
Kachivache, 105
KB Tours, 125
Khipus Restaurant, 104
Kintaro Japanese Restaurant, 94
Kitsch, 197, 202
kkinacoperu-lodge, 187
Korma Sutra, 103
KTM Peru Adventure Tours, 185
Kusicoyllor Café-Bar, 122, 129

L
La Carreta, 163
La Casa Barranco, 199
La Casa de Kishkashta, 87
La Casa Verde, 164
La Casona Real, 92
La Catedral Restaurant and Bar, 179
La Dalmacia, 192
La Isla del Mono, 193
La Muralla, 178-179
La Noche, 197, 201
La Pampilla, 183
La Posada del Ángel, 201
La Posada del Márquez, 178
La Quinta de Allison, 199
La Rosa Náutica, 193
Laguna Dorada, 178
Lalo's, 164
Language, 15, 16
Larco Museum / Museo Larco, 154
Larcomar, 182, 244
Lares Valley Trek, 110-111
Las Brujas de Cachiche, 194-195
Las Hamacas, 201
Las Portadas, 122, 126
Le Nomade, 95
Learn Spanish, 42, 229-234

Librería El Virrey, 169
Lima, 146-209
Lima Activities, 153-157
Lima Airport, 204
Lima Airport Lodging, 204
Lima Apartment Rental, 212
Lima Art Museum / Museo de Arte de Lima, 156
Lima Cathedral / Catedral de Lima, 172
Lima Flights, 147, 150
Lima Lodging, 152
Lima Municipal Tourism Information Office, 168
Lima Museums, 154-157
Lima Overview, 146
Lima Restaurants, 162-163, 173-179, 190-195, 200-201, 203
Lima Services, 151-152
Lima Tours, 152-154
Lima Travel Lodge, 204
Lima Visión, 154
Lingua Cusco, 231-232
Living in Peru, 210-249
Llama Path, 73
Loki Hostel Cusco, 88
Loki Hostel Lima, 186
Lori Berenson: An American Behind Peruvian Bars, 17-18
Los Apus Hotel and Mirador, 102
Los Escribanos, 177
Los Perros Wine and Couch Bar, 100
Los Vitrales de Gemma, 179

M
Machu Picchu Activities, 141-143
Machu Picchu and the Inca Trail, 136-145
Machu Picchu History, 141
Machu Picchu Lodging, 144
Machu Picchu Overview, 136
Machu Picchu Pueblo Hotel, 134
Machu Picchu Restaurants, 144-145
Machu Picchu Sanctuary Lodge, 144
Machu Picchu Spanish School, 231
Machu Picchu Suites, 204
Machu Picchu Tours, 143-144
Macondo, 104
MacPlanet Internet Café, 181
Magdalen House Tourist Hostel, 205
Magdalena del Mar, 205
Magdalena del Mar Lodging, 205

Magdalena Del Mar Restaurants, 205
Maikhana The Indian Restaurant, 95-96
Makaha, 183
Mama Africa, 98
Mami Panchita, 174
Mana's Grill - Pizzeria Resturant, 104
Manchego Turismo, 181-182
Manco Capac - Lake Titicaca and the Founding of Cusco, 63
Mandela's Bar, 99
Manhattan Inn, 204
Manu Expeditions, 75
Manuel Chávez Ballón Site Museum / Museo de Sitio Manuel Chávez Ballón, 132
Map Cafe, 107
Matseui, 163
Máximo Nivel, 223-224, 229
Mayuc, 42
Mayupata, 122, 128
Media in Peru, 54-55
Mercado Central, 241
Mercado Mollina, 84
Mijn Bestemming Peru, 233
Minor Health Problems, 52-53
Mirador de la Nusta, 101
Mirador Hanan Qosco, 86
Miraflores, 180-195
Miraflores Things to See and Do, 182-185
Miraflores Lodging, 185-190
Miraflores Overview, 180
Miraflores Park Hotel, 189
Miraflores Restaurants, 190-195
Miraflores Services, 181-182
Miraflores Tours, 185
Miski Mijuna Wasi, 118-119
Miski Wasi, 179
Moloko, 94-95
Money and Costs in Peru, 56-58, 217
Monterrico, 205-206
Monterrico Lodging, 205-206
Monterrico Restaurants, 206
Monumento Y Mirador Pachacuteq, 81
More Serious Health Problems, 53
Mountain Biking, 38-39
Mullu, 116, 118
Munay Wasi, 187
Mundo Verde Spanish School, 229-230
Murphy's Irish Pub, 191, 195
Museo De Arte Popular, 83
Museo de Arte Religioso, 82

Museo de Arte y Monasterio de Santa Catalina, 83
Museo de Historia Natural UNMSM, 160
Museo de la Electricidad, 197, 198
Museo de los Descalzos, 155-156
Museo de Sitio Qoricancha, 82
Museo Galería Arte Popular de Ayacucho, 198
Museo Histórico Regional, 82
Museo Inka, 83
Museo Municipal De Arte Contemporaneo, 83
Museo Taller Hilario Mendivil, 82-83
Museum of the Inquisition / Museo de la Inquisición, 156
Museums in Peru, 21
Music in Peru, 20-21
Mythology, 76, 105

N
National Archaeology Museum / Museo Nacional de Arqueología, 154
National Museum / Museo de la Nación, 147, 155
News Café, 163
Nexos Voluntarios, 221

O
Ollantay Bar and Restaurant, 122, 129
Ollantaytambo, 121-130
Ollantaytambo Activities, 124-125
Ollantaytambo Adventure Center (OAC), 122, 125
Ollantaytambo Fortress, 124
Ollantaytambo Heritage Trail, 122, 124
Ollantaytambo Lodging, 125-128
Ollantaytambo Overview, 121-123
Ollantaytambo Restaurants, 128-130
Ollantaytambo Tours, 125
Organic Market (Bioferia), 182

P
Pacha-Papa, 104
Pachacámac, 209
Pachacútec, 99
Paddy Flaherty's, 98
Palace Concert, 173
Palacio de Gobierno, 172
Palacio de la Esmeralda, 169
Palacio de las Maletas, 169
Palacio de Sancochado, 178
Panadería El Buen Pastor, 103
Pantanos de Villa, 202
Pardo's Chicken, 178
Parque Combate de Altao, 160
Parque de la Cultura, 170
Parque de la Exposición, 147
Parque de la Muralla, 147, 168
Parque del Amor, 183-184
Parque Kennedy, 184-185
Parque Principal, 197, 198
Patagonia Art-Bar, 190
Pay Purix Backpackers Hostel, 204
Paz y Luz Bed and Breakfast, 118
Pepe Zeta Bistro Lounge, 98
Peru Adventure Tours, 185
Peru Border Crossings, 30-31
Peru Car Rental, 32
Peru Dance, 21
Peru Theater, 21-22
Peru Food and Drink, 46-50
Peru Geography, Climate, Flora and Fauna, 12-13
Peru History, 13-14
Peru Internet, 56
Peru Mail, 54-55
Peru Overview, 12
Peru Phones, 55-56
Peru Trains, 31, 66, 85-86, 124, 139-141
Peru Transportation-Getting To and Away From Peru, 29-30
Peru Trek 4 Good, 74
Peru Treks and Adventure Tour Operator, 73
Peru-Chile Border Crossings, 29-31
Peru-Ecuador Border Crossings, 29-31
Peruvian Comedy, 22
Peruvian Culture, 19-23
Peruvian Departure Tax, 29
Peruvian embassies & consulates, 27-29
Pescados Capitales, 193
Photography in Peru, 59
Pikillacta and Rumicolca, 79
Pinculluna, 113
Pirwa Hostel Bed and Breakfast, 87
Pisac, 114-119
Pisac Activities, 114-117
Pisac Lodging, 117-118
Pisac Market, 114-116
Pisac Overview, 114
Pisac Restaurants, 118-119
Pisac Ruins, 116-117

Pisco Sour, 47, 49
Pl@net.Com, 119-120
Plaza Bolívar, 206
Plaza de Acho, 170
Plaza de Armas, 147, 170-171
Plaza San Martín, 171
Politics in Peru, 14-15
Population, 15
Prasada, 94, 105
Presidente Hotel, 131, 134
Prince Hotel Suites Spa, 207
Principal Temple, 1-2, 142-143
Proyecto Peru Language Centre, 231
Pub Cubano 443, 195
Puca Pucara, 79
Pueblo Libre, 152, 206-208
Pueblo Libre Activities, 206-207
Pueblo Libre History, 206
Pueblo Libre Lodging, 207-208
Pueblo Libre Restaurants, 208
Puente de los Suspiros, 198
Pumamarca Ruins, 113
Punta Hermosa Beaches, 210
Punta Negra & Punta Rocas, 211
Punta Sal, 165
Puntarenas Restaurant, 203
Punto Blanco, 200
Punto Italiano, 163
Putucusi, 132

Q
Q'ewar Project, 222
Q'enqo, 79
Qoricancha Templo del Sol and Santo Domingo, 78-79
Quad Bike Tours, 75
Quechua Blues Bar Café, 129

R
R.H. Atlantic, 176
RadioShack, 181
Raulito's, 177-178
Real McCoy, 98, 249
Redondo, 183
Religion in Peru, 15, 16-18
Residencial el Faro, 187
Responsible Tourism in Peru, 58-59
Restaurant Aldea Yanapay, 97
Restaurant Aries, 194
Restaurant Doña Clorinda, 116, 119
Restaurant Miranda, 122, 129
Restaurant Narguila, 97
Restaurant Samana Wasi, 119
Restaurant Valle Sagrado, 116, 119
Restaurante La Rana Verde, 203

Restaurante Vida, 201
Rey Antares Mystic Hotel, 90
Rincón Cervecero, 177
Rincón Chileno, 176
Royal Tomb, 1, 142
Rusti Bar, 177

S
S.I.I.E School, 234
Sacred Valley Mountain Bike Tours, 120
Sacred Valley Trekking, 109-113
Sacred Valley—Acclimatization, 108-109
Sacred Valley--Trekking Fees, 109-110
Sacred Valley--What to Bring Trekking, 109
Sacred Valley--When to Go, 108
Sacsayhuamán, 80
Safe in Lima, 199
Safety in Cusco, 62
Safety in Peru, 239-240
Salapunco, 80-81
Salcantay, 111-112
Salcantay alternative route, 112
San Blas, 100-105
San Blas Lodging, 100-102
San Blas Restaurants, 102-105
San Blas Spanish School, 232
San Borja, 208-209
San Borja Activities, 208-209
San Borja Lodging, 209
San Borja Overview, 208
San Borja Restaurants, 209
San Francisco, 171
San Isidro, 152, 158-165
San Isidro Activities, 160
San Isidro Lodging, 160-162
San Isidro Restaurants, 162-165
San Isidro Services, 159-160
San Paolo, 177
Scena, 192
Second Home Cusco, 102
Second Home Peru, 200
Señoritas, 209
Services in Barranco, 197
Services in San Isidro, 159-160
Shehadi NYC, 191
Shopping at Manay Raqay (Square of the Request), 124-125
Shopping in Peru, 50-51
Shopping in San Isidro, 159-160
Sidrik's Peruvian Handicraft, 207
Six things to see in Lima, 147
Social and Environmental Issues in Peru, 24
Sol Innka Plaza, 89
Sonccollay Restaurante Café

INDEX

Bar Pizzeria, 128
Sonesta Lima Hotel El Olivar, 162
Sonesta Posada del Inca, 93
Soul Mate Inn Hotel, 188
South American Explorers, 51-52, 221, 223
South American Spanish School, 231
Southamerican Quality, 185
Spanish in Peru, 16
Spanish Schools, 229-234
Spanish, Quechua and Aymara, 16
Stop & Drop Lima Backpacker Hotel & Guest House, 186
Suites Antique, 161
Suites del Bosque, 161-162
Sumac Wasi, 90
Sumaq Machu Picchu Hotel, 131, 134
Sun Gate Tours, 74
Sun God Expeditions Tours, 35
Super Rueda, 192
Surfing Lima's Waves, 208
Sushi Ito, 206
Sweet Temptations, 99
Swissôtel, 162

T
T'anta, 164, 179
Tai Lounge, 163
Talleres Los Andenes, 122, 125
Tambo Machay, 80
Tampu Restaurant Bar, 145
Tasca Bar, 190
Tatoo Adventure Gear, 182, 241
Tayta Pizzeria-Trattoria, 128
Teatro Inka Bed and Breakfast, 91
Teleperu Telephone, 166
Temple of the Moon, 2, 143
Temple of the Sun, 1, 142
Teqsiqocha Hostal, 88-89
Terra Andina, 74
The Chaksi Inn Hostal, 90
The Cross Keys Pub, 98
The Discovery Internet Café and Snack Bar, 130-131
The Economy of Peru, 15
The Fair Trade Association in Ollantaytambo, 125
The Film Lounge and Danish Café, 95
The Garden House, Cusco, 93
The History of Barranco, 196-197
The History of Miraflores, 180-181
The Inca Trail, 137-141
The Mandor Gardens and Waterfalls, 132

The Mirabus, 153
The Muse Too, 103
The National Library, 209
The Niños Hotel, 91
The Old Pub, 191
The Point, 87, 197, 199
The Sacred Valley, 108-114
The Sacred Valley Activities, 109
The Sacred Valley Lodging, 114
The Sacred Valley Overview, 108
The Sacred Valley Tours, 113-114
The San Francisco Catacombs, 147, 172
The Shark Hostel, 185-186
the Small Luxury Guest House, 93
The Stone Puma, 81
The Thermal Baths of Aguas Calientes, 132
The Wiracocha Hotel, 173
Three-Windowed Temple, 1, 142
Tika Bistro Gourmet, 102
Tinkuy Buffet Restaurant, 144-145
Tipón, 80
Toqokachi, 104
Toto's House, 135
Tourist Information, 67-72
Traditional Dance – Qosqo Center Of Native Art, 84
Train Cusco to Puno, 85-86
Trattoria San Ceferino, 163-164
Travel Insurance In Peru, 25
Traveling with Kids in Lima, 150
Trek in the Chicón Valley, 85
Trekperu, 73
Truco Restaurant, 96
Tumbao VIP, 195
Tupana Wasi, 103
Turismo Inkaiko, 73

U
Ulrike's Café, 119
United Mice, 73
United Planet, 222
Urubamba, 119-121
Urubamba Activities, 120
Urubamba Lodging, 120
Urubamba Overview, 119
Urubamba Restaurants, 120-121
Viajeros, 131, 133

V
Victor Victoria, 97
Viento Sur, 120
Vilcabamba, 111
Villa Mayor, 90
Villa Natura, 179
Visas, 26-27
Volunteer Visions, 221
Volunteering or Working in Peru,

INDEX

43
Volunteers for Peace, 219
VolunTourism, 220
Vuelto, 103

W
Waikiki, 183
Wasijaus, 186
Wayki Trek, 73
Wayruro's Backpackers, 186
When to Go, 62, 108, 137-138
Wiñay Wayna, 143
Wines of Peru, 49-50
Wiracocha Spanish School, 232
Witches' Garden, 104-105

Y
Yakumama II Restaurant, 135
Yin Yang Massage, 84
Yma Sumac - Pop Life of an Andean Princess, 23
Youth Hostel Malka, 160
Yucay, 121
Yucay Overview, 121
Yucay Restaurants, 121

PACKING LISTS
(* indicates something that might not be available in Peru)

GENERAL PACKING LIST
There are a number of items that every traveler should consider bringing to Peru as follows:

- ☐ **Medicines and prescriptions** (Very important. Bringing all relevant medical info and medicines may well save you a lot of grief in Peru)
- ☐ **Photocopies of passport** and other relevant ID documents
- ☐ Paperback novels (sometimes you'll be sitting on buses, in airports, or some where else for a long time. Bring some books with you so you're not bored. It is possible to find and / or exchange books in several places in Peru, but don't count on much selection)
- ☐ Plug converter
- ☐ A good camera (see photography section)
- ☐ Water bottle (bottled water is readily available in Peru, but you may want your own bottle)
- ☐ Sunglasses
- ☐ Motion sickness medicine
- ☐ Lip balm
- ☐ *Tampons (difficult to find outside the major cities)
- ☐ Sun hat
- ☐ Condoms and other contraceptives
- ☐ *Foot powder
- ☐ Antacid tablets, such as Rolaids
- ☐ Mild painkillers such as aspirin or ibuprofen
- ☐ *GPS device (especially for hikers)
- ☐ Watch with alarm clock
- ☐ Diarrhea medicine (i.e. Imodium)
- ☐ Warm clothes (the highlands are cooler than you think)

BACKPACKER PACKING LIST:
- ☐ All of the above, plus,
- ☐ Rain poncho
- ☐ Plastic bags
- ☐ *Swiss army knife / leatherman
- ☐ Toilet paper
- ☐ *Antibacterial hand gel
- ☐ Small padlock

RAIN FOREST PACKING LIST
- ☐ Rubber boots (most jungle lodges have them, call ahead)
- ☐ *Bug spray (with Deet)
- ☐ Flashlight
- ☐ Waterproof bags
- ☐ Rain poncho
- ☐ First aid kit
- ☐ *Compass
- ☐ Whistle
- ☐ Long-sleeved shirt and pants
- ☐ Malaria / yellow fever medicine
- ☐ Original passport
- ☐ Mosquito net (if your destination does not have one; call ahead)
- ☐ Biodegradable soap

APPENDIX

ADDITIONAL ITEMS

- ☐
- ☐
- ☐
- ☐
- ☐
- ☐
- ☐
- ☐

ANTI-PACKING LIST: THINGS NOT TO BRING TO PERU

- ✗ Expensive jewelry. Just leave it home.
- ✗ Nice watch or sunglasses. Bring a cheap one you can afford to lose.
- ✗ Go through your wallet: what won't you need? Leave your drivers' license (unless you're planning on driving), business cards, video-club membership cards, 7-11 coffee club card, social security card and anything else you won't need at home. The only thing in your wallet you'll want is a student ID, and if you lose it you'll be grateful you left the rest at home.
- ✗ Illegal drugs. You didn't need us to tell you that, did you?
- ✗ Stickers and little toys for kids. Some tourists like to hand them out, which means the children pester every foreigner they see.
- ✗ Really nice clothes or shoes, unless you're planning on going to a special event or dining out a lot.

Useful Spanish Phrases

Conversational

Hello	Hola
Good morning	Buenos días
Good afternoon	Buenas tardes
Good evening	Buenas noches
Yes	Sí
No	No
Please	Por favor
Thank you	Gracias
It was nothing	De nada
Excuse me	Permiso
See you later	Hasta luego
Bye	Chao
How are you (formal)	¿Cómo está?
" " " (informal)	¿Qué tal?
I don't understand	No entiendo
Do you speak English?	¿Habla inglés?
I don't speak Spanish.	No hablo español.
I'm from England	Soy de Inglaterra
" " " the USA	Soy de los Estados Unidos

Food and Drink

Breakfast	Desayuno
Lunch	Almuerzo
Dinner	Cena
Check please	La cuenta, por favor
Main Course	Plato Fuerte
Menu	La Carta
Spoon	Cuchara
Fork	Tenedor
Knife	Cuchillo
Bread	Pan
Fruit	Fruta
Vegetables	Verduras
Potatoes	Papas
Meat	Carne
Chicken	Pollo
Beer	Cerveza
Wine	Vino
Juice	Jugo
Coffee	Café
Tea	Té

Health/Emergency

Call a....	¡Llame a...!
Ambulance	una ambulancia
A doctor	un médico
The police	la policía

It's an emergency	Es una emergencia
I'm sick	Estoy enfermo/a
I need a doctor	Necesito un médico
Where's the hospital?	¿Dónde está el hospital?

I'm allergic to...	Soy alérgico/a a
Antibiotics	los antibióticos
Nuts	nuez
Penicillin	la penicilina

Getting Around

Where is...?	¿Dónde está...?
The bus station?	la estación de bus?
The train station?	la estación de tren?
A bank?	¿Un banco?
The bathroom?	¿El baño?

Left, right, straight	Izquierda, derecha, recto
Ticket	Boleto
Where does the bus leave from?	¿De dónde sale el bus?

Accommodation

Where is a hotel?	¿Donde hay un hotel?
I want a room	Quiero una habitación
Single / Double / Marriage	Simple / Doble / Matrimonial
How much does it cost per night?	¿Cuanto cuesta por noche?
Does that include breakfast?	¿Incluye el desayuno?
Does that include taxes?	¿Incluye los impuestos?

HEALTH/EMERGENCY

Call a....	¡Llame a...!
Ambulance	una ambulancia
A doctor	un médico
The police	la policía

It's an emergency	Es una emergencia
I'm sick	Estoy enfermo/a
I need a doctor	Necesito un médico
Where's the hospital?	¿Dónde está el hospital?

I'm allergic to...	Soy alérgico/a a
Antibiotics	los antibióticos
Nuts	nuez
Penicillin	la penicilina

GETTING AROUND

Where is...?	¿Dónde está...?
The bus station?	la estación de bus?
The train station?	la estación de tren?
A bank?	¿Un banco?
The bathroom?	¿El baño?

Left, right, straight	Izquierda, derecha, recto
Ticket	Boleto
Where does the bus leave from?	¿De dónde sale el bus?

ACCOMMODATION

Where is a hotel?	¿Donde hay un hotel?
I want a room	Quiero una habitación
Single / Double / Marriage	Simple / Doble / Matrimonial
How much does it cost per night?	¿Cuanto cuesta por noche?
Does that include breakfast?	¿Incluye el desayuno?
Does that include taxes?	¿Incluye los impuestos?

APPENDIX

V!VA TRAVEL GUIDES BRINGS YOU A TEAR-OUT LIST OF USEFUL CONTACTS IN PERU

Feel free to photocopy this sheet for your use, to give to your dog, or to wallpaper your room.

EMERGENCY NUMBERS

General Emergencies	116	Police	105
Fire	116	Medical	117

HOSPITALS / DOCTORS

Lima: Clínica El Golf
Av. Aurelio Miro Quesada 1030
San Isidro
Tel: 264 3300, 319 1500

Cusco: Essalud Clinic
Av. Anselmo Alvarez s/n, Cusco
Tel: 51-84-234724
24 hr emergency room

ENGLISH-SPEAKING LAWYERS

Garcia de Piccetti, Consuelo
Jr Carabaya 1011 of 208
Lima
Tel: 428-1647, Cell: 9-630-2029
E-mail: cpiccetti@yahoo.com

Benites, Forno y Ugaz
Jr. Jiron Guillermo Marconi 165
San Isidro, Lima
Tel: 444-4966, 615-9090
E-mail: bmu@bmu.com.pe

TRAVELER GUIDANCE:

V!VA Travel Guides: www.vivatravelguides.com

South American Explorers' Club:

Lima contact details: Calle Piura 135, Miraflores, Lima, Peru, Tel/Fax: (51-14) 453-306, E-mail: limaclub@saexplorers.org.

Cusco contact details: Atoqsaycuchi 670 San Blas, Mailing Address: Apartado 500, Cusco, Peru, Tel: (51-84)245-484, E-mail: cuscoclub@saexplorers.org

Post Offices:

Lima's Main Post Office: Plaza de Armas at Camaná 195, Tel: 427-0370
Lima DHL/Western Union: Nicolás de Piérola 808, Tel: 424-5820

Cusco's Main Post Office: Av. El Sol 802, Tel: 224-212
Cusco DHL/Western Union: Av. El Sol 627-A, Tel: 244-167

Taxis

Lima:
Taxi Plus: 578-4555, 24-hrs

Cusco
Cusco Taxis: 422-2222

Pharmacy: Pharmax, Av. La Encalada 1541, Monterrico, Lima (across street from Embassy), Delivery: 434-1460

APPENDIX

EMBASSIES & CONSULATES

[handwritten: Caracol Bella fer skin,]

Canada
Bolognesi 228, Miraflores Lima
Tel: 51-1-319-3200
E-mail: lima@international.gc.ca
http://geo.international.gc.ca/latin-america/peru/

France
Av. Arequipa 3415, San Isidro, Lima
Tel: 51-1-215-8400, Fax: 51-1-215-8441
E-mail: france.embajada@ambafrance-pe.org
URL: www.ambafrance-pe.org/

Germany
Av. Arequipa 4210, Miraflores, Lima
Tel: 51-1-212-5016, Fax: 51-1-422-6475 / 51-1-440-4048
E-mail: kanzlei@embajada-alemana.org.pe
URL: www.embajada-alemana.org.pe

Japan
Av. San Felipe 356, Jesús María, Lima 11
Tel: 51-1-219-9550 / 219-9551
Fax: 51-1-219-9544
URL: http://www.pe.emb-japan.go.jp/
Email: consjapon@embajadajapon.org.pe

Netherlands
Torre Parque Mar, Av. José Larco 1301, 13th floor, Miraflores, Lima
Tel: 51-1-213-9800 / 51-1-213-9800
Fax: 51-1-213-9805
E-mail: nlgovlim@terra.com.pe
URL: http://www.nlgovlim.com/

Switzerland
Av. Salaverry 3240, San Isidro, Lima
Tel: 51-1-264-0305
Fax: 51-1-264-1319
URL: www.eda.admin.ch/lima

Spain
Calle Los Pinos, 490, San Isidro, Lima
Tel: 51-1-513-7930, Fax: 51-1-422-0347
E-mail: cog.lima@mae.es
URL: www.consuladolima.com.pe/

United Kingdom
Torre Parque Mar, 22nd floor, Av. Jose Larco 1301, Miraflores, Lima
Tel: 51-1-617-3000, Fax: 51-1-617-3100
Consular: consular.lima@fco.gov.uk
URL: http://ukinperu.fco.gov.uk/es

United States of America
Av. La Encalada, block 17, Surco, Lima
Tel: 51-1-434-3000, Fax: 51-1-618-2397
URL: http://lima.usembassy.gov/

Complete the sections below for your convenience:

My Tour Operator:

My Hotel Address:

Taxi Directions to
the hotel:

APPENDIX